America's Uncivil Wars

America's Uncivil Wars

*The Sixties Era
from Elvis to the Fall of Richard Nixon*

MARK HAMILTON LYTLE

New York   Oxford
OXFORD UNIVERSITY PRESS
2006

Oxford University Press, Inc., publishes works that further Oxford University's
objective of excellence in research, scholarship, and education.

Oxford New York
Auckland   Cape Town   Dar es Salaam   Hong Kong   Karachi
Kuala Lumpur   Madrid   Melbourne   Mexico City   Nairobi
New Delhi   Shanghai   Taipei   Toronto

With offices in
Argentina   Austria   Brazil   Chile   Czech Republic   France   Greece
Guatemala   Hungary   Italy   Japan   Poland   Portugal   Singapore
South Korea   Switzerland   Thailand   Turkey   Ukraine   Vietnam

Published by Oxford University Press, Inc.
198 Madison Avenue, New York, New York 10016
http://www.oup.com

Oxford is a registered trademark of Oxford University Press

Library of Congress Cataloging-in-Publication Data

Lytle, Mark H.
America's uncivil wars : the Sixties era : from Elvis to the fall of Richard Nixon / by
Mark Hamilton Lytle.
p. cm.
Includes bibliographical references and index.
ISBN-13: 978-0-19-517496-0 — ISBN-13: 978-0-19-517497-7 (pbk.)
ISBN 0-19-517496-8 (acid-free paper) — ISBN 0-19-517497-6 (pbk. : acid-free paper)
1. United States—History—1953–1961. 2. United States—History—1961–1969. 3. United
States—History—1969–4. United States—Social conditions—1960–1980. 5. Nineteen sixties.
I. Title: Sixties era. II. Title.

E839.L98 2005
973.923—dc22   2004063585

Printing number: 9 8 7 6 5 4 3 2 1

Printed in the United States of America
on acid-free paper

For the Koesters—Bill, Audrey, Lindsey, and Rob

Contents

Preface

Who needs another book on the sixties? Certainly bookstore shelves and Web sites are already filled with relevant titles. But every time we think we have made peace with that contentious era, it commands our attention once again. Our understanding of what the sixties were all about is not yet free of the political and cultural passions the era inflamed. In the 1980s, veterans of the New Left and antiwar movement produced important histories and memoirs. While recognizing the excesses of many activists, they celebrated the era's efforts to overcome racial and gender inequality, to end what they saw as an unjust war, and to liberate people from a repressive culture. At the same time, conservatives led by Allan Bloom launched a powerful counterattack on an era they blamed for every social and moral disorder, from welfare to street crime and teenage pregnancy. Ronald Reagan, as their public spokesperson, condemned affirmative action, drug use, and permissive culture. In facing the world, he urged Americans to put Vietnam in the past, "stand tall again," and renew their efforts to defeat Communism's "evil empire." His administration supported a right-wing counterinsurgency in Nicaragua that his critics called a potential Vietnam.

The debate over the sixties grew more heated in the 1990s. For the first time, a number of historians too young to have "been there" began to interpret what it all meant. Earlier histories had focused on the New Left, the antiwar movement, and the counterculture. For this younger generation, those movements were only part of the story. Conservatives could look back on that era as the genesis of their movement's rise to power. Any comprehensive history of the sixties had to explain how a movement declared dead in 1964 could come to define the nation's political agenda less than twenty years later. At the same time, the generation who came of age in the sixties began to define public policy. Former Young Americans for Freedom (YAF) members played key roles in the Reagan and first Bush administrations. The American military leaders who planned Desert Storm, the invasion to drive Saddam Hussein out of Kuwait, had Vietnam very much on their minds. Almost all were veterans of that conflict. For this war, they insisted on overwhelming force, broad domestic and international support, and an exit strategy—precisely those factors missing during Vietnam. In the wake of the allies' crushing victory, President George H. W. Bush exulted, "By God, we've kicked the Vietnam syndrome once and for all." Yet the failure to topple Saddam Hussein left the outcome much in doubt. The United States had snatched "a modest victory from the jaws of triumph," a marine corps general groused.

The 1992 election was in some ways a referendum on the sixties. Tipper Gore and Marilyn Quayle, wives of the Democratic and Republican vice presidential candidates and mothers of teenagers, condemned the excessive sex and violence in popular culture—a legacy of the sixties. Sixties veterans viewed such comments as a call for censorship. George H. W. Bush represented the generation who held power in the 1960s. His conservative allies turned their harshest invective on Bill and Hillary Clinton. The first couple embodied everything that the Right hated about the sixties. Republican House speaker Newt Gingrich derided them as "McGoverniks." They were, above all, liberals who, despite Clinton's very Baptist upbringing, seemed to be the ultimate secular humanists. The Right's constant battering turned the "L" word into a label few politicians were willing to embrace. It came to connote a host of discredited ideas—weakness on national security, permissiveness on sex, drugs, and crime, affirmative action, a green agenda for the environment, and an indifference to traditional family values. As president, Clinton could do little more than defend against efforts to repeal the sixties. For example, he vetoed laws to ban "partial birth abortions" as pro-life forces maneuvered to overturn *Roe v. Wade*. The impeachment effort was in some ways another attempt to defeat the sixties. Hillary Clinton, echoing the rhetoric of sixties, blamed a right-wing conspiracy.

The election of George W. Bush might have consigned the sixties to the nostalgic echoes of the 1950s and *Happy Days*. Bush has done all he can to obscure his personal history from those years, though the evidence suggests he was not immune to the allure of sex, drugs, and rock and roll. But rather than douse the sixties' political and cultural fires, Bush has reignited them. He exploited the events of September 11 to advance the long-term conservative drive to overturn liberal achievements of the sixties by restricting civil liberties, reducing access to government information, opening the environment to development, limiting women's right to choice, and seeking once again to impose American values on non-Western cultures. The election of 2004 virtually exploded over the meaning of the sixties. John Kerry trumpeted his war record as a reason for the voters to choose him. George Bush hid his. His campaign, however, charged that the liberal Kerry had shamed his fellow veterans by opposing the war. Once again, Americans confronted the contested legacy of Vietnam.

So if debate about the sixties continues to shape our political and cultural divisions, we should certainly have a clearer idea what the uproar was all about. That is, I believe, a sufficient reason for another book on the sixties. Within that period, American society fractured more completely than it had at any time since the Civil War era. That fracturing seemed almost infinitely compound, as society broke along generational, racial, class, ethnic, regional, ideological, aesthetic, and gender lines. Upheaval of one kind or another touched almost every aspect of private and public life. As public debate devolved into anger, confrontation, and recrimination, civility was lost. Protestors called Johnson and Nixon fascists, murders, pigs, and worse. Government officials dismissed the protestors as traitors, cowards, and Communists.

Such intolerance produced a spirit of recrimination that provoked America's uncivil wars. The circumstances within which people experienced that tumult certainly colors the way they remember it today. Former participants in the counterculture, New Left, civil rights, feminism, environmentalism, Brown Power, or a host of other movements tend to privilege their own experience in reconstructing the history of the era. As insiders in one cause, they often have a more limited perspective on other movements of the times.

My own experience, I believe, allows me to adopt a somewhat detached, though far from objective or unbiased, point of view. I came alive socially, politically, and intellectually during the uncivil wars. Buffalo, my hometown, was perched precariously between the East and Midwest. Its population was largely blue-collar, ethnic, and Catholic. My father was a conservative Republican; my mother, a liberal Democrat; and our neighborhood, almost exclusively Jewish. Until I reached high school, I thought Protestants were a disadvantaged minority. During the late 1950s, I discovered cool jazz, though like most of my adolescent friends I dug rock and roll. Elvis was a musical and cultural revelation, though my real hero was Ray Charles. Through his music I became more aware of the segregated world in which I lived. Civil rights thus became the first of the 1960s protest movements to capture my attention.

A second awakening came on a visit to my brother at Cornell University in the early 1960s. Walking through the center of campus, I noticed a gathering of students who had held an all-night vigil to protest the nuclear arms race. Small groups of fraternity types occasionally jeered at them. I was surprised to see such open political expression and discomforted by the intolerance it provoked. When I arrived at Cornell in 1962, the student body was almost exclusively white, and most students of color came from abroad. Politics remained pretty conventional—largely devoted to campus offices and debates over the policies of the Kennedy administration. The fraternities that dominated the campus often had bylaws restricting membership on the basis of race and religion. All the same, the winds of change were blowing. Most students I knew supported civil rights, pushed to remove the exclusionary restrictive fraternity and sorority bylaws, and demanded more freedom from university rules.

I was scarcely aware of Vietnam before entering college. Cornell was fortunate to have George Kahin, a Southeast Asian specialist, on its faculty. He taught us that many of the claims the Johnson administration used to justify escalation of war in Vietnam were false. Historian Walter LaFeber explained how the atomic bombing of Japan might not have been necessary. For the first time, my friends and I began to question many of the received truths of our lives. That growing political enlightenment coincided with a cultural awakening. Cosmopolitan students had already discovered protest music, especially Joan Baez and Bob Dylan, who had links to both pacifism and civil rights. By the fall of 1964, almost everyone listened to the Beatles, the Rolling Stones, and other British invasion bands. That's when hair became longer (for men and women) and clothes became less formal.

By the time I graduated in 1966, the elements of 1960s consciousness were largely in place. Cornell was far more integrated, black radicalism and feminism were stirring, black music was widely popular, the war in Vietnam was more unpopular, Students for a Democratic Society (SDS) had become prominent, and my roommate showed an unusual protectiveness toward a stained sugar cube he kept in the refrigerator. The following year, the world turned upside down. Antiwar protest became more frequent and intense. When I revisited Cornell in the spring of 1967, my former beer-swilling fraternity brothers were all stoned out of their minds. The campus had also become heavily politicized over issues such as feminism and Black Nationalism.

After a year of teaching in an inner-city junior high school, I decided that the study of history was an effective way to engage the issues dividing the nation. That was not a widely held view at the time. Enrollments in college history courses were falling even at Yale, where I entered a doctoral program. Like many of my peers, I dabbled in Marxist ideas and quantitative analysis. Neither stuck. What did make an enduring impression was the antiwar passion of members of the Yale community, such as the Reverend William Sloane Coffin. Unfortunately for me, I became vulnerable to the draft. What to do? I had just discovered my calling in life and had no intention of supporting the war. A pragmatist at heart, I became a "conscientious acceptor" and joined the National Guard. I would serve my country, but not in Vietnam. The National Guard at that time was being trained to combat civil disorders. Newark and Detroit had exploded the previous summer. More rioting followed the assassination of Martin Luther King, Jr., and the Democratic convention in Chicago. By the time Richard Nixon was elected in November 1968, it truly felt like America was at war with itself.

In May 1970, the uncivil wars came to New Haven. Bobby Seale and several other Black Panthers faced trial for the murder of a member thought to be a police informant. A loose coalition of radicals, led by yippies Jerry Rubin and Abbie Hoffman, decided to come to New Haven to protest. Many of my graduate school friends became heavily involved in planning the weekend. Yale girded for trouble as some of the more outspoken radicals promised to burn the university to the ground. My National Guard unit called me to active service. Rather than joining my friends on the barricades I would be facing them from the other side, or so I feared. Anticipating that confrontation was one of the most morally wrenching weeks of my life. By some quirk of bureaucratic inanity, I was sent home minutes after I arrived at the Armory, so spent most of the weekend watching events from the sidelines as New Haven seethed but never exploded. Then on May 4, National Guardsmen killed four students at Kent States University. Ten days later, state police in Mississippi killed two students at Jackson State.

The events of early May forced me to reconsider the direction in which sixties protest seemed headed. All the hue and cry had done little to stop government harassment of dissent, ease racial inequality, or end the war in Vietnam. Too often, I saw radical activists who as they experienced power for the first time became impatient with the group consciousness building that had shaped earlier protests. As the Vietnam War wound down and the draft ended, protest lost much of its urgency. And then came Watergate. Seldom have I ever been so mesmerized by politics. Every time it seemed like we had heard the worst some new bomb went off— John Dean accused Nixon, Alexander Butterfield revealed the White House tapes, and Vice President Agnew pleaded nolo for corruption. Quick on the heels of Watergate came the Yom Kippur War and the OPEC oil boycotts. Once Richard Nixon resigned, the economy went into a tailspin, and as the American phase of the Vietnam War ended, the country no longer felt so polarized, though few of its divisions had healed. The uncivil wars seemed to be over.

For me they never really ended because they became part of my work as a historian. From the time I began teaching at Bard College I have offered a course called "From Camelot to Watergate." Even when the sixties seem to fall out of favor, student interest has never waned. Some students, I suspect, want to know more about the events that had such a formative impact on their parents. Others seemed to think the sixties had a moral and political engagement their own times lack. I try to explain that the sixties made moral clarity deceptively easy. In those supercharged times, even the most mundane gesture, such as lighting a joint, seemed fraught with social and political import. Put another way, many people in the sixties passed off self-indulgence and arrogance as moral and political commitment. That is a perspective I hope readers will take from this book.

Students also study the sixties because many feel they missed out on something really big and important. The sixties, unlike any other postwar era, was where it was happening. "If you remember the sixties, you weren't there," or so goes a well-worn aphorism. It suggests more than the dope-addled ambiance of smoke-filled rooms and rock concerts. For most people the sixties were not only an era, but also a set of places and experiences. A person did not simply live in the sixties. The events of the decade were so tumultuous, intrusive, and overwhelming that each person had to decide at some level—whether to be on or off the bus—to use novelist Ken Kesey's metaphor for a new consciousness. That gave to those who embraced the movements of the era a sense of membership, and hence to those who did not, a sense of exclusion. By listening to Dylan, smoking dope, marching for civil rights, wearing long hair, and protesting against the war in Vietnam, anyone could claim to have joined, though what they belonged to was far from clear. Conversely, those who didn't inhale or protest or drop out were not in the club.

This sense of inclusion and exclusion has had a significant impact on the writing about the era. Some of the best and earliest histories, written while the wounds were yet to heal, came from participant observers. Todd Gitlin, Sara Evans, and Tom Hayden can write with authority on the New Left and Students for a Democratic Society because they were "present at the creation." Similarly, Emmett Grogan, author of *Ringolivio*, helped the Diggers conceive of some of their more outrageous theatrics. Their proximity to the action gives them an air of authority—a position much challenged by those who came of age at the time. It tends to make readers feel like outsiders who, having not been there, will never quite get it. My students and many people who lived through the sixties without getting on the bus seem to think they will never truly understand what the tumult and shouting was all about. This book is an effort to include them.

The sixties that I try to capture in this book, despite their divisiveness, excesses, and incivility, were also a time of hope. The era's youthful rebelliousness sometimes invites comparison to the 1920s, and so in thinking about them I am reminded of F. Scott Fitzgerald's peroration in *The Great Gatsby*, when he described mankind standing for a transitory moment, "Face to face for the last time in history with something commensurate to its capacity for Wonder." Many activists shared that sense of possibility. They had sufficient confidence in the resilience of our national fabric that they felt free to test its limits. That plus trust in the ultimate good sense of the American people gave them a faith their conservative critics do not seem to share.

The first historians writing about the sixties generally chose a topical approach. I have adopted a more chronological structure. Separating the counterculture from the New Left or antiwar movement might provide more clarity about each topic, but it masks the ways in which those movements interacted and influenced each other. Chronology also communicates the sense of mounting chaos that characterized the times. By 1967, events seemed to cascade upon us. The Summer of Love was also the summer of the Detroit and Newark riots. Soon after Lyndon Johnson announced he would not run in November 1968, James Earl Ray assassinated Martin Luther King. In a world of such tumult we were barely afloat, rushing downstream with no sense where we would end up. If readers come away with a sense of both the exhilaration and desperation of that experience, then another book on the sixties will have been worthwhile.

Acknowledgments

Historians write as solo practitioners, but history is a corporate enterprise. No matter how much digging we do in archives, each of us is dependent on the work of others. We may disagree, even vehemently at times, but each new book builds on those that preceded it. This is particularly true for *America's Uncivil Wars*. As much as I have drawn on my own research and personal experience, this book also synthesizes what I have learned from my fellow scholars. I have tried to acknowledge that debt in the notes accompanying the text. Nonetheless, some historians deserve special thanks, because they influenced my thinking in ways notes can never fully recognize. Among them I would mention Terry Anderson, John Andrews III, Michael Kazin and Maurice Isserman, Ruth Rosen, Winnie Breines, David Farber, Geoffrey Hodgson, Lisa McGirr, Edward P. Morgan, Martin Duberman, Barry Adam, Susan Douglas, Stephen Whitfield, Allan Matusow, David Steigenwald, William Rorabaugh, Doug Rossinow, Doug McAdams, Melvin Small, Bruce Schulman, Tom Wells, and Milton Viorst. Recently, when I saw Country Joe McDonald perform, I remembered him as a regular on the H-Sixties list I subscribed to. That site and the current H-1960s@H.Net.MSU.edu have been valuable sources for ideas, information, and lively debate.

My personal obligations are legion. They begin with Chris Rogers, who conceived the idea for the book at McGraw-Hill and welcomed it to Oxford. At McGraw-Hill, Peter LaBella was an early and incisive reader and Lyn Uhl encouraged the project. My life and the life of this book became much easier when Peter Coveney and June Kim got involved. No author could ask for better editorial support. Archivists at the Kennedy and Johnson Presidential Libraries and the Sterling and Beineke Libraries at Yale were always accommodating. Jane Hyrshko and Jane Dougall at Bard College have helped out whenever I asked. Now almost two generations of Bard students have sat through my class on the Sixties, challenged me, turned up interesting sources, and forced me to clarify my thinking. Faculty seminars at Bard, University College Dublin, the University of Connecticut, Corpus Christi College Oxford, and the American Studies Center at Keele University gave me an opportunity to test out my ideas and offered the most constructive kinds of criticism. My colleagues at Bard have been equally generous. Myra Young Armstead and Aureliano DeSoto read and commented on parts of the manuscript. James Chace was a constant source of fresh ideas about history and politics, especially in the course we co-taught on Vietnam. Similarly, Gennady Shkliarevsky gave me new perspectives on the Cold War.

I had the good fortune to study history at both Cornell and Yale during the Sixties. My mentors in both places not only trained me to become a historian, but also helped me understand the events that roiled both universities. Walter LaFeber and Michael Kammen inspired me to become a historian and then taught me how to read and think about history. My conversations with them over the years are reflected in this book. Donald Kagan bridged my experiences, having been my freshman adviser at Cornell and friend at Yale. Over lunch at Silliman College Don led a group of us through a three-year debate over what the Sixties signified. We seldom agreed, but we never tired of disagreeing. John Morton Blum may not even remember his most significant contribution to my education. On the eve of the May Day demonstrations at Yale, several us went to his office for advice. Unlike our friends who were going to demonstrate, we'd been called up by our National Guard units and were confused and nervous. As a World War II veteran, he had a more detached view. He advised us to take stock of the worst things we imagined might happen and then, afterwards, take inventory of what actually occurred. Somehow the idea of seeing May Day through a historian's eyes made the threat seem less ominous. I should add that his book, *Years of Discord*, has been an important source for this book.

Perhaps my largest debt is to my friends and family, who have put up with this project through the years of its gestation. Jim Davidson has influenced my thinking and writing as a historian more than any other person. During our morning jogs, he has heard more about this book than is good for a person. Mike Stoff lived through the late Sixties with me in ways only he and I can fully appreciate. Who could forget Chuck's Steakhouse? Two friends I've lost, Bill Gienapp and Kevin Simon, made significant contributions. I miss them both. And then there are the Pros from Dover, all Sixties veterans, all politically engaged, and all appropriately skeptical about my claims to historical understanding. To Dod, Norm, Warren, Richard, Chuck one and two, Mike, and our patron Richard Strain, I give thanks for your forbearance. My wife Gretchen and I have been fortunate to have a circle of friends who, contrary to the liberation ethos of the time all got married in the late Sixties and stayed married. For having shared so much then and since, I'd like to thank Mike and Lindy Keiser, Dave and Margie Carney, and Ethel and Rick Berger. Other friends who followed that same path have been equally generous— Dod and Dorothy Crane, Norman and Ida Brier, Warren and Andrea Replansky, Greg Barker and Susan Phillips, James Steinberg and Lyn Itzkowitz, Barb and Bill Maple, George and Evelyn Constable, Tim and Barbara Schweizer, Chuck and Sharon Griffith, and Dave and Pam Wetherill.

I have an enormous debt to my family. My brother James, aka Torch, introduced me to jazz, blues, and the politics of urban education. As Peace Corps volunteers and teachers, he and his wife Susan modeled the constructive side of Sixties idealism. My sister Fran Clay and her husband Bob brought the Vietnam experience home to our family. They reached a peace before our government did. My son Jesse and daughter Kate discovered the music of the Sixties without parental pressure. Their enthusiasm reminded me how much of value the Sixties had actually produced. I met my wife Gretchen in 1968, so for me it wasn't such a bad year after all. To-gether, we made a decision that many of our generation also made to seek a high quality of life rather than success in conventional terms. Despite the current cele-bration of wealth as the measure of all good things, I've never regretted the choices we made. Her support for this book has made all the difference.

Finally, a note about the dedication. Bill Koester is one of my oldest friends. In the 1950s he introduced me to the bohemian side of Buffalo, which given the blue collar nature of that city was not easy to find. After college our lives went in differ-ent directions until the 1980s when we rediscovered each other. His family, Audrey, Rob, and Lindsey have been a vital part of our lives ever since. When I was looking for the perfect reader for my manuscript I turned to Rob. He protested that he had never studied history so would not have much to offer. In fact, he was the perfect reader—interested, candid, sensitive to the nuance of language, and alert to my fail-ures of explanation. For whatever clarity my narrative has achieved, I have Rob to thank. Those who know the Koesters will understand what resolve it took for Rob to make his contribution. He could not have done it without the unflagging devo-tion that Bill, Audrey, and Lindsey have shown. The four of them have demonstrated for their circle of friends the real meaning of family. No one I know better embod-ies the very best qualities of the Sixties. That is why I am dedicating this book to them.

Introduction

At a 1960 political gathering, humorist Art Buchwald gently poked fun at presidential candidate Richard Nixon. Nixon took the remarks with good humor. Shortly after, however, Buchwald heard from his outraged father who "couldn't believe that I would make fun of the vice president of the United States." Some thirteen years later in the midst of Watergate, Nixon was still the butt of political humor, but now it had more bite. "Heard about the new Watergate watch? Both hands point to Nixon," a comedian joked. David Frye, while doing an impersonation of Nixon, declared, "There's a bright side to Watergate. My administration has taken crime out of the streets and put it in the White House where I can keep an eye on it."

Something had happened in the United States during those intervening years that made the propriety of Buchwald's father seem quaint, as if it had come from another time and place. In a sense it had. Buchwald senior was at home in a 1950s America in which a sense of decorum framed public discourse. Parents in the 1950s expected children to respect authority, work hard in school, fear Communism, and love God and country. Historian Kenneth Cmiel observed, "As the 1960s opened, civility was, quite literally, the law of the land." The Supreme Court extended no First Amendment protection to speech deemed "lewd," "profane," or "obscene."

Then came the sixties, the most deeply factionalized period in American history since the Civil War. Once Vietnam turned the cold war hot, the level of public vitriol rose. "Hey, Hey, LBJ how many kids have you killed today?" war protestors came to chant. Black Power advocates attacked the white use of social etiquette to reinforce the Jim Crow system of racial inequality. Members of the counterculture dismissed traditional notions of social behavior as barriers to authentic relationships. By the time Richard Nixon resigned, the "F" word had become part of everyday speech for many Americans. Pornographic sex and violence were common in Hollywood movies. Faced with a multifaceted assault on the conventional idea of civil society, the Supreme Court greatly extended the range of civil liberties and protected speech, overturned laws banning the dissemination of birth control information, and gave women abortion rights.

Many Americans welcomed these new boundaries as a sign of a more tolerant society. Others condemned them as subversion of traditional authority and standards of acceptable behavior. As the fight over fundamental values intensified, the combatants became increasingly unrestrained in condemning each other. Rising incidences of intolerance, disrespect, and violence produced America's uncivil wars. Ever since, historians have struggled to make sense of what the national upheaval was all about. How and why did civility give way to confrontation, moderation to the radicalism of Left and Right, and conformity to a proliferation of lifestyles?

One barrier to our understanding has been a preoccupation with what one historian called "the good sixties / bad sixties" treatment of the period. Either approvingly or disapprovingly, historians constructed a narrative that went something like this:

> Once upon a time, Americans lived in a world of social conservatism and political consensus. Preoccupied with the Communist menace, the nation's leaders refused to acknowledge fundamental domestic problems, including the second-class status of African Americans, Latinos, homosexuals, and women. Along came a generation of grassroots social, political, and cultural movements. Inspired by John Kennedy and their own youthful idealism, they insisted that the nation live up to its democratic, egalitarian ideals. While the power elite tried to accommodate and channel these movements, it got the country bogged down in a morally ambiguous Southeast Asian war. Everything came to a head in 1968. Protest brought down some of the war makers and made the war increasingly unpopular. After that, the extreme behaviors of political and social protest groups provoked widespread resentment and government repression. Unable to achieve their idealistic goals, movements became increasingly frustrated, fragmented, and polarized. Richard Nixon, the enigmatic man who ruled by dividing the nation, saw his presidency collapse from its abuse of power. After that everyone was so tired, they had to take a break.

Veterans of New Left activism recounted this story with a sense of regret. Conservatives told it more as a morality tale of how liberal values tore the nation from its political and spiritual roots.

Obviously, this summation is a caricature of a complex reality. No historian has treated the sixties so simplistically. Still, early histories followed its broad contours. The story they told focused largely on national movements inspired by liberal and radical activists. That perspective ignored certain key facets of the era. For one, neither the consensus nor conformity of the 1950s was ever as entrenched as the conventional wisdom assumed. Dissent and discontent were widespread, though muted. For another, much of the sixties activism was local in nature. No national organization ever directed the antiwar movement. The best protestors could do was create an umbrella structure under which each organization tended to do its own thing in its own way. Nor did any national organization inspire the civil rights movement that swept the South by the early 1960s. Indeed, organizations such as the NAACP opposed many of the tactics employed at the grass roots by religious leaders and student protestors.

Like so much of 1960s protest, African-American confrontation with the white social order was as much spiritually as politically inspired. That is another important perspective the conventional narrative tends to ignore. By the 1960s, many clergy sought ways to make religion more vital. Some of the more reform minded among them, heirs of the social gospel, found their path in the civil rights movement. As religious historian Mark Silk noted, "Civil rights, the supreme cause of the day, was to a striking degree a religious affair." Folk singers turned songs like Bob Dylan's "Blowin' in the Wind" into hymns of protest. In his "Letter from a Birmingham Jail," Martin Luther King, Jr., confronted his detractors with the real religious issue they faced. "If today's church does not recapture the sacrificial spirit of the early church," King wrote, "it will lose its authenticity, forfeit the loyalty of millions, and be dismissed as an irrelevant social club with no meaning for the twentieth century."

Historian Sydney Ahlstrom explained that Americans had come to feel deeply "the need for reexamining fundamental conceptions of religion, ethics, and nationhood." As a consequence, Ahlstrom believed the American religious establishment had fractured by the 1960s. King represented the growing prominence of the black churches. The "ancient Eastern Churches" (Greek, Russian, and other orthodox branches as well as the Polish National Catholic and Armenian) had joined the ranks of the Federal Council of Churches, founded in 1908 by Protestants. By embracing such diversity, the council lost its standing as the "one surviving institutionalized symbol" of Protestant preeminence, according to religious historian Winthrop Hudson. Increasingly, Americans looked for spiritual guidance to movements outside the traditional religious denominations. Fundamentalism, ancient faiths, the occult, mysticism, and Asian religions all attracted widespread adherence.

Religion was at the center of a conservative resurgence the traditional sixties narrative overlooked. If the sixties were all about the politics of the Left, how can we explain the prominence of the conservative movement since the 1970s? A number of historians have shown conclusively that the New Right had its origins during the uncivil wars. Rather than trying to reform the state and society, radicals on the Right wanted to revive earlier religious and social values while freeing Americans from the oppressive hand of the state. Their targets included not only liberals and socialists on the Left, but also the GOP establishment they believed had stolen the 1952 Republican presidential nomination from their hero, Robert Taft. To that end, they concentrated on grassroots organizing, with the goal of gaining control of the Republican Party. Throughout the 1960s, Young Americans for Freedom, a conservative campus organization, had a larger student membership than more visible groups such as Students for a Democratic Society. The vast majority of conservatives, like the majority of Americans, supported the war in Vietnam, believed government had a limited role in guaranteeing equal rights, and found the manners and mores of the counterculture morally offensive.

That points to yet another aspect of the sixties that the conventional narrative slighted. The rise of the New Right occurred as both population and cultural influence began to flow from the North and East to the South and West. By the 1960s, the South and Southwest had begun to redefine the national culture. Conservatives had their greatest organizational successes in those regions that came to be known as the Sunbelt. Southern churches provided the moral center of the civil rights movement. At the same time, the battle over civil rights drove the traditionally Democratic South into the conservative wing of the Republican Party. Southern politicians such as George Wallace used populist rhetoric to make their brand of racial conservatism palatable to both northern blue-collar Democrats and rural Southerners. Following the enormous popularity of Elvis Presley, southern musicians introduced rhythm and blues, country and western, and gospel to national audiences. In the process, they redefined popular music.

As the South was moving into the cultural mainstream, California produced a bicoastal national culture. Los Angeles came to rival New York as a media center. Surfing produced a lifestyle that influenced fashion, music, and popular jargon. The Bay Area and Berkeley would become home to almost all the sixties disparate phenomena, from powerful conservatives to the free speech movement to LSD and acid rock, to communes and vegetarian food, to the Black Panthers and antiwar protest.

Yet another problem with the conventional narrative is that it offers no compelling explanation for how and why America's uncivil wars occurred when they did and in the way that they did. Historical interpretation requires nothing less. Over the past two decades, historians have offered important studies of individual movements within the era. What remains less certain is the bigger picture—how consensus and social conformity gave way to conflict and rebellion along cultural and political fronts. At first, historians gravitated toward a generational theory. Most simply, they conflated the sixties with the coming of age of the baby boom generation. The popular sixties notion that "you can't trust anyone over thirty" gave that theory credence.

Historian Arthur Schlesinger, Jr., offered a more complex view of the generational dynamic. Drawing on the work of his father, a distinguished social historian, Schlesinger suggested that in alternating periods of about thirty years, or the length of a generation, the United States undergoes cycles of reform. Preoccupation with private interest gives way to a concern with public purpose, only to reverse again. Certainly, such a case could be made in the twentieth century, where progressivism gave way to the hedonism of the twenties, which in turn brought on the reformism of the New Deal, just as the conformist fifties and middle-of-the-road Republicanism preceded the New Frontier and the Great Society. Despite his conservative instincts, Richard Nixon found that "the liberal tide of the sixties, still running strong, shaped his early domestic legislation."

Several problems arise in using the generational theory to explain the activism of the 1960s. For one thing, it is largely political. Yet much that made the sixties so contentious was cultural or social in nature. Indeed, the broad scope of public confrontation led some sixties activists to coin the phrase "The personal is political." Historian Terry Anderson identified a second difficulty. Most of those who inspired the early civil rights, antiwar, countercultural, and identity activist movements were not, in fact, part of the baby boom generation. Elvis Presley, Martin Luther King, Jr., the Beatles, Bob Dylan, Joan Baez, John Lewis, Robert Moses, Ralph Nader, Ken Kesey, Timothy Leary, David Dellinger, William Sloane Coffin, Richard Viguerie, Cesar Chavez, Betty Friedan, Gloria Steinem, Abbie Hoffman, and Tom Hayden were among the shapers of the sixties born before or during World War II.

That list suggests an alternative way to explain the social and political uprising of the 1960s. With the exception of the Reverend Coffin, no one in that group would have been mentioned in a 1950s list of the nation's elite. Sydney Ahlstrom's description of the fracturing of the religious establishment provides another useful clue. In *America's Uncivil Wars*, I will argue that just as the church establishment fractured, so did the elite that in the 1950s framed the cold war consensus and arbitrated the nation's moral and cultural standards. That elite was almost exclusively white and male, Protestant, middle and upper middle class, and socially and culturally conservative. It controlled business organizations, media, churches, colleges and universities, and government at both the local and national level. If it had a symbolic leader, it was Dwight D. Eisenhower, but its most powerful figure was FBI director J. Edgar Hoover. The uncivil wars undermined that elite. By the time the wars ended, every person on the list above became a part of a new national leadership.

In a prescient book published in 1964, sociologist E. Digby Baltzell anticipated that transformation. A crisis had arisen, he argued, because of the unwillingness or inability of the WASP establishment "to share or improve its upper-class traditions by absorbing talented and distinguished members of minority groups into its privileged ranks." Had he been even more prescient he would have appended male to WASP, though his concept of minorities did not exclude women. Baltzell's "establishment," while easily recognizable, was not a precisely defined group. It was comprised prior to the turn of the twentieth century by patrician Protestants who held positions of political and institutional power and "set the style in arts and letters, in the universities, in sports, and in the more popular culture, which governs the values and aspirations of the masses."

Drawing on de Tocqueville's analysis of the decline of the Ancien régime in France, Baltzell observed that in the twentieth century, America's Protestant patricians had shifted their energy largely from the management of power and leadership to the protection of privilege. The Republican Party ceased to function as an agency of opportunity and reform. By the 1930s, it had lost its majority status and the authority to define the national agenda. That explains to some degree why the Liberty Leaguers and other conservatives of their ilk heaped such vituperation on Eleanor and Franklin Roosevelt. Rather than restoring the prestige of the WASP establishment, the New Deal opened the corridors of power and authority of Catholics, Jews, ethnics, and women.

Sociologist David Reisman argued that by the 1950s, the American social elite had ceased to lead. Power groups promoted their own interests rather than advancing a national agenda. "Veto groups exist as defense groups, not as leadership groups," Reisman observed. They built their defenses along the lines of prep schools, colleges, and, above all, private clubs. When in the 1950s the admissions office at elite colleges and universities relaxed the social qualifications for entrance, the fraternity and sorority systems served to reassert the patterns of social hierarchy and exclusivity. Max Weber noted forty years earlier, "Affiliation with a distinguished club was essential above all else. He who did not succeed in joining was no gentleman."

Over the course of time there came to be many successful Americans who, because of race, religion, gender, or ethnicity, were denied entrance into exclusive clubs. Baltzell used gentlemanly anti-Semitism to exemplify this growing tension of class and caste in American society. He in no way meant to suggest that Jews were the sole victims of discrimination. Rather, he used anti-Semitism to demonstrate the effort of WASP elites to preserve their privilege by making birthright, rather than talent, the key to position. By the 1950s, Jews had achieved success in almost all sectors of American life. But that success did not readily turn into social acceptance in elite circles. Most WASP institutions either barred Jews or restricted their access. Many of the patricians who voted for Barry Goldwater in 1964 would have denied him membership in their clubs because he had a Jewish ancestor. Thus what had begun as a meritocracy in the late nineteenth century had by the 1950s threatened to ossify into a caste system.

In the class society de Tocqueville commended and Baltzell analyzed, the aristocracy has several vital functions. It preserves traditions, which give society cohesion, and it arbitrates the issues of the day. If, however, the aristocracy ceases to represent the major elements of a society or if it becomes divided, it loses its ability to arbitrate. Or as Baltzell put it, "for an upper class to maintain a continuity of power and authority especially in an opportunarian and mobile society like ours, its membership must, in the long run, be representative of society as a whole." In the 1960s, I will argue, as did Baltzell, this was not the case. The elite was inadequately inclusive to address the aspirations of a more socially diverse population. Groups such as African Americans, Latinos, gays, political dissenters, and women, who demanded more rights, recognition, and opportunities, found the paths into the elite blocked.

Baltzell's choice of anti-Semitism to dramatize his point had particular resonance for the 1960s. A number of historians have commented on the unusual prominence of Jews in the civil rights, antiwar, and other radical movements. So, too, Jews had attained high visibility in the arts, media, and academia—the very centers that had come to arbitrate public tastes and values and which, not coincidentally, became the special targets of conservatives who saw the male WASP elite and the American way as synonymous. To many of those in authority, such as J. Edgar Hoover, an attack on one was an attack on the other. They associated dissent not with traditional American perfectionism or egalitarianism, but with Communism. In essence, they sought to preserve their power and authority not only through social institutions, but also under the ideological mantle of the cold war consensus. They frequently charged that those who would make America more pluralistic, egalitarian, and democratic were either dupes or agents of the Communists.

In order to explain the rise of dissent against the consensus and the culture of civility that reinforced it, I have reconsidered the time frames of the era. Those who lived through the sixties know they did not simply begin with the election of John F. Kennedy and end with the ringing in of the New Year on January 1, 1970. The period is better understood as a set of experiences that stretch over twenty years, beginning somewhere in the mid-1950s and drawing to a close in the mid-1970s. For that reason, *America's Uncivil Wars* divides the sixties into three phases: the era of consensus, from 1954 until the assassination of John F. Kennedy in November 1963; the years from 1964 to 1968, during which most of phenomena associated with the sixties emerged; and finally the era of essentialist politics, from 1969 until the fall of Richard Nixon in 1974.

The roots of America's uncivil wars lie in the first phase. It began around the mid-1950s, when Senator Joe McCarthy was hunting Reds, and the cold war consensus was at its peak. Established after World War II, the consensus defined the nation's mission to contain Communism at home and abroad. In this phase, rising wages brought an unprecedented prosperity, as the children of the baby boom generation passed into puberty and on to young adulthood. Historian Thomas Hine commented, "the decade from 1954 to 1964 was one of history's great shopping sprees," as Americans stocked up on all the accoutrements of a consumer culture.

Despite widespread prosperity, authorities feared that teenagers and their culture had become a threat to the consensus. They investigated comic books, rock and roll, and teen movies as potential sources of subversion. Another form of dissent emerged from intellectuals and cultural rebels such as the Beats. By the early 1960s, they had subjected the cold war consensus and social conformity to a penetrating critique. Pressure came from both the Left and the Right. In 1960, the Student Nonviolent Coordinating Committee (SNCC), Students for a Democratic Society (SDS), and Young Americans for Freedom (YAF) organized to crusade for a redefinition of American values.

The 1960 election reaffirmed the cold war consensus but also called it into question. While John Kennedy and Richard Nixon ran as ardent cold warriors, Kennedy pledged to move the United States vigorously in new directions. His appeal to youthful idealism highlighted by the creation of the Peace Corps unleashed the energies of social and political activists. At the same time, events inspired the rise of independent political movements. The Cuban missile crisis increased the determination of peace advocates to reduce the nuclear peril. Led by Martin Luther King, Jr., civil rights advocates forced the nation to confront the Jim Crow system of racial segregation. Although Kennedy at first resisted their appeals for federal support, he could not ignore repeated acts of violence against peaceful protestors. He did manage to turn the march on Washington into a demonstration of support for his administration's civil rights bill. All the same the day belonged to King, who shared with the nation his dream for an integrated future. The spirit of that dream died with John Kennedy in Dallas, bringing the United States toward the brink of its uncivil wars.

The period from Kennedy's death until the ascendancy of Richard Nixon marks the second phase of what is popularly thought of as the 1960s. The uncivil wars began during this phase. Preoccupation with the tumult of 1968 has caused many historians to discount 1964 as an equally transformative year. In 1964, America discovered the Beatles, and Bob Dylan established himself as the poet laureate of his generation. Lyndon Johnson steered his civil rights bill through Congress. But as the reforms of his Great Society rolled into high gear, Johnson escalated the war in Vietnam. From the Right, Barry Goldwater offered a trenchant criticism of the liberal consensus while challenging Johnson to escalate the war against Communism. The civil rights movement, having gained ground in the South with nonviolence, adopted a more confrontational style as it turned to the North and West. There, the entrenched patterns of de facto segregation and white resistance proved more formidable. Frustration turned increasingly to rage. In the summer of 1964, American cities began to burn as small, racially charged incidents exploded into outbreaks of rioting, arson, and looting.

On college campuses, the rising tide of dissent at first took an orderly course. Most common were the earnest gatherings of students at teach-ins to hear their professors debate the course of American involvement in Vietnam. The free speech movement at Berkeley that brought protesting students to surround police cars was a glaring exception. It was also a precursor of the confrontational style that would undermine the traditional practice of political civility. A more subtle form of protest coincided with the increasing militancy of antiwar and anti-apartheid movements. Among the baby boomers were those who inherited the sense of spiritual malaise that the Beats dramatized in the fifties. They began to heed the call of LSD guru Timothy Leary, who urged them to "tune in, turn on, and drop out." By the summer of 1967, Americans were fully engaged in their uncivil wars. They came to a head in 1968, a year marked by assassinations, rioting, and increasingly violent protest.

The Nixon era marked the third phase of the sixties. Richard Nixon came to office promising to bring the nation together. If anything, he divided it more deeply. Protest became more strident, government repression of dissent more determined, and demands for social justice more insistent. A host of movements pressed for equality along gender, sexual, racial, and ethnic lines. Latinos and Native Americans asserted their right to an equal place within the national community. Consumer advocates armed ordinary citizens with new means to promote their safety and protect their rights. Environmentalists organized the largest mass protest in the nation's history. As the Vietnam War dragged on, increased violence and especially the killing of students at Kent State in Ohio and Jackson State in Mississippi introduced a sobriety alien to the dionysian spirit of the earlier phases of the sixties. Widespread prosecution of dissenters pitted their meager financial and legal resources against the machinery of a government that did not have to win conviction to stifle its opposition.

Sometime in the early seventies the uncivil wars ended. That is not to say that protest stopped completely, that rioting ended, that all hippies deserted their communes, that hair became short and skirts long, or that all dreams of a better society ended. A number of vital reform groups—environmentalists, Native Americans, feminists, consumer advocates, gay rights activists, the New Right—continued to press their causes. But in 1973, the last American troops left Vietnam, and, after Richard Nixon resigned, the country no longer seemed so polarized. Facing a declining economy, those leaving college once again made career choices rather than lifestyle decisions. Most adults no longer found sex, drugs, and rock and roll so shocking, since they had become the fashion of the times.

Historians understand that power never changes hands without resistance. That was certainly true during the sixties era. Activists demanded nothing less than that those in authority live up to the nation's highest ideals or cede power to those who would. They had the support of many people whose position among the nation's elite made them influential. Opposing them were others from that elite who remained committed to the consensus culture they established in the 1950s. No one better personified the old consensus than Richard Nixon. After all, he had used it to build his career. With his downfall, a measure of civility returned to the public arena.

America's uncivil wars left much unresolved and battles yet to be fought. They left scars that would be long in healing, but they also led to the rise of a new, more inclusive elite, better able to "set the style in arts and letters, in the universities, in sports, and in the more popular culture, which governs the values and aspirations of the masses."

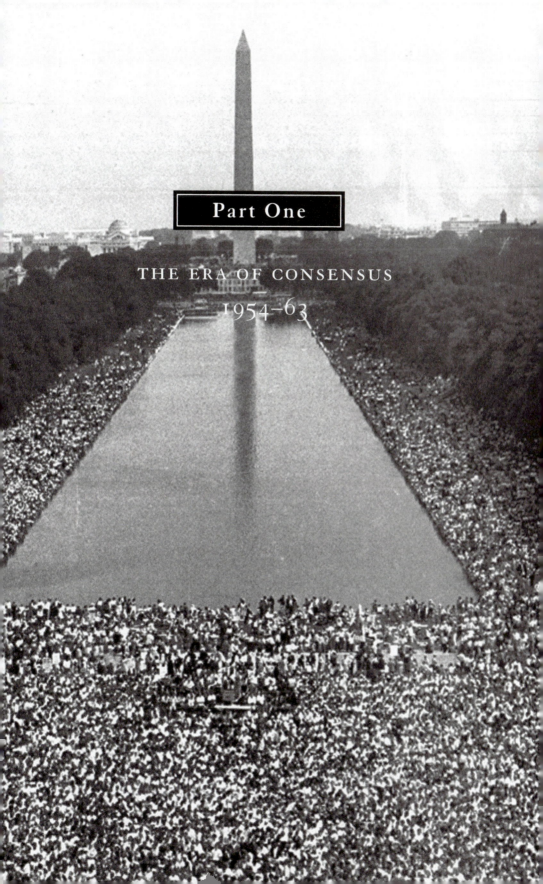

Part One

THE ERA OF CONSENSUS

1954–63

I

The Consensus

In the 1950s, many schools worried more about producing good citizens than able learners. Classroom lessons emphasized that proper manners were as important as grades and that popularity mattered more than classroom performance. Public speaking programs showed how to project a positive personality. Banking day instilled the virtue of thrift. And students learned that a good citizen was also a safe one. Fire drills assured an orderly exit in an emergency. Then there were the air raid drills, an occasional reminder that the nation stood on the brink of Armageddon. Teachers warned that far away in Russia, evil leaders plotted to attack America with nuclear weapons. During the drills students learned to "duck and cover," mindful to stay clear of windows and doors to avoid flying glass after an explosion. To all but the most innocent children, the advice seemed quaint. They had heard enough about atomic bombs to know that if the big one dropped, broken glass would be the least of their worries.

Back in the classroom, the morning might begin with seatwork—a brief assignment to quiet the class or to allow the teachers another moment to plan the day and finish a cup of coffee. Finally all the students would rise together to pledge the flag: "I pledge allegiance to the flag of the United States of America and to the republic for which it stands, one nation, indivisible, with liberty and justice for all." It was a patriotic ritual learned by rote and intended to inspire both patriotism and loyalty. For many cold war crusaders, it was not enough. At a Washington church service in 1954, Rev. George Docherty told the congregation that the pledge lacked a vital element. It failed to address "the characteristic and definitive factor in the American way of life." Where the Communists were atheists, Americans cherished their religious freedom. But, as Docherty explained, "the pledge as now written could just as easily be recited by little Soviet children to—"their hammer and sickle flag." To rectify that shortcoming, the rector proposed adding the phrase "under God." His plea had a special importance, for among those in his congregation that morning were President Dwight D. Eisenhower and his wife, Mamie.

Docherty was not the first to avow the central place of the deity in America's cold war crusade. Other patriotic and religious groups had made the same pitch for the same phrase. They owed their inspiration to Abraham Lincoln, who at Gettysburg had said, "this nation, under God, shall have a new birth of freedom." During the cold war, Americans had developed a consensus that gave the phrase a meaning Lincoln never intended. According to President Eisenhower, the phrase "under God" would serve the United States as another of "those spiritual weapons" in the battle against Communism, whose "materialistic philosophy of life" had deadened millions "in mind and soul." Congress embraced the pledge modification. Congressman Overton Brooks of Louisiana identified belief in God as separating a "free people of the Western World from the rabid Communists." Representative Louis Rabaut, who sponsored the pledge amendment, asserted, "the Soviet Union would not, and could not, . . . place in its patriotic ritual an acknowledgement that their nation exists 'under God.'" And to nail the divine coonskin to the wall, Congress added a requirement that rather than "E Pluribus Unum," all U.S. currency would bear the motto "In God We Trust." In that way, faith in God joined the A-bomb on the frontline of the nation's defenses.

The phrase "under God" was an essential ingredient in the cold war consensus that by the mid-1950s had become an American orthodoxy. Never again would the nation be so clearly united in its determination to contain the Communist menace at home and abroad. At the heart of the consensus was the belief shared by liberals and conservatives alike that America had a mission to fight the international Communist menace. The job of planning that mission fell to the National Security Council (NSC). The Truman administration had established the NSC in an effort to coordinate policies of the various defense and intelligence agencies charged with keeping the nation safe. By 1948, the NSC had begun to weave the various strands of containment policy into a coherent program. It is worth considering more closely the NSC's assumptions, for they largely define central tenets of the cold war consensus.

These assumptions appeared in a series of "top secret" reports that culminated with NSC-68. NSC-68 introduced a series of recommendations that would shape American domestic and foreign policy until the cold war ended in the late 1980s. The policies the NSC recommended included a curious blend of positives and negatives. In some ways it served to identify the enemy and the steps needed to contain it. The United States should vastly increase military spending and increase surveillance on potential enemies at home and abroad. In other ways, the NSC identified those positive values it loosely construed as "the American Way of Life."

The cold war consensus had at its core an assertion that was as self-evident to most Americans as any they have ever held: "The ultimate objective of Soviet-directed world Communism is the domination of the world." Given that assumption, Americans had concluded that wherever Communism existed, it was controlled from Moscow and hence constituted a monolith. Further, Moscow had an ambition to take over the world. Did it have the means to do so? The NSC argued that the Communists had a plan that involved "aggressive pressure from without and militant subversion from within." The result of Moscow's march to conquest was a cold war "in which our national security is at stake and from which we cannot withdraw short of eventual national suicide."

In explaining the sources of Communist behavior, the NSC used a curious blend of psychological and demonic metaphors. The Satanic forces of Communism were "something new in history," one NSC analysis argued. Operating through fifth columnists, the Communists set about "frustrating foreign policy, dividing and confusing the people of a country, planting the seeds of disruption in time of war, and subverting the freedom of democratic states." Like Satan, the Communists were often difficult to identify, for they operated "under a multitude of disguises." Against such an enemy, the democracy that made us strong also made us weak by opening our society to those who would undermine it. "The democracies have been deterred in effectively meeting this threat," the NSC observed, "in part because communism has been allowed to operate under the protection of civil liberties." Domestic Communists had "the ability to exploit the margin of tolerance accorded the communists and their dupes in democratic countries by virtue of reluctance of such countries to restrict democratic freedoms merely in order to inhibit the activities of a single faction and by the failure of those countries to expose the fallacies and evils of communism."

NSC strategists had a plan to fight that evil. The United States would restore its military strength and mobilize the non-Soviet world to join its crusade. Ever so briefly, the NSC recognized, this call to arms created the possibility that to fight Communism more effectively, the United States would have to become more like its enemy. With a "vast armed camp within its borders," the United States could easily develop "rigid economies, regimentation, and a fear psychosis [that] might easily promote the very conditions in the United States that we are trying to eliminate in the world." For that possibility the NSC had no answer. It merely went on to describe the means it proposed to win the cold war at home and abroad. These included a peacetime draft, the reconstitution of the wartime military-industrial complex, acceleration of the nuclear arms race (development of the hydrogen bomb), further legal steps to suppress Communism, and a "domestic information program, designed to insure public understanding and non-partisan support of our foreign policy." Propaganda would ensure right thinking. The ends, if not the means, of foreign policy would no longer be a proper subject for public debate. In short, the NSC never seemed to appreciate the irony that it proposed using the instruments of a totalitarian state to preserve American freedoms.

In fighting Communism abroad, the NSC believed the battle in Europe must have top priority. That seemingly reasonable assumption proved to be a fault line along which Americans split into rival camps. The two major hot wars, Korea and Vietnam, were both fought in Asia. And among the staunchest of America's cold warriors were those conservative Republicans like *Time* magazine publisher Henry Luce who gathered behind World War II hero General Douglas MacArthur to press for an Asia-first policy. In the late 1940s, however, the NSC anticipated no such disagreement. Its foreign policy recommendations covered programs that became the mainstays of America's containment policy: the Truman Doctrine, the Marshall Plan, NATO, and military assistance to non-Communist nations. In addition, the United States would look to export whatever programs it developed for "suppressing the domestic communist menace." The NSC even wanted to enlist private American citizens in an attempt to foster non-Communist trade union movements, to the extent of rewarding their efforts with income tax deductions. Here too propaganda would promote American goals, and once again the imperatives of the cold war made partisan debate undesirable.

The domestic side of the consensus blended "family values," anti-Communism, and what President Eisenhower called modern Republicanism. Eisenhower sought to capture the consensual middle and thereby shun ideologues of either the Left or the Right. Or, as he put it, he was "conservative when it comes to money and liberal when it comes to human beings." For that reason, Eisenhower resisted pressure from conservatives to dismantle New Deal Programs like Social Security or to destroy organized labor. In his jumbled style of "Ike speak," he acknowledged, instead, the responsibility of the federal government to see "that the productivity of our great economic machine is distributed so that no one will suffer disaster, privation, through no fault of his own."

Like most business leaders, Eisenhower believed the nation owed its blessings to the free enterprise system. That system worked best when the government practiced fiscal restraint and preserved a sound dollar. Whenever possible, he hoped to put the nation's problems "in the hands of localities and the private enterprise of states." Decentralized authority in Eisenhower's view freed the people from the oppressive hand of centralized government favored by Socialists. Yet such sentiments echoed the state's rights philosophy of social conservatives who supported racial segregation. Eisenhower remained largely silent on the fractious issue of civil rights. The Supreme Court in the *Hernandez* and *Brown* decisions of 1954 had begun to dismantle the Jim Crow system. The Montgomery bus boycott led by Martin Luther King, Jr., indicated the growing impatience of the nation's African-American and Latino minorities with the government's indifference to their demands for greater equality. Eisenhower saw civil rights as a state not a federal matter. He had expressed his reluctance to involve the federal government in the effort to end segregation when he explained his belief that "you cannot change people's hearts merely by laws." Only with reluctance had he sent federal troops into Little Rock, Arkansas, in 1957 when Governor Orval Faubus defied a federal court ordered to integrate previously all-white Central High School. While Eisenhower's reticence may have offended civil rights leaders, it reflected the mainstream American view on race relations. The great white majority favored racial justice but was not yet willing to have federal authorities force it upon their southern neighbors.

Segregationists frequently charged that Communist agents were behind the new racial activism. That was the conviction shared by the great Red-hunter J. Edgar Hoover, for whom racial integration was only slightly less menacing than Communism. During the 1950s, no person commanded more widespread public respect (and private fear) than J. Edgar Hoover. Few people sensed the demons that haunted the czar of the FBI. One historian described his office on Pennsylvania Avenue in Washington as "the headquarters of the domestic cold war." From that position, Hoover helped promote a level of intolerance not seen since World War I. The Bill of Rights suffered extraordinary abuse. At home, the United States established an array of political, legal, and cultural institutions to fight Communism without regard for the rights of the accused. High-profile groups like The House Committee on UnAmerican Activities (HUAC) grilled an array of major and minor celebrities. Loyalty review boards at the local, state, and federal levels investigated government employees. Seldom did the investigators discover a Communist, much less a legitimate threat to national security. More often than not those dismissed from their jobs had committed the sins of human weakness, not political disloyalty. Alcoholism, sexual infidelity, gambling, and bad debts exposed people to dismissal. Homosexuals became a special target for investigators, based on the assumption that they were vulnerable to seduction and blackmail by deviant Communist agents. Indeed, some anti-Communist crusaders were so preoccupied with sexual orientation that prurience rather than political purity seemed their primary concern.

Hoover insisted that winning the cold war required more than stamping out Communism. His propaganda mill churned out endless platitudes about the sanctity of moral character, family, patriotism, and respect for God. To join the FBI, Hoover wrote in the introduction to a Landmark Book about the FBI, a young man did not need brains so long as he "respects his parents, reveres God, honors his flag and loves his country." Given Hoover's prejudices, that young man also had to be a white male, preferably an Irish Catholic or southern Protestant. In his 1958 best-seller *The Masters of Deceit*, Hoover reiterated his principles of consensus. He condemned Communism as "a false, materialistic, 'religion'" that undermined for an individual "his belief in God, his heritage of freedom, his trust in love, justice and mercy." For Hoover, as for so many Americans of the 1950s, religious faith stood as the key to the American way of life. "The truly revolutionary force of history," he assured his readers, "is not material power but the spirit of religion." Popular culture reinforced that sermon. Each Friday at the close of the *Howdy Doody Show*, Buffalo Bob Smith reinforced the importance of religion in America. He told all young baby boomers in the television audience "to attend the church or synagogue of your choice."

In that spirit, my own experience is somewhat revealing. I came of age as a child of the cold war. Movies, radio, and television taught my generation the virtues of America and the dangers of Communism. We learned that Communists wanted to steal our land, that masturbating would make us blind, that one puff of marijuana could make us drug addicts, and that if we worked hard, respected our parents, and attended school regularly, we would succeed. Commercial breaks reminded us that benevolent corporations like General Electric were promoting the progress that made America great.

But we also learned how to spot potential Communists. In that endeavor, the TV series *I Led Three Lives* was especially instructive. This series, which ran from 1953 to 1956, told the story of Herb Philbrick, a respected businessman (life 1) who secretly belonged to the Communist Party (life 2), and, even more secretly (life 3), was an agent for the FBI. From Herb's experiences we learned the sneaky ways Communists practiced subversion. They operated in tight cells and regularly

I Led 3 Lives *taught a generation of American television viewers how to recognize the evil ways of Communist subversives. F.B.I. Director J. Edgar Hoover encouraged such anti-Communist propaganda.* (Source: Wisconsin Center for Theater Research)

transferred their leaders to avoid detection. Most wore heavy glasses and seemed vaguely ethnic—a cross between intellectuals and gangsters. What we never learned and what patriotic zealots never could explain is why they feared Americans would find such people and their ideas appealing.

One day I Led Three Lives opened my eyes to a potential conspiracy right in my own family. It seems my mother and grandmother were both members of a group that to my childish mind was mysterious at best. Each month they attended sessions of "Great Books." Worse yet, my grandmother was a group discussion leader. Several times she had transferred to a new group. Now, anyone familiar with Great Books knows it catered largely to college-educated women who discovered that full-time mothering left their brains largely unengaged. My grandmother was also somewhat unusual for women of her generation. She had gone to college, and after her husband died she earned a graduate degree so she could start a career. The pain of her husband's early death had also destroyed her faith in God. My grandmother was an atheist. Under the spell of Hoover and Herb Philbrick, I, of course, saw something far more sinister. Great Books, I concluded, was really the front for

Communist cells. And since all Communists were atheists, was it not likely the case that all atheists were Communists? As a youngster of the cold war, I was ready to do my patriotic bit. Had the FBI come to my door, I would have felt it my duty to report my mother and grandmother as Communist agents.

Such distortions would ultimately undermine for many young Americans the credibility of the cold war consensus. But the process by which I, and many others, began to question the platitudes and certitudes of that public creed was a long and uncertain one. No single person, event, or idea suddenly turned our heads. Rather, along a number of major fault lines the consensus began to crack. By the mid-1950s, the sharpest dissent came ironically from the political Right, not the Left. Most liberals accepted anti-Communism as a worthy cause, though they objected to the domestic excesses such as loyalty oaths, witch hunts, and threats to civil liberties. Liberals challenged modern Republicanism mostly because they found it insipid and preferred more dynamic presidential leadership, a revival of New Deal–style federal activism, and greater commitment to civil rights.

Traditional conservatives, by contrast, argued that liberalism threatened the values of Western civilization by "the strengthening of the state and the diminution of the person." Those on the Right had profound objections to liberal programs like the New Deal. They chafed at Eisenhower's pragmatic modern Republicanism because it accepted much of the New Deal legacy. In 1955 they found a powerful new voice when William F. Buckley, Jr., began publishing *The National Review.* Buckley and *The National Review* editors sought to vitalize a "New Right." They believed that for too long liberals had used the state to promote policies for human perfectibility. Religious faith, not reason; adherence to tradition, not progress, paved the road to a good society. Thus, principle rather than pragmatism would define the political agenda of the New Right. "It has been the dominating ambition of Eisenhower's Modern Republicanism to govern in such a fashion as to more or less please everybody," Buckley wrote. "Such government must shrink from principle: because principles have edges, principles cut, and blood is drawn, and people get hurt. And who would want to hurt anyone in an age of modulation?" In some ways, conservative values anticipated the agendas of the New Left and counterculture in the 1960s. Conservatives rejected the vapid materialism of the present age in favor of "the spiritual essence of human existence." In short, they quested for authenticity steeped in tradition.

On one issue *The National Review* came down off its lofty perch into the realm of politics. Buckley charged that liberals and modern Republicans lacked sufficient commitment to fight Communism effectively. The nation sorely needed, in his view, a more muscular brand of anti-Communism. In Senator Joseph McCarthy of Wisconsin, Buckley found his caped crusader. Only too late would conservatives realize that McCarthy was a blunt instrument whose antics would cause them considerable political embarrassment. The junior senator from Wisconsin in fact had few organized political ideas or deeply held beliefs. At some level he probably did oppose Communism in so far as he understood it. But he seized anti-Communism as an issue that would thrust him into the public spotlight, not from the kind of principled position that inspired Buckley. What made McCarthy so effective was his combination of outrageous political behavior and the support of powerful conservatives like Buckley, Senate Republican leader Robert Taft, and J. Edgar Hoover. Though it was not publicly known at the time, Hoover and the FBI supplied McCarthy with much of the material he used to sustain his crusade.

With conservative support, McCarthy operated for four years with near impunity. He destroyed innocent lives, ruined careers, silenced political foes, and even intimidated members of his own party. His perfection of the "multiple untruth" kept the news media from seriously analyzing the content of his endless stream of accusations and innuendoes. Political analyst Richard Rovere, who coined the term, pointed out that the multiple untruth avoided the need for a big lie, which might be exposed as false. Instead, as Rovere recognized of McCarthy's distortions, they could be "a long series of loosely related untruths, or a single untruth with many facets." Anyone seeking to correct McCarthy faced the problem that "the whole is composed of so many parts that . . . it is utterly impossible to keep all the elements of the falsehood in mind at one time." And whenever a critic had the temerity to raise questions, McCarthy branded him the dupe of the Communist conspiracy.

Drunk on power, publicity, and notoriety, McCarthy began to attack basic institutions and ideas upon which the consensus rested. He charged that Communists had infiltrated the nation's churches, the hydrogen bomb program, the CIA, and other centers of authority. He even accused members of his own party. That made him a growing source of discomfort to President Eisenhower. But reluctant to risk splitting the GOP between its moderates and the conservatives who applauded McCarthy's crusade, the president remained publicly silent. In March 1954, the news media finally fired a timid shot in McCarthy's direction. Edward R. Murrow, a respected CBS news commentator, decided to make McCarthy the subject of his widely viewed television program *see It Now*. Murrow made no direct attack on McCarthy. Rather, through judicious use of news clips, he let McCarthy expose his own excesses: blustering, contradicting himself, and scowling more like a hoodlum than a senator. In his program summary Murrow took a rather Olympian tone. The senator, he implied, had struck a blow against civil liberties. "We cannot defend freedom abroad by deserting it home. The actions of the junior Senator from Wisconsin have caused alarm and dismay among our allies abroad and given considerable comfort to our enemies, and whose fault is that," Murrow wondered. "Not really his. He didn't create the situation of fear; he merely exploited it, and rather successfully."

Curiously, the program probably damaged Murrow more than McCarthy. Conservatives sponsored a program that gave McCarthy a chance to reply. The senator in his typical fashion denounced Murrow as "a symbol, the leader and cleverest jackal of the pack which is always found at the throat of anyone who dares expose individual communists and traitors." An opinion poll suggested that one-third of those who saw McCarthy's rebuttal believed he had either raised questions about Murrow or proven him pro-Communist. Within a year, Alcoa, Murrow's sponsor, quietly withdrew from the show and CBS reduced Murrow's airtime.

An emboldened McCarthy moved on with his most audacious attack so far, an attack on the United States Army. In doing so, he seemed to have forgotten that Dwight D. Eisenhower, the president and leader of his party, had devoted his life to that army. For McCarthy, the army was but one more target for his ever more outrageous political show. The incident that ultimately destroyed McCarthy and did much to discredit McCarthyism arose from rather trivial circumstances. It involved Irving Peress, a New York City dentist drafted into military service. Peress had entered the medical corps as a captain and in due course been promoted to major. He had also at one time been the member of the liberal, but not Communist, American Labor Party and had invoked the Fifth Amendment rather than answer a question about membership in organizations listed on the attorney general's subversive list. After that modest act of defiance came to light, Peress's commander at Fort Monmouth, New Jersey, General Ralph Zwicker, turned his name over to McCarthy's Government Operations Subcommittee. McCarthy's young assistant, the smarmy and pugnacious Roy Cohn, decided to make Peress an example, not of a subversive, but of the army's porous defense against subversion. When the army resisted some of McCarthy's demands for information, the senator became outraged at Zwicker, and the tension between the army and the committee mounted.

At that time another McCarthy aide, G. David Schine, received his draft notice. Schine would prove to be no ordinary draftee. His family owned one of the nation's largest theater chains. Before the army called him, he lived a playboy's life under the bright lights of New York, where he maintained a private suite in one of the city's poshest hotels. Such wealth seduced many with whom Schine readily shared it, especially Roy Cohn. Cohn cultivated the friendship, while the debonair Schine brought his somewhat reclusive pal into the social whirl. The friendship also had an aspect that would much influence the anti-Communist crusade. "[David] and Roy became such fast friends and neither one thought the rules applied to them," Roy's Aunt Libby observed. "[The rules] were for the other man."

By 1954, Cohn, Schine, and McCarthy faced a more serious problem. The committee had run out of promising cases to investigate. That is what led them to Fort Monmouth and the infamous question, "Who promoted Major Peress?" As that investigation stumbled forward, Schine received his draft notice. To Roy, it was a matter that required simple fixing. If Schine could not be excused from service altogether, then the army could put him on special assignment to New York City. When Cohn's arm-twisting failed, he repeatedly berated senior army department officials for not living up to the "agreement" he believed had been struck. But as in the cases of other celebrities, the army refused to favor Schine out of fear of exposing the inequities of the Selective Service system. McCarthy did not share Cohn's fixation with Schine or his service obligation. He at one time told an official, "send him wherever you can, as far away as possible. . . . Korea is too close. But don't tell Roy."

Perhaps, McCarthy sensed that Schine had become his Achilles' heal. The senator's own erratic behavior—excessive drinking and possibly drug abuse—made him more dependent on Cohn. And Cohn, unhappy about the army's refusal to do his bidding with Schine, pressed ahead with his investigation of Peress and Fort Monmouth. It soon became clear that the committee had precious little of a case. Peress had been honorably discharged before the rumors came to light. And Cohn continued his efforts to intimidate army officials to give Schine special treatment. The Eisenhower administration finally decided Cohn and McCarthy had gone too far.

When the Senate Judiciary Committee held hearings on April 22, 1954, on the battle between McCarthy and the army, ABC decided to televise them. It was not that the network was especially courageous or public spirited. ABC lacked adequate daytime programming to compete with CBS and NBC. The army-McCarthy hearings had special appeal because they cost so little to put on the air. And to the amazement of all three networks, over four weeks the hearings attracted a large and devoted following. What the public saw was part spectacle, part disgrace, and part political suicide. To present its case, the army had hired Boston attorney Joseph Welch. Behind his folksy, grandfatherly manner, Welch was a shrewd trial lawyer with an understated flair for the dramatic.

McCarthy never stood a chance. Given his sloppy methods, his baseless charges, and his bullying manner, he exposed himself as a mean-spirited slob. Cohn was by turns evasive and obsequious. Whatever public favor the two had accumulated through uncritical newspaper accounts of their anti-Communist witch-hunts dissolved before the unblinking TV eye. McCarthy was intermittently long-winded, rambling, obnoxious, belligerent, but mostly boring. Nor did his foes on the Judiciary Committee and among the army brass cover themselves with glory.

Only the army's lawyer, Joseph Welch, distinguished himself. He sat for much of the hearings slouched in a posture that suggested a mixture of boredom and bemused skepticism. But on several occasions he came alive to ensnare McCarthy and Cohn in traps they set for themselves. McCarthy had long asserted his right to receive information of any kind from any source. That often included top-secret government files. When challenged about the legality of his files, McCarthy claimed immunity from rules of evidence and investigation because his anti-Communist crusade served a higher national good. In fact, McCarthy and Cohn seldom based their accusations on actual evidence and never uncovered a single real Communist. Welch had a field day making just that point at Cohn's expense. With Cohn on the witness stand, Welch pressed him to give actual numbers of Communists in defense plants. A clearly uneasy Cohn finally claimed 130 in sixteen plants. In mock alarm, Welch then asked Cohn if he would not "before the sun goes down give those names to the FBI and at least have those men put under surveillance?"

Welch now truly had Cohn cornered. He knew something Cohn could not admit publicly: the FBI and not the committee was the source of that information. Senator

The Army-McCarthy hearings provided ABC with a surprisingly successful daytime soap opera. Army counsel Joseph Welch proved so effective he was given a major role in the movie Anatomy of a Murder. (Source: Associated Press)

McCarthy leapt to Cohn's defense. The FBI had access to all his committee files, he assured Welch. "Then they have got the one hundred thirty, have they Mr. Cohn?" Welch asked. When Cohn assured him Hoover did, Welch replied, "Then what is all the excitement about if J. Edgar Hoover is on the job chasing these one hundred thirty communists?" What more could Cohn say? To imply in any way that J. Edgar Hoover had not taken adequate steps to meet this danger might outrage the nation's most vindictive bureaucrat. And in that way Welch laid bare to those who cared to notice the emptiness of McCarthy's claim that he was the frontline of the nation's defense against Communism.

Further, Welch found a way to expose another of McCarthy's more outrageous tactics—his constant implication that homosexuality was linked to Communists in government. McCarthy referred regularly to the "lavendered boys" in the State Department with their "perfumed" notes. On this account Cohn was himself vulnerable, and his relationship with Schine had been the subject of considerable snide commentary. At one point in the hearings, Cohn produced a photograph that showed Army Secretary Robert Stevens smiling at Private Schine. What the picture did not show was the presence of Colonel Kenneth Bradley, the base commander who was the object of Stevens's friendly smile. Cohn had an assistant crop the picture to remove Bradley to make it appear that Stevens and Schine were friends. If that was the case, then the secretary needed no pressure to help Schine.

This evidence of tampering gave proof positive that McCarthy and Cohn had been doctoring evidence. Now McCarthy compounded his misfortunes. When one

McCarthy aide denied any knowledge of where the doctored picture came from, an incredulous Welch wondered for him, "Did you think it came from a pixie?" McCarthy interrupted in his own snide way to ask if Welch "might for my benefit define—I think he might be an expert on that—what a pixie is?" With his eyes fixed on Cohn, Welch retorted, "Yes, I should say Mr. Senator, that a pixie is a close relative of a fairy. Shall I proceed? Have I enlightened you?" Even if much of the audience missed the import of Welch's imputation of Cohn's homosexuality, neither McCarthy nor Cohn did.

McCarthy's political death was not immediate, and McCarthyism took longer to fade. Even after the Senate condemned McCarthy for his financial irregularities and abuse of other senators, the public continued to believe that domestic Communism remained a threat. J. Edgar Hoover continued on the job. Still, the witch-hunters would never again command such wide and uncritical public acceptance. In supporting McCarthy, they had inflicted on themselves a serious blow. The public began to distinguish between responsible anti-Communism and the politics of paranoia of the far Right.

The existence of groups like the John Birch Society compounded the conservatives' problem. The society became best known for its outrageous conspiracy theories impugning the loyalty of public officials of both parties. When Robert Welch, Jr., formally launched the society in 1958, it represented the most extreme expression of McCarthyism. The society derived its name from an army officer and Baptist missionary killed by the Chinese Communists after World War II. Welch proudly proclaimed, "Our enemy is the Communist—nobody else." At the height of his Red-baiting, McCarthy had drawn a line from Alger Hiss to general of the army George Marshall, the leader of America's armed forces during World War II and former secretary of state for Harry Truman. If Hiss had been a Soviet agent, McCarthy reasoned, why couldn't one assume that General Marshall had been part of that conspiracy? Welch went a step further. He charged that Dwight D. Eisenhower, the man Marshall had promoted to lead American forces in Europe, was "a dedicated, conscious agent of the Communist conspiracy." Worse yet, Eisenhower had adopted many of the ideas of his brother Milton, the president of Johns Hopkins University. "The chances are very strong," Welch surmised, "that Milton Eisenhower is actually Dwight Eisenhower's superior and boss within the Communist Party." Welch went so far as to suggest that the Kremlin leaders were wearing "I Like Ike" buttons.

Welch and his conspiracy theories were an embarrassment to leading conservative intellectuals. A billboard outside Dallas, Texas, calling for the impeachment of chief justice of the Supreme Court Earl Warren helped popularize an image of the conservative Right as extremists and political deviants. In such ways the excesses of witch-hunting etched themselves into the minds of the nation's youngsters. If a hero like McCarthy proved to be a bum and if what we learned about the Communist menace was warped, who or what could we trust? What about the danger of drugs? About sex? About religion? About the American way of life?

The army-McCarthy hearings forced many Americans to recognize the excesses of the anti-Communist crusade. This witch-hunt had been as much or more a reflection of political partisanship and self-promotion as of any effort to protect the national interest. By no calculation could the record of McCarthy and his kindred witch-hunters compensate for their abuses of civil liberties. In the years that followed, ever-fewer thoughtful people could still believe that the war on domestic Communism had been worth the price. McCarthyism had eroded the willingness of many young Americans to enlist in the domestic cold war. By the late 1950s, the cold war consensus began to face challenges from the Left as well as the Right. Sporadic demonstrations broke out against atom bomb tests and the threat of nuclear war. More shocking yet, protestors began to heckle HUAC when it took its inquisition on the road to major cities. Civil rights activists protested that the American way of life was a segregated one. The Beats rebelled against the spiritual bankruptcy of a nation dedicated to materialism. If ever so subtly, the times, they were a changin.'

2

The Cultural Cold War

Communism was not the only menace vexing the defenders of the cold war consensus in the 1950s. The popular culture of teenaged America aroused much anxiety. The self-appointed custodians of culture took steps to suppress behaviors that they found at best unappealing and at worst subversive. Writing in the late 1950s, sociologist Edgar Friedenberg commented that "the 'teen-ager' seems to have replaced the Communist as the appropriate target for public controversy and foreboding." Indeed, no less a personage than J. Edgar Hoover ranked what he called the "juvenile jungle" as a threat to American freedom every bit as grave as Communism. An article in *Cosmopolitan* asked, "Are Teens Taking over?" and, tongue in cheek, referred to them as "a vast, determined band of blue-jeaned storm troopers, forcing us to do exactly as they dictate." During the 1950s, the custodians of culture launched a sustained attack on those media—advertising, comic books, popular music, and television—that both catered to and popularized teen culture. In that way they sought to suppress what for them represented a threat to the American way of life. In their crusade they had not reckoned on the vitality of that culture or its appeal to mainstream America.

In a sense this public outcry was nothing new. Popular culture had long been a battleground between generations or between traditionalists and rebels. Nor was teen culture a discovery of the 1950s. Traditionalists in the 1920s had railed against the flaming youth whose outrageous styles, casual sexuality, and cosmopolitan ways offended their morality. That reaction mixed fascination and anxiety. According to one observer, parents, teachers, and other concerned adults found teenage mores as strange as "the social customs of Mars." Teens in the 1920s most commonly developed their distinctive style in the nation's high schools. As sociologists Helen and Robert Lynd observed in *Middletown*: "The high school with its athletics, clubs, sororities and fraternities, dances and parties, and other 'extra curricular' activities is a fairly complete social cosmos in itself, and about this city within a city the social life of the intermediate generation centers." In the 1950s, the teen years became a more distinctive phase than in previous eras. Those entering adolescence moved into a group that defined itself quite apart from adults and society as a whole. Social distance created tensions between teens and the family, thus posing a particular problem during an era in which the media reinforced the ideal of the family as the primary agency of social control. The family in question was most often portrayed as hierarchical, with two parents firmly in charge of their children, whatever their ages. Traditionalists reacted most strongly against styles of behavior teens adopted to mark their separation or independence.

∾

Most critical to the rise of a distinctive teen culture were sheer numbers. The return of prosperity during World War II triggered an increased birthrate. The number of children between the ages of five and nine increased by 24 percent between 1940 and 1950. And as the war babies entered adolescence by the mid-1950s, their numbers turned their fads and fancies into national concerns. The high school continued to serve as an incubator for a teen culture. The majority of American teenagers attended comprehensive high schools, which adults saw as a place to teach social and cultural values. Themes of patriotism, team play, and community responsibility dominated extramural activities.

Adults, whether parents, teachers, or community leaders, never fully controlled the high schools or the subculture they nourished. Teens appropriated schools as an oasis surrounded by adult institutions and demands. Here teens sampled new fads and fancies generated by the media or invented styles of their own. This separation between adult and teenage domains generated considerable tension. Adults were most disturbed by the social class values of teen culture. In their clothing styles, heroes, and entertainments, teens behaved in ways many adults viewed as lower class. One report on youth behavior warned of the danger "that the standards of the lowest class can through children reach some of the boys and girls of other social groups." Or as another anxious commentator said of the Elvis phenomenon, "His striptease antics threaten to 'rock 'n' roll' the juvenile world into open revolt against society. The gangster of tomorrow is the Elvis Presley type of today."

This association of class conflict and juvenile delinquency was at the center of the controversial 1953 movie *The Wild One*. The movie was based loosely on an actual incident in which a motorcycle gang terrorized a small California town. Over time, the movie became a cult classic. Its star, Marlon Brando, became one of the major teen icons of the era, and the dress and language of the bikers heavily influenced teen styles. The producers claimed to have made the movie to arouse public concern with delinquency. "This is a shocking story," a scroll title warns. "It could never happen in most American towns—but it did in this one. It is a public challenge not to let it happen again." And with that, Marlon Brando and his leather-clad bikers roar into view. Despite the menace of his gang and their rivals, led by a psychopathic Lee Marvin, the movie suggests simplistically that these alienated rebels sought only a little love, understanding, and freedom from hassles. When a townie asks gang leader Brando what he's rebelling against, he shoots back, "Whad'a ya got?" Yet he also has moments of caring and shows hints of tenderness, suggesting that youthful rebellion was neither as deep nor as dangerous as some adults feared.

Just as alienation defined the bikers in *The Wild One*, it was a central theme in another influential film of the era, *Rebel without a Cause*. The movie models all three factors that promoted a distinctive and threatening teen culture: mobility, affluence, and numbers. But where the rebels in *The Wild One* are lower class, the delinquents in *Rebel* are middle-class teens adopting lower-class styles. The movie's star, James

Dean, would become every bit as much a teen icon as Brando. Dean plays the troubled son of a dysfunctional family. Each time Jimbo's antisocial behavior creates an embarrassment, the family moves. In the opening scene, he lies stupefyingly drunk in a local police station until his well-heeled parents arrive to take him home. Affluence and mobility offer this teen no shield from youthful angst. A less-affluent teen, the movie suggests, would become another police blotter statistic. Though Jimbo has all the requisites for social acceptance, among them a cool car and an attitude, he struggles to fit into the tight cliques that dominate his affluent suburban L.A. high school. The school's leaders are delinquents who force Jimbo into a knife fight and a suicidal game of automobile chicken before he gains some acceptance. And while the movie reconciles some of the family and community tensions it exposes, the overarching theme is one of teenage alienation from a world of insensitive and incompetent adults.

The Wild One and Rebel without a Cause are just two examples of how the media exploited public anxiety about teenage delinquency and at the same time promoted the very behaviors they pretended to condemn. Teenaged audiences thrilled at the blend of sensitivity and menace both Brando and Dean portrayed. So, too, teens adopted the jive lingo and delinquent fashions these movies glamorized. In similar ways, all the major media of the 1950s made teens both a subject to explore and a market to exploit. Indeed, it was undoubtedly the media that made teens aware that the subculture they inhabited in their schools and communities was part of a national phenomenon. At the same time, that subculture generated fads and tastes the media were quick to commercialize.

Certainly this was the case with advertising. By the late 1950s, advertisers had recognized teens as a discrete market sector. Agencies used sophisticated research methods to determine what teens would buy and what appeals would instill teen loyalty to brand names. In that spirit, the R. J. Reynolds tobacco company sponsored the popular Alan Freed rock music show, The Camel Rock 'n' Roll Dance Party, and American Tobacco used the popular TV music show Your Hit Parade to promote Lucky Strikes. New products like Clearasil, small transistor radios, and portable typewriters were created specifically for a teen market. Acquisition of such products thus became part of the rite of passage through the teenage years.

But the media themselves gave teen culture its clearest expression. Teens were the major consumers of comic books, rock music (and top forty rock radio), television, and a genre of movies called teenpics, or teen exploitation films. From these media teens derived a common set of cultural experiences that were more egalitarian and antiauthoritarian than the adult world from which the younger generation separated themselves. Thus, the teen-oriented media defined a fault line along which consensus broke down. Commercial reality limited the efforts of concerned adults and cultural custodians to censor those media. Put more simply, the teen media were profitable in a society that venerated the bottom line. Hence, industries that made money catering to teen tastes resisted efforts to sanitize their products.

The Subversive World of Comic Books

Comic books provoked the opening salvo in the attack on teen media. Some adults charged that comics debased conventional culture. By emphasizing pictures over words, they discouraged reading. Teachers objected that students assigned a Shakespearean play or famous novel like *Moby Dick* often read the Classics Comics version instead. Worse yet, most teens preferred horror, crime, and romance comics that depicted mindless gore, lurid affairs, satanic rituals, and other sinister themes. In the late 1940s, psychologist Fredric Wertheim launched a crusade to save young Americans from this invidious influence. Wertheim was persuaded, and confirmed the fears of many adults, that exposure to comics triggered violence and other forms of antisocial behavior. Indeed, he believed comics were responsible for the youthful crime wave reported to be sweeping the nation.

Those who condemned comics did have a point. Crime and horror accounted for the large majority of comics sold—some sixty million a month by the early 1950s. Wertheim singled out for special mention one issue of *Crime Does Not Pay* with the story of Paul Chretien (a pun on the term "cretin," or mental defective). For the first forty-seven of the story's forty-eight frames, crime did indeed pay. The villain's death in frame forty-eight could not in any meaningful way atone for the carnage that preceded it: ten guillotinings, seven stabbings, six shootings, one murderous push off a ladder, two shockings, one drowning, and one crushed skull. While such mayhem would little disconcert fans of recent action movies, it did distress many parents groups in the 1950s. But Wertheim went further in his exposé. In his 1953 book *The Seduction of the Innocent*, he charged that Batman and Robin had a homosexual relationship and that Wonder Woman was a lesbian role model.

Wertheim was not a prude lobbying for censorship. Much of his life he fought for liberal causes and supported civil rights. His liberalism did not, however, make him tolerant of comic book content that he believed promoted fascism, sexism, racism, and ethnocentrism. And the manner in which children read comics with eyes moving up and down rather than across the page caused a condition he labeled "linear dyslexia." Among those drawn to his argument were defenders of traditional culture such as librarians, teachers, and women's groups. Unfortunately for him, his complaints also attracted a number of right-wingers, whom he found uncongenial bedfellows. Where Wertheim was concerned almost exclusively with comic books, groups like the American Legion and Catholic Legion of Decency advocated a broad censorship that he opposed. For many of those crusaders, comic books were yet another instrument of the Red menace. "Would it not be simple for the Kremlin conspirators to put comic books to 'the cause' by infiltrating the ranks of the writers and artists, if nothing else?" one conspiracy theorist asked an unsympathetic Wertheim.

The attack on comic books was part of a larger assault on mass media. Criticism came from both sides of the political spectrum. Many liberals like Wertheim feared that film, radio, television, magazines, and comic books debased culture and in that way made possible the appeal of totalitarian ideas. Conservatives were more likely to see an assault on traditional moral values or the Communists at work. Hence, HUAC had in 1948 opened its assault on Reds in Hollywood. As the McCarthy era peaked in 1954, so did the assault on comic books. One newspaper referred to comic books as "the filthy stream that flows from the gold-plated sewers of New York." The Book-of-the-Month Club made *Seduction of the Innocent* a monthly selection. Congress realized that if it investigated comic books, it could attract widespread public attention.

The Senate committee that took up the anti–comic book crusade had earlier won acclaim for exposing the influence of organized crime in city government. Its chair, Senator Estes Kefauver of Tennessee, gained such prominence questioning mob boss Frank Costello before the television cameras that he became the Democrats' 1956 vice presidential candidate. Now the Subcommittee to Investigate Juvenile Delinquency tested Wertheim's claim that comics provoked youthful violence. After hearing a parade of "decent" comic book artists and the ubiquitous Dr. Wertheim, the committee turned to its star witness, Bill Gaines.

Gaines had taken over the family publishing business after the death of his father, Max. He was, by his own admission, an eccentric, "a behavior problem, noncon-formist, a difficult child" with a taste for practical jokes. When he inherited Educational Comics, the business was failing. But his offbeat humor had led him to horror and suspense stories. So, too, did the diet pills that kept him awake at night plotting macabre and ghoulish stories for EC to publish. What most critics saw as an assault on decency was to Gaines broad parody. And teen readers loved it. By 1953, Gaines had changed the name of Educational Comics to Entertaining Comics, since the company that published *The Haunt of Fear, Tales from the Crypt, Shock SuspenStories, Weird Science,* and *Two-Fisted Tales* could hardly claim to have an educational mission. But it did have monthly sales in the millions and a host of imitators. As a consequence, Gaines became a prime target for Wertheim and the Senate cultural watchdogs.

Before the committee, Gaines tried to take the moral high ground. His comics used "the best writers, the finest artists; we spare nothing to make each magazine, each story, each page, a work of art." And if the prices paid now for what have become collectors' items are any gauge, Gaines was correct. The committee wasn't buying it. The members wanted fireworks, not aesthetic debate. They zeroed in on one EC story of a young victim of foster home abuse. It is hard to keep a straight face when reading the record of the hearings.

Gaines: Most foster children, I am sure, are not in homes such as were described in those stories. Those were pretty miserable homes.

Committee Counsel: You mean homes that had vampires in them, those were not nice homes?

Gaines: Yes.

Counsel: Do you know anyplace where there is any such thing?

Gaines: As vampires?

Counsel: Yes.

Gaines: No, sir; this is fantasy.

Gaine's irreverent wit dressed up as mock sincerity did not play well to this crowd. Brandishing an especially startling cover from *Crime SuspenStories*, Kefauver closed in on Gaines:

Kefauver: This seems to be a man with a bloody ax holding a woman's head up which has been severed from her body. Do you think that is in good taste?

Gaines: Yes sir; I do, for the cover of a horror comic. A cover in bad taste, for example, might be defined as holding the head a little higher so the neck could be seen dripping blood from it and moving the body over a little further so the neck of the body could be seen to be bloody. . . .

Sen. Hendrickson: Here is another one I want to show him.

Kefauver: This is a July one. It seems to be a man with a woman in a boat and he is choking her to death with a crowbar. Is that in good taste?

Gaines: I think so.

Committee Counsel: How could it be worse?

Gaines had actually asked his cover artist to tone down the original, so it could have been worse. But the reference to taste is more to the point. Horror comics of any kind clearly offended the middle-class, middle-aged sensibilities of these senatorial custodians of culture. Where Gaines saw the horror as so exaggerated as to be funny, they took these ghoulish depictions rather literally. Nothing Gaines might say could assuage them, for they wanted a scapegoat, not a defense of what they thought was indefensible.

The committee and other critics of comic book mayhem worried, too, because unlike other media, no censoring apparatus existed to protect young readers from dangerous or subversive materials. Radio and television presented less of a problem to the cultural custodians, since both required federal licenses to operate. The fear of losing a license was sufficient to keep both electronic media relatively tame. Comic books were quite another matter. Since they cost little to produce or distribute, publishers could enter the business with little capital and small financial risk. In that way an eccentric like Bill Gaines was able to reach an audience in the tens of millions. That may explain the intensity of the attack against the comic book industry. With little ability to censor comic book content, cultural watchdogs viewed the medium as especially dangerous. Certainly the sensationalist content excited their worst fears.

But by 1954, the critics had found that distribution was the industry's vulnerable link. Under intense political pressure, distributors agreed to handle only those comics bearing the industry seal on their covers. To Gaines's dismay, they went so far as to ban in their titles such words as "crime, horror, terror, and weird, even weird!" Facing opposition both in- and outside the industry, Gaines suspended publication. Rather than produce comics, he turned to a new vehicle of irreverent wit, *Mad Magazine*. By the simple expedient of calling it a magazine rather than a comic, he evaded the code. Under the gaze of super-nebbish Alfred E. "What-Me Worry?" Newman, *Mad* lampooned almost every aspects of 1950s convention, from

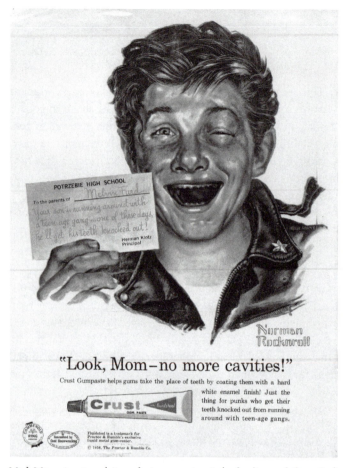

Mad Magazine turned its sardonic eye on America's ad culture and the nation's preoccupation with juvenile delinquency. Mad readers would never again feel the same about Crest toothpaste.   (Source: Courtesy of Doug Gilford, Doug Gilford's Mad Cover site: www.collectmad.com/madcoversite)

advertising to McCarthyism to "high-brow" culture, to TV shows and movies, to suburban lifestyles. *Mad's* readers learned from its parodies and satires how to recognize the pomposity and self-serving rhetoric of authority. Other cartoonists and artists with a flair for the macabre and iconoclastic went underground. By the 1960s, new low-budget publications and small distribution comics would be in vogue among teenagers and young adults. And this time their message would become even more irreverent, and in many cases politically subversive.

The Rock Revolution

In attacking comic books, the cultural custodians had fended off only the first wave of popular culture shock troops. A more profound assault was already forming. In the words of one popular song, "baby, that was rock and roll." Until the mid-1950s, popular music was safely in the hands of mainstream media controlled by large corporations. Hit songs came out of Broadway and Hollywood musicals, nightclubs, and network radio and television. Most of the performers were white, and their songs almost antiseptically upbeat. Who could complain about "Mr. Sandman," who brought true love with a complexion of "peaches and cream," or the insufferably cute "Doggy in the Window?" The seemingly suggestive "Naughty Lady of Shady Lane" who "hit the town like a bomb" turned out to be a baby girl. Such music was welcomed in even the most staid suburban homes.

Only on the fringes of society did other forms of music attract significant audiences. The most substantial, country and western, had a somewhat restricted regional audience in the South and West. Folk music, popular during the Depression era, declined after the late 1940s, especially after Red hunters attacked the Weavers, a popular group who included songs of social relevance in their repertoire. And as families fled to suburbs, nightclubs began a serious decline, and downhill with them went the big band jazz so popular in the 1930s and 1940s. Many jazz musicians turned to a progressive style, which while musically innovative, tended to alienate traditional fans. African Americans in the South and those who had migrated to the northern cities had two styles distinctly their own—gospel and rhythm and blues (R&B). Occasionally whites might hear gospel as performed by the legendary Marian Anderson or the Fisk University Jubilee Singers. R&B, however, remained taboo for most white audiences. Critics dismissed it as "race" music, whose thumping rhythms and suggestive lyrics smacked too much of dirty sex.

Billboard, the official magazine of popular music, recognized the segmentation of popular music by keeping three separate charts for hit songs—popular, country and western, and R&B. Yet while the United States remained tightly segregated along racial lines, musical tastes began to shift. Some white teenagers began to discover the small R&B radio stations that catered to African-American audiences. In 1954 "Sh-Boom," an R&B song by the Chords, an African-American group, appeared on the Billboard popular song list. Where before an occasional black artist such as Nat King Cole made the list with a conventional song, "Sh-Boom" marked the first R&B crossover. White artists moved quickly to cover the song, so most audiences heard the version sung by the white Crew Cuts.

All the same, a fault line in American culture, one no less substantial than the "separate but equal" concept struck down in the Supreme Court's 1954 Brown decision, had been breached. The trickle soon became a torrent. In 1955 a white group, Bill Haley and the Comets, came out with "Rock around the Clock." Since Haley was under contract to a major record company, the song reached an audience never before exposed to music that had become known as rock and roll. In 1956 "Rock around the Clock" became part of the sound track for Blackboard Jungle, a controversial film about juvenile delinquents in an urban high school. The film established vividly in the public mind the connection between the new music and youthful rebellion against authority.

In promoting Haley and "Rock around the Clock," Decca Records chose not to fight the rock revolution but to ride the wave and exploit its commercial possibilities. Companies with no rock performers under contract did not have that option. They either had to revive pop or face extinction as "semiliterate hillbillies and black ex-dishwashers on upstart labels usurped their place in the music industry." Older performers frequently resisted a music form that overnight made them old fashioned. Some, like fundamentalist Christian singer Pat Boone, performed the new songs as if they were old pop tunes. Others voiced despair. As nightclub entertainer Sammy Davis, Jr., lamented, "if rock 'n' roll is here to stay, I might commit suicide." The most unreal response came from some groups in the music industry who tried to supplant rock and roll with polkas and "commercial corn music" as the new dance crazes. For reasons they could not fathom, the Steve Wolowic Polka Band did not drive Haley from the top of the charts.

To many teens, the overwrought response seemed another example of adult excess. To them, rock and roll was about fun and excitement. The words of early rock songs usually addressed teen concerns—broken hearts, first love, or cars. Indeed, many critics marveled at the inanity of rock lyrics like "Do-wop-do-wah" or "A-wop-bop-a-loo-mop-a-lop-bam-boom." But after 1955, no matter how much adults might condemn the new music, they could not ignore it. It was then that the ultimate teenager and the quintessential delinquent burst onto the national scene. The slicked-back hair, flashy shirts, lascivious sneer, pink Cadillac, and thrusting hips all belonged to Elvis Presley. Elvis became by far the most popular celebrity for the teens of the 1950s. Both Brando and Elvis radiated a kind of raw sexuality that adults found menacing. Indeed, one promoter called Elvis "Brando with a guitar." And with his long sideburns, "greaser" hair, and blue jeans, Elvis projected an image that was self-consciously lower class. Worse yet, since he sounded black, he was mainstream America's worst nightmare.

In February 1956, Elvis's first RCA record, *Heartbreak Hotel*, went to the top of both the country and pop charts and to number five in R&B. Never before had a song had such crossover appeal. And Elvis repeated his success with a whole string of records, including *Hound Dog* and *Love Me Tender*. When popular TV show host Ed Sullivan invited him to appear on his Sunday night variety show, Elvis became both a celebrity and a symbol. The symbolism arose from Sullivan's decision to censor Elvis's famous pelvic swivel. Elvis combined his sensual singing with a raucous hip-swinging style that dripped sexuality. Sullivan assuaged Middle American sensibilities by forbidding the camera to show his performance below the waist. Once again, the effort to censor teenage culture proved foolish. Any kid who did not know what was going on below the camera was determined to find out.

Despite the furor, Elvis never moved very far from his country roots. As his fame soared, he quickly shifted into a more traditional entertainment career. RCA sweetened his style by subduing the guitars and playing Elvis off against the smooth harmonies of the Jordanaires. He also became one of Hollywood's top box office draws and a regular on the Las Vegas nightclub scene. And when the U.S. Army drafted him in 1958, Elvis meekly traded his delinquent slick-backed hair and sideburns for the army crew cut.

Elvis's patriotism saved him from the cultural backlash that struck rock and roll just as it had comic books. Nothing in the 1950s had done more to draw battle lines or demarcate the terrain of teenage subculture than rock music. Conservative Americans saw this phenomenon, too, as subversive. In their worldview, a subversive movement must have at its core a cabal of conspirators responsible for spreading its invidious message. They found their conspirators among the gurus who did most to popularize rock culture, the radio disc jockey and, chief among them, Alan Freed, the self-acclaimed "Father of Rock and Roll."

In some ways Freed was an unlikely candidate to become a symbol of cultural rebellion. He came to radio as a classically trained musician who gained his first fame as a popular music DJ on an Akron, Ohio, station. But like Bill Gaines, Freed was prone to eccentricity, accentuated by a significant drinking problem. His turbulent career landed him in 1951 on a late-night classical music show at WJW in Cleveland. A record storeowner tipped Freed off that local white teens had a craving for R&B records. What about a late-night radio show doing nothing but black music? Finally, taken in by music where "the beat is so strong that anyone can dance to it without a lesson," Freed launched his show in June 1951. *The Moondog Show* opened with a wailing sax solo going out over WJW's powerful 50,000-watt signal. As he played blues, Freed sat with an open mike rhythmically pounding a Cleveland phonebook and screaming "Go, Go, Gogogogogogo, Go, Go." When his show took off, Freed recognized that teens who loved R&B records would be eager to hear the performers at live concerts. So he briefly traded in his mike to become an R&B concert promoter. Teens flocked by the thousands to his shows. His popularity landed him a spot at WINS, 1010 AM in New York, where he proved that R&B had huge appeal to white audiences. In that way, he and a host of other DJs who followed his success with R&B paved the way for the "Sh-Boom" crossover and Elvis.

Before Elvis, many people assumed that rock was just another fad, much like the craze in coonskin caps and other Davy Crockett paraphernalia that followed a Walt Disney series on the legendary Tennessee frontiersman. By 1957, the enduring popularity of rock and roll over popular music was so self-evident that network television began giving it airtime. No show was more a rite of passage for the sixties generation than *American Bandstand*. As opposed to the frenetic, erratic, and Jewish Freed, *Bandstand* host Dick Clark was the model of white Protestant propriety. Under Clark's reserved eye, Philadelphia high school students came each weekday afternoon to attend an after school record hop. Soon the regulars on *Bandstand*, Kenny and Arlene and the inimitable Justine, had become national teen celebrities. Their popularity with television audiences seemed to confirm the American democratic faith that fame could happen to even ordinary kids.

American Bandstand welcomed teens from all over the nation into a world of their own. It modeled new dance styles, showcased fashion trends, and introduced slang

Dick Clark's American Bandstand *turned ordinary kids into stars. The show also introduced a generation of teenage Americans to the world of rock and roll.* (Source: Associated Press)

terms. Indeed, by 1957 almost all the elements of the rock and roll culture were in place—celebrity performers, high-visibility promoters like Freed, cheap record players, and exposure on national television. Then came the final ingredient, top forty radio wedded to new transistor technology. Transistors made possible the miniaturization of radios so they no longer required bulky vacuum tubes. The top forty format provided radio station owners with an inexpensive way to program without relying on high-paid DJs. Two radio station managers got the idea one night in a bar. They noticed that the patrons played the same forty songs on the jukebox all night long. So did the waitresses after the patrons went home. Might that approach not work on the air, they wondered?

Top forty and similar formulas soon grabbed high ratings around the country. It also provoked disc jockeys to rebellion. Many DJs saw themselves as the gatekeepers who determined which songs would actually receive airtime. Like Freed, they had an avuncular relationship with the teen radio audience. Formula programming took away their creative role and more than a little of their potential income. Many received under-the-table payments, or "payola," from record promoters eager to assure hits for their labels. This system of payola was the breach through which rock's critics launched a frontal attack on music they believed threatened society's values.

The first sign of serious trouble came when Alan Freed's *The Big Beat Show* played Boston on May 3, 1958. A frenetic young white woman leapt from the audience onto the stage and grabbed a black performer's crotch. Boston's finest were not then (or after) known for their racial tolerance. An outraged white policeman who saw the act shoved through the audience toward the stage. Pandemonium erupted as security forces rushed in to clear the auditorium. As the exiting teens hit the streets, more cops set on them. In the retelling to the press, however, the police riot became a teen riot. Stories flew around about dope smoking, sexual violence, and lewd behavior. The real cause for the violence was Boston's hostility to racially integrated events and to rock and roll. Even before the show began, an angry cop had snarled at Freed, "We don't like your kind of music here" as he pushed him off the stage.

As controversy swirled around Freed and *The Big Beat* tour, Congress once again took issue with a popular media that many Americans thought was corrupting the nation's youth. Just a year before, hearings had exposed a pattern of cheating in popular television quiz shows. Many congressmen now made the simple deduction that if popular television was rigged, so, too, was popular music. They concluded that for teenagers to become so agitated by rock and roll, someone, DJs most likely, must have seduced them into listening to it. How else could anyone explain why such distasteful music could be so popular?

Freed was, of course, a particularly vulnerable target. He had a finger in every aspect of the business—publishing, song writing, recording, producing, as well as promoting concerts and television and radio shows. Evidence linked him financially to several record industry executives. The New York state attorney general grilled him about financial improprieties. But Freed was not alone. The seemingly squeaky clean Dick Clark was as deeply entangled in a dubious web of self-serving financial arrangements. A number of DJs, some who admitted accepting payola, were abruptly fired.

The house subcommittee, chaired by Congressman Oren Harris of Arkansas, chose Cleveland (now home to the Rock and Roll Hall of Fame) as the symbolic setting for its opening hearings. It was here that Alan Freed had first aired his *Moondog Show*, and Cleveland remained critical as a "breakout market," an area in which a song's popularity usually meant success elsewhere. Just as in the comic book hearings, committee members revealed through their questions that they were more interested in moral posturing than in legislative oversight. Harris described two popular Cleveland DJs as pathetic young men. He rejected their argument that the quality of a song rather than bribes determined what they chose to play.

These little fish did not long satisfy the committee. Publicity came from big names, and that meant Alan Freed and Dick Clark. The difference in how the two fared speaks volumes about the intention of those seeking to put rock and roll on trial. Where the Middle America–styled Clark emerged with his image and empire largely in tact, the eccentric Freed was destroyed by a combination of persecution and his own self-destructive habits. New York district attorney Frank Hogan indicted Freed and seven others for accepting payola. As his career dwindled, Freed spent the better part of his energy and his money defending himself. In 1962 he was convicted, fined a token $300, and given a suspended six-month sentence. Such penalties were beside the point, because he could no longer find work. All the same, just two years later the IRS indicted Freed for failing to declare payola income he earned from 1957 to 1959. He died in January 1965 a thoroughly broken person, but in the process became a minor martyr of the 1960s, eulogized among the young as one who sacrificed so that rock and roll could live.

Dick Clark suffered no such martyrdom. In some ways he was simply too smart or too slick to provide the forces of cultural purity another victim. As both Clark and the committee knew, payola had in fact existed in the music industry since the days of sheet music. In the face of hostile questioning, Clark, in a most businesslike way, denied any wrongdoing. Perhaps he had been too quick to seize any deal that came his way, but in popular music success was so transient that a person had only a brief moment to cash in, he explained. Besides, he had since divested himself of his entangling deals. Congressman Harris was so impressed with Clark's performance and his mastery of the music business that he praised him as an unusually "attractive and successful young man" who had recognized the error of his ways.

More important, by refusing to kowtow to his inquisitors, Clark not only saved his own skin but kept faith with his teenaged audience. While he was far from forthright about his business arrangements, not once had he shown any lack of commitment to the music that had built his fortune. Support from teen groups indicated that Clark had not violated the trust of his fans. The committee members revealed in the questions they asked that they were as much or more concerned about why rock and roll was popular than how Clark made his money. They simply could not believe that the music had any inherent value:

Congressman Derounian: [quoting a music critic's put-down of Fabian, a singer whose career Clark had shaped] Here is what he had to say about your Fabian "Reeling like a top, snapping his fingers and jerking his eyeballs, with hair like something Medusa had sent back, and a voice that was enormously improved by total unintelligibility." And Mitch Miller—

Clark: Wishes he had him. [meaning under contract to his record company]

Derounian: No.

Clark: Excuse me; I'm sorry.

Derounian: He said "You would not invite those unwashed kids into your living room to meet your family, why thrust them into the living rooms of your audience?" Mr. Clark, I think what you are saying is this: the singer appears on your program physically—and apparently this is your format, you get a big hunk of young man who has got a lot of cheesecake to him and the kids are thrilled by this on the television program—and then you play his records, but you don't have him sing too often. That is the way you sell records and that is a pretty cute way to do it. And all I want you to do, if that is the case, is to admit that the singing part of his talent is not the all-important part, but his physical appearance plays a great part in whether or not you are going to let him appear on your show.

Clark: No, it is not factual.

Derounian: You would then have an ugly person appear on your show?

Clark: Mr. Derounian, do you want me to say I have had a lot of ugly people appear on my program?

Actually, as Clark fully understood, Derounian, like most committee members, wanted him to denounce rock and roll. According to the Derounian vision, teens responded to the "cheesecake," or sexual sell, of the music, not any intrinsic merit. That was the point Clark refused to concede, though he was too clever to contradict Derounian.

Ironically, in choosing Fabian as an example, Congressman Derounian had identified a near fatal disease that had infected rock culture, but hardly for the reasons he thought. Fabian was more a pop performer than a rock and roller. Worse yet, he had remarkably little talent. He succeeded because promoters like Clark knew how to showcase his persona. By the late 1950s, other performers like Neil Sedaka, Paul Anka, and Bobby Vinton with more talent than Fabian (if less sex appeal) had so much redirected rock toward pop tunes and ballads that much of its vitality was lost. The untimely deaths of some of the most influential talents such as Buddy Holly further weakened rock. Richard Pettyman, better known as Little Richard, gave up rock and roll to follow the voice of God. Others, like Freed and rock and roll pioneer Chuck Berry, fell victim to their personal weaknesses, made worse by the hostile forces arrayed against them.

More important, rock by the late 1950s had begun to fragment. A music that had once transcended differences among teens now began to reflect the larger patterns of adult society. Regionalism rebounded as record producers exploited a Texas or Philadelphia sound that did not often produce national hits. Styles as diverse as black vocal groups (the Drifters with "Up on the Roof"), a cappella, surfing, folk, the twist, Motown, and even a singing nun attracted record buyers. No longer could teens claim popular music as something distinctly their own. But as with comic books, rock and roll had not simply disintegrated after its meteoric rise; it had gone underground, in this case to clubs in England. From there it would soon return with a force that would give the 1960s much of their distinctive style.

Teen Flicks

Teens were somewhat less influential in shaping more-sophisticated media such as magazines and movies. Since those media required more extensive (and expensive) production systems, the creators exercised more control over style and content. On the other hand, teenage consumer preferences still determined which products succeeded and which died for want of an audience. Here, too, the producers of media designed products aimed at teens. The most popular teen magazines of the

1950s appealed primarily to female readers. If the teen-oriented magazines of early decades offered adult guidance into the adult world, *Teen World, Confidential Teen Romance, Teen Today*, and forties holdover *Seventeen* addressed the issues that concerned teens: fashion, peer pressure, dating, and other essentials of popularity. None of these magazines had as wide circulation as comic books or as large an audience as rock and roll. Still, in creating magazines aimed at teens, publishers recognized them as a distinct market sector.

So, too, did Hollywood. The film industry discovered the teen audience almost out of desperation. Much like AM radio, the movies had lost much of their traditional audience to television. Cinemascope, drive-in theaters, and gimmicks to attract young suburban families had done little to stop the decline in box office receipts. In 1956, the popularity of *Rock around the Clock* tipped some Hollywood producers off to the potential of the teen audience. The match between teens and movies made sense. Theaters and drive-ins offered a semi-private, public place teens could escape to. *Rock around the Clock* had an appealing formula: a rock and roll musical with a story about teenagers. Among its featured performers were Bill Haley and the Comets and Alan Freed. And, of course, it provoked the predictable outcry from the usual quarters. James Finley, writing in *Catholic World*, complained that "catering to teenagers' taste has leveled our song standards to the point of vulgarity, banality, infantilism ["The Doggy in the Window" may not have been vulgar, but what could have been more banal or infantile?]. . . . Can this happen to movies under the prospect of their getting hungry enough to start indulging the banal, untrained, irresponsible tastes of the average teenager?"

The question must have been rhetorical, for Hollywood never saw a dollar it did not like. The producer of *Rock around the Clock*, Sam Katzman, was among the first in the industry to see the potential of the teen market. Not coincidentally, he was one of the least pretentious and most commercially successful Hollywood moviemakers. Before *Rock around the Clock* he made such forgettable, though profitable, low-budget films aimed at adolescents as *Captain Video* and *Betty Co-ed*. He recognized in the 1950s that "We got a brand new generation, but they got the same old glands." *Rock around the Clock* proved him right, for it became one of the most financially successful films of 1956. More telling in Hollywood terms, it spawned a host of imitations such as *Shake, Rattle, and Roll, Love Me Tender*, and *Don't Knock the Rock*. Almost all of these films had the same story line: hostile adults seek to prevent teens from enjoying the new music, a wise disc jockey reminds them that other music crazes once provoked similar concerns, and the adults finally agree to let the kids be kids, just as they once were.

Rock and roll may have been at the core of teen culture, but Hollywood discovered other lines along which teens shared a common identity. Just as cars defined the suburban culture of the 1950s, they shaped the teenaged world. Within the teen culture, a male-dominated subculture of street or drag racing thrived. Mechanically inclined male teens and young adults turned cars from the 1930s and 1940s into street racers that were "chopped, blocked, and channeled."

Both *The Wild Ones* and *Rebel without a Cause* succeeded at the box office in part because they recognized the racing cult. Drag racing came to symbolize for most adults both a reckless independence and morbid courtship of death. Similarly, popular songs like "Teen Angel" and "Tell Laura I Love Her" told stories about racing and tragedy. In 1956, *Newsweek* condemned drag racing for attracting "crowds of riotous teenagers mocking the forces of law and order." Such hostility did not stop Hollywood from producing a cycle of movies such as *Hot Cars*, *Hot Rod Girl*, and *Speed Crazy*. These were movies specifically targeted for teen audiences. However, Americans so loved their cars that this genre never provoked the same level of anxiety as rock and roll or other teen movie genres such as crime and horror.

Adults leveled their sharpest attacks on juvenile delinquent films that followed in the mode of *Rebel without a Cause*, *The Wild One*, and *Blackboard Jungle*. Most of those who criticized Hollywood believed these films contributed to the problem of teen criminality by glorifying it. The same Kefauver committee that confirmed the connection between comic books and crime issued a similar report on movies. While Hollywood promised to take such criticism to heart, financial needs dictated otherwise. A whole cycle of horror and crime films flourished. As always, J. Edgar Hoover stood vigilantly by, ready to condemn "trash mills which spew out celluloid poison destroying the impressionable mind of youth."

Hoover was even more disturbed that the troubled youth of the 1950s movies bore more resemblance to the hardcore 1930s gangsters than street-tough Bowery boys. Most 1930s films offered a socioeconomic explanation for youth crime. Poverty and slums more than defective character led youth astray. Clean up the environment and you could clean up the kids. By the 1950s, psychodrama had preempted environmental explanations. Young Jim Stark from *Rebel* came from an affluent suburban home, not any slum. The teens who menaced him acted from alienation and boredom, not material and social deprivation. They were often the victims of parental abuse who longed for love and authority they could respect. In a pivotal scene in *Rebel*, Jim Stark must accept a challenge to a "chickee run." Each contestant races a jalopy toward a cliff. The first to bail out is "chicken." When Jim asks, "Why do we do this?" Buzz, his ill-fated opponent, replies, "You gotta do somethin', don't ya?" Jim comes home from this deadly encounter to find his father in an apron doing the housework for his domineering wife. Not until Dad acted like a man by assuming control of his own house and family, the film suggests, would Jim have a model for ordering his own life.

Hollywood did not limit itself to tales of tormented and tormenting teens. The industry produced a number of popular films such as *Gidget*, *Tammy and the Bachelor*, and *April Love* about happy, well-adjusted suburban kids. Sanitized stars such as Pat Boone, Debbie Reynolds, and Tommy Sands oozed a kind of sweet moral sensibility no parent could help but love. Yet even these films spoke almost exclusively to teen sensibilities. As film historian Thomas Doherty observed, "Their real focus was the self-contained world of the teenager, where adults were inconvenient but more often peripheral or superfluous." Sometimes the issues were real enough—an unwanted pregnancy or going all the way before marriage, but in the end middle-class family values triumphed. Women paid a high price for that victory, since the clean films almost always treated them as moral vessels who found fulfillment in romance, marriage, and family.

By the end of the 1950s, the battles over popular culture and crime had been so often fought they had become less provocative. And in the period after Stalin's death, the cold war had thawed enough so that conspiracy theories no longer had such sway over the public imagination. Perhaps more telling still, advertisers and other media managers had come to recognize the enormous potential of teens as consumers. One survey predicted that the number of thirteen- to twenty-one-year-olds would grow from 22.4 million in 1958 to 30 million by the mid-1960s. That could and would have meant an increase in the number of impressionable minds for the media to lead into delinquency. But as historian James Gilbert pointed out, behavior that "once seemed clearly to be delinquency" had become "confused in a burst of enthusiasm for youth culture." When the controversies over youth culture erupted anew, the terms would be more explicitly political and the threat to consensus far more overt.

As important as teen culture was in establishing generational boundaries, it would be misleading to see this issue as central to the 1950s. The controversy over rock and roll and other media always remained a somewhat peripheral issue, and the rebelliousness it presaged more latent than overt. America's political leaders did have more important matters to worry about as they continued their crusade against Communism. The shock of the Russian satellite *Sputnik*, a revolution in Cuba, and the collapse of the Geneva summit after the shooting down of an American U-2 spy plane were among those reminders of the thin line between cold wars and hot ones. For the members of the Kefauver and Harris subcommittees, however, the idea of a separate teen world threatened the idea of a unifying national culture, so especially important in a time of crisis. In tying the popularity of teen media to conspiracy theories, they adopted the same model of historical causality invoked by Joe McCarthy, J. Edgar Hoover, and the defenders of the American way of life. Since much teen culture was different and disturbing, drawn from the lower classes and other peripheral subcultures and generated by minorities and outcasts, it must be subversive.

The majority of teenaged Americans paid little attention to such gnashing of teeth. Only when the army sent Elvis to Germany did outside events enter seriously into their lives. For them, the popularity of rock and roll required no pained explanations. They liked it because "it had a good beat and they could dance to it," and because, like comics and teen films, it demarcated a separate teen world. As one influential historian of rock concluded, it was "a music they could use to define themselves while they themselves were defining it." Ironically, the teenaged domain defined by popular culture was more biracial and egalitarian than the adult domain that disdained it. The cold war consensus used the illusion of an egalitarian society to maintain a host of inequities along fault lines of race, class, ethnicity, gender, and religion. By contrast, the world of *American Bandstand* and Alan Freed's *Big Beat* shows bound "together teenagers from all walks of life under the banner of rock and roll."

In its fashion, rock and roll broadened the definition of what American popular culture encompassed. Lawrence Wright spoke for much of the baby boom genera-tion when he recalled his first encounter with rock. The son of a banker, Wright came from a politically conservative and religious Dallas family. He recalls that until the mid-1950s, he shared the same musical tastes as his family. Each week they enjoyed the sappy renditions of popular songs on the television show *Your Hit Parade.* Like many kids, Wright could sing every verse of the Disney show's "Ballad of Davy Crockett." But when Elvis sang "Hound Dog," Wright "began to give way to the tidal pull of rock and roll." His parents reacted with such "contempt and bewilderment that the music became defiant." More important, he sensed that because the churches and politicians were so scandalized by rock, they "gave the music a political importance it had never aspired to have." Todd Gitlin, a New York–bred leader of SDS who has written a history of the decade, came from a cultural realm far removed from the conservative suburbs in which Wright was reared. Yet he had a similar sense of the impact of popular media: "In a world that adult ideologies had defined as black and white—America versus totalitarianism, respectability versus crime, obedience versus delinquency, affluence versus barbarism, suburbia versus degradation and filth—they did help to establish the possibility of gray." Having come of age under the banner of youth culture, restive young Americans were ready to march under it when the trumpets sounded.

3
Cracks in the Consensus

Popular culture did not alone inspire the upheavals of the uncivil war. Dissent on the Left was for many rebels a style they learned in the late 1950s and early 1960s from performers, artists, and intellectuals who provided both points of view and language with which to launch attacks on consensus culture. While much dissent did have substantial intellectual and cultural roots, many rebels of the sixties did not read widely or think deeply. They were consumed with the present and the need to change the world now. A clenched fist or a poster of revolutionary Che Guevera, much like popular ad slogans, embodied a cluster of values, sensibilities, and feelings that put them at odds with the mainstream. Hippies in particular rejected the scientific rationalism that characterized much of the academic discourse of the 1950s. So too, political radicals dismissed most orthodox ideas as the products of a hopelessly corrupt capitalist order they sought to undermine.

Still, it is clear that ideas mattered. Whether expressed superficially in slogans and cultural icons or systematically as sustained cultural and political analysis, those ideas helped dissenters define their opposition to the cold war consensus and the establishment that defended it. The work of writers and artists gradually disturbed the foundations on which the received orthodoxy stood. If their dissent had an overarching theme, it was alienation—the antithesis of the liberal corporate ethos that the consensus embraced.

Along three broad lines intellectuals and artists depicted individuals in varying degrees of alienation. Sometimes feelings of distance, despair, and hopelessness were rooted in the interior self, most often in struggle over identity and sexuality. At other times those feelings came as reaction against the repressive mechanisms of society, especially the corporate culture that seemed to dominate the 1950s. And finally, they informed a sardonic rejection of the optimistic rationalism that defined officially sanctioned culture. This dark mood gave rise to black humor, a style that pierced the smug self-assurance of the military-industrial-university complex. How could alienated young Americans celebrate a culture that seemed all too willing to plunge the world into nuclear Armageddon in order to make the American way of life safe from godless Communism?

What follows is a sampling of ideas that inspired dissent in the 1960s. Since the paths to the uncivil war were so idiosyncratic and varied, few people could ever agree on what works most shaped their emerging consciousness. No single book or individual stands out as the wellspring of inspiration for 1960s dissenters. Each historian would construct a completely different list of intellectuals and artists who had a profound impact. Those I have chosen meet certain criteria: their ideas were controversial, they provoked hostility from critics in both academia and the media, they were popular, and they intermingled, to some degree, elements of all three themes of alienation: the problem of sexuality and identity, anti-corporatism, and irreverence.

The Sexual Struggle

Many intellectuals and artists in the postwar era recoiled from the evils of Nazi and Soviet totalitarianism, the horrors of the Holocaust and atomic bomb, and a sense of the dehumanizing ways in which mass society suffocated the individual. Theologian Paul Tillich suggested that sin in modern societies came from the temptation to make "the other person into an object, into a thing." How else could we understand the excesses committed by modern bureaucratic, war-making civilizations? Out of this concern came a crisis of faith in which the progressive optimism of the early century gave way to "anxiety about the meaning of our existence, including the problems of death, faith, and guilt." Conventional society responded with bromides about faith in a Christian God and the American way of life.

Such nostrums could not satisfy students cutting their intellectual teeth on Nietzsche or the French existentialists. They were more likely drawn to those thinkers influenced by the psychoanalytic thought of Sigmund Freud, who located the crisis of individual identity in sexuality. Freud's view of the human condition was essentially a tragic one: repression of our sexual natures was the price humans paid for civilization. The ruling conscience of the superego repressed the destructive impulses of the id, leaving the ego, or self, conflicted. Mature or healthy individuals adjusted to that conflict. But those unable to get in touch with their true sexual natures could not function normally in the world. From that emerged an absurdist trap. Individual freedom required sexual liberation, but society bound sexuality to its collective purposes, leaving individuals with no way out. The totalitarian or dehumanizing power of mass society made it virtually impossible to discover the sexual self.

That was the terrain explored by the reclusive J. D. Salinger in *The Catcher in the Rye*. First published in 1951 and popular ever after, it was among baby boomers one of the most widely read novels. As poignantly as any author of the era, Salinger defined the landscape of psychological discontent. Who could have been more profoundly alienated than preppy Holden Caulfield? *The Catcher in the Rye* caught the insecurities of those born into the atomic age. It mirrored the dark world of the postwar film noir genre, in which sexuality and betrayal are commonly linked, time is disoriented, space is claustrophobic, and good and evil are hopelessly confused. Salinger drew heavily as well on the intellectual domains of Freudian psychology and French existentialism. While few American teenagers ever read Freud, Salinger and other popular writers exposed them to the psychosexual terrain that preoccupied post–World War II intellectual life. In that way, young readers encountered ideas and attitudes that linked their own exploding sexual energy to a sense of alienation and despair.

In narrating his own story, Holden taught an entire generation to recognize a "phony." At first reading, Holden's phonies are those teens and adults who cover their superficiality with airs of social ease, self-confidence, and worldliness. Yet on closer reading, it becomes evident that what actually disturbs Holden is not the "phoniness" of those around him, but confusion over his sexuality. All the characters Holden sees as phonies are those like his brother D.B. or the randy Stradlatter, who have passed through puberty to heterosexual adulthood. Holden idealizes only his brother Allie, who died before puberty, and his prepubescent sister, Phoebe. As the "catcher in the rye," Holden imagines a field full of running little kids and "nobody's around, nobody big I mean—except me. And I'm standing on the edge of some crazy cliff. What I have to do, I have to catch everybody if they start to go over the cliff."

To fall off that cliff is literally to die and figuratively to fall from innocence—that is, to become sexually active. In Holden's estranged mental universe, sex does not mean love or the giving of life, but the onset of death. And it is from that consequence that he seeks to save those innocent children. Significantly, immediately after revealing his dream to Phoebe, Holden calls on his old English teacher Mr. Antonelli, with whom he has an ambiguous but sexually wrought encounter. Whether Holden properly understands Mr. Antonelli's gestures as a homosexual advance or is projecting his own fears is never clear. What is clear is that Holden's problem comes from his own associations of sex with violence and death.

That association becomes evident in the episode that made the book a cult experience for many young readers and anathema to proper adults. Given the casual way in which people use profanity today, it is difficult to convey the mixture of shock and prurient delight with which teen readers of the 1950s discovered "fuck you" in print. Indeed, for that single transgression many libraries and schools banned *The Catcher in the Rye*.

In reality, Salinger uses the episode not so much to shock, but to underscore the sexual nature of Holden's psychological confusion. Holden clearly fears what the onset of sexual knowledge does to innocence: "Somebody had written "Fuck you" on the wall. It drove me damn near *crazy* [italics mine]. I thought how Phoebe and all the other kids would see it, and how they'd wonder what the hell it meant, and then some kid would tell them—all cockeyed, naturally—what it meant, and how they'd all think about it and maybe even worry about it for a couple of days." Here is the same protective, almost mother hen sensibility that underlies Holden's image of the catcher in the rye. Then, in a recurring linkage of sex to violence, he adds, "I kept wanting to kill whoever'd written it." And for one of the few times in the book, Holden acts upon a thought rather than running from reality—he rubs the offending words off, despite his fear a teacher might see him and conclude he had written it.

If this example does not confirm the connection of sex and violence in Holden's mental universe, consider how the episode concludes. Upon leaving Phoebe's school, Holden discovers another "Fuck you" on the wall. That leads him to conclude that the world offers no place "that's nice and peaceful": "You may think there is, but once you get there, when you're not looking, somebody'll sneak up and write 'Fuck you' right under your nose. Try it sometime. I think, even, if I ever die, and they stick me in a cemetery, and I have a tombstone and all, it'll say 'Holden Caufield' on it, and the year I was born and the year I died, and then right under it'll say 'Fuck you.' I'm positive in fact." In that brief passage are many of the qualities that account for the book's appeal: Holden's morbid preoccupations, his sense of insecurity bordering on paranoia, his antic view of a world in which no one and no place was safe, and his irrepressible sarcasm.

The cult of *The Catcher in the Rye* suggests that if the fifties had a central preoccupation besides the cold war and nuclear peril, it was sex. Purveyors of popular culture had long understood the insatiable appetite Americans had for anything with even a hint of the erotic. Many American intellectuals gave Freud's tragic view an optimistic spin. To them, psychoanalysis offered a therapeutic response to sexual maladjustment. To find freedom, one had only to become adjusted to one's sexuality, meaning of course heterosexuality. Increased leisure gave Americans more time to nurture their sexual impulses. Advertisers used sex to sell products such as refrigerators that had no evident erotic possibility. And predictably, those who sought to preserve the nation's moral traditions found that preoccupation with sex a further symptom of loosening moral standards. This was the era after all which turned Alfred Kinsey's two social science reports on male and female sexuality into runaway bestsellers. Just as they fought against comic books and rock and roll, the cultural traditionalists promoted crusades against materials they found obscene or that undermined family values. Increasingly, the sexual became political.

By engaging that controversy, *Playboy* became a publication many serious people took somewhat seriously, rather than into just another dirty picture magazine more often seen than read. It would be easy and not unfair to dismiss *Playboy* as the commercialization of male sexual fantasies. Its founder, Hugh Hefner, came from a background in advertising and cartooning. With a mere $10,000 and rights to a nude photograph of Marilyn Monroe, the 1950s most sexually charged female symbol, Hefner launched a magazine aimed at swingers. The formula was a curious mix of sophistication—racy cartoons and reprinted articles—and relatively modest (by contemporary standards) nude photographs of women.

Playboy sold so well that even without advertising it made a profit its first year and turned the magazine's bunny in a tuxedo into one of the era's most recognized icons. Two years later, Hefner persuaded his subscription manager, Janet Pilgrim, to pose nude. Her layout gave birth to the "Playmate of the Month." Eventually, Hefner would pay major creative and intellectual figures to contribute to the magazine that in 1959 reached a circulation of about 800,000 (which surely translated into a far larger viewing audience). That year he spun off a *Playboy Penthouse Show* for television, and a year later opened his first Playboy Club in Chicago. Hefner built his small empire by catering to a seemingly unslakable male thirst for sexual fantasy. Yet despite his suave, almost continental airs, Hefner exuded a Middle American quality. He in many ways epitomized the American preference for style over substance. His concept of liberation promoted a largely male ideal of sexuality. It was cool rather than passionate and embraced a hedonistic enjoyment of transitory pleasure without emotional commitment. On questions of sexual liberation for women, Playboy was largely silent, and for gays it was, if anything, retrograde.

Within those limits, Hefner did become a voice, perhaps not of rebellion, but at least of resistance. Playboy crusaded for sexual liberation and the elimination of many legal barriers to free sexual expression. In that way, Hefner opened one of the frontiers along which 1960s rebels would assert their independence from conventions. Inspired in part by Playboy and its "philosophy" they, too, would reject the repressive sexual mores of the adult world in favor of a male ideal of liberation. Healthy sexual adjustment promised them relief from their sense of alienation. But no more than in the realm of comic books and rock music did the conventional standards on sexuality give way without a struggle. In 1963, an Illinois prosecutor charged that Playboy's nude bedroom photographs of a voluptuous Jane Mansfield violated obscenity laws. Hefner's victory in that case contributed to a judicial climate that eased laws on contraception and obscenity.

The subterranean sexual terrains Playboy ignored were the domains of bohemian movements. During the 1950s they flourished on the fringes of the nation's larger cities, especially New York's Greenwich Village and San Francisco's North Beach area. Unconventional approaches to sexuality explained the arrival of police officer William Hanrahan at San Francisco's City Lights bookstore one June evening in 1957. The store's proprietor, Lawrence Ferlinghetti, was on his way to becoming a celebrated poet. City Lights had become a refuge for a subculture of dropouts—artists, musicians, poets, homosexuals, runaways, drug addicts, and misfits who inhabited the North Beach area. Sometimes Ferlinghetti published the work of struggling poets like Allen Ginsberg, an expatriate from the East Coast. The arrival of Ginsberg and other eastern refugees hinted at the increasing importance of the West Coast in shaping American culture.

Among its eclectic titles, City Lights sold Howl, a poem Ginsberg had first read, actually chanted, in 1955. Howl drew its inspiration from peyote, amphetamines, and wine as well as the poet's own vision of a world gone mad. From his opening lines, Ginsberg rejected the more cerebral and academic forms that had captured poetry in the postwar era:

> I saw the best of my generation destroyed by
>   madness, starving, hysterical naked,
> dragging themselves through the Negro streets at dawn
>   looking for an angry fix,
> angelheaded hipsters burning for the ancient heavenly
>   connection to the starry dynamo in the machinery
>   of night.

Had Ginsberg limited his vision to drugs and the celebration of black urban hipsters, Hanrahan would have had little reason to invade City Lights. But Ginsberg openly advertised his homosexuality in an era that stigmatized gays as much or more than Commies. If Salinger's "Fuck you" opened eyes, imagine the reaction to these lines in which Ginsberg celebrated friends,

> who howled on their knees in the subway and were
> dragged off the roof waving genitals and
> manuscripts,
> who let themselves be fucked in the ass by saintly
> motorcyclists, and screamed with joy,
> who blew and were blown by those human seraphim,
> the sailors, caresses of Atlantic and Caribbean
> love,
> who balled in the morning in the evening in rose
> gardens and the grass of public parks and
> cemeteries scattering their semen freely to
> whomever come who may.

For Hanrahan this rhapsody of gay love made Ferlinghetti and City Lights the target of an anti-obscenity crusade. Ultimately, that crusade failed when a judge ruled that Howl was not obscene, since it had "social importance." Foiled in court, the police resorted to harassing both the gay and Beat communities that Ginsberg had embraced.

In reality, something far more spiritual than hedonistic or obscene had driven the Beats to the fringes of society. They, like earlier religious utopian communities,

Lawrence Ferlingetti's City Lights bookstore became a center for the Beat culture in San Francisco. Allen Ginsberg introduced Howl there.   (Source: Allen Ginsburg/CORBIS)

searched for authenticity and spiritual transcendence that would overcome their profound sense of alienation from the conventional world. That search became the stuff of legend in the writings of one of the 1950s major cult novelists—Jack Kerouac. Kerouac had been among those who gathered in 1955 to hear *Howl* when Ginsberg first read it in public. Through Kerouac's novels—*Visions of Cody, The Subterraneans, Dharma Bums*, but most of all *On the Road*—many young Americans discovered the exotic, urban world of the Beats.

On the Road celebrates the restless quest for "IT," the transcendent moment when mind and experience mesh. At times IT was personified in Dean Moriarty, modeled on Neal Cassady, Kerouac's real-life alter ego. And through Cassady/Moriarty, Kerouac attempted, in the verbose way beat writers seemed to prefer, to explain IT:

> Here's a guy and everybody's there, right? Up to him to put down what's on everybody's mind. He starts the first chorus, then lines up his ideas, people, yeah, yeah, but get it, and then he rises to his fate and has to blow equal to it. All of a sudden somewhere in the middle of the chorus he gets it—everybody looks up and knows; they listen; he picks it up and carries. Time stops. He's filling empty space with the substance of our lives, confessions of his bellybotton strain, remembrance of ideas, rehashes of old blowing. He has to blow across bridges and come back and do it with such infinite feeling soul-exploratory for the tune of the moment that everybody knows it's not the tune that counts, but IT—

However vaguely defined, Kerouac's IT would become a central part of the 1960s ethos. It dismissed rational analysis and conventional ethics in favor of ethereal flights of fancy and a commitment to authentic experience, immediacy, sensuality, and community, defined in this instance as those who when that saxophone blew IT, knew IT when they heard IT.

Cassady would become a legend twice—as the road companion for Kerouac's fictional persona, Sal Paradise, and again as the manic, madcap driver for Ken Kesey's Merry Pranksters, chronicled in the 1960s by Tom Wolfe in The Electric Kool-Aid Acid Test. Through Cassady, both Kerouac and Ginsberg connected with the working-class world they idealized as free of suffocating middle-class culture. Neighborhoods of workers, blacks, Indians, and Mexicans preserved communal folkways that kept them in touch with their essential humanity. In this the Beats anticipated the way 1960s cultural and political rebels would romanticize those same groups. In one nostalgic passage, Kerouac recalled how after a hard day's manual labor,

> At lilac evening I walked with every muscle aching among the lights of 27th and Welton in the Denver colored section, wishing I were a Negro, feeling that the best the white world had to offer was not enough ecstasy, not enough life, joy, kicks, darkness, music, not enough night. . . . I wished I were a Denver Mexican, or even a poor overworked Jap, anything but what I was so drearily, a "white Man" disillusioned. . . . I passed the dark porches of Mexican and Negro homes; soft voices were there, occasionally the dusky knee of some dark sensuous gal. . . wishing I could exchange worlds with the happy true-hearted, ecstatic Negroes of America. The raggedy world reminded me of Dean and Marylou, who knew these streets so well from childhood.

Seldom did Kerouac or those who took up this refrain acknowledge the anger and desperation behind the faces of those "ecstatic Negroes."

The Beats focused on the sexual rather than political in their identification with nature's noble people. "Real life was sexual," one of Kerouac's lovers recalled. Sex served the Beats as an antidote to the desperation and loneliness that overwhelmed them when they faced themselves alone. Set adrift without spiritual refuge, Sal Paradise and Dean turn to each other, much as the Beats sought to construct communities on the fringes of a world they rejected. This rejection was aesthetic, even religious, not political. Above all, they turned away from the materialism that inhibited spiritual enlightenment. *On the Road* chronicles their search for Dean Moriarty, Sr., the father whose absence denied his son both authority and love and who ultimately was nowhere to be found. What Sal did discover instead was the energizing power of the road and the raw beauty of the land. The book ends with Dean and Sal having parted, and Sal contemplating "all that raw land that rolls in one unbelievable huge bulge over to the West Coast, and all that road going, all the people dreaming in the immensity of it."

Here was a blend of celebration and resignation that issued no clarion call to action. Yet for beat literature, as with rock and roll, some sense of its significance can be discovered in the venom that it provoked from its enemies. Conservative critic Norman Podhoretz savaged it as "a revolt of all forces hostile to civilization itself." Podhoretz ranted that "what juvenile delinquency is to life, the San Francisco writers are to literature." That linking of the Beats to youth culture was prescient in a way Podhoretz almost certainly did not recognize at the time. And his hostility to Beat literature was so profound as to introduce a polarization of values that would become more distinctive as the uncivil wars emerged.

The prosecution of Lawrence Ferlinghetti was a more drastic attack on Beat culture. Yet rather than crushing this incipient rebellion, it brought the Beats notoriety few actively sought. As the news media descended on North Beach to revel in the novelty of the Beat subculture, they inadvertently turned this isolated domain into an incubator for attitudes that would provoke the uncivil wars that few Americans at that time saw coming. By the late 1950s, nearly every large American city had an area that attracted self-acclaimed social outcasts, the intellectually curious, and the simply prurient. College towns and campus cafeterias affected their own mini-versions of North Beach or Greenwich Village. Student intellectuals and the culturally avant garde gathered to talk about foreign films, poetry, classical music, jazz, and even politics. They discovered in the Beat style an exotic alternative to the buttoned-down world around them. Mainstream America looked curiously on these demimondes from a distance, but few people other than the Beats, their critics, their student admirers, and the police vice squads took them very seriously. It seems they should have.

The Attack on Corporate Culture

Above all, the Beats called into question the corporate ethic of work and career. Novelist William Burroughs once told Kerouac, "I am shitting out my educated Middle West background once and for all." That background was in many ways at the heart of consensus. It had prepared Burroughs to enter the managing class of a corporate society. According to the prevailing wisdom purveyed by advertising, the modern corporation afforded its employees and customers the opportunity to enjoy the materially expansive lifestyle that its technological innovation and productive efficiency made possible. To reach the top of the corporate ladder was to realize the American dream and join the band of enlightened executives who managed this world. In a spirit of cooperation, they joined with government leaders to steer the country down the road to prosperity and freedom. Or as General Motors chairman Charles Wilson assured a congressional committee, in a phrase that sixties radicals often used to illustrate the power of big business over government, "what is good for our country is good for General Motors, and vice versa."

Such smug assurance did not rest easily with a number of the nation's academics and intellectuals. Like the Beats, they regretted the ways in which contemporary culture suffocated individuals with any independence of spirit or thought, but unlike the Beats, they located their discontent in a historical context and expressed it in more traditional ways. Without the outrageous sexual agenda, their ideas may have seemed less shocking, but they were generally more powerful and disturbing. When these intellectuals struggled to reconcile traditional Western notions of progress with the horrific legacies of fascist and Stalinist totalitarianism, they found an explanation in the herd mentality nurtured by corporate culture and the manipulations of the media. To many, it seemed the United States had sold out its democratic culture in favor of a numbing materialism.

That may account for their positive reaction to *The Organization Man*, a book that viewed corporate culture as an attack of society against the individual. Witchhunters normally treated such critical ideas as subversive, but they could not easily dismiss its author, William Whyte, as a discontented "pinko." Whyte was a conservative writing for the impeccably establishment *Fortune* magazine. His analysis of corporate culture and suburbia was based on anecdotal observations that connected his laboratory (Forest Park, Illinois—a Chicago suburb) to the reader's world. In this brave new world, "there should be, then, no conflict between man and society."

As Whyte examined the organizational world, he observed that it operated with a therapeutic model in which "conflicts are misunderstandings, breakdowns in communication. By applying the methods of science to human relations we can eliminate these obstacles to consensus and create an equilibrium in which society's needs and the needs of the individual are one and the same." Under such a therapeutic model, the individualist, the dissenter, and the eccentric were seen as maladjusted; the possibility that fault might lie within society or the organization simply did not arise. Individual discontent did not reveal flaws in that society. Rather, problems arose when individuals failed to adjust personal needs to the larger good of the group.

Whyte had not reached that conclusion because he saw the organization and its ethos as bad. Quite the opposite: the danger lay in its "very beneficence." Going along to get along paid well and provided considerable security. Such comfort often seduced the individual into a loss of selfhood. Where the old labor boss demanded "your sweat," the new corporate manager wanted something more precious: "The new man wants your soul." Herein Whyte discovered the irony of the organizational society. On the one hand, it seduced its members with the promise of security; on the other, it venerated "progress." In the 1950s, corporate spokesperson Ronald Reagan reminded Americans that at General Electric, "Progress was our most important product." Yet qualitative progress required innovation—the special province of the nonconformist. In a society where everyone conforms, progress would become simply a matter of producing the same things in greater quantity. If society crushed nonconformity, from whence would innovation spring?

Despite the scathing tone of his critique, Whyte had no heroic remedy to offer. He concluded that with evasion rather than confrontation, individuals could survive the world of George Orwell's *1984* with some humanity intact. Young Americans could scarcely find that a prescription for dissent, but in laying bare the hollowness of corporate culture and its departure from the nation's individualistic traditions, Whyte raised a sensitive issue. Where advertisers spent huge sums to create images of corporations that were dynamic and progressive, Whyte revealed them as cautious and bumbling. Further, the hypocrisy of corporate culture would alienate young Americans, who increasingly insisted on authenticity in their relationship to the world around them. And his style anticipated the "new journalism" of the 1960s, in which the narrative voice becomes first person and engaged rather than coolly detached, seemingly objective, and utterly impersonal, as was the style of most academic writing in the 1950s.

In a similar way, force of personality distinguished John Kenneth Galbraith from many 1950s social critics. On one level, Galbraith could be seen as a pillar of the establishment. He shuttled regularly between his teaching position at Harvard to roles in national politics and journalism. He even did an editorial stint for Henry Luce at *Fortune*. But Galbraith had a side that detested smugness and pomposity. He seemed to have assumed the personal mission of deflating orthodoxy, save, perhaps, the preference of Keynesian economists for activist public policy. Galbraith was in his way every bit as irreverent, iconoclastic, and disturbing as *Mad*. Indeed, he was probably one of the few academics of the era who would have been flattered by such a comparison.

In 1958, Galbraith achieved something of an anomaly for an academic when his book, *The Affluent Society*, became a bestseller. Like Whyte, Galbraith's impact came as much from style and tone as from content. Galbraith contended that economic thought derived from a world of scarcity and poverty, a world that had little relevance to Americans in the affluent 1950s. He also rejected the popular idea that wealth somehow measured wisdom or the notion, so comforting to those without wealth, that it brought its own burdens:

> Wealth is not without advantages and the case to the contrary, although it has often been made, has never proved widely persuasive. But, beyond doubt, wealth is the enemy of understanding. The poor man always has a precise view of his problem and

its remedy: he hasn't enough and he needs more. The rich man can assume or imagine a much greater variety of ills and he will be correspondingly much less certain of their remedy. Also, until he learns to live with his wealth, he will have a well-observed tendency to put it to the wrong purposes or otherwise to make himself foolish.

As with individuals so with nations.

Hence Galbraith believed the United States, having recently achieved affluence, had failed to use it in a way that guaranteed prosperity in the future. Indeed, the possibility of nuclear holocaust threatened the future itself.

Galbraith understood that the 1950s were not receptive to unorthodox thinking: "These are the days when men of all social disciplines and political faiths seek the comfortable and the accepted; when the man of controversy is looked upon as a disturbing influence; when originality is taken to be a sign of instability; and when, in minor modification of the scriptural parable, the bland lead the bland." More than any particular political ideology, it was the suffocating "conventional wisdom" Galbraith sought to disturb. Most people, he argued, associate the truth "with convenience, with what most closely accords with self-interest and personal well-being." And where in personal relations, familiarity may breed contempt, in the realm of social ideas "it is the touchstone of acceptability." Even among those who traffic in ideas, being an advocate of new ideas was more important than actually articulating them.

Galbraith believed that conventional wisdom created the inertia and resistance to change to which people of all political persuasions succumbed. Among the ideas Americans of the 1950s clung to most tenaciously was that "the increased production of goods is, . . . a basic measure of social achievement." Indeed, that was a pillar upon which consensus rested. Galbraith suggested that such productivity was not enough. What was needed he called "social balance." Increases in consumer goods in the private sector required a comparable increase in services rendered in the public sector. What good did shiny new cars do if roads, parking places, and traffic regulation were all inadequate? He singled out for mention Los Angeles, where failure to regulate exhaust emissions resulted in "the agony of the city without useable air." Juvenile delinquency could be explained as much by the lack of good schools, recreation facilities, and police as by the baneful influence of media.

But no more than Whyte or others who attacked consensus culture did Galbraith propose radical remedies. In his unabashedly liberal agenda, he called for improved opportunity through better education, a renewed commitment to public service, and the emergence of a more critical public able to resist "the want creating power [to wit, advertising] which is essential to the modern economy." Galbraith proposed to achieve those ends by reinvigorating the activist state. He showed his real courage in criticizing fundamental assumptions of the consensus. Even if massive defense spending, especially on nuclear weapons, might improve security in the short term, he believed it threatened long-term security. Rather than create weapons "designed to destroy all life," Americans could better assure their future affluence through technological innovation in consumer products and public services.

Galbraith also made a case for the nation's poor and unemployed. He did not believe an affluent society should ignore those in need. Given the level of prosperity, every citizen had a right to "decency and comfort." Such ideas indeed ran against the grain of the "conventional wisdom," just as Galbraith knew they did. Only in times of national emergency had Americans ever tolerated the kind of public activism he recommended.

Another critic seems especially worth mentioning, perhaps because he came to the intellectual realm of Columbia University and New York from Texas; or perhaps because of the image he projected when driving to class on a huge Harley; or possibly because his premature death in 1962 at the age of forty-five enshrined him, along with James Dean, Alan Freed, Che Guevera, and others, in the hall of youth culture martyrs. Whatever the explanation, C. Wright Mills provided the New Left with much of its political rhetoric and identified for dissenters of the 1960s the connection between politics and culture. Neither a Marxist nor a liberal, Mills drew upon the social critic Thorstein Veblen to analyze how hierarchies of power in the nation's elites and bureaucracies undermined democracy. He rejected Marxism because its focus on capitalism ignored the critical role of the state and military. Liberals, Mills believed, failed to see that the mechanisms of democratic elections had little impact on the managers and bureaucrats who actually made and carried out critical decisions.

The Power Elite, the most influential of his books, argued that World War II and the cold war had produced a merger among the leaders of the great political, economic, and military institutions. Authority rested atop those large, centralized organizations. Hence real power lay with the presidents and managers of the giant corporations; the president, his circle, and agency heads; and the Joint Chiefs of Staff. While each group had its own domain in which it wielded ultimate authority—the business corporation, the government, and the military defense community—they acted in partnership to enhance their power. At the center stood the president and his national security managers, responsible for coordinating and maintaining the "interlocking" interests of the elite. Through their shared control over power, they made the decisions of national and international consequence that determined the fate of the people. Or as Mills observed, those who sense the existence of an elite "know that the bomb was dropped over Japan in the name of the United States, although they were at no time consulted about the matter."

The elite constituted itself through the American social and educational systems, which identified individuals with the proper constellation of character and background to manage power. Mills discovered that those chosen shared a psychological profile, professional connections, educational experiences, club memberships, and links through marriage, career tracks, and even vacation preferences. Having such common cultural experiences, members of the elite naturally thought and acted much alike. From those similarities they gained the sense of common purpose and entitlement that made them comfortable with power and gave them an "internal discipline" that ensured their control. Their common purpose was made all the more coherent by the ease and regularity with which leaders moved back and forth from the military to the government to Wall Street and the corporate world.

This concentration of power was not simply the results of a conspiracy among capitalists or eastern power brokers, as radicals of the Left and Right often charged. Nor did Mills share E. Digby Baltzell's fear that the elite class would threaten democracy by hardening into a caste system. Even with its proscribed channels of access, the elite he described was something of a meritocracy, expanding and contracting to meet the exigencies of governing. What made it dangerous was its remoteness— its shadowy membership was impersonal, distant, anonymous, and, above all, inaccessible. These were not the congressmen and senators who asked for votes, or the low-level functionaries who staffed public agencies, or the union officials, farm bloc leaders, and business lobbyists who came to government seeking favors for their constituents. Individuals did not have power; institutions did, and among them the great institutions, not these small ones, controlled real power. The little fry saw only the small picture. And as competing interests, their power remained fragmented, their influence limited to their own narrow domains.

This reading of power rejected the prevailing 1950s idea of pluralism. Leading pluralist theorists saw a society structured on a horizontal plain. The many affiliational bodies—political parties, voluntary associations, professional and religious organizations, and other informal political groups—created a balance in which power divided relatively equally, much along the lines described by James Madison in Federalist 10. Mills dismissed this as an illusion. Membership in affiliational bodies in no way mediated between individuals and the state. In a society with a vertical axis of power, none of those groups had any significant impact on critical decisions, since democracy in the modern state had nothing to do with the distribution of power. Outside the elite, individuals faced the state alone: insecure, unprotected, and alienated.

The media enhanced that powerlessness, for as Mills argued, they "not only give us information; they guide our very experience." For those in mass society, the sense of self comes from the media, not some inner light: "(1) the media tell the man in the mass who he is—they give him an identity; (2) they tell him what he wants to be—they give him aspirations; (3) they tell him how to get that way— they give him technique; and (4) they tell him how to feel that he is that way even when he is not—they give him escape." Here is a vision of the world not much at odds with George Orwell's 1984. Individuals lead inauthentic lives without the will or ability to shape their own destiny. In such a world, the distinction between democracy and totalitarianism was no longer clear.

Such a radical critique did not afford Mills, any more than Whyte or Galbraith, with a substantial agenda either to revive democracy or to restructure society. He hoped largely that intellectuals might once again become a source of dissent. In the recent past they had been co-opted by the elite that used their ideas to legitimize the hierarchy of power. By freeing themselves from that subservient position, intellectuals might once again become an independent "moral conscience." As they raised their private malaise to the level of public issues, they could alert the public to the ways in which the elite used the media to manipulate public opinion in support of the reigning order. Properly educated, the public could gain the consciousness necessary for autonomous political behavior. In essence, Mills's vision was so conservative it seemed radical. He embraced a political system envisioned by Ralph Waldo Emerson in which political parties debated the real issues and an enlightened citizenry made informed and meaningful political choices.

The radicals of the 1960s learned much from Mills. He was brash, when most academics were timid. There was something delightfully naughty in hearing him dismiss McCarthy and his ilk as "a small group of political primitives" who had succeeded largely in having "emptied domestic politics of rational content, and decisively lowered the level of public sensibility." His rejection of orthodox categories, either Marxist or liberal, satisfied their desire to see their rebellion as something new. In the *Port Huron Statement* of 1962, which gave official birth to the New Left, SDS virtually paraphrased Mills (echoing Emerson): "The goal of man and society should be human independence: a concern not with image [or] popularity but with finding a meaning in life that is personally authentic." As their own critical skills grew, the new radicals could imagine themselves as dissenting intellectuals seeking to raise the public's awareness (as well as their own) of the ways in which the elite stifled critical commentary.

Corporate culture shielded itself from such attacks in part by the sheer bounty it produced for American society. There seemed to be no material need the modern corporation could not meet. And when problems arose like the acrid smog over Los Angeles, the automakers had legions of public relations specialists to deflect criticism and lobbyists to defeat unwanted government regulations. Among those harnessing technology to improve the human condition, none in the postwar era could claim greater success than the agricultural chemical producers. Against insect hordes pictured in advertising as remarkably similar to Communist subversives, they had created a vast new arsenal of chemical weapons. They replaced primitive poisons such as arsenic and mercury with carbon-based pesticides such as chlordane and DDT. These new chemicals did not appear to pose a threat to those who applied them. But some scientists began to suspect that hydrocarbon-based pesticides and herbicides might have unrecognized long-term effects. Sudden mass kills of fish and birds suggested something was rotten in the kingdom of "better living through chemistry" (a popular DuPont ad slogan). That concern led Rachel Carson in 1962 to publish *Silent Spring,* a best-selling book about DDT and other pesticides.

A furor over the fallout of strontium-90 from nuclear tests had preceded the publication of *Silent Spring,* a book with an impact much like Harriet Beecher Stowe's *Uncle Tom's Cabin* and Upton Sinclair's *The Jungle.* It provoked outraged denials from those interests it criticized. And like Stowe and Sinclair, Carson inspired a reform movement, in this case giving rise to popular environmentalism. Prior to the publication of *Silent Spring,* the public learned that fallout from nuclear tests had irradiated mother's milk. Carson raised similar concerns about the indiscriminate spraying of pesticides.

Already a well-known naturalist writer, Carson had what was rare for a woman of that era, a career as a scientist. Her research into chemical pesticides revealed that their indiscriminant use posed a danger. Where chemical companies touted the power of insecticides to exterminate pests, Carson thought the term "biocide" better described their impact on the natural world. This chemical warfare threatened "the contamination of man's total environment with such substances of incredible potential for harm—substances that accumulate in the tissues of plants and animals and even penetrate the germ cells to shatter or alter the very material of heredity upon which the shape of the future depends." Ignorance and apathy, encouraged by the deceptive claims of farm interests, scientists, and chemical companies, prevented an effective public response. As William Whyte had also suggested, these were the institutions that embodied the ideal of beneficial progress that made America great.

Silent Spring did not reach its audience simply by playing on popular fears. As a writer, Carson had the descriptive gifts of other great naturalist writers like Henry David Thoreau and John Muir. She introduced in simple terms the concepts of ecology that placed human activities within, rather than above or outside, the processes of nature. Her analysis of the chemistry of pesticides, while expressed in terms accessible to a lay audience, was based on solid scientific evidence. To make sure she reached her audience, Carson did raise her voice a bit louder and, perhaps, more sharply than the available evidence justified. But then again, she believed the danger of inaction was equal to the threat of extinction through nuclear war. In the face of ever-increasing use of chemical sprays, insects, she pointed out, had vindicated Darwin's theory of the survival of the fittest by evolving superraces resistant to current pesticides. "Destructive insects often undergo a 'flareback,' or resurgence, after spraying, in numbers greater than before," she noted. Hence the demand arose for even heavier spraying with ever more deadly chemicals. As a consequence, "the chemical war is never won, and all life is caught in a violent crossfire." In time, pesticides like DDT accumulated in the food chain, where they began to kill off birds and other creatures while posing an increasing danger to humans.

Powerful interests, including the farm bloc, its allies in the Department of Agriculture, the petrochemical industry, and the male-dominated research sciences, tried to discredit Carson. In 1964, *Science* magazine argued that she could "be legitimately charged with having exceeded the bounds of scientific knowledge for the purpose of achieving shock." The chemical companies and their scientists charged that since the evidence did not prove her point, she did a disservice to valuable economic interests by raising public hysteria and to organized science by abusing the scientific method. As *Science* concluded, "Rachel Carson's stretching of scientific points is not easily excused." What was it about this shy and gentle woman that provoked otherwise civil men to condemn her so? Ezra Taft Benson, a Mormon elder who had been Eisenhower's secretary of agriculture, wondered "why a

SAVE THAT COTTON!

During periods of national emergency cotton is vital. It goes into uniforms, gun covers, pup tents, duffle bags and a thousand other items essential to the well equipped soldier. Leave it to the boll weevil and there would not be nearly enough cotton. But cotton we must have in unbelievable quantities and that means death to the weevil.

Benzene Hexachloride is the lethal chemical in most of the dust and spray insecticides which today are destroying these pests and saving cotton for the big defense job.

Whether you have weevil trouble or not, there are many ways in which your own daily life is made safer and more comfortable with chemicals from Tennessee . . . and industry serving all industry.

TENNESSEE
PRODUCTS & CHEMICAL
Corporation
NASHVILLE, TENNESSEE

PRODUCERS OF: FUELS • METALLURGICAL PRODUCTS • TENNEALOY BUILDING PRODUCTS • AROMATIC CHEMICALS • WOOD CHEMICALS • AGRICULTURAL CHEMICALS

Agricultural chemical manufacturers used Cold War themes to promote pesticides. Ads evoked the spirit of a nation at war against hordes of subversive insects to boost sales. (Source: Agricultural Chemicals)

spinster with no children was so concerned about genetics?" He concluded that she was "probably a Communist."

Carson did have her defenders, but they generally lacked the authority of the technical and scientific establishment. So, for example, the respected *Saturday Review of Literature* paid Carson tribute when it acknowledged that she had "wagered her entire reputation (and it is considerable despite the omission of her name from the American Men of Science) against an army of propagandists richly paid by chemical manufacturers and provided free and respectable lecture platforms by societies of chemists." Scientists eventually had to grant the virtue of her cause, for in 1964 a report from the President's Science Advisory Council largely vindicated her case and her reputation.

During the 1950s, advertising for the chemical companies described the insect world as a danger every bit as invidious as the aliens of horror movies or the godless Communists. Hence they portrayed themselves as warriors on the frontline of the nation's defenses, bringing to bear all the weapons of science and industry against an invading foe. It was as if to say that we were in an arms race with the insect world—their hereditary adaptability against our chemical arsenal. Carson challenged their dubious assumptions that insects posed a clear and present danger and that pesticides were harmless to humans. Further, as she pointed out, many of the crops they so heroically defended were generally grown in surplus and stored at public expense. In questioning the science establishment's presumption of infallibility, Carson was in their eyes guilty of sedition. In fact, several chemical company PR types agreed with Benson that Carson might be a Communist.

Her writing did not simply evoke the dangers of science run amok. In her reverence for the mysteries of nature and the intricate web of life, she was something of a romantic. Empirical science has often tried to dismiss the romantic sensibility as "shrill," "irrational," and "emotional." These same terms distinguished the masculine from the feminine. In that way, male scientists used Carson's gender to discredit her ideas. As a *New York Times* editorial remarked, "Among the mildest rejoinders of the chemical industry is the charge that she is 'a fanatic defender of the balance of nature'—as if the balance of nature were equivalent to nudism or skin diving." In a televised debate, a scientist from the American Cyanamid Corporation argued in defense of the chemical industry that "man is steadily learning to control nature." To that, Carson replied that the big challenge was to prove "our maturity and our mastery, not of nature, but of ourselves." Maturity meant thinking of "ourselves as only a tiny part of a vast and incredible universe." With more humility, humans might better ensure the future for themselves and their fellow species. Such a biocentric idea contradicted the anthropocentrism of a generation of scientists who preached the conquest of nature, whether through manipulation of the atom, synthetic materials, or deadly pesticides. As environmental historian Donald Worster concluded, that idea became "the central creed of the ecology movement: a vision of the unity of life, as taught by science, and a moral ideal of living cooperatively with all members of the natural community."

In another way, Carson challenged the authority of corporate and scientific elites. If, as she charged, the dangers of pesticides were real, through silence or, even worse, deceptive claims on this issue, science and industry had abdicated their responsibility. "This is an era of specialists, each of whom sees his own problem and is unaware of or intolerant of the larger frame into which it fits," she observed. Carson wanted an informed public with a holistic view of nature, rather than self-serving businesses or narrowly trained specialists, to decide the future. As she argued, "It is the public that is being asked to assume the risks that the insect controllers calculate. The public must decide whether it wishes to continue on the present road, and it can do so only when in full possession of the facts. In the words of Jean Rostand, 'The obligation to endure gives us the right to know.'" In essence, Carson's determination to have the public rather than the experts decide would require a radical transformation in public policy. She advocated nothing less than "power to the people," the ideal of participatory democracy that inspired much of the political dissent during the uncivil wars.

Iconoclasts

Those with a scientific or rationalist temperament have long tended to see people such as Carson as romantic subversives. Where they preach the power of reason, romantics appeal to the emotional self. And where science might look for order in the world, anarchy and upheaval have more appeal to romantics. On its darker side, the romantic sensibility falls into a pessimism and despair at odds with the scientific faith in progress. Increasingly, by the late 1950s and early 1960s, such a dark streak intruded into the dissenting style. Hints of it are evident in Carson's apocalyptic view of "the endless spiral" of chemical spraying and "flareback." Carson was a subversive for yet another reason: she was a public figure in an era that consigned women to the kitchen, not the laboratory. Why, after all, when many people thought her worthy of a Nobel Prize did the men of science refuse to list her among their elite? Were not the terms "shrill," "emotional," and "irrational" the common pejoratives men used to dismiss values they saw as feminine?

That the public culture of the 1950s was almost exclusively a male domain was a point not lost on Betty Friedan. Just as the attack on Carson reached a crescendo in 1963, Friedan published her epochal book *The Feminine Mystique*. Because most people connect Friedan to the emergence of the women's liberation movement, they are less concerned with her ties to dissent in the 1950s and 1960s. Friedan's writing has an obvious connection to those like Salinger, who defined the crises of the postwar era in terms of sexuality and identity or who, like Whyte, took on the suburban, corporate consensus. The corrosive style in which Friedan delivered her critique and the absurdist trap in which she found women ensnared link her to yet another tradition, the iconoclastic irreverence of the black humorists. Even if she did not manifest their inclination to devolve terror into comedy—as if to say "in a world this bad, you might as well laugh"—she did share their sense of moral outrage and personal anguish.

As a journalist and a housewife, Friedan had come to doubt the image of domestic bliss purveyed in the popular women's magazines of the 1950s. Her own discontent, as well as that of women she knew and interviewed, alerted her to what she called, "the problem that has no name." Where conventional authorities might dismiss women's sense of discontent as typical female neurosis, Friedan saw it as profoundly existential. As one woman told her, "There is no problem you can put a name to. But I'm desperate. I begin to feel I have no personality. I'm a server of food and a putter-on of pants and a bedmaker, somebody who can be called on when you want something. But who am I?" It was a discontent Friedan had discovered in herself: "I, like other women, thought there was something wrong with me because I didn't have an orgasm waxing the kitchen floor." The sexual text of this identity crisis was unmistakable. Indeed, Friedan made it explicit: "Encouraged by the mystique to evade their identity crisis, permitted to escape identity altogether in the name of sexual fulfillment, women are living once again with their feet bound in the old image of glorified femininity."

Who then was responsible for setting this trap? Friedan, to some degree, blamed women themselves. In the era after World War II, the American woman had made what Friedan believed was a "mistaken choice. She ran back home to live by sex alone, trading in her individuality for security." But that was only part of the answer. Friedan uncovered what she saw as a massive conspiracy within the functionalist social sciences, education, and, above all, the media to promote the feminine mystique. These were bastions of established authority, almost exclusively controlled by men. Masculine domination, Friedan believed, was the major reason the feminine mystique reflected an idealized male view of women as housewives, mothers, and lovers.

The media offered substantial evidence of how men had sold women on the mystique. One advertising executive told Friedan without any evident self-consciousness that "properly manipulated, . . . American housewives can be given that sense of identity, purpose, creativity, the self-realization, even the sexual joy they lack—by the buying of things." What clearer admission was needed that the feminine mystique served to assure that women's lives lacked authenticity? For advertisers, the mystique was a means to an end to guarantee consumption; for women, it became an end unto itself.

What then was this mystique that had so enslaved women? And for the purpose of identifying the sources of rebellion in the 1960s, what did this have to do with the attack on established authority that runs through texts we have thus far examined? The mystique, as Friedan defined it, was the consensus that the "housewife-mother, who never had a chance to be anything else" should serve as "the model for all women." Domesticity defined the idealized world in which women existed, "confined by necessity to cooking, cleaning, washing, bearing children." Over time the consensus had become "a religion, a pattern by which all women must now live or deny their femininity." So here for Friedan was what amounted to an absurdist trap. To be a fulfilled woman was to be fully feminine. To be fully feminine was to be blissfully domestic. To be blissfully domestic was to submerge one's identity in the lives and needs of others. To live for others was to deny one's own existence and thus to have no identity. To have no identity was to give way to alienation and despair. Hence, for most women society offered no way out. To be happy they had to embrace the feminine mystique, but to embrace the feminine mystique was to guarantee their self-destruction.

In attacking the stifling tyranny of male authority, Friedan was more persuasive in identifying and condemning the mystique than in offering a new course for women. She recommended careers, more purposeful education, and a higher sense of identity to enable a woman "to find herself, to know herself as a person by creative work of her own." Yet as historian Nancy Wolloch concluded, "the power of The Feminine Mystique was not in its remedies, which seemed quite meager compared to the enormity of the conspiracy against women Friedan described. Rather, it was in the revelation of the 'mystique' itself." By raising women's consciousness, as she had raised her own, Friedan invited them to take control of their own destinies. In the 1960s, that is just what a generation of women began to do.

Among those at whom Friedan pointed a finger, none stood more properly accused than male media executives, and among them advertisers, who had been shameless promoters of the "feminine mystique." Advertising agencies of the 1950s were almost exclusively male domains governed by strict corporate hierarchies and a devotion to a scientific approach to arousing consumer desire. Indeed, advertising men seemed to epitomize "the man in the grey flannel suit." All the same, advertising was far from monolithic in its structure and was often its own harshest critique. A number of best-selling books, led by Vance Packard's *The Hidden Persuaders*, exposed the industry's use of manipulative techniques to sell to a gullible public inferior products that filled no essential need. "They think we are dopes," Packard told his readers.

Historian Thomas Frank has argued persuasively that a few advertisers in the early 1960s unleashed a powerful critique of their industry that echoed the era's concern with mass society and in many ways anticipated, even shaped, the countercultural upheavals of the era. Bill Bernbach, the force behind the Doyle Dane Bernbach agency, produced advertisements that turned Packard's critique of the 1950s consumer culture into a "creative revolution of the sixties." He did so by injecting the "public mistrust of consumerism" that writers such as Whyte and Galbraith had identified into what Frank called "anti-advertising." Unlike the established leaders of the advertising industry, Bernbach believed "advertising is fundamentally persuasion and persuasion happens not to be a science, but an art."

More than any other product, automobiles defined the consumer culture of the 1950s. The Big Three automobile companies (Chrysler, Ford, and General Motors) designed a product to become obsolete in a year, engineered to drive like a mattress, and built to fall apart within two years or 60,000 miles. With never a hint of their product's deficiencies, advertisers touted cars as the ultimate status symbol. One Buick ad made the case: "What a wonderful sense of well-being just being *seen* behind the wheel. No showing off. Just that Clean Look of Action which unmistakably tells of your success." To Bill Bernbach, the conventional approach to selling cars epitomized all that was wrong with conformist society of the 1950s. Television commercials placed cars on pedestals to be worshipped.

Among Doyle Dane's clients was one that defied the conventions of the automobile industry. Rather than status or ephemeral styling, Volkswagen was prepared to give consumers something they claimed to want, a "better car . . . made for less money." Bill Bernbach set out to sell it. That was no small achievement, given that the car had been originally conceived in part by Adolph Hitler as the ultimate vehicle of mass society. Worse yet, the Beetle was small, with a spartan interior and an underpowered engine. Doyle Dane succeeded by breaking every rule of the advertising industry. Rather than adopt the scientific sell, their ads used humor and treated the consumer as someone who understood the game. Rather than promote glitz and fancy accessories, VW sold reliability, economy, quality manufacturing, and low-cost maintenance. Ads regularly admitted that the car was ugly, that it looked like a bug, or that it was funny looking. A particular target was the auto industry's practice of designed obsolescence. One ad, done in sober black and

The '51 '52 '53 '54 '55 '56 '57 '58 '59 '60 '61 Volkswagen.

Ever since we started making Volkswagens, we've put all our time and effort into the one basic model.

You can see we've had lots of practice. We've learned to make every part of the VW fit every other part so well, the finished car is practically air-tight.

The engine is so carefully machined and assembled, you can drive a brand new VW at top speed all day.

We don't make changes lightly. And never to make the VW look different, only to make it work better.

When we do make a change, we go out of our way to make the new part fit older Volkswagens, too.

With this result: An authorized Volkswagen dealer can repair any year's Volkswagen, even the earliest. (Why not? They use mostly interchangeable parts!)

If you had to decide between a car that went out of style every year or two and a car that never did, which would it be?

With visual irony, Volkswagen parodied the planned obsolescence of Detroit's automobile culture. The Beetle, pictured here, became an icon of the counterculture.
(Source: Courtesy of Doyle, Dane, Bernbach and Volkswagen of America)

white, showed a single Beetle featured under spotlights as the year's new model. The caption read with obvious tongue-in-cheek: "The '51, '52, '53, '54, '55, '56, '57, '58, '59, '60, '61 Volkswagen." The print copy assured readers Volkswagen changed their car "never to make the VW look different, only to make it work better."

By the middle of the 1960s, Doyle Dane had turned the VW Beetle into the ultimate anti-car and the vehicle of choice (along with the VW bus) for the counterculture. How could hip consumers not respect a company that admitted it was a capitalist venture, "since we have the burning desire to stay in business." Such "truth in advertising" began to refashion the entire industry. It appealed to consumers who respected authenticity and wanted to be treated like intelligent beings. Doyle Dane Bernbach unleashed the advertising industry's creative potential by addressing, rather than evading, the issues raised by the critics of the liberal corporate consensus.

The absurdist flavor of ads for "a car so ugly you have to love it" links the advertising of Bill Bernbach to Joseph Heller and the black humorists. The sense of entrapment in a world of corporate conformity was at the core of Heller's gothic tale of institutional life, *Catch-22* (1961). Heller imagines a world gone mad in which it is insane to be sane and vice versa. Yossarian, Heller's protagonist, began World War II as the military equivalent of Packard's manipulated consumer or Friedan's domesticated housewife. He was a good soldier, expert at laying bombs on the target. But as those around him die, Yossarian begins to change, first into a resister and then into the worst nightmare the organization world could imagine, a troublemaker. Survival becomes his obsession. He would rather save his life than bomb the targets as he once did: "He had decided to live forever or die in the attempt, and his only mission each time he went up was to come down alive."

The focus for Heller's nightmare reality is the corporate culture that the Detroit auto industry embodied and Whyte and Mills dissected. Where Mills exposed the inequities of power in corporatized America, Heller shattered the organizational mystique. Where Whyte provided an analytical perspective to reveal the arbitrary nature of authority, Heller stripped that authority of its very legitimacy. Much of the prestige large organizations acquired stemmed from the success that the military-industrial-university community claimed in winning World War II and managing the cold war. Thus, Heller showed particular satirical insight by setting *Catch-22* in what Americans thought of as the "good war." Against the nation's crusade Heller juxtaposed the twentieth century's most destructive impulses. By the time the cynical smoke cleared, all the sacred cows of American life—patriotism, religion, military heroism, service to country, loyalty, government, and authority—had been pilloried.

The pessimism of *Catch-22* comes from its depiction of life as controlled and manipulated from outside. The army air corps in which Yossarian serves as a cog is little more than a machine that in the process of killing others devours its own soldiers. What distinguishes Yossarian from those around him is his growing refusal to accept the dehumanization that organizational life imposed. To his superiors, he is just a cipher to send on missions that have no higher purpose than a "tighter bomb pattern." Yossarian, however, chooses to cling stubbornly to life in face of dangers spiraling hopelessly out of control.

His immediate enemy is Colonel Cathcart, who for no reason other than his own career ambitions continues to raise the number of missions his crews must fly. Yossarian responds at first by resisting and looking for a way out. He tells his superior, Major Major Major, "I don't want to be in the war anymore." "Would you like to see our country lose?" the major asked. To which Yossarian responds with the moral relativism that has become his credo:

"We won't lose. We've got more men, more money and more material. There are ten million men in uniform who could replace me. Some people are getting killed and a lot more are making money and having fun. Let someone else get killed."
"But suppose everybody on our side felt that way?"
"Then I'd certainly be a damned fool to feel any other way. Wouldn't I?"

Even after Yossarian chooses resistance, he finds his peril ever increasing. In desperation he turns to his friend Doc Daneka, who, as the squadron doctor, has the authority to ground him. All that stands in the way is "Catch-22," which states "a concern for one's own safety in the face of dangers that were real and immediate was the process of a rational mind." And then the madness begins: "Orr was crazy and could be grounded. All he had to do was ask; and as soon as he did, he would no longer be crazy and would have to fly more missions. Orr would be crazy to fly more missions and sane if he didn't. If he flew them he was crazy and didn't have to; but if he didn't want to he was sane and had to." The simplicity of this convoluted concept left Yossarian in awe. "That's some catch, that Catch-22," he tells the doctor. "It's the best there is," Doc Daneka replies.

Yossarian finally moves beyond quiet resistance to outright defiance; he becomes a troublemaker. His defiance begins to disrupt the organizational routines that mask the insanity of the war. Besides standing in the nude at formation to receive a medal, he walks around backward with his gun on his hip and refuses to fly any more missions. For Colonel Cathcart, this rebellion from the ranks poses a serious problem. "Morale was deteriorating and it was all Yossarian's fault. The country was in peril; he was jeopardizing his traditional rights of freedom and independence by daring to exercise them." Before Yossarian began to refuse, Colonel Korn points out, "The men were perfectly content to fly as many missions as we asked as long as they thought they had no alternative. Now you've given them hope and they're unhappy."

In the end, Yossarian has gone beyond resistance to act as our conscience. When he declares his intention to run away, Major Danby accuses him of escaping from his responsibilities. To which Yossarian replies, "I'm not running away from my responsibilities. I'm running to them. There's nothing negative about running away to save my life." The true escapists, as he points out, are those who stay to fight in the name, not of their country, but for Colonel Korn and Colonel Cathcart, which they claim is the same thing—"You're either for us or against us. There's no two ways about it." But in choosing to run, Yossarian has defined his own choice, the choice to live for himself, not for the "odious" deal they have offered to keep the system functioning.

By his example Yossarian inspires the chaplain to take a stand, to "nag and badger Col. Cathcart and Col. Korn every time I see them. I'm not afraid." And in some sense Yossarian had a similar impact on young readers of the 1960s. He became the model of a troublemaker who by saying "no" confronts the absurdities and arbitrariness of the power that created the Vietnam War. His refusal to be co-opted earns our admiration. As the Vietnam War escalated, the madness of Catch-22 became real: Lyndon Johnson increased the bombing to promote peace and American soldiers burned a village to save it. The idealism that Kennedy called into the service of America's cold war crusade devolved into an "odious" choice. "You're either for us or against us" became "My country; love it or leave it." With no middle ground, sanity became elusive. Resistance became a powerful moral choice against political authority that seemed hopelessly self-serving and corrupt. But even more, Catch-22 stripped the official voices of the nation of their authority. To hear the echo of

Colonel Cathcart in Lyndon Johnson or General Westmoreland aroused in a vocal minority a skepticism so profound that patriotism in the "one nation under God" sense was no longer possible.

Catch-22 by itself could not have inspired the revulsion with consensus that swept the college communities, but the sensibility it contained was widely shared. Certainly, that helps explain the popularity of sick jokes, of the cartoonist Jules Feiffer with his mordant images of neurosis, of comedians like Mort Sahl, Lenny Bruce, and Woody Allen, and novelists like Philip Roth, Thomas Berger, and Kurt Vonnegut. But of all the examples of black humor, none was more popular nor more devastating to the cold war consensus than Stanley Kubrick's *Dr. Strangelove, Or How I Learned to Stop Worrying and Love the Bomb* (1964).

Throughout the 1950s, movies like *Strategic Air Command* and *Bombers B-52* had reinforced official assurances that our nuclear deterrent was working to keep Communism contained. Toward the end of the decade, enthusiasm for nuclear deterrence began to slip. The movie *On the Beach* (1959), made over the opposition of the Pentagon, suggested the possibility that nuclear war might destroy human life. In reaction, strategic air command (SAC) leader General Curtis LeMay encouraged the making of the pro-SAC 1963 movie *Gathering of Eagles*. The film was only a modest success, as its deferential documentary style could no longer persuade skeptics that current nuclear doctrine assured the nation's future survival. The very acronym used to describe that doctrine, MAD, or "mutually assured destruction," seemed to many people a concept straight out of *Catch-22*. It was that insanity Kubrick captured in *Dr. Strangelove*. From the novel *Red Alert* he had gotten the idea for a film about a rogue officer who on his own initiative ordered a preemptive nuclear attack on the Soviet Union. The Pentagon assured Kubrick that no officer could launch such an attack. Only the president possessed the attack code, and only he or a surrogate could convey the necessary order to SAC.

Kubrick remained unconvinced, as well he should have. Only a few years earlier the National Security Council had created the Gaither Commission to appraise the nation's civil defenses and especially the need for a vast fallout shelter program. The commission became persuaded the real issue was not civil defense, but the ability of SAC to survive a Soviet nuclear attack with a second-strike capacity intact. To learn about SAC's plans, they visited its headquarters in Omaha. There General LeMay, often called "Bombs Away" for his passionate belief in strategic bombing, had boasted to the commission that SAC was untouchable, that Soviet missiles posed no threat, and that SAC's B-52 bombers could solve any defense problem. When the commissioners expressed skepticism, LeMay explained that the Russian accusations about American spy planes penetrating their airspace, the ones we so vigorously denied, were all true. The United States had spy planes over the Soviet Union twenty-four hours a day, monitoring military radio traffic. Hence LeMay would have ample warning of any preparation for a massive attack. "If I see that the Russians are amassing their planes for an attack, I'm going to knock the shit out of them before they take off the ground," he told commission member Robert Sprague.

Sprague was dumbfounded. Here was an American general prepared on his own initiative to launch a preemptive nuclear attack on the Soviet Union: "But General LeMay, that's not national policy," he objected. "I don't care. It's my policy," LeMay insisted. "That's what I'm going to do." Instead of a plan to survive a nuclear attack, LeMay had armed SAC with a secret plan for a preemptive attack. That plan contradicted the standing orders of the Joint Chiefs of Staff approved by the president.

Did Kubrick have any inkling of what Sprague learned? There is no evidence that he did. On the other hand, Kubrick was something of a nuclear war junky, having read most of the literature on the subject. Further, by the time *Dr. Strangelove* went into production, the Soviets had launched *Sputnik* and captured U-2 pilot Francis Gary Powers. The army had also relieved General Edwin Walker of his command in Germany for proselytizing his troops with right-wing literature. Walker was something of an extremist, but others in the military, including LeMay, were known to be sympathetic to his ideas of a preemptive war against godless Communism.

So it was not much of a stretch to meld Walker and LeMay to create General Jack D. Ripper. Kubrick had intended to treat seriously Ripper's crusade against the Soviet Union. But as he worked on the screenplay, the situations seemed just too absurd. "How the hell could you have the President ever telling a Russian premier to shoot down American planes?" Kubrick wondered. As a result, *Dr. Strangelove* spun into hysterical satire. The opening shot sets the tone as we watch a B-52 refuel in the air in what Kubrick shows as a graceful mating ritual, with the song "Try a Little Tenderness" in the background. The movie then cuts to General Ripper, who seals off Burbleson Air Force base and orders his bomb wing to attack targets in the Soviet Union. His action forces the chairman of the Joint Chiefs of Staff, General Buck Turgidson, another LeMay type, to abort a tryst with his voluptuous secretary. Off he goes to the War Room, where the nation's security managers join President Merkin Muffley in an effort to save the world from nuclear holocaust.

Just two alternatives exist. Either Ripper can be persuaded to issue the recall code to his bomber squadron or the president can give the Russians information needed to shoot the planes down. British exchange officer Captain Mandrake attempts to talk sense into Ripper but succeeds only in provoking the general into right-wing ruminations. Ripper believes that women are trying to sap him of his essence and that fluoridation of drinking water is part of a Commie conspiracy to corrupt "the purity and essence of our natural fluids." To the president falls the task of breaking the news to Soviet premier Kissof. With the help of Soviet ambassador de Sadesky, he reaches Kissof in the midst of a drunken orgy with his mistress. "Our Premier is a man of the people," de Sadesky assures President Muffley. The conversation between Muffley, a dead ringer for Adlai Stevenson, and Kissof is priceless. After soothing the premier's ruffled feelings—"Of course I like to talk to you, Dimitri"— Muffley must break the bad news: "'Look, Dimitri. You know how we've always talked about the possibility of something going wrong with the bomb? . . . The bomb? The HYDROGEN BOMB! . . . That's right. One of our base commanders did a silly thing. He, uh, went a little funny in the head. You know, funny. He ordered our planes to attack your country. . . . Let me finish Dimitri.' "

All hell then breaks loose. General Turgidson proposes, à la LeMay, that since there is no turning back, the United States should launch an all-out attack. "I'm not saying we won't get our hair mussed," he admits. Meanwhile, forces under Colonel Bat Guano have managed to break into Burbleson headquarters, where Ripper has committed suicide rather than face torture and Mandrake has figured out the recall code. With all military communications cut off, Mandrake has no way to reach the War Room. His only recourse is a pay phone, but he does not have the right change. As the world's survival hangs in the balance, he tries to persuade Colonel Guano to shoot open the change compartment of a Coke machine. "That's private property," an outraged Guano responds. When Mandrake insists, Guano warns, "You'll have the Coca Cola Company to answer to."

The recall code almost works, except the plane piloted by Major Kong does not receive the message. In the War Room, everyone awaits the outcome. President Muffley turns for advice from the scarcely rehabilitated former Nazi scientist, Dr. Strangelove. Strangelove, like Muffley and Mandrake, is played by British actor Peter Sellers. Sellers blends into Strangelove character traits of some of the day's leading nuclear theorists: refugee Nazi rocket scientist Werner Von Braun, who Walt Disney turned into a celebrity; nuclear theorist (On Thermonuclear War) Herman Kahn, a man famed for his prodigious IQ and enthusiasm for thinking the unthinkable about nuclear war; and Harvard political scientist and future national security advisor and secretary of state for Richard Nixon, Henry Kissinger, then best known for his book Nuclear Weapons and Foreign Policy. Confined to a wheelchair, with an arm ever eager to swing on its own initiative into a "Seig Heil," Strangelove learns from de Sadesky that the Soviet Union has secretly built a doomsday machine. If a nuclear bomb explodes in Russia, the doomsday machine will poison the earth with radioactivity lasting ninety-nine years. What was the point of keeping it a secret, Strangelove asks, because "the whole point of the Doomsday Machine is lost if you keep it secret! Why didn't you tell the world, eh?" To which de Sadesky lamely replies that Kissof "loves surprises." As the movie ends, the screen lights up with nuclear explosions, while a soothing female voice sings the pop ballad "We'll Meet Again (Don't Know Where, Don't Know When)."

Predictably, Kubrick's irreverence unleashed a critical storm. Lewis Mumford, one of the most insightful critics of modernity in America, saw the movie as one of the first breaks in "the cold war trance." For that very reason, other critics savaged Kubrick. The New York Times complained that the movie was "too contemptuous of our defense establishment." Granting the comic genius of its "devastating satire," the Times reviewer still found its delight in mocking matters of "gravest consequence" was "more charged with poison than wit." And in the backhand style of finding a way to turn criticism of the United States into praise, Newsweek argued that Dr. Strangelove demonstrated the freedom filmmakers had to explore controversy, even though "most of them have not dared use it."

Shortly after the release of Dr. Strangelove, a historian compounded the debate over nuclear policy. In his book Atomic Diplomacy, Gar Alperovitz suggested that the United States bombed Hiroshima and Nagasaki not to end the war quickly, as Truman and others claimed, but to send a warning to Stalin. Indeed, Alperovitz argued that Truman delayed the Potsdam Conference of 1945 in order to be assured that the bomb would be operational when he went to negotiate postwar issues with Stalin. Many historians have since found fault with both Alperovitz's evidence and his conclusions. But the truth of his argument was less consequential than the fact he raised it at all. Until then, few Americans had ever doubted the wisdom or justice of dropping the bomb. It never occurred to practically anyone that alternatives existed.

Alperovitz pointed out that Japan was on the verge of defeat and the American military knew it. Further, Roosevelt and Truman had rejected recommendations from physicist Niels Bohr and others to establish international controls over atomic energy. Some Manhattan Project scientists had urged that the United States demonstrate the bomb before using it. Had the American people been lied to all these years? Was the bombing of Hiroshima and Nagasaki justified? Had the war ended immorally, rather than with an affirmation of technological genius? Had racism influenced the decision to use the bomb on the Japanese? For many college students, such questions shook the foundations of some of the unexamined truths they had long accepted. And those issues had special resonance because they arose as the escalating war in Vietnam raised similar questions.

∾

All of these figures, from Salinger to Alperovitz, had in some way challenged the orthodoxy that young Americans inherited in the 1950s and early 1960s. Certainly, other writers and ideas could be added to this list. What of Michael Harrington, who in The Other America (1961) focused the nation's attention on the persistence of poverty amidst affluence? Of Paul Goodman, who in Growing Up Absurd linked the spiritual emptiness of the age to corporate, technocratic culture? Did not the psychoanalytic writings of Carl Jung and Norman O. Brown and novels of the German writer Herman Hesse arouse interest in Asian philosophy? Did not many students rediscover the Romanticism and civil disobedience of Henry David Thoreau?

Obviously, the dissenters of the uncivil war drew on a rich and varied heritage. But certain underlying values and concerns recurred. Almost all the dissenters had an irreverent view of authority, which while it arose from many sources, in some way reflected a growing disenchantment with the cold war consensus and especially its attendant threat of nuclear holocaust. As an alternative to remote, bureaucratized power, they embraced a populist impulse to empower the people. Most argued that in gaining control over their lives, people would begin to fulfill their spiritual need for more authenticity. To that end, sexual liberation would connect people to their true selves and, hence, help them discover a meaningful personal identity. So, too, people would gain new meaning from work and leisure that led to quality experience rather than simple material advantages. These ideas were not so thoroughly developed that they constituted a coherent ideology. Nor were they so widely adopted that they formed a new consensus. Instead, they embodied a set of attitudes that would shape the way many disaffected Americans responded to growing divisions in American society.

Even if ideas did not alone inspire dissent in the 1960s, they did color the way people read events as they unfolded. So to understand the 1960s, we must also look at the events that gave shape to the era. As in all periods of political and social upheaval, some of the events would be self-consciously instigated. The Freedom Rides of 1961 were no more spontaneous than John Brown's raid on Harper's Ferry. But as is also true in history, fate played its unforeseen hand. Who could have known that Martin Luther King, Jr., would be jailed on the eve of the 1960 election, that Lee Harvey Oswald would be along President Kennedy's motorcade route in Dallas, or that students would seize a police car on the Berkeley campus? To these events, both contrived and unexpected, we must turn to find the path to the uncivil wars.

4
The New Generation

The Russian launching of *Sputnik* in 1957 spread fear across America. Missiles that could place a satellite in space could also strike targets anywhere in the United States. A growing number of Americans wished for a safer world. Some advocated nuclear disarmament and an end to cold war hostilities. One group of peace advocates with ties to the old socialist Left and pacifists of the 1930s created a group called the Committee for a Sane Nuclear Policy. It soon became know simply as SANE. The organizers believed that rising public concern with radioactive fallout and strontium-90 in foods would help them pursue their larger goals: a nuclear test ban and disarmament.

SANE's very existence in the late 1950s indicated that political activism was on the rise. No group with its leftist ties and critique of the nuclear arms program could have long survived when Senator McCarthy was in his prime. Now, even in Hollywood, so recently ravaged by the House Committee on Un-American Activities (HUAC) and blacklists, celebrities joined SANE. Historian H. Stewart Hughes saw in the unexpected vigor SANE demonstrated "the sign that the McCarthy pall was really lifting." All the same, SANE struggled to balance its commitment to pacifism with the obvious radicalism of some of its members. As a loosely formed national coalition, SANE could not easily screen Communists or Soviet sympathizers from its local affiliates. In 1960, flush with new members and increased donations, SANE planned a May rally at Madison Square Garden in New York. It was no coincidence that President Eisenhower and Soviet premier Nikita Khrushchev were scheduled to hold a summit meeting at that very time in Geneva, Switzerland. But then the Soviets shot down an American U-2 spy plane over Russia and Khrushchev canceled the summit. SANE held its rally anyway.

By almost any measure it was a great success. Twenty thousand peace advocates (and an undetermined number of FBI agents) gathered to hear such distinguished citizens as Eleanor Roosevelt, the most admired woman in America, speak out against the perils of fallout and nuclear war. A celebrity roster headed by Harry Belafonte entertained, and prominent politicians sent telegrams congratulating the nuclear pacifists for their humanitarian efforts. As one observer commented, "for a moment it looked as though SANE might grow into a really powerful force in American politics."

That was precisely what many ardent cold warriors and arch anti-Communists feared. Senator Thomas J. Dodd (D-CT), the acting chair of the Senate version of HUAC, charged that a major organizer of the rally "was a veteran member of the Communist Party," that "Communists were responsible for a very substantial percentage

of the overflow turnout," and that he had evidence "of serious Communist infiltration at chapter level." Dodd, besides being a rabid anti-Communist, worried that if
SANE succeeded, a nuclear test ban might weaken the nation's key strategic deterrent.
Whatever his motives, he succeeded in wreaking havoc within the organization. The
furor over Communist influence drove many members out.

Curiously, what most offended some of those who quit was not the potential
stigma of association with Communists, but the authoritarian way in which SANE
leaders purged its ranks of members under suspicion. One who left wrote that he
preferred a "broad peace movement to be run democratically and open to everyone." A group of Brooklyn student members likened the purge to the "grand tradition of Cold War hysteria and McCarthyism." The organization's democratic charter
should compel SANE, they believed, "to accept anyone who has a contribution to
make to the struggle for peace." When the leadership persisted, many of those
students quit to join the Student Peace Union, a group with ties to the aborning
Students for a Democratic Society (SDS).

Across the continent, students with a similar distaste for McCarthyism made
their own news. That May, HUAC came to San Francisco to stage an exposé of Communists in the Bay Area. A contingent of some 500 people, mostly Berkeley students
who sought to attend the hearings at City Hall, was denied admission. Forced outside, protestors chanted "What are you afraid of?" sang the spiritual "We Shall Not
Be Moved," and staged a sit-in in the rotunda. Police used high-pressure fire hoses
and clubs to disperse them. In the melee that ensued, some 64 were arrested. The
committee called them "well-trained Communist agents," the press called them
"unruly," the police charged them with rioting, but old leftist labor leader Harry
Bridges said, "This is a hell of a note washing them down the steps like that." The
next day, some 5,000 or more Berkeley activists and students confronted HUAC
with chants of "Sieg Heil." The size of the crowd suggested that here, too, the cold
war consensus was losing some of its power to silence and that on some campuses,
many of the apolitical students of the fifties were embracing a new activism.

❧

Leftist students and peace activists were not the only Americans who questioned
the cold war consensus. In the wake of *Sputnik*, many public figures charged that
weaknesses in American education, especially in science and math, explained the
failure to keep pace with the Russians in the space race. In response, Congress in
1958 passed the National Defense Education Act to strengthen American schools.
Among its provisions, the law required student recipients of loans and grants to assert they neither belonged to nor supported organizations advocating the overthrow of the United States government and to swear an oath of loyalty. Liberals
found the provision a throwback to McCarthyism and a threat to civil liberties. By
1959, they gained President Eisenhower's support for an initiative to eliminate the
loyalty oath. Two young conservatives, Douglas Caddy and David Franke, saw the

initiative as another case of growing weakness in the face of the Communist menace. To them, the danger to freedom had never been greater. In a war for freedom, they believed that patriotic students should have no qualms about pledging their allegiance and that disloyal students had no right to receive public funding. The two joined together in the fall of 1959 to create the National Student Committee for the Loyalty Oath. The committee claimed that repeal would not only undermine internal security and embolden "the enemies of the American way of life," but would "promote the worldwide Communist conspiracy." Their expressed purpose was to defeat the repeal, but their larger goal was to organize conservative students.

∾

To four young students at North Carolina A&T, an all-black college in Greensboro, freedom had quite another meaning. Ezell Blair, Jr., Franklin McCain, Joseph McNeil, and David Richmond entered North Carolina A&T in the fall of 1959 with the typical eagerness and anxieties of first-year students. They talked of future careers in science and the ministry. They complained about the dining halls and the inaccessibility of the women on campus. And late at night they talked about larger issues, like freedom and equality. Inevitably their conversations came back to the same question: what should be done to bring an end to Jim Crow, the system of racial segregation that stigmatized all black Americans as second-class citizens? More immediately and personally, what were they going to do about it?

Slowly, a plan emerged. The lunch counter in the Woolworth's Department Store was the single largest moneymaker in downtown Greensboro. While blacks were welcome to spend their money anywhere else in the store, the lunch counter was strictly segregated. The four students decided they would change that. So on February 1, 1960, they headed downtown. As a locale in which to trigger a revolution in race politics in 1960, few places would have been less promising than Greensboro. The city had a reputation for progressive approaches to race relations. The local business elite provided African Americans with decent community facilities and relatively good schools. In return for their support, they expected African Americans to maintain the same deference to their paternalistic control that had long defined race relations in Greensboro. As historian William Chafe observed, "So deep was the need of whites to believe in 'good race relations' that they took ritualistic deference as an authentic expression of black attitudes towards them."

After making a few purchases to establish themselves as legitimate customers, the four sat down at the counter and asked for coffee. They planned to stay until they were served, though as Ezell Blair warned, "that might be weeks, that might be months, that might be never." An astonished policeman paced menacingly behind them, not quite sure how to react. A few white customers cursed them. Others reminded them that they did not belong at the "whites only" counter. One of the angriest comments came from a black dishwasher, who called them "ignorant, stupid." "That's why we can't get any place today, because of people like you, rabble-rousers, troublemakers," he told them. They stayed anyway. The white manager simply

Franklin McCain, Ezell Blair, Jr., David Richmond, and Joseph McNeil had no idea they might start a civil rights revolution when they headed off to the lunch counter at Woolworth's. They simply wanted to turn talk into action. (Source: Bettman/CORBIS)

ignored them, as if this affront to white supremacy did not exist. A few white women even encouraged them. "You should have done it ten years ago," one said. That afternoon, the four young men returned to the campus without their coffee.

The response was beyond their wildest imagining. A&T students greeted them as heroes. The college president, despite his previous deference to white community leaders, proved unexpectedly sympathetic. When whites demanded he expel or suspend the troublemakers, he refused. All he wanted to know is why they had picked Woolworth's lunch counter, since the food there was no better than the campus cafeteria. By February 2, a fever gripped the campus. Some twenty students came to Woolworth's to sit-in. On the fourth day, the first white student joined. Soon the movement had spilled over to other states and other communities. In South Carolina, Cleveland Sellers, who would become a leading student activist, felt "a shot of adrenaline" that left him "a burning desire to get involved." Up in New York City, a young high school math teacher, Robert Moses, saw in newspaper photos of the four Greensboro students defiance rare among southern blacks.

In their determination to make a difference, Blair, McNeil, McCain, and Richmond touched a chord in young African Americans across the nation. Within months, Moses had headed south to join the student movement, and Sellers was leading a protest in Denmark, South Carolina. And in Nashville, Tennessee, another group of students who had anticipated the prospect of nonviolent protests and had already staged sit-ins the previous fall knew their time had come. So, too, did students like Lonnie King and Julian Bond in Atlanta, Georgia. When King saw the headlines from Greensboro, he shoved the paper in front of Bond and said, "Don't you think it ought to happen here?" And soon enough it did.

~

These three stories—the Greensboro sit-ins, student protests against SANE and HUAC, and the National Student Committee for the Loyalty Oath—were each connected to the creation in 1960 of an organization that would have a powerful impact on the future uncivil wars. Greensboro and the sit-ins that followed in its wake lead to the founding of SNCC, the Student Non-violent Coordinating Committee. Many of the students who left SANE or rolled down the City Hall steps in San Francisco would become members of SDS, Students for a Democratic Society. The National Student Committee for the Loyalty Oath would transform themselves into YAF, Young Americans for Freedom.

Each movement had a distinctive cast of characters and separate, though sometimes intersecting, histories. SDS and SNCC were organizations that helped create the New Left; YAF identified itself with the New Right. White students from northern, midwestern, and West Coast campuses initially dominated YAF and SDS. SNCC began as a distinctly southern group of black students with a regional focus on fighting Jim Crow. Jews were prominent among SDS's founders and Catholics were conspicuous in the founding of YAF, while SNCC began with close ties to Martin Luther King's Southern Christian Leadership Conference, and most of its early members were Protestants. On the other hand, where religion played a central role in the worldview of SNCC and YAF members, SDS was distinctly secular. SDS and SNCC quickly achieved a high public profile, only to fall into factionalism that left them in disarray by the end of the decade. Largely unnoticed on or off campus, YAF struggled early on with internal factionalism, out of which a coalition emerged that contributed to the conservative ascendancy in the 1970s and 1980s.

Yet for all their differences, these three groups had much in common. Their members were largely middle class. They chose to become political when most students cared far more about social life, careers, and marriage. Politics for them required the mobilization of people at the grass roots, and they agreed that students were uniquely situated to promote that process. Beyond that, they were idealists and sometimes ideologues in a society where politics tended to be ruled by pragmatism and compromise. All criticized the dominant consensus of the day, though seldom for the same reasons. In that way they called into question the legitimacy of contemporary government. Their determination to upset the political and social status quo and to forge a new consciousness brought them self-consciously into conflict with the elders of their own movements.

In seeking to explain the upheavals of the 1960s, historians at first concentrated on SDS, SNCC, and the New Left. They wanted to understand how political forces on the Left mobilized in the face of McCarthyism and the cold war consensus. More recently, they have come to see the New Right's shift from extremist fringe groups such as the John Birch Society to the mainstream of American politics as an equally unanticipated phenomenon. Possibly even more than SNCC or SDS, YAF demonstrated the activism of the sixties student generation that challenged the cold war consensus. All three organizations remained smaller in membership than traditional student groups such as the National Student Association, but they had a disproportionately larger impact on other students and the general public. By comparing their early initiatives and their articulation of political programs, we gain a better sense of the coming of the uncivil wars.

SNCC and the Struggle for Racial Justice

While southern civil rights activists were surprised by the level of protest in the wake of the Greensboro sit-ins, they were not totally unprepared. Some sixteen sit-ins had taken place in the three years before Greensboro. Students in Nashville, Tennessee, had been preparing themselves to launch such a movement. At the core of their emerging movement were a Christian devotion to the idea of a "Beloved Community" and a Ghandian commitment to nonviolent protest. The person who brought the Nashville students together was James Lawson, a northern black minister and a divinity student at Vanderbilt University. Lawson first came to Nashville at the behest of the pacifist Fellowship of Reconciliation to lead a workshop on nonviolence.

In Nashville, he met a number of young activists who shared his faith-based approach to protest and racial equality. These were people who would provide SNCC with much of its early leadership. Twenty-year-old John Robert Lewis, a sharecropper's son, came to Nashville from rural Troy, Alabama. John showed even before he was four a flare for preaching and a deep evangelical piety. Radio broadcasts of the sermons of Martin Luther King, Jr., provided him an early model. King's leadership of the Montgomery, Alabama, bus boycott linked religion to the civil rights struggle. Lewis saw in King "a Moses, using organized religion and the emotionalism within the Negro church as an instrument, as vehicle toward freedom." Entering the American Baptist Theological Seminary in 1957, Lewis began to think about a faith-based protest movement against segregation.

For Diane Nash, the fight against Jim Crow was a form of "applied religion." It could "bring about a climate in which there is appreciation of the dignity of man and each individual is free to grow and produce to his fullest capacity." Having grown up as a Catholic in Chicago, Nash, unlike Lewis, had little firsthand experience with the stifling effect of legalized segregation. But after she became a student at Fisk University, she felt herself "boxed in since so many areas of living were restricted." "Race hatred," she believed, kept the South backward and undermined American prestige abroad.

Marion Barry entered Fisk as a graduate student in chemistry. As a scientist, he did not share the same depth of religious feeling that drew Nash, Lewis, and others to Lawson. His beliefs had an existential tone. Unless he was a free man, he said, "I was not a man at all." That conviction led him to protest an anti-black remark by a white trustee of Le Moyne College, where he earned his undergraduate degree. He continued to attack segregation as a graduate student at Fisk, even though he risked losing his fellowship.

Lawson brought Barry, Nash, Lewis, and other socially committed students from black colleges into his Beloved Community. Together they worked out the fundamental principles that would guide their actions. Among them were "Don't strike back or curse if abused"; "show yourself courteous and friendly at all times"; and "remember love and nonviolence." In the fall of 1959, they organized their first sit-ins against local restaurants and lunch counters. Rather than provoke arrest, they stayed only until they were refused service. That action did not cause any change in policy, nor did it attract much attention from the local media and other students. Still, they had made a beginning.

In April 1960, Lawson led a delegation of Nashville students to Raleigh, North Carolina, to what proved to be the founding conference for SNCC. The conference was the inspiration of Ella Baker, the executive director of King's SCLC. After college she had moved to New York City. Although arriving in the midst of the Great Depression, she found work as a community organizer while taking courses at the New School for Social Research. She then became a field secretary for the NAACP. In 1958, the NAACP sent her to Atlanta to help the newly formed SCLC organize a series of mass meetings. She was still there when the sit-in movements erupted. Here she discovered an exciting alternative to what she saw as the excessive caution of King and the ministers who ran the SCLC.

As a graduate of a southern black college, Baker understood how little prepared young civil rights activists were for the uncertain future they faced. One challenge for the students, Baker believed, was to overcome the political apathy of their peers, most of whom entered college eager to join the black middle class. Their conservative families viewed protest, much less the possibility of arrest or jail, as anathema. John Lewis remembered his mother warning him "to get out of that mess before you get hurt." The parents of most students had learned to get ahead by getting along. Like the older generation of civil rights leaders from the NAACP and even SCLC, they thought change should come, but through moderation and small incremental steps.

Baker believed that the major civil rights organizations wanted to capture the activists' energy and channel it into their own programs. The NAACP, SCLC, and CORE all sent observers to the Raleigh convention, as did sympathetic northern groups such as the Young People's Socialist League, the National Student Association, and Students for a Democratic Society. Baker urged students to cooperate with those traditional organizations on terms of equality, but not to tolerate "anything that smacked of manipulation or domination." Julian Bond, a student activist from Atlanta, recalled, "NAACP wanted us to be NAACP youth chapters, CORE wanted us to become CORE chapters, SCLC wanted us to become the youth wing of SCLC." With Baker's encouragement, the delegates "finally decided we'd be our own thing." The thing they chose to be was the Temporary Student Nonviolent Coordinating Committee. It would have no formal connection to any of the existing organizations but would cooperate with all of them.

One source of inspiration for the delegates came from Martin Luther King, Jr. King's decision to attend the convention had guaranteed heavy attendance. He urged the students to become more assertive in their protest, but also to expand their understanding of nonviolence. Rather than pay fines when arrested, King thought they should go to jail and thereby draw attention to injustice. If they took the "freedom struggle" all over the South, the federal government could no longer avoid involvement. Where King offered the delegates a future agenda, James Lawson gave them a moral and spiritual foundation. Their "radically Christian methods," Lawson asserted, laid bare the sinful nature of segregation. No longer would white Southerners be able to manipulate "law or law-enforcement to keep the Negro in his place."

Like so many of the 120 black students at Raleigh, Lawson saw the anti-colonial movements in Africa as an inspiration to black Americans. Unless the pace of reform accelerated, he warned, "all of Africa will be free before the American Negro attains first class citizenship." Lawson also highlighted the distance between the student program and the "middle-class conventional half-way efforts to deal with radical social evil." He specifically criticized the NAACP, which because of its "preoccupation with fund-raising and court action" had ignored the development of the black race's capacity for disciplined social action.

The question finally arose whether SNCC should adopt a platform on the "goals, philosophy, future, and structure of the movement" or first enunciate a statement of principles. A majority of the delegates saw SNCC as an action-oriented organization. Lawson pressed them to accept a statement that reflected his religious commitment to nonviolence. "Love is the central motif of nonviolence," Lawson explained. "Such love goes to the extreme; it remains loving and forgiving even in the midst of hostility." He then concluded, "Nonviolence nurtures the atmosphere in which reconciliation and justice become actual possibilities."

Inspired by King and Lawson, the delegates agreed that the pace and scale of protest should increase. Their organization would be assertive and confrontational, but also nonviolent. Recognizing the influence of the Nashville delegates, the convention elected Marion Barry to be their first chair. One other point remained to be resolved. They finally determined that the Beloved Community would be inclusive. That meant opening SNCC up to whites as well as blacks. In time, however, that commitment to inclusiveness would tear apart the Beloved Community envisioned at Raleigh.

Over the next months, SNCC struggled to establish itself. Short of funds and staff, it had no role in the few demonstrations that did occur. Ella Baker was determined to see that the organization survived. Baker had a vision of SNCC not simply as an agency to coordinate the autonomous activities of local protesters, but more as a vanguard of an ever-widening movement. She arranged office space at SCLC's Atlanta headquarters, while the NSA provided additional resources. She also gained the support of Robert Moses. News of the sit-in movement had persuaded Moses to leave his position as a math teacher in New York to work for SCLC in Atlanta. There, through Ella Baker, he discovered SNCC.

Moses was an unlikely person to have a determining influence on the organization. There was little that was imposing about him. Slight of build, light in complexion, somber in manner, he led by quiet example rather than charisma. People found him accessible, more a listener than a talker. Moses was, as one reporter noted, "an outstandingly poor speaker." He would urge SNCC to practice what was known as "participatory democracy"—allowing those most directly affected a central role in discussions and decision making.

In the summer of 1960, Moses found the project that would define SNCC's future. He had gone to Mississippi with the idea of recruiting local leaders to attend a SNCC conference scheduled for October. Among those he met was Amzie Moore. Cleveland, Mississippi, Moore's hometown, was in the heart of the segregated South. Moore agreed to come to Atlanta in October, but made clear to Moses that desegregation was not his concern. Voter registration was. Why didn't SNCC send students to Cleveland to help him register local blacks? Moore asked. Impressed by both Moore and his appeal, Moses said he would return to Mississippi in the near future. That promise would put voter registration at the top of SNCC's agenda.

In October, 140 people and about 80 observers from northern colleges came to Atlanta to reconsider SNCC's agenda. Although there had been little protest activity that fall, the mood in Atlanta had a new militancy. The invitation stressed that SNCC would be "action-oriented," because "[we are] convinced that only mass action is strong enough to force all Americans to assume responsibility" for the nation's racial injustice. Once again, the delegates affirmed their commitment to nonviolence. James Lawson, though no longer an active SNCC member, insisted that a "jail, no bail" strategy would have the most powerful impact. Lawson called it the start of a "nonviolent revolution" to destroy "segregation, slavery, serfdom paternalism." Finally, the delegates agreed that "Temporary" should be dropped from SNCC's title. SNCC would be a permanent organization in which local groups would retain their autonomy while the central office would speak for them collectively and maintain communications among them.

Historian of SNCC Clayborne Carson called the October conference a turning point. After it, the movement turned away from the religious orientation urged by King and Lawson to a focus on political issues. That shift would bring SNCC to Mississippi as Amzie Moore had suggested. Carson concluded that "only when SNCC workers were prepared to initiate protests outside their own communities could they begin to revive and extend the social struggle that had already become the central focus of their lives."

SDS and the New Left

As Todd Gitlin, an SDS founder and a historian of the sixties, asked somewhat rhetorically, "Why a New Left? Why not a new liberalism?" And he then added, "Why not a revival of the old left?" More than any other group, Students for a Democratic Society defined the New Left. The Point Huron Statement it issued in 1962 summarized the core values that mobilized student political activists on the Left, particularly in the early 1960s. Over the decade, movements would emerge that outstripped the organizational resources of SDS or moved beyond the concerns of its founding generation. Opposition to the war in Vietnam is an example of a movement too large and complex for SDS to shape. Environmentalism, consumerism, and feminism would later engage major elements of the New Left, but those issues were not on the SDS agenda in 1962. They emerged with the support of other organizations and constituencies.

Two types of students were instrumental in the founding of both SDS and, more broadly, the New Left. First were those who had parents loyal to the New Deal liberalism of Franklin Roosevelt. They favored an activist state committed to social justice, greater economic equality, and the containment of Communism and other totalitarian forms of government. Organized labor served, for them, as a major instrument of reform. Almost all were stridently anti-Communist but saw Joseph McCarthy and McCarthyism as a danger to both civil liberties and freedom of thought. At the same time, they supported the articulate though barely liberal Adlai Stevenson as the politician who in the presidential races of 1952 and 1956 best represented their values. Most were disappointed when Stevenson lost the 1960 Democratic nomination to John Kennedy. At first suspicious of Kennedy, his family's ties to Joe McCarthy, and his hawkish cold war rhetoric, they preferred him to Richard Nixon, the politician they most loved to hate. Many found hope in Kennedy's inaugural address that his administration would revive Roosevelt's liberal activist spirit for a new generation. Along with their college-aged children, they saw the Peace Corps as a thrilling example of the kind of humanitarian politics they favored.

A second group of student leftists had parents who had actively participated either in the Communist party or socialist and progressive politics. Many of those old leftists had quit the party in the 1930s when it proved too authoritarian and beholden to Moscow, or when they learned of Stalin's purges, or in the 1940s when the anti-Communist witch-hunts flourished, or after Khrushchev denounced Stalin in 1956. Almost all of them had suffered from McCarthyite denunciations and repeated harassment by the FBI. Out of embarrassment or fear of exposure, most old leftists had given their children little if any information about their former political activities. Yet as Gitlin pointed out, many preserved much of the culture of the old Left. They championed the cause of the working class, sent their children to socialist and Communist summer camps, and introduced them to populist folk music. Singers such as Woody Guthrie, the Weavers, and Paul Robeson taught them to sing "If I Had a Hammer," "This Land Is Your Land," or "Amazing Grace." Within the New Left, the children of old leftists were popularly known as "red-diaper babies."

Where the old Left had arisen out of ideologies and bitterly debated the ideas of Marx, Lenin, and Trotsky, issues gave rise to the New Left. That is not to say that the New Left was without ideas. From a wide variety of social critics and writers such as C. Wright Mills, French existentialist Albert Camus, and theologian Reinhold Niebuhr they learned about the nondemocratic distribution of power, alienation, and how human imperfectability created moral limits to reform. All the same, the New Left discovered its self-definition in the issues it took up. The opening of this chapter introduced some of those issues—the opposition to McCarthyism and oppressive anti-Communism, the peace movement and disarmament, and, above all the effort of African Americans to overcome the Jim Crow system of racial apartheid in the American South. Campus governance also aroused student activists. They challenged campus rules, ranging from compulsory participation in the Reserve Officer Training Corp (ROTC) to limits on political activities to a host of in loco parentis rules that restricted student behaviors and subjected students to arbitrary punishments. At most colleges or universities, for example, women could not live off campus. Those who returned to their dormitories after curfew could be confined on weekends or suspended. Such rules suggested a basic disregard for personal freedoms and, to some politically minded students, a governance structure designed to ignore their rights in order to suit the biases and whims of administrators.

Those were precisely the kinds of issues that concerned the Berkeley students who protested against HUAC in February 1960. Many of them belonged to SLATE (the initials stood for nothing), a campus political organization formed to oppose the fraternity system's control of student government. From its founding in 1957, SLATE had confronted the vestiges of McCarthyism in the California university system. The Board of Regents, for example, banned any Communist from speaking on a UC campus. SLATE welcomed left-wing students, opposed mandatory ROTC training, and favored the creation of a cooperative bookstore. When a SLATE member won an election upset over the fraternity-backed candidate, the university chancellor's office threw SLATE graduate students out of the student organization. The university also allowed the student government to use extralegal means to eliminate SLATE activists who had gained editorial control of the campus newspaper, the *Daily Californian*.

SLATE survived because Cal was changing. Graduate students had become a larger part of the university population. Fewer undergraduates joined fraternities and sororities, in part because they found the Greek traditions outmoded and in part because they objected to the system's discriminatory practices. Few fraternities or sororities were open to blacks, Latinos, or Jews at a time when the student body was becoming more heterogeneous. The city of Berkeley was also becoming racially mixed. That made Cal students far more sensitive to the civil rights activism in the southern United States. They objected in 1961 when the university banned Malcolm X from speaking on campus. Officials claimed he was promoting a religion, even though they welcomed conventional religious figures.

At northeastern universities, student dissidents focused their energies on the threat of nuclear holocaust. In May of 1960, a group of students at New York's City University (CCNY) organized a demonstration against a "duck and cover" air raid drill. Rather than the usual bunch of old leftists, the event attracted a new group of students. When a dean showed up to gather names, rather than flee to hide their identities, these protestors crowded around to make sure he collected their registration cards. In the fall of 1961, Harvard and Brandeis Universities peace advocates joined together to organize a protest march in Washington. At Brandeis, a heavily Jewish university near Boston, the red-diaper babies dominated the student SANE chapter. They had already raised fundamental questions about American responsibility for the cold war. Neighboring Harvard students retained more faith in the system. They believed that pressure from the political Left would encourage Kennedy to resist the military and "bomber liberals" who took a hawkish view of national defense policy.

Together the Harvard and Brandeis organizers hoped to expand their regional base to a more national one. To that end they contacted the Student Peace Union, Student SANE, and a small organization with Midwestern roots and a New York City office called Students for a Democratic Society. SDS at that time had just three chapters—Columbia, Yale, and the University of Michigan—and possibly a few hundred members. It had begun as the Student League for Industrial Democracy (SLID), with the purpose of promoting "greater active participation on the part of American students in the resolution of present-day problems." Funding came from the League for Industrial Democracy, a social democratic political organization from the 1930s that in turn received its budget from liberal labor unions such as the International Ladies Garment Workers Union.

By early 1960, a few of SLID's members decided the organization needed a new orientation. They sensed that before a New Left could emerge, it had to separate itself from its liberal and old Left parentage. "Industrial Democracy" struck them as an idea whose time had come and gone. Organized labor had by then lost most of its crusading energy. They wanted to capture what they saw as a growing political restlessness among leftist students. After kicking around such new names as "Student Liberal Union" and "Students for Social Democracy," the membership in January 1960 warmly embraced Students for a Democratic Society. Armed with a new name, the organization looked for new ways to make an impact. The Harvard-Brandeis initiative offered one possibility. And just then, the four North Carolina A&T students chose to sit-in at Woolworth's. As the sit-in movement attracted wide support among whites at northern colleges, political activism gained energy and moral purpose.

SDS seized the moment. It had already scheduled a conference on human rights for the coming May; now it shifted the conference focus to civil rights. For three days, representatives of some of the established organizations such as CORE and the NAACP met with leaders of the newly formed Student Nonviolent Coordinating Committee and SDS. Michael Harrington, a crusading Catholic social activist who would soon reveal the depths of poverty in Appalachia in *The Other America*, attended on behalf of the Young People's Socialist League. While the meeting produced little in the way of plans, it did create a heightened sense of goodwill between northern and southern students, a commitment among SDS members to focus on civil rights, and a sense that students could effect change.

The person most responsible for the shift in SDS was University of Michigan graduate student Robert Alan Haber. Haber was a faculty brat whose father taught at Michigan and had been involved in the Democratic Party and the League for Industrial Democracy (LID). As an undergraduate, Haber had been active in liberal campus politics and a leader in SLID. He began looking for ways to capture for SDS the new political energy he sensed on campus. "I know that if any really radical liberal force is going to develop in America," he wrote the LID office, "it is going to come from the colleges and the young." LID had little interest in the kind of broad-based campus movement Haber envisioned. The League preferred small campus groups whose activities did nothing to threaten its tax-exempt status.

Haber had other ideas. He believed that most student activists responded to a single cause—peace, civil rights, or student rights. SDS could act as liaison among these groups, coordinating their programs and organizing conferences that would give local groups the sense of participating in a wider movement. Haber further believed SDS should move away from its traditional educational role and become a direct action organization. Members would picket, boycott, march, and protest when promising situations arose. Most of all, SDS would not have any ideological guidelines for determining what groups were eligible to join. It would reach out to all social activists and try to help them recognize how their individual grievances were a by-product of an overarching American system. Haber believed that the power elite that supported Jim Crow in the South also championed McCarthyism and promoted the cold war arms race. As he put it, "the various objects of protest are not *sui generis* but are symptomatic of institutional forces with which the movement must ultimately deal." According to SDS historian Kirkpatrick Sale, Haber's perception "of a group which connects and operates on otherwise isolated issues" accounted "for much of SDS's early success."

An SDS conference held in Ann Arbor over Christmas vacation in 1961 revealed to Haber the limits of his laissez-faire approach. Personally, he believed SDS would be most effective if it identified a single cause that mobilized the Left on campus. Civil rights had been an obvious choice. Those who came to Ann Arbor had ideas of their own—indeed, a wealth of ideas. A Southerner proposed that SDS sponsor conferences to educate southern whites about civil rights. A Cornell student suggested campus reform, while a woman from Michigan thought campus peace centers would be a worthy cause. As a result, even as the delegates were inclined to agree that SDS should focus on a single issue, they could not agree on what that issue would be.

Despite the diversity of views, the Ann Arbor conference ended harmoniously. Those who attended thrived in the company of like-minded people. As one woman recalled, "We talked about a new life, a new world—no one had ever put down on paper what it would look like, though we all had a notion about it." Together with Haber, the conference put in place a national executive committee to give SDS a more defined organizational structure. And finally, Haber determined that SDS did not so much need a single cause, but rather a fundamental statement of the values and ideas that gave its members a shared sense of commitment.

From that desire came *The Port Huron Statement*, a manifesto that created a blueprint for the New Left. Primary responsibility for producing the working draft fell to Tom Hayden, an activist who gained his political voice as editor of the *Michigan Daily*. Hayden grew up in a middle-class community in Royal Oak, Michigan, fifty miles east of Ann Arbor. His father, an Eisenhower Republican, and mother, a Stevenson Democrat, shared the populist resentment of privilege and elitism. High school introduced him to journalism and school politics, but his real education in radicalism came at the University of Michigan. His work on the *Michigan Daily* exposed him to the impersonal bureaucracy that ran the university. Recognizing Hayden as a leftist BMOC, Haber tried to draw him into SDS. Hayden chose, instead, to pursue his activism as editor of the *Daily*, though he was much impressed by Haber's political and intellectual passion. In time, however, he decided that he would commit himself to SDS's program for building a national student movement on the Left.

In the summer after graduation in 1961, Hayden with his new wife, Casey, were on their way to Atlanta, Georgia, for their first jobs. Sandra Cason shared her husband's passion for social justice. As a student at the University of Texas, she had joined the Christian Faith and Life Community, an integrated group who formed what they called an "intentional community." Hayden first met her at a National Student Association meeting, where she transfixed the delegates with an eloquent defense of civil disobedience as a weapon against segregation. Though sympathetic to those convictions, Hayden's parents worried about their decision to go to the South. "I don't know what you're doing," his mother had said. A newspaper career she could understand, but her only child had decided to help Negroes. It just didn't make sense to her that he had agreed to become the field secretary in Atlanta for SDS.

By the fall of 1961, Hayden and Cason had settled in an apartment to begin their new careers. Both had links to SNCC, which at that time was pursuing its most daunting campaign—the registration of African-American voters in Mississippi. Voting could be a life-and-death proposition for black Mississippians. Shortly after the Haydens arrived in Atlanta, Eugene Hurst, an elected Mississippi official, walked up to NAACP member Herbert Lee in broad daylight and shot him dead. Lee's crime: he was black and had helped SNCC with the registration efforts. No court would find against Hurst. One potential witness to the Lee murder was himself shotgunned to death before he could testify.

Hayden immediately sensed the contrast between SNCC's battle-scarred veterans and the somewhat abstracted political activists from the North. He recalled his initial exposure to SNCC's plans for voter registration in Mississippi as "akin to a religious conversion." Here was the revolution radicals had been searching for. That did not mean that Hayden was prepared for the harsh reality of the Mississippi battlefront. His first field assignment took him to McComb, at that time possibly the most violent place in America. Along with his SDS colleague Paul Potter, he planned to observe the threats to SNCC workers and black voter registrants, report to federal officials on what he saw, and try to stir up media interest.

Hayden soon discovered these plans were more than a little naive. The McComb sheriff explained without a hint of irony that local blacks were "better treated down here than anyplace in the world. We pay'em, support their schools with taxes, work'em. But they know they're niggers. They know their place." The sheriff then produced newspaper photos of several SNCC organizers, including Bob Zellner, who just coincidentally happened to one of Hayden's good friends. Pointing at Zellner, the sheriff said, "they'll kill that one if he comes back down here. We can't keep him protected. We don't go for that mixing stuff."

The next day Hayden saw his first demonstration by local blacks, experienced his first beating, faced his first jail time, and sounded his first retreat. He and Potter had driven their rental car that morning to SNCC's Freedom School. A group of local whites had gathered to threaten a SNCC organizer. Hayden admitted that it was the first time he had "heard people threatening openly and loudly to kill someone on the spot." He and Potter then moved on to observe a demonstration by local black high school students. A police officer ordered them to go instead to the police station to establish their identities. "We can't protect everyone around here," he warned, "'specially outsiders like yourselves." Several blocks away they stopped briefly at a traffic light. Suddenly, they were yanked from the car, kicked, punched, and beaten. A sheriff's deputy finally stepped in. One of their assailants explained that Hayden and Potter had fallen from the car onto their heads. The deputy then arrested them and sent them to City Hall for booking. A sympathetic photographer warned them to leave town because the locals planned to drag them out of their motel that night. When given the choice of death, jail, or a quick exit, they fled to the airport at Jackson and flew off to Washington. At the Justice Department they received a sympathetic hearing, but no hint that federal officials had any plans to protect SNCC workers in Mississippi. "From that point on," Hayden concluded, "I began to feel we had been officially abandoned."

That first experience sobered Hayden but did not undermine his commitment to the civil rights struggle. In the fall of 1961, he went to jail in Albany, Georgia, for his role in a nonviolent protest there. The failure of the Albany movement led him to doubt the effectiveness of nonviolence as a tactic for change. From his jail cell, Hayden began to reevaluate the future for SDS and his role in it. "I didn't want to go from beating to beating, jail to jail, a lone field representative for an organization that was little more than a mailing list," he decided. The system that excused terror in McComb and Albany, that sent people to jail for insisting on their constitutional rights, could not simply be reformed. Hayden concluded that he could be most useful "in galvanizing students nationally to confront the system and change it."

Two weeks after he left the Albany jail, Hayden joined forty SDS activists in snowy Ann Arbor. They decided that the organization needed a "manifesto of hope" that would serve as an "agenda for a new generation." Hayden, with his newspaper experience, was the logical choice to create the first draft. In the process he read C. Wright Mills, Russian novelist Fyodor Dostoyevsky, philosopher John Dewey, and French existentialist Albert Camus. From Camus he learned that ethical action did not require pragmatic outcomes. Mills informed him about the undemocratic nature of power held by an elite over an apathetic and uninterested public. SDS would invade what Mills called the private "milieu," in which people felt a sense of helplessness and blamed themselves for their misfortunes. Hayden concluded that political apathy was an even more serious issue than war or racism.

The following summer, sixty SDS delegates gathered on June 11 at a United Auto Workers camp in Port Huron, Michigan. Hayden had a document prepared for debate. "The Port Huron Statement of the Students for a Democratic Society" asserted what in a general sense would become the spirit of the New Left. It identified a new generation "bred in at least modest comfort, housed now in universities, looking uncomfortably to the world we inherit." For this generation, silence and apathy would give way to a new sense of activism. Urgency came from the sense "that we may be the last generation in the experiment with living." Two issues created this imperative for action: "the Southern struggle against racial bigotry" and the threat of nuclear destruction "greater than incurred in all wars of human history."

Drawing on Mills, Hayden described how even as technology destroyed old and created new forms of social organization, "men still tolerate meaningless work and idleness." Major nations continued to exploit the earth's physical resources, yet left two-thirds of mankind suffering from undernourishment. Rather than provide the necessary "revolutionary leadership, America rests in national stalemate, . . . its democratic system apathetic and manipulated rather than 'of, by, and for the people.'" These realizations introduced a sense of disillusionment and ultimately tested "the tenacity of our own commitment to democracy and freedom and our abilities to visualize their application in the world in upheaval." SDS was determined that each individual would realize "human independence" by "finding a meaning in life that is personally authentic." And beyond that, the young radicals sought nothing less than to understand and to change "the conditions of humanity in the late twentieth century."

In the light of history, *The Port Huron Statement* seems both brash and naive. These young radicals condemned the spiritual, political, and moral bankruptcy of the world they had inherited from their elders. They intended to harness the energy and idealism of a new generation of students to save the world from its corruptions. That sixty well-intended radicals could imagine achieving such grandiose ends defies reasonable expectations. They could not even reasonably expect to stir the consciousness of their fellow students, who remained far more preoccupied with careers and conventional living than with issues of human betterment. Hayden later recognized that his "infatuation with the 'new'" made it difficult to for him to recognize legitimate elements in the old Left's critique of the SDS platform. In his passion to create a new movement, he failed to recognize that revolutionary fervor could produce "the crimes of communism described in Orwell and Kafka," or cultivated intellectuals who rationalized heinous acts, or idealistic leaders who became Frankenstein's monster. As Hayden confessed, he had believed "those horrors won't happen to us; we are too good."

Port Huron was also indifferent to environmental issues and sexist in its rhetorical structures. Rather than talk of people and persons, Hayden spoke of "men," "mankind," and "brotherhood." Failure to acknowledge the environment or gender as categories of social analysis was but one of many ways in which "Port Huron" simplified the realities of the world it intended to reform. Those causes had yet to enter into the group's radical consciousness. Nor did the statement at first reach a wide audience. SDS printed some 20,000 copies priced at $.35. (In this era, photocopying was not readily available.) Hayden called it "the most widely read pamphlet of the sixties generation." Perhaps so, but it certainly never reached the broad American public, much less the large majority of college students.

Whatever its shortcomings, *Port Huron* did express the aborning spirit of the New Left. That spirit was optimistic, idealistic, and inclusive in the spirit of SNCC's Beloved Community. The delegates had sharply rejected the political sectarianism of their old Left forebears and the anti-Communism of their social democratic sponsors in the labor movement. Several socialist delegates tried early in the convention to prevent the seating of an observer from a group set up by the Communist Party. The convention rejected that move by a large majority. One delegate observed that to social Democrats, accepting such an observer was "like recognizing Cuba"; to the large majority, however, "it wasn't anything." In a similar vein, SDS recognized the cold war as bipolar rather than a battle of good and evil. Soon enough, the excesses of the cold war consensus that SDS condemned would lead to escalation in Vietnam. The call for individual autonomy, personal authenticity, and political empowerment would inspire a host of movements to achieve greater gender, class, ethnic, and racial justice.

Young Americans for Freedom

Conservatives seeking to change America in the late 1950s had their own elders to contend with. Dwight D. Eisenhower's middle-of-the-road approach to politics deeply disturbed many conservatives but proved highly popular with the voters. Ike and Republican moderates accepted the broad contours of the New Deal and showed scant appetite for confrontation with the Communist bloc. Worse yet, the general public had come to associate conservatism and aggressive anti-Communism with extremist organizations like the John Birch Society. Founded in 1958 by a wealthy businessman, the society gained widespread notoriety for its charge that Eisenhower was "a dedicated, conscious agent of the Communist conspiracy." Even some anti-Communist conservatives found the Birchite message paranoid. All the same, the John Birch society was not alone in promoting its vision of a nation awash in conspiracy. Oil tycoon H. L. Hunt was among a number of right-wing elements that believed sinister forces plotted to "convert America into a socialist state and then make it a unit in a one-world socialist system." They spewed hatred toward Jews, race mixers, labor unions, liberals, and supporters of the United Nations.

Deep ideological divisions in the conservative ranks further compounded the difficulty of generating a significant movement. Historian Godfrey Hodgson has identified three major strands of serious conservative thought in the 1950s. These were not coherent poles to which large numbers of people gravitated, but clusters of ideas and values that attracted faithful followings. Traditionalists, sometimes called the New Conservatives, railed against the rootlessness of modern mass society. To them the rampant individualism of the times threatened to devolve into anarchy. Bernard Iddings Bell of Bard College spoke for many traditionalists when he warned against the "complacent, vulgar, mindless, homogenized, comfort-seeking, nouveau riche culture of the common man." By contrast, their conservatism was "the community of spirit." It addressed the spiritual crisis in society through adherence to a transcendent moral order. Religious and military institutions embodied the order they embraced.

Diametrically opposed to the traditionalists was a second cluster of conservatives—the Libertarians. Where the traditionalists wanted to impose order on an atomistic society, the Libertarians sought to maximize individual freedom to an extent that bordered on anarchy. Novelist Ayn Rand became a spokesperson through such works as *The Fountainhead* and *Atlas Shrugged*. Her heroes pursued their personal visions no matter what the social or economic cost. Other Libertarians targeted the intrusive hand of the state. Free-market economists such as Milton Friedman from the University of Chicago defended the power of unrestrained capitalism and denounced the dominant Keynsian school of economists for its advocacy of government management of the economy. Such views appealed to the conservative business community that chafed against New Deal regulations and the power of organized labor.

Many Libertarians believed that traditionalists favored a European-styled elitism and held to ideas that had lost their currency in the eighteenth century. Traditionalists saw in economic Libertarianism a thinly veiled defense of business-class self-interest. Both did, however, have an affinity for the third pole of conservatism—anti-Communism. All the same, anti-Communists were no more unified than the traditionalist and libertarian factions. Their movement included many ex-Communists who, having seen the error of their ways, rejected their youthful involvement with the party but held liberal or moderate views on many issues. On the other extreme were the John Birchers and groups such as the Christian Crusade of the Reverend Billy James Hargis, who toured America warning his faithful that treason and Communism had become epidemic.

Perhaps the cornerstone of the anti-Communist wing of conservatism was William F. Buckley and his journal of conservative ideas, *The National Review*. As a young man, Buckley had gained notoriety for his witty and caustic denunciations of what he saw as a hegemonic liberal consensus. Through *The National Review* he attracted new adherents to the conservative crusade. While Buckley's fervent support for morality and faith appealed to traditionalists, his mania about Communism struck many of them as extreme. Never, for example, did Buckley criticize McCarthy or the "ism" he embodied, despite the assault on civil liberties and traditional

institutions. Buckley believed the threat of Communism was so extreme that it justified almost any means to combat it. After a Catholic journalist questioned the
excesses of his anti-Communism, Buckley responded, "when we stand together, as
well we may, in that final foxhole, you will discover, as we pass the ammunition,
that all along, we had the same enemy."

Buckley's combative style appealed to young conservatives in much the way
Kennedy's calls to service attracted their more liberal peers. Pat Buchanan, later a leading conservative politician and journalist, recalled that The National Review took "the term
conservatism, then a synonym for stuffy orthodoxy, Republican stand-pat-ism, and economic self-interest," and converted it into "the snapping pennant of a fighting faith."
By 1960, Buckley determined that the time had come for conservatives to resolve
some of their ideological differences and speak with a more unified voice against
their common enemies. The 1960 Republican presidential convention gave him an
opportunity to reach out to young conservatives. The students who organized the
loyalty oath campaign admired Buckley, but their real hero was Senator Barry Goldwater from Arizona. His book The Conscience of a Conservative served them as a political
bible. Young Americans believed that "the radical or Liberal approach has not worked
and is not working," Goldwater asserted. "They yearn for a return to Conservative
principles." The Conscience of a Conservative challenged the liberal tenets of the cold war
consensus and pulled together the three major strands of conservative thought.

To Goldwater, freedom, not security or material well-being, was the end point of
politics. As he put it, politics was the "art of achieving the maximum amount of
freedom for individuals that is consistent with the maintenance of the social order."
Goldwater had two particular targets—statism, or what he defined as the "first principle of totalitarianism," and the international Communist threat. Statism had
reared its ugly head during the New Deal as the federal government assumed
increasing responsibility for the welfare of its citizens. Social Security, aid to education, subsidies to farmers, and other federal programs preempted the rights and
responsibilities of both individuals and states. As the federal government extended
its reach, it eroded freedom and promoted totalitarianism. Goldwater argued
instead for a government limited to "maintaining internal order, keeping foreign
foes at bay, administering justice, [and] removing obstacles to the free exchange of
goods." Proper public officials were those who understood their primary duty was
"to divest themselves of the power they have been given."

Possibly even more threatening to freedom than statism was any accommodation with the Soviet Union or Communism. For that reason, Goldwater rejected the
containment strategies of both Truman and Eisenhower. Neither had shown the will
to defeat Communism. As "alien forces" threatened the United States, fear had replaced faith on the frontline of America's defenses against the Communist menace.
The moment of danger had never been greater, Goldwater believed. Worried about
war and beset by a "craven fear of death," American leaders favored compromise
with Moscow. Without using the exact phrase "better dead than Red," Goldwater
preached that death was preferable to life under Communist tyranny. Coexistence

was neither desirable nor possible. To him, only one outcome guaranteed both peace and freedom, and that was victory. Where containment was defensive and left the United States no prospect but "to surrender or accept war under the most disadvantageous circumstances," a war of attrition against the enemy might "bring about the internal disintegration of the Communist empire." Americans had to replace fear with faith, summon the common will, and create the military means necessary to wage that war.

Having embraced those views, young conservatives saw their liberal peers as a threat to national survival. SANE's proposals for a nuclear test ban and disarmament amounted to capitulation to the Communists. One conservative saw the Berkeley HUAC "riots" as a "frightening example of how guileless students can be manipulated by Communist agents." In his eyes, HUAC served on the frontline of the nation's defenses against Communism. When HUAC commissioned a film documentary on the riots called *Operation Abolition*, conservative groups used it to "alert viewers to the dangers of internal Communism" and as a tool to recruit new members.

Mobilized by their opposition to SANE, the battles over the loyalty oath, and the defense of HUAC, young conservatives turned their energies to the upcoming GOP convention scheduled for July. Goldwater was their choice for the vice presidency, since they knew Richard Nixon had sewed up the party's presidential nomination. "Senator Goldwater carries the torch which fell from the hands of the late Senator Robert Taft as the leading spokesman for American conservatism," they announced. Their advocacy came with a warning to both parties: "American youth is turning away from the dogmas of the left and will not devote its loyalties to candidates who espouse the blatantly paternalistic policies of the New Deal or even the somewhat milder statism that Nelson Rockefeller would impose on us."

Imagine then the betrayal these young conservatives felt when they learned just before the GOP convened in Chicago that Nixon and Rockefeller had struck a deal. What the two agreed on was not the vice presidency—Rockefeller did not want it in any case (it went to Massachusetts moderate Henry Cabot Lodge)—but on the future direction of the Republican Party. The ever-pragmatic Nixon wanted the 1960 party platform to endorse the record of the Eisenhower administration and, hence, his association with the popular president. For that position he wanted Rockefeller's support. Such moderation and accommodation to the statism of the New Deal was the approach that mobilized Senator Goldwater and his young conservative supporters to transform the Republican Party.

At this time, Youth for Goldwater organizers Douglas Caddy and David Franke first met their spiritual mentor, William Buckley. The two so impressed Buckley that he offered Franke an internship at *The National Review*, while Caddy joined a prominent conservative public relations firm. Together, they viewed the Rockefeller-Nixon détente as an "American Munich" or the "Compact of Fifth Avenue." Disappointed but not defeated, the young conservatives turned their energies to creating a new organization. Through it they hoped to promote both Goldwater in 1964 and the principles that he had spelled out in *The Conscience of a Conservative*.

That September, Buckley invited some 120 young conservatives to gather at his family's Great Elm estate in Sharon, Connecticut. The invitation stressed the millennial spirit of the event: "America stands at the crossroads today. Will our Nation continue to follow the path towards socialism or will we turn towards Conservatism and freedom?" Resolution of that question, the organizers asserted, "lies with America's youth." The project for those who attended, much as for those who gathered to create SNCC that fall, was the adoption of a statement of principles. The main responsibility for drafting a document fell to M. Stanton Evans, a recent Yale graduate who had already gained considerable exposure writing for conservative journals. The essence of what Evans and his collaborators produced reflected the conservative synthesis Buckley had been promoting.

Unlike *The Port Huron Statement*, which it preceded by almost two years, the *Sharon Statement* was about ideas, not issues. The delegates declared themselves living in a "time of moral and political crisis." Echoing traditionalists, they asserted their responsibility "to affirm certain eternal truths." Chief among the "transcendent values," they asserted, "is the individual's use of his God-given free will." Drawing on Goldwater, Friedman, and the Libertarians, they then emphasized "that liberty is indivisible, and that political freedom cannot long exist without economic freedom." The government envisioned by those at Sharon was a limited one. Its purposes were "to protect these freedoms through the preservation of internal order, the provision of national defense, and administration of justice." Whenever government reached beyond "these rightful functions," it became a threat to "order and liberty." The genius of the constitution was the restraints it imposed on "the concentration and abuse of power." Again turning to Friedman, they championed the free market economy as on the one hand "compatible with the requirements of personal freedom," and on the other "the most productive supplier of human needs."

The guests at Great Elm were not unmindful of their debt to their host and patron, William Buckley. They concluded by echoing his belief that freedom could only exist "when free citizens concertedly defend their rights against all enemies." No greater threat to liberty loomed at the present time than "the forces of international Communism." And in another nod to Goldwater and repudiation of Eisenhower, they agreed "that the United States should stress victory over, rather than coexistence with, this menace." Buckley repaid his acolytes with a glowing endorsement of the Sharon Statement. "Even now," he told his *National Review* readers, "the world continues to go left, but all over the land dumbfounded professors are remarking the extraordinary revival of hard conservative sentiment in student bodies." One YAF leader summed up that "conservative sentiment" as a "declaration of war against the forces of campus collectivism who would impose upon us fascism in the name of liberalism, and a national purpose as a substitute for freedom."

Like their counterparts in SDS and SNCC, the young radicals of YAF understood the need to move from ideology as spelled out at Sharon to activism. They proceeded, however, in quite a different spirit. Both SNCC and SDS were skeptical of power embedded in the system and traditional political organizations. They resisted creating hierarchy within their own ranks and placed more emphasis on process than on outcomes. For them, a democratic society would flow from democratic procedures where all voices received a hearing. They self-consciously distanced themselves from both major parties, established civil rights organizations, or old Left groups. YAF reversed those priorities. As Buckley observed, "what is so striking about the students who met at Sharon is their appetite for power." A central committee of four decided the issues on which YAF would take positions. Their ultimate target was to control the Republican Party and through it to change the course of history. Where leftist students defined their politics through peace symbols, YAF expressed their aspirations with Goldwater buttons. When they wore them, as one conservative recalled, they felt "the thrill of treason." Nixon's defeat in the 1960 election opened new prospects for Goldwater and the conservatives.

Two factors complicated the new conservative insurgency. Again like SDS and SNCC, YAF's numbers were so small that few students on the nation's campuses were aware the organization existed. Recruiting and organizing demanded more resources than it possessed. The second problem stemmed from the generalities in the Sharon Statement. Seeking to appeal to all three strands of conservatives—traditional, libertarian, and anti-Communist—the delegates glossed over the sharp differences among them. Traditionalists had dominated the Sharon convention. To them, freedom was inseparable from a "belief in an absolute and moral law" given by God and impervious to scientific or rational demonstration. What then to make of Ayn Rand and her Objectivist followers among the Libertarians? Rand was an atheist. Could she or other atheists be true conservatives? Buckley rejected her "materialism of technology" as contrary to conservatism built on "transcendence, intellectual and moral."

Ideological rifts drained away energy that might have gone into organization building. So, too, did the leadership's taste for palace intrigue. Ambitious young men dominated the organization. Their efforts to gain power were often personal as well as ideological. There were those drawing the organization toward the John Birch wing of conservatives. That angered the Buckley acolytes. They suspected others of secretly plotting to steer YAF toward Rockefeller and the moderate wing. All the same, YAF did make progress. Its attacks on the Kennedy administration, the Peace Corps, and Communism gained valuable publicity. To streamline operations and direct local chapters, the executive committee also decided to appoint an executive director. The person they chose was Richard Viguerie.

Viguerie would transform not only the conservative movement, but the Republican Party and American politics as well. Born a Catholic, raised and educated in Texas, and employed in the energy sector, he defined himself as a Goldwater conservative. Before taking the reins at YAF, he led his county GOP organization and helped fellow Texas Republican John Tower win a Senate seat. Viguerie quickly learned that he preferred to work behind the scenes. He did so in part because he hated one of the essential jobs that came with organization building—face-to-face fund-raising, the lifeblood of politics. Viguerie discovered he could raise money even more effectively by adopting new computer technologies. He developed donor databases and solicited money by direct mail. In that way he gave the conservative movement an enormous advantage over its political opponents.

SDS and YAF first seriously confronted each other in a 1961 battle over the direction of the National Student Association. YAF challenged the organization's liberal bias without knowing that it was secretly financed by the CIA. One YAF delegate suggested that NSA spoke for no one but its "coterie of liberal" officers. YAF demanded that NSA confine its activities to apolitical matters on college campuses. SDS was not unaware of its fledgling conservative rival that by then had a membership of about 30,000. "What is new about the new conservatives," Tom Hayden had warned, "is their militant mood, their appearance on picket lines." On the NSA convention floor, Al Haber charged, in language that became a New Left trademark, that YAF consorted with "racist, militarist, imperialist butchers." Liberal NSA officers attacked YAF as an autocratic organization, "threatening to democratic student government," that paralleled "the authoritarian pattern of the Soviet Union and its satellites."

The NSA meeting was but an opening skirmish in what would soon become a wider battle to control the hearts and minds of future generations. The real battleground in 1961 was in the South and the issue was civil rights. For SDS and SNCC, the struggle for racial equality was an essential Left cause. SDS associated racial injustice with a host of other issues such as poverty and economic inequality that demanded the overthrow of the hegemonic capitalist system. As it confronted the entrenched power of formal segregation in the South and de facto racial barriers everywhere else, SNCC moved ever leftward to challenge racist structures of power. Militancy replaced nonviolence, and the struggle for integration gave way to Black Power.

The civil rights struggle created special problems for YAF. Many conservatives at least condoned segregation and opposed integration. William Buckley once argued that the white race was entitled to maintain supremacy even where outnumbered by blacks because "for the time being, it is the advanced race." Certainly after the 1954 *Brown* decision, racist fears and prejudices attracted significant support for conservative causes. Whether racist or not, leading conservative leaders like Barry Goldwater and Buckley stridently opposed federal measures taken to eliminate legalized forms of segregation. They argued in favor of states' rights, or "home rule," and denied that government could change the feelings that lay in people's hearts, much less the laws that protected them. Volunteers for SNCC often complained about the indifference of federal law enforcement to the violence they faced. YAF and the new conservatives also attacked federal law enforcement, not for its ineffectiveness, but for its intrusion on individual liberties. Defense of racial protest, they claimed, deprived "private citizens of the protection of their property; of enjoining, under threat of federal armed power, the police from preserving order in our communities." That southern police sometimes kept the peace by turning high-pressure hoses and dogs on peaceful demonstrators did not for conservatives invalidate their larger principle.

Between the egalitarian, leveling principles of SDS and SNCC and the ideology of tradition, individual liberty, and anti-Communism of YAF, there could be no common ground. All three groups sought a radical transformation of American society. All three sought power—SDS and SNCC claimed it for the people; YAF demanded it for the right people. Each sought to build a mass movement and saw young Americans as the frontline troops in the battle that lay ahead. That battle, the first in the uncivil wars, took place across the South as African Americans and their liberal allies challenged the system of racial apartheid that made American two nations, separate and unequal.

5

The Cold War on the New Frontier

The simmering youthful activism that would give rise to the tumult of the uncivil war gained considerable heat from the 1960 presidential election. Most political scientists recognize that election as a point of departure in American political life. What made the choice in 1960 so epic had as much to do with generational politics as with issues. Kennedy and Nixon were the first two major party candidates born in the twentieth century and the first who were too young to have fought in World War I. Along with their running mates, Lyndon Johnson and Henry Cabot Lodge, they brought into power the generation that would dominate American politics until the 1990s. While Kennedy would become the first Roman Catholic president, Johnson would become the first Texan and first southern state president since before the Civil War. Nixon would be the first president from California.

Cold War Politics: The Election of 1960

If some 60,000 Americans had switched their votes from John Kennedy to Richard Nixon, the 1960s would certainly have had a different flavor. The closeness of the election—34,227,096 for Kennedy versus 34,107,646 for Nixon—reflected the partisan fervor the two opponents inspired. The turnout of some 64 percent was the highest since 1908. Kennedy attracted those Americans who saw themselves outside the political mainstream: Catholics, Jews, ethnics, Latinos, and African Americans. Nixon linked his politics with quite another America, one more traditional, small town, white, Protestant, and middle class.

Image had much to do with this electoral intensity and much to do with the 1960s. Where Kennedy and his wife, Jacqueline, radiated the glamour of Hollywood, Harvard, and Newport, Nixon identified himself with the emerging middle class of service providers, professionals, and small business. Where Kennedy talked about the need for change, Nixon, as heir to Eisenhower's legacy, defended the administration's record. And where Kennedy called for sacrifice and new challenges, Nixon spoke to those seeking security and convention. The writer Norman Mailer in his overblown fashion observed that "the people might know (since these candidates were not old enough to be revered) that they had chosen one young man for his mystery or his promise that the country would grow or disintegrate by the unwilling charge he gave to the intensity of the myth, or had chosen another young man for his unstated oath that he would do all in his power to keep the myth buried and so convert the remains of Renaissance man as rapidly as possible into mass man."

A majority of people who heard the Kennedy-Nixon debates on radio thought Nixon had the edge, but television viewers saw something presidential in John Kennedy. (Source: Associated Press)

That the two candidates could arouse deeply partisan responses from the voters is somewhat surprising. For all their efforts to construct opposing images, Kennedy and Nixon were not so very different. Both were political pragmatists, calculating and self-promotional, secretive, often remote, and frequently devious. Television commentator Eric Sevareid dismissed them as "two packaged products devoid of conviction or passion (but both with sharp tempers and a sense of aloofness)." There was, for example, Kennedy's youth. At forty-three, he would be the youngest president, but Nixon was only four years older. Much has been made of Kennedy's Irish-Catholic background. Nixon was also Irish on both sides of his family and, as a Quaker, hardly from the religious mainstream. Lawrence Wright observed, however, that "California washes away such distinctions, which are nurtured in Boston. The Kennedys were social upstarts; they threatened the social balance by being too successful. The Nixons, on the other hand, were quiet failures who threatened no one."

Even more has been made out of Kennedy's good looks and celebrity appeal. Campaign reporters discovered what they called "jumpers." Wherever Kennedy's motorcade passed, women in the crowds would begin jumping up and down with the intensity with which female fans responded to Elvis. After years of

Nixon's sagging jowls, forbidding eyebrows, and ski-jump nose, it is difficult to believe that in 1960 many people actually argued that he was better looking than Kennedy. Some magazines likened him to a matinee idol. He too had his female fans spurred on by the pert "Nixonettes." Political reporter Theodore White for one saw a sharp contrast between the scowling Nixon of political cartoons and the candidate in person. "He was attractively slim, as lithe as Kennedy, a fine and healthy American, almost an athlete," White observed. "His face as he spoke to this friendly audience was a smiling one—and Nixon has a broad, almost sunny smile when he is with friends." The problem for Nixon was television. The cameras that were so good to Kennedy were cruel to Nixon. As White noted: "the deep eye wells and the heavy eyebrows cast shadow on the face and it glowered on the screen darkly; when he became rhetorically indignant, the television showed ferocity; when he turned, his apparently thick brush of hair showed in a glimmering balding widow's peak."

On the issues, the candidates differed little more than Tweedledum and Tweedledee. Much has been written, for example, about how the Kennedys late in the campaign called Coretta Scott King, the wife of the great civil rights leader, to express concern about her husband's arrest. They received gratitude from black voters when a Georgia judge released King. In actuality, neither Kennedy nor Nixon had an interest in civil rights issues beyond the possibility of electoral advantage. Nixon had supported the strong civil rights plank introduced at the Republican convention by the more liberal factions pledged to Nelson Rockefeller. With that approach, he hoped to hold the African-American vote that went to Eisenhower in 1956. But when he received an unexpectedly warm reception in the South, until then an impregnable Democratic stronghold, he began to wonder whether he could get both the southern and the African-American vote. The potential hypocrisy in this position cost him no sleep.

The cold war consensus was at the heart of the election of 1960. That did not mean the candidates debated the assumptions of the consensus in any significant way. Quite the opposite was true. Both John F. Kennedy and Richard Nixon portrayed themselves as ardent cold warriors. Soviet premier Nikita Khrushchev likened them to "a pair of boots—which is better, the right boot or the left boot?" Nixon's aggressive anti-Communism had earned him a place on the Republican ticket in 1952. In that campaign, GOP strategists had assigned him the low road of slinging mud at the Democrats for losing China, for stalemate in Korea, and for being ineffective in rooting out the domestic Communist menace. As simplistic and misleading as such charges were, they succeeded in painting liberal Democrats if not red, at least a bright pink. For such excesses, liberals would never forgive Nixon.

Over the next eight years, Nixon moved to reconstruct himself as more of a statesman and less of a gutter fighter. Given that he never had the confidence or respect of President Eisenhower, he had few opportunities to play a visible role. So Nixon concentrated on strengthening his position with the party regulars and on foreign policy. In 1959, Nixon used a trip to Moscow to burnish his image as a statesman and a skillful foe of Communism. The occasion was the opening of a cultural exchange between the United States and the Soviet Union. To dramatize the advantages of free enterprise capitalism, the Americans had set up an exhibition of recent technological marvels, including the latest television equipment. While touring the exhibit, Khrushchev and Nixon began a debate triggered by the premier's anger at a Republican-sponsored Captive Nations Resolution, proclaiming a week of prayer for all people living under Communist tyranny. When at one point the Soviet premier wagged his finger in Nixon's face, the vice president jabbed his finger back at Khrushchev: "You must not be afraid of ideas . . . ," he insisted. "You don't know everything."

From there they moved on to a model American home, replete with the latest gadgetry. Nixon would later claim that what would be known as the "Kitchen Debate" had erupted spontaneously. All the same, a cameraman just happened to be stationed at the model kitchen, ready to capture the Nixon-Khrushchev exchange. Nixon told Khrushchev that any American, even a steel worker, could afford a house with a kitchen like this one. "This house costs about $100 a month to buy on a contract running twenty-five to thirty years," he explained. The irritated Khrushchev, taking a shot at America's throwaway consumer culture, retorted that after a century the house would no longer be standing. By contrast, he insisted, "we build firmly. We build for our children and grandchildren." When Khrushchev denounced the American obsession with consumer goods and homemaking, Nixon quickly played to the American television audience (and a Russian one, he hoped, as well): "I think that the attitude towards women is universal. What we want to do is to make easier the life of our housewives." The sexism so blatant in Nixon's (and Khrushchev's) attitudes was lost on the 1950s American audience. Americans appreciated instead his ability to match wits with the head of the Communist world. Nixon would henceforth claim that he was the candidate in 1960 who had already shown that he could "stand up" to the Russians. A large majority of Americans polled in 1960 said they would prefer to have him rather than any of the Democratic presidential hopefuls represent the United States at a summit with the Soviet Union.

To win the presidency, John Kennedy would somehow have to contest Nixon's image as the candidate best equipped to confront the Soviets. More generally, Kennedy would have to retrieve for the Democrats the anti-Communist mantle they lost in 1952 after Nixon, Senator Joe McCarthy, and the other witch-hunters successfully made the Republicans the party of anti-Communism. But after eight years holding the White House, the Republicans were now themselves vulnerable to charges that they had mismanaged the cold war. Had not the Russians beaten the United States into space with the launching of *Sputnik* in 1957? Who was responsible for the string of missile failures that led some to describe American launches as "flopniks" and "kaputniks"? On whose watch had Communists led by Fidel Castro seized power in Cuba? So Kennedy could charge that the Republicans had "lost" Cuba and were responsible for a "missile gap" that threatened the nation's security. Further, Kennedy argued that three brief recessions in the last five years demonstrated the Republicans had mismanaged the economy. Weak economic performance, in turn, damaged the nation's ability to maintain free-world defenses against the Soviet Union.

In taking that tack, Kennedy kept the cold war consensus at the center of the campaign. Voters could chose Nixon, a veteran cold warrior and anti-Communist, or Kennedy, a candidate who promised to infuse the cold war crusade with new energy. Substantively, neither candidate offered any specific proposals on how the cold war might be won or American advantage secured. In their televised debates, they engaged only in a meaningless exchange about whether the United States should defend Quemoy and Matsu, two inconsequential islands within artillery range of the Chinese Communist coast. But in staking his candidacy on a reinvigorated cold war, Kennedy had made a devil's deal. To win the election, he had promised that his administration would succeed where the Republicans had failed. Hence there could be no more Chinas, no more Cubas. In fact, Kennedy had essentially committed himself to retrieve Cuba and to strengthen American alliances around the globe. The price for redeeming that pledge would lead to embarrassment in Cuba and tragedy in Southeast Asia.

If cold war rhetoric defined the candidate's political ends, television provided the means to win the election. The networks had televised earlier conventions, and candidates had used television advertising since 1952. But in 1960, television not only expanded a politician's capacity to reach voters, it determined the outcome of the election. John Kennedy concluded, "it was television more than anything else that turned the tide." As a relatively new face on the national political scene, Kennedy had two major hurdles to overcome, his Catholicism and his age. The religious issue, however, cut two ways. On the one hand, in combination with support for civil rights, his religion alienated some Protestant voters, especially in the South. Kennedy sought to offset that disadvantage by naming Lyndon Johnson, a Southerner, as his running mate and by openly addressing the issue of his Catholicism before potentially hostile audiences.

Leading Protestant clergy like Norman Vincent Peale, the apostle of "positive thinking," publicly wondered whether a Catholic president would be "free to exercise his own judgment" if the pope ordered otherwise. Associating such views with bigotry, Kennedy framed the religious issue in cold war rhetoric. "The great struggle today," he told a Los Angeles audience, "is between those who believe in no God [i.e., Communists] and those who believe in God." And before the Greater Houston Ministerial Association, Kennedy defused the potentially damaging issue by declaring his absolute commitment to the separation of church and state. He believed in an America "where no Catholic prelate would tell the President (should he be Catholic) how to act, and [in an implicit rebuke to Peale and other skeptical Protestant clergy] no Protestant minister would tell his parishioners how to vote."

The Houston performance turned a potential liability into a plus. Sam Rayburn, a seasoned Texas political leader, was so impressed with Kennedy's performance, he burst out at one point, "My God! . . . He's eating them blood raw"—a real accolade in cattle country. Seeing Kennedy score points off the religious controversy, Nixon and the GOP dropped the issue from the campaign. The Democrats did not. They televised film clips from the Houston speech to audiences around the country. Kennedy's brother Robert played the issue another way: "Did they ask my brother Joe whether he was a Catholic before he was shot down [during World War II]?" Election analysis indicated that most of the votes Kennedy lost on the religious question he gained back with greater support from Catholics. One voter, when asked if he voted Democratic because Kennedy was a Catholic, replied, "No, because I am."

Age for Kennedy created a problem of image. Many voters did not find in the youthful Kennedy the stature or maturity they sought in a national leader. That is why Nixon made so much of his own experience. And that is why the Kennedy forces sought televised debates. They believed, quite correctly, that if Kennedy stood next to Nixon before the television audience, their candidate would win over reluctant voters. The more interesting question is why Nixon agreed to the debates. As the frontrunner, he had more to lose and less to gain. Evidence from his own recollections suggests that he wavered before finally agreeing. His staff, however, was convinced that as a skilled debater, Nixon would destroy Kennedy with a knockout blow. As a result, they asked for a single debate. Eager for as much exposure as possible, the Kennedy team demanded five and settled for four.

The two candidates first met on September 25, 1960, in a Chicago television station. In his opening statement, Kennedy, not Nixon, delivered the knockout blow. Kennedy said nothing new or dramatic—his statement was pure political rhetoric. "In the election of 1860," he began, "Abraham Lincoln said the question was whether this nation could exist half slave or half free. In the election of 1960, the question is whether the world will exist half slave or half free." Election analyst Theodore White argued that at that moment Kennedy had won the debates. There he stood before 65–70 million viewers looking every bit as mature and presidential as Nixon.

It did not hurt that Kennedy had switched from a white to a blue shirt to soften the glare of studio lights, the same lights that threw dark shadows over Nixon's craggy face. Nor did it help that the Lazy Shave used to cover Nixon's heavy beard ran, exposing a five o'clock shadow. The well-rested and tanned Kennedy stood coolly, almost detached behind his lectern. Nixon appeared by contrast pale and tense. He had come to debate. And that, even more than runny makeup, proved to be his undoing. Nixon systematically responded to Kennedy, addressing each point he had made. Kennedy, in turn, ignored Nixon. Recognizing the nature of television, he instead addressed his comments to the unseen audience. People who heard the debate on the radio considered it close or gave the nod to Nixon. Polls showed, however, that among the vast viewing audience, Kennedy was the decided winner. As historian Thomas Reeves commented, "To many Americans Kennedy became the hero, Nixon the villain."

After the first debate, money poured into the Kennedy campaign, crowds became larger and almost frenzied, and politicians jumped to get on his bandwagon. Nixon managed in the next debates to correct many of the mistakes he made, but the damage had been done. The Kennedy campaign had the momentum it needed to overcome Nixon's lead. Some 110 million Americans had watched at least part of one of the debates. What they heard would do little to inform them about a candidate's character or political priorities. As one disgruntled voter complained, "It's all phony. This has become an actor's election." But what the viewers saw did matter greatly. Even a member of the Nixon campaign staff admitted begrudgingly that at least superficially, Kennedy could stand shoulder-to-shoulder with Nixon. Never again would political professionals doubt the power of television to shape the outcome of an election. And television, more than any other medium, would dominate the public culture of the 1960s.

If the story of the television debates indicates the trivial character of presidential politics in 1960, one other campaign incident revealed a deep fault line that the election obscured. The incident did not involve Kennedy at all, but his vice presidential choice, Lyndon Johnson. Kennedy did not particularly like Johnson, and to members of his campaign, Johnson was, as Lawrence Wright quipped, "a hard-shell Southern conservative, a native racist, a drawling, backslapping political whore with no guiding light other than the oil depletion allowance." Kennedy strategists feared that whatever votes Johnson gained among Southerners, he would lose by alienating northern liberals who viewed Kennedy as at heart a conservative with few convictions. Over their resistance, Kennedy had chosen Johnson to shore up his shaky support in the South.

Dutifully accepting his role as second banana, Johnson had gone about lining up reluctant southern politicians. He had urged Kennedy to give the speech to the Greater Houston Ministerial Association that neutralized the religious issue. Johnson, in turn, personally took up the civil rights question. The way he did so revealed just how deeply civil rights tortured his southern soul. Publicly, he spoke "as an American to Americans—whatever their region, religion, or race." Privately, he is rumored to have warned the politicos that they had to elect Kennedy so that he, Johnson, "your fellow-Southerner, can defeat this integration proposal." Knowledge of Johnson's duplicitous posture would only have confirmed the liberals' worst suspicions. On the other hand, any other course would have been suicide for Johnson, a man not noted for being careless with his political life.

On November 4, just days before the election, Johnson concentrated his energies in Texas. No Democrat since the Civil War ever won the presidency without carrying the Lone Star state. Few people in the Kennedy camp understood, however, that the contempt most liberals felt toward Johnson paled compared to the hatred Texas conservatives harbored toward him. To them, Johnson was "a closet socialist, a leftover New Dealer, a bleeding heart on domestic matters and [in macho Texas the worst kind of slur] a weak sister when it came to standing up against Communist aggression." The public figure who most personified this right-wing fury was the only elected Republican in Texas at that time, Congressman Bruce Alger of Dallas. Even in a land of extremists, Alger was off the charts. His most notable achievements as a congressman were to drive federal projects out of Dallas and to oppose free milk for schoolchildren. Besides his formidable extremism, the key to his popularity was his movie-star good looks. They won him the devoted following of an energetic cadre of Dallas club women. These right-wing Texans practiced the paranoid politics of superpatriotism evoked by the John Birch Society. They were ever on the lookout for Communist plots, which to them meant school integration and fluoridated drinking water. These Texans liked Nixon because he had destroyed Alger Hiss and stood up to Khrushchev in the Kitchen Debates.

The day Johnson and his wife, Lady Bird, came to Dallas, the Alger women were out canvassing for the Republicans. Despite their stylish Junior League appearance, hatred for Johnson transformed them into a mob. As Lady Bird emerged from a limousine, one of the women actually snatched her white gloves and threw them in the gutter. Such incivility was at that time rare in American politics and unheard of among socially prominent women. Soon after the first confrontation, the Johnsons left their hotel to attend a political luncheon across the street. Under normal circumstances, the walk would have taken less than five minutes. Instead, the Johnsons passed into what would become known as the "Mink Coat Mob." Leading them was the grinning Alger with a sign proclaiming, "LBJ SOLD OUT TO YANKEE SOCIALISTS." "We're gonna show Johnson he's not wanted in Dallas," Alger announced.

As the Johnsons struggled across the street, the jeering women closed in on them and began to curse and spit. The scene reminded one observer of the mobs that assaulted Nixon's motorcade in Venezuela, except these were not radical leftists, but Dallas socialites decked out in patriotic red, white, and blue. When Lady Bird tried to respond to a heckler, Johnson covered her mouth and steered her into the hotel lobby. They were then but a short walk to the elevators and safety. Towering over his tormentors, Johnson could easily have pushed through. But some political sixth sense told him otherwise. He slowed down so that five minutes turned into thirty.

Before that moment, few northern liberals had any understanding of either Johnson or Texas politics. Now, as Lawrence Wright concluded, they saw Johnson "as he understood himself. He was a liberal—in the Southern context." And many decent, God-fearing, and socially respectable Americans saw an extremism in that Dallas mob that they had not known existed in the era of consensus politics. In that context, the Kennedys and Johnsons appeared to them much closer to the mainstream of American life. This event may not have swayed many votes, but Kennedy did carry Texas and could not have won the election if he had not done so.

In understanding the 1960s, it is worth noting that this harbinger of the political extremism associated with the decade came in the heartland of the South, not on a college campus or in some urban bohemia. The fury in Dallas was in some way an omen of the political violence that would strike there three years later. Yet these political agitators were not the long-haired, bomb-throwing anarchists. These fashionable, neatly coifed, and financially secure inheritors of the American dream were J. Edgar Hoover and Barry Goldwater's people who worried about Communism and racial integration. Nixon's election would have brought their values to Washington.

Through him they, not the liberal eastern establishment, would have determined the nation's manners and mores.

Camelot

History has not been kind to John Kennedy or his presidency. The mystique of Camelot that surrounded his administration has been eroded by the relentless disclosure of his cynicism, womanizing, links to organized crime, ambiguous Vietnam policy, and the tepidness of his liberal convictions, especially on civil rights. Typical of the posthumous revelations was the discovery that his Pulitzer Prize–winning book, Profiles in Courage, was largely ghostwritten by his speechwriter, Theodore Sorensen. The book extolled the heroic devotion to principle demonstrated by a handful of congressmen and senators. Detractors of Kennedy's politics liked to quip that he showed far more profile than courage.

In 1960, all the Kennedy debunking lay in the future. To understand the 1960s and Kennedy's substantial contribution to the spirit of the era, it is essential to recapture the aura of excitement and expectation that greeted his ascension to the White House. Compared to the grandfatherly Eisenhower, "you had a young guy who had kids, and who liked football on the front lawn." The public thrilled to pictures of Caroline and John Jr. playing in the oval office. They loved stories about Jackie's ever-so-tasteful redecoration of the White House, and the celebrity guest list of artists, movie stars, and intellectuals who lent their aura to a growing Kennedy mystique.

In that way, the same attention to image that made Kennedy's election possible also guided his presidency. The process began even before he entered the White House. During the interval between the election and his inauguration, he formed the youngest and one of the most energetic cabinets in the nation's history, filling it with what became known as "action intellectuals." Certain traits distinguished Kennedy's people. They were intensely loyal to the president and his political future. They came ready to serve Kennedy, not to outshine him. As one reporter said of appointments secretary Kenny O'Donnell, "Nobody who knows Kenny doubts for a moment he would die for the President if need be." In addition, Kennedy chose people who were nonideological. They shared his ambition for practical results rather than large visions. Joseph Kennedy had weaned his boys on competition. The Kennedys would never be "satisfied with anything but first place. The point was not to try; the point was to win." Hence, Kennedy had advisors who, like the president, admired toughness and strove to demonstrate that they had "the right stuff." They came into the Cabinet persuaded that they understood power: how to gain it, and how to use it. In that way, arrogance became another of their common characteristics.

Yet not a single one had wide experience in electoral politics. They came from the bureaucracy, academia, corporate management, finance, and law firms. Defense Secretary Robert Strange McNamara exemplified this new breed. As president of Ford Motors, McNamara had imposed his cost-cutting and efficiency regime on a company that had lost its edge. He just exuded energy, a person who ran rather than walked, even "running up and down escalator steps". McNamara embraced the new era of computers, statistics, and cost-benefits analysis. Once, when challenged on a policy recommendation, McNamara reportedly shot back, "Where is your data? Give me something I can put in the computer. Don't give me your poetry." As reporter David Halberstam concluded about McNamara, he was "the can-do man, in the can-do society, in the can-do era."

For all their brilliance, many of the elite Kennedy appointed would be wrong on some of their most crucial decisions, especially on Cuba and Vietnam. Their lack of political experience was not lost on some of Washington's more seasoned insiders. Lyndon Johnson grumbled to whomever would listen about all "the Harvards." Once, as Johnson recited the list of their credentials to veteran representative Sam Rayburn of Texas, the savvy house speaker replied, "Well, Lyndon, you may be right and they may be every bit as intelligent as you say, but I'd feel a whole lot better about them if just one of them had run for sheriff once."

The excitement with which the Kennedys swept into Washington gave his inauguration the feeling of a coronation. Kennedy spared no effort to make this a memorable event. So potent was his image that even some of his small gestures had a major impact. Despite bitter cold, Kennedy stood before the crowd without a hat or coat. Until that moment, hats had been one of the central accessories of men's fashion. Following Kennedy, many men would now adopt a preppy look that was youthful and hatless. The ceremony included a recitation by the celebrated poet Robert Frost and the rendition of the "Star Spangled Banner" by the black opera star Marian Anderson. Some twenty years before, the patriotic Daughters of the American Revolution (DAR) had barred an Anderson concert in their Washington hall. Eleanor Roosevelt had interceded to arrange the concert at the Lincoln Memorial. So Kennedy had made the symbolism of that early civil rights event part of his inauguration.

As in his presidential campaign, the cold war crusade was the essence of his inaugural address, certainly one of the most inspired and inspiring ever delivered. It was a clarion call to action and sacrifice, though in what ways Kennedy never specified. He observed the generational significance of his election: "Let the word go forth from this time and place, to friend and foe alike, that the torch has been passed to a new generation of Americans . . . unwilling to witness or permit the slow undoing of those human rights to which this nation has always been committed and to which we are committed today at home and around the world." Lest America's enemies underestimate this generation's determination to carry on the cold war battle, Kennedy assured them that Americans would "pay any price, bear any burden, meet any foe to assure the survival and success of liberty." Returning yet again to his theme of challenge and sacrifice, he declared, "In the long history of the world, few generations have been granted the role of defending freedom in its hour of maximum danger. I do not shrink from that responsibility; I welcome it."

Kennedy seemed at this moment to personify the American nation's promise to reform the world. The New Frontier, as his program would come to be known, echoed the Puritan notion of the "errand into the wilderness." Kennedy asked the members of his generation to support "a struggle against the common enemies of man: tyranny, poverty, disease, and war itself." And he called on them to take up this task in the most selfless manner: "ask not what your country can do for you; ask what you can do for your country."

Praise for the speech was almost universal. Even some Kennedy detractors found it "eloquent, inspiring—a great speech." Something beside the content must have aroused their enthusiasm, for much of what Kennedy said had been said before. His "struggle against the common enemies of man" had striking similarity to FDR's idea of the four freedoms. Warren Harding, certainly no crusader, had asked his generation to "think more about what you can do for your government than what your government can do for you." A few cynical observers noted that Kennedy's call for selfless devotion to country had a rather discomforting similarity to fascism. It was not, however, so much what people heard but what they saw that made the speech such a stirring success. There, coatless and hatless on a bitter January day, stood a vibrant young leader looking steadfastly into the future and challenging the nation to realize its destiny. That was the kind of authenticity so many young Americans yearned for. And the fact that it was so cleverly contrived for the media speaks volumes about the politics of the decade to come.

The Cold War President

In reaching the White House, Kennedy had made two commitments which more than any others would define his presidency. One was more implicit than explicit— that was to advance the cause of racial justice. Black votes had made a critical difference in his victory. But, like Lyndon Johnson, Kennedy recognized that if he got out in front on civil rights he could destroy the Democratic Party and his own political future. There was no way to compromise the demands of the civil rights movement with the traditional apartheid policies of white, southern Democrats. The slender electoral majority indicated that Kennedy would face stiff opposition to an activist domestic policy in almost any area. As a consequence, his administration allowed events to shape his civil rights policy.

Kennedy had promised repeatedly to infuse the cold war crusade with new energy. As a consequence, he intended to make foreign policy the focus of his administration. The logic of that political strategy was compelling. The crisis atmosphere engendered by the cold war had shifted the balance of power within the government to the executive branch. Trouble anywhere in the world required the kind of quick decisions only the president could make. Hence, an activist foreign policy most embellished the presidential image. Fighting the cold war had also enhanced the power of major executive agencies like the CIA, FBI, National Security Administration (NSA), as well as the State and Defense Departments.

In his campaign, Kennedy seized on the two events that suggested the balance might be tipping in favor of the Soviet Union—Sputnik and Cuba. But since he knew the missile gap did not exist, Kennedy meant to concentrate on Cuba, not only containing Castro, but reclaiming what threatened to be a Soviet outpost in America's backyard. In the broader scheme of world politics, Kennedy identified with the ideas of the cold war liberals. While liberals had traditionally opposed the excesses of capitalism and championed the cause of the downtrodden, in the cold war era they began to see capitalism as the antidote to militant Communism. Like Galbraith, they had come to believe that the economic system no longer required major reforming, only a shift away from the consumption of private goods toward the creation of public goods. *Sputnik* dramatized their complaint that the nation had squandered its technical and scientific advantages.

Walt Whitman Rostow in many ways epitomized this thinking among Kennedy's action intellectuals. Few people have ever had Rostow's sublime confidence in the correctness of their ideas, and few people have been so consistently wrong about important issues. Rostow, like Kennedy, was something of an outsider among insiders. He had gone to Yale as a scholarship student. While there, he was a social and academic success, but as a Jew, many of the doors of the elite organizations such as Skull and Bones (which included WASPs like the Bushes among its distinguished membership) were closed to him. Somehow, Rostow managed not to notice. He was too busy promoting his own success that led him from Yale to Oxford and then to a position with the bombing survey during World War II. When later asked if he recalled any anti-Semitism at Yale, an institution where it abounded, he remembered vaguely only one incident in the English Department involving a tenure case.

After the war, Rostow went on to join the economics faculty at MIT, where he made the economics of development his specialty. His theory of the stages of economic growth opened for him a possible new approach to the cold war. If material privation made people receptive to Communism, then economic growth was a remedy. Obviously, the United States lacked the resources to promote growth everywhere. But Rostow believed that national economies went through stages. Under the right circumstances, they reached what he called a takeoff point, where they had the resources to make growth self-sustaining. By recognizing when conditions were ripe, the United States could provide foreign assistance that would promote the takeoff. Advancing industrial economies would naturally gravitate toward the Western bloc. Rostow's ideas were so well received that he gained a hearing in the Eisenhower administration.

Sometime around 1957, Kennedy had discovered Rostow and the liberal view of the cold war. Liberals considered their strategies to be more activist, more interventionist, and more subtle than the militant anti-Communism of conservatives. Instead of seeing the Communist bloc as a monolith, the liberals recognized the possibilities of exploiting the deep tensions between the Russians and the Chinese. By 1960, the cold war liberals had embraced a liberation scheme to replace what they saw as the crude "brinkmanship" advocated by Eisenhower and Dulles. They recognized that the balance of power in Europe had taken on an uneasy permanency. As a result, the cold war struggle had shifted to the Third World, where nationalism, decolonization, rapid population growth, and widespread poverty created chronic instability and potentially fertile soil for Communism. Based on the Rostow model, foreign aid could be judiciously applied to promote economic growth and political reform. With greater stability in the Third World, Communism would lose its appeal. Rostow and others also became fervent champions of counterinsurgency as opposed to conventional warfare. In that way, the United States could contain leftist revolutions without the risk of a major war. And by unleashing the enormous potential of its own economy, the United States could inspire a drift toward the West within the Third World. It would lead by example.

Kennedy found a position for Rostow in the State Department. But when he appointed the reserved Dean Rusk as secretary of state, he served notice he would personally conduct foreign affairs from the White House. Beyond his determination to lead, Kennedy came to the White House with few concrete plans for foreign policy. He admitted to John Kenneth Galbraith that his only new idea was for a "peace corps"—an organization that would send young people and their American know-how to nations of the Third World. The Peace Corps in many ways reflected the gulf between the idealistic image and practical realities that the guided the Kennedy administration. When Kennedy created it in March 1961, just over a month into his term, he captured the ideal of service and sacrifice about which he had spoken so eloquently in his inaugural address. Even though it cost little money and involved only a few thousand volunteers in its first years, the Peace Corps generated much favorable publicity for the new administration. Americans liked the idea of helping people to help themselves. The volunteers included teachers, agricultural and sanitation advisers, and technicians. As a legacy of their efforts, they left behind irrigation projects, sewer systems, rural schools, and other small-scale public works.

For all the fanfare surrounding it, the Peace Corps remained largely a symbolic initiative. Kennedy himself had had no great enthusiasm for it until he noticed how warmly college students responded to the idea. He reportedly once quipped that he appointed his brother-in-law Sargent Shriver to head the new agency so it would be easier to fire the director when the program failed. Its modest projects could not begin to dent the enormous problems of material privation that burdened most of the world. Too often the well-intended volunteers learned that they lacked the language skills, cultural knowledge, or material resources needed to overcome the problems they encountered. They discovered, too, that in places like Latin America and the Philippines, American interests contributed to the political corruption and economic exploitation responsible for much of the poverty they encountered. Worse yet, in many areas the Peace Corps fell under a cloud of suspicion that it was a cover for United States imperialism. That suspicion was fully warranted. Whatever its humanitarian purposes, Kennedy saw the Peace Corps as another weapon in the cold war crusade. The largest numbers went to Latin America as part of the effort to contain Castro. In April 1963, Peace Corps director Sargent Shriver personally asked the president to stop the CIA from planting agents among the volunteers.

The Peace Corps probably had more impact in the United States than it did in the Third World. In creating it, Kennedy unleashed the idealistic energies of many young

The idea of serving the Third World in the Peace Corps struck a responsive cord among idealistic young Americans of the sixties era.   (Source: Associated Press)

Americans. Tom Hayden, who would soon apply that energy to the creation of Students for a Democratic Society, admitted that the concept of the Peace Corps and its mission of service had especially captured him with its humanity. From Kennedy, he gained the hope that great visions might actually be realized. Hayden was far from alone. And the Peace Corps, like the civil rights movement, proved to be an incubator of political radicals. The University of California at Berkeley produced more volunteers than any other campus. By the time they returned home, many had grown cynical about their own government and its responsibility for Third World poverty. Volunteers also learned to organize in new ways. As one Peace Corps veteran remarked, "I still think it's a good way to approach problems—at the grass roots level—unlike policymakers who never understand things at the grass roots." That idea of empowering the people would become central to New Left politics.

World politics gave young Americans another reason to be cynical. They had grown up under the threat of imminent nuclear destruction. John Foster Dulles may have meant to frighten the Russians with his talk of going to the brink, but his message had just as much impact at home. Air raid drills offered a constant reminder that each day might be the last. Among Kennedy's earliest initiatives was an article in *Life* magazine encouraging the building of home bomb shelters. The most popular book of 1961 was a Defense Department pamphlet called *The Family Fallout Shelter*. Lawrence Wright tells the story of a friend whose mother had prepared him for the worst. "If I ever come to school to get you," she had told him, "don't listen to your teachers or principal; just come." So one day as he gazed out the school window he saw his mother's car arrive. He immediately jumped out the window and ran to her, only to discover she had brought his lunch money.

In such an environment, foreign policy had a special immediacy. Each confrontation carried with it the possibility of disaster. That may explain why Kennedy's first major cold war initiative came as such a shock. Predictably, it involved Cuba. Kennedy had made clear in his campaign that he would end the threat that Castro posed. More-thoughtful observers felt that Kennedy exaggerated the problem. J. William Fulbright, chair of the Senate Foreign Relations Committee, remarked, "The Castro regime is a thorn in our flesh, but it is not a dagger in the heart." Nonetheless, Kennedy was determined to show his mettle by removing the thorn.

He did not have to look far for a means. During Eisenhower's last year, the CIA had begun training a force of exiles to invade Cuba. Intelligence experts assured Kennedy that at the first sign of the invasion, the Cuban people would overthrow Castro and a CIA assassin would kill him. That persuaded Kennedy to put any reservations aside. He stipulated only that no American forces would become directly involved. Even before the invasion force left its training centers in Guatemala, the operation went badly. American newspapers published reports that a "secret" invasion was in the works. As the 1500 troops waded ashore at the Bay of Pigs on April 17, 1961, they found themselves caught in a swamp with no route inland. The promised air and naval support never materialized. Within hours, over 100 were dead and the rest prisoners.

Here was a clear warning that there was a serious flaw in the theory of counterinsurgency. Cuba was not seething with discontent, and Castro was firmly in control. Aggression against a small neighbor tarnished the moral armor Kennedy donned at his inauguration. The sheer incompetence of the operation raised serious questions about how bright the best people were. And a nagging feeling arose that the United States had been caught behaving like its enemies. Sadly, this failure left the administration unchastened, though in public Kennedy shouldered blame for the fiasco. In private, he condemned the so-called experts who had had such confidence in success: "How could I have been so stupid, to let them go ahead?" Rather than question their own assumptions, the Kennedy advisers assumed that the next time the job would be done right. Worried that the Russians might think of them as weak, they looked forward to new confrontations. As Walt Rostow assured a dejected Kennedy, "we would have ample opportunity to prove we were not paper tigers in Berlin, Southeast Asia, and elsewhere."

True to the spirit of his inaugural address, Kennedy followed the Cuban fiasco by rapidly increasing the nation's preparedness. The defense budget jumped 15 percent in his first year. "Flexible response" was the term Kennedy adopted. That meant having the forces available for any eventuality. Against wars of national liberation, the United States would have its new special forces, or Green Berets, trained to fight in any climate or terrain. United States military personnel at that time were training security forces in some seventy-two countries. But the key to defense was the strategic nuclear force. That meant the buildup of the triad—a three-legged force of strategic bombers, land-based ICBMs (Inter-continental Ballistic Missiles), and nuclear missile submarines. Kennedy even extended the cold war race into space when he declared that the United States would put a man on the moon before the decade was out. Though this enormously expensive undertaking had little scientific or military justification, it served Kennedy's sense of the dramatic by extending the "New Frontier" into the realm of science fiction. It also created a more optimistic vision to offset the sense of menace from nuclear weapons.

The next major crisis Kennedy faced made the possibility of nuclear Armageddon seem all too real. The setting was Berlin, divided into East and West zones since World War II. For all their talk of the Third World, American policymakers recognized Western Germany as the key to the security of Western Europe and, by extension, the United States. The Allied zone in West Berlin thus became a symbol of NATO's determination to contain Communism. For the Soviet Union and East Germans, West Berlin was the thorn in their side. Each month some 30,000 east bloc refugees poured from East Germany into West Berlin. When Kennedy first met Soviet premier Khrushchev at Vienna, Austria, in June 1961, the future of West Berlin was one of three issues they discussed (Laos and a nuclear test–ban treaty were the others). Khrushchev told Kennedy that the West must leave Berlin. If not, the Soviet Union would sign a treaty with East Germany, ending the postwar occupation. On one level, Khrushchev was just testing Kennedy. He knew that Berlin had symbolic importance to the West far beyond its strategic or economic value. In the earthy style for which he was so well known, he joked to a comrade, "Berlin is the testicles of the West. Every time I want to make the West scream, I squeeze Berlin."

And scream Kennedy did. He feared the Vienna meeting had gone badly, that the Soviet premier had found him weak. If Khrushchev thought he could push Kennedy around, then he might miscalculate the West's resolve. In the nuclear age, such errors could have tragic results. So Kennedy decided to raise Khrushchev's bet on Berlin. He got authority to call up the military reserves, asked Congress for a major increase in defense spending, and stated publicly that Berlin was "the great testing place of Western courage and will." Instead of folding, the Russians and East Germans raised the bet one wall. They constructed a massive concrete and barbed wire barrier that effectively shut off the refugee flow. The United States commander in Berlin, General Lucius Clay, prepared to raise the bet again. He had ten tanks take up positions to bulldoze the wall. The Russians responded with tanks of their own. Chastened by the crisis they had precipitated, Kennedy and Khrushchev privately negotiated an end to the showdown. The wall remained up, the West stayed in Berlin, and Europe narrowly averted a nuclear disaster. At the same time, both sides resumed tests of ever more powerful nuclear weapons.

Shortly before the Bay of Pigs disaster, some 25,000 Americans had staged the largest peace demonstration since World War II. As they marched, Soviet and American negotiators at Geneva struggled to find some basis for a mutually acceptable nuclear test ban. The Berlin crisis shattered any immediate possibility a test ban might succeed. Without some compromise, SANE (the National Committee for a Sane Nuclear Policy) warned, Berlin might instead "touch off a nuclear war." SANE leadership proposed that rather than face "extermination without representation," the United States could allow the United Nations to solve the problem of Germany reunification. That position provoked some predictable outrage from anti-Communists. "Better Dead Than Red," was a typical response. More significant was the widespread approval for SANE's peace initiative. Though Kennedy did placate the right wing and military by resuming underground tests, he also spoke for peace. At the United Nations General Assembly in September 1961, he challenged the Soviet Union to a "peace race" rather than an "arms race." In that spirit, Congress approved the creation of the U.S. Arms Control and Disarmament Agency.

The residue of anti-Communist hysteria complicated the efforts of peace advocates to promote disarmament. No such compunction restrained a group of Washington, D.C., area suburban housewives. Desperate to do something to ease the threat of nuclear Armageddon, they decided to call on women to express support for a nuclear test–ban treaty and international disarmament. SANE and the Women's International League for Peace and Freedom provided mailing lists. On November 1, 1961, over 25,000 women heeded the call to demonstrate on behalf of the Women's Strike for Peace (WSP). The media treated them not as strikers but as mothers. Their rallying cry was "End the Arms Race, Not the Human Race." The surprising strength of the turnout encouraged them to continue their efforts. A spokesperson among them rejected the idea that they marked a reemergence of feminism. "I am not now or never have been a feminist, but one thing I will say for women, they know that there are no miracles except the one ultimate miracle of the seed of life," a WSP activist commented.

Their fragile hopes that Kennedy would resist pressure to match the Soviets' atmospheric tests ended in March 1962. Goaded by the military and nuclear arms advocates, he announced that the United States would resume its tests in April unless the arms negotiations deadlock at Geneva was broken. SANE continued to resist. It had by then found among its contributors Dr. Benjamin Spock, whose book *Baby and Child Care* had served as a bible to a generation of anxious parents. Dr. Spock agreed to speak publicly against atmospheric testing. As he explained, "I thought of all the children who would die of leukemia and cancer, and the ultimate possibility of nuclear war, and I joined SANE." SANE bought a full-page ad that appeared in the *New York Times* and was then reprinted in 700 other newspapers. The ad showed a pensive Dr. Spock, a young child, and the caption, "Dr. Spock is worried."

SANE's efforts had no real effect on the decision to resume atmospheric testing. What the ad had done, however, was to recruit to the peace movement a person who would become one of its most visible public figures. It also broaden SANE's support throughout the country. SANE then shifted its attack to the issue of radioactive fallout. That campaign received a powerful boost after the publication of Rachel Carson's *Silent Spring* raised awareness of these threats to public health.

Cuba: The Nuclear Showdown

Whatever progress SANE made toward nuclear disarmament was suspended for a perilous moment in the fall of 1962. Once again, the eyes of the world turned toward Cuba. The Bay of Pigs disaster had in no way deterred the Kennedy administration from its efforts to be rid of Castro. Plans abounded for invasions and assassinations. U.S. troops held major training operations in the Caribbean. Kennedy even made secret efforts to enlist organized crime in an assassination plot. Fully aware of these threats, Castro strengthened his links to Moscow. After the Bay of Pigs, Khrushchev had begun to supply Cuba with conventional weapons, including MIG fighter planes and anti-aircraft missiles (SAMs). At the same time, Kennedy had finally confessed publicly that rather than facing a missile gap, the United States had such superiority in strategic weapons that it could successfully initiate a preemptive attack.

As a result, Khrushchev had several compelling reasons to defy Kennedy's warning against installation of offensive nuclear weapons in Cuba. Above all, it had become clear that a buildup in conventional weapons would not save Cuba from invasion. The loss of Cuba would have been a serious blow to Soviet prestige among Communist bloc nations at a time of intense rivalry with the Chinese. In addition, the presence of nuclear weapons in Cuba would quickly narrow the missile gap in the Soviets' favor. As Khrushchev told his advisors, "we must pay them back in their own coin . . . so they will know what it feels like to live in the sight of nuclear weapons." The first inkling that an arms buildup was underway came in August 1962. On the 14th, an American U-2 spy plane flying over Cuba photographed operational SAM sites. Two days later came photos of medium-range bombers with nuclear capability.

At first, the administration discounted these sightings. Kennedy had assurances from Khrushchev that he would do nothing to disturb East-West relations before the contentious mid-term elections in November. Some Republican congressmen seeking a campaign issue publicly charged that an arms buildup was underway, which Kennedy vigorously denied. He twice warned Khrushchev in the most unambiguous terms that the United States would treat the placement of nuclear weapons in Cuba as a warlike act. On September 19, an intelligence board assured the president that in fact the Soviets had not and would not install offensive missiles. So the combative Kennedy reacted with outrage when he learned that Khrushchev had betrayed his trust. Intelligence photographs from October 14 and 16 left no doubt the Soviets were constructing offensive missile sites in Cuba. "That son of a bitch," Kennedy shouted, "he can't do that to me."

Khrushchev had done it; the question now became what would the United States do in response. Four major options existed, each carrying grave strategic and political risks. Kennedy might have done nothing. Robert McNamara pointed out that the missiles in Cuba scarcely tipped the strategic balance. The United States could live with them; Kennedy could not. Khrushchev might become emboldened to take even riskier steps, and the Republicans would gain immense political capital. Diplomacy was an option favored by liberal members of the administration. Kennedy's more hawkish advisors thought that approach was too soft and would leave the initiative with the Soviets. They pushed for a "surgical air strike" that would take out the missiles. The risk with this option, and it was an enormous one, was that the strike might kill Soviet personnel at the sites. And if missiles survived and were fired, an escalating nuclear exchange was virtually unavoidable. As a compromise, a group of Kennedy's closest advisors, led by his brother Bobby, pushed for a naval blockade. Such a course left future options open. If negotiations for the removal of the missiles broke down, an air strike remained possible.

For a week, Kennedy and his advisers met almost nonstop in efforts to avert disaster. So careful were they to disguise their activities that few people outside the administration had any idea a crisis was at hand. The president continued his routine of speeches and public appearances. That only magnified the impact of his announcement to the nation on October 22, 1962, that the Soviets had created "a nuclear strike capability against the Western Hemisphere." In response, the United States would impose a "quarantine on all offensive military equipment" shipped to Cuba. For many of the young Americans who heard the president that night, their lives would never be quite the same. Their seemingly secure world stood on the eve of destruction. As Todd Gitlin recalled, "For six days, time was deformed, every day life suddenly dwarfed and illuminated, as if by the glare of an explosion that had not yet taken place."

Fortunately for humankind, the blockade worked. While an anxious world waited, Kennedy and Khrushchev negotiated a bargain that publicly saved face for both. The Russians removed their missiles and bombers in return for a pledge from Kennedy that the United States would not invade Cuba. It is almost impossible to exaggerate the sense of relief that swept the administration and the nation as the crisis abated. Praise for Kennedy and his cool handling of the confrontation was nearly universal. His approval rating in the Gallup poll reached 74 percent. While gratified by the success of his diplomacy, Kennedy was also chastened to have stood so perilously on the brink of disaster. In June of 1963, Kennedy gave a speech at American University in Washington that may have been the finest of his career. He called upon the two superpowers to seek the basis for a "genuine peace."

Talk of peace in the highly charged atmosphere of the cold war carried great political risks. Hard-core cold warriors assumed that those who sought peace lacked the manliness to face down the enemy. Real "peaceniks" were either soft on Communism, fellow travelers, or dupes of the Kremlin. Thus, Kennedy assured his audience that he still recognized that Americans "find Communism profoundly repugnant" and that "the Communist drive to impose their political and economic system on others is the primary cause of world tension today." Nonetheless, the time had come for the superpowers to think about each other in new ways in order to "help make the world safe for diversity. For, in the final analysis, . . . we all inhabit this small planet. We all breathe the same air. We all cherish our children's' future. And we are all mortal." Kennedy ended his speech with the assurance that the United States would never start a war.

The response from Khrushchev was most favorable. To ensure against a nuclear accident in the future, a "hot line" was installed that established a direct link between the White House and the Kremlin. Within a month, both sides agreed to a Limited Test Ban Treaty that prohibited either atmospheric or underwater nuclear tests. The missile crisis seemed, in that way, to ease cold war tensions. Yet in other ways, the opposite was true. The crisis revealed to Soviet leaders the consequences of their nuclear weapons inferiority. They embarked soon after on a program to increase their missile strength. The Kennedy administration, having pledged not to invade Cuba, continued plotting to assassinate Castro.

Many of those who planned American policy during the crisis came to recognize just how close they had come to disaster. McGeorge Bundy, the national security advisor, remembered his sense of events "so near spinning out of control." Yet somehow the experience led most of Kennedy's advisors to behave more, not less, aggressively. They concluded that success in Cuba showed they knew how to use the right levels of power, in the right ways, in the right places, at the right time. The threat of limited military action had been sufficient to force the Communists to back down. If it worked in the case of Cuba, would military confrontation not work elsewhere? What, for example, about Vietnam, where the American-installed regime of Ngo Dinh Diem faced growing opposition from what it glibly described as Communist forces. That has led a number of historians to agree that success in Cuba served as the precedent for growing American involvement in Vietnam.

The missile crisis also had a transformative impact on the small but growing student radical movement. Kennedy's speech announcing the crisis triggered numerous demonstrations on college campuses across the nation. The hecklers often outnumbered the demonstrators. At Cornell, where two professors spoke against Kennedy and American imperialism, counter-demonstrators pelted them with mud and eggs. All the same, it became clear to Tom Hayden, Todd Gitlin, and other activists on the aborning student Left that "when push came to shove, the powers in Washington—and in Moscow—couldn't care less what a darling bunch of articulate college students thought. The great powers could drag the world to the brink of annihilation whenever they damned well pleased." Hayden expressed the shock of SDS at how close the Washington "war party" had come to provoking nuclear disaster. Only a thread of hope remained that Kennedy might move in a more progressive direction. The time had come, Hayden concluded, to transform the system.

6

The Second Civil War

Dorothy Dawson grew up in a religious southern community, albeit a segregated one. Her quest for an active faith aroused a longing for a higher purpose for herself and American society. At the University of Texas she moved into the Christian Faith and Life Community. There she met Sandra "Casey" Cason, who would marry Tom Hayden several years later. The Christian Faith and Life Community attracted both women not only because it had more intellectual vitality than any other place at UT, but also because it was the one place on campus where black students could live. Integrated living awakened in Dawson a passion for racial justice. "It was pretty insulting to go where other students that we lived with couldn't go," she recalled.

Work in the civil rights movement provided Dawson with some exceptional female role models. She formed a tight circle with Casey Cason and other white activists who rejected the traditional role of southern womanhood. Through Constance Curry, the head of the National Student Association Southern Race Relations Project, they became aware of the broader movement for racial justice in the South and came to love and admire black women like Ella Baker and Fannie Lou Hamer who had dedicated their lives to the civil rights cause. Curry hired Dawson to work on a voter registration project in Raleigh, North Carolina. Since the office was integrated by gender as well as race, women compromised half of the project staff.

The civil rights movement radicalized Dorothy Dawson. She had come to believe that the battle against institutionalized racism was essential to "pulling down all the fascist notions and mythologies and institutions in the South." Dawson's radicalism took on a dimension, however, missing from the SDS analysis of the system of oppression in America. She came to believe that within that system the church, "as guardian of public morality, mostly women's morality," served as a means to shape women as "anti-intellectual, irrational about politics and economic questions." So the burden on women in the civil rights struggle was that much greater. Southerners condemned integration for both blacks and women. Dawson had to jettison the racial and gender stereotypes she had inherited as a southern woman. In that process, she and others like her would place feminism on the reform agenda.

Anne Moody came from the same South as Dorothy Dawson but from a different world. She grew up in the backwoods of Mississippi that Dawson, Hayden, and the SNCC volunteers hoped to drag into the twentieth century. Most black children were born at home with the help of a midwife or neighbors. Plumbing, telephones, and appliances, where they existed at all, existed almost exclusively for the better class of white folks. Moody once recalled the time she had spent with a lower-middle-class white family. They had the first indoor plumbing she had ever seen: "I used to go to the bathroom and sit on the stool even if I didn't have to use it. I would just sit there and look at that big beautiful white tub, the pink curtain that hung over it, the pink washing powder in the big beautiful glass container, the sink with the pink soap in the soap tray. It all looked so good to me." As a child, Moody saw nothing of the world beyond rural Mississippi. For her, like Dawson, the church was the center of social life. She recalled one Sunday when her mama "pointed out about fifty people who she said were our 'cousins' or something. It seemed like just about everybody out there was kin to us one way or another." Evidence of the willful streak that would bring Moody to the civil rights movement came when she resisted her mother's pressure to join the rural family church. Where others felt the presence of the Lord at baptism, she remembered only the stink of wet mud and feeling "shitty all over."

Circumstances began to separate Moody from her insular Mississippi world. The problem of racial inequality first struck her as a young high school student. Walking home from school one day in 1954, she heard several boys talking about the murder of Emmett Till, a fourteen-year-old black Chicago boy who had whistled at a white woman while visiting family in Mississippi. His temerity had earned him the death penalty from the self-appointed defenders of the South's racial code. News of his death reached a national audience as tens of thousands of people in Chicago passed by his casket. What they saw was a body beaten so badly that his face was unrecognizable. Until that moment, Moody knew nothing about Till and did not fully appreciate the power of the racial terrorism that had led to his death. Over time, the lessons sank in. Gossip about interracial sex in Centreville would often give way to violence.

Then one day, a shotgun blast shattered the ties binding Moody to the community. Unknown assailants shot Samuel O'Quinn in the back from close range. Moody learned that the murderers were black men paid by local whites to commit the crime. No one was ever arrested. What had O'Quinn done to make himself a target? Rumors had spread that on a trip up North he had been infected with the civil rights bug. He might even have joined the NAACP. After his return, he had spoken about race issues to a few local blacks he thought were trustworthy. That confidence had proven misplaced, since several reported his activities to the local white authorities. The shock of that betrayal so disturbed Moody that she became "a real loner," avoiding both her schoolmates and her former white employer.

Summer jobs in Baton Rouge and New Orleans opened her eyes to an urban lifestyle. College provided her with the escape she sought. Following two disappointing years at a provincial junior college, more a finishing school than a place to learn, Moody looked at four-year colleges. At first she thought about Louisiana State in Baton Rouge. But LSU had only recently integrated, and Moody feared the competition and derision of white students. Instead she chose Tougaloo, an all-black college. Even that decision confronted her with subtle racial prejudices, for as one friend warned, "You're too black. You gotta be high yellow with a rich-ass daddy." In 1961, Moody went anyway.

At Tougaloo, her civil rights impulses escalated from passive to active. Despite fears of violence against herself or her family, she joined the local NAACP chapter. During her first summer at Tougaloo, Moody met Joan Trumpauer, a white college student who had come to Mississippi to work for SNCC. Their friendship, the first interracial friendship Moody had ever formed, provided a channel into civil rights protest. The two endured the abuse of angry white students—ketchup in their hair, cigarette burns, taunting, and beating—during a sit-in to integrate the local Woolworth's lunch counter. Undaunted, Moody committed herself to the cause of voter registration. For the next year, she lived under a cloud of fear and frustration. Racial terrorism left most Mississippi blacks too intimidated to risk their lives to achieve a taste of freedom they had never known. Rumors of her political activism reached her hometown. The family warned that civil rights involvement had put their lives in danger. An uncle died when he was shot-gunned by unknown white assailants. Moody realized that she could never go home again.

All the same, her experience did not radicalize her in the ways that it had Casey Cason, Dorothy Dawson, and Tom Hayden. White college students who came to Mississippi in 1964 to register voters could leave the South. Moody remained a Mississippian. For all the distance she had traveled from her rural roots, she lacked the broader cultural exposure Northerners took so much for granted. So when she encountered male chauvinism, she did not become disenchanted as Cason and Dawson did. On her first organizing trip she had to share a house with her male coworkers. When she walked into the kitchen on her first morning, a young man announced, "All right girls, take over. Us boys have been cooking all week." She and the other women prepared the meals without complaint, for that was the way they had been raised. Moody worried more about the shortage of food than who had to prepare it.

Not that the privileges and restrictions of gender escaped her notice. She was fully aware of the special burdens women in the movement faced. When things went badly for her friend George, she noted, "he could go out and drink beer every night or so, and he always had lots of girls. His life was pretty normal in many ways." Not so for the women: "We weren't allowed to go anywhere, and there wasn't anything we could do to relax. People were always overprotecting us." That view drove Moody more to resignation than to feminism. "I had gotten so tired of seeing people suffering, naked and hungry." The recurring violence, "the Taplin burning, the Birmingham church bombing, Medgar Evers' murder, the blood gushing out of [her friend] McKinley's head, and all the other murders" took a deadening personal toll. When civil rights workers sang "We Shall Overcome," Moody could only wonder if it could ever be so. At least on one point, she shared the growing disenchantment of the northern radicals nurtured on civil rights. All, whether black or white, had come to sense that whatever was needed to quiet violence in the America of the 1960s, "'the Vote' was not the way to end it."

Civil Rights at the Grass Roots

Through the civil rights movement, Dawson, Moody, and tens of thousands of other young Americans encountered the deeply entrenched forces that kept the United States divided along racial lines. Television showed the nation some of the events they experienced firsthand. Viewers saw images of unruly white mobs, vicious dogs, and police with billy clubs and high-pressure fire hoses attacking nonviolent demonstrators who had crossed some arbitrary line. Stirred by such sickening sights, more Northerners, especially idealistic college students, took up the civil rights cause. That meant that even though they often tried, national politicians could not ignore the racial revolution sweeping out of the South. The burden proved especially heavy for the Democratic Party and John Kennedy. If they failed to address the civil rights agenda, they would alienate liberals in the party. Yet almost any racial accommodation might drive out Southerners, who as Dixiecrats of 1948 had bolted from the party once before on the race issue. Federal activism on civil rights also provoked conservatives to attack his administration on either ideological or racist grounds. Either too strong or too weak a stance on civil rights threatened to cost Kennedy the White House in 1964 and to return the Democrats to the status of minority party. No wonder that its leadership waffled on race issues during the early sixties.

The divided counsels in the White House reflected the deep divisions the civil rights movement exposed. Race has always been the major fault line in American society. But the question here is not just how the nation dealt with its race problem in the 1960s. Rather, we must ask how the civil rights movement contributed to the upheavals of the era. As important as were the march on Washington in 1963, the Civil Rights Act of 1964, and the Voting Rights Act of 1965, they alone do not explain the racial revolution and the consequences it had for the nation in the 1960s.

To understand the upheaval, we must look at the grass roots. Pressure from local organizations, church congregations, and neighborhood groups in southern towns and cities rather than national leadership created the civil rights movement. In some ways, this process paralleled the rock and roll phenomenon in popular culture. It, too, had roots among southern blacks, had links to southern churches, and appealed most to alienated young Americans while provoking puzzlement or hostility among their elders. The courage of those who sat-in, marched, or risked their lives registering voters in the Mississippi countryside excited the admiration of liberals in general and, in particular, students such as Dorothy Dawson and Tom Hayden. As Todd Gitlin, a leader in SDS, recalled, "northern supporters were swept into SNCC's force field. SNCC moved us, seized our imaginations." And, he might have added, drew many of them to the South.

SNCC was just one of several organizations pressing for desegregation and equal rights. The leadership in those organizations, even established ones like the NAACP or Martin Luther King's SCLC, came from outside the traditional centers of power. Dorothy Dawson and Anne Moody, while exceptional in their energy, courage, and leadership, were more representative of those who created the movement. Neither had any real contact with formal politics before they became involved. Most of the civil rights activists shared their apolitical background. In that regard, Hayden was something of the exception.

The events that triggered the civil rights movement may have been modest at first, but they tapped into a deep reservoir of discontent. The 1960 sit-in at Woolworth's in Greensboro, North Carolina, loosened a storm of demonstrations across the South and the border states as well as Nevada, Illinois, and Ohio. In 1960, some 70,000 people participated in various protests and acts of civil disobedience. Demonstrations targeted public transportation—buses, trains, and planes—and public facilities such as parks and swimming pools as well as churches, restaurants, and stores. The initial results of the sit-in movement were hard to measure. Certainly, most of the nation took notice. At least in public, President Eisenhower expressed his sympathy for those who sought to "enjoy rights" granted by the Constitution. And as we have seen, both political parties had civil rights planks in their platforms in 1960, and both candidates, Richard Nixon and John Kennedy, saw the possibility of using the issue to advantage.

Ministers and students were among those most attracted to and supportive of the movement. Dorothy Dawson in some ways exemplifies those whose quest for spiritual renewal brought them to the civil rights cause. It spoke to their need to bear witness, or in Ghandian terms, to "put your body on the line." Ministers saw the question of equal rights in Christian terms. The eminent evangelist Billy Graham called it "the most burning issue of modern times." Graham's endorsement, however, was more pragmatic than principled. In that way he demonstrated how little the movement had as yet influenced the thinking of Middle America. For Graham, racism threatened to erode the nation's strength in its struggle with Communism. When white racists humiliated the Christian leaders of Africa who visited the United States, he warned, they alienated the very people whose hearts and minds he viewed as essential to victory in the cold war.

Such a practical approach was also typical of moderate Southerners, who sought compromise on the divisive issues protestors raised. These moderates were drawn heavily from the business communities. Civil rights boycotts cut deeply into the profits of downtown merchants. Communities seeking to attract new businesses from the North did not want the stigma of racial violence driving potential newcomers away. Compromise generally meant desegregation of a few facilities and a promise to open more doors in the near future. In Nashville, Greensboro, and other cities, mostly in border states rather than the Deep South, business leaders supported the creation of community groups to plan phased desegregation. Woolworth's even announced that it would serve blacks at its Greensboro store.

These token concessions did not resolve deeper issues of economic, social, or political inequality. Nor had the many demonstrations much shaken the complacency of Middle America. One newspaper service rated the sit-in story only the eighth most significant of the year, barely ahead of Hurricane Donna. In fact, the sit-ins had polarized race relations, especially in the deep southern states. The severity of that polarization would become increasingly apparent. While the protestors remained committed to the principle of nonviolence, segregationists readily used terrorism to protect white supremacy. In most places, they had the overt or covert support of police, who were frequently members of the Klan or other racist organizations. During many demonstrations, the police, took a leading role in beating demonstrators.

The cold war issue added to the polarization. Where Graham saw harmonious race relations as critical to building support among Third World leaders, white supremacists linked the demonstrators to the Communist menace. Since the days of abolition, southern politicians readily blamed any sign of black discontent on "outside agitators." In making that case in the 1960s, they had the support of the FBI and J. Edgar Hoover, one of the nation's leading racists. Hoover knew from FBI COMINFIL (an acronym for Communist infiltration) investigations from the 1950s that Communists had no significant role within civil rights groups. But rather than dismiss the assertion of Communist influence as baseless, he pressed his subordinates to intensify their efforts to make the connection. Since most FBI agents shared the director's prejudices on both racial and ideological grounds, they needed little prompting. Many people who witnessed violence against civil rights demonstrators could report that FBI agents stood by passively, taking notes and often retiring from the scene in the company of local police. So even when the White House showed sympathy to the civil rights movement, the Justice Department's police agency covertly warred against it.

Riding to Freedom

In May of 1961, the Freedom Rides introduced a more aggressive phase of civil rights action. Conceived by CORE director James Farmer, these integrated bus trips into the Deep South were meant to provoke confrontations. In that way, they would dramatize the failure of desegregation in the wake of the Supreme Court's 1954 *Brown* decision. On a deeper level, Farmer expected to create a headache for federal officials, who would have to react to violence against the riders. "We felt we could count on the racists of the South to create a crisis," Farmer admitted, "so that the federal government would be compelled to enforce the law." Traditional civil rights leaders in organizations like the NAACP preferred a more gradual and legalistic approach. Others, like Mississippi NAACP leader Medgar Evers, feared that Farmer's direct action strategy would undermine current initiatives. All the same, national NAACP chairman Roy Wilkins had grown disenchanted with the caution in his organization and the Kennedy administration's tepid approach to civil rights. He saw Farmer's tactic as a way to put the feet of Kennedy's timid New Frontiersmen to the fire.

More even than Martin Luther King, Jr., James Farmer was a disciple of Ghandi's nonviolent direct action. In 1947, he had initiated a "Journey of Reconciliation" across the border states that anticipated his plan for the Freedom Rides. After a stint with the NAACP, Farmer had returned to CORE in 1961 with the intention of revitalizing that organization. A large, charismatic figure with the voice of Darth

Vadar, Farmer believed nonviolent confrontation was a way to energize the civil rights cause. He followed the Ghandian program "of advising your adversaries or people in power of just what you were going to do, when you were going to do it, and how you were going to do it, so that everything would be open and above board." Before initiating the Freedom Rides, CORE sent letters to President Kennedy, his brother the attorney general, J. Edgar Hoover, the chairman of the Interstate Commerce Commission, and the presidents of Greyhound and Trailways bus companies, all of which went unanswered.

Farmer went ahead anyway. He recruited thirteen people—seven blacks and six whites—all committed to integration and nonviolence. The plan was to have the whites in the back of the bus and blacks up front. At each stop, blacks would enter the "whites only" sections and attempt to use the restrooms. Then it was up to local whites to determine what would happen next. The buses carrying the Freedom Riders left Washington, D.C., on May 4, 1961, scheduled to reach New Orleans by the 17th. Few demonstrators before or since had so self-consciously "put their bodies on the line." So sure were they of a hostile reception along the way that they "prepared for the possibility of death."

In Virginia and the Carolinas, the Riders faced sporadic hostility. In Rock Hill, South Carolina, several local hoods blocked John Lewis as he tried to enter the "white only" bathroom. The idealistic Lewis reminded them that he had a constitutional right to use the facility. Such niceties of principle were lost on these paragons of social progress. They punched Lewis, clubbed him, and knocked him to the ground. But far worse threats faced the Riders as they entered Anniston, Alabama. There a crowd of thirty to fifty men carrying baseball bats and metal bars awaited

Violent crowds encouraged by local police authorities attacked Freedom Riders at almost every stop. Anniston, Alabama, was the most frightening moment. (Source: Associated Press)

their arrival. No police were anywhere to be seen as the first bus pulled into the terminal. The mob slashed its tires, hurled stones, and tried to board. A white passenger held them off with a pistol. He turned out to be an Alabama state trooper sent in plainclothes by Governor John Patterson. Patterson hoped to limit violence without besmirching his segregationist credentials. An uneasy standoff ensued until someone shoved a bundle of rags through a broken bus window. It was an incendiary device, which quickly filled the bus with deadly smoke and flames. As the passengers fled, the mob set upon them. Suddenly a gunshot cooled the mayhem. The trooper warned the mob to cease, giving the riders a chance to seek safety.

The second bus was similarly assaulted when it arrived that afternoon. Some of the Riders were so severely beaten that an FBI agent standing aloof at the scene reported that he "couldn't see their faces through the blood." Alabama police commissioner Eugene "Bull" Connor told reporters with a hint of a smirk that since it was Mothers' Day, none of his officers had been available to protect the buses. In fact, FBI director Hoover had known from an informant what the mob intended to do. Connor had even promised the mob fifteen minutes to beat the Riders as badly as they could. Yet Hoover had not even warned Attorney General Robert Kennedy. In response to the violence, the White House sent the attorney general's aid, John Seigenthaler, to Alabama to ensure the safety of the Riders. So badly beaten was this first group that CORE halted its campaign. The initiative then passed to SNCC, which sent new volunteers to Birmingham.

President Kennedy wanted the rides stopped. He feared a domestic crisis would complicate his position during his upcoming meeting with Premier Nikita Khrushchev of the Soviet Union. The youthful Kennedy was determined to prove to Khrushchev that he was a serious adversary. Civil rights agitation at home might weaken his image as an effective leader. "Tell them to call it off," he told his civil rights assistant Harris Wofford. "Stop them!" The SNCC volunteers refused to quit. Beaten by police in Birmingham and driven to the Tennessee border, they returned to resume the journey. Their determination made the situation all the more difficult for the Kennedys. They had done little to protect the Riders and were determined not to offend local sensibilities by sending federal troops as Eisenhower had to do in Little Rock. That restraint did little to appease segregationists, who saw the Kennedys as sympathetic to the protestors. Seigenthaler did manage to extract a promise from Governor Patterson that the state of Alabama would protect the Riders. When pressed to say so publicly, Patterson promised protection for all travelers in his state, but then added, "We don't tolerate rabble rousers and outside agitators."

With that qualified assurance, the new Freedom Riders left on the next leg of their trip, from Birmingham to Montgomery. At Montgomery, all state police presence disappeared. One Freedom Rider remembered "white people everywhere" with clubs and bricks, crying, "Niggers. Kill the Niggers." Seigenthaler, following in his own car, saw a mob of whites beating the Riders as they tried to leave the bus. When he intervened, someone knocked him out with a pipe. Now that a federal official had been assaulted, the Kennedys were forced to act. The *Atlanta Constitution* reflected the shock of many moderates, "If the police, representing the people, refuse to intervene when a man—any man—is being beaten to the pavement of any American city, then this is not a noble land at all. This is a jungle." The president sent plainclothes federal marshals to Montgomery to protect the Riders, including those in the hospital. From his hospital bed, a badly beaten Jim Zwerg, a white pacifist from Wisconsin, told a television audience, "We will take hitting. We'll take beatings. We will accept death. But we are going to keep coming until we can ride anywhere in the South to anyplace else in the South, as Americans, without anyone making any comment." Just as determined as the Freedom Riders were to go on, the segregationists were prepared to stop them.

The following night, Martin Luther King, Jr., addressed a Montgomery church rally in support of the Freedom Riders. Outside a mob gathered. One group torched a car; tear gas drifted into the church; Molotov cocktails burned on the lawn. It was not clear the marshals could protect the people inside. An anxious King called Robert Kennedy in Washington. Is there any law and order in America? King asked. Arguing that the administration had done the best it could under the circumstances, Kennedy snapped at King that "if it hadn't been for the United States marshals, you'd be dead as Kelsey's nuts right now." President Kennedy, in fact, had decided to bring in federal troops, but before he took that politically charged step, Governor Patterson declared martial law and sent the Alabama National Guard.

An uneasy stalemate set in. Patterson blamed the Kennedys for the violence. The Kennedys, though disgusted with Patterson's duplicity, urged the Freedom Riders to let matters cool down, ostensibly for the Riders' safety, but in reality because they still had the Khrushchev summit meeting foremost in their minds. To them, managing the cold war took precedence over domestic injustice. The Ride leaders in Montgomery would not be deterred. James Farmer replied that his people had "been cooling off for 350 years." On one matter the Freedom Riders were uncertain as they prepared to leave the shoals of Alabama for the reefs of Mississippi. Would King and Farmer share the risks with them? Farmer at first demurred. He had been away from his office too long, he explained. But when a CORE worker appealed, "Jim, please," he changed his mind. How could he face his workers if they were hurt and he had deserted them?

For King, the matter was more complicated. Since the trip to Mississippi would violate his current probation, he had decided not to go. Several disappointed SNCC riders replied that they too were on probation and were going anyway. King's failure to get on the bus opened a subtle crack between moderate and radical elements of the nonviolent movement. That schism would grow wider over the next several years. Had King simply admitted that he was afraid, "I would have respected him more," one SNCC member complained. That was a harsh and largely unfair judgment of a person who had for five years faced jail and the probability of murder. At the same time, it suggested that the younger elements of the civil rights movement were growing impatient with moderation and nonviolence.

Few who boarded the bus in Montgomery on May 24 had the luxury of contemplating political differences. An uncertain reception awaited them in Mississippi. Contingents of state police and National Guard forces lined the road all the way through Alabama to the border. The Riders could not know that in private the Kennedys had sold out their crusade. Determined to avoid both the use of federal force and televised violence, they turned to Senator James Eastland of Mississippi. Segregation was the cornerstone of a system that had made Eastland rich and powerful. On his large plantations in the Mississippi delta he kept hundreds of black families in virtual peonage. Seniority and political skill made him one of the barons of the U.S. Senate. From his position as head of the Judiciary Committee, he would force the Kennedys to appoint several arch-segregationists to the federal courts.

As a political realist, Eastland knew the time had come to cut a deal. He guaranteed that the Freedom Riders would be safe in Mississippi. In return, he extracted from the Kennedys a pledge that the federal government would not interfere if Mississippi arrested the Riders for "inflaming public opinion." It was a savvy political strategy. As the Riders got off the buses in Jackson, police escorted them through the terminal into police vans waiting to cart them off to jail. As one historian has commented, "Harassment of freedom riders now shifted from attacks in the sunlight and the glare of news cameras to abuse within the confines of Jackson's prisons." A judge sentenced them to sixty days, some at Parchman, a notorious maximum-security prison. But as one load went off to jail, another arrived. Eventually some 300 Freedom Riders found themselves in Mississippi prisons.

Many of those who went to jail had an experience at once degrading and politically liberating. Conditions were abominable, with a dozen or more people packed into cells meant for two. When the prisoners sang freedom songs, guards beat them or had hardened inmates do the beating for them. At night, prison officials opened windows to let in the cold, and closed them in the day to raise temperatures to over 100 degrees. Some prisoners were hung with wrist chains from the walls as if they were in a medieval dungeon. Food was disgusting and scarce. Under this regimen, James Farmer lost thirty pounds. As bad as it was, jail had its benefits. Middle-class protestors lost some of the fear of being arrested and jailed. With time to kill, Riders from diverse backgrounds and points of view had an opportunity to confront their conflicting beliefs. The biggest gap existed between political radicals like Stokely Charmichael of SNCC and religious activists like James Bevel and John Lewis from Nashville. By the time both groups left prison, they had learned at least to respect each other's views. Still, the gap would never close, nor would the movement ever have a truly unified front.

Though many fewer people participated directly in the Freedom Rides than in the sit-ins the year before, they impacted the civil rights movement and the nation more forcefully. For one thing, the protest achieved its stated goal. Across the South, the offensive "whites only" signs came down in transportation terminals. By late 1962, interstate facilities became technically integrated. Given the depths of white resistance, that was no small accomplishment. Success deepened the movement's faith in direct action. "We . . . created a crisis situation," James Farmer observed. "It was worldwide news and headlines and everybody was watching it—people all over the world. The Attorney general had to act; and he did." The Freedom Rides suggested that a small number of people with conviction and courage could have a disprorpotionately large impact. Further, no matter how limited their civil rights agenda, the Kennedys had proven themselves highly sensitive to criticisms from the racial battlefront. Whether moderates in King's SCLC and Wilkin's NAACP or radicals in CORE and SNCC, civil rights leaders sensed that the administration could not back away from the struggle they intended to press. Many SNCC members had put their lives on the line. Having survived, they adopted an even more militant moral posture that would brook none of the wheeling and dealing the Kennedys had employed to save the situation in Jackson, Mississippi. That created the likelihood of more extreme polarization both in- and outside the movement.

On to Mississippi

The Kennedys realized that the civil rights movement was becoming more militant, something like a stallion they tried to lasso but could not break. More demonstrations could only lead to more violence, in which federal intervention would further alienate the Democratic Party's southern wing and lessen the president's chances for reelection. So as the Freedom Riders left jail, Robert Kennedy began an effort to redirect SNCC and SCLC to voter registration. Moderate civil rights leaders knew his point was valid; even a small increase in black voting could have a major impact on southern elections. Through the ballot, blacks might weaken Jim Crow without the same fear of violence. More militant elements, especially in SNCC, correctly sensed that Kennedy was trying to deflect them from a more confrontational course. At the same time, they too saw voter registration as a legitimate goal and a possible way to turn their small organization into a mass movement.

The turn to voter registration occurred in 1962 when Robert Moses left SCLC to join SNCC. Moses had already begun his own voter project in McComb, Mississippi. Nowhere in America was segregation more deeply embedded and racial violence more endemic. And no one in the civil rights movement would have the same quiet influence on his peers as Robert Moses. Moses was almost the antithesis of Martin Luther King. Where SNCC members somewhat irreverently called King "d'Lawd," Anne Moody had a common reaction to Moses, whom she came to think of "as Jesus Christ in the flesh." Despite his diffident manner, he had huge reservoirs of moral and physical courage. Few volunteers were so often exposed to the murderous intent of Mississippi white supremacists. Moses was often threatened and shot at. Nonetheless, he attracted a growing number of students to the registration drive.

Still, as the Kennedys anticipated, voter registration lacked the dramatic appeal of the sit-ins and Freedom Rides. It provoked few confrontations that attracted national media attention. And it was a slow process. As white supremacists practiced in the arts of terrorism understood, murder of several activists stalled the project for several years. As of 1964, the SNCC had successfully registered only a few thousand out of Mississippi's almost 400,000 African Americans. All the same, this phase of the movement would have a subtle and enduring effect on the political consciousness of both black Mississippians and the college students who came to liberate them. The experience stirred the political consciousness of people who were becoming soldiers in the uncivil wars.

SNCC's shift to voter registration did not mean an end to direct action. Too many groups had taken up the battle on too many fronts to keep the revolution out of the news. In Mississippi, for example, the NAACP field secretary, Medgar Evers, had been looking for a way to integrate the University of Mississippi, whose law school had rejected him in the 1950s. Ol' Miss provided an ideal target. It was the core of the state's all-white, good old boy network. Evoking the spirit of Dixie, its mascot was "Colonel Reb." Academics took a back seat to football and fraternity life. Where some universities might boast of Rhodes scholars and Nobel Prize winners, Ol' Miss could proudly claim that in just four years it produced two Miss Americas, two Miss Mississippis, and one Miss Dixie. The only African Americans on campus were custodial help and servants.

Evers found in James Meredith an ideal candidate to challenge this bastion of white supremacy. Inspired by the rhetoric of Kennedy's inaugural address, Meredith had decided he wanted to transfer from all-black Jackson State to Ol' Miss. When he applied in 1962, Meredith was already twenty-eight, having served a hitch in the U.S. Air Force. The university rejected him. A federal court then ruled that such an able student could not be turned away solely on the basis of race. But in September when he tried to enroll, Governor Ross Barnett personally blocked the way to the admissions office. Barnett's inflammatory speeches put Meredith's life in jeopardy. The Justice Department stepped in to protect Meredith and assure his admissions. Some 500 federal officers came to the Oxford campus as Meredith moved into his dorm room. That day, September 30, a student mob, reinforced by off-campus segregationists, gathered to taunt Meredith, denigrate blacks, and condemn Kennedy.

With Barnett doing all he could to stir opposition, President Kennedy appealed to the whites for order. Instead, the mob grew in numbers and vitriol. Tear gas fired by the marshals had little affect. By nightfall, a riot had erupted. Gunfire killed 2 bystanders and wounded 28 marshals. Kennedy had no choice but to order in 5,000 federal troops, who restored order without further violence. Dismayed faculty members then overruled the governor. Meredith registered the next morning and remained on campus, though under close guard. He even managed to graduate the following August.

Almost single-handedly, Meredith had attracted more attention to the civil rights cause than any other protest. That is not to demean the importance of other initiatives on behalf of racial equality. Rather, it explains much about American political culture in the early 1960s. The Meredith case had provided the civil rights cause with an ideal media event. Other civil rights strategies were often too complex for the media to present easily. Most Americans opposed direct-action civil disobedience, even though they sympathized with the ends demonstrators sought. A vaguely radical and foreign aura clung to the idea that people would provoke violence to achieve their political goals. Political action rather than civil disobedience was the American way.

Meredith, however, personified the injustice of segregation. Here was a deserving veteran who asked only for something he had earned. Millions of Americans knew firsthand how important it was to get into a good college. Mississippi's decision to bar him was an affront to the nation's egalitarian and opportunarian ideals. Television footage made it clear that Governor Barnett and white Mississippi hoodlums, not Meredith, had broken the law and resorted to mob violence. In that way, the Meredith case reduced the issues to a Manichean simplicity the media could easily portray: Meredith had behaved with calm dignity and great courage; Governor Barnett and his mobs had challenged the constitutional authority of the United States. When Robert Kennedy had asked Barnett, "Are you getting out of the Union?" Barnett replied, "It looks . . . like we don't belong to it."

The reaction to Meredith also forced Kennedy to recognize how obstructionist and uncompromising the segregation forces could be. Where Patterson had resorted to deception, Barnett openly flouted federal authority and threatened public safety. Hence, moderate Southerners accepted Kennedy's use of federal troops, not as an affront to local southern authority, but as a necessary evil. As a result, the Meredith episode taught the Kennedys that they could afford, even benefit from, a stronger civil rights posture.

On to Birmingham

John Kennedy was not the only leader struggling to harness the forces of the racial revolution. During the early 1960s, Martin Luther King, Jr., had experienced a marked weakening of his leadership within the movement. In part, others like Farmer and Meredith had captured the spotlight. Secular organizations like the NAACP and SNCC often resented the preachers of SCLC, who seemed to prefer sermons to strategy. That division had been most evident in the aborted effort to push integration in Albany, a small city in southwest Georgia. A coalition of local African-American groups had formed an Albany movement to support SNCC and push the Freedom Riders' agenda. In November of 1961, nine SNCC volunteers had been arrested as outside agitators. More demonstrations and arrests followed.

In December 1961, King and SCLC decided to take command of the movement already underway. Certainly, as a former center for the slave trade, Albany offered symbolic promise. African Americans accounted for 40 percent of its population but 0 percent of the its police, fire department, or local officials. All public facilities were strictly off-limits to African Americans. King's arrival brought national attention to the local civil rights coalition's efforts to desegregate the city. SNCC's student volunteers welcomed King's ability to mobilize the masses, but they had made considerable progress on their own. When two King aids, Wyatt Walker and Ralph Abernathy, assumed total authority for directing strategy, they showed little regard for the views of local leaders and openly opposed SNCC as too confrontational.

In the end, SCLC suffered a major setback. Not only did Walker and Abernathy alienate most local civil rights activists, but also their strategy of nonviolent protests failed to produce significant concessions on desegregation. Despite mass arrests, including King himself, few incidents captured national attention. Local white authorities saved their viciousness for the privacy of the jails. The visible violence that did occur erupted when blacks threw rocks, bricks, and bottles at police in protest against the beating of a black woman. "Did you see them non-violent rocks?" the local police chief asked reporters. To the dismay of SNCC, King called for penance and a moratorium on demonstrations. Dismayed SNCC members tried to persuade the SCLC clergy that if nonviolence failed to win concessions, then, perhaps, more confrontational methods were necessary.

Though King would make numerous trips to Albany, the demonstrations never cracked the stubborn resistance of local segregationists. Having assumed they could overcome that resistance by filling the local jails, the activists conceded that "we ran out of people, before [the sheriff] ran out of jails." At best, the Albany coalition could claim that because of their protests, many local blacks were far less willing to abide the daily indignities they suffered under Jim Crow. One local activist learned from the movement "that if someone puts you down, you have to fight against it." King had little such comfort. He had expended considerable time, energy, and prestige without any appreciable gain.

The setback at Albany left King hungering to restore momentum to his crusade. Birmingham, Alabama, provided him an inviting target. The city had given the Freedom Riders one of their most violent welcomes. Among segregationists, local commissioner of public safety Eugene "Bull" Connor's neck glowed more scarlet than any. After a series of unsolved bombings in black neighborhoods, some people called the city "Bombingham." The NAACP chose not to organize there. When several local businesses voluntarily desegregated, Connor had them cited for building-code violations. Back up went the "colored only" signs. And rather than comply with a federal court order on integration, the city closed its parks and recreational facilities.

King timed the Birmingham protest with an eye on the Easter shopping season. Local merchants profited heavily from the holiday clothing purchases of the black community. Somewhat coincidentally, Birmingham voters had just ousted the old segregationist regime and with it, Bull Connor. In a special election, racial moderate Albert Boutwell had handily defeated Connor for the newly established post of mayor. That complicated the picture for King. Local business leaders appealed to the Kennedy administration to call him off. Given time, they hoped to fashion accommodations that would make the protest unnecessary. But King had staked too much on Birmingham to back off now. Across the nation, civil rights efforts had stumbled after initial successes. A rather tepid civil rights act Kennedy had submitted to Congress died in committee. And while Boutwell might be a moderate on race issues, he was a segregationist nonetheless. "Just a dignified Bull Connor" was how King described him. Connor himself refused to step down as commissioner of public safety until the courts validated the new government.

On "B-Day," April 3, 1963, SCLC mobilized for its confrontation at the citadel of segregation. About sixty-five pickets began marching to downtown stores and lunch counter sit-ins. An unexpectedly restrained Connor immediately had twenty arrested and thrown into jail. But Connor's fuse was as short as his neck. On Palm Sunday he sent police dogs into a downtown prayer march lead by A. D. King, Martin's younger brother. A few days later, Connor won a court injunction banning King and other civil rights leaders from organizing any further demonstrations. Failure to comply with the court could cost King imprisonment and stiff fines that SCLC could not afford, since bail money had run out. Yet at that point, only about one hundred fifty volunteers had gone to jail, and few more seemed willing to make the sacrifice. In Albany, compliance with a court injunction had crippled the movement. King had reached his Rubicon. Either he had to confront the Alabama authorities, or the civil rights movement would face a potentially crippling defeat. Facing the divided counsel of his supporters, King decided—"I don't know whether I can raise money to get people out of jail. I do know that I can go to jail with them." He asked his closest supporter, Ralph Abernathy, to join him. That would mean missing Easter, the most important day in the pulpit for southern ministers.

Miss it they would. Their Good Friday march had gone barely a half-mile before Connor's police arrested King, Abernathy, and about fifty fellow marchers. Photographers snapped away, and black spectators jeered as officers manhandled their eminent prisoners. At Birmingham jail, Connor ordered King separated from the other prisoners and kept in "the hole"—solitary confinement. With King silenced, the national press brought comfort to his enemies. The New York Times and Washington Post called the demonstrations ill-timed and suggested they had been inspired more by rivalry among civil rights factions than by the real needs of the movement. The Times pointedly contrasted the goodwill at the swearing-in ceremony for Mayor Boutwell with the rancorousness of the demonstrations. Many local black leaders joined the chorus of complaints against King. But none of these rebukes disturbed King as deeply as did a statement from a coalition of liberal clergy condemning civil disobedience. Joining the chorus of Boutwell apologists, they denied "extreme measures" were justified in Birmingham.

Isolation afforded King both the time and energy to reply. Over the next days, writing with unbridled moral fervor on the margins of newspapers and scraps of paper, King produced one of the most compelling testaments to the civil rights cause. His "Letter from a Birmingham Jail" secured his role as the most powerful voice of the movement. Its many ideas and arguments cut the moral ground from under the apostles of moderation, who, as King suggested, were "more devoted to 'order' than to justice" and who "set the timetable for another man's freedom." To those in the news media and the White House who found the Birmingham demonstrations ill-timed, King showed chilly disdain. In what is one of the letter's most often quoted lines, King remarked, "I have yet to engage in a direct action campaign that was well-timed in the view of those who have not suffered unduly from the disease of segregation." To those who admonished the Negroes to "Wait," King replied "this 'Wait' has almost always meant 'never.'"

What then followed was one of the longest (300 words) and most powerful sentences in American writing. In it, King shifted from searing examples of individual pain to the historical experiences of black Americans to the philosophical problems of identity and existential despair:

> But when you have seen vicious mobs lynch your mothers and fathers at will and drown your sisters and brothers at whim; when you have seen hate-filled policemen curse, kick, and even kill your black brothers and sisters; when you see the vast majority of your twenty million Negro brothers smothering in an airtight cage of poverty in the midst of an affluent society; when you suddenly find your tongue twisted and your speech stammering when you try as you seek to explain to your six year old daughter why she can't go to the public amusement park that has just been advertised on television, and see tears welling up in those eyes when she is told that Funtown is closed to colored children, and see ominous clouds of inferiority beginning to form in her little mental sky . . . when you have to concoct an answer for a five year old son who is asking, "Daddy, why do white people treat us so mean?"; when you take a cross-country drive and find it necessary to sleep night after night in the uncomfortable corners of your automobile because no motel will accept you; . . . when you are forever fighting a degenerating sense of "nobodiness"—then you will understand why we find it difficult to wait.

That was language that middle-class American families with young children could understand. Once exposed to King's compelling indictment, tens of thousands of Americans would find moderation increasingly indefensible.

It took more than King's eloquence, however, to turn momentum in favor of the protestors. Connor would have to play his part. Rev. James Bevel, a veteran of the sit-in movement, had recognized a weak point in the protest strategy. Adults marched reluctantly because they could not afford the economic consequences of time in jail and lost jobs. Children had no such vulnerability. And would not the sight of children being carted to jail shift public opinion outside Birmingham? Bevel asked. While King fought in court, Bevel and SCLC organizers recruited children to their cause. Connor dutifully performed, as Bevel had anticipated he would. During the first march on May 2, Birmingham police hauled 959 children off to jail. The next day almost a thousand more, ranging in age from six to sixteen, gathered at the Sixteenth Street Baptist Church. Connor decided to stop the marchers before they left the churchyard.

Black businessman A. G. Gaston witnessed the brutality. Talking on the phone to David Vann, a lawyer for the white business community, Gaston had explained that he had never supported King's decision to demonstrate against segregation. Gaston favored the less divisive strategy of private mediation. He suddenly interrupted the conversation. "But lawyer Vann," he cried. "They've turned the fire hoses on a little black girl. And they are rolling that girl right down the middle of the street." When other protestors sat down to resist the force of the hoses, firefighters resorted to tripod-mounted monitor guns, normally used to fight fires at long range. These devices had the power to knock bricks out of a wall from one hundred feet away.

Images of firemen and police attacking neatly dressed and orderly civil rights marchers shocked the nation's sense of complacency about race relations.   (Source: Associated Press)

People caught in the stream rolled down the street like tumbleweeds. Amidst the onslaught, other marchers managed to leave the churchyard. For them, the police had in store their K-9 units.

The images of these vicious and often unprovoked assaults forced Gaston, the Birmingham business community, and the nation to recognize the violent impulses harbored by the foes of integration. President Kennedy spoke for millions of Americans when he claimed the sight of dogs tearing at well-dressed and nonviolent bystanders sickened him. The president sent several top Justice Department officials to Alabama to serve as mediators. The black community of Birmingham, having been divided between those like Gaston who favored negotiations and those who supported demonstrations, now stood firmly behind King. Connor had done for King what he could not have done alone.

The stage was set for compromise. Ongoing protest hurt downtown sales and darkened Birmingham's reputation outside the South. Abetted by Kennedy aide Burke Marshall, moderates struck a deal with SCLC. King would call off the protests in exchange for desegregation of stores and jobs for African Americans. The agreement outraged extremists on both sides. Those in King's camp believed they had lost their leverage in exchange for token concessions and empty promises. Segregationist governor George Wallace, denying that any settlement existed, sent his brutal state troopers in to terrorize Birmingham's black neighborhoods. Arch-segregationists had a more traditional Birmingham response. One of their bombs leveled the home of A. D. King; another damaged a wing of the Gaston motel where

Martin Luther King was staying. Miraculously, neither bomb claimed any lives. As outraged blacks rioted, seven stores went up in flames. President Kennedy finally sent federal troops to nearby Fort McClellan. That tactic, plus a court decision that turned power over to Boutwell and ousted Connor, had a calming effect.

Greenwood, Mississippi

Birmingham marked a sharp reversal in King's fortunes. The combination of courage, conviction, and sheer eloquence established him as the recognized national leader of the civil rights movement. But before Birmingham, SNCC, not SCLC, and Mississippi, not Alabama, had been the focus of the Kennedy administration's efforts to manage civil rights protest. Kennedy actively discouraged the efforts of his own Civil Rights Commission to investigate the racial situation in Mississippi. If anything, Mississippi segregationists were more blatant in their use of intimidation, legal obstruction, police brutality, and terrorism. Greenwood, Mississippi, had become the target of SNCC's voter registration project. To discourage blacks from registering, state authorities in February 1963 cut off federal food aid to some 22,000 destitute sharecroppers around Greenwood and surrounding LeFlore County. Arson aimed at the local SNCC headquarters destroyed four nearby black businesses. When Sam Block, a local SNCC volunteer, described the fire as a bungled attempt to intimidate local blacks, Greenwood police arrested him for breach of the peace. Choosing jail rather than a fine, Block inspired blacks to register in increasing numbers. The local registrar turned most of them down.

As in Birmingham, events in Mississippi captured national media attention. On an isolated stretch of highway, seven miles outside of Greenwood, three white gunmen shot Jimmy Travis, the driver of a car carrying Bob Moses and Randolph Blackwell. Blackwell had come to Greenwood to investigate the future prospects of the voter projects in the delta area. The shooting galvanized both SNCC and local blacks. New volunteers arrived, and the national media picked Greenwood as a breaking story. That forced the Kennedy administration to send investigators. And folksinger Pete Seeger, once the target of McCarthyite Red-baiting, brought young Bob Dylan to the South to see the southern civil rights struggle firsthand. By then, Dylan had attracted a large and enthusiastic national audience of folk music aficionados. His version of the song "Blowin' in the Wind" became an anthem for supporters of liberal causes such as nuclear disarmament and civil rights. He chose Greenwood as the one place he would perform on his southern trip.

Local authorities had perpetuated apartheid by avoiding the glare of national publicity. But under this growing siege, they resorted ever more aggressively to the usual segregationist strategy—blame outside agitators, harass and intimidate local blacks, and commit random acts of violence. Night riders shotgunned a car carrying Sam Block and a friend. Greenwood mayor Charles Sampson suggested SNCC had done the shooting to arouse sympathy. Three weeks later, arsonists finally succeeded in torching SNCC headquarters. Two days later, assassins hiding in the dark of night murdered Dewey Greene, Sr., one of the black community's most popular figures and the father of the second black (after James Meredith) to apply to Ol' Miss. That death brought 150 marchers to city hall. Police were ready with an attack dog and such taunts as "Kennedy Is Your God."

How wrong they were. Neither Jack nor Robert Kennedy had an appetite for confrontation in Mississippi. Only the Greenwood dogs, the media coverage, and the convergence of celebrities caused them to overcome their hesitation. Greenwood police threw eight national civil rights figures in jail. The Civil Rights Commission warned the president that in the face of violence and blatant constitutional excesses in Greenwood, they could no longer remain silent. Comedian Dick Gregory lent his star aura to the cause. He told an enthusiastic crowd that they would march through Greenwood's dogs. "And if you get some elephants, we'll march through them!" After three days in which the media featured Gregory's taunting of local officials, the administration finally sought an injunction to free the SNCC leaders, to stop the harassing of those who sought to register, and to provide adequate police protection. Several days later, the eight were free; Greenwood had caved in, or so it seemed.

Freedom had come at a heavy price. The Justice Department agreed to drop its other demands in order to get the SNCC prisoners out of jail. With that, federal officials left matters largely in local hands. The celebrities returned to busy lives elsewhere. Local politicians adopted a law-abiding posture, so that few outside Greenwood and SNCC noticed that of the 1,500 prospective voters brought to the LeFlore registrar, he turned down all but fifty of them. The pen had proved mightier than the police dog. Perhaps a worse setback for SNCC came not from the evasions of Greenwood officials or the desertion of the Justice Department, but from within the civil rights movement itself. On his way to Atlanta from Greenwood on April 3, James Farmer had stopped off in Birmingham to add SNCC's support to what had been until then the faltering effort of the SCLC to stir up local support. Wyatt Walker immediately kicked him out. Birmingham would remain a SCLC operation, and that meant that while Greenwood faded into the background, Birmingham brought SCLC and King into the center of the civil rights spotlight. What might have seemed a triumph for the movement as a whole instead obscured a deep and widening breach.

On to Washington

SNCC and SCLC had forced the Kennedys to give civil rights a higher priority. To push that agenda further, they needed to find new ways to cooperate. One possibility could have been concerted action to help assure passage of the civil rights bill President Kennedy introduced in June of 1963. This was not the usual token measure designed to placate the civil rights movement without offending moderate Southerners; Kennedy's bill attacked the very heart of Jim Crow. It would outlaw segregation in all public interstate facilities, authorize the attorney general to initiate school desegregation cases, and deny funds to federal programs which involved discrimination. And as a blow against literacy tests as a barrier to voting, a key provision declared literate a person who had a sixth grade education.

The introduction of the civil rights bill coincided with plans for a major march on Washington. The original idea came from movement veteran A. Philip Randolph. Randolph had planned a march for Negro jobs and economic opportunities in the early years of World War II. Franklin Roosevelt had dissuaded him by issuing an executive order on discrimination in employment and adopting a Fair Employment Practices Commission. But in 1963, Randolph brought his idea back. Jobs for blacks were still hard to find. Other civil rights leaders persuaded him to make passage of Kennedy's bill an additional rationale for the march. The White House convened a gathering of civil rights leaders at which Kennedy declared his firm opposition. It would risk violence, harden segregationist opposition, and undermine his own political fortunes, he contended. Vice President Lyndon Johnson argued forcefully that the way to move Congress was not through demonstrations, but the traditional practices of pressing the flesh and twisting arms in private. King and the others would not back down. Their restive organizations demanded the kind of gesture the march would provide. So in a compromise, civil rights leaders agreed that the theme of the march would be broadened to include support for the Kennedy bill. Few of them had any great illusions about the Kennedys' commitment to the civil rights cause, but they understood that the movement could not succeed without federal cooperation.

The one significant holdout was John Lewis of SNCC. Too many times Lewis had seen workers harassed, beaten, and murdered while their demands for federal protection went largely unheeded. In January 1963, Robert Moses and his staff filed suit against Robert Kennedy and J. Edgar Hoover. They charged that these officials had failed to protect SNCC workers from those in Mississippi who repeatedly violated their constitutional rights. Though the suit failed, as Moses knew it would, it reflected the profound impatience SNCC had with federal civil rights policies and the Kennedys' efforts to work with southern moderates.

Out of growing frustration, SNCC grew cynical and more militant. In Cambridge, Maryland, in June 1963, a SNCC demonstration turned into a violent clash with local police. The governor sent some 400 National Guardsmen to restore order. Such eruptions had become increasingly common. In an estimated 930 protests in eleven southern states, some 20,000 demonstrators were arrested. Such direct action strategies contrasted sharply in intent, if not so clearly in consequence, from King's nonviolent approach. Liberals who supported the movement saw nonviolence as an alternative to SNCC's growing militancy. King, too, had experienced his share of disillusionment, but he was more inclined to work through, rather than against, the system. For those reasons and for the simple differences of age and personal temperament, the movement began to diverge ever more sharply at the moment of its most apparent triumph.

SNCC leaders saw the march on Washington not as an opportunity to support the Kennedy civil rights bill, but as a chance to criticize the Justice Department. On the eve of the march, southern authorities began a number of legal actions designed to stifle desegregation and voting rights efforts. The Justice Department had actually joined one of the suits against SNCC demonstrators. Lewis planned to address these injustices at the Washington march. In the draft of a speech, he asked rhetorically, "which side is the federal government on?" Reflecting SNCC's frustration, he warned, "We will not wait for the President, the Justice Department, nor Congress, but will take matters into our own hands and create a source of power outside of any national structure that could and would assure us victory." Civil rights leaders were most troubled that Lewis wanted to call for a "revolution." Even the militant Randolph found the idea excessive. "John, for the sake of unity, we've come this far," he argued. "For the sake of unity, change it."

And change it Lewis did, if ever so reluctantly, and if only to take out the most offending passages. He and his SNCC comrades remained deeply ambivalent about the march. Yet all this behind-the-scenes maneuvering was invisible to most of the nation. Other than the victory parades after World War II, few Americans ever experienced the inspiration of the march that took place on August 28, 1963. Organizers had worried that only a few thousand might show up; they hoped for as many as 100,000. That day some 250,000 marchers, perhaps 60,000 of them white, joined in peaceful witness to the cause of civil rights. Until that moment, few Americans probably appreciated the force of the movement. For millions of Americans, especially among the young, this was a moment of awakening.

The voice that captured their attention belonged not to Lewis, though his fervor stirred the crowd, but to Martin Luther King, Jr. This was the first time most Americans had seen or heard King. Much that he said that day had been anticipated in his "Letter from a Birmingham Jail." He spoke of his people, "crippled by the manacles of segregation," of their poverty, and of "the horrors of police brutality." His message, however, was not about past wrongs, but about his dream of a new beginning, "where sons of formers slaves and the sons of former slave owners will be able to sit down together at the table of brotherhood, when even the state of Mississippi will be transformed into an oasis of freedom and justice." Rather than complain of past divisions, he called for a new unity. As he swept into his peroration, he shaped a great vision for the future: "And when this happens and we allow freedom to ring, when we let it ring from every village and hamlet, from every state and city, we will be able to speed up that day when all God's children, black men and white men, Jews and gentiles, Protestants and Catholics, will be able to join hands and sing together in the words of the old Negro spiritual: 'Free at last, Free at last. Thank God Almighty, we are free at last.'" In that moment, King offered the nation a vision in which the spirit of brotherly love healed the wounds of race and slavery.

The size of the demonstration for civil rights in Washington surprised even march organizers. Martin Luther King, Jr's eloquence stirred the crowd. (Source: Associated Press)

In many ways, August 28 marked an end, not a beginning. Most SNCC workers had by then lost all faith in the gospel of nonviolent reform King preached. Yes, the civil rights act would make its way through Congress, but under the guidance of Lyndon Johnson, not John Kennedy. And yes, voting rights would become a reality. But for the militants on either side of the race issue, the real battle had just begun. In New York City, an obscure Black Muslim, who called himself Malcolm X and called on blacks to arm in self-defense, dismissed the event as the "Farce on Washington." "Whoever heard of angry revolutionists swinging their barefeet together with their oppressor in lily-pad park pools, with gospels and guitars and 'I Have A Dream' speeches?" Malcolm asked with naked sarcasm.

Eighteen days after the march, arch-segregationists in Birmingham devised their special way to commemorate the spirit of racial harmony. Their target was the Sixteenth Street Baptist Church, which had served as the center for desegregation protests. On a peaceful Sunday, with the children attending Bible school classes, a powerful explosion ripped the church. Four young girls had left class to gossip in a downstairs bathroom. When the smoke and rubble cleared, they were dead. That same day, two white Eagle Scouts on their way home from a segregation rally shot and killed a thirteen-year-old black riding on the handlebar of a bike. During racial disturbances that erupted, police shot a black man in the back of the head as he tried to flee a melee with whites.

Dallas

Birmingham, more than Washington, presaged the future of racial politics. In place of orderly and neatly dressed civil rights demonstrators would stand angry SNCC workers, urban rioters, and menacing Black Panthers brandishing shotguns. One event, more than any other, marked the transition from moderation to extremism and from nonviolence to violence. That was the assassination of John F. Kennedy. Kennedy's death did not cause the ensuing turmoil so much as it eroded faith in traditional politics.

John Kennedy went to Dallas in November 1963, in part, to repair the political damage inflicted by civil rights. In the wake of the march on Washington, the South no longer stood so solidly for the Democratic Party. Many Southerners blamed Kennedy for what they saw as a conspiracy to undermine their way of life. All the same, Kennedy's reelection prospects seemed bright. He had overcome many of the early setbacks to his administration such as the Bay of Pigs. In both domestic and foreign policy, he had taken the reins of power more firmly. The civil rights issue, which cost him significantly in ethnic neighborhoods and the South, earned him the support of liberals and African Americans.

Kennedy's appeal was in many ways more personal than political. Young Americans, the types who supported civil rights and joined the Peace Corps, especially admired Kennedy. His rhetoric had stirred their dreams to have lives that mattered in new and important ways. Through him, the nation learned the definition of "charisma," that mysterious brew of physical vitality, manliness, and sex appeal. Kennedy was a celebrity for the television age. His young children, his beautiful and sophisticated wife, and his own photogenic image flowed from the TV screen into the nation's living rooms. Jackie exuded good taste, whether entertaining leading artists and musicians, speaking French, or hosting a television tour of the redecorated White House. She defined cosmopolitan for a nation rapidly becoming more educated and affluent. And Camelot had an innocent and wholesome side, too. Kennedy urged the nation to stay physically fit, while his aides played football on the White House lawn. Then there were images of Caroline and John-John playing under the president's desk. As one writer remembered, "We knew the Kennedys in the same way we knew the Nelsons, the Ricardos [I Love Lucy], and the Cleavers [Leave It to Beaver]."

In the fall of 1963, the world reverberated with the promise of Kennedy's New Frontiers. Most Americans ignored the hooded Klansmen, the John Birchers, and other extremists who lurked on the fringe of American life. Their paranoia seemed more amusing than frightening. That was far less true in the South and especially in Texas, where the John Birch Society flourished. Texas was also home to Lyndon Johnson and his pragmatic Democrats, around whom Kennedy hoped to sustain his party's southern majority. Theodore Sorensen, a chief Kennedy adviser, described the trip as a "journey of reconciliation to harmonize the warring factions of Texas Democrats, to dispel the myths of the right wing in one of its strongest citadels, and to broaden the base for his own reelection in 1964." After a warm welcome in San Antonio and meetings with Lyndon Johnson in Houston, Kennedy went on to Fort Worth and Dallas.

Dallas, despite its reputation as a right-wing citadel, gave the presidential motorcade an enthusiastic welcome. Cheering crowds lined the route. Almost every American old enough to remember November 22, 1963, can tell you where they were and what they were doing at the moment the Kennedy motorcade passed the Texas Schoolbook Depository. In Ithaca, New York, it was a dreary late fall Friday, shortly before Thanksgiving vacation. I had just finished washing the lunch dishes at a Cornell University fraternity where I worked. A member came in, the kind of annoying person who relished bringing bad news that bursts your bubble. That moment was nirvana for him. "The president has been shot," he told us. At first we thought it was a bad joke; then we turned on the radio. Shortly after one o'clock we learned the president was dead. Nothing in our generational experience prepared us for this. We had lived through Ike's operations and the shock of *Sputnik*. But Ike got better, and the space program had reasserted American technological supremacy. Nothing really bad, nothing that couldn't be fixed or made better, had ever happened to our America. As much as we might have worried about the bomb, Kennedy had taken some critical steps—the nuclear test–ban treaty, the hotline to the Kremlin, and his American University speech on peaceful coexistence—that had eased cold war tensions. We had even beaten the mighty Russians in hockey at the 1960s Olympics.

For us, Kennedy reaffirmed a sense of possibility and promise. And now he was dead. That afternoon we gathered in small, aimless groups on the campus quad. Knowing nothing at first about Lee Harvey Oswald, we assumed that right-wing, racist Texans had killed the president. Nobody said much; many people broke into periodic bouts of sobbing. We cried, I think, as much for ourselves as for Jackie, Caroline, and John-John or for Rose Kennedy, Bobby, and Ted. We knew that day that something in our futures had been killed by that assassin's bullet—that we would never again be so hopeful or confident about the future. And when Jack Ruby shot Oswald two days later, the act seemed part of the chaos that threatened to engulf our world. The idea that our futures rested in the hands of Lyndon Johnson deepened our sense of desperation. He was one of them, we assumed, tainted by the southern extremism that had killed Kennedy.

That reaction was far from universal. Apolitical and Republican students did not feel the same sense of loss. The assassination shocked them, but they did not grieve. Left-wing students like Tom Hayden assumed, with ample justice, that right wingers would blame the killing on the radicals. Oswald did have vague ties to Communists, Cuba, and leftist politics. For young Lawrence Wright, an apolitical student from Dallas, the event mixed shock and shame. The news had made his friends giddy with excitement, because something so extraordinary had happened. "All I knew," he remembered, "was that life could change, it had changed at last. . . . I was grateful for the loss of innocence." Later he would be shocked to discover how much the world came to hate Dallas—"no matter who had killed him, we had willed him dead." Judge Sarah Hughes, herself a prominent Texan who swore in Lyndon Johnson aboard Air Force One, called Dallas "a city of hate, the only city in which the President could have been shot."

The anger was understandable even if the accusation was unfair. Oswald had nothing to do with Dallas or the hatreds that seethed there. But Dallas had tolerated, even nurtured, a climate where extremism flourished. The city was a bit like television, built more on fantasy and dreams than on realities. In such a world, demons and conspiracies seemed to make some sense. And Dallas, again like television, suggested not so much where the nation had been, but where it was headed. As Wright pointed out, Lee Harvey Oswald was television's first real death. Before tragedy struck there, people turned on television for escape, not information or news. Only in 1963 had CBS picked Walter Cronkite for the network's new thirty-minute format. Until then, the news was limited to fifteen minutes of superficial sound bites in which John Cameron Swayze would spend no more than a minute or two "hopscotching the globe" to offer little capsule comments about world events.

For the days after the assassination, millions of Americans remained fixed to their television sets. Television took them to Dallas, it focused on Jack Ruby as he shot Oswald, and it persuaded us that what we wished to deny was really true—John Kennedy was dead; Lyndon Johnson was president. Together, the entire nation grieved. All three networks cancelled their regular weekend programming to cover events from Dallas and Washington. Through television, we shared the image of young John-John saluting, the funeral cortege with the riderless horse, and the flag-draped caisson. During the funeral service, I saw my older brother cry for the first time I could ever remember. Death conferred on Kennedy a mystique akin to that which surrounded Abraham Lincoln. Yet no more than Lincoln had Kennedy willingly embraced the racial politics that would be for many Americans their most enduring legacy. And only later would we learn about the dark side of Camelot, with the political wheeling and dealing, the womanizing, and the growing canker of Vietnam. For now, Kennedy's death marked a rite of passage into a world full of tumult and tragedy.

Part Two

THE SIXTIES

1964–68

7
1964: Welcome to the 1960s

Historians often look at certain years as pivotal. Certainly 1929, with the onset of the Great Depression, was a turning point in American history. Most historians treat 1968 as a similarly significant year, marked by war, assassinations, and political turmoil. Preoccupation with the events of 1968 has caused historians to underestimate the significance of 1964. In that year, the fifties ended and what most of us think of as the sixties began. Even though the nation remained unusually prosperous, the optimism of the *Happy Days* or *Populux* era had begun to erode in the face of Kennedy's assassination, the civil rights upheaval, and ongoing cold war tensions. Many of the issues that exposed the factionalism of the uncivil wars were by then apparent.

During 1964, the civil rights movement reached its apotheosis but also began to fracture as radical elements demanded more than the political system was prepared to give. Urban race riots shook the nation. The United States commitment in Vietnam escalated, as President Lyndon Johnson Americanized what had begun as a Vietnamese civil war. Not only had McCarthyism lost the power to intimidate, it had inspired a powerful leftist backlash. On some college campuses, a more radical political culture blossomed. Among adventurous and sophisticated young people, drug use began to spread. And as the first wave of baby boomers went off to colleges and universities, women were granted more social freedom, while the widespread availability of birth control pills eased inhibitions against premarital sex.

The Rock Revolution

The cultural ferment of the era was evident to anyone with a radio. Since the 1950s, rock had dominated the airwaves, but in the early 1960s it had ceased to define a separate teen world. By 1963, rock and roll had become so trivialized that Elvis Presley released what would be his last top ten hit for the next six years, a pop song called "Bossa Nova Baby." The white country boy who sounded black but could really sing had traded in his blue suede shoes for a Las Vegas tuxedo. Elvis was not alone in producing music for the mainstream. Such saccharin and silly tunes as Bobby Vinton's "Blue Velvet," the Singing Nun's "Dominique," Leslie Gore's "It's My Party," and Allan Sherman's "Hello Mudduh, Hello Fadduh! (A Letter from Camp)" topped the charts.

Only in pockets did popular music retain some of the vitality of earlier rock and roll. In Detroit, Berry Gordy had begun to mix rhythm and blues, gospel, and pop into a style that would become known as Motown. Out of the surfing subculture of Malibu, California, came the music of Dick Dale, Jan and Dean, and the Beach Boys.

The production values of the music were high, while the lyrics reflected the affluent and isolated world of young California suburbanites searching for endless summer. The civil rights movement, with its songs of resistance and change, also had a powerful influence on the devotees of folk music. As Robert Zimmerman made his way to Greenwich Village from rural Minnesota in 1961, he changed his name to Bob Dylan (in honor of poet Dylan Thomas) and began performing in small folk clubs. By 1963, he was in the process of becoming the poet laureate of the sixties.

Motown, the surf sound, and Bob Dylan would all influence 1960s culture, but in 1964, the phenomenon that exploded the conventions of popular music came from abroad. That January, Capitol Records released a recording by a group popular in England but largely unknown in the United States. Much to the label's astonishment, "I Want to Hold Your Hand" by the Beatles became an instant hit. Ed Sullivan, the host of a popular television variety show, had already previewed the Beatles' magic. While at the London airport, he had seen British teenyboppers stage a near riot welcoming the Beatles back from a trip to Stockholm. The hysteria reminded him of Elvis. And having played a key role in bringing Elvis to the mass market, he had signed the Beatles to his show. In February 1964, a frenzied crowd of young teenage girls greeted Paul, John, George, and Ringo as they arrived at New York's Kennedy Airport. The enthusiasm that followed the Beatles stunned the music world. By April 1964, they had five songs in the *Billboard* top forty.

The Beatles, as we now know, were far more than a passing pop fad. They impacted American music and popular culture in ways far more profound than had

After Ed Sullivan introduced the Beatles to a national television audience, their mod look set a new style in fashion, while their music transformed popular culture. (Source: Bettmann/CORBIS)

earlier teen idols like Elvis and Frank Sinatra. For one thing, unlike the vast majority of popular performers, they played their own instruments and wrote and arranged most of their own songs. Creative control made them seem more authentic to their audience. That same quality distinguished early blues musicians and contemporary folk artists like Bob Dylan. Further, the Beatles were in many ways more familiar with the varieties of American rhythm and blues than many American musicians. That allowed them to transcend the derivative sound suffocating American popular music in 1963. As rock historian Charlie Gillett said of the Beatles: "Musically the Beatles were exciting, inventive, and competent; lyrically they were brilliant, able to work in precisely the right kind of simple images and memorable phrases that distinguished rhythm and blues from other kinds of popular music."

The Beatles not only made way for a flood of British groups to succeed in the United States, they also helped open audiences to black performers, whose best music had until then largely been preempted by whites. After the Beatles, American popular music became far more integrated, in part because British groups exposed white fans to black styles. Whenever critics claimed the Beatles had invented a distinctly British version of rock and roll, the Fab Four (a popular nickname for Paul McCartney, John Lennon, George Harrison, and Ringo Starr) were quick to acknowledge their debt to such rock and roll veterans as Chuck Berry, the Miracles, or Bo Diddley. From hard rockers like Little Richard they picked up driving rhythms and the use of nonverbal vocal effects. From Ben E. King, the Shirelles, and some of the Motown groups they learned a gospel-influenced call-and-response style. In essence, they recycled black music back to an America that was finally prepared to hear it.

America embraced the Beatles almost as much for their style and personalities as for their music. They exuded a boyish enthusiasm, tempered by a hint of ironic detachment. "We know this is all about fame and fortune," they seemed to say, "but isn't it fun while it lasts?" For Americans grown disenchanted with conformity and convention, that was a refreshing notion. It also lacked the hard edge of another British export—movies with a socialist sensibility that exposed the seething resentments of working-class slums. Class was for the British almost as impenetrable a barrier to social mobility and opportunity as race was in the United States.

The Beatles never hid their working-class origins; rather, they seemed to transcend them. Their longish hair, mod clothes, and zaniness made them different without being threatening, modern without being weird. They were more about youth and good feelings than about race, sexuality, class, or politics. Their androgynous effect defined a new masculine style. It was youthful rather than macho, irreverent without being overtly rebellious. Male students who imitated the Beatles' mop-top look often faced hostility and even suspension from school.

Traditional men thought long hair was feminine; rock stars saw it as sexy. And in the 1960s, rock stars displaced movie stars as the public figures who most defined the male image. Mick Jagger of the Rolling Stones rejected the idea that "being masculine means looking clean, close-cropped, and ugly." Men, too, could be beautiful, even if they had to exchange their barbers for hairstylists in order to achieve the new look. African-American men and women found an alternative way to make long hair into a cultural statement. They gave up wavy processing or short cuts that mirrored Anglo hair and let their hair grow into bushy Afros. Many whites with naturally kinky or curly hair imitated the Afro look.

The Beatles also redefined the concept of love. Popular songs of the fifties and early sixties tended to treat love in romantic, neurotic, or morbid ways. These were the stories of teenage relationships, the good and bad feelings men and women held for each other, and the narcissistic celebration of self. To the Beatles, love had more to do with identity and spiritual well-being, almost an existential quality. Being loved by a woman made a man feel good about himself as a person: "With a love like that you know it can't be bad." Such a love brought to the world a higher sense of harmony and goodwill, a sense of brotherhood and communal feeling not unlike the ethos advocated by the integrationist faction of the civil rights movement. Eventually the Beatles, especially John Lennon, introduced explicit references to peace, though without any particular political or ideological edge. Not that the Beatles would ever have made any claim that their music or ideas had any significant intellectual content. They were too ironic and playful for such pretense. Like much of the British lower classes, they had an instinctive suspicion of highbrow culture. That put them very much in tune with American anti-intellectualism that was a salient characteristic of the 1960s.

Intellectuals in the United States responded to the Beatles phenomenon with a mixture of fascination and disdain. Arthur Schlesinger, Jr., a Pulitzer Prize–winning historian and Kennedy advisor, was at first dismissive, "knowing only the idiotic hairdo and [to him] melancholy wail." Schlesinger adopted a far more approving tone after he saw the Beatles in their smash movie hit of 1964, *A Hard Day's Night*. Its director, Richard Lester, had made just one forgettable rock film, *It's Trad Dad*, with twist star Chubby Checker. But Lester had a feeling for contemporary visual media. *Hard Day's Night* had the look of a documentary, shot in grainy black and white, as it followed the Beatles through a typical day in their new lives as celebrities. Would they make it through their endless encounters with the press, disapproving adults, and adoring fans in time to perform a scheduled concert? Since the plot scarcely mattered, Lester used the fast-cutting and episodic technique found in television commercials.

What he had to sell was not a story but a product—the Beatles. They came across as charmingly bemused by all the fuss they managed to stir up. The film also succeeded in giving the audience a sense of their individual personas. As John Lennon commented about the film's screenwriter, David Owen, "he stayed with us for two days and wrote the whole thing based on our characters then: me, witty; Ringo, dumb and cute; Paul, this; George, that." Audiences loved it. *Hard Day's Night* was one of the top box office hits of 1964. Teenagers went to theaters over and over to sing along and to eye their favorite Beatle. More cerebral critics liked it as well. Schlesinger applauded it as "smart and stylish film, exhilarating in its audacity and modernity."

With the success of *A Hard Day's Night*, the Beatles had wrought a small cultural miracle. They appealed simultaneously to the naive and sophisticated, to the unthinking and the cerebral, and to mainstream America and the cultural avant garde.

Their movies and songs anticipated many of the themes of the 1960s—the celebration of youth, the search for spiritual grace, the pricking of intellectual and cultural convention, and the removal of barriers to human fraternity and sorority. And in what became a defining moment for popular culture, the Beatles met Bob Dylan in August 1964. Dylan had by then established himself as something of a musical messiah. Rather than sing the traditional folk songs, he wrote his own music and lyrics in a folk manner. Like the Beatles, his personal style contributed heavily to his popularity. He too was irreverent and iconoclastic, in his case a mixture of bohemian, folky, and biker, inspired largely by the movie star James Dean. But while some of Dylan's songs had become major hits, he had not yet achieved the same level of popularity as the Beatles.

Dylan was, however, considerably more sophisticated. Despite his stories of his days as a runaway and a hobo, he grew up in a solidly middle-class family against which he had rebelled. In Greenwich Village in the early 1960s, folk music, not rock and roll, was the idiom of alienation. Folk musicians favored old blues, social protest songs, and traditional ballads. Dylan modeled his career after the legendary Woody Guthrie, who gave voice to the struggles of the Depression era. The Village, however, was not just about music. It was a haven for all manner of artists, writers, and bohemian counterculturalists. Its jazz and folk musicians had long been pioneers in drug use, especially hallucinogens. By 1964, Dylan had begun composing under the influence of LSD. His songs took on a far more cynical, abrasive, and cryptic quality than the early Beatles music. The Beatles decided they wanted to meet the person who was fast becoming a legend among the musical avant garde. Once Dylan and drugs entered their lives, the Beatles moved their music in directions that would once again redefine popular culture.

Lyndon Johnson and Civil Rights

Though they were white, the Beatles and the other bands of the British invasion exposed through their music the racial tensions afflicting the nation. Signs of conflict appeared in other unexpected places. One was the New York World's Fair of 1964. America has long had a love affair with world's fairs and international expositions. These episodic extravaganzas were as much about urban boosterism and tourism as they were about celebrating the cutting edge of American technology and commerce. In 1964, the United States had a great deal to celebrate in those areas. Its economy dwarfed those of other nations. Whether in military or consumer goods, the United States led the world. Neither Germany nor Japan had quite completed its economic revival from the destruction of World War II. A strong dollar, cheap airfares, and growing cosmopolitanism drew Americans to all parts of the globe. Wherever they went, they could find no city with greater cultural, financial, and human resources than New York.

In 1964, New York put on a fair that brought the world to its doorstep. This fair was about the future. At its center stood the Unisphere, a giant metal sculpture of the earth being orbited. Dotting the grounds were towers that one observer described as "flying saucers on a stick." The General Motors Pavilion imagined a future of underwater cities in which the family submarine replaced the family car. General Electric had one exhibit at which visitors stared in awe at the simulation of a nuclear fusion reaction. But the biggest splash came from Ford Motors. Ford used the fair to introduce the Mustang, its most successful car since the Model A.

Prior to the Mustang, most American cars could be described with three Bs: big, boxy, and boring. Market surveys had suggested to Ford that the mass market was ready for a car targeted at youthful buyers. Sporty, with clean lines and a low-slung look, the Mustang evoked the image of a European sports car, though mechanically, it was actually a clone of Ford's doughty compact Falcon. A low price made it affordable to a broad range of consumers. Americans of all ages, not just young drivers, rushed out to buy Mustangs. The car became the apotheosis of the consumer and automotive culture of the 1950s. Affluence allowed millions of Americans to buy a product that was more a toy than a useful consumer product. What better place to show it off than at a world's fair?

Civil rights leaders had other ideas about the occasion. Before the fair opened they had warned that protestors would block the roads to Flushing Meadows. That had not occurred, but the crowds who flocked to see the Mustang saw the object of their desire turning on a pedestal—surrounded by civil rights demonstrators. A movement once seen as largely confined to the South had come North. And in this protest at the commercial center of the United States, civil rights leaders had found a new way to intrude their demands into the consciousness of Americans accustomed to images sanitized by Hollywood, Madison Avenue, and Washington politicians. Nothing, not the playfulness of the Beatles nor the ultimate consumer appeal of the Mustang, could shield Americans from the increased polarization of their society.

That summer, a white New York City policeman shot a fifteen-year-old black whom he claimed had threatened him with a knife. Urban ghetto dwellers were all too familiar with such officially sanctioned violence. The civil rights movement, however, had created a higher level of race consciousness and frustration. Protest demonstrations followed and then boiled over into rioting. One person was killed, some 100 injured, and 200 arrested before an uneasy calm returned. Similar rioting occurred in nine other northern cities. An FBI report concluded that the riots had been spontaneous, not part of some systematic attack on authority. Still, the explosion of violence had a sobering effect on the nation. Until that summer, most Northerners had been largely unaware of or indifferent to the nearby ghettos. Some white families had black maids or gardeners; a few owned ghetto businesses, but at night these workers returned to their separate worlds. After the riots, racial inequality and the sorry state of the nation's ghettos could no longer be ignored.

The burden for dealing with the racial division in American life fell to President Lyndon Johnson. Most Americans tend to exaggerate the importance of the presidency. They like to credit or blame presidents for events such as wars and depressions over which they often have little control. All the same, it is reasonable to argue that the uncivil wars that swept America after 1964 would not have been so wide-spread, violent, or extreme had Kennedy rather than Johnson been president. Some-thing about Johnson and his personality aggravated the divisions in the nation. That must stand as the ultimate irony of the era, because Johnson defined himself as a practical idealist—forging compromises and holding the middle ground. But the uncivil wars raised issues over which compromise proved increasingly difficult, if not impossible. What was the middle ground between the equal rights for minori-ties and women and the realities of institutionalized racism and sexism? How did one reconcile the differences between those who saw any step toward integration as a step too far and those who demanded absolute equality now? Between those who believed in liberal reform and those who saw a need to overthrow a system rotten to its core?

Further, even though Johnson was in many ways a political genius, he practiced the politics of another era. Where Kennedy built his career through skillful manip-ulation of the media, Johnson had operated as the ultimate political insider, wheel-ing and dealing in the Senate corridors outside the public limelight. Not that Johnson did not appreciate the importance of media, especially television. He had built his personal fortune largely from radio and television stations. Inside the oval office he had a console with three televisions so he could watch the major network news simultaneously. One historian remarked that "no President before Lyndon Johnson had worked so hard to cajole, control, and neutralize the news media. . . . In the end his hopes seem to hang entirely on keeping television in line." That often meant throwing a veil of secrecy over policymaking that sometimes appeared to cover up a conspiracy or some other villainy. On television, he came across as awk-ward, manipulative, and contrived. Something about his southern accent struck much of the national audience as foreign.

Certain character defects compounded that image problem. One prominent columnist described Johnson as a "proud, cruel, . . . insecure . . . and bitterly driven man." Ambition and insecurity combined to produce in him excesses of rhetoric and boasting. He took all criticism, even when fairly given, as a personal affront. So when he received unfavorable press, he would chew out reporters, try to manipu-late the news, and succeed only in alienating those in the media whose uncritical approval he craved. So, too, he tyrannized subordinates in his administration. In his earthy idiom, he once explained that he wanted people around him "who would kiss his ass in Macy's window and say it smelled like roses." That meant that save for a few intrepid advisers, Johnson surrounded himself with yes-men who would not speak the unpopular truth, even if the president needed to hear it.

Between Johnson the Senate majority leader and the Kennedy camp there had been no great love lost. Theirs was a marriage of political convenience. Johnson hungered for the presidency, but the Kennedy organization simply outmaneuvered him in the 1960 campaign. In winning the nomination, however, Kennedy knew he had not won over the Democratic Party's southern wing. Hence, he had offered the vice presidency to Johnson. And Johnson had accepted, knowing full well that the office, in the words of an earlier Texas vice president, John Nance Garner, "wasn't worth a bucket of shit." The deal had worked for Kennedy; he won the election. For Johnson it had meant frustrating years of obscurity and the erosion of his power base.

When the unthinkable happened, Johnson was ready to be president. All the same, he had the good sense not to contest the Kennedy mystique. Instead, he presented himself as the caretaker of his predecessor's legacy. Kennedy said in his inaugural, "Let us begin"; Johnson told the nation, "Let us continue." A civil rights bill, a tax cut bill, aid to education, care for the elderly, and the space program— these had been Kennedy's agenda; they would be Johnson's, too. Most Americans had not expected to like Lyndon Johnson. They knew little about him, and what they did know did little to endear him. His sensitivity to the Kennedy legacy and forceful assumption of the presidency at first overcame that popular skepticism.

On no issue was skepticism greater than on civil rights, and on no issue did Johnson so forcefully demonstrate his leadership. African Americans had experienced Kennedy's death as a major blow to their growing hopes for racial justice. No matter how much Kennedy may have equivocated in private, many civil rights leaders had come to see him as the champion of their cause. On the day of his death, Martin Luther King's son asked innocently, "Daddy, President Kennedy was your best friend, wasn't he?" Coretta King found herself thinking, "In a way, he was." By contrast, blacks saw Lyndon Johnson as a veteran obstructer of the civil rights cause. Yes, he had steered a civil rights bill through Congress in 1957, but not before its opponents stripped it of any effective provisions. Johnson excused his behavior on that occasion as a necessary bow to political reality: "One heroic stand and I'd be back home defeated, unable to do any good for anyone, much less the blacks and the underprivileged." With Kennedy dead and a Southerner in the White House, civil rights advocates feared their cause was stymied.

Johnson's critics had misjudged their man. For one thing, Johnson was no bigot. As a New Deal administrator in the 1930s, he had an unusual record of treating blacks and Mexican Americans on an equal footing with whites. He had, while serving on Kennedy's Committee on Equal Employment Opportunities, been "face to face with the deep-seated discrimination against blacks." The time had come, he understood, for the South to exorcise itself of its traditions of racial demagoguery and terrorism. Johnson also sincerely championed the downtrodden and needy. Preoccupied with how history would judge him, he saw his legacy as making a difference for those who for whatever reason were ill-equipped to help themselves. Of course, for Johnson, there was a political consideration. Just as Catholicism had been a defining issue for John Kennedy, civil rights would be the test of Johnson's ability to hold his party together. As he admitted, "I knew that if I did not get out in front on this issue, they [liberals] would get me. They'd throw my background against me; they'd use it to prove that I was incapable of bringing unity to the land I loved so much." And if that happened, Johnson believed, "I'd be dead before I could even begin."

Not one to commit political suicide, Johnson used all his formidable legislative skills to produce the most sweeping civil rights legislation since Reconstruction. When southern opponents tried to delete two critical provisions calling for equal access to public accommodations and equal job opportunities, Johnson refused to compromise. This bill was all or nothing. And that meant overcoming the opposition of some of the Senate's most skilled political operators. At one point, Senator Richard Russell of Georgia tied the Senate up in a dizzifying debate on "whether a motion to debate the bill was debatable." Johnson made it clear that no strategy of delay, no crippling amendments, and no amount of filibustering would keep his bill from passing.

The House of Representatives got the message first. While gaseous clouds of oratory engulfed the Senate, the House passed a strong bill, though not before defeating over 100 potentially crippling amendments. One amendment, intended to kill the bill, proved particularly nettlesome. Representative Howard Smith of Virginia had offered what he referred to as a "perfecting" amendment that would extend to women the ban on discrimination in employment. Did not women outnumber men by at least two million? Smith asked his House colleagues. Since they were so disadvantaged in seeking spouses, should they not at least have equal pay?

Smith knew that women faced every bit as much discrimination in the job market as did blacks. Women's work was in fact equally segregated, and their pay rates similarly inequitable. Those realties had been pointed out both by the Commission on the Status of Women created by President Kennedy in 1963 and by Betty Friedan in *The Feminine Mystique*, published in 1963. Representative Smith, a long-time ally of Alice Paul and the National Women's Party, had supported an equal rights amendment for many years. He was also an arch-racist who had used the chairmanship of the powerful Rules Committee to frustrate progressive causes in general and desegregation in particular.

Smith undoubtedly relished the consternation his strategy caused, especially among the more liberal supporters of civil rights. Some liberals did not want to impede the cause of black rights by intruding the separate issue of women's rights. Others feared that the amendment would be used to erode special provisions for women such as alimony and child custody. Many, however, worried because they did not want to "endanger traditional family relationships." For them, a woman's place remained in the home. Though legislators divided over the amendment, it did pass but soon disappeared as an issue. No more than the Congress was the country ready for a full battle over women's rights. That became apparent over the next several years when the Equal Employment Opportunity Commission, charged with enforcing the employment provisions of the Civil Rights Act, largely ignored the complaints brought by women.

Johnson used his political savvy to break segregationist resistance in the Senate. For every diehard obstructionist like Strom Thurmond of South Carolina, who tried to undermine the bill by delay, he relied on a Richard Russell of Georgia, who bowed to the new racial climate. When one liberal senator tried to goad Thurmond to permit action on one section of the act, the South Carolinian tried to punch him. Russell, by contrast, told the South to accept the Civil Rights Bill as "the law of the Senate" by which they must abide. Yet within a few months, the nation was engulfed in racial turmoil. Riots erupted, civil rights leaders made new demands and organized new demonstrations, and the Mississippi Freedom Democrats confronted the Democratic presidential convention with an issue that defied simple compromise. After the Civil Rights Bill passed, the racial divide seemed to widen, not narrow.

Mississippi Freedom Summer

For all its provisions against racial discrimination, the Civil Rights Bill did not address the issue of voting rights. The many devices by which southern states denied blacks the right to vote in state and local elections remained largely unaffected. As a result, Martin Luther King shifted the emphasis of the SCLC from integration to voting rights. He focused his efforts in Alabama and Georgia, not Mississippi, the most deeply segregated state in the union. Only SNCC and its beleaguered band of crusaders had the temerity to take on the heart of the Confederacy. Mississippi, which pioneered the disenfranchisement of blacks during the 1880s, had the nation's most entrenched system of racial caste. While millions of blacks labored in cotton fields for peons' wages, the state's white elite controlled both wealth and political power. Mississippi ranked lowest in the United States in per capita income, and black income there was only a third of what the average white person earned. Some 86 percent of all blacks lived below the federal poverty level, and 68 percent were rural, as opposed to 39 percent nationally. A secret white supremacist commission enforced the state's racial codes.

Responsibility for voter registration in Mississippi rested with COFO—the Council of Federated Organizations—a civil rights coalition that included SCLC, CORE, the NAACP, and SNCC. SNCC, however, with some support from CORE, provided almost all the volunteers and funding for the voter registration drive. For three years, a handful of SNCC volunteers like Robert Moses, Anne Moody, and John Lewis risked their lives to turn poor rural blacks into voters. By 1964, they were largely frustrated and exhausted; they were also more cynical about white America and more radicalized. As Doug McAdam, a historian of the movement, observed, "It wasn't simply the succession of unpunished attacks by segregationists that had produced this effect. Or the frustration of having achieved so few tangible victories to weigh against their sacrifices. Just as important was their growing awareness of the depths of federal complicity in Mississippi's *system* of racism." Increasingly, they came to question the ideals of nonviolence and the goals of integration that had originally directed their efforts.

At its founding, SNCC had decided to be a racially inclusive organization. In the summer of 1963, it began to use white volunteers in COFO's Jackson, Mississippi, headquarters. Among those who showed up at the office was political activist Allard Lowenstein. Lowenstein, by training a lawyer, by experience a university dean, came to Jackson to protest the murder of NAACP leader Medgar Evers. He stayed around long enough to recognize that SNCC needed a more effective strategy. On that point he and Robert Moses agreed. They conceived a "freedom vote," in which Mississippi blacks would hold their own election in November. That would allow them to vote for their own candidates and to avoid the polling places where whites would exclude them. Since the Freedom Party candidates favored civil rights, blacks demonstrated their desire for suffrage by voting for them. Lowenstein recruited some eighty white volunteers from Stanford and Yale Universities to help organize the campaign. The 80,000 ballots were only symbolic, but in casting them, many blacks lost their fear of involvement in civil rights activities.

For Moses and Lowenstein, the success of the freedom vote gave birth to a bolder idea. Why not recruit an even larger force of white college students to support the voter registration campaign in the summer of 1964? That idea was not without its complications. Over the summer of 1963, racial tensions had grown within SNCC. SNCC had traditionally been a black organization led and staffed by blacks. Its increased visibility had attracted increasing numbers of white civil rights activists. By upbringing and education, these activists had skills and self-confidence that allowed them to dominate the decision-making process. Some SNCC members feared whites would take over their organization. And would not the presence of interracial teams antagonize local whites and intimidate local blacks? Lowenstein recognized the problem: "Here were kids who had been risking their lives in Mississippi for a long time, and nobody even noticed. I mean the white people who came down got the publicity. It would have taken an angel not to have resented that."

Increased racial consciousness compounded the problem. John Lewis, a supporter of nonviolent integration, noticed that southern blacks had begun to think more along color lines. "They're conscious of things that happen in Cuba, in Latin America, and in Africa," Lewis observed. "Even in SNCC, we talk about integration, about the beloved community, but . . . there's been a radical change in our people since 1960; the way they dress, the music they listen to; their natural hairdos—all of them want to go to Africa . . . I think people are searching for a sense of identity, and they are finding it." Whites in SNCC found no effective way to reconcile this tension. Race consciousness was as much embedded in those who fought segregation as in those who fought to preserve it. As a compromise, the white members established a parallel organization, the Southern Students Organizing Committee, to promote civil rights among whites.

Moses recognized that the presence of self-confident whites complicated the development of black leaders within SNCC. But on a practical level, he realized that northern volunteers would provide an infusion of energy and much-needed visibility. For all their efforts, he pointed out, the current volunteers had achieved little success in breaking down the fear that kept blacks away from the registrars' offices. And despite early assurances from the Kennedys, they had seen precious little in the way of support or protection from Washington. Lyndon Johnson actively discouraged SNCC's efforts in Mississippi, which he feared would polarize the Democratic

Party on the eve of the passage of the Civil Rights Bill and his own election campaign. Most of all, Moses was unwilling to work in a segregated organization. To some fellow COFO staff who wanted to marginalize the role of whites, Moses argued that "the only way you can break that [a racist movement] down is to have white people working along side you—so then it changes the whole complexion of what you're doing, so it isn't any longer Negro fighting white; it's a question of rational people against irrational people. . . . I always thought that the one thing we can do for the country that no one else could do is be above the race issue." Out of the esteem in which his comrades held him, Moses carried the day, but for SNCC the race issue would not go away.

In private, Moses was more cynical about the decision to bring in white volunteers. Only with whites around was it likely the federal government would intervene to protect SNCC workers. So SNCC made sure that the volunteers included the children "of some of the most powerful people in the country over there, including Jerry Brown [son of California governor Pat Brown and later a governor and presidential candidate]," Moses recalled. Whites would also attract the attention of the national media. If SNCC workers were murdered, Moses recognized, the "death of a white college student would bring more attention to what was going on than for a black college student getting it." Moses knew that such reasoning seemed "cold" but explained it as "the language of this country."

Other issues, both tactical and ideological, faced SNCC as it planned for the summer of 1964. The organization had assumed in its democratic fashion that its primary objective was civil rights reforms. More-radical elements found that program naive. They argued that integration and voting rights initiatives only served to distract the black masses from their real grievances. What did it mean to integrate a restaurant if blacks could not afford to eat there? Since voting rights did nothing to help feed a poor family, SNCC should concentrate more on issues like unemployment and poverty. Under attack for his failure to establish an economic agenda, Moses countered that SNCC workers did not have the economic sophistication to plan a revolution. He urged that they stick to stopgap measures until they had time and energy to think long term.

The radicalism behind this critique exposed SNCC leaders to another dilemma. What would they do about Communists? As on so many other questions, the organization had no formal position. It practiced what was known as "freedom of association," an extension of its practice of welcoming people and ideas of all stripes and of preferring direct action to ideologically conceived strategies. Still, McCarthyism was not such a toothless tiger that they could simply ignore segregationist allegations that Reds had infiltrated the organization. Similar charges planted by J. Edgar Hoover had seriously damaged Martin Luther King and SCLC. Some SNCC members had chastened King for firing a valued adviser for his prior associations with the Communist Party. But SNCC, like SCLC, depended heavily on the financial support of northern liberals, many of them ardent anti-Communists. So this argument, like the argument over integration, came down to principle versus practical realities. Here, too, Moses prevailed with his view that SNCC would consider the issue if it was relevant, but would otherwise continue its policy of openness—in essence, they made a decision not to decide.

As troubling as these issues proved to be, SNCC did not have time to resolve them, assuming that was even possible. The organization was focused, instead, on its preparations for the summer freedom campaign. Fund-raising in the North, though never adequate to the organization's growing needs, expanded SNCC's financial resources and its visibility. In Mississippi, local blacks proved more receptive to the work SNCC sought to do. In response, SNCC, with the help of 50 northern clergy, organized the Hattiesberg Freedom Day. That activity inspired some 500 blacks to try to register and instigated more local "freedom days" around the state.

Freedom days gave way to "freedom registration." SNCC organizers recognized that the Democratic Party in Mississippi was effectively closed to blacks. Inability to vote in Democratic primaries in a one-party state effectively disenfranchised even those few who managed to register. So SNCC created a separate party, the Mississippi Freedom Democratic Party (MFDP), with its own registration requirements. The idea was to have MFDP delegates challenge the regular Mississippi delegation at the Democrats' 1964 convention scheduled for Atlantic City, New Jersey. One local black attorney found the prospect of taking on the Democratic establishment so preposterous he dismissed it as "ridiculous by any standard other than that of SNCC." Yet that was just SNCC's appeal. The organization never shied from thinking the unthinkable or attempting the improbable. By June 1964, MFDP had qualified four candidates for the Democratic primary. To complement the Freedom Party, SNCC inaugurated "freedom schools," intended to overcome the inadequacies of Mississippi's schools and to raise the political consciousness of poor blacks. Beside the standard academic fare, student volunteers would teach current events, black history, and the politics of liberation. Northern liberals gave enthusiastic support. Staughton Lynd, son of the sociologists Helen and Robert Lynd of *Middletown* fame and himself a noted historian, agreed to direct the freedom schools program.

SNCC, however, had put itself on a crash course with the nation's most powerful Democrat, Lyndon Johnson. Johnson believed he was entitled to gratitude for his civil rights initiative. Instead, he discovered growing insistence on more federal intervention in the southern struggle. Johnson also determined that his party's 1964 convention had but one purpose—to inaugurate him as the unchallenged leader of the Democrats as he assumed control of the presidency in his own right. Having pressed civil rights leaders for a moratorium on protests prior to the 1964 election, he had little patience with SNCC's activism in Mississippi. SNCC, in turn, saw no reason to defer its program simply to assuage Johnson's political vanity. When SNCC leaders sought a meeting, the White House informed them that the president was too preoccupied with Vietnam to see them. So the two major strands of 1960s unrest, the Vietnam War and civil rights, began to entwine.

Freedom Summer opened in Oxford, Ohio, once an important location along the underground railroad. On June 13, some 300 volunteers gathered for a week of orientation for the COFO voter registration projects. These students constituted the vanguard of the uncivil war. Of the some 800 who went to Mississippi that summer, most had completed college or entered their last two years. In screening the applicants, SNCC interviewers sought to weed out those deemed too "paternalistic," who had "fixed ideas about what they wanted to do and what they hoped to achieve." "A student who seems determined to carve out his own niche, win publicity and glory when he returns home," the interview guidelines warned, "can only have harmful effects on the Mississippi program." Instead, SNCC wanted those who would "work with local leadership, not to overwhelm it."

SNCC faced Freedom Summer with a limited budget and a determination to increase its visibility. Those priorities dictated that the students chosen would be both affluent and elite. To qualify, students agreed to work without pay, to provide their own transportation, and to have adequate funds to make bond, if arrested. Almost

At Western College in Oxford, Ohio, volunteers for Freedom Summer learned the essential steps for non-violent self-defense. (Source: Herbert Randall, The University of Southern Mississippi, McCain Library and Archives)

60 percent came from Yale, Berkeley, Michigan, Princeton, Harvard, Wisconsin, and Stanford. In general, both they and their parents were themselves highly educated, liberal, and politically active. Many had strong ties to churches and campus religious organizations. One historian of the 1960s aptly described their view of themselves as the "counter power elite."

About one-quarter of those who wanted to come bowed out, often discouraged by parental pressures or personal fears. Those fears were amply warranted. One nationally syndicated columnist warned in early June that "Southern Mississippi is now known to contain no fewer than sixty-thousand armed men organized to what amounts to terrorism." So, too, were the Mississippi authorities. Jackson mayor Allen Thompson warned that "We are going to be ready for them. . . . They won't have a chance." To give credence to his threat, he bought 250 shotguns and built an armored vehicle, dubbed "Thompson's tank." State legislators tried to outlaw the freedom schools and made it illegal to distribute leaflets calling for boycotts. Charles Brenner, a state Klan leader, boasted that "this is going to be a long, hot summer. But the 'heat' will be applied to the race mixing trash by the decent people. . . . When your Communist-oriented goons get to Mississippi, I hope they get their just dues."

Women faced additional resistance, mostly from parents who worried about the fate that awaited the volunteers in Mississippi. All women but only men under twenty-one had to have parental approval. One young woman recalled the thrill she felt after a SNCC recruiter spoke on her campus. She hurried to her dorm to call her parents about this newfound sense of mission:

> So what happens? My mom starts crying. Then my dad gets on and starts yelling about how he's not paying $2,000—or whatever my tuition was—for me to run off to Mississippi; that I'm there to get an education and that if I have anything else in mind he'll be glad to stop sending the check. End of discussion.

Another young woman faced emotional rather than financial resistence:

> I can only hope you have the sensitivity to understand that I can both love you very much and desire to go to Mississippi. . . .
>
> I hope you will accept my decision even if you do not agree with me. There comes a time when you have to do things which your parents do not agree with . . . I think you have to live to the fullest extent to which you have gained an awareness or you are less than the human being you are capable of being.

The second woman went; the first did not.

Women also encountered the double standard that applied to gender relationships during that era. Some women received negative comments because they were physically unattractive. One woman who wanted "to work with people" and to "learn something from the summer" was rejected, in part, because she refused to do clerical work. Another woman's parents opposed her participation because "it was not a woman's place really." Men were far less often asked about their willingness to take particular work assignments. And as always, the specter of interracial sex complicated the decision of women to participate. One woman was rejected after she said she might have sex with a black man who asked her, even if she had been told that "as a staff member, that sexual activity would endanger everyone, and not to do it." Sex between a white male and black woman posed no similar threat.

Among the approximately one thousand volunteers chosen, about 75 percent went to Mississippi. Men outnumbered woman about two to one. Whatever illusions the volunteers entertained about privilege or power were quickly tempered by the menace of what lay before them. At Oxford, volunteers found themselves immersed in one of the most intense personal experiences of their lives. At general meetings, SNCC veterans recounted war stories about Mississippi and bore jagged scars that spoke more vividly than words. John Doar, speaking on behalf of the Justice Department, warned the volunteers that they could expect little in the way of federal protection.

In workshops, participants learned the basics of their responsibilities in the project. Dramatic role playing subjected volunteers to verbal abuse and physical punishment. They learned to roll into a ball to protect vulnerable parts of their bodies from kicking and clubs. SNCC trainers insisted that no one should drive at night or travel alone. R. Jess Brown, a black lawyer from Mississippi, added some advice informed by experience: "If you're riding down somewhere, and a cop stops you and starts to put you under arrest, even though you haven't committed a crime, go to jail. Mississippi is not the place to start conducting constitutional law classes for policemen, many of whom don't have a fifth-grade education."

The volunteers found their lives transformed in just one week. Trailed by reporters and television cameras, they could not help but sense they had embarked on a history-making mission. Nor had they ever before encountered people like the SNCC veterans. "SNCC is not populated with Toms who would wish to be white," one woman remarked. Another had a more romanticized view: "You can always tell a CORE or SNCC worker—they're beautiful." For those "beautiful" SNCC and CORE workers, the encounter at Oxford was more complex. Some volunteers noticed "they tend to be suspicious of us, because we are white, northern, urban, rich, inexperienced." Some Mississippi blacks had been so conditioned to hating whites or avoiding them that they found the intimacy at Oxford threatening. Moses used open discussions to mitigate some of the tension, but never fully closed the racial divisions. As SNCC historian Clayborne Carson observed, "The ambivalence of black staff members working with white volunteers was complicated by the staff's awareness that only further violence—against the volunteers rather than black Mississippians—would promote federal intervention."

That violence would not be long in coming. On June 20, the first volunteers left Oxford for Mississippi. The following day, as Moses addressed the next volunteer group, a staff member passed him a note. Three COFO workers were missing. Andrew Goodman from Queens College in New York City had left Oxford just the day before. Upon arriving in Mississippi, Goodman had gone off with James

Chaney and Michael Schwerner to look into the bombing of a black church in the town of Philadelphia. The twenty-one-year-old Chaney was a black Mississippi native. After working as a plasterer's apprentice, Chaney decided to dedicate himself to the civil rights struggle. Membership in CORE allowed him to "do something for myself and somebody else too," he told his worried mother. "Ain't you afraid of this?" she asked him. "Naw, mama," he assured her, "that's what's the matter now—everybody's scared." At CORE's Meridien headquarters he met Mickey Schwerner, who had given up his position as a social worker in New York City to join the struggle in Mississippi. Schwerner's welcome outside CORE was a chilly one. The one rabbi in Meridien told him that his efforts were "not helping Negroes but hurting Jews." Local whites called him "that goddamned bearded atheist communist Jew." But Schwerner had stayed, and with his wife, Rita, and people like James Chaney helped build a community house to serve local blacks.

Philadelphia, Mississippi, would never be mistaken for the city of brotherly love. No COFO worker ever stayed there past four in the afternoon. As the three prepared to leave Meridien for Philadelphia, Schwerner told his fellow workers, "If for any reason we aren't back by four P.M., you should alert [the COFO office] in Jackson and begin checking every city jail, county jail, sheriff's office, police station and hospital between Meridien and Neshoba [County]." No one in Meridien ever saw any of the three alive again. At four, the COFO office began its inquiries and found nothing. At Oxford, a new sense of fear and urgency settled on the volunteers. A few left for home. "We know the blood is going to flow this summer and it's going to be our blood. And I'm scared—I'm very scared," a volunteer admitted, but like the vast majority, she stayed.

Word of the disappearance reached Washington and went on the national news as well. Nothing else that happened over the summer would have the same impact as this single event. Just as SNCC organizers had anticipated, violence to whites had brought national attention to the local struggle. Walter Cronkite told a CBS evening news audience that the whole world was watching Mississippi. Lyndon Johnson dispatched former CIA director Allen Dulles as his emissary to COFO, and the FBI opened a new Mississippi office. Dulles revealed just how little sympathy the administration had for the freedom struggle. Johnson, he explained, was more determined to keep the peace in Mississippi than to protect civil rights workers. The federal government had no plans to increase its involvement. Johnson, instead, would concentrate his efforts on the Civil Rights Bill, at that time still bogged down by the Senate filibuster. The president did dispatch several hundred sailors and some FBI agents to search for the missing bodies. Washington, it seemed, had more interest in these young men dead than alive.

The intensive hunt for Chaney, Goodman, and Schwerner first turned up the bodies of other blacks who had previously disappeared without notice. More than a few black civil rights leaders observed that their discovery did not arouse significant outrage. Finally, on August 4, the searchers uncovered the three bodies buried in an earthen dam. Goodman and Schwerner had each been shot once. Chaney had been shot three times, and the pathologist who examined his body testified that in twenty-five years he had "never witnessed bones so severely shattered." Investigation would later make clear that the crime was the handy work of Philadelphia deputy sheriff Cecil Price. After the three were arrested on trumped-up charges, Price had arranged their release just so local whites could capture and murder them. Eventually, Price and five others involved were convicted, not for murder for which local juries would surely have acquitted them, but on a federal charge of violating the victims' civil rights.

The murder of Chaney, Schwerner, and Goodman was not an isolated act of violence. Cleveland Sellers spoke for many of the SNCC workers when he described the summer of 1964 as "the longest nightmare I have ever had: three months." Over the course of the summer the volunteers faced more than a thousand arrests, thirty-five shootings, thirty bombings, eighty beatings, the three murders, and three more violent deaths. More discouraging, perhaps, was the reticence of local blacks. They generally greeted the volunteers politely, but few showed much enthusiasm for confronting Mississippi's deeply entrenched caste system. Some volunteers came to recognize that reluctance as "a highly rational emotion, the economic fear of losing your job, the physical fear of being shot at. Domestic servants know they will be fired if they register to vote; so will factory workers, so will Negroes who live on plantations. In Mississippi, registration is no private affair."

Still, the volunteers persevered. Some forty-one freedom schools introduced ideas and values once foreign to blacks. Many volunteers lived in black communities with families who had never before known or been on a first-name basis with whites. Seventeen thousand blacks attempted to register to vote, though only some 1,600 succeeded. Given the status of blacks in Mississippi, that could be seen as a breakthrough. On the other hand, that was scant results considering the enormous personal sacrifice the volunteers had made. Some 300 volunteers did stay on as the summer ended. By then most suffered from severe burnout. For too long they had endured the hostility of whites and the reluctance of blacks to accept them or their message. Little of the spirit of Freedom Summer remained.

MFDP at Atlantic City

Even as SNCC nursed its wounds on the Mississippi home front, it suffered perhaps its most demoralizing setback in national politics, this time at the hands of its supposed friends and allies. By early August 1964, sixty-eight Freedom Party delegates were on their way to Atlantic City and the Democratic Convention. For some, it was their first trip outside Mississippi. They left with much the same moral fervor as Saint George on his dragon-slaying foray: they intended to unseat the regular Mississippi Democratic delegation. The regulars had already repudiated Lyndon Johnson, the Civil Rights Act, and the party platform. Could a delegation that denied membership to over half the state's population claim in any real sense to be representative?

Fannie Lou Hamer emerged as the heart and soul of the Mississippi Freedom Democrats when they sought to become official state delegates at the 1964 Democratic Convention in Atlantic City.   (Source: Associated Press)

No one better conveyed the spirit of the insurgents than Fannie Lou Hamer. Once a sharecropper, a grandmother, and several times the victim of white brutality, she had been reborn in the civil rights movement. No one believed more deeply in the ideals that propelled the Freedom Democrats. "When we went to Atlantic City, we didn't go there for publicity;" she explained, "we went there because we believed America was what it said it was, 'the land of the free.'" That was before she met the battle-hardened veterans of traditional party politics. Lyndon Johnson had no intention of turning the spotlight of his convention on these rural upstarts. Veteran civil rights leaders like Roy Wilkins of the NAACP simply resented them as potential rivals. He told Hamer that she and her people "have put your point across, now why don't you back up and go home?" They, of course, had no more intention of leaving without being heard than Johnson had of seeing his convention disrupted. At first he had indicated he would accept a compromise in which both Mississippi delegations would be seated. But the regulars, supported by the governors of Texas and Georgia, threatened to walk out.

Johnson assigned his designated vice president, Hubert Humphrey, a person with solid civil rights credentials, to work out a new deal—the Freedom Party would get just two seats elsewhere on the convention floor, but the regulars would have to swear loyalty to the party ticket. Even that was too much for the regulars, who stormed out, and two seats was too few for the Freedom Democrats. They had come too far to settle for so little. Prospects for the Freedom Democrats brightened when they were called to testify before the convention credentials committee. To a national television audience they described the shocking patterns of terror and police brutality they faced in Mississippi. No one was more compelling than Hamer. For eighteen long years she had toiled faithfully as a sharecropper. Then in 1962, she registered to vote. That was the end of her farm. When she urged other blacks to register, state police arrested her. At the jailhouse, police ordered other prisoners to beat her. "I began to scream," she recalled, "and one white man got up and beat me on my head and tell me to 'hush.'" The beatings left Hamer with permanent kidney damage.

Her testimony threatened to steal Johnson's political stage. So even as the witnesses testified, he called his own press conference to preempt the TV coverage. Soon after, he sent an honor guard of national civil rights leaders to persuade the Freedom delegates to accept the Humphrey compromise. First came Bayard Rustin, then Martin Luther King, followed by Walter Reuther of the United Auto Workers, a stalwart civil rights supporter, and finally James Farmer of CORE. Each in his way pressed the insurgents to take the deal. As Rustin argued, protest with its moral imperative must give way to politics rooted in reality and compromise. To which an angry Moses responded that they had come to put morality back into politics not to trade in their ideals. Or as Hamer retorted, "We didn't come all this way for no two seats!" With that, the delegates voted again to reject the compromise.

In the end, the Freedom delegates were simply outmaneuvered. By rejecting the compromise, they kept their principles in tact; Johnson, by keeping them out of the spotlight, preserved the surface impression of a unified convention. Most of the MFDP delegates returned to Mississippi embittered by the experience. John Lewis admitted they had been "naive to go on believing that somehow the Democratic Party in 1964 would have unseated the Mississippi regular Democrats." To compromise, another SNCC veteran argued, would have been to concede that "people should have to sit down with racists to discuss their humanity." Charles Sherrod, while pleased they had not "bowed to 'massa,'" believed that SNCC must take a more radical course, even if meant seizing power through "rioting and blood." To Stokely Carmichael, Atlantic City proved that blacks could not rely on their "so-called allies." Labor, liberals, and civil rights leaders all proved more loyal to the party than to justice.

As bitter as those comments were, no one took this setback harder than Robert Moses did. Perhaps, it was the culmination of a long, stressful crusade with so few positive results. Possibly, he was more emotionally spent than the rest. After returning to Mississippi, he lost interest in the MFDP and championed a more radical course. "Why can't we set up our own government. . . . And say that the federal government should recognize us?" Such notions would seem far less radical in the near future. That may have been one of the most enduring legacies of Freedom Summer. Certainly, despite the many disappointments from the summer of 1964, SNCC's efforts had forced the nation to recognize the depth of the apartheid system in Mississippi. The refusal of registrars to enroll black voters had a major influence on the passage of the Voting Rights Act of 1965.

Yet given the vision of those who had hoped to transform Mississippi, Freedom Summer had largely failed. Most of the freedom schools would close within a year.

Mississippi remained virtually as segregated as it had been since the beginning of Jim Crow. As one white volunteer acknowledged that December, "In Mississippi an autocratic and powerful minority rules, through organized violence, to suppress the vast, virtually powerless majority." By August of 1964, SNCC had become so disillusioned with liberal politics that a radical turn became inevitable.

Lyndon Johnson and Vietnam

For Lyndon Johnson, the confrontation with SNCC at Atlantic City was a sideshow. He had managed to stem the insurgency while keeping his major civil rights coalition in tact. That, in turn, shored up his support among the party liberals, who still viewed Johnson with uneasiness though also some begrudging respect. So he had left Atlantic City just as he intended—as the unchallenged political leader of his party and the nation. The Republicans had earlier chosen as their candidate a favorite of the party's right wing, Senator Barry Goldwater of Arizona. Goldwater's views proved so out of step with the liberalism and optimism of the era that his candidacy doomed the Republicans to one of the most crushing defeats in American political history.

Yet in ways not at all clear at the time, Goldwater more than Johnson represented the future direction of American politics. His Libertarianism had much in common with New Left suspicion of the system. Nor was there a categorical difference between his Libertarian beliefs and the "do your own thing" ethos of the emerging counterculture. In his way, Goldwater mistrusted big government as much as the radicals in SDS, especially the shift of power from the state and local to the federal level. He believed the government in Washington had no business desegregating schools, building housing, subsidizing farmers and the poor, or imposing progressive income tax. His proposal to end Social Security proved too radical for most voters.

In foreign affairs, Goldwater attacked "one world" notions such as the United Nations and viewed much of the world outside America's borders with suspicion. He was above all an arch–cold warrior who indicated he would use nuclear weapons to stop the Reds. Anticipating the slogan "Better Dead Than Red," he preached that "our job, first and foremost, is to persuade the enemy that we would rather follow the world to Kingdom Come than consign it to Hell under communism." Such views sold particularly well in what would soon be known as the Sunbelt, where Johnson's support for civil rights and affirmative action programs would alienate one of the Democratic Party's major constituencies. As a result, Johnson's crushing defeat of Goldwater in the election of 1964 would prove to be more an end than a beginning. It marked the last time a majority of white males voted for a Democrat for president.

Johnson's presidency also marked the last stand of New Deal liberalism. On matters that counted to liberals, Johnson delivered. He drove the Civil Rights Act through Congress. He launched his war on poverty, which sought to attack some of the grosser forms of inequality. The Great Society, as Johnson labeled his domestic legislation initiatives, vastly extended the reach of federal government programs to assist the poor, to aid public education, to improve the environment and protect the wilderness, and to benefit the elderly through Medicare and Medicaid. In his war on poverty, Johnson was politically shrewd enough not to attempt anything so radical and politically divisive as income redistribution. Rather, as one economist noted, "nearly all of the early Great Society and war on poverty programs were manpower training programs and not income maintenance programs." In short, Johnson sought more to change the poor rather than to fund them.

One overriding factor made all of this federal largesse feasible—economic growth. Liberals and conservatives alike worshipped at this altar. Growth was a weapon in the cold war crusade. Soviet premier Nikita Khrushchev had called it "the battering ram with which we shall smash the capitalist system." The race to expand the economy became even more vital to victory in the cold war than the arms and space races. Kennedy and Nixon made improved economic performance a central theme of their 1960 presidential contest. A major tax cut that Kennedy proposed in 1963 and Johnson legislated the following year produced an increase in the gross national product of over 5 percent a year. Sustained prosperity also altered the worldview of the postwar generation. Unlike the Depression generation, one journalist observed, they were "brought up to believe, either at home or abroad, that whatever Americans wished to make happen, would happen." That was certainly reflected in the volunteers who participated in Freedom Summer, who had both the affluence to give up their summer to a noble cause and the faith they would succeed. And prosperity allowed Lyndon Johnson to launch the Great Society, fund NASA's race to the moon, and expand the nation's defense effort, including its involvement in Vietnam.

When John Kennedy had assumed the presidency, he was stunned to learn that the United States had almost no capacity to meet military emergencies around the world. If he sent just 10,000 troops to Southeast Asia, he would have no strategic reserve left. To overcome what he saw as a deficiency, he vastly expanded the budget for national defense. That not only meant more planes, ships, and divisions, it meant a more flexible military. The army special forces (Green Berets), for example, were trained in jungle and counter-guerrilla warfare so they could be deployed to quell revolutions in the Third World. In 1961, adviser Walt Rostow urged Kennedy to "bring to bear our unexploited counter-guerrilla assets on the Vietnam problem: armed helicopters, other Research and Development possibilities; our Special Forces units." Rostow added that he thought it "wrong to be developing these capabilities but not applying them in a crucially active theater. In Knute Rockne's [a legendary football coach] old phrase, we are not saving them for the Junior Prom."

Vietnam had remained somewhat on the back burner for most of Kennedy's term. Kennedy, however, like Eisenhower before him, was determined that South Vietnam would not fall to the Communists while he was president. He knew from personal experience how dearly the Communist takeover in China in 1949 had cost Harry Truman and the Democrats. Out of frustration with the corruption and repressive politics of Ngo Dinh Diem, Kennedy had endorsed a coup that cost the

South Vietnam president his life. At the time of Diem's assassination, Kennedy had sent 16,000 military advisors to shore up South Vietnam's effort to defeat Communist rebels. The defense buildup and general prosperity made such a commitment both militarily feasible and easily affordable. When Johnson became president, he believed he had the means both to build the Great Society at home and fight the cold war abroad. As he warned, "Let no one doubt for a moment that we have the resources and we have the will to follow this course as long as it may take." And at that moment, South Vietnam's government was in chaos as seven regimes rose to power, three between August and September alone. The various conspirators seemed more bent on enriching themselves than on fighting the Communists.

Johnson knew Vietnam was a potential disaster. He likened himself to a catfish who "just grabbed a big juicy worm with a sharp hook in the middle of it." But Johnson feared that if he showed weakness on Vietnam, Goldwater would accuse him of appeasing the Communists. Goldwater had a simple policy for Vietnam: "Let's win." So Johnson looked for some way to neutralize Vietnam. Secretly, the United States was already more involved than Johnson would admit to the public or the Congress. Under O Plan 34-A, the American navy was supporting South Vietnamese commando raids against the North. That brought the destroyer *Maddox* into the Gulf of Tonkin. On August 2, 1964, the *Maddox* cruised off some islands during a commando attack. As three North Vietnamese gunboats closed in, the *Maddox* opened fire, hitting at least one. The North Vietnamese launched torpedoes which missed, then fled to port to repair the damage inflicted by the *Maddox*.

When news of the incident reached Washington, Johnson met with his National Security Council. Did this mean Hanoi wanted war? he asked. His advisers assured him that Hanoi was only "reacting defensively to our attacks on the off-shore islands." Secretary of State Dean Rusk saw this as an opportunity not to ease tensions with the North, but to step up the raids. Johnson then ordered a second destroyer, the *Turner Joy*, into the Gulf. On the night of August 4, sonar men on both ships claimed to have contacts with North Vietnamese ships. A pilot flying overhead, "with the best seat in the house to detect boats," in fact saw nothing, even though the guns on the U.S. ships blazed into the night. Privately, Johnson doubted the navy's claim of an attack. "For all I know our navy might have been shooting at whales out there," he admitted. Publicly, he informed a national television audience that American ships had been attacked, and that he ordered U.S. planes to retaliate against selected targets in the North.

At this time, he asked Congress for a resolution authorizing him to take any necessary steps to halt aggression in Southeast Asia. The attacks were totally unprovoked, he assured congressional leaders. Defense Secretary Robert McNamara similarly claimed, "our navy played no part in, was not associated with, was not aware of, any South Vietnamese actions, even if there were any." In the Gulf of Tonkin Resolution, the House voted unanimously and the Senate 88-2 to give the president virtually unrestricted authority to halt aggression in Vietnam. Ernest Gruening of Alaska and Wayne Morse of Oregon, who voted against the resolution, would become early heroes of the antiwar movement that emerged as Johnson Americanized the war. So at the very moment the Mississippi Freedom Democrats headed to Atlantic City and the same day searchers found the bodies of Schwerner, Chaney, and Goodman in Mississippi, Lyndon Johnson cast the United States far deeper into the abyss of Vietnam.

Several characteristics of the Tonkin Gulf incident anticipate the future conduct of the Vietnam War and its role in fracturing American society. First, the Johnson administration lied about the extent of American involvement. Even as the United States was conducting secret military operations, Johnson blamed the North Vietnamese for escalating the war. Further, there was at that time no clear pattern of North Vietnamese aggression. Much of the early unrest in the South was provoked by the corruption and political repression of the Saigon government. That pattern of secrecy and misinformation would be repeated throughout the war, first by Johnson and later by Nixon. It would ultimately create suspicion of official claims and increase the intensity of domestic opposition.

Fallout from Freedom Summer

In the aftermath of the Tonkin Gulf incident, Vietnam faded into the background. Civil rights tensions, not the war, continued to command more publicity, even though both candidates in the presidential campaign avoided playing the race card. Barry Goldwater might well have exploited the backlash against civil rights. Alabama's segregationist governor, George Wallace, ran a brief campaign that revealed a deep resentment among elements of the white electorate. Goldwater, no racist, chose to emphasize his libertarian beliefs and credentials as a cold warrior. Most civil rights leaders had doubts about Johnson, but the prospect of a Goldwater victory genuinely frightened them. Many broke with a tradition of nonpartisanship and openly endorsed the president. Even some of the Mississippi Freedom Democrats campaigned for Johnson. In response, Johnson made equality for blacks a central theme of his campaign. In his landslide victory in November, some 95 percent of registered blacks voted for Johnson. And the much-feared white backlash failed to materialize, at least in this election.

The presidential election meant little to the veterans of Mississippi Freedom Summer as they left the South for college campuses. There they would become central figures in the growing radical political movement initially inspired by civil rights activism, but increasingly focused on antiwar activities. Most of them had become cynical about traditional politics. Those who stayed behind were left to cope with the bitter legacy of the summer's many defeats and frustrations. The SNCC office seethed with racial friction.

Another source of tension had quietly arisen. Women who participated in Freedom Summer had found themselves struggling to fill conflicting roles. On the one hand, the decision to come to Mississippi and face all the attendant dangers instilled a new sense of self-confidence. Most had overcome family pressures and broken with traditional stereotypes. They had become more assertive and independent. Yet in Mississippi, men often assigned them secondary roles as freedom school teachers, librarians, and office staff. Voter registration, where the action was, remained a largely male responsibility, since it exposed workers to more violence. Some women came to resent this traditional division of labor. "We didn't come down here to work as maids this summer," one woman protested. "We came down here to work in the field of civil rights." Possibly, women would have been more effective as field workers, because southern conventions on womanhood might have restrained white Mississippians from harassing them in the way they did male SNCC workers. Whatever the reason, a number of women in the movement began to challenge the male commitment to traditional gender roles.

Their challenge was made more problematic by matters of sexuality. Interracial sex remained one of the most potent taboos in all of southern society. In what more dramatic way, then, could a black male assert his equality in racist America than by having a white woman as a sexual partner? In what better way could a white woman demonstrate her commitment to true racial equality than by sleeping with a black man? That notion imposed a difficult sexual burden on many women, for it was "much harder to say no to the advances of a black guy because of the strong possibility of that being taken as racist." That is not to say that among the men and women of SNCC that all sexual relations were charged with racial and political significance. Many mixed-racial couples formed loving and lasting relationships. Among those for whom sex was more recreational or experimental, taboos about sexuality sometimes added a certain erotic appeal. And much like sex for soldiers, sex for SNCC volunteers offered a welcome escape from the constant threat of violence.

For black women, the issue posed special problems. The attraction of black men for white women affronted their own sense of femininity. As one woman phrased it, "If white women had a problem in SNCC, it was not just a male/female problem. . . . It was also a black woman/white woman problem." Certainly, many white women sensed just that. One admitted, "I was very afraid of black women, very afraid." She found intimidating the forceful personal strength that allowed these women to face constant danger in the field. At the same time, she sensed that her sexual relations with black men had formed a barrier that she could not overcome. Black women within the movement felt a special need to appear tough, almost as "superwomen," as one of them put it. That toughness came at considerable personal cost, since it tended to distance them from black males and deny them the opportunity to build relationships. White women paid a price, too, for over the summer, they lost standing within the movement, while the stature of black women grew.

A group of women led by Casey Hayden tried to raise the issue of gender equality. Out of frustration, Hayden and several other female co-workers prepared a position paper, "Women in the Movement," that they finally presented at a November SNCC strategy retreat. So uncertain were they of their position in SNCC as both whites and women that they presented the paper anonymously. Even if the organization seemed to welcome them, they saw themselves in "positions of relative powerlessness." Male leaders generally excluded them from major policy decision making. What influence they did have came through personal relationships and their strenuous work responsibilities.

Of all the discussions SNCC held, this one was probably taken the least seriously and was among the most prophetic. The women understood all too well when they presented their list of grievances that they faced an unsympathetic audience. We know that "this list will seem strange to some, petty to others, laughable to most," they acknowledged. Yet they wanted people to recognize the many ways women, like blacks, faced systematic discrimination. The problem, they concluded, stemmed from the "assumption of male superiority . . . as widespread and deeply rooted and every much as crippling to the woman as the assumptions of white supremacy are to the Negro."

Experience in SNCC opened the women volunteers to a more radical political agenda. In a system that conspired to promote inequality, integration by race or gender was not enough. In entering the system on an equal footing as proposed by Betty Friedan in *The Feminist Mystique*, liberated women would serve only to perpetuate its class, racial, and gender hierarchies. The SNCC women believed that only a thorough purging of that system would suffice. So the same radical-liberal division that fractured the civil rights movement in 1964 underlay the women's rights movement, even before it had achieved political visibility.

Not even the radical males in SNCC were prepared to give this issue serious consideration. Some ridiculed the paper, and even more ignored it. Stokely Carmichael, in an offhand comment that would prove as divisive as any ideological posture ever adopted in SNCC, remarked ironically, "The only position for women in SNCC is prone." In the end, Hayden and her comrades proved more prescient when they predicted that "women in this movement will become so alert as to force the rest of the movement to stop the discrimination and . . . come to understand that this is no more a man's world than it is a white world."

The Free Speech Movement

After the intensely personal atmosphere in SNCC, the return to university campuses jolted many civil rights activists. At the University of California, their unease was especially intense. Berkeley had by then grown into one of the mega-institutions of the postwar era. By the 1960s, at least fifty university centers around the country had enrollments over 30,000. Berkeley's 27,000 students might actually be considered modest compared to the University of Minnesota, with over 40,000. (Fifteen years earlier not one university was larger than 15,000.) One Minnesota psych class had 2,000 students. Management of such huge campuses required a large bureaucracy, imposing elaborate rules and regulations. Administrators searched for ways to make education efficient. They computerized student records and used other technologies like televised lectures. "They always seem to be wanting to make me into a number," one "megaversity" student complained.

Lost in the crowd, students had to contend with a maze of rules and regulations, especially those dictating social behavior for women. Many colleges had dress codes and set curfews by which women had to be in their dorms each night. When men visited, three of four legs had to be touching the floor at all times. The president of Vassar warned that girls who had sexual intercourse need not apply to her school. One university fired a professor for publicly condoning premarital sex among mature students. A woman might need permission from a dean if she wanted to get married. Since colleges and universities assumed the right to act in loco parentis, students had almost no rights. A carelessly thrown snowball, an amorous touch at the wrong moment, or too many curfew violations could lead to suspension or expulsion without the right of appeal. Most often administrators tried to manage student behavior rather than take student complaints seriously. They treated unhappiness as a sign of maladjustment, not a legitimate objection to the university's shortcomings. If the problem became severe, health service psychologists were there to help students adjust to norms as the university defined them. Students could not help but sense that the university sought not to educate them, but to turn them into conventional adults ready to fill a niche in a bureaucracy—"a cookie-cutter approach," as some disgruntled students called it.

Had administrators been more sensitive to their students, they might have seen trouble coming. Even before protest erupted at Berkeley in the fall of 1964, there were signs of student discontent. Political activism, spurred by the civil rights movement, had increased in both size and intensity. In 1962, Cornell student government ended compulsory ROTC. Students at Indiana persuaded the university to reject restrictions on political speech. In the spring of 1964, several hundred students at Brandeis protested the arbitrary imposition of stricter dorm visitation rules. Progressive campuses had already begun to bow to student pressures to reduce or eliminate parietal rules for women. Campus newspapers became more openly critical of bureaucratic regulations designed for the convenience of administrators rather than the best interests of students.

That did not stop the Berkeley administration in the fall of 1964 from extending its ban on campus political activities. Traditionally, student activists had a 26' by 96' area off Sproul Plaza where they set up tables, solicited funds, and disseminated literature. The new rule denied them that space, most likely because administrators were embarrassed by radicals and beatniks hanging around the main entrance to the campus. Many students saw the ban as an attack on civil rights groups, who most often used the space to raise funds and recruit. Throughout September, some twenty-two groups actively protested that decision. When activists defied the ban, deans penalized them for violating campus rules. During a "mill-in" inside the administration building, Mario Savio and seven other protesters were indefinitely suspended.

Prior to that summer, Savio was an undergraduate who transferred to Berkeley from Manhattan College. He failed to impress one SNCC interviewer who described him as "not very creative" and "not exceedingly perceptive." Mississippi sparked something new in him. That fall, "there was this single-mindedness of purpose and moral certainty that pushed him . . . and it came from Mississippi," a fellow Berkeley volunteer speculated. Savio now articulated the sense of anger and alienation many students had begun to feel.

On October 1, CORE activist and former student Jack Weinberg set up a table in the contested area of Sproul Plaza. Administrators called the police. But when the police tried to take Weinberg for booking, someone yelled, "Sit down!" Several hundred students surrounded the car, leaving the police in a quandary about what to do next. The sit-in continued for thirty-two hours before an agreement was reached. Several times, Savio removed his shoes so he could climb on the roof of the police car to address the crowd. And it was Savio who presented the movement's demands to the administration. When negotiations broke down, he led students into Sproul Hall for a second sit-in. After the administration agreed to terms, Savio was one of nine students to sign. He then returned to Sproul Plaza and his police car perch to urge the demonstrators to go home.

The mass defiance stunned university president Clark Kerr, an administrator more skilled as a manager than a leader. Kerr thought of himself as a liberal on most matters, but adopted a rather high-handed approach to governance. He suddenly found himself surrounded by angry students, a restive faculty, and conservative trustees who expected him to maintain order and protect the university's reputation. Kerr once joked that a successful college president had to provide just three things: sex for the undergraduates, winning football for the alumni, and parking spaces for the faculty. Such a managerial ethos did not prepare him to handle the country's first major campus upheaval. His goal was to end the demonstration, not to address the issues the students raised. When faced with student protest, he invoked the authority of the administration and the sanctity of campus regulations. If that failed, he threatened to turn loose hundreds of police called to the campus.

Free speech leaders showed repeatedly that they were far more adept at organizing protest than Kerr was at quelling it. By opposing the ban on political activity as a denial of the right to free speech, radicals appealed to moderate student groups. Nor were the protestors much bothered by Kerr's threat to use the police. Freedom Summer veterans like Savio had faced far worse in Mississippi. As one movement member remarked, "a student who has been chased by the KKK in Mississippi is not easily scared by academic bureaucrats." The protestors also understood from the civil rights movement that police violence against a nonviolent demonstration would embarrass the university. So they calculated that as long as the demonstrators sat in Sproul Plaza, they could extract compromises from Kerr. In return for an end to the sit-in, Kerr finally agreed to drop charges against Jack Weinberg. The students facing punishment for the mill-in would go before a faculty committee, and another committee with student members would negotiate new rules for campus political activities.

That compromise got students out of the plaza, but the trouble was far from over. The governor along with conservative politicians and trustees pressured Kerr to bring order to his campus and punish rule breakers. Kerr believed that he could stifle dissent simply by dragging his feet while student interest waned. Student activists sensed that neither Kerr nor his compromise was to be trusted. So they created an umbrella organization, much in the spirit of COFO, to maintain solidarity. Eventually some fifty individuals and group representatives joined the executive committee. They in turn picked a steering committee to manage day-to-day activities. The members agreed that mass student support was essential; with that support, faculty would then have to choose between the students and the administration. Savio impressed on them that given the importance of publicity, all meetings should be public. At the first meeting they adopted a name; they would become the free speech movement (FSM).

Rhetoric inspired by civil rights protest resonated with broad groups on campus. Free speech leaders held daily rallies in Sproul Plaza attracting up to 5,000 students. By late November, Kerr had voided every condition of the original compromise. He packed the committees with his sympathizers, reaffirmed the ban on political activities, and, on the 29th, announced that the administration would press new charges against Savio and other FSM leaders for their role in the October demonstrations. Kerr might just as well have set off a bomb among moderate students and faculty, many of whom had been until then uncomfortable with FSM tactics. Now they saw the administration as at best incompetent and at worst dishonest. On December 2, thousands of students gathered in Sproul Plaza to voice their outrage and demand amnesty for FSM leaders. Folk singer Joan Baez led the crowd in

When police forced Mario Savio from the microphone, they turned many moderate students into supporters of the Free Speech Movement.   (Source: Time Life Pictures/Getty Images)

singing Bob Dylan's "The Times They Are a Changin'" and the civil rights anthem "We Shall Overcome".

Once again, Savio gave voice to the anger and alienation so many students felt. In a speech to the crowd, he compared the autocracy running the university to those who dominated Mississippi. In this corporate enterprise, with Kerr as the manager and the trustees as its board of directors, "the faculty are a bunch of employees and we're the raw material." Savio then evoked an image from Charlie Chaplin's movie *Modern Times*: "There is a time when the operation of the machine becomes so odious, makes you so sick at heart, that you can't take part . . . ; and you've got to put your bodies upon the gears and upon the wheels, upon the levers, upon all the apparatus and you've got to make it stop. And you've got to make it clear to the people who run it, to the people who own it, that unless you're free, the machine will prevent you from working at all." In response, some 1,000 students moved into Sproul Hall to stage a sit-in. Once inside, FSM leaders organized "freedom classes" as part of what they called a "free university," very much in the spirit of the Mississippi freedom schools. The governor of California, decrying anarchy on the campus, insisted that Kerr have the activists jailed. At 4:00 A.M., with students settled in for the night, 600 police entered the building and began to make arrests. It took them until almost 5:00 the next afternoon to clear the building. This operation, netting almost 800 students, constituted the largest mass arrest in California history and attracted media coverage across the nation. Stunned Berkeley faculty, after voting to condemn the use of police on campus, declared their support for FSM. A student strike shut down at least half the classes on campus.

Support for FSM was not universal among students and faculty. Most fraternity members and Goldwater supporters remained openly hostile. Many Libertarian students who supported FSM goals objected to the use of illegal tactics. But the majority on campus had embraced FSM and its insistence on civil rights for students. Whatever support Kerr retained soon dissipated. At a December 7 meeting, attended by 16,000 faculty and students, he offered clemency to FSM leaders and "new and liberalized political action rules." As Kerr left the microphone, Savio crossed the stage to announce a rally for the next day. Campus police grabbed him before he reached the podium and dragged him backstage. As others leapt to his defense, police wrestled them offstage. The crowd was outraged. Chants went up: "We want Mario! We want Mario!" Eager not to antagonize the crowd, Kerr quickly consented, and Savio made his announcement. Kerr's gesture had come too late. Almost everyone there agreed with the judgment of one radical FSM leader who said "that episode more than any other single event revolutionized the thinking of many thousands of students." The faculty passed a motion that "speech or advocacy should not be restricted by the university." By this time, Kerr was so out of touch he did not realize that many of the trustees actually supported that position. The campus returned to an uneasy calm, soon to be disrupted by new waves of protest and unrest.

After the free speech movement, neither the university nor the nation would ever be the same. Perhaps what was most shocking was not the issue of free speech, but the idea that students had protested. Across the country administrators began to wonder what had happened to those orderly, clean-cut students of the 1950s. Kerr was as much or more offended by the protestors' behavior as by their demands. These students did not respect their elders. They freely broke rules, even the law, and a faction known as the "Filthy Speech Movement" sprinkled their speeches with obscenities. Critics of student protestors focused on a few who smoked dope or retired to a roof for recreational sex. These were behaviors society did not condone, even on college campuses. Bob Dylan was right: the times were changing.

∽

The free speech movement anticipated many aspects of the uncivil wars. As Freedom Summer historian Doug McAdam suggested, it applied the tactics and ideas of the civil rights movement to a broader array of issues. The sit-in tactic at Sproul Plaza and then in Sproul Hall was the trademark of nonviolent civil rights protest, though some radicals also identified it with the labor struggles of the 1930s. FSM also borrowed from the civil rights movement many of its anthems and protest songs. Music often expressed the spiritual yearning and identification with the oppressed that students might otherwise have been unable to articulate. On the simplest level, the act of singing together turned motley crowds into congregations. When FSM held press conferences to explain its side of the story, few in the media bothered to attend. Only the *New York Times* and *Los Angeles Times* bothered to present both sides of the confrontation. Media bias provoked many activists to begin their own newspapers and publications. In that way, FSM inspired a flourishing underground press that would include the Berkeley Barb, Los Angeles Free Press, and East Village Other.

FSM had a moral passion that a generation of alienated students came to embrace. Within a matter of months, that passion would have new targets, most especially the war in Vietnam and the corporate, capitalist culture that many protestors linked to the oppression of blacks in Mississippi, to the killing of peasants in Vietnam, and to the restrictions of free speech on university campuses. Some students chose not to protest but to move into subcultures that freed them from what they saw as a corrupt and spiritually dead world. Their protests, added to the civil rights unrest, would evoke sympathy among many college faculty and clergy, arouse a mixture of concern and puzzlement among their parents, and provoke outright hostility from those wedded to traditional notions of patriotism, social convention, and morality. After 1964, these tensions triggered the uncivil wars.

8

Teach-in, Strike Out:
The Uncivil Wars Heat Up

The idealism of the early 1960s evokes certain images: Peace Corps volunteers building schools in Third World villages, civil rights protestors braving enraged crowds, hippie communes, or, perhaps, antiwar protestors burning their draft cards and chanting "Hell No; We Won't Go." There were, however, other styles of idealism that shaped the era every bit as much. Without them, the uncivil wars could never have become so fractious. Throughout the 1960s, for example, the majority of Americans still embraced an uncritical patriotism. The conservative Young Americans for Freedom (YAF) had a far larger (though probably less visible) membership than leftist groups like Students for a Democratic Society (SDS). These clean-cut young Americans seldom marched or demonstrated. They attacked the Peace Corps as "a grand exercise in self-denial and altruism, paid for by the American taxpayers and administered by the United Nations." To YAF, those behind the free speech movement and antiwar protests at Berkeley were a motley crowd of beatniks, liberals, and Commies who needed to learn manners and to bathe more regularly. Sponsors of YAF included such flag-waving patriots as John Wayne, Ronald Reagan, and Senator Strom Thurmond.

Unlike YAFers and FSMers, most young Americans entered the 1960s without any political agenda at all. They became activists only when the era's conflicts caught them up or when boredom with the dullness of suburbia made them quest for windmills to tilt against. Young Philip Caputo was one such apolitical product of postwar American affluence. Caputo described his hometown as having everything a suburb should have: "sleek new schools, smelling of fresh plaster and floor wax; supermarkets full of Wonder Bread and Bird's Eye frozen peas, rows of centrally heated split levels that lined dirtless streets on which nothing ever happened." Oh, how Caputo longed for something important to do with his life. In the woods near his house, he found arrowheads and other fragments of the frontier past. Gazing on them, he began to "dream of that savage, heroic time" and wished he had lived then, "before America became a land of salesmen and shopping centers." John Kennedy's call for sacrifice stirred in him a desire for patriotic sacrifice.

Like many young men before him, Caputo found the challenge he sought, not in political or social activism, but in the U.S. Marine Corps. A chance encounter with recruiters on his college campus filled his head with heroic visions. "I saw myself charging up some distant beachhead, like John Wayne in *Sands of Iwo Jima,* and then coming home a suntanned warrior with medals on my chest," he recalled. Something else pushed him as well, the need "to prove something—my courage, my toughness, my manhood, call it what you like." Through the Marine Corps, Caputo would take quite another road from the one chosen by civil rights activists who went to Mississippi, yet he shared with them more than most observers of the sixties would ever recognize. Like them, he had "done something on my own; that it was something that went against my parents' wishes made it all the more savory. And I was excited by the idea that I would be sailing off to dangerous and exotic places after college rather than riding the 7:45 to some office." Caputo had become a rebel, albeit without a cause.

Dreams of glorious charges across bullet-swept beaches quickly gave way to the tedious realities of military training. Only the desire to succeed kept Caputo from succumbing to the mind-numbing repetition of close-order drill and classroom lectures on such topics as the M-14 rifle, "a handheld, gas-operated, magazine-fed, semiautomatic shoulder weapon." At Officer Candidate School, he was offered the opportunity to join the growing cult of counterinsurgency warfare specialists (Kennedy's military alternative to the Peace Corps). He rejected this clandestine calling for more routine service. By January 1965, as a young lieutenant, he was assigned to a marine infantry battalion stationed in Okinawa. This isolated Pacific island induced boredom so severe it inflicted both physical and psychological pain. Those in the military who experience it often develop a heightened desire for action, even if that means war and personal danger. Caputo wanted to go to Vietnam, not as a crusader against Communism, but as a soldier eager for the thrill of battle.

In January 1965, rumors began to circulate: the battalion was heading for Southeast Asia, maybe the Philippines, maybe . . . Then in late February it was official. Caputo and his men were headed for Danang in South Vietnam. They were part of a troop deployment to protect airbases. Vietcong rebels had recently attacked a U.S. helicopter base at Pleiku. The raid resulted in what were then considered heavy casualties—8 dead, 126 wounded, and 10 aircraft destroyed. In response, U.S. bombers unleashed heavy retaliatory raids against the North.

Service in Vietnam would change Caputo and other young American soldiers in ways none of them could have anticipated. Caputo would become almost addicted to the intensity of combat and the lurking sense of danger. Years later, he found himself hungering for the excitement he left behind. But fighting in a war in which the body count of suspected enemy dead, not territory captured, would measure success quickly disillusioned him. So, too, did the realization that many of his fellow officers saw Vietnam primarily as an opportunity to advance their careers. Like their leaders in Washington, they had scant concern for Vietnam or its people.

Even before he left Vietnam in 1966, Caputo had come to believe the war was unwinnable. "Every American life lost was a life wasted," he concluded. "Sir," one rear echelon clerk had countered, "if we pull out now, then all our efforts would have been in vain." That kind of thinking just made Caputo angry. He had barely survived court martial, profound bouts of depression, and suicidal despair. "In other words," he snapped back, "because we've already wasted thousands of lives, we should waste a few thousand more. Well, if you really believe that 'not in vain' crap, you should join a rifle company and go get yourself killed, because you deserve it." Such talk in 1966 constituted "borderline treason" Caputo recognized, but by then he was beyond caring. Back in the United States, he would join thousands of other disgruntled vets who formed Vietnam Veterans against the War. He even mailed his combat ribbons to the White House. They were returned with the ominous comment that his views would be communicated "to the attention of the proper authorities."

Lyndon Johnson's War

Presidents from Truman to Kennedy had deepened American involvement in Vietnam's civil war, but it was Lyndon Johnson who Americanized it. Vietnam was truly Lyndon Johnson's war. The expanded mission in Vietnam had in reality less to do with circumstances in Saigon than with politics in Washington. To civilian leaders, Vietnam was a small part of the larger cold war struggle. In January 1965, Assistant Secretary of State William Bundy had warned Johnson that the government in South Vietnam was coming apart. Fearing that the United States "was looking for a way out," Saigon leaders had no incentive to prosecute the war. In fact, intelligence revealed that key government groups were "starting to negotiate covertly with the Liberation Front [Vietcong] or Hanoi." Bundy worried less that South Vietnam would go Communist than that its neighbors would lose "any confidence at all in our continued support." A Communist Vietnam might actually serve as a bulwark against Chinese Communist expansion in the region. But a local Communist victory would look to Laotian, Cambodian, and Thai leaders and to conservatives at home as an American defeat.

That was an outcome Johnson would not countenance. As a result, Bundy recommended a stronger military policy in South Vietnam, in essence "to hold the next line of defense, namely Thailand." Put another way, Johnson and Bundy would shed Vietnamese and American blood to protect national prestige on the presumption that their actions in Vietnam would determine the fate of the government in Thailand and possibly elsewhere in Southeast Asia. An internal memorandum quantified the American objectives:

- 70 percent—To avoid a humiliating U.S. defeat (to our reputation as a guarantor).
- 20 percent—To keep SVN [South Vietnam] (and then adjacent) territory from Chinese hands.
- 10 percent—To permit the people of SVN to enjoy a better, freer way of life.

Such was the cruel calculus that would devastate much of Vietnam and cost in excess of three million lives.

The assignment to Vietnam that Caputo had seen as a stroke of fate had actually been foreordained by American policy. The attack at Pleiku gave Johnson and his advisers the excuse they needed to expand the American military role. Those who study foreign policy talk of the notion of "a search for a useable crisis." National leaders look for an event that will solidify popular opinion behind a course of action that might otherwise provoke widespread opposition. Until Pearl Harbor, the American people had opposed entry into World War II. After the Japanese attack, Franklin Roosevelt was able to lead a united nation into the war. Pleiku served Lyndon Johnson in somewhat the same way. Publicly, he called the Vietcong action an outrage against Americans. Privately, McGeorge Bundy (William Bundy's brother) admitted that the attack served as a pretext to bomb the North. The administration had long intended to implement an operations plan labeled Punitive and Crippling Reprisal Actions on Targets in North Vietnam. "Pleikus are like street-cars," Bundy remarked. The first one is not so important, because "there's one every ten minutes."

The Pentagon did not believe that stepped-up military operations would have a decisive impact on the course of Vietnam's civil war. General Maxwell Taylor had gone to Vietnam in December 1964 to survey the situation. While having few illusions about Saigon's ardor for fighting, he advised Johnson against sending ground troops. The presence of American combat forces would turn the Vietnamese against the United States, Taylor cautioned, "until like the French, we would be occupying an essentially hostile country." But since some action seemed necessary, Taylor had supported the bombing as "an old recipe with little attractiveness."

Why, then, did Johnson proceed down the path of escalation toward disaster? Again, the answer lies partially in history and partially in the defects of his character. As president, Johnson had scant interest in foreign policy or in Vietnam, but he remembered all too well the price that his generation of Democrats had paid for China's fall. He wanted to prosecute the war without endangering his domestic programs. So rather than openly present the administration's options for Vietnam, the ever-Machiavellian Johnson wanted to force the North to negotiate a settlement without provoking a major debate on the administration's Vietnam policy. Advisers like the Bundys supported the policy of gradual escalation. Johnson most feared that any show of weakness on Vietnam would mobilize his critics on the Right and their allies in the Pentagon.

The president also suspected that the war would be unpopular with the American public. He recalled that as the Korean War dragged on, public support quickly eroded. To avoid arousing popular opinion, administration officials avoided using the word "war" at all, even after Johnson secretly authorized the marines to begin combat operations. Pressure on the North could not work, however, if Saigon failed to prosecute the war or fell into chaos. Johnson believed that bombing would address all his concerns at the lowest risk, both politically and militarily. The North would learn the cost of continued hostilities, this sign of American commitment would bolster Saigon's leaders, hawks would applaud Johnson's toughness, while low casualty numbers would discourage domestic opposition.

In urging the bombing, the generals and admirals had an agenda that had more to do with bureaucratic politics than with Vietnam. Since 1961, Secretary of

Defense Robert McNamara had taken the reins of national defense policy ever more securely in his own hands. McNamara was a human dynamo obsessed with numbers and efficiency. He had appointed to the Joint Chiefs of Staff a "new breed" of "planners and thinkers, not heroes, team men, not gladiators." These officers understood the complexities of national security policy in a nuclear age. And far more than the war heroes they replaced, they were willing to defer to civilian authority.

Expansion of the war gave the fighting generals an opportunity to restore their influence over defense priorities. McNamara might still seem to be calling the shots, but it was the generals who picked the targets and the weapons. So when Johnson and McNamara asked for a way to fight the war more aggressively without a full-scale deployment, the Joint Chiefs of Staff had backed the use of retaliatory air strikes. In February 1965, Johnson authorized operation Rolling Thunder, a sustained bombing campaign against the North, but he left the timing of its implementation in the hands of his generals. They did not tell him, since he did not ask, that bombing would require more bases, and more bases, meant more ground troops. Hence, the generals understood that Caputo and his men were part of a trickle that would most likely become a torrent.

By choosing to escalate the war in this fashion, Johnson had failed to develop a public consensus for his Vietnam policy. Few Americans understood what stake their nation had in this remote Asian land. In the wake of the "hot line" to the Kremlin and the nuclear test–ban treaty, the cold war had lost much of its menace. Thus, Johnson escalated the war on a fragile base of domestic support. As the American role expanded and the fighting dragged on, opposition to the war mounted. The nation's attention shifted from the civil rights movement and the Great Society to a fundamental debate over the war and the ways it reflected on the character of American society. Was Vietnam an essential battlefront in America's crusade to preserve democracy by containing Communism, as supporters of the war argued? Or was the war a wanton assault by a technological giant against a rural peasantry in order to sate the imperial appetites of a permanent warfare state, as some critics claimed? Inability to reconcile those two points of view did much damage to the cold war consensus.

The Home Front

When Lyndon Johnson assessed the state of the union in late January 1965, he had reason to be optimistic. Americans had never had it so good. National wealth was growing at an annual rate of about 5 percent. Income was up, unemployment down, and inflation barely over 1 percent a year. Economists believed they could now eliminate downturns in the business cycle. The real issue was how to spend all the new wealth. One rash economist worried that the nation would run out of problems to solve before it had used all the means available to solve them. He had not reckoned on the grandiose visions of Lyndon Johnson.

As Johnson addressed the nation that night, he understood two critical realities of his political situation. The goodwill that had swept him into office would soon dissipate. He had to move quickly to realize his ambition to be one of the greatest presidents in history. Johnson also recognized that his aggressive support of civil rights had eroded support among ethnics and Southerners for the Democratic Party. So to preserve his party's majority, he proposed a legislative agenda that offered something for almost every potential constituency. For the young, there was aid to education and college scholarships; for the elderly, there was Medicare; urbanites would have mass transit; the cultural elite would have endowments for the arts and humanities; ethnics would have an immigration policy that no longer insulted their national origins; business would have tax cuts; labor, a revision in the much-despised Taft-Hartley law; for the emerging environmental movement, new park lands and cleaner water; and for the politicos, a feast of pork barrel projects.

This Great Society cornucopia was not just about politics. The liberal in Johnson truly hoped to level the playing field and lift the disadvantaged onto it. The sheer affluence of the moment allowed him to pursue that end without asking for sacrifice. The cost could be paid, not by reducing individual shares of the economic pie, but by making the pie bigger. Johnson invited the nation to ask "not how much, but how good; not only how to create wealth, but how to use it."

Almost no one who heard the president that night had any idea that the United States might be on the verge of crises at home or abroad. About the only comment that might have applied to Vietnam was Johnson's assertion that "to ignore aggression would only increase the danger of a larger war." That was, however, a standard cliché endlessly reiterated by cold warriors since 1945. In reality, cold war tensions had abated. One prominent analyst reported in early 1965 that both the Pentagon and the State Department "no longer fear the Communist power, nor do they expect the cold war to last forever." Here was a golden opportunity for the United States to play upon the divisions between its Communist foes. It would then stand unchallenged as the economic, political, and military leader of the world. "This then is the State of the Union," Johnson concluded, "free, growing, restless, and full of hope."

Out in Berkeley, the nation looked restless, indeed. On February 2, the *Daily Cal* at Berkeley ran an article that declared the free speech movement "for all practical purposes dissolved." In escalating the war, however, Johnson gave the rebels at Berkeley and at campuses across the nation a new cause. Even before the onset of Rolling Thunder, the *Daily Cal* reported, "student groups have conducted marches, pickets, rallies, and debates on the subject [of the American attacks on North Vietnam]." The paper also reported with a sniff of disdain that some "moronic individuals" had used red spray paint to scrawl on campus walls "Get the troops out of Vietnam" and other similar phrases. Three days later, Art Goldberg, a FSM activist, led 100 students in a protest at the Oakland Army terminal. Eighty Berkeley faculty members joined other prominent Bay Area residents in signing a full-page *New York Times* ad opposing American involvement in Vietnam.

Dissent against Vietnam did not begin at Berkeley, though the campus remained a major center of antiwar protest. The first critics of the war came from old pacifist groups, leftists, and the emerging New Left. At its December 1964 meeting, SDS had decided to organize a national demonstration against the war. That was an ambitious notion, considering that SDS had no more than a few thousand members and Vietnam was far from the organization's most burning concern. SDS organizer Todd Gitlin confessed that at the time he was more preoccupied with apartheid in South Africa. Over the summer of 1964, more than a hundred SDS volunteers had moved into the slums of Chicago, Philadelphia, Newark, and other cities to build a class-conscious interracial movement among the urban poor. The Economic Research and Education Project (ERAP), as this effort was called, took up much of the organization's energies and resources. But by late 1964, other groups on the Left had begun to seize the antiwar position. One Maoist group, M2M (the May 2d movement that splintered from the Communist Party), was circulating a "We Won't Go" petition that appealed to many SDS members. To preempt rivalry on the Left and to address growing opposition to the war, SDS decided to organize an antiwar rally in Washington for April 17.

A number of prominent liberals had already expressed doubts about the bombing. Democratic senators Frank Church of Idaho and George McGovern of South Dakota (a veteran of the World War II strategic bombing campaign) joined Senators Morse and Gruening as opponents of the retaliatory attacks. Johnson, who had little tolerance for criticism, especially from within his own party, reportedly told Church that "the next time you need a dam in Idaho, Frank, ask Walter Lippmann for one." Lippmann, an editorial writer for the *Washington Post* and the most influential foreign policy opinion maker outside of government, had doubts about the bombing, but had not yet become a vocal critic of Johnson's Vietnam policy. U Thant, secretary general of the United Nations, was more outspoken. Johnson, or more likely Secretary of State Dean Rusk, had rebuffed Thant's efforts to initiate peace negotiations. But in general, Vietnam at that time provoked little sustained dissent. By and large, Johnson's critics were civil in tone as was the president in his responses.

The civility began to erode in March of 1965 with the advent of teach-ins. No event more clearly reveals the process by which the Vietnam War divided the nation's elite. As activities at Berkeley suggested, significant numbers of students had already begun to worry about the morality of the war. Even more had anxieties because of their vulnerability to the military draft. Many faculty members shared their moral qualms and sympathized with their anxieties. At the University of Michigan, some faculty had grown increasingly uneasy with the bombing. How would they make their views more widely known? they began to wonder. William Gamson, a professor of sociology, had some experience in the civil rights movement. As a CORE officer in Boston, he had helped organize a school boycott by African-American children. Rather than just ask them to stay away from school, the organizers set up freedom schools, modeled on those in Mississippi, to teach black history and civil rights issues. This experience gave birth to the teach-in.

Looking for an effective way to voice their opposition to the bombing, a group of faculty suggested that they cancel classes and, instead, hold a day-long symposium based on the model of the freedom schools. Thirty-five agreed to participate. Many state legislators objected to what they saw as the politicizing of a public university for an unpatriotic activity. Chastened by the Berkeley experience, university administrators pressed Gamson and his group to modify their plans. The campus paper then announced that "Faculty Group Cuts Off Walkout, Plans Teach-in." In an ad addressed to the community, the protesting faculty explained that they were "deeply worried" (not opposed) to the war and sought alternatives. To that end, "we are devoting this night, March 24–25, to seminars, lectures, informal discussions, and a protest rally to focus attention on the war, its consequences, and ways to stop it." The moderate tone of the ad attracted many who would never before have thought of themselves as political activists. In a concession to the gender rules of the day, the ad announced that "women may obtain overnight permission from their house directors" if they wished to attend. Some three thousand students and faculty participated, along with two spokespersons from the State Department.

Nothing very radical happened at Michigan. The tone was earnest and generally without rancor. Still, the sit-in had struck a responsive cord. Students mixed on an equal footing with faculty they previously only saw in lecture halls. Education became relevant in a striking new way. One student recalled that "on that night, people who really cared talked of things that really mattered." Here was a small step toward a more democratic or egalitarian university culture. But as FSM and the spreading impatience with arbitrary campus rules had shown, a movement to liberalize the campus community was already underway. By late April and May, the teach-in strategy had spread to hundreds of campuses. Where civil rights had once dominated the conversation of socially committed students and faculty, they now debated the merits of escalation in Vietnam.

Equally significant, the media had noticed. Always on the lookout for something new and unusual, newspapers and television publicized this outbreak of political fervor at the nation's leading schools. Much of the commentary was hostile, since most leading journalists accepted the premises of the cold war consensus. Many critics implied that "Communists and crypto-Communists" had inspired campus debate. The media also noticed on April 17 when an SDS-sponsored march against Vietnam attracted some 15,000–30,000 protestors to Washington (crowd estimates are notoriously flawed because they reflect the bias of the counter). The crowds came despite efforts to discredit the demonstration as a "pro-Communist production." Yes, there was subversion afoot, but it was pure New Left, not old leftist Communism. SDS leader Paul Potter defined the New Left position when he attacked "the system," a vague though powerful concentration of economic and political power, manifest in such diverse forms as "war in Vietnam," "murder in the South," and "atrocities that worked on people all over—all the time." For Potter, the mission of the protestors was clear: "We must name the system," he demanded, and then concluded that "all our lives, our destinies, depend on our ability to overcome that system." As one student observed, such opposition was about something more than the war: "Vietnam was for some, then, a symbol of the deeper ills of society."

These early protests were significant not so much for the numbers they attracted (which were relatively small though large by past standards), but for who the people were and where they came from. That is a major reason Lyndon Johnson paid attention to them. Johnson had a politician's contempt for "pointy headed intellectuals." Yet the sensitive side of him craved their approbation. Many of his advisors with close ties to academia were also sensitive to this unprecedented upsurge in protest from the university community. So, too, was J. Edgar Hoover. He refused to see the protests as either spontaneous or sincere. Instead, he fed Johnson's suspicions that Communist agents with funds from Hanoi and Moscow had organized the protest. At Hoover's direction, the FBI began systematically infiltrating the student movement. Hoover understood that investigation served as a form of intimidation.

Most of the administration's efforts to silence protest backfired. A white paper issued in February made a seemingly well-documented case that North Vietnam had launched a "concealed aggression" against the "sovereign people" of South Vietnam. Critics quickly punctured its central arguments. I. F. Stone, a highly regarded independent journalist who had courageously attacked McCarthyism at its height, pointed out that the United States had militarized South Vietnam's government and escalated the violence, while the North and the Chinese had been willing to abide by the Geneva Accords of 1954. McGeorge Bundy admitted the white paper had been a disaster. Truth squads, with speakers sent from the State Department to make the administration's case, succeeded largely in provoking the wrath of war protestors.

In a speech at Johns Hopkins University in April, Johnson had sought to silence domestic opposition by offering Hanoi "unconditional discussions" and a grand plan for a TVA (Tennessee Valley Authority)–styled regional development project for the Mekong delta. As he spoke, planes from Rolling Thunder continued to pummel the North. And Johnson's "unconditional" offer had many hidden conditions. The North, in fact, did agree to talks, but on the condition that the United States pledge to withdraw and the Vietnamese people be allowed to settle their dispute without foreign interference. That meant holding elections under the terms of the Geneva Accords, elections that the administration knew its allies in the South would lose.

Johnson's advisers urged him to reject Hanoi's proposal. Negotiations, they argued, must take place from a position of strength, and that meant an improvement in the military situation in the South. When critics pointed out that Hanoi would not negotiate as bombs fell, Johnson in May ordered a brief bombing halt. That left Hanoi with a devil's choice: to call off a war it had not started or to face continued bombing. Hanoi refused to negotiate on the terms Johnson dictated. In fact, his intention was not so much to open negotiations, but to shore up domestic support by making Hanoi appear unreasonable. And so the war continued and domestic criticism in the United States mounted.

Even more damaging to Johnson's credibility than the white paper and the phony bombing halt was the decision he made in late April to send marines into the Dominican Republic. In this, one of the poorest nations in the western hemisphere, a liberal democratic coalition led by Juan Bosch had attempted to overthrow a repressive and corrupt right-wing military dictatorship. Liberal and conservative Dominicans alike opposed the dictatorship, but it had the backing of the United States. The American embassy inaccurately portrayed the uprising as a Castro-like revolution. Violence, an official claimed, threatened American lives. So once again, the marines poured into the island. Most Americans accepted Johnson's rationale that Communism had again reared its menacing head. Those in the antiwar camp thought otherwise. American forces had been sent to kill Dominicans, who were "fighting and dying for social justice and constitutionalism," so that another corrupt military dictatorship could rule. Todd Gitlin remembers being so disturbed he thought "for the first time that I belonged to a 'we' that had no choice but to fight against America's armed power." Unfortunately for Johnson, those in the antiwar camp were not alone in condemning his decision to send the marines. Senator J. William Fulbright, a sponsor of the Tonkin Gulf Resolution, believed Johnson had deceived the Senate and the American people. Once he broke with Johnson over the Dominican intervention, Fulbright began to criticize the administration on Vietnam.

As antiwar sentiment spread within the political establishment, it also grew widely within the cultural elite. Johnson's court intellectual, Eric Goldman, a Princeton history professor, had organized a White House Festival of the Arts as a way to signify the administration's support for culture. This apolitical event suddenly became political. In early June, poet Robert Lowell refused to attend because he opposed the president's Vietnam policy. The *New York Times* featured Lowell's action in a front-page news story. Letters of support came from other prominent artists and writers. During the festival, novelist John Hersey pointedly read from *Hiroshima*, even though Lady Bird Johnson had tried to dissuade him. Critic Dwight Macdonald used the occasion to circulate an anti-Johnson petition. Johnson felt the intellectuals had betrayed him. "I don't think I'll ever get credit for anything I do in foreign policy," he complained to Goldman, "because I didn't go to Harvard." So rather than hear his critics, the thin-skinned Johnson chose to demean them personally or to ignore them. Fulbright, for example, he dismissed as a "little old lady" disappointed he had not been named secretary of state.

Summer brought a lull in antiwar protest as students left their campuses. It did not bring any respite in the war. Instead, on July 28, Johnson announced he would send an additional 50,000 troops, bringing the total to 125,000. In fact, he sent closer to 100,000, but misrepresented the number to lessen the political backlash. He also turned down a Pentagon request to mobilize the reserves and, instead, chose to double the draft. Johnson calculated that a call-up of reservists would stir opposition since they often had jobs, homes, and families. By contrast, the pool of eligible draftees, swollen by the baby boom, would minimize the impact of the increased inductions. Almost anyone who cared to could find a way to avoid the draft. Johnson also decided not to ask for a tax increase to pay for the rapidly rising cost of the war. Once again, his attempts to depoliticize escalation misfired. Higher draft calls increased the skepticism of many college-aged young men about the purposes of the war. Those without moral or political cause to question the war now had a self-interested reason to do so.

From the perspective of the antiwar movement, perhaps the most critical decision that summer was not one that it made, but one it did not make. The success of the April 17 march in Washington had left SDS as the logical organizer of future protests. This was not the role SDSers envisioned. They saw themselves as a force for domestic change, though most of them had been pleased by the success of the Washington march. That did not mean, however, they were prepared to organize antiwar efforts in a systematic fashion. Besides, antiwar sentiment had grown so rapidly that they had no idea how to capture it. Many of them were depressed that the march had no impact on Johnson's war policies. They saw future antiwar demonstrations as a liberal political strategy that achieved nothing, while the war ground on. Those involved in anti-poverty work resisted turning the organization over to foreign policy protest. So, too, did a new crowd of SDS members, who first showed up at the Michigan convention that summer.

The founding members of SDS had tended to be intellectual in their analysis of politics. The new breed of "prairie power" radicals took a non-cerebral and anarchic approach. Many of them came from staid midwestern and western communities and had rebelled against conservative, often Republican parents. They believed in direct action, not analysis, and had no interest in formulating a strategic vision. Most preferred getting stoned to debating politics. In those ways, they had more in common with the underground hippie movement that emerged around this time. So the combination of dissent within SDS, the more spontaneous approach of the prairie radicals, and the reluctance of SDS veterans to redefine themselves as an antiwar group resulted in a decision to let antiwar protest develop on its own. So by default, responsibility for organizing shifted to a loose coalition of leftists and peace groups which called itself the National Coordinating Committee to end the War in Vietnam (NCC). Deep divisions existed within this group between factions of the socialist and Communist Left. So at the moment of its coming of age, the New Left was barely organized and often deeply divided.

A New World for Catholics

American conservatives and Catholics were particularly sensitive to the social change sweeping the nation. They feared that the secular trends of modernity threatened Christian faith. Pope John XXIII worried instead that the Catholic Church had failed to address the issues of the modern world. Despite his advancing cancer, Pope John called together the Church Council, Vatican II, to deal with issues ranging from the use of Latin in church services to poverty, nuclear war, atheism, and birth control. Having begun in October of 1962, Pope John did not live to see the council concluded. His successor, Paul VI, finished his work when the council concluded in 1965.

Vatican II transformed the Catholic Church. On a superficial level, some changes seemed small, though they altered church practices in fundamental ways. Certain traditions were gone: fish on Friday, confession on Saturday, and compulsory church attendance on Sunday. More consequentially, American priests would now face the congregation and conduct the mass in English rather than Latin. The laity or church members would have a greater role in implementing the faith. Local bishops gained more control over church matters. Vatican II also encouraged the spirit of ecumenicalism by which Catholics would seek greater understanding with other Christians. The council even indicated that it might alter its strict ban against artificial means of birth control.

All of these steps were intended to keep the church in tune with the spiritual needs of Catholics in the modern world. Vatican II called on the faithful to embrace as their own the "griefs and anxieties of the men of this age, especially those who are poor or in any way afflicted." That spirit inspired a new commitment to social action among many nuns and priests such as the Berrigan brothers, Daniel and Philip, who became crusaders for social justice and outspoken foes of the war in Vietnam. Eventually, the church would rein in these activists, as conservatives tried to limit the impact of Vatican II. All the same, historian Garry Wills concluded, "Catholics live in a different world since the council."

Riot and Ruin: Racial Politics

The same spirit that moved some Catholic clergy to social activism similarly affected Jews and mainline Protestant denominations. They saw the unfinished civil rights revolution and the concentration of poverty and discontent within the ghettos of the nation's cities as a cause for moral witness. In that spirit, the Reverend Martin Luther King had recently won the Nobel Peace Prize. With his prestige high, King had turned his efforts to voting rights in Alabama. Civil rights activists there showed tremendous courage in facing the violence of Governor Wallace and the police of Alabama. With support from Lyndon Johnson, SCLC organized a five-day march from Selma to the capitol in Montgomery. On March 21, clergy were prominent among the some 3,200 people who left Selma and the over 20,000 more people who joined them for the final three and a half miles. Inspired by the marchers' example, Congress passed the Voting Rights Act of 1965 that eliminated many of the barriers southern states had erected to deny blacks the suffrage.

Despite that stunning success, not all was well within the civil rights community. King had attracted white support and neutralized moderate segregationists by emphasizing nonviolence and integration. The strength of his movement lay in the South. But since World War II, millions of blacks had migrated to urban areas in the North, upper Midwest, and West. There they encountered forms of de facto

Catholic, Jewish, and Protestant Clergy were among the leaders of the crowd who marched to Selma, Alabama, in 1965 to promote voting rights. (Source: Associated Press)

segregation that were harder to attack through legal and political means. As blacks poured into the cities, economic and political power was draining out to the suburbs. So vast numbers of blacks found themselves effectively disenfranchised politically and marginalized economically. To them, King's doctrine of nonviolent protest and integration held out little hope for improvement.

Impatient with the gradualist tactics of mainstream civil rights, many northern blacks turned to leaders who preached a doctrine of racial pride, solidarity among blacks, and separation or independence from an oppressive white society. The popularity of Marcus Garvey in the 1920s indicated the appeal of Black Nationalism. After World War II, the most influential among these separatists was the Lost-Found Nation of Islam. Its leader, Elijah Muhammad (born Elijah Poole), had migrated in the 1920s from a dirt-poor sharecropper's farm in Georgia to find work in Detroit's booming auto industry. The Depression cost him his job and left him searching for an explanation for the misfortune of blacks in America. He found it in the preaching of an Arab silk merchant who blamed black misery on scheming whites. Using a variety of Eastern texts, Poole developed a set of religious doctrines vaguely linked to traditional Islam and adopted the surname Muhammad. Elijah Muhammad's brand of Islam rejected the Christian faith of most blacks, arguing that "blue-eyed devils" had converted them to Christianity to make them more submissive.

Muhammad preached to blacks that they were God's chosen who would one day see Allah destroy white civilization. His vision of racial pride and self-improvement appealed to all ranks of ghetto society, but especially to its lowest elements among the poor. Black Islam demanded of its adherents a new kind of discipline and hard work. Vice was out; marital fidelity, education, and economic initiative were in. Among those who heard this message of racial uplift was a bright young convicted thief, pimp, and dope dealer named Malcolm Little. Little had watched helplessly as the Depression and the general indifference of whites to the well-being of blacks destroyed his family. In prison, he embarked on a course of self-education, reading widely and learning foreign languages. His younger brother introduced him to the ideas of Elijah Muhammad, with whom he began a correspondence. Seven years after entering prison, he emerged as an eager convert to Black Islam with the name Malcolm X.

Few public figures of the 1960s aroused more curiosity and fear in white America than Malcolm X. On the one hand, he and the Black Muslims adopted behaviors that were decidedly middle class. On the other, Malcolm had a message most whites found menacing. "Our enemy is the white man!" he preached. When criticized for calling all whites devils, he countered, "You cannot find one black man, . . . who has not been personally damaged by the devilish acts of the collective white man!" Malcolm dismissed all civil rights initiatives as nonsense. He called on blacks to separate from white society into "a land of our own, where we can reform ourselves, lift up our moral standards, and try to be godly."

The black civil rights establishment also came to fear Malcolm. Where they called for reform and integration, he preached revolution: "Who ever heard of angry revolutionists harmonizing 'We Shall Overcome Suum Day . . .' while they were tripping and swaying along arm-in-arm with the very people they were supposed to be angrily revolting against?" Even the exalted Dr. King with his Nobel Prize was not immune. "If I'm following a general, and he's leading me into battle," Malcolm remarked, "and the enemy tends to give him rewards, or awards, I get suspicious of him. Especially if he gets a peace prize before the war is over." Such outrageous comments attracted eager, though hostile, attention from the white media. Malcolm's growing celebrity became the envy of other black leaders, who could not help but notice that black audiences of all classes applauded his barbed commentary. When they called him extremist or irresponsible, he shot back, "you show me a black man who isn't extremist and I'll show you one who needs psychiatric attention!" When they accused him of playing on emotions, he asked with derision, if "a man is hanging on a tree and he cries out, should he cry out unemotionally?"

Unfortunately for Malcolm, moderate civil rights leaders were not the only black leaders who saw him as a threat. The conservative Elijah Muhammad had no desire to immerse the Nation of Islam in racial politics. Over time, Malcolm grew ever more disillusioned with a disengaged approach and with revelations that his spiritual leader had quite ordinary carnal appetites. The two split in March of 1964.

A trip to Africa and Mecca introduced Malcolm to varieties of Black Nationalism and a more tolerant form of Islam. His many engagements on college campuses revealed to him that not all whites were inherently evil, even if a racist society promoted evil behavior. In time, Malcolm tried to meld his growing acceptance of whites with his revolutionary fervor. "If you attack a man because he is white," he told one reporter, "you give him no way out. He can't stop being white." He also attended the 1964 NAACP convention with the idea neither of accepting integration nor rejecting separatism. His goal now was "a society in which people can live like human beings on the basis of equality."

Malcolm's ghetto audience preferred his splenetic assault on white America to this more nuanced worldview. His former Nation of Islam brethren tracked him everywhere. On February 21, 1965, three Black Muslims in the front row of his audience gunned him down. Malcolm X joined the ranks of martyrs who had died, as he came to believe, "in the cause of brotherhood."

The assassination silenced one of the most astringent voices in black America; it did not, however, alleviate the ghetto misery and discontent to which his message appealed. Nor did the many initiatives of the Great Society, its war on poverty, or the successes of the civil rights movement. Younger civil rights activists had grown increasingly restive with the doctrine of nonviolence. They had faced too many lunging dogs, baton-swinging police, and armed night riders to believe they should still turn a beaten cheek. On a sweltering August day in Los Angeles, only five days after Lyndon Johnson signed the Voting Rights Act, the smoldering remains of racial civility burst into flames. A white police officer arrested Marquette Frye for speeding. The officer was polite; Frye was drunk. A small crowd gathered to watch as Frye bantered pleasantly with the officer. His mother chided him for being intoxicated and urged him to cooperate. Suddenly, at the thought of jail, he panicked. Too often, he had seen what white police did to black men. His string of obscenities attracted more bystanders and his brother Ronald. Another officer arrived, took one look at the crowd, saw the angry Frye brothers confronting his fellow officer, and radioed for help.

One thing led to another. Somebody spit; the police arrested a woman who was trying to get away from trouble and shoved her roughly into a patrol car. Rumors spread that the police had assaulted a pregnant woman and taken her away. Soon rocks and bottles filled the air. This was, after all, Watts, not some pleasant residential neighborhood. Behind the facades of stucco houses, Watts was as desperate as any ghetto community in America. Each block had four times as many people as any other section of Los Angeles. Over a third of the men were unemployed. City services scarcely existed. Residents viewed the police as an occupying army more than a form of law enforcement. No matter how guilty Frye might have been, his arrest seemed like another in an endless string of indignities. With the heat, the rumors, the frustrations, the community snapped. Some 5,000 Watts residents set out in a frenzy of rioting, looting, arson, and gunfire. When comedian Dick Gregory appealed for calm, someone shot him in the leg.

Though their neighborhood lay in ruins, many young African-Americans saw the Watts riots as a triumph, since white authorities could no longer ignore them. (Source: Associated Press)

It took six days, 14,000 National Guardsmen, and several thousand police to quell the rioting. By the time the shooting stopped and the fires were out, 34 people had died (32 of them black), 900 people were injured, 4,000 were arrested, hundreds of families were left homeless, and most businesses were destroyed. The rioting had not spared black businesses either, even when the owners put signs in their windows saying "owned by a brother" or "soul brother." Many of the rioters had no higher purpose than to express anger or to seize a little piece of American materialism. White Americans predictably condemned the violence. Lyndon Johnson spoke for much of the nation when he argued "neither old wrongs nor new fears can justify arson and murder."

For Martin Luther King the riots presented a problem of another kind. A smoldering Watts was a rebuke to his doctrine of nonviolence. Touring the ruins, he came to understand something of the despair that had provoked the rioters. Still, he was taken aback when a band of young blacks announced defiantly, "We won!" "How can you say you won," King asked, "when thirty-four [sic] Negroes are dead, your community is destroyed and whites are using the riot as an excuse for inaction?" None of that mattered to them: "We won because we made them pay attention to us."

In that remark, King confronted the depth of alienation in black urban America. He now understood that the successes of the civil rights movement did not address the despair that defined the ghetto. Even the more radical elements in SNCC seemed for the time being unable to respond to the rapidly changing racial climate. Beleaguered by charges they harbored Communists, wearied by beatings and long days in jail, and uncertain whether to take a stand on Vietnam, SNCC entered the period after Watts without a sense of direction. That became most evident when Robert Moses changed his name to Robert Parris, left SNCC, and returned to the North. More radical figures like Stokely Carmichael and H. Rap Brown would give SNCC new energy, but the Beloved Community was dead. In the future, both SNCC and CORE would exclude whites.

Patriots to the Fore

From the summer of 1965 until the spring of 1967, the violence of the American war effort in Vietnam escalated. Troop levels rose to over 400,000, the number of targets in North Vietnam expanded, while the total tonnage of bombs dropped exceeded that of World War II in Europe. Casualty levels rose too. Fourteen hundred Americans died in 1965; around 5,000 died in 1966. The strategy of combat guaranteed indiscriminate killing of Vietnamese peasants. American "search and destroy" units would scour the countryside, hoping to find the enemy. Sometimes they would draw sniper fire; sometimes they would walk into an ambush. If that had happened in Korea, the patrol would have grouped, opened fire, and charged. Not in Vietnam. The patrol leader would halt his men in place before calling in air strikes and artillery fire from distant bases. Such indiscriminate firepower was certain to destroy Vietcong and civilians alike. American troops began to realize they were being used not as warriors, but as bait.

Try as they might, American military leaders could not draw the enemy into large-scale battles. The Vietcong might study the lure, but they never tried to swallow it. When American troops arrived, the VC would fade into the jungle or blend in among the peasants. GIs on patrol learned to walk jungle paths with a slow shuffle and cautious eye, on the lookout for a wire or a piece of vine that seemed unnaturally straight. "We took more casualties from booby traps than we did from actual combat," one frustrated medic recalled. "It was very frustrating because how do you fight back against a booby trap? You're just walking along and all of a sudden your buddy doesn't have a leg. Or you don't have a leg." Yet the villagers would walk the same paths, seemingly oblivious to danger. "It's very easy to slip into a primitive state of mind," one marine admitted, "particularly if your life is in danger and you can't trust anyone." Many American soldiers focused their fears and anger on the peasants. Atrocities and accidental deaths became commonplace.

The air war was equally frustrating. Unlike Germany or Japan, Hanoi had no centralized industrial economy. Most of its war goods were shipped from China or came on Soviet ships through ports in Cambodia. What industry Hanoi had it scattered and moved underground. So, too, it hid its major supply routes such as the Ho Chi Minh Trail under the jungle canopy. Eventually, the Americans began to make war on the jungle itself. By spraying large areas with defoliants such as Agent

Orange, they sought to deny the enemy the cover of triple canopy growth. Jellied gas bombs, or napalm, burned everything and everybody in its path. Daisy cutters sprayed lethal clouds of metal fragments. With such ghoulish devices, the American military adapted its deadly arsenal to the special circumstances of jungle warfare.

"Search and destroy" turned the land campaign into a war of attrition in which Americans used the number of enemy dead or body count as the measure of their success. Those who died in fire fights and massive bombing raids were often the same peasants whose "hearts and minds" the Americans needed to win if they wanted to isolate the enemy. That meant, just as Hanoi calculated, the war would be a long one, and the American role an increasingly unpopular one both at home and among the Vietnamese. And that proved Lyndon Johnson's undoing, for he had assumed, as many of his military and civilian advisers assured him would be the case, that American military might would quickly bring the Vietcong to its knees and Hanoi to the bargaining table. Instead, the war dragged on and the casualty figures mounted.

The antiwar movement did not escalate as rapidly as the war did. Protestors remained a vocal though somewhat isolated group. The president continued to worry about them, because the idea of protest was itself so exceptional and because he understood that the war would grow increasingly unpopular if it was not resolved quickly. The vast majority of Americans backed the war effort, though they had little understanding of the scale of American involvement or the reasons Americans were fighting. Instead, they rallied behind their president, their boys in battle, and their nation's fight to contain Communism. Prominent Americans took out newspaper ads expressing their support. By any measure of status or influence, the prowar elite at this time outranked the antiwar elite.

The existence of protest did lead to increased media coverage of the war. While the Pentagon did not directly censor news footage from Vietnam, it did pressure reporters to give their stories a positive spin. Those who told the truth or filed controversial stories found themselves isolated from privileged sources. In August 1965, CBS reporter Morley Safer discovered the price of candor. Safer and his camera crew had accompanied a marine platoon on patrol. They moved into a village reported to have given aid to the Vietcong. To make an example of them, the marines did a Zippo job, that is, they used cigarette lighters to set fire to the thatched huts as Safer's camera rolled. "We had to burn the village to save it," was the rationale they offered for their actions. Back home, viewers saw the footage after hearing administration officials assure reporters that such things never happened. The next morning, an irate Lyndon Johnson was on the phone with CBS president Frank Stanton. "Frank," Johnson bellowed into the phone, "are you trying to fuck me? Frank, this is your president and yesterday your boys shat on the American flag."

Such pressures encouraged self-censorship by the media, especially television. Almost the only place Americans could learn about the war was in the newspapers and journals that generally adopted a pro-administration stance. So it behooved Johnson to understate war issues and avoid turning demonstrators into martyrs, since the public generally viewed them with hostility or as outright traitors. That was the case with the International Days of Protest held on October 15 and 16. The *New York Times* reported that as many as 100,000 people had demonstrated in over ninety cities. As many as 10,000 came out in Berkeley alone. Media reports, instead, stressed the role of radicals, especially SDS, in organizing the event and promoting scattered acts of civil disobedience. In fact, SDS had played only a secondary part.

November brought several events that indicated the fragility of support for the war. On the one hand, The National Coordinating Committee (NCC) had fallen into factional warfare among old leftists and new antiwar radicals. That left traditional pacifist groups like SANE to organize protest. Somewhere between 20,000 and 40,000 protestors marched in Washington on November 27. What was striking about this group was its middle-class and establishment character. Among its most notable figures was Dr. Benjamin Spock, the baby boomers pediatrician. Joining Dr. Spock was Coretta Scott King, the wife of Martin Luther King. Her appearance indicated the growing convergence of mainstream civil rights and antiwar groups. The *New York Times* did manage to deflate the modest success of the protest by running a story that the organizers had received a grateful message from the Vietcong.

The impact of that news was offset by a story published in *Look*, a popular family magazine, about Adlai Stevenson's troubled last days. The author was highly respected television news analyst Eric Sevareid, so it had the stamp of authenticity. Stevenson until his death in 1965 had been the darling of the Democratic Party's liberal wing. What troubled Stevenson was his knowledge that UN secretary general U Thant had initiated peace talks with Hanoi in late 1964. Stevenson believed that Thant's initiative might have brought about productive negotiations, except the United States had refused to talk. So the story suggested that Washington, not Hanoi, was the obstacle to peace. Johnson did not deny the story; he claimed, instead (and probably honestly), that he had never heard about the peace proposal. Episodes like this one helped split the liberal establishment into a peace faction that mistrusted Johnson and cold war liberals who saw the Vietnam War as essential to containment.

Johnson's decision to call a bombing halt did indicate that protest was having an impact. No one in the administration believed the halt would have an effect on Hanoi, which still insisted on an end to bombing and American withdrawal as essential peace terms. Rather, Johnson and his advisors hoped the pause might divide Communist bloc nations and convince the American public of the administration's sincerity. "The weakest link in our armor is public opinion," Johnson told his advisers. On the other hand, Johnson had pretty much written off the liberal peace establishment. As his press secretary Jack Valenti put it, "the minute we resume [bombing] . . . the doves, the Lynd-liners [radical historian Staughton Lynd], and the *Times* will shriek." With the Left gone, Johnson worried more about the hard Right. His good friend and mentor Senator Richard Russell, the Georgian heading the Armed Services Committee, had told Johnson, "go all the way. . . . This is an unpopular war but the people want us to win it." So to show his toughness to the Right and to Hanoi as well as his independence from the doves, Johnson in late January 1966 resumed the bombing.

As Johnson anticipated, protests followed, though not in great numbers. What he had not expected was the overt opposition of Senator Fulbright. Fulbright was truly a Senate anomaly. Like Johnson a Southerner, he hailed from Arkansas, at the time one of the most culturally backward states in the union. Fulbright, by contrast, was a Rhodes scholar who had made foreign policy his specialty, though few Arkansans shared that interest. He may be best remembered for the exchange program that sends American scholars to foreign universities. Fulbright retained his political base at home by maintaining an impeccable record as a segregationist. His independence in foreign policy meant that the administration seldom sought the approval of the Foreign Relations Committee. By 1965, he was convinced Johnson had deceived him on the Dominican intervention and now had serious doubts about the administration's policy for Vietnam. The day Johnson announced he would resume the bombing, Fulbright announced his committee would hold hearings on the war. Not that he expected to change Johnson's mind; rather, he saw hearings as a way to change public opinion and a few senatorial minds.

Johnson was infuriated—and not without cause. The clash of antiwar Senate doves and expert witnesses with prowar administration spokespersons was the stuff of public drama. The three major networks, recalling earlier successes with the army-McCarthy hearings, decided to put them on the air. At one point, however, CBS suspended coverage of the hearings in favor of an *I Love Lucy* rerun. The head of the news division was so outraged he resigned, though the network claimed its decision was a response to local affiliates and not an attempt to suppress unfavorable views. Johnson certainly was capable of trying to intimidate the media. No doubt he called a hastily arranged meeting with South Vietnam's president Nguyen Cao Ky to divert attention.

Still, the witnesses came and the public—some twenty-two million—watched. Most of those who spoke before the committee such as Secretary of State Dean Rusk defended administration policy. They did so, however, under intense and sometimes hostile questioning from the committee. Two unfriendly witnesses, George Kennan and General Maxwell Taylor, questioned current policy rather than the decision to escalate. Antiwar forces took heart that two such pillars of the cold war establishment had registered even a partial dissent. Nonetheless, a favorable public response generally comforted the administration. For the moment at least, it had bested its critics.

No amount of presidential jawboning could cover up one harsh reality: the human cost of the war was rising, even for Americans. By 1966, few families did not know someone with a son in Vietnam or who might soon go. Increasingly, young Americans had friends who had been killed, wounded, or returned from the war like Philip Caputo, strangely changed. The America they returned to was in the midst of a social revolution that would deepen the divisions of its uncivil wars.

9
The Great Freak Forward

In 1958, Mao Tse-tung organized "the great leap forward" to mobilize the peasant masses of China's countryside. Six years later, a group from La Honda, California, set off on a cross-country trek to disorganize the America masses. "Get them into your movie before they get you into theirs," Ken Kesey told his motley crew. The set was America; the cast—the Merry Pranksters and anybody in their path. The vehicle was a 1939 International Harvester schoolbus laid out with bunks, a refrigerator, and a sound system amplified to blow your socks off. If the sound failed to make an impression, the bright, swirling Day-Glo paint job certainly would. A hole in the roof allowed the passengers an unimpeded view of the world.

The crew, in their long hair, costumes, masks, body paint, and irreverent swatches of American flag, looked as outrageous as the bus. Kesey financed the coast-to-coast acid bacchanalia with proceeds from his critically and commercially successful novel, *One Flew over the Cuckoo's Nest*. That novel had featured Chief Broom, a precursor of the counterculture's fascination with Native Americans, and McMurphy, the rebel who blew the minds of the authoritarians who tried to suffocate his irrepressible spirit. Along with Kesey, who called himself "the Swash-buckler," the crew included such acid luminaries as cameraman Mal Function, the Intrepid Traveler, Gretchen Fetchin the Slime Queen, Doris Delay, and at the wheel and fresh out of San Quentin prison, the amphetamine-chewing "holy primitive" of the Beats, Neal Cassady. On board to record the story of this antic odyssey was Tom Wolfe, a leading practitioner of the "new journalism." Unlike reporters whose traditions of objectivity prevented them from revealing themselves in a story, the new journalists and their experiences were the story. And this story of Ken Kesey and his Merry Pranksters became *The Electric Kool-Aid Acid Test*, one of the bibles of the emerging counterculture.

After a stint as a laboratory guinea pig in which he sampled hallucinogenic and psychedelic drugs, Kesey had settled near the coast in La Honda. There, he contin-ued to initiate a band of friends, faculty from nearby Stanford, beatniks, and dropout kids into the mind-bending properties of LSD. Never one short of words, Kesey described the early, untutored trips as "shell-shattering ordeals that left us blinking kneedeep in the crack crusts of our pie-in-the-sky personalities. Suddenly people were stripped before one another and behold: we were beautiful. Naked and helpless and sensitive as a snake after skinning but far more human than that shin-ing nightmare that had stood creaking at parade rest. We were alive and life was us."

In that outburst, Kesey captured the link between LSD and the cultural upheavals of the uncivil wars. First, Kesey had spoken of the idea of personal revelation and

Ken Kesey's 1939 International Harvester bus, Further, *became a visual icon of the new acid-inspired psychedelic subculture.* (Source: Courtesy of Don Williams/New Millenium Writings)

transformation. Most trippers thought that LSD had the power to liberate people from the repressive forms of society and return them to a state of nature. Drug-induced visions inspired transcendence to a higher creative and spiritual plain. LSD was not about thinking, but about feeling; it moved people into "the ever widening Present." In short, psychedelics had the power to remake consciousness and thereby to redefine reality, or so Kesey and his Pranksters believed. There was a touch of neo-religious proselytizing in their enthusiasm for drugs. "The purpose of psychedelics," Kesey once commented, "is to learn the conditioned responses of people and then to prank them. That's the only way to get people to ask questions, and until they ask questions they're going to remain conditioned robots." Of course, with the Pranksters, you never knew when they were simply pulling your leg or, as Kesey put it, "tootling the masses."

No matter what higher purpose the Pranksters might claim, they were above all about fun. In July of 1964, they drove the bus into Phoenix to help the Republicans celebrate their convention. GOP conservatives were in the process of anointing Barry Goldwater while humiliating Nelson Rockefeller as a symbol of the eastern, internationalist liberal establishment. Imagine, then, the sight of the Merry Pranksters, decked out in American flag outfits and body paint, descending on these pillars of tradition. What planet had these aliens descended from? The sign on the back of their bus warned "Caution: Weird Load." The banner they waved announced, "A Vote for Berry Goldwater Is a Vote for Fun." Goldwater, while no stuffed shirt, was about as much fun as a glass of club soda.

Upon their arrival in New York City, cool Beat collided with hot Prankster as Cassady brought Jack Kerouac to meet Kesey and cohorts. All that West Coast madness—lights flashing, rock blaring, and an American flag–adorned sofa—was too much for Kerouac. Were they Communists? he asked as he folded the flag. He soon retreated to Massachusetts, where he lived with his mother. Tom Wolfe saw the meeting as a passing of the guard: "Kerouac was the old star. Kesey was the wild new comet from the West heading Christ knew where." So then it was on to Millbrook, where the eastern and western acid all-stars would meet for their first attempt to mind meld.

Millbrook, about seventy miles north of New York City, was the center of hunt country, where wealthy New Yorkers came to their weekend estates to ride to the hounds in the scenic hills of Dutchess County. At one of the grander estates, William Hitchcock had turned his mansion over to former Harvard professor Timothy Leary and a band of psychedelic experimenters called the International Federation for Internal Freedom (IFIF). IFIF saw LSD as a means to achieve their goal of returning "to man's sense of nearness to himself and others, the sense of social reality that civilized man has lost." Leary first discovered psychedelics as a faculty member at Harvard, where students and faculty had participated in CIA-funded experiments in the 1950s. Leary's research dealt with psilocybin, the chemical agent in magic mushrooms. In 1960, he first tried psilocybin while on vacation in Mexico. The mushroom sent him on the "deepest religious experience" of his life. "I discovered that beauty, revelation, sensuality, the cellular history of the past, God, the Devil— all lie inside my body outside my mind," he reported.

Back at Harvard, he became a combination of experimenter, missionary, revolutionary, and huckster. In his lab, he and his research team explored both the consciousness altering and religious effects of the drug. LSD proved far more potent, and to Leary's mind more "consciousness expanding," than psilocybin. It soon became a central part of his research agenda. He doled it out to almost any colleague or student who expressed an interest. One of his early converts was a prominent Washington socialite and wife of a senior CIA official, Mary Pinchot. Pinchot reported to Leary that through her, "top people in Washington are turning on." Among her romantic liaisons was the president of the United States, John Kennedy. It is not impossible that Kennedy, who apparently smoked dope in the White House and received amphetamine-laced injections from a New York doctor, also tried LSD. Certainly, both Harvard and the CIA came to question the loose way in which Leary administered his experiments. Eventually, both the government and the university began to restrict his use of either psilocybin or LSD. Leary countered that no one who had not experienced these drugs could properly judge the importance of his work or methods. As he once joked, "These drugs apparently cause panic and temporary insanity in many officials who have not taken them."

In May 1963, Harvard fired Leary's collaborator, Richard Alpert, when he defied a ban on giving LSD to students. Alpert was the first Harvard faculty member dismissed for cause in the twentieth century. Leary soon followed him out of the groves of academe. As a parting shot, he told reporters that LSD was "more important than Harvard" and spoke disparagingly of the university as "the establishment's apparatus for training consciousness contractors" for an "intellectual ministry of defense." The whiff of scandal in Cambridge caught the attention of major news media, for whom Leary provided an intriguing story. As they publicized his run-in with the university, they informed the nation about a drug that had entered America as a potential "truth serum" for the CIA. In fact, a CIA agent provided Leary with much of his experimental drug supply. Leary's indictment of Harvard, though not overtly political, had much the same spirit that inspired the FSM at Berkeley a year later. Both challenged authority, chafed at arbitrary rules that restricted personal freedom, and flaunted convention. LSD and marijuana helped protestors pass the night in Sproul Hall during the FSM sit-in. And both movements involved members of the nation's elite dissenting from established cultural norms.

After retreating to Mexico and being expelled from there, Leary and IFIF settled in Millbrook. His group established as their goal the discovery and nurturing of the divinity in each person. The idea was to incorporate the acid high into normal consciousness. A hint of academia carried over as participants carefully recorded and discussed their insights. Some participants tripped occasionally; some stayed stoned for days on end. Rumor had it that the children and dogs were high as well. Such an environment inevitably took on the aspect of a permanent party. Like the Pranksters, Leary and his band were having fun. To pay the bills, they invited guests to weekend workshops where they explored non–drug induced mind-altering techniques such as yoga, Zen meditation, and encounter groups. Leary discovered in *The Tibetan Book of the Dead* what he thought was a remarkable appreciation for the "nature of experiences encountered in the ecstatic state." He transformed it into a psychedelic manual and began to proselytize with his mantra "tune in, turn on, and drop out."

About the time Dylan met the Beatles in New York, Kesey and the Pranksters descended on Millbrook. Their reception, while polite, was not especially warm. Leary never even appeared to greet them. In time, it became clear to the Pranksters that IFIF was in a different orbit. They found the academic tone incredibly stuffy. Goofing on *The Tibetan Book of the Dead*, they dubbed it "the crypt trip." It lacked the frantic energy that drove the bus commune. Kesey's band preferred raucous rock to Beethoven and Bach, face paint and costumes to country scenes, adventure and spontaneity to genteel contemplation. Where Leary turned on the elite, Kesey intended to democratize the acid trip. "It only works if you bring other people into it," he believed.

The Pranksters returned to the West Coast to launch the "electric Kool-Aid acid tests." Under pulsating strobe lights, with videos playing on the walls and the Grateful Dead improvising drug-induced rock, they initiated crowds of Freaks into the world of acid. Kesey even invited the notorious Hell's Angels motorcycle gang to attend an acid picnic at La Honda. "We're in the same business," he told some

Angels. "You break people's bones; I break people's heads." While locals locked their doors and the police called in reinforcements, the event proved relatively mellow. Acid subdued the normally rambunctious bikers. For two days, they wandered about in a befuddled drug stupor, grooving on the gay poet Allen Ginsberg and nodding at Kesey's collection of professors and dropouts. This was the ultimate freak, without any of the cerebral restraints that alienated the Pranksters from the Millbrook scene.

Just as the New Left would emphasize action over analysis, so too Kesey and his initiates saw experience as an end unto itself. The acid tests were a combination of rock concert and dance hall party in which the audience was a critical part of the performance. The participants sought no special insight into the cosmos, though they were open to the possibility of spiritual transformation. Over time, many of the features of the acid tests would become ritualized and commercialized, but in the early years of the 1960s, the scene Kesey helped create was about spontaneity with no end in sight.

The Counterculture

Before 1967, few people outside the Bay Area knew much about the acid tests or the cultural revolution of which they were a harbinger. Most students who graduated from college before 1967 had an experience akin to that of the 1950s generation. They continued to do what students had traditionally done: go to football games, join fraternities and sororities, drink too much, and worry about careers and marriage. Surveys from that time indicate that the majority of young Americans generally shared the values of their parents' generation. Certainly, at major universities with adjoining progressive college towns, small groups of bohemian and radical students pushed beyond conventional cultural and political boundaries. They might read Herman Hesse, Freud, and Marx, listen to jazz, folk music, and acid rock, experiment with sex and drugs, organize political protest, or do all those things and more. All the same, the rebelliousness that defined the sixties remained on the fringe, except when the media focused on some particularly unexpected event like Greensboro sit-ins, Berkeley's free speech movement, or Leary's departure from Harvard. Only at those moments did the vast majority of young Americans begin to get an inkling that the times were changing in ways that began to prick their interest.

Between the free speech movement and the summer of 1967, the elements of the cultural upheaval percolated into the mainstream. Many parents and politicians began to see young Americans, certainly those under thirty, as a discreet political and cultural force. Whether marching for civil rights, protesting the Vietnam War, or engaging in outrageous behaviors, the young seemed increasingly determined to challenge authority and convention across a broad front. Most adults lumped all the rebels together into something they loosely identified as a counterculture, often mistaking a common preference for long hair, beards, outlandish clothes, and other badges of difference as the uniform of a coherent movement. But what many worried and outraged adults condemned as a movement lead by long-haired hippie radicals (undoubtedly seduced by Communists) was in reality an amorphous trend spontaneously generated. It swirled around three poles: Black Power, the New Left, and the hippies. Individuals generally gravitated toward one of those poles but adopted styles and values from all three.

The criticism of hippies as dirty, degenerate, and depraved masked a subtext about race, social class, and gender. Youth behaviors upset the inherited order in all those categories. If you took the most negatively stereotyped groups in America in the early 1960s—Commies, blacks, the poor, and homosexuals—youth culture contained elements from all of them. Aggressive egalitarianism and rejection of the capitalist ethos smacked dangerously of Marx and other radical isms. Casual sex, substance use and abuse, loud music, and scanty material possessions are all traits associated with the poor. And though there were few black or Latino hippies, the hippie style owed a great debt to minority culture. In an essay about the Beats, Norman Mailer observed that the "source of Hip is the Negro," for "in this wedding of white and black it was the Negro who brought the dowry." Long hair and androgynous dress styles blurred traditional gender lines. All those behaviors repudiated inherited class, gender, and racial advantages. In a society where children were supposed to improve on the status of their parents, these young people had chosen to be downwardly mobile. Americans have always viewed downward mobility as at best a sign of defective character and at worst as a major social pathology.

Black radicals had far more in common with the New Left than with the hippies. To a large degree, they demanded access to the middle-class materialism hippies rejected while at the same time calling for racial pride and separatism. They self-consciously flaunted their masculinity in part to confound old Uncle Tom and Sambo stereotypes. Hence, the hippies and black radicals were seldom bedfellows, strange or otherwise. Still, the hippies, by rejecting social hierarchies and embracing tolerance of human difference, implicitly accepted blacks as their equals. The New Left, which shared with black radicals a view of establishment culture as imperialistic and saw the black poor as a potential revolutionary proletariat, viewed the counterculture with ambivalence. Most on the Left criticized the hippies' flight from politics as irresponsible and naive. Yet radicals also found mainstream culture repressive and were enthusiastic about the revolutionary possibilities of sex, drugs, and rock and roll. The ground occupied by the cultural rebels was as bitterly contested by mainstream Americans as the political terrain claimed by the New Left and Black Power movements. Despite the significant differences within and among these rebel groups, adult authorities concluded, sometimes with near hysteria, that hippies represented a danger to consensus culture every bit as threatening as Soviet-directed world Communism. That similar signs of rebelliousness had swept across Europe and even Asia underscored the degree of danger the counterculture seemed to pose. Like Communism, it had a subversive countenance and links to foreign movements.

Sex, Drugs, and Rock and Roll: The Hippies

From the vantage point of those caught up in 1960s rebellion, the term "counter-culture" more accurately applies to hippies. These were generally young people who chose to turn their back on 1950s suburban culture. Americans in the postwar era had staked much of their claim to moral and political leadership on the sheer bounty of their nation's production and consumption. By rejecting that blessing, hippies attacked a core American value. Their credo, if they could ever truly have been said to have any body of ideas at all, was summarized by *Time* magazine in 1967:

> Do your own thing, wherever you have to do it and whenever you want
> Drop out. Leave society as you have known it. Leave it utterly.
> Blow the mind of every straight person you can reach. Turn them on, if not to drugs, then to beauty, love, honesty, fun.

Those who found the hippies disturbing summarized this credo as a recipe for immediate gratification, escapism, and degeneracy.

Yet the counterculture did include a wide variety of dissenters who questioned the conformism, racism, sexism, and materialism of the 1950s and who wanted to make the world more humane. Historians have linked them to Thoreau and the Romantics, to social reformers and utopian communities, and to religious revival-ists. In their quest they, too, struggled to perfect democracy, to protect individuality, to create community, to find spiritual renewal, or, more simply, to live the good life—whatever that might be. The antics of more extreme factions like the Merry Pranksters attracted many dropouts and social misfits who had no agenda whatso-ever. Probably, the majority of those in the counterculture were part-timers who either passed through a hippie phase on their way between school and the real world or those in the 9 to 5 rat race who dropped out on weekends. Whether full- or part-time, spiritually motivated or self-indulgent, creative or self-destructive, hippies appeared alien and subversive to their real-world critics.

Since hippies seldom articulated their values, their cultural critique had to be inferred from their behavior. The three lines along which they most directly flaunted convention can be encapsulated as sex, drugs, and rock and roll. Of those, drug use most clearly marked the cultural divide both by age and by values. As historian Timothy Miller argued, "The commitment to—as opposed to the furtive use of—dope was the single largest symbol between the counterculture and the establishment culture." For young Americans, the decision to take drugs went beyond getting high. It began an initiation into an entire culture, with elements of permissiveness, pleasure, and noncompetitiveness that repudiated middle-class expectations. Each drug had its proper setting, its distinctive high, and its appropri-ate musical accompaniment. Authorities, who regularly condemned sexual permis-siveness and denounced rock and roll, brought the full force of their moral outrage against the drug culture. In the early years of the counterculture, arrests, even for recreational drug users, often led to long prison terms.

Hippies distinguished between "drugs" and "dope." To them, "drugs" was a more inclusive term that covered substances that were both good and bad—from marijuana to heroin. "Dope" applied to those substances hippies favored—marijuana, LSD, peyote, psilocybin, hashish, mescaline, and even banana peels. Bad drugs included amphetamines (especially speed or methadrine), opiates (heroin, morphine, opium), and possibly cocaine, though that is where the line often blurred. Many hippies approved of all drugs; a few rejected them altogether. Generally, the distinction followed medical lines, with dope applying to the largely nonaddictive drugs. That meant that most hippies rejected alcohol, the establishment's drug of choice. Alcohol and the other addictive drugs tended to inhibit consciousness—in reality to make the user stupid. Good drugs or dope expanded consciousness and in that way helped promote a new mindset free of the acquisitive and repressive features of the old one.

The dope culture had several features that explained its appeal. Those who turned on discovered that dope enhanced the pleasures of food, sex, and music. Even more, dope appealed to rebels because its use flaunted authority. For decades, adults had warned the young of the perils of narcotics, a category in which they lumped soft drugs like marijuana and hard drugs like heroin. The antidrug movie *Reefer Madness* (1935) predicted that flirtation with dope would lead inevitably to a life of addiction and crime. As drug use became more popular, a shrill public outcry accelerated law enforcement efforts to repress the drug epidemic. As a result, the decision to smoke marijuana or drop acid was not just a deviation from convention, but a decision to break the law. Those who turned on joined a secret society that practiced its illicit rituals with shades down, windows open, incense burning, and towels across the door jamb to avoid detection. Loud music heightened the communal experience. That marijuana proved so much less potent or addictive than claimed only served further to erode the credibility of the authorities. As one FSM veteran observed, "When a young person took his first pull of psychoactive smoke, he . . . inhaled a certain way of dressing, talking, acting, certain attitudes. One became a youth criminal against the state."

Drugs posed a special problem for political radicals. Like hippies, many on the Left took up dope because it was fun and made a powerful antiestablishment statement. On the other hand, the dope culture was the antithesis of the revolutionary culture radicals envisioned, "the ultimate giggle," as one called it. Politics required discipline, organizaton, and action. Radicals discovered that after smoking dope, "the tension of a political life dissolved; you could take refuge from the Vietnam War, from your own hope, terror, anguish." So radicals and hippies coexisted in an uneasy relationship. The liberation aesthetics of the hippie universe was appealing for the spiritual freedom it conferred, but was too frivolous for those committed to the politics of liberation. Conversely, the discipline required of successful political action was too severe for the free spirits of the counterculture.

The tension between the political and cultural wings of the youth rebellion became evident at the Berkeley Vietnam Day rally in October 1965. The organizers had planned an around-the-clock teach-in on the war and a protest march against the nearby military base. Among those asked to speak was Ken Kesey. No one among the organizers knew anything about his politics, but they were certain that he shared their antiestablishment values. Besides, as a celebrity author and local legend, his presence would swell the crowd. Coinciding with demonstrations around the world, the rally attracted some 15,000 people. Kesey and the Pranksters prepared for quite another kind of event. They loaded the bus with guns and adorned it with swastikas, iron crosses, an American eagle, and other military symbols. They also recruited some Hell's Angels to escort their band. Cranked up on acid, they paraded off to Berkeley. As antiwar speakers warmed up the crowd for their march on the Oakland Army terminal, Kesey grew ever more impatient. He and the Pranksters found all this earnestness pathetic. Where was the fun and good humor? Why did these people take themselves so seriously? Didn't the speaker up there have a resemblance to Mussolini, he asked one of the organizers.

When Kesey began to speak, the Pranksters plugged in electric guitars and began to tune up. What he had to say was not what the crowd expected to hear: "You know you're not going to stop this war with this rally, by marching . . . That's what they do . . . And that's the same game you're playing . . . their game." As the stunned crowd tried to figure out if they had heard Kesey right, he pulled out a harmonica and began to play *Home on the Range*, backed up by the Pranksters doing an imitation of music. The crowd grew uneasy. Kesey finished his rambling speech, not with a call to march, but a call to nihilism: "There's only one thing gonna to do any good at all. . . . And that's everybody just look at it, look at the war, and turn your backs and say. . . . Fuck it." The profanity stunned the crowd as its moral fervor drained away.

Politics was simply not Kesey's thing; acid and goofing were. Leary may have been the media's "Dr. LSD," but Kesey was the messiah of acid. So, like a preacher, he organized the psychedelic equivalent of tent meetings, or what he called the acid test. As much as any emergent phenomenon of the 1960s, the acid tests anticipated the cultural style of what would become the era's youth rebellion. That style was distinctly West Coast—part San Francisco bohemian and part Hollywood. The costuming was highly eclectic, mixing elements of buckskin and Indian paint, circus performers and harlequins, military and Salvation Army surplus, and Flash Gordon sci-fi. Multimedia sound and lights accompanied by the raucous music added to the sensory overload. Around 5 or 6 P.M., the folks would start dropping acid to prepare for a 9 o'clock party. Tom Wolfe described the scene at the last acid test: "a ballroom surrealistically seething with a couple of thousand bodies stoned out of their everlovin' bruces in crazy costumes and obscene makeup with a raucous rock 'n' roll band and stroboscopic lights and a thunder machine and balloons and heads and streamers and electronic equipment and the back of a guy's coat pleading *please don't believe in magic* to a girl dancing with four inch eye lashes so even the goddam Pinkerton guards were contact high."

Wolfe makes a plausible case that the acid tests gave birth to the psychedelic look that defined the public perception of the counterculture. Poster art dominated by swirling Day-Glo paints often adorned the walls. The use of sound and light effects to complement the music made multimedia a counterculture staple. One critic defined acid rock as pioneered by groups like Big Brother and the Holding Company, the Jefferson Airplane, and the Grateful Dead as "turned on music" or "old-timey stretched out blues songs performed by people who were themselves stoned for the dancing and tribe-gathering pleasure of an audience that was likewise." Rather than follow the usual concert format of two- to three-minute covers of well-known songs performed over four or five sets of eight songs, the Dead might play one of their own songs for ten to thirty minutes. They acquired the most exotic, state-of-the-art electronics, with which they produced the weird sounds and special effects that came to define acid rock.

The Dead could afford expensive gear not because of any commercial success; in fact, they often played for free. Rather, they had a financial patron who, as much as Kesey, any Freak, or any band, would make San Francisco an incubator for the counterculture. That was Augustus Owsley Stanley III. Owsley, as he was known, hailed from Kentucky, where part of his family's fortune came from distilling bourbon. Though he was brilliant and from a distinguished family, his prep school expelled him from ninth grade for bringing alcohol to school. By age eighteen, he was on his own. After stints in engineering school and the Air Force, he migrated to the Berkeley area, where in the Kentucky tradition, he became a bootleg chemist. His first batch of LSD entered the market around the time Kesey began to plan the acid tests. Though LSD was not at that time illegal, Owsley chose to live the life of a recluse. Occasionally, he would appear on the Freak circuit in Millbrook or at an acid test. That is where he heard the Grateful Dead and was so impressed he underwrote their early career.

Owsley, for all his eccentricities, was too much the wiseguy and too sophisticated to fit comfortably into the West Coast scene. Still, his product was revered by the heads. He became celebrated as "the unofficial mayor of San Francisco," even after police harassment drove his operations to L.A. No one was ever sure with Owsley whether he operated from the profit motive or out of reverence for LSD. He

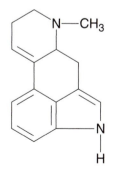

The molecular structure of LSD was less complex than the drug's cultural impact.

gave away as much as he sold. The popularity of his goods rested part on quality and part on mystique. To distinguish each batch, Owsley color-coded the tabs. Heads who believed each color had a particular quality had special affection for the blues—the perfect compromise between edgy greens and mellow reds. (In fact, the quality of Owsley's product resulted largely from its purity and uniformity.) An assistant captured the messianic spirit of their acid empire: "Every time we'd make another batch and release it on the street, something beautiful would flower, and of course we believed it was because of what we were doing. We believed we were the architects of social change, that our mission was to change the world substantially, and what was going on in the Haight was a sort of laboratory experiment, a microscopic example of what would happen world wide."

Eccentrics like Owsley or charismatic gonzos like Kesey had no trouble finding a following in the Bay Area. San Francisco had long attracted a mixture of political radicals, cultural bohemians, and crazies. In the late fifties, the Beats had gathered in the North Beach area, until a combination of gawking tourists, police harassment, and changing times had driven them out. Some had drifted across town to the Haight-Ashbury area, where run-down Victorian houses were available at low rents. There, they were joined by disaffected radicals and academics dropping out of Berkeley, a new generation of artists, writers, and musicians, and various street urchins, runaways, and social misfits. In Haight-Ashbury, they did not simply transplant the Beat scene, but produced the essence of the counterculture. Rejecting the Beats' nihilism, the new generation celebrated good times and good feelings. Where the Beats gravitated toward downer drugs including heroin, the hippies favored hallucinogens, especially marijuana and LSD. The Beats had tended to isolate themselves and to gather in intimate little clubs; the hippies loved the community street and the spirit of medieval fairs. They often formed tribes or families for communal living. Members generally viewed sex as a source of pleasure and a means to engender goodwill between people. To that end, they encouraged nonexclusive sexual relations and open marriages.

But what most distinguished the hippies from the Beats was music. The Beats liked music for listening—folk, classical, and cool jazz. Hippies wanted to dance. On the night Kesey rained his rhetorical water on the Vietnam Day parade, an organization called the Family Dog threw a party for the people of Haight-Ashbury. The Family Dog party was the inspiration of Chet Helms, a defrocked Baptist minister who had fled the stifling conservatism of Texas for the freedom of the Bay Area. With him, he brought a raw blues singer named Janis Joplin. While Joplin hooked up with the local music scene, Helms promoted the antic notion that people should turn on and dance at rock concerts. So the Family Dog rented a large union hall off Fisherman's Wharf and invited the neighbors to what was called "A Tribute to Dr. Strange." Among those attending were radicals from the Vietnam Day demonstrations, neighborhood Freaks decked out in weird costumes, and a few zonked-out Hell's Angels. To entertain, the Family Dog invited a number of local bands, highlighted by the psychedelic sound of the Jefferson Airplane (pre–Grace Slick).

Those in attendance that night sensed that the forces of the Haight scene had converged into something powerful. Kesey's acid tests, Owsley's blues, and the Bay Area's rock underground had been united with the neighborhood's motley bohemians to form what looked and sounded like a counterculture. Kesey saw in that gathering a way to further his quest to turn on the masses. Two months later, the Pranksters decided to throw a free three-day party called the Trips Festival. This bash was the apotheosis of the acid tests. The idea actually came from Stewart Brand, a biologist, who would pass on to fame and fortune by publishing *The Whole Earth Catalogue*, a guide to the goods and ideas critical to alternative lifestyles. Much of the organizing was done by Bill Graham, a refugee from New York. Graham was a veteran of the San Francisco Mime Troupe, a group frequently busted by police for doing agitprop theater (inflammatory political theater) in public places. In that way, he had the respect of the heads (cultural rebels) and the fists (political rebels).

The Trips Festival was a coming-out party for Freaks and LSD—thousands showed up, everyone obviously stoned. For the first night, Brand chose the theme "America Needs Indians." The revelers displayed all manner of Indian and southwestern apparel, including one who advertised himself as "Under Ass Wizard Mojo Indian Fighter." The second night belonged to the Pranksters. At the center of the hall they had erected a tower of platforms and pipes on which they arrayed the electronic gear used to produce the multimedia effects. Lights flashed, multiple movie projectors shone on the walls, huge speakers blared, and women in leotards pranced about blowing dog whistles. Kesey observed all the madness from a balcony, dressed in a space suit to avoid detection. Jerry Garcia of the Dead, who performed at the festival along with Big Brother, struggled to find words for the three-day freakout: "Thousands of people man, all helplessly stoned, all finding themselves in a room of thousands of people, none of whom any of them were afraid of. . . . It was," he concluded, "magic, far out beautiful magic."

Spreading the Word

By January 1966, word of the "magic" brewing in San Francisco was spreading across the land. The sheer mobility of American youth guaranteed that no phenomenon as colorful and compelling as the counterculture would remain isolated. Hitchhiking, cheap youth airfares, travel to colleges and universities, and the restless tradition of Americans encouraged movement from coast to coast. People who visited the Bay Area brought the word back across the nation. In addition, other bohemian communities around the country had subcultures of their own. Greenwich Village continued to spawn its own harsher version of the ferment on the West Coast, though the scene there was livelier in art and theater than in music. Los Angeles and Austin, Texas, each produced new groups and hit songs. Perhaps the closest rival of the Haight as a counterculture incubator was not in the United States at all. London had become the center of the mod phenomenon that produced its own distinctive counterculture.

No element did more to spread the word than rock musicians. Media innovations played a part in promoting that music revolution. The solid-state technology that made the modern computer possible also helped create smaller and less expensive radios and stereos as well as new recording and sound equipment. Until the early sixties, cheap 45 records dominated the pop music scene. Their short (2–3 minute) length suited the purposes of commercial AM radio. By playing more songs, stations appealed to a broader audience and hence attracted more advertising. During the folk music phase of the early 1960s, many people acquired long-play 33-rpm equipment, previously favored for classical and jazz listening. The availability of a longer-play format allowed folk and rock performers to break out of the restrictive time limits of 45-rpm records.

FM radio also played a critical role. The FM band had a more limited range than AM but higher-quality reception. Most radio networks simply reproduced AM programming on their FM stations. In 1966, the FCC decreed that FM stations must have their own programming. Some responded by appealing to niche markets for jazz, classical, ethnic, or rhythm and blues. Garage bands, inspired by the Beatles and other British groups, filled one niche that opened in the mid-1960s. Since many garage bands like the Dead played their own songs to live audiences, their music tended to have a local following. That plus the greater length of their songs disqualified them for AM top forty radio. As a result, few people outside the Bay Area actually heard acid rock before 1967. By then, a new breed of counterculture disc jockeys had begun to feature these groups on FM stations. They also featured music by the Beatles, Rolling Stones, or Bob Dylan, who had large followings with hip audiences. Since those audiences were primarily white, programming remained largely segregated. Hip stations played little rhythm and blues, or what was by then known as "soul music." With the exception of a slicker pop sound coming out of Detroit's Motown, black performers were limited largely to stations targeted at black listeners.

Beginning in 1965, Bob Dylan, the Beatles, the Rolling Stones, and a host of other British-invasion bands began to introduce counterculture themes into mainstream popular culture. No one more powerfully addressed the sixties ferment or influenced the music of the era than Dylan. By the time he appeared at the Newport Folk Festival in the summer of 1965, he had emerged as the leading songwriter and performer of the folk music circle. Peter, Paul, and Mary had turned two of his songs, "Blowin' in the Wind" and "Don't Think Twice, It's All Right," into top-forty hits. The political edge of songs like "Masters of War" and "A Hard Rain's A-Gonna Fall" added to Dylan's standing with leftist students and civil rights activist. His songs also captured the romantic yearnings and alienation prevalent in the emerging counterculture.

Several factors shifted Dylan from the world of folk music to both folk and acid rock, perhaps the single most defining style of the era. In the early sixties, Bay Area groups had begun to develop a folk-rock style with an acid twist. LSD also helped propel Dylan's shift toward a rock sound. His initiation to acid occurred in early 1964, though he had been smoking dope well before then. A friend discovered several acid tabs in a refrigerator and decided the time had come to turn Dylan on. First trips are often harrowing, but, as his friend recalled, "actually, it was an easy night for Dylan. Everybody had a lot of fun. And if you ask me, that was the beginning of the mystical Sixties right there." Certainly, it was the beginning of a new phase for Dylan. After that, his lyrics became more poetical and less political, more imagistic and less narrative. His next album opened with "Johnny's in the basement / mixing up the medicine," which drifted into "Better jump down a manhole / light yourself a candle / don't wear sandals." Drugs would increasingly dominate Dylan's life and music until an accident sidelined him in 1966.

British bands influenced Dylan much as he did them. In 1964, Dylan toured England, where his second album, Freewheelin', was a bigger hit than in the United States. Dylan's talent for putting teeth into his lyrics impressed British songwriters. Here was a musician who could express alienation and disdain and still appeal to a popular audience. What Dylan discovered in Britain was a music culture steeped in the rock and roll idiom of his youth. One song in particular impressed him. A group called the Animals had taken "The House of the Rising Sun," a traditional song Dylan had included on his first album, and added percussion and rhythmic organ. The result was a more powerful bluesy version. When Dylan returned to the States, he decided to end his solo career and add backup musicians. And that is what blew away (or, more properly, blew up) the crowd at Newport in July 1965. Until then, Dylan fans were largely folk purists. Dylan by contrast was an ambitious performer, eager to go where the action was, and that was folk rock, not pure folk music. In little more than a year, he produced three albums that redefined popular music: Bringing It All Back Home, Highway 61 Revisited, and Blonde on Blonde.

Several songs stand out as of particular importance. "Like a Rolling Stone," the lead track on Highway 61 Revisited, became Dylan's first chart-topping single. To fit it into the AM commercial format, DJs broke the six-minute song into two parts. Unlike the usual pop fare, the lyrics really mattered: "How does it feel / to be on your own? / No direction known / like a complete unknown / Like a rolling stone?" Most of the songs on the album came across with a cynical sneer and a "fuck you" bite: "Something is happening and you don't know what it is do you, Mr. Jones?" An even more seminal song actually appeared earlier on Bringing It All Back Home. That was "Mr. Tamborine Man," which became a huge hit for the Byrds, a Los Angeles–based band inspired by the Beatles and who, like Dylan, began as folk performers. The Byrds popularized the song by draining off its menace. As one critic noted, "when Dylan sang it, 'Mr. Tamborine Man' was mysterious, private—and perhaps a little threatening. In the Byrd's lush and soaring harmonies, it became an invitation." As Dylan sang "Let me forget about today until tomorrow" or "the jingle jangle morning," many listeners now recognized that he was singing about drugs. "Rainy Day Women #12 & 35" released in 1966 made the drug theme explicit as Dylan urged his audience to "go get stoned." Some radio stations censored the song, along with the Byrd's "Eight Miles High."

Dylan and the Byrds connected folk rock to the pop audience that until then belonged largely to the Beatles. Into this circle came such groups as the Lovin' Spoonful, Simon and Garfunkel, Sonny and Cher, and Buffalo Springfield, who would dissolve and reform as Crosby, Stills, Nash, and (sometimes) Young. The Beatles, it just so happened, were headed that way themselves. Almost no popular cultural phenomenon in history equals the worldwide excitement the Beatles inspired. By the end of 1965, they had sold some 140 million records. Their songs continued to dominate the pop charts. A second movie, *Help!*, had substantial box office success. Frenzied crowds still swarmed around them on their concert tours. So enormous was their appeal that revenue from their music helped offset the British international trade deficit.

In 1965, the Beatles still performed largely catchy ballads, love songs, and danceable tunes within the standard 2–3 minute pop time frame. Their personal style, despite conservative objection to their longish hair and mod clothes, was relatively tame. They still wore matching suits during their concert tours. Adults liked them almost as much as teenagers did. Hip fans sometimes contrasted them rather snidely to major British rivals, especially the Rolling Stones, who by 1965 had begun to challenge the Beatles command of the pop charts. Where the Beatles seemed cuddly and cute, the Stones snapped and snarled. Their music was distinctly black, drawing heavily on Chuck Berry and Little Richard. Mick Jagger projected sexual ambiguity in a way that appealed to rebels and offended most adults. Their provocative pelvic thrusts and vamping caused Ed Sullivan to issue a public apology after they appeared on his TV show. "I was shocked when I saw them," he confessed. Ironically, in private the Beatles were the more honestly low rent of the two groups. While the Beatles were honing their music in sleazy Hamburg clubs, the Stones were in college.

Acid affected the British music scene every bit as decisively as it did Dylan and the Bay Area bands. After a rather frightful introduction to LSD in early 1965, John Lennon soon began dropping acid routinely, and it began to show in his songwriting. Hints of the psychedelic mood began to surface on the Beatles' late 1965 *Rubber Soul* album. Several tracks, especially "Norwegian Wood," played with a sitar, and "I'm Looking through You (Where Did You Go?)" evoked drug images, if only by double entendre and implication. By 1966, the impact of both drugs and Dylan were more obvious. On *Revolver*, the cover has a psychedelic image, the Beatles in dark granny glasses look decidedly hip, and they sing more bitingly about drugs and alienation—as in *Eleanor Rigby*, with its refrain, "look at all the lonely people, where do they all come from." Even the seemingly innocent *Yellow Submarine*, which inspired a zany feature cartoon, was a sly allusion to amphetamines. As the Beatles became more countercultural, the Stones became more outrageous, appearing in full drag on one album sleeve. They, too, made drug imagery a central part of their music in such songs as "Paint It Black," "19th Nervous Breakdown," and "Lady

Jane." British authorities eventually struck back by infiltrating a police informer into the Stones' inner circle and busting them for illegal possession.

Drug imagery and alienation were more a subtheme than a preoccupation of mass culture before 1968. Songs with conventional themes and styles still filled the charts. In the fall of 1965, a few DJs featured the battle of the two Barrys (McGuire and Sadler). Listeners voted on whether they preferred McGuire's sharply cynical "Eve of Destruction" ("Violence flarin', bullets loadin' / You're old enough to kill but not for votin'") to Sgt. Sadler's patriotic "Ballad of the Green Berets" ("Fighting soldiers from the sky"). Out of Motown came a succession of slickly produced, gospel influenced, rhythm and blues hits by groups like the Four Tops, the Temptations, and the Supremes. From 1965 to 1966, six straight Supremes songs reached number one. The Beach Boys continued to turn out their bright pop harmonies. Even "old blue eyes," Frank Sinatra, the teen idol of the 1940s, had his first million-selling record.

Backlash

Most Americans remained only vaguely aware of the cultural ferment in their midst as the Baltimore Orioles crushed the L.A. Dodgers in the World Series. Many had been dismayed when heavyweight boxing champion Cassius Clay changed his name to Muhammad Ali and embraced the Nation of Islam. All the same, far more were concerned with whether Mr. Phelps would accept his impossible mission or Captain Kirk and the crew of the starship *Enterprise* would best the Klingons on the new *Star Trek*. In real life, NASA's *Gemini* launches achieved a series of successful space missions that brought the nation closer to realizing President Kennedy's promise to land a man on the moon before the decade was out. Enjoying a widespread prosperity, consumers lapped up such new products as Gatorade and Spaghetti Os. Kids bought Whamo superballs and tabletop slotcar racers. While the term "acid" did enter popular speech in 1966, so too did "beach bunny," "dove" and "hawk," and "integrated circuit" or "chip."

Word about LSD was not confined to rock musicians, drug gurus, and underground newspapers, however. As more Americans began to discover recreational drugs, the mass media publicized the acid scene. Rather than take a sober look at pharmacological and psychotropic issues, the media reacted with something akin to hysteria. "A Monster in Our Midst—A Drug Called LSD," ran one shrill headline. "Thrill Drug Warps Mind, Kills," raved another. Henry Luce, the influential editor of *Time-Life* magazines and an early experimenter with LSD, warned his magazine's readers that a person "can become permanently deranged through a single terrifying LSD experience." Two claims, neither validated, buttressed the case against acid. One was the notion of "flashbacks." Some medical authorities suggested that LSD induced psychotic states of mind that often resulted in violence. Worse yet, the episode could recur at any time in the future, in essence suggesting LSD induced long-term insanity. Then there was the worrisome claim that LSD caused permanent chromosome damage. Those contemplating turning on now had to conjure the image of mutant children. Even after government scientists failed to substantiate that claim, they remained silent about their findings while the media issued dire warnings.

Once the media discovers an issue, can the politicians be far behind? By 1966, the Senate had begun hearings on legislation to deal with the "LSD problem." That there was a serious public health issue requiring legislation was not so clear. LSD was still a fringe phenomenon, though its use was spreading. So the "LSD problem" was far more emotionally than statistically compelling. Classification of a substance as a drug is most often a cultural and political issue, not a pharmacological one. Those drugs most heavily stigmatized are those associated with the poor, ethnic minorities, or subcultures—for example, opium with Asians, cocaine with blacks, marijuana with Latinos and beatniks, and peyote with Native Americans. The substances that cause the most serious public health problems—alcohol and tobacco— have not been similarly proscribed because they are the drugs of choice of the dominant culture.

LSD created a special problem of demonization. Use and abuse was growing most rapidly not among dangerous minorities, but among children of the affluent white middle class. Once the media conflated drug use and political protest, politicians realized that by discrediting the drug culture, they could attack all the troubling currents flowing out of the counterculture. As Octavio Paz, a guru of mind-altering drugs, observed, "The authorities do not behave as though they were trying to stamp out a harmful vice, but as though they were trying to stamp out dissidence." Noting the ideological zeal of the crusade against LSD, Paz observed that "they are punishing a heresy, not a crime." Who was more of a heretic than Timothy Leary? And whose outrageous opinions were more likely than Leary's to discredit the counterculture in the eyes of mainstream America? If not Leary, then how about Allen Ginsberg, an admitted homosexual? And if that did not suffice, why not introduce the public to Arthur Kleps, who called himself "Chief Boohoo," founder of the Neo-American Boohoo Church? The Boohoos claimed for LSD the same sacramental role as peyote served for some Indians. A judge rejected that claim on the grounds that a group that used "Row, Row, Row Your Boat" as its anthem could not be serious enough to qualify as a church.

These were the three "friendly" witness called by the Senate Subcommittee on Juvenile Delinquency headed by Senator Thomas Dodd of Connecticut. Dodd had earned his spurs in the McCarthyite congressional posse of the 1950s. Echoing earlier Red scare themes, Dodd specifically condemned the "pseudo intellectuals" (read Leary and Ginsberg) who associated drug use with "imaginary freedoms." Imagine then how impressed the sanctimonious senators of the committee were when Kleps likened being born in America in 1948 to being "born into an insane asylum." Or when he contested one expert who had denounced the idea that LSD was "mind expanding." "If I were to give you an IQ test," Kleps supposed, "and one of the walls of the room opened up giving you a vision of the blazing glories of the central galactic suns, and at the same time your childhood began to unreel before your inner eye like a three dimensional movie, you would not do well on an intelligence test." His inquisitors were neither persuaded nor amused. As Martin Lee and Bruce Schlain argued in their history of LSD, "it was a lot easier to discredit the radical cause if the rest of society could be convinced that those uppity radicals were out of their minds."

Criminalization of LSD only added to the growing polarization of American society. Many of those in the counterculture embraced the spiritual and reforming possibilities Ginsberg and Leary claimed for psychedelics. Now those who dropped acid, even in search of spiritual uplift, would become outlaws. That put them in company with the martyrs of earlier religious inquisitions. And for those for whom acid was just a good high, criminalization only dramatized the hypocrisy of a society addicted to alcohol, tranquilizers, and nicotine.

Coming Together

C'mon people now
Smile on your brother
Ev'rybody get together
Try to love one another right now
—The Youngbloods (1966, © 1963 Irving Music)

Several historians have referred to the early period of the counterculture as a first wave. As this wave crested, mind-altering drugs, sexual freedom, and the new sound of rock and roll unleashed a spirit of exuberance and hope. The lyrics in "Get Together," popularized by the Youngbloods, captured the era's vision of brotherly love. Many people, no matter how naively, believed that the counterculture might contain a blueprint for a more harmonious world. Official hostility only confirmed for cultural rebels that they had found a new way. They chose to ignore or at least discount corrosive forces working to undermine what they envisioned as a new world order dawning in the age of Aquarius. While they preached peace and love, the Vietnam War continued to escalate. As they tried to build egalitarian communities, racial violence rocked the nation's cities. As they sought to expand their minds, authorities cracked down on drugs. But commercialism proved the most invidious of all the forces arrayed against them. Their efforts to build a more authentic society based on real human needs fell before the onslaught of American consumer culture that did so much to define and popularize it. The media, drug dealers, record companies, greedy landlords, fashion designers, and a host of consumer goods manufacturers discovered there was gold in them thar countercultural hills.

A certain commercial streak had always coexisted with the counterculture's free spirit. New lifestyles required accoutrements. Entrepreneurs opened shops to sell bongs, pipes, psychedelic posters, Indian bedspreads, Mexican serapes, records, vegetarian food, army-navy surplus, or love beads. These were mostly low-budget affairs, taking advantage of empty urban storefronts deserted in the suburban boom of the fifties. As quickly as they sprouted, most hip businesses withered and died, the victims of the traditional forces of capitalism: lack of capital, excess competition, changing fashions, and slim profit margins. Hostile merchants pressured the city to enforce zoning regulations requiring expensive improvement. Hippie values—a lack of ambition, a mañana attitude that made regular hours a problem, a spirit of sharing that included the ever-popular five-finger discount, and a desire to pursue more spiritual goals—contradicted sound business practices. One store, the Psychedelic Shop in the heart of Haight-Ashbury, embodied the uneasy balance between commercialism and spiritualism. Owners Ron and Jay Thelin made their store into a gathering place for LSD culture. Their shelves held any drug-related paraphernalia a head might desire. But the brothers were as concerned with promoting a way of life as with making money. They envisioned a neighborhood with "fine tea shops with big jars of fine marijuana and chemist shops with the finest psychedelic chemicals." A bulletin board offered a place to publicize local events. Most people came to the store just to hang out and talk or to buy and sell dope. Hippies generally viewed dope trafficking more as a service than as a business, though there was money to be made.

Every hip community had at least one underground newspaper, often distributed for free. The alternative press allowed hippies to circumvent the biases and censure with which the mainstream media treated the counterculture. Underground papers gave the kind of attention to music and drugs that the commercial press lavished on sports and politics. *Rolling Stone* magazine turned music coverage into a huge commercial success. The magazine pioneered rock criticism, and through its stories word about new performers reached across the nation. A vibrant counterculture comic book industry produced such offbeat cartoonists as Robert Crumb of Zap Comix. In Detroit, musician John Sinclair joined other cultural activists to create Trans-Love Energies Unlimited, or what they called "a total tribal living and working commune." An underground newspaper called the *Sun* became a voice through which they promoted rock concerts, psychedelic art shows, and guerrilla theater. Police harassment drove the commune out to Ann Arbor, where it transformed itself into the White Panther Party, dedicated to subversion "by any means necessary, including rock and roll, dope, and fucking in the streets."

Consistent with that spirit was the array of free goods and services spawned by the counterculture. Free universities and alternative schools became commonplace. Hip legal aid clinics defended those busted for drugs. Volunteers staffed drug hotlines, mental health clinics, and treatment centers for such missteps as venereal disease, bad trips, and unexpected pregnancies. Food and clothing co-ops helped hippies survive almost without income. Communes offered housing, sometimes with a spiritual theme. Every street corner became a potential stage for musicians, jugglers, dancers, and improvisational theater. No group more flamboyantly proselytized the ethos of the free than the Diggers. "Every brother should have what he needs to do his own thing," a Digger manifesto declared. To that end, they proposed "Free Families" (ranging from Black Panthers to radical street gangs to love communes) who would "develop Free Cities where everything that is necessary can be obtained for free by those involved in the various activities of the various clans."

The group, an offshoot of the San Francisco Mime Troupe, derived its name from a seventeenth-century English radical agrarian cult. The original Diggers viewed money and private property as instruments of the Devil. Adopting an early form of Communism, they squatted on the commons and gave free food to the poor until church authorities loosed mobs against them. Around 1966, the new Diggers deserted the political scene in Berkeley to bring their own brand of freewheeling Robin Hoodism to the Haight. The Digger scene was an "all for free" free-for-all. With money from Owsley Stanley and food liberated from stores or donated by sympathetic merchants, they operated a soup kitchen. Every day at four P.M. they provided a free meal to anyone who came to their corner of Golden Gate Park. They occasionally gave out free dope, "free" money, and "liberated" goods from their Free Store.

At the heart of the Diggers' activities was a form of performance art designed to put on the system. As dusk settled over the Haight one day, hundreds of street people climbed to the rooftops armed with rear-view mirrors the Diggers had liberated from local junkyards. Their mission—to reflect the sunset into the streets. At the same time, a chorus of women began a chant that was picked up by thousands in the streets below. The police soon arrived to clear the crowds away and unwittingly became part of the performance. Reflecting the sunset was but one of many Digger-inspired "rituals of release" designed to reclaim "territory (sundown, traffic, public joy) through spirit." For the Diggers this was participatory theater, or what they described as "a poetry of festivals and crowds with people pouring into the streets."

Those who saw the Diggers as a hippie Goodwill misunderstood them. They were significantly older than most of the radicals and hippies, and several, like former junkie Emmett Grogan, had considerable experience with the criminal justice system. Unlike the New Left or the innocent spirits who drifted into Haight-Ashbury, the Diggers had no illusions that the "system" could be reformed. "Free" was not about charity, but a way to subvert the money game that dominated straight society. In a world of bounders and thieves, only an anarchist culture could liberate the human spirit from the shackles of the system. Nor did the Diggers share the hippie faith that acid would offer salvation by moving people to a better place. The Diggers liked acid, but as an end unto itself. Transcendence was only possible when people could acquire life's essentials—food, clothing, housing, and art—from outside the system.

Unlike the Diggers, most elements of the counterculture welcomed publicity as a way to spread their message. Antiwar demonstrations were planned to maximize press coverage. Similarly, Timothy Leary and other drug gurus seldom shunned an opportunity for media celebrity. Many of the acid rock bands began to covet the fame and fortune that Dylan and the Beatles had achieved. The popularity of the Trips Festival inspired Bill Graham to book the Fillmore ballroom, where he staged regular light shows and dance concerts—for a fee. Prior to then, most of the bands saw themselves much in the Digger spirit as community performers. They gave free concerts, where they played for drugs or just for the fun of it. Graham's chief competitor, Chet Helms, tried to keep that spirit alive. He ran his concerts at the Avalon ballroom more like community socials. Since many people came for free, he could not always pay the performers. Not that they minded that much. The rapport between audiences and the band was a distinctive quality of the San Francisco music scene. Business skills and ticket receipts, however, gave Graham the upper hand in attracting top groups to the Fillmore. He could sign the big-name local bands because he was able to pay them. He also developed a direct line to the record companies. Many of the companies who had missed signing the Beatles and the other English invasion bands were determined to cash in on the new West Coast acid rock. But the bands that turned on San Francisco crowds often had to add new performers and a different sound to make successful records.

In such ways, an uneasy tension between community and commerce troubled the Haight, even as it planned the event that announced the counterculture to the world. That was the first "Human Be-in." The moving spirit behind this communal gathering was Michael Bowen, an agent for a group called the Psychedelic Rangers. Bowen and the Rangers had close ties to the *Oracle*, an underground paper dedicated to Timothy Leary's vision of an LSD nirvana. Together they percolated an idea to take the Trips Festival / acid test concept to a higher orbit of spiritual energy. They would call a "gathering of the tribes." In particular, they hoped to ease the tension between the heads and fists by turning the radicals on to LSD. In that way, as the *Oracle* put it, they would create a "union of love and activism previously separated by categorical dogma and label mongering." To assist their efforts, they enlisted the help of Vietnam Day–organizer Jerry Rubin, a hardcore Marxist who had recently discovered the joys of acid. An underground press release, designed to alert the mainstream media, announced "Berkeley political activists and the love generation of the Haight-Ashbury will join together . . . to powwow, celebrate, and prophesy the epoch of liberation, love peace, compassion and unity of mankind." Organizers secured a permit from the city to hold the Be-in on a polo field in Golden Gate Park. At one end, they erected a small bandstand from which the entertainment—poetry, music, chanting, mime—would just happen. Beat poet Gary Snyder opened the day by blowing mellow tones out of a conch shell.

And the crowds came—some 25,000 people of all ages wandered by to be swept up in the good vibrations of doing and protesting nothing in particular. The Hell's Angels were there to provide security and round up lost children. The scent of dope mingled with incense, while free acid, courtesy of Owsley and the Diggers, flowed all day. An all-star lineup of hip gurus was on hand to bless the occasion. Timothy Leary, decked out like a Buddhist holy man in white pajamas, highlighted the celebration of acid. Leary understood how to preach to a stoned audience. He limited himself to pithy aphorisms about altered consciousness—"the only way out is in," whatever that might mean. As the founder of the League of Spiritual Discovery (get it—LSD), he shared his two holy injunctions: (1) "Thou shalt not alter the consciousness of thy fellow man"; (2) "Thou shalt not prevent thy fellow man from altering his own consciousness."

Many of those gathered found Leary's brew of religious revival and psychedelic liberation old news. They had already entered or rejected the psychedelic revolution. The Diggers, in spite of themselves, catered the Be-in with free food and drugs. They resented the idea of an organized event with planned performances that distanced the crowd from participation. The elevated stage, they felt, spoke of the old hierarchical fashion with them—celebrities like Leary and Ginsberg—looking down on the rest of us. The media predictably had a field day. Seldom had they ever had an event so given to producing memorable images. All three networks sent camera crews and followed up with stories on the "flower children" and "love generation." Herb Caen of the *San Francisco Chronicle* made perhaps the most enduring contribution when he called them all "hippies" and the label stuck. California governor Ronald Reagan, with his ear for Middle American sensibilities, scornfully dismissed a hippie as a person who "dresses like Tarzan, has hair like Jane, and smells like Cheetah."

The reaction of Helen Swick Perry captured a sense of what people experienced that day. As a mental health researcher from Berkeley, Perry welcomed the prospect of seeing the spirit of the Haight "up close and personal." The crowds streaming into the park "all seemed enchanted, happy, and smiled like a welcoming committee, upon us as they trundled along with baby carriages and picnic hampers." Each person, whether in costume or regular clothes, carried some sign of participation— "a young boy with a nasturtium behind his ear, a gray-haired woman with a flower tied on her cane with a ribbon." Upon arriving, Perry was immediately struck that this corner of the park had been turned into a medieval fair, with banners streaming in the breeze. All day people gathered on their blankets, occasionally wandering to the stage to hear the music, the poetry, and the speeches. Sometime in the afternoon a parachutist drifted unannounced into the midst of the crowd. When it was over, the organizers asked the gathered tribes to "leave the park clean" and they did, much to the amazement of the police. San Francisco's finest had kept a benevolent distance from the whole scene, despite the proliferation of drugs. There was safety in numbers, the hippies noticed that day. To Perry, something had happened which she had difficulty describing. It was not the drugs, for her group had not done any. "It was," she thought, "a religious rite in which nothing in particular had happened."

As for political radicals, the Be-in left them in a quandary. They generally found Leary's message hopelessly naive and irresponsible. Leary openly rejected political revolution in favor of a religious one. "You can't do anything about America politically," he warned. Whether right wingers or Communists, capitalists or Marxists, political people were, at least to his expanded consciousness, all trapped in a competitive struggle for power. Such pronouncements so outraged Bay Area radicals that the *Berkeley Barb* urged readers to demonstrate against him. Some organizers on the Left tried to bridge the gap between the counterculture's indifference to social injustice and their own moral engagement. In the spring of 1967, Jerry Rubin ran for mayor of Berkeley on a platform of ending the war and legalizing marijuana. Across the country, antiwar activists in New York, lead by Abbie Hoffman, among others, staged "Flower Power Day," meant to look like a Be-in to attract the hip community, but in reality a march against the war.

Ultimately the two communities could do little more than coexist. The New Left continued to respect the hippies' "peace and love" ethos. And most of the New Left adopted the long hair, costuming, drugs, and antimaterialist lifestyles that became the outward manifestation of the counterculture's dissidence. Hippies, for their part, shared much of the New Left's political agenda, even as they rejected political activism. They opposed the war not by marching, but by refusing to participate. And they, too, were determined to change the world, though by private inaction rather than by public protest.

10

A Very Bad Year Begins

Most historians view 1968 as the year that defined the 1960s. *The Year of the Barricades; 1968: The Year That Rocked the World; 1968: Rip Tides* are just some of the many descriptions they have used. Unfortunately, such conventional wisdom distorts the chronology of the era. To understand the uncivil wars that engulfed the nation, we must step back from the focus on 1968 and return to the summer of 1967. That is when the uncivil wars gripped the nation, as trends that had been developing in isolation began to merge into the mainstream of American life. In particular, the counterculture spilled from communities like Haight-Ashbury and Greenwich Village into college towns and cities across the nation. Black Power displaced nonviolent resistance as the cutting edge of the struggle for racial equality. Political activists, driven by both the desire for a greater voice on campuses and an end to the war in Vietnam, mobilized large numbers of dissidents.

The uncivil wars began symbolically, on June 30, 1967, when President Johnson issued an executive order placing nineteen-year-olds at the top of the draft list. That decision guaranteed that baby boomers would bear the major burden of fighting the war in Vietnam. It also enlisted the energy of more young Americans in the antiwar and draft resistance movements. Then race riots exploded in Newark, New Jersey, and Detroit, Michigan. As violence escalated, President Johnson had to order federal troops into Detroit. The war in Vietnam compounded the tensions dividing American society. Great Society programs spent $50 per person on the war on poverty at home; the government spent $300,000 to kill each Vietcong (many of them noncombatant peasants). Between July and December, almost 5,000 Americans would die in combat. Senator William Fulbright, a leading critic of the Vietnam War, suggested that "each war [the war at home and the war in Vietnam] feeds on the other, and, although the president assures us that we have the resources to win both wars, in fact we are not winning either of them."

The link between escalating violence at home and in Vietnam was not lost on those seeking to end the war. Frustration rose as troop levels and casualties increased on both sides. In October, antiwar groups organized a week of draft resistance and a march on the Pentagon that brought somewhere around 50,000–100,000 protestors to Washington. Though publicly the administration discounted the march, in private many officials were impressed by the size and nature of the demonstration. Press Secretary George Christian saw it as a turning point—the beginning of the end for the Johnson administration. It troubled the president deeply and helped inspire Senator Eugene McCarthy to enter the presidential race as an antiwar candidate. So even before the ball fell in Times Square on January 1, 1968, the uncivil wars were fully engaged.

The Counterculture Blooms

In the short period from 1966 to the summer of 1967, the counterculture rede-fined mass popular culture. Over the summer of 1967, a hippie invasion swept across America. Those who once associated drugs with addiction and depravity began to turn on routinely. The ideals of peace and love, spiritual and sexual free-dom, and the sheer celebration of good feelings attracted large numbers of Americans across generational lines. Whether a person rejected the counterculture, embraced it, or fell somewhere in between, it had become by then a central fact of American life. It polarized the country every bit as much as the civil rights and antiwar movements. Many Americans felt profoundly threatened by the countercul-ture's assault on religious, political, and social authority, the critique of middle-class lifestyles, and the irreverent use and abuse of traditional icons.

Three events over the summer of 1967 heralded this cultural transformation: the Beatles' *Sgt. Pepper's Lonely Hearts Club Band* album, the Monterey International Pops Festival, and two movies, *The Graduate* and *Bonnie and Clyde*. These events signified that hippie values and style had begun to flood into the cultural mainstream. *Sgt. Pepper's* must stand as the popular culture event of the year, if not the entire era. The album was four months aborning, and by the time it came out, Beatles fans anticipated that it would somehow be different. Two proceeding albums, *Rubber Soul* and *Revolver*, had

Just three years after their triumphant appearance on Ed Sullivan, the Beatles had transformed themselves into hip icons of the counterculture. (Source: Getty Images)

indicated that the Beatles were moving with the countercultural tide. *Sgt. Pepper's* did not disappoint expectations. From its symphonic production values to its psychedelic cover, to the lyrics printed for the first time on the liner, to the electronic sound effects, the album was innovative. Previous Beatles albums were generally recorded quickly and cheaply out of the bits and pieces of music available at the moment. *Please, Please, Me*, their first album, took 585 minutes to record; *Sgt. Pepper's* took over 700 hours! "The Beatles definitely had an eternal curiosity for doing something," their producer George Martin recalled.

The cover announced that these were the "new" Beatles. Decked out in psychedelic band uniforms, looking decidedly hip, they stand next to four wax figures of the original Beatles enshrined in their mod suits at Madame Toussaud's Wax Museum. Around them are arrayed the people they selected as those they would most like to have as an audience, including pop culture icons (Oliver Hardy, Mae West, Fred Astaire), cultural rebels (Oscar Wilde, Bob Dylan, Marlon Brando), Mohandas Ghandi and several Indian gurus, Albert Einstein, and a Shirley Temple doll with a sweatshirt saying "Welcome Rolling Stones, Good Guys." In *Sgt. Pepper's*, the Beatles added substance to what had been largely a skilled pop and rhythm and blues style. They took their listeners on a fantasy tour through the history of popular music of dance halls, the circus, folk festivals, and rock and roll. One critic described it as a summing up as much as a new departure. The album also announced the Beatles' embrace of the counterculture, especially its rhapsodies of drug use. The lyrics make the drug themes clear. Some fans literally wore out the album grooves, listening in a drug-mellowed reverie to John Lennon's evocation of "tangerine trees," "newspaper taxis," and "marmalade skies," though Lennon claimed that "Lucy in the Sky with Diamonds" came from a child's drawing and was not an allusion to LSD.

One measure of *Sgt. Pepper's* success was the number of places it was banned—a first for the Beatles. The BBC refused to play "A Day in the Life" because of the line "I'd love to turn you on." Vice President Spiro Agnew later added the Beatles to his list of cultural outcasts because they got "high with a little help from friends"— presumably psychedelic. One John Birch Society expert on musical subversion determined that the songs "show an acute awareness of the principles of rhythm and brain washing." Whether the Beatles actually had intended to subvert their audience or were, as one myrmidon of the law claimed, agents of the entertainment section of the Communist Party, criticism from the cultural Right testified to the power of their music: "The Beatles are the leading pied-pipers creating promiscuity, an epidemic of drugs, youth consciousness, and an atmosphere of social revolution." To that, Beatles' fans could only say "Amen."

Sgt. Pepper's served as the anthem for what was called in 1967 the Summer of Love. The story had gone out that spring through the underground press and word of mouth that "the youth of the world are making a pilgrimage to our city [San Francisco], to affirm and celebrate a new spiritual dawn." The *East Village Other* wrote of the creation of a Bay Area "love-guerrilla training school for drop-outs from mainstream America." Pop balladeer Scott McKenzie crooned in a song that swept the charts in Europe and America, "If you're going to San Francisco, be sure to wear some flowers in your hair." These were the "gentle people, from across the nation, a new generation." The San Francisco authorities looked forward to their arrival with open hostility. One local politician likened the hippie pilgrims to "thousands of whores waiting on the other side of the Bay Bridge." Despite the warnings of the mayor to stay away, some 100,000 hippies and probably an equal number of tourists descended on San Francisco to "search for the holy grail of sex, drugs, and rock and roll."

These cultural forces inspired the Monterey International Pops Festival. The first Human Be-in had raised the possibility of forming the masses of the Haight into a spiritual community. Monterey, an idyllic seaside site, had previously hosted folk and jazz festivals. A young L.A. rock promoter, Ben Shapiro, nurtured the idea that the Summer of Love would provide an unprecedented opportunity to showcase the rock underground before a mass audience (and to turn a big profit). Shapiro and a partner signed several lead acts and booked the Monterey County Fairgrounds for June 16. When they realized that their $50,000 budget would not attract enough good acts to fill a three-day program, they turned to John Phillips of the Mamas and Papas, who also happened to have written the McKenzie ballad "San Francisco."

Phillips had the connections in the music business necessary to turn vision into reality. By virtually any measure, the festival proved an overwhelming success for its promoters, the performers, and the several hundred thousand rock fans and hippies who managed to attend. Woodstock 1969 certainly made more of a splash, but as one rock historian observed, "Monterey was a seminal event: It was the first rock festival ever held featuring debut performances of bands that would shape the history of rock and affect popular culture from that day forward." The festival also inducted untold thousands into the counterculture. One young attendee from rural California had seen nothing like it before:

> "But Monterey! Hippies everywhere! Bearded and long-haired guys and beautiful little hippie girls every where Man, we just knew we were in for the time of our lives. Volkswagen buses and old cars painted up with peace symbols and flowers all over them. One group was (living?) in a big old bus that was painted all psychedelic looking. People walking and hitchhiking everywhere with big backpacks. People wearing furs and skins and moccasins and beads and feathers and flowers. It looked more like a fur trappers' 'ron-day-voo' from the 1800's than a music festival."

By the time this young Californian left Monterey, his world looked different. "That weekend at Monterey gave us a sense of belonging to a family that extended outside of our closed in borders," he recalled.

The world of music expanded as well. On the eve of the festival, pop music retained a regional flavor. Fans could readily distinguish the sounds of L.A. from those of San Francisco and Detroit, or those of Austin, Texas, from Nashville and Muscle Shoals, Alabama. The dominance of British groups on the pop charts stymied the efforts of many American musicians to break out of regional markets to reach national audiences. The Beatles, Stones, Dave Clark Five, Pink Floyd, and others had until then defined the hip sound in music.

The motley collection of thirty bands performing at Monterey represented the range of regional styles from country and pop, to soul and folk, to acid rock and Indian sitarist Ravi Shankar. Almost all the performers achieved newfound popularity, and for a number of them, major new record contracts, but four acts really stole the show at Monterey. Janis Joplin with Big Brother and the Holding Company belted out an R&B set that earned her a huge new following. Before Monterey, Otis Redding, the festival's only true soul singer, had limited success crossing over from the R&B to the pop charts. Afterward he stood at the top of mainstream pop in Europe and the United States until his tragic death six months later.

Joplin and Redding performed for the Saturday crowd. Sunday evening truly brought the house down. The crescendo began with the Who, until then an English band virtually unknown to American audiences. The crowd was at first polite and curious, but grew increasingly more enthusiastic as the group moved toward its finale, "My Generation." This performance literally exploded. Shattering the "good vibes, mellow" mood, the band, in what became their trademark, smashed equipment all over the stage. The dubious prospect of following this performance fell to Jerry Garcia and the Grateful Dead. They warmed-up the crowd by opening the gates to fans stuck on the outside, while soothing those inside with their amiable boogying.

Then came Jimi Hendrix. Though American born, at the time Hendrix was largely unknown in the United States. He did have a major following in England, especially among other musicians. Paul McCartney had insisted that the promoters include Hendrix on the program. He did not disappoint either them or the audience. His playing redefined both music and performance in what was a pyrotechnic show. Where the Who smashed their equipment, Hendrix set his on fire. Rock historian Ed Ward captured the import of their performance. "Hendrix," he wrote, "had decided to offer more of everything—more volume, more distortion, more grimacing, more erotic gymnastics, more I-am-a-star-and-you'll-never-forget-it-strutting." In this performance Hendrix had revolutionized the electric guitar, for other musicians and the rock audience.

Despite the enthusiastic audience response, the festival provoked some hostile comment from both cultural conservatives and radicals. The magazine *Rolling Stone* in its November inaugural issue charged that the organizers had exploited the event for commercial gain. Monterey was "a combination trade show and shopping spree where [record company executives] might browse 'til they saw something they liked, then inquired about the price." The number of new contracts inspired by the festival gave some credence to that comment. Reviews did not spare the performers, either. Ralph Gleason, the dean of West Coast critics, found Hendrix's performance boring, while *Esquire* dismissed Hendrix as "a psychedelic Uncle Tom." Another critic, in words he would soon eat, observed that Hendrix's "chicken choke handling of the guitar doesn't indicate a strong talent." Filmmaker D. A. Pennebaker, more than the critics, caught the countercultural spirit that infused Monterey. His documentary released two years after the festival exposed a national audience to the hip scene of the Summer of Love.

Just as Monterey was bringing new blood into the recording industry, Hollywood stumbled into the commercial possibilities of the counterculture. Two offbeat comedy dramas, The Graduate and Bonnie and Clyde, became huge box offices successes at a time when the film industry had lost much of its audience to television. Neither film, at first glance, has any obvious appeal to the hip audience that conferred on both something of a cult status. At least in the case of The Graduate, the Simon and Garfunkel folk-rock sound track and Dustin Hoffman's offbeat portrayal of an alienated middle-class dweeb gave the movie some countercultural resonance. The story follows recent college graduate Benjamin Braddock, whose lack of commitment after graduating from Columbia University hints at clinical depression. For much of the opening moments of the film, Ben hides in his room or floats aimlessly in the family pool while his father presses him to get off his butt and into a career. At one point, Ben dons scuba gear and escapes to the bottom of the pool to avoid the suffocating goodwill of his family's suburban friends.

Director Mike Nichols showed his gift for social satire when a smarmy businessman informs Ben that one word, "plastics," holds the key to the future. Ben's revival comes from an unexpected source. Mrs. Robinson, one of his parents' close friends, decides to seduce him. The idea of sex between a middle-aged woman and a callow young man was rather bold for American movies of the 1960s. Their sexual encounters fill Ben with anxiety, then guilt, and finally self-loathing. When he suggests to Mrs. Robinson that a little human interaction might be appropriate before sex, she rebuffs him with a coldness that gives a harsh edge to what until then has been handled as comedy. The harshness extends to Ben's attempts first to offend and then to win the affections of Mrs. Robinson's sweet, loveable daughter, Elaine. In pursuing Elaine, Ben rebels against Mrs. Robinson, his sexual dominatrix. The movie hits its dramatic climax when Ben is forced to tell Elaine that the married woman with whom he has admitted having an affair is her mother. As Elaine lets out a primal scream, Mrs. Robinson shows a look of pain that gives the movie a moment of authentic emotion.

Two aspects give the film its sixties resonance. The phrase "plastics," at which hip audiences howled, implicitly condemned the artificiality of middle-class suburban life. In that way, Ben's alienation mirrored the discontent of many of those flocking to the counterculture. His efforts to win Elaine's love offered a romantic twist to his psychological despair. Unfortunately, the relationship between Ben and Elaine has so little substance that it is far less interesting than the relationship between Ben and Mrs. Robinson. Only with the older woman does Ben seem alive. Her predatory sexual nihilism contrasts sharply to her daughter's innocence.

The battle between Ben and Elaine's blond Adonis fraternity boyfriend pits an unconventional and alienated (though hardly rebellious) outsider against the embodiment of corporate conservatism. Will Elaine choose Ben and romantic uncertainty, or will she follow her mother into the world of material comfort and lost innocence? At first convention wins out, but as she stands before her bridal alter, Ben races into the church and cries out her name in an existential wail that mirrors Elaine's earlier primal cry. His pain reaches Elaine, who flees the church with him. With the snarling wedding party in pursuit, Ben holds them off with a large golden cross that he then uses to bar the church doors. In a final populist gesture, Ben and Elaine escape on a local bus. The skeptical glances of their fellow passengers, as well as Elaine's final quizzical glance at Ben, make us wonder what if anything the future has in store. Nichols offers no 1960s style assurance that "all you need is love."

Bonnie and Clyde shared with *The Graduate* an offbeat idea of what love can be and a populist, democratic sensibility. It has a comic, almost lyrical pace, supported by a lively banjo score which, like *The Graduate*, slowly shifts into a dark nihilistic mood. The historical Bonnie Parker and Clyde Barrow were illiterate sociopaths. Warren Beatty as Clyde and Faye Dunaway as Bonnie are simply too glamorous to give any historical authenticity to their portrayals. Director Arthur Penn sought instead to create a mythological landscape against which he explores themes of violence and moral ambiguity. Here Penn blends the Robin Hood mythology surrounding Bonnie and Clyde with those of populist Depression era criminals like Pretty Boy Floyd and John Dillinger. Besides its links to the populist Western genre, Penn's *Bonnie and Clyde* also appealed to the sixties' audience taste for nonconformity. No authority figure in the film inspires even modest sympathy. Frank Hamer, the Texas ranger who tracks the Barrows down, radiates an aura of sadistic cruelty. Various bankers and lawmen come across as greedy, selfish, or manipulative.

By contrast, Bonnie and Clyde and the various members of the Barrow gang are painfully human. They create an extended family, loyal even in the face of death, save perhaps for Clyde's shrewish sister-in-law, introduced for comic effect. What drives the movie is Bonnie's simmering passions set against Clyde's sexual ambiguity. When she first tries to bed him, he recoils and tells her, "I'm not one of those glamour boys." Instead, Clyde expresses his masculinity through his guns and his audacious behavior. In the process, he and Bonnie lift themselves above the bleak prospects of Depression-America's losers to become celebrities, even if ill-fated ones.

The final scene marked a point of departure for Hollywood. As the police emerge to ambush Bonnie and Clyde, the camera moves into a close-up. Their bodies sway rhythmically from the impact of the bullets; death serves as an orgasmic conclusion. Critics damned this scene as disturbingly explicit. In a sense, they were correct. The intimacy of this final shot made the violence almost pornographic. Yet that was the point of the movie. Throughout, Penn had developed the link between sexuality and violence. As he and the younger elements of his audience recognized, sex, violence, and celebrity were staples of American popular culture. Television news offered images of murder, urban riots, and the war in Vietnam with levels of violence no less obscene, though perhaps less humanized. *Bonnie and Clyde* introduced a frankness about sexuality and violence that paralleled the frankness of *The Graduate*. In future films, Hollywood would often exploit sex in such a way that the ideas these films explored with wit and candor would become increasingly pornographic. For the moment, however, audiences of the 1960s discovered vitality in the work of Penn and Nichols that helped restore to Hollywood a central role in defining popular culture.

Move to Suppress

While these films explored themes of concern to cultural rebels, their dark undercurrents contradicted the sense of celebration that underscored *Sgt. Pepper* and the Monterey Pops. That darkness was linked to the growing violence in American society. It takes two sides to make a war, even an uncivil one. By the summer of 1967, the army of official America was already in the field. Like the dissident movements it opposed, its forces were seldom organized into battalions or dressed in recognizable uniforms. Rather, the armies of the republic fought a largely counter-guerrilla campaign using double agents, agents provocateurs, riot squads, campus police, National Guardsmen, and on a few occasions, the regular forces of the United States military. Nearly every major police department had undercover operations to penetrate the hippie drug culture and political protest groups. One reporter wrote in 1967, "The ghetto teams with espionage, codes, and double agents. One would think the police were readying for war. Or waging it." The CIA, IRS, military branches, and other government agencies began systematically spying on American citizens. The nation's courtrooms became battlefields, where prosecution became persecution. Through police harassment and arrests, law enforcement officials forced dissidents to shift meager resources from organizing protest to defending their freedom from criminal indictments.

Most of this domestic intelligence activity exceeded the authority of the agencies involved and was blatantly unconstitutional. That mattered little to the person most determined to stifle dissent, FBI director J. Edgar Hoover. By the mid-1960s, Hoover sought "to break the back of social protest." FBI programs "were designed in a way that circumvented due process requirements in an era when the administration of criminal justice procedure and civil rights were enhanced by Congress and the courts." Such covert operations became a means by which official America sought to preserve the cold war consensus.

So great was Hoover's reputation, as well as that of the FBI, that the agency operated with almost complete autonomy. Within the FBI, Hoover acted as tsar. His word was law; his authority, unchallenged. He could order illegal "black bag jobs" (breaking and entry to collect evidence), wiretaps, and domestic surveillance; fire agents without cause; and require them to live in FBI-approved housing under FBI-approved rules, which forbade all manner of sexual indiscretion. Insulated from accountability, the agency transformed itself, as one historian explained, "from a bureau of internal security into an agency resembling more a political police and an independent security state within a state."

In the 1960s, the FBI disrupted dissidents through its Cointelpros, or counterintelligence programs. Liberals joined conservatives in approving the Bureau's broad mandate, because Hoover shrewdly chose among his first targets the Ku Klux Klan. The excesses of southern segregationists in resisting the civil rights movement created a growing demand among liberals for federal intervention. Hoover was more than willing to establish counterintelligence programs against groups he saw as "extremists." The FBI had earlier established a precedent for such initiatives when it organized Cointel operations against the Communist and the Socialist Workers Parties. In 1964, subsequent to the passage of the Civil Rights Act, the FBI launched its White Hate Cointelpro, a program specifically targeted at disrupting, and thereby neutralizing, the Klan. The FBI viewed the Klan and other hate groups as "subversive in that they hold principles and recommend courses of action that are inimical to the Constitution." Most liberals agreed. This step was, however, as historian William Keller has observed, "the first instance in which the FBI moved against a group that did not have ties to a foreign government and that was entirely the product of endogenous factors in American history." White Hate was thus a point of departure. The FBI soon launched similar internal security operations against a wide range of dissident groups, most of whom were liberal or leftist in their politics, who opposed the Vietnam War or who championed civil rights.

By 1965, some 600 FBI agents and informants had penetrated the Klan to identify members and keep the Bureau apprised of Klan activities. Given Hoover's prurient obsessions, agents often collected information on sexual practices that would disgrace Klan leaders or on financial irregularities that invited action by the Internal Revenue Service. Above all, the FBI wanted to create dissension in the ranks. Efforts began with a smear campaign, planting rumors and disinformation about Grand Wizard Robert Shelton. Hoover told his agents that "this proposal can be moved through informants, established news sources, anonymous communications, the Bureau-controlled fictitious anti-Klan organization, the National Committee for Domestic Tranquillity, chain letters, cartoons, compromise of Klansmen and other means too numerous to mention."

The FBI operation was generally a success, despite an occasional black eye. Investigation later revealed that one FBI informant was present at the murder of civil rights worker Viola Liuzzo, though he denied participating. But the FBI did penetrate every major Klan organization. Klan membership declined from a high of about 10,000 in 1965 soon after the Civil Rights Act to about 6,800 in 1969. Attorney General Nicholas Katzenbach once congratulated Hoover for the effectiveness of the FBI operation, though Katzenbach regretted that the matter was too sensitive to acknowledge publicly. For the Justice Department, such extralegal initiatives were essential to avoid violence. Like many moderates and liberals, Katzenbach equated the Klan's extremist positions with those of the Communists: "They were lawbreakers of the most vicious sort—terrorists who intimidated, bombed, burned, and killed, often under the watchful and protective eye of their brethren in the local enforcement agencies."

The substitution of "extremist" for "subversive" in the internal security lexicon opened wide the door for future abuses. Hoover had a more idiosyncratic, socially conservative, and racist view of what constituted an extremist threat. When he informed Katzenbach in September 1965 that the Bureau had several thousand informants collecting data on "racial matters," he did not mention that many of them had targeted legitimate civil rights organizations. No one more deeply and profoundly disturbed Hoover than Martin Luther King, Jr., the recent recipient of a Nobel Peace Prize. During the 1964 Democratic Convention, the FBI had bugged King's hotel suite (it had earlier bugged SCLC offices) as well as the local office of SNCC. Undercover agents spied on the Mississippi Freedom Democrats. Hoover took these steps with the tacit approval of Lyndon Johnson, who wanted to insure that civil rights groups did not disrupt HIS convention. All these activities were illegal. Hoover compromised the Bureau to gain favor with Johnson, but he also knew he had the president cornered. If Johnson ever tried to dismiss him, he could threaten to reveal the damning truth about political spying.

Perhaps the sense of invulnerability went to Hoover's head. Various bugs and wiretaps had already alerted the director to King's sexual appetites. The civil rights leader's philandering included white and black women. Nothing could have done more to raise Hoover's sense of moral outrage, save perhaps his undying conviction that the civil rights movement in general and King in particular were heavily influenced by Communists. In November 1964, Hoover lashed out at those who criticized the Bureau for its failure to pursue civil rights violence. He called King "the most notorious liar in the country." The New York Times suggested that perhaps Hoover's sensitivity to public criticism indicated it was time for him to step down. A week later, Hoover struck again. He charged that criticism of the Bureau's civil rights record was the work of "zealots or pressure groups" who were "spearheaded at times by Communists and moral degenerates." Such intemperate remarks would have doomed the career of almost any other Washington figure. But Hoover survived because he had Johnson's full support. The president placed a high value on the political intelligence Hoover provided, and preferred, he admitted in his earthy Texas way, to have "Hoover on the inside of the tent pissing out rather than outside pissing in." Though King and Hoover declared a public truce in December 1964, the FBI's efforts to destroy the civil rights leader politically and personally continued unabated, even after his assassination. Hoover privately described King as "a 'tom cat' with obsessive degenerate sexual urges." Agents sent anonymous letters and tape recordings, seeking to destroy King's marriage and drive the civil rights leader to suicide.

Hoover's vendetta against King was just one of the more egregious of the FBI's efforts to monitor and suppress dissent. By 1967, the Bureau had in excess of twenty domestic security intelligence programs in operation. They most often targeted student radicals, antiwar groups, and Black Nationalists. Almost none of them were legal, and some had been initiated without the direct knowledge of either the president or the attorney general. By 1965, for example, traditional investigations of potential Communist subversion had been extended to include SDS and other leftist organizations. While SDS did embrace a range of Marxist ideas, it did not have formal links to the Communist Party nor to foreign governments. The New Left, for which SDS was a major voice, had self-consciously rejected the doctrinaire creeds of the party and cold war Stalinists. That distinction seemed largely lost on Hoover and his agents. When they saw dissent, they saw Red.

With the onset of ghetto riots, Bureau agents began to monitor the possibility of further racial explosions. A similar rationale, however, caused Hoover to extend such investigations to antiwar demonstrations. The director never recognized the spontaneous nature of most protest. He assumed, instead, that manipulative leaders were behind most of the upheavals. In the 1960s, he expanded the Bureau's list of 100,000 "radically inclined individuals" to cover Black Nationalists, antiwar spokespersons, and student activists. These were people marked for detention in certain national security emergencies. Other FBI operations went beyond maintaining lists to active investigation conceived to neutralize troublemakers even in the absence of any emergency. Most of those targeted on the "Rabble Rouser Index" were considered to have a "propensity for fomenting racial discord." By 1968, the Bureau renamed it the Agitator Index, to include leaders of anti-government demonstrations such as the march on the Pentagon.

In 1966, the FBI added to its program Black Nationalist–Hate Groups Cointelpro to cover SCLC and SNCC, followed in 1968 by New Left Cointelpro and another for the Black Panther Party. These programs were all conceived within the FBI and known only to Bureau officials. Congress exercised no oversight, nor does any evidence exist that the attorney generals knew about them. Agents were, in fact, cautioned to keep knowledge of the programs strictly within the FBI. As the level of dissent and civil disturbances increased throughout 1967–68, so too did the efforts of the FBI to crush political activism.

Black Nationalism

Well before the Newark and Detroit riots erupted, the struggle over racial equality had shifted out of the South. The tone of protest had become more radical and less nonviolent. By then, Martin Luther King had become an outspoken critic of the war in Vietnam. Leaders in SNCC and CORE increasingly identified their struggle with those of Third World people throwing off the shackles of colonialism. This combination of racial pride and demands for political empowerment came to be known as Black Nationalism. In the spring of 1966, James Meredith once again played a role in redirecting racial politics. Meredith, who had earlier integrated Ol' Miss, marched by himself some 220 miles from Memphis, Tennessee, through rural northern Mississippi. He wanted to assure blacks in the region they could vote without fear. Near the Mississippi-Tennessee border, a lone assassin fired a shotgun at point-blank range, wounding Meredith, though not critically. From his hospital bed, Meredith regretted he had undertaken his march unarmed. When a friend chided him for forgetting his nonviolent ethos, Meredith retorted, "Who the hell ever said I was non-violent? I spent eight years in the military and the rest of my life in Mississippi."

Civil rights leaders of all stripes flocked to Meredith's bedside. They gained his support to renew the "James Meredith March against Fear." Immediately it became clear that two issues divided the coalition. Many members of SNCC and CORE had renounced nonviolence. Others also repudiated interracialism. "This should be an all-black march," one proclaimed. "We don't need any more white phonies and liberals invading our movement. This is our march." Roy Wilkins of the NAACP and Whitney Young of the Urban League, both mainstream civil rights groups, were so angered by the disrespect younger protestors had shown them and their ideas they left Memphis. Only when Martin Luther King threatened to leave did Stokely Carmichael of SNCC and Floyd McKissick of CORE agree to have the march go ahead, interracial and nonviolent. Under goading from Charles Evers, brother of the slain Mississippi NAACP leader, the march became a voter registration program.

Large crowds greeted the marchers at each town along their route. Many had come to see Martin Luther King. But what looked on the surface like a show of unity masked profound and growing differences over goals and tactics. At Greenwood, Mississippi—the heart of SNCC's voter efforts—anxious police arrested Carmichael and other marchers. With King back in Memphis, SNCC organized a protest demonstration. One spokesman fired the crowd with the demand for Black Power. Carmichael, freed on bail, returned to the meeting where the crowd was already angry about his arrest. On taking over the microphone, he declared, "This is the twenty-seventh time I've been arrested, and I ain't going to jail no more." Then Carmichael turned the subject from the traditional civil rights focus on righting old wrongs to the New Left's concern with power—in this case, Black Power. "The only way we gonna stop them white men from whuppin' us is to take over," he declared. "We've been saying freedom for six years—and we ain't got nothing. What we gonna start saying now is 'Black Power!'"

The difference in tone between "freedom now" and "Black Power" was unmistakable. The one spoke of the trials and tribulations of long-suffering African Americans. The other was fraught with racial pride and self-assertion. Carmichael at times defined the new slogan in innocent terms. He saw Black Power as "a call for black people in this country to unite, to recognize their heritage, to build a sense of community." Blacks would take charge of their own organizations and "reject the racist institutions and values of this society." Yet in the context the slogan was often used—before angry crowds bitter at recurring acts of white violence, lawlessness, and abuse—the repudiation of nonviolence was clear. Carmichael and other Black Nationalists often linked their slogan to the prospect of blood flowing in the streets and revolution against the white power structure.

Certainly, Martin Luther King understood the slogan's threatening tone. King had no problem with the idea that blacks should develop race pride, political unity, and economic power. He recognized, all the same, that "Black Power" was inflammatory, because it suggested "black domination rather than black equality." Why, he asked Carmichael, should they adopt a slogan likely to "confuse our allies, isolate the Negro community and give many prejudiced whites, who would otherwise be ashamed of their anti-Negro feeling, an excuse for self-justification?" In the short run, King prevailed. The march continued with the SNCC coalition agreeing not to use the cry of "Black Power" and the SCLC faction dropping their slogan of "Freedom Now." And in the long run, history would suggest that King was right to be concerned. Black Nationalism tended to alienate traditional liberal allies and inflame the deeply embedded prejudices of the white majority.

But the near future for civil rights belonged to Carmichael and the Black Nationalists. "Black Power" stirred racial pride and activism, especially among northern and urban African Americans who would take up the struggle over race. By the time the march ended in Jackson, the divisions had become irreparable. While SCLC workers handed out American flags to symbolize their ongoing commitment to a national movement, SNCC handed out placards with the symbol of a black panther and the warning: "Move on Over or We'll Move on Over YOU."

Stokely Carmichael was white America's nightmare come true. The son of a Trinidadian immigrant, Carmichael was bright, handsome, articulate, charismatic, and proud. He would become for Black Nationalists the kind of leader Robert Moses and John Lewis had been during the voter registration. Whites came to fear him and the Old Testament retribution implicit in the idea of Black Power. From his father, Carmichael learned about the West Indian struggle for independence. As a student at Bronx High School of Science, he met the public school intellectual elite of New York City, including Todd Gitlin, a future founder of SDS. Carmichael eagerly absorbed their leftist politics, but quickly noticed they had little awareness of the plight of African Americans. Then he met Bayard Rustin, who would become a force behind the student sit-ins and freedom rides. Rustin showed Carmichael how to turn socialist ideas and racial concerns into an action-oriented political program. "At that point in my life," he later recalled, Rustin "appeared to be the revolution itself, the most revolutionary of men."

In 1961, Carmichael answered SNCC's call to become a Freedom Rider. It was then he experienced his first beating, his first arrest, and his first stay in a southern jail (Parchman Prison in Mississippi). His initial commitment to nonviolence began to erode. During one demonstration in Nashville, he helped organize an attack by blacks on group of harassing white hoodlums. He was not, however, prepared to abandon nonviolence until he believed the idea was bankrupt. Voter registration next captured his energies, not because he thought the vote mattered, but because it helped blacks defy the white system of oppression. Carmichael was also one of those in SNCC who opposed the use of white volunteers during the 1964 Freedom Summer. He thought SNCC should be an exclusively black organization that would create a black society without contact with whites.

Finally, discouraged with SNCC, Carmichael left Mississippi for Lowndes County, Alabama. Here, four-fifths of the people were black and none could vote. To some degree, the Voting Rights Act of 1965 had encouraged blacks in Lowndes to register. But Carmichael saw no advantage for blacks to compete for power with the local Democratic machine, dominated by those aligned with segregationist George

Wallace. He persuaded some local blacks to establish the Lowndes County Freedom Organization. For their symbol they chose a black panther. Just as Carmichael would become a voice for Black Nationalism, the black panther came to symbolize the racial divide in America.

Ghetto Violence

By the summer of 1966, white liberals had begun to read the Black Nationalists out of the civil rights coalition. Speaking to the NAACP, Vice President Hubert Humphrey condemned "calls for racism whether they come from a throat that is white or one that is black." Robert Kennedy warned that Black Power could set back the civil rights cause. But by then the action had shifted from the South to the streets of the nation's cities. There, the long-standing grievances of the black ghettos clashed with deeply embedded white racism. Just as southern whites had explicitly racialized social inequality, de facto segregation in northern cities racialized economic and political inequality. Put another way, all of the symptoms of social pathology—poverty, crime, disease, and despair—were worst in the black ghettos. The white elites who managed the cities and divided the spoils tried to ensure the perpetuation of that system. The slogan "Black Power" threatened whites in part because it spoke so directly to the plight of African Americans.

The racial front of the uncivil wars had begun with small outbreaks in 1964 and the eruption in Watts a year later. Over the summer of 1966, small riots in cities around the nation took a heavy toll in property, though they did not approach the magnitude of destruction in Watts. Cleveland, Ohio, offers a good example of the volatile brew created by white racism and growing black racial assertiveness. Most Cleveland blacks lived in Hough, a once-fashionable middle-class area that had deteriorated after the influx of southern blacks during World War I. By the 1960s, unemployment in Hough was four times the city average. Of the 11,500 workers with jobs in the high-wage building trades, only 13 were black. Few blacks held city jobs; almost none served on the police force. When ghetto residents complained about substandard housing, city officials ignored them. Black welfare recipients were given benefits at a lower rate than whites.

Inequality thrived in Cleveland in part because the city was blessed with a racially insensitive set of white politicians. The mayor ignored local black leaders and dismissed Martin Luther King as an "extremist." Police officials routinely ignored complaints about unwarranted arrests and brutality. So when the inevitable incident between a black man and police triggered a riot in July 1966, city hall had no lines of communication to the Hough community. Instead, the police chief ostentatiously cruised the streets, even using his own hunting rifle to exchange fire with snipers. Police officers shot a young mother desperately searching for her children on the streets. Rather than apologize, the chief showed the sensitivity of a Bull Connors. "There was a similar occurrence in the Chicago riots [a month earlier]," he told the media. "They sacrifice one person and blame it on police brutality." Under such astute leadership, it is no surprise that the Cleveland police could not contain the violence. After five days of rioting, the Ohio National Guard finally restored order. Of the four people who died, all of them black, two (including the mother) were shot by police, one by a white vigilante, and another by a group of white hoodlums.

Cleveland and other urban riots should have served as a warning. Instead, they combined with the rise of Black Nationalism to provoke a white backlash. A Gallup poll determined that by late 1966, a majority of Americans worried more about racial unrest than racial inequality. Among Republican politicians, in particular, "Law and Order" became a counterpoint to "Black Power." Each slogan carried potent racial baggage. Georgians elected as governor Lester Maddox, a man so acutely racist he even publicly joked about hunting blacks in Atlanta. Maddox gained notoriety in 1964 by using an ax handle to threaten blacks who entered his diner. "You're dirty Communists and you'll never get a piece of fried chicken here," he told them. More ominously, Republicans in Congress saw an opportunity to attack Great Society programs designed to fight poverty in the nation's cities, just as the cities had begun to explode.

In the summer of 1967, major battles in the uncivil wars broke out on the streets of Newark and Detroit. Like so many riots before and after, these began with seemingly minor police incidents. Ghetto dwellers looked on "the men in blue" as at best a hostile presence and at worst an occupying army. Violence, brutality, and arbitrary arrest initiated by police were commonplace. Yet the police were not inherently worse than the white America they sought to protect. Among whites, the police had the most contact with the African-American community. A Michigan judge and former Detroit police commissioner noted that while police saw themselves as public servants responsible for law and order, they adopted a more hostile posture in black communities. "There," he wrote, "they tend to view each person on the street as a potential criminal or enemy, and all too often that attitude is reciprocated. Indeed, hostility between the Negro communities in our large cities and the police department, is the major problem in law enforcement in this decade." And, the judge concluded, "It has been a major cause of all recent race riots."

Certainly, tension between police and African Americans played a major role in the riots that devastated Newark and Detroit. After World War II, Newark had become a heavily African-American and Latino city run by white politicians. From 1960 to 1967, the city shifted from 65 percent white to 52 percent black and 10 percent Puerto Rican and Cuban. Yet seven of the nine members of both the city council and board of education were white, as were the mayor and police chief. Most of the police were Italians; most of those they arrested were black. The Mafia reputedly controlled the bulk of lucrative criminal activities. Charges of police brutality went largely uninvestigated. When the black community objected to plans to turn a neighborhood into a medical college campus, the all-white planning board showed little concern, even though the public schools in Newark were overcrowded and underfunded. Almost half the black teenagers dropped out of school. SDS organizers had found a community frustrated by its lack of political power. Tensions rose so high that the state police made contingency plans for riot control.

On July 12, 1967, officers stopped John Smith, a black cab driver, for tailgating a police car. Smith's behavior was certainly suspect. In four years he had been in nine accidents and his license had been revoked. Thus, he was driving both illegally and erratically. Neighbors who saw police drag Smith into the precinct house claimed he was being beaten. A crowd gathered in a nearby housing project. A senior police official rushed to the scene and agreed to allow community leaders to interview Smith, whose injuries were serious enough to require medical attention. As more police arrived at the station, the crowd grew increasingly hostile. Several Molotov cocktails (gasoline-filled bottles that burst into flames upon breaking) erupted against the walls. Some civil rights leaders tried to organize the crowd into a protest march, but a shower of rocks from the housing project fell onto the marchers and broke police windows. An old car burst into flames. Helmeted police then rushed out to disperse the crowd. Despite a few incidents of arson and looting, the crisis seemed to have passed.

The next day, the mayor met with community leaders and agreed to appoint a black police captain. Newark, however, had a highly vocal Black Nationalist movement that included the well-known playwright LeRoi Jones (later Imamu Amiri Baraka). A march organized the next day to protest police brutality brought cries of "Black Power" before dissolving into an ugly confrontation with police. Neither side showed any sympathy for the other. That night, there were more incidents of looting and arson. Bands of young blacks roamed the central business area, smashing windows and breaking into groceries, liquor stores, and pawnshops. Looting begat more looting as people poured into the streets. The crowds proved discriminating, however, because they spared black businesses. State police arrived in the city, and National Guard units set up roadblocks to contain the crisis.

That was when the counter-riot began. This time it was the police and National Guardsmen who did the damage. Among the 17,523 Guard members in New Jersey, just 303 were black. Poorly trained and unprepared for the hostile urban terrain, the Guardsmen worried about rooftop snipers. No evidence suggests that serious danger actually existed. All the same, the Guard started shooting indiscriminately with high-powered rifles and machine guns. Shots on one block often frightened nearby police and Guard units. The head of the Newark police later concluded that "Guardsmen were firing on police and police were firing back at them. . . . I really don't believe there was as much sniping as we thought." One Guard unit sprayed a building with machine-gun fire. When the shooting stopped, three women lay dead. Police and Guard units then moved down the street, shooting into black-owned stores the rioters had spared. One Chinese business owner had saved his store by putting up a sign saying "Soul Brother," only to look on in disbelief as the state police ruined his shop. The battle became so desperate that the governor finally sought advice from radical SDS community organizer Tom Hayden. Hayden warned that if the governor did not withdraw the National Guard, "the troops are going to

Michigan Governor George Romney compared the riot-devastated neighborhoods of Detroit to a bombed-out war zone. (Source: Associated Press)

massacre more people, and you're going to go down in history as one of the biggest killers of all time." Once the Guard left, order returned to Newark. Of the twenty-three deaths, just two were white—a policeman and a fireman. The remainder, including six women and two children, were mostly innocent bystanders shot by police and Guardsmen.

During the riots, Newark sustained relatively little property damage. That was not the case in Detroit. There, too, a police incident mushroomed into disaster. A week after the Newark riot, the Detroit police had decided to raid a series of "blind pigs," after-hours joints that offered drinking and gambling. At the fifth spot, raided around 3:30 Sunday morning, the officers expected a handful of patrons. Instead, they came upon a large party celebrating the return of two black servicemen from Vietnam. Had this been a party at a suburban country club, the police would have looked the other way. But this was inner-city Detroit, and the police hauled eighty-two people off to jail. With so many people to handle, the operation took almost two hours. By then a crowd had begun to gather, and a few incidents of vandalism brought police reinforcements. Rumors swept the ghetto that police had used excessive force on those arrested.

Around 5 A.M., a bottle smashed the window of a police car; someone threw a litter basket through a storefront. A young man, known to police only as "Mr. Greensleeves," shouted, "we're going to have a riot," as he urged the growing crowd to begin vandalizing stores. More police arrived. Heavily outnumbered, they sought only to confine the crowds of looters to a small area. A fire broke out but was extinguished without incident. Still, the number of looters grew. Most were not simply the down-and-out elements of the ghetto, but people with jobs. Some whites joined in the looting as well. A few professional criminals seemed to be systematically cleaning out stores. The festive crowd did not spare "soul brothers" any more than white merchants. Most police made no attempt to interfere. As investigators later put it, "a spirit of carefree nihilism was taking hold. To riot and destroy appeared more and more to become ends in themselves." One observer remarked that the young people "were dancing among the flames."

Sunday afternoon, a young man threw a Molotov cocktail into a store as a policeman looked on. Summer heat had whipped up winds of 20–25 miles per hour. As flames shot up, winds blew them from roof to roof, including the roof of the arsonist who started the fire. Other fires broke out across a wide area. When firefighters arrived, crowds sometimes pelted them with rocks and bottles. Over and over the trucks withdrew and then returned. But even without harassment, Detroit had too few fire squads to fight the growing conflagration. Before the rioting ended, flames would consume an area of almost 100 blocks. Governor George Romney on Sunday evening said, "it looked like the city had been bombed on the west side and there was an area two-and-a-half by three-and-a-half miles with major fires, with entire blocks in flames."

By Monday, the situation was so desperate Governor Romney decided to ask for federal troops. Lyndon Johnson would agree only if Romney declared "a state of insurrection" existed in that state and local forces could not control it. While Romney hesitated to make such a sweeping claim, more of the city went up in smoke. He finally called for federal troops, but before they could be deployed, nervous National Guard troops and police repeated many of the excesses of Newark, spraying buildings with machine-gun fire in an effort to drive out snipers. Disciplined federal troops proved far more effective. They contained the rioting with a minimum of force. Where police and Guardsmen killed as many as thirty people, the army was responsible for only one death. In the end, forty-three people died, including thirty-three blacks and ten whites, seventeen looters (two of them white), fifteen bystanders (four white), one National Guard soldier, one firefighter, and no police. A number of those killed were possibly murdered. By Thursday, five days after it began, the riot had largely ended, and as of Saturday, federal troops finally withdrew.

The riots confounded most Americans and outraged many. What particularly disturbed whites was that some middle-class blacks seemed to approve of the rioters' behavior. Certainly the traditional civil rights leadership condemned the riots. But other articulate spokespeople treated the rioting as retribution or even as the sign of incipient urban revolution. One such person was the new head of SNCC, H. "Rap" Brown. If whites feared the Black Nationalism of Stokely Carmichael, they came unglued when confronting the revolutionary bravado of Hubert Geroid Brown. Ironically, SNCC had chosen Brown as its leader because he had a low profile and, hence, promised to be less controversial than Carmichael. Carmichael knew better. When he introduced Brown to the press, he predicted, "You'll be happy to have me back when you hear from him—he's a bad man." (The term "bad" as Carmichael used it was new to whites at that time.)

SNCC comrades called Brown "Rap" because, having grown up in Baton Rouge, Louisiana, he was cool with urban blacks. As a nonviolent civil rights worker in Washington, Brown became convinced that college students had to build a bridge to "the brothers in the street." Students could "begin to legitimize the brother's actions," he suggested, "begin to articulate his position, because the college student has the skills that the blood doesn't have." Brown had been only marginally involved with SNCC until 1966, when he joined Carmichael's voter registration project in Alabama. Once chosen to head SNCC, Brown managed at first to maintain his low profile. *Newsweek* described him as "far less assured" as a speaker than Carmichael "and far less flammable." Nonetheless, he did give his support to the new Oakland, California, Black Panther Party for Self Defense because he believed black people had the right to protect themselves. And he himself often carried a gun. Alabama police arrested him in 1966 for carrying a concealed weapon. He refused to give up his gun because, he would argue, "The only thing 'the man' is going to respect is that .38 or .45 you got."

By the summer of 1967, Brown had become an advocate for black assertiveness. His public statements provoked a mixture of disbelief and outrage among whites and embroiled SNCC in controversies from which it would never recover. He told one white interviewer that "if America chooses to play Nazis, black folks ain't going to play Jews." The remark was certain to alienate Jewish Americans, who had been among the leading supporters of civil rights. Brown did not care, because he was moving into territory well outside the traditional civil rights domain. When angry black protestors exchanged gunfire with Klansmen in Prattsville, Alabama, Brown told the press that SNCC would "no longer sit back and let black people be killed by murderers who hide behind sheets or behind the badge of the law." "Racist white America" had declared war, he claimed, which would bring "full retaliation from the black community across America." A month later, with Newark still shaking from its riots, he told blacks in nearby Jersey City they should "wage guerrilla war on the honkie white man."

A week later, with smoke billowing from Detroit's burning ghetto, Brown went to Cambridge, Maryland, to support blacks responding to increased segregationists activities. His message was militant, violent, and anti-white. "If America don't come around were going to burn it down," he told his audience. To him, poverty and draft calls of young men to fight in Vietnam were means by which whites practiced genocide on blacks. So the brothers needed to seize economic power. "You got to own some of them [white-owned] stores," he shouted. "I don't care if you have to burn him down and run him out." Within an hour after Brown finished, blacks and police began shooting. Someone burned a black elementary school that Brown had complained was inferior to the white schools. By the next morning, seventeen buildings had been damaged or leveled before Governor Spiro Agnew sent in the National Guard. Brown was himself lightly wounded by police, though he claimed he had taken no part in the rioting. Before police could arrest him he left town.

Agnew reflected the growing antagonism Brown inspired from whites. Having been elected with support from black voters, Agnew had a reputation as a liberal on race issues. The disorder in Cambridge and his revulsion against Brown turned him into a law and order man. "I hope they pick him up soon, put him away, and throw away the key," he told reporters. Even if Brown bore some responsibility for rioting in several communities, his role was largely symbolic. Few urban blacks needed to be told they were victims of white racism, and by the summer of 1967, little provocation was necessary to trigger racial violence. Nor could Brown do much to back up his militant threats. SNCC was by then in such disarray that it was no longer capable of sustained organized action. Brown himself became a target of the repression orchestrated by J. Edgar Hoover. After Maryland indicted him for arson, the FBI entered the case. Agents of the Justice Department arrested him on a trumped-up weapons charge. Henceforth, as the government intended, he would spend his energies and resources in court rather than on the streets. In that way, he lost his ability to promote what he envisioned as a revolutionary struggle.

The role as the symbol of militant Black Nationalism then fell to California's Black Panther Party. Founded by Huey Newton and Bobby Seale in October 1966, the Black Panthers began as a tiny fringe group with a flare for self-dramatization that distinguished many sixties dissidents. Newton was then just twenty-four and a college dropout who made his living off petty crimes. His education gave him a smattering of revolutionary ideas that he thought could be used to advance the cause of ghetto blacks. In most regards, the manifesto he and Seale composed for their party was a standard rehearsal of nationalist rhetoric about white exploitation of blacks and the need for racial self-determination. On one point, however, they made explicit the profound ghetto animosity toward the police. "We believe we can end police brutality in our black community by organizing black self-defense groups that are dedicated to defending our community from racist police oppression and brutality." Taking a cue from the Muslims, Newton had party members dress neatly but provocatively, in black pants, black leather jackets, dark sunglasses, and black berets—a uniform that captured the image of the emergent ghetto man. Their job was to monitor the police, but they did not simply follow the detested "pigs" through the streets. They openly brandished guns, since California made it illegal to conceal them. The sight of these cool, audacious figures brandishing shotguns and rifles captured the imagination of Oakland's ghetto.

So, too, did the Panther's bravado. In February 1967, the party ostentatiously provided an armed escort when Betty Shabbaz, the widow of slain Muslim leader Malcolm X, visited the Bay Area. A large police contingent arrived to challenge the Panthers. At one point, Newton and four comrades decided to face the enemy down. As one burly cop loosened his holster, Newton pumped a round into his shotgun and shouted, "OK, you big fat racist pig. Draw your gun!" That incident drew only local attention. On May 2, 1967, Newton pulled off a caper that put the Panthers in headlines across the nation. Thirty heavily armed party members walked coolly into the California State Assembly chamber in Sacramento. They came to protest a revision of the gun law that Newton believed would restrict the black community's capacity for self-defense. Newton would later explain that "only with the power of the gun can the black masses halt the terror and brutality perpetuated against them by the armed racist power structure." In an even more provocative statement, he asserted that "when the masses hear that a Gestapo policeman has been executed while sipping coffee at a counter, and the revolutionary executioners fled without being traced, the masses will see the validity of this type of approach to resistance."

Newton had failed to calculate what would happen if the "revolutionary executioner" did not escape. On October 28, 1967, two policemen stopped him at 5 A.M. What occurred then is unclear, but once the shooting stopped, a policeman lay dead and Newton and the other cop both suffered critical wounds. Rather than lead the revolution, Newton would spend the next three years in jail. Without its charismatic leader, the Black Panther Party floundered. The new California gun law stripped the Panthers of their power to bear arms. Party membership dropped to fifteen. But then Eldridge Cleaver took charge. If anything, Cleaver was more charismatic than Newton. He had honed much of his persona during long stays in prison. There he had discovered Islam before the excommunication of Malcolm X disillusioned him with Elijah Muhammed. After finishing a nine-year term in California's maximum-security Soledad Prison, Cleaver joined the staff of the radical political magazine *Ramparts*. As a reporter, he had been at the scene when Newton ("the baddest motherfucker ever to step foot inside history") had first faced down the "big fat racist pig." After that, he joined the Panthers as their minister of education.

Cleaver vitalized the Panthers, not so much through political action, but through exploitation of the media. He developed two major themes—the martyrdom of Huey Newton and the imminence of a ghetto revolution. In 1967, he even engineered a strategic alliance with SNCC, whose leaders adopted Newton's cause. The alliance never led to a formal merger, however, because SNCC leaders were wary of the Panthers and too deeply divided by their own internal disputes to form a united front. Unlike SNCC, the Panthers were willing to create ties to white radicals. Both the links to SNCC and the enthusiastic endorsement of radical groups like the California Peace and Freedom Party greatly increased their visibility. Radicals cheered the Panthers' revolutionary ideals and saw them as a critical link to the black community. By the end of 1968, Panther chapters had formed in two dozen cities outside Oakland, and membership rose to about 2,000.

The prominence of Carmichael, Brown, Newton Cleaver, and other radical advocates of Black Nationalism nurtured the conviction of many conservative whites that a widespread conspiracy lay behind the turmoil in the nation's ghettos. This was little more than a contemporary version of myths perpetuated by southern planters in the antebellum era. So it was in the 1960s. Conservative politicians, like the planters before them, sought to look outward for a conspiracy and preferred to perpetuate the racial status quo that advantaged whites and spared them the burden of addressing the reality of life in the ghettos. An editorial in a Detroit newspaper at the height of the riots claimed that local police were "trying to unravel the vicious pattern of deadly sniping that prolonged Detroit's racial maelstrom." They had concluded, "there is already strong evidence of a national conspiracy." The president of the Los Angeles Police Association told a national convention that the riots were caused by "travelling agitators, perhaps hundreds of them." And national Republicans, beginning to develop their "law and order" campaign, struck out at "hatemongers" (read Rap Brown) who went "from community to community inciting insurrections."

Conspiracy theorists did not seem at all concerned that there was virtually no evidence to support their claims. Even if a Rap Brown was in the neighborhood or endorsed looting and violence, investigators inevitably identified spontaneous events and local conditions as the cause of rioting. Neither in Newark nor Detroit did anyone find any systematic pattern of sniping. Most of those killed in the riots were blacks shot by police and the National Guard. In Detroit, police charged twenty-seven people with sniping, but the courts dismissed twenty-four of the cases and convicted no one. Ironically, radicals and Black Nationalists adopted their own conspiracy theories. At times they charged that white leaders or the white power structure had laid plans for racial genocide, using the police as an occupying army to keep the ghettos in bondage. In response, the radicals adopted a theory of revolutionary insurrection. They saw the riots in Detroit and Newark as the opening phase of a popular and spontaneous rebellion to overthrow the white oppressor. Black Nationalist leaders had the responsibility to give this uprising shape and direction—"to legitimize the brother's action," as Rap Brown had said.

Unfortunately for the radicals, the riots lent no more support to their theories than they did to the conservatives'. Most of the damage in the riots was confined to black neighborhoods; most of the victims were black. Analysis of who participated also undermined the insurrection theory. Few rioters had any purpose beyond looting or settling grievances against local merchants. Hence, the riots were often aimless and, as in Detroit, targeted black businesses and property as well as white. The violence left in its wake no community organization and no plan to take a next step. In fact, the riots did more to unify whites than blacks and encouraged the police to arm themselves ever more heavily. J. Edgar Hoover used the riots as an excuse to step up FBI infiltration of black organizations. So in reality, the riots led to more repression than liberation.

The Kerner Commission, appointed by Lyndon Johnson in the immediate aftermath of Detroit, offered a more persuasive explanation of the rioting. The commission was comprised of what one observer described as "representatives of the moderate and 'responsible' Establishment." That meant that neither southern segregationists nor Black Nationalists were among its members. Instead, it drew on the old civil rights organizations and centrist business and political groups. That made its conclusions all the more surprising. The commission identified the root causes of rioting in the "hopelessness" of the ghetto and its residents. These were communities of "men and women without jobs, families without men, and schools where children are processed instead of educated, until they return to the streets—to crime, to narcotics, to dependency on welfare, and to bitterness and resentment against society." These conditions had been brought about by patterns of racial seg-regation and discrimination, black migration from the South to northern cities and white flight to the suburbs, and the growing pathology of the ghettos. All these factors had created an explosive mixture that the commissioners reduced to a salient cause: "white racism." In every case, the match that lit the fuse was the "arrests of Negroes by white police for minor offences." To the ghetto community, the police had come "to symbolize white power, white racism, and white repression."

Laying the blame at the feet of white society did little to gain support for the programs for jobs and education that the commission recommended to alleviate the causes of ghetto tensions. Even Lyndon Johnson rejected his own commission's prescriptions. Gone now was the commitment Johnson had made in the heady first days of his Great Society to end poverty in America and close the racial divide. Gone, too, was the unity of sentiment that had led nonviolent civil rights workers to face white mobs, club-wielding police, and snarling dogs. Black Nationalism and the violent rhetoric of its radical wing shattered the civil rights coalition and drove many white liberals to find new causes. That would leave the nation divided along racial lines into "two societies, one black, one white—separate and unequal," as the commission concluded.

Race was a major fault line along which America had divided during its uncivil wars. After all, the wars began with the civil rights movement. The counterculture in its antic fashion proved almost equally divisive. But by the fall of 1967, disagree-ment over the American role in Vietnam had begun to rip the nation apart.

I I

A Bad Year Gets Worse:
The Domestic War Front

In the summer of 1967, Stokely Carmichael toured socialist nations. Like many Black Nationalists, he had come to identify the struggles of African Americans at home with those of Third World people abroad. Among those with whom he expressed the strongest sympathies were the North Vietnamese. Speaking in Hanoi in September 1967, Carmichael declared that like the North's Communist regime, Black Nationalists "are revolutionaries. We want to stop cold the greatest destroyers of humanity, the American leadership." Like Carmichael, many leaders of SNCC and CORE had become outspoken opponents of the war.

So too was Martin Luther King. While King rejected much of the radical's critique, he shared their sense of moral outrage. He grieved publicly at the bombing raids that took the lives of "little brown children." And King saw a link between the war and the loss of commitment to social justice at home: "I watched the program broken and eviscerated as if it were some idle political plaything of a society gone mad on war, and I knew that America would never invest the necessary funds or energies in rehabilitation of its poor so long as adventures like Vietnam continued to draw men and skills and money like some demonical suction tube." King's comments so angered Johnson that he urged J. Edgar Hoover to escalate investigations of the civil rights leader. Much of the mainstream media condemned King as they also criticized the Black Nationalists, for abetting Hanoi's cause. Like Johnson, the media chose to shoot the messenger.

Vietnam Again

Attacks from the civil rights community were only one sign of the growing disenchantment with the administration's Vietnam policy. The longer the war dragged on, the more unpopular it became. Lengthening casualty lists began to impact more homes and communities. Few people did not know at least one person killed or wounded. So Black Nationalists were among a growing chorus of voices raised against the war. No longer was criticism of the war confined to elite universities and colleges. Draft resistance was also on the increase. To those raised on the verities of World War II and patriotic sacrifice, opposition to military service seemed akin to treason. By the fall of 1967, a quick victory might have saved the nation from the growing strife, but news from Vietnam suggested that no end was in sight. As 1968 approached, disagreement over the war became ever more contentious.

Critics from the Right and the Left agreed on one point: the United States was not winning the war. Hawks like Senate minority leader Everett Dirksen suggested that "someone in Washington is putting the reins on military commanders." A free hand for the military to take any steps necessary to win (even to use nuclear weapons) was the most common policy hawks supported. Or as General Curtis "Bombs Away" LeMay put it, "We are just swatting flies when we should be going after the whole manure pile." Most doves believed the war was not winnable. Pacifists and radicals were especially vocal about the futility of bombing and its destructive impact on civilians. An increasing number of people within the Johnson administration shared those views, but with little prospect of influencing the president and his policies, they began to leave the government.

Johnson understood that public support for the Vietnam War had eroded. He responded in ways that proved unfortunate for his administration and the nation. First, he nurtured a conspiracy theory. Rather than take seriously the Left's critique of the war, the administration treated dissenters as subversives with possible links to Moscow or the Communists. In that spirit, a conversation at Lyndon Johnson's Cabinet meeting in September 1968 is instructive. By then, Johnson groped for some persuasive explanation of the forces that had so disrupted his term of office. For the veteran cold warriors in his Cabinet, one conclusion seemed unavoidable: domestic unrest and Communist influence must go hand in hand. Unfortunately for those who suspected subversion, CIA director Richard Helms reported that his agency had found "no convincing evidence of Communist control, manipulation, or support for student dissidents." Secretary of State Dean Rusk was incredulous. "No support?" he replied. When Helms assured Rusk that was so, Johnson insisted "that there is support." But his insistence reflected more a need for reassurance than conviction, because he immediately added, "there is, isn't there?"

As always, there were those in the Cabinet ready to give the president the assurance he sought. Secretary of Labor Henry Fowler likened the role of the Communists in student unrest to their earlier role in the labor movement. "I'm travelling around this country and all kinds of people tell me about Communist involvement in this thing," Fowler insisted. Secretary of State Rusk added that one ivy league college trustee claimed to have "30 Communists on his faculty." Johnson followed their lead: "I just don't believe this business that there is no support. . . . I've seen them provoke and advocate trouble. I know that Students for a Democratic Society and the DuBois Clubs are Communist infiltrated, Communist led, Communist supported and aggravated." Then Johnson conceded the possibility of the indigenous roots of dissent. "Maybe they are not Communist led," he concluded, "but they are Communist agitated and aggravated."

While the administration tried to discredit antiwar groups, it took the erosion of public opinion as a serious matter. Many Johnson advisers warned that criticism of the war encouraged Hanoi to fight on. Demonstrations suggested to Ho Chi Minh that American "will is weakening." The need to bolster public opinion led to a second misguided strategy—the overselling of the war. One army official recalled that "as the antiwar movement grew there was a growing need to demonstrate success." Optimistic reporting led to suppression of information from CIA agents in Vietnam that enemy troop strengths were far greater than official army estimates. National Security Adviser Walt Rostow told one CIA official, "the President needs your help. He is depressed about the progress being made in the Vietnam War and needs encouraging news." In that spirit, Johnson pressed General Westmoreland, the head of American forces in Vietnam, and other military leaders to produce evidence that the United States was making headway toward winning the war. On September 29, 1967, Johnson also made a somewhat conciliatory speech offering a cessation of bombing to induce Ho Chi Minh to begin negotiations.

The battle over public opinion deepened the antagonism between the administration and the antiwar movement. That conflict is what made the march on the Pentagon in October such a pivotal event. March organizers were reasonably confident that they could attract an impressive crowd to Washington. Optimistic forecasts went as high as a million. The administration did what it could to keep the numbers lower, including pressure to limit the number of rental buses available. Stories leaked to the press suggested that organizers of the march were mostly Communists and extremists. Johnson pressed his attorney general and the head of the Selective Service to make plans to prosecute those who were organizing a mass burning of draft cards. And the Defense Department moved 25,000 troops into the Washington area to protect the White House and the Pentagon. A week before the demonstrators arrived, a siege mentality gripped White House officials.

Events outside the capitol added to the administration's anxiety. The march on the Pentagon actually culminated a week of nationwide antiwar activities loosely coordinated by a group called the National Mobilization Committee, or MOBE for short. At the heart of these activities was a resistance effort known as Stop the Draft Week (STDW). During that week, more than a thousand students would burn their draft cards. The most dramatic moments came, not surprisingly, in Oakland, California. So many factions wanted to lead the protests there that the STDW assigned each group its own day. Monday opened quietly with several dozen pacifists blocking the entrance to the Oakland army induction center. A sign proclaimed, "Girls Say Yes to Men Who Say No." Police then arrested over a hundred people, but since the media paid scant attention, the results disappointed the protestors. Tuesday belonged to Berkeley antiwar factions who planned a teach-in on campus. Outraged conservatives got a court injunction banning the event. "We are at war with reds wherever they exist," one hawkish official remarked. As lawyers wrangled, several thousand protestors attempted to block the induction center. Oakland police plunged into the crowd, clubbing anyone in their way.

Tuesday's bloodshed was followed by several days of mild protest. Then came the Friday finale. Some 10,000 demonstrators found the induction center ringed by nearly 2,000 police, many of them citizen volunteers totally untrained for crowd control. As in Newark and Detroit, much of the violence that ensued came from the police rather than the protestors. Police repeatedly attacked and then drew back. The incensed demonstrators slashed tires on patrol cars, blocked intersections, immobilized buses, and totally halted traffic through downtown Oakland. Witnesses thought they had stumbled on a battle zone, though despite the furor no one was killed or seriously injured.

The protestors at first were elated by their success in confronting police violence and in stopping "business as usual," but they were frustrated as well. Demonstrations did little more than polarize public opinion, while the war and its destruction continued to escalate. In reaction, some radical elements of the New Left lost their faith in nonviolent protest. They would soon adopt more-violent forms of resistance and civil disobedience. Authorities sensed the growing militancy. The Oakland district attorney brought conspiracy charges against the leaders of STDW, who became known as the "Oakland Seven." Over a year later all were acquitted, though at considerable emotional and financial expense.

On Saturday the nation's eyes turned to Washington, where somewhere between 50,000 (government estimates) and 150,000 (march organizer estimates) protestors poured into the mall. From the administration's perspective, the question of how many people protested was less consequential than who they were. Among those leading the marchers were luminaries of the academic, literary, and social establishment, including baby doctor Benjamin Spock, Yale chaplin William Sloane Coffin, novelist Norman Mailer, and poet Robert Lowell.

The presence of such celebrated figures put the lie to claims that dissenters were a radical fringe element. Indeed, the majority came from college campuses and mainstream political action groups. They included children of high-placed administration officials. To outsiders, the motley uniforms of the counterculture might have given the impression of organizational unity. In reality, no consensus existed about the purposes or strategies of the march. Some wanted a peaceful demonstration; others called for active resistance, whatever that might mean. Moderates worried that illegal actions would undermine the effectiveness of the demonstration. SDS rejected the protest altogether, arguing "that these large demonstrations . . . can have no significant effect on American policy in Vietnam."

Perhaps the most antic approach came from a faction lead by counterculturalist Abbie Hoffman and his political sidekick Jerry Rubin. Hoffman had learned his politics as a radical in Berkeley and as a SNCC volunteer before moving into the hip underground of New York's Lower East Side. Rubin had been an active organizer of antiwar protest in the Bay Area, where he received over 20 percent of the votes in the mayoral election of 1966. Together they used guerrilla theater to con the media into advertising the cultural politics of the hippie and New Left communities. They understood that it was better for the "hip-Left" to be reported unfairly than not to be reported at all. "Recognizing the limited [attention] span of someone staring at a lighted square in their living room," Hoffman explained, "I trained for the one-liner, the retort jab, or sudden knock out put-ons." Rubin had earlier realized the potential of the put-on when he appeared stoned before HUAC in a Revolutionary War uniform and proceeded to blow soap bubbles.

In August, Rubin came east to help organize the march on Washington. Inevitably, he met Hoffman. "Jerry Rubin and I were destined to join forces," Hoffman remarked. Both "had a willingness to go beyond reason." Their first act took place at the symbolic heart of the establishment—the New York Stock Exchange. From the gallery, they organized a group of hippies to drop dollar bills onto the trading floor. As the agents of capitalism scrambled to capture the cascading bills, the market briefly came to a halt. Later, before disbelieving reporters, Hoffman burned money as a response to their questions. Suddenly the yippies had become news.

As October 21 approached, MOBE, as much as it was in charge of the Washington march, opted for a sixties-style resolution of the question of who would have responsibility for events that day—groups would do their own thing in their own manner. Saturday morning brought perhaps as many as 100,000 people together before the Lincoln Memorial. After listening to speeches and protest songs, the crowd slowly moved toward the Arlington Memorial Bridge and the Pentagon. Several groups split off, broke through fences (so people could get to "their" Pentagon), and gathered outside the building. Several dozen then actually sprinted through a lightly guarded door and raced down the corridors before angry soldiers drove them out. Army sharpshooters crouched on the roof. High-ranking officials, including Defense Secretary McNamara, looked out anxiously at the crowd around the building. McNamara later admitted to being frightened. "You had to be scared," he recalled. "A mob is an uncontrollable force. It's terrifying." Paul Nitze, a senior Pentagon official also looking out that day, did not realize that the mob contained three of his own children. But Nitze, one of the chief architects of cold war policy, had himself developed doubts about the war and fed McNamara's growing disenchantment.

Toward the end of Saturday, the majority of the protestors began leaving the Pentagon, but a few thousand stayed on, mostly more militant elements. Some female protestors offered soldiers a few moments bliss if they would switch sides. When one protestor shouted for a "piss call," a group urinated en masse toward the Pentagon. By midnight the crowd settled in. The Diggers provided food and blankets as protestors gathered around campfires. Government officials then decided the time had come to clear the plaza. Soldiers in a V formation marched steadily into the crowd, pushing those who were standing and kicking those seated on the ground. Federal marshals grabbed some protestors and clubbed others, targeting women for their special rage. "The brutality by every eyewitness account was not insignificant," novelist Norman Mailer reported, "and was made doubly unattractive by its legalistic apparatus." A witness described a particularly gruesome beating:

> One soldier spilled the water from his canteen on the ground in order to add to the discomfort of the female demonstrator at his feet. She cursed him—understandably I think—and shifted her body. She lost her balance and her shoulder hit the rifle at the soldier's side. He raised the rifle, and with its butt, came down hard on the girl's leg. The girl tried to move back but was not fast enough to avoid the billy club of a soldier

in the second row of troops. At least four times that soldier hit her with all his force, then as she lay covering her head with her arms, thrust his billy club swordlike between her hands into her face. Two more troops came up and began dragging the girl toward the Pentagon. . . . She twisted her body so we could see her face. But there was no face there.

By early the next morning, the final few hundred protestors had left to lick their wounds while the administration weighed the cost of its dubious victory over a ragtag army.

The immediate media reaction seemed to vindicate the administration's hard line. Johnson pointedly contrasted the "outstanding performance" and "restraint" of the nation's uniformed forces with "the irresponsible acts of violence and lawlessness by many of the demonstrators." The newspapers were almost vicious in denouncing the protestors. James Reston of the *New York Times* condemned the "the ugly and vulgar provocation of many of the militants." Like many Americans, he was morally outraged at the marchers' use of obscenities and had contempt for the "theatrical performances put on by the hippies." As Mailer noted, few in the press deigned to address the marchers' notion that it was the war itself that was obscene. Instead, "emphasis was put on every rock thrown and a count was made of windows broken. (There were, however, only a few.)" Of the wedge, illegal arrests, and random acts of violence against the marchers, the news media made no mention. Americans, in so far as the media reflected their values, were more preoccupied with proper dress, good manners, and the sanctity of property than with the possibility their government was conducting an immoral action in their name.

The administration's claim of victory proved premature. Perhaps it was mere coincidence, but as historian Melvin Small observed, a little more than a week after the march, Defense Secretary McNamara first openly expressed his opposition to Vietnam policy. On November 1, he resigned, though he remained as a lame duck until the following February. Critics on the Left and Right both became more outspoken. Robert Kennedy led a group of senators who openly questioned Johnson's handling of the war. And on November 30, Minnesota senator Eugene McCarthy announced he would run as an antiwar candidate against Johnson in the Democratic primaries. Worse yet from the administration's perspective, in December a group of distinguished moderates from the military, the press, and the Foreign Service issued recommendations on how to end the war.

Johnson's advisors now warned him that he must regain control of the debate over Vietnam. His one trump card, McGeorge Bundy observed, was general public "distaste for the violent doves," but "discontent with the war is now wide and deep." The people, Bundy concluded, "are really getting fed up with the endlessness of the fighting." So Johnson and his team went on the offensive. As always, the president wanted to crack down on the Communists, who planned to "take this government and they're doing it right now." With no Communists to attack, government agencies went after dissenters. The FBI reinforced its Cointelpros, the

CIA created "Project Resistance" against those who interfered with government recruiters, ROTC instructors used student cadets to spy on campus radicals, and the military services accelerated their domestic intelligence operations. Over strong opposition from many advisors, Selective Service director Lewis Hershey urged local draft boards to remove deferments from war protestors. Thousands of dissenters would be drafted before the courts ruled the Hershey directive was illegal. In the administration's most aggressive move, the Justice Department in January 1968 indicted five leading dissenters, including Dr. Spock, Rev. Coffin, and lawyer Marcus Raskin, for conspiring to counsel violation of the draft law. Many on the Left saw these actions as evidence that fascism had taken root in Washington.

Ignoring Bundy's warning to avoid hype, the president renewed his efforts to sell the war. He suggested that the public should line up behind him, so Hanoi could not use the war in America's streets to assist its cause. To lead the prowar campaign, General William Westmoreland, the head of MACV (Military Assistance Command, Vietnam), returned to the United States in November 1967. The administration had three primary audiences in mind: television networks and news weeklies that were not providing a favorable view of the war, skeptical senators and congressmen, and, last of all, the general public. Upon his arrival in Washington, Westmoreland told reporters, "I have never been more encouraged in the four years I've been in Vietnam. We are making real progress." Later he claimed the war had reached "an important point when the end begins to come into view." The United States would be able to begin its withdrawal "within two years or less."

Tet and After

For all the blood and treasure spent in Southeast Asia, few Americans, even those planning the war, cared much about Vietnam or knew much about its history. For most in Washington, it was a piece in a larger cold war puzzle made consequential only because of its links to Communist China and the Soviet Union. Had the administration taken more time to study Vietnamese history, it might have been spared the pain it now came to endure. The Christmas holidays and Tet, the Vietnamese lunar new year, traditionally brought a ceasefire to allow time for celebration. Ambassador Ellsworth Bunker seized upon the occasion to throw a New Year's party, where guests would "see the light at the end of the tunnel." Bunker ignored the wry observation of poet Robert Lowell that the light at the end of a tunnel might be the headlight of an oncoming train. Neither Bunker nor his guests probably knew that during the Tet holiday in 1789, Vietnamese armies had launched a surprise attack that drove invaders back to China.

Ho Chi Minh and his commanders had not forgotten. For long months they had carefully laid their trap. Most of the fighting in late 1967 took place at remote rural outposts like Khe Sanh, where entrenched marines withstood bombardment from Viet Cong forces in the surrounding hills. To meet this threat, General Westmoreland had moved many of his troops away from South Vietnam's cities. All that time,

Viet Cong forces had been quietly headed in the opposite direction, dressed as civilians and even occasionally as South Vietnamese soldiers. On January 30, 1968, they sprung their trap. In almost every major city and town across South Vietnam, the Viet Cong attacked key government installations. Some of their most audacious assaults came in and around Saigon. Guerrilla forces temporarily entered the grounds of the airport, the presidential palace, and government communications centers. After blasting a hole in the wall of the American embassy compound, nineteen Viet Cong rushed into the grounds. Television cameras showed bloody embassy personnel shooting from windows. After fierce fighting, all nineteen commandos lay dead, but one reporter compared the courtyard to "a butcher shop in Eden."

The worst fighting took place at Hue, the old capital city of Vietnam. Viet Cong held the city and its ancient palace for almost three weeks. Before marines drove them out, the Viet Cong executed hundreds (official U.S. sources claimed thousands) of Saigon officials and supporters. South Vietnamese hit squads retaliated by executing untold numbers of reputed Viet Cong sympathizers. Americans at home saw televised footage of haggard-looking marines shooting over stone rubble at an invisible enemy. The destruction at Hue and around the country was almost beyond calculation. In Saigon alone, officials estimated that some 6,300 civilians had died and another 206,000 became homeless. Around the country as a whole, at least 14,300 died, 24,000 were wounded, and over 600,000 had become refugees.

Despite the carnage of Tet, General Westmoreland would claim with justification that the enemy had suffered a major defeat. Compared to 1,100 American and 2,300 South Vietnamese soldiers killed, the Viet Cong lost at least 40,000. It would be several years before they could remount a sustained offensive of any kind. American forces and their ARVN allies had recaptured all of the centers the Viet Cong briefly held. The Americans had not been driven into the sea nor forced to withdraw, as Ho's commanders had hoped. Nor had Saigon's government fallen. Yet those had not been the sole objectives of Tet. Ho and his commanders gambled that the offensive would undermine American determination to continue escalating the war. The evidence of Viet Cong strength would "force the United States to de-escalate the war against the North and to go to the negotiating table." With the war in a new phase, the United States would withdraw. And to a large degree, that is what happened.

Not that American military efforts slackened appreciably in the wake of Tet. Genereal Westmoreland's forces made a concerted effort to exploit the opportunity afforded by the heavy Viet Cong losses. Nor did the American news media interpret Tet as a major setback for Americans. What reporters did seem to conclude was that no matter how great a victory the Americans and ARVN had won, the Viet Cong were in no way defeated and unlikely to give up their fight. As one analyst suggested, reporters now realized that "regardless of who won or lost [Tet], that the war was not under control." Certainly, the events as presented on television broadcasts supported that skepticism about American prospects for victories. Only a month before, an American officer had assured reporters that the local Viet Cong were "poorly motivated, poorly trained," and that South Vietnam's army now "has the

Among the many images that made Americans question the Vietnam War, this summary execution of a young Vietcong was one of the most shocking. Few viewers understood that the young man was also a terrorist. (Source: Associated Press)

upper hand completely." What American could not wonder then who the marines were shooting at in Hue or who blew the hole in the wall at the embassy in Saigon?

Having won the military battle in Vietnam, the Americans lost the psychological war at home. One humor columnist compared Westmoreland's claims of success to optimistic reports from General Custer at the Battle of Little Big Horn. "We have the Sioux on the run," he spoofed. "Of course we still have some cleaning up to do, but the Redskins are hurting badly and it will only be a matter of time before they give in." American television viewers were appalled by news footage of Tet that showed the chief of Saigon's dreaded police summarily shoot a handcuffed Viet Cong prisoner in the head. In this case, image obscured reality. The story made no mention that the prisoner was a terrorist. Instead, the audience saw an armed man, dressed in American fatigues, execute what looked like a young peasant. Were Americans in Vietnam to support murder?

More telling yet was the sobering appraisal offered by TV commentator Walter Cronkite. In 1968, TV anchors seldom editorialized on any subject. Cronkite was well known for what one historian described as his "impeccably non-partisan voice." After a February trip to South Vietnam, he told his audience that the United States was "mired in stalemate." "To say that we are closer to victory today," he concluded, "is to believe, in the face of the evidence, the optimists who have been wrong in the past." When Lyndon Johnson heard Cronkite, he knew the public opinion war was lost.

Tet brought a new sobriety to the Pentagon. International incidents involving North Korea and Berlin warned that Vietnam was distracting the United States from other, strategically more consequential cold war commitments. War planners decided the time was ripe to gamble on a knockout offensive. That meant calling up the reserves and requesting 206,000 new troops. On March 10, the *New York Times* revealed the plan to escalate further and mobilize the reserves. The shock was palpable. In January, public opinion polls had shown hawks outnumbering doves 60 to 24 percent, but by March the doves were ahead 42 to 41 percent.

And then came the New Hampshire primary. Few political pros believed the antiwar candidacy of Senator Eugene McCarthy had the faintest prospect of success. McCarthy was a notoriously dull speaker, and his campaign seemed painfully disorganized. Lyndon Johnson did not even formally enter the primary, though a slate of delegates supported his candidacy. As Johnson stood aloof in his role as leader, thousands of college students poured into the state to work for McCarthy. Shaving beards or putting on full-length skirts, they got "clean for Gene." Students ran the McCarthy campaign. They rang doorbells, organized public meetings, and stuffed envelopes to get McCarthy's message across. The leading candidate in the Republican primary, the "new" Richard Nixon, recently returned from the political graveyard, also attacked Johnson. On primary day, McCarthy won 42 percent of the Democratic vote; Nixon handily won the GOP primary. The press reported McCarthy's near victory against his party's presidential incumbent as a repudiation of Johnson's management of the war.

Perhaps nothing galled Johnson more than the announcement four days later that the man he hated most in politics, Robert Kennedy, had announced his candidacy. McCarthy supporters denounced Kennedy as an opportunist—a "Bobby-come-lately." All the same, Kennedy generated political passion that McCarthy could never muster. He also appealed more broadly to key ethnic, blue-collar, and Catholic elements of the old Democratic, New Deal coalition. A beleaguered Johnson began a period of painful reappraisal. The hardest task fell to the new secretary of defense, Clark Clifford. Clifford had long been a supporter of the Vietnam War and a pillar of the cold war establishment.

Clifford's efforts to appraise Pentagon strategy for Johnson left him in a muddle. The Joint Chiefs of Staff insisted they needed 206,000 more troops but could not promise success even if they had them. "How long would it take?" Clifford wanted to know. "They didn't know." Might they need more troops? he asked. "Yes, they might need more," they told him. "So what was the plan to win the war?" he asked. Well, they thought attrition might wear the Communists down. "Was there any indication that we've reached that point?" "No there wasn't," they replied. Clifford concluded that the time had come to deescalate. The war, he believed, had severely damaged the nation's international financial situation. Even more, he worried that the defection of business and educational leaders threatened the broader consensus on which American cold war foreign policy had been built.

How then to persuade Johnson to accept what amounted to defeat? Clifford called together a panel of the leading cold war architects, like former secretary of state Dean Acheson, to review Vietnam policy. The "Wise Men," as they were known, had once been united in support of the war. Now they told Johnson that he should "take steps to disengage." "The establishment bastards have bailed out," an angry Johnson remarked after the meeting. Still, he told Clifford, "I've got to get me a peace proposal." On March 31, he laid out his plan to a national television audience. The United States would limit future bombing to a narrow area north of the demilitarized zone. Even that bombing could be ended "if our restraint is matched by restraint in Hanoi." Beyond that, Johnson declared that the United States was ready to discuss peace any place, any time. He then dropped one of the great bombshells of modern American political history. "I shall not seek, and I will not accept, the nomination of my party for another term as your president," he announced. Johnson would spend the rest of his term trying to salvage his strategy for establishing an independent South Vietnam. If he succeeded in that regard, he would at least vindicate the policy that had destroyed his presidency. As of March 31, the military escalation phase of the Vietnam War had come to an end.

Toil and Trouble

Antiwar groups celebrated Johnson's announcement. "The hawk is dead," they chanted. McCarthy campaign workers in Wisconsin cheered, "we did it." That moment would probably mark the high point of 1960s optimism on the Left. The forces for change had pulled off what seemed an enormous coup. They had in some sense defeated one of the savviest politicians ever to hold the presidency. After that achievement, anything seemed possible. And then came Memphis and the beginning of what seemed an endless spiral into the abyss.

Civil rights leaders were not among those who celebrated Johnson's defeat. From their perspective, America had become more divided than ever before. Antiwar demonstrators had largely preempted the public stage. Energy that might have taken civil rights to another plateau went into the antiwar movement and other emerging rights crusades. A powerful backlash had turned traditionally Democratic, urban ethnics against federal initiatives to assist the African-American poor. Without Johnson, the prospect for new initiatives to help African Americans dimmed even further.

No one had found the shoals of civil rights politics more difficult to navigate than Martin Luther King. Both traditional moderates and radical nationalists had challenged his leadership. His opposition to the war closed his access to the White House. Waves of urban rioting made nonviolence an untenable position. Somehow King had persisted. If anything, his commitment to nonviolence deepened as he shifted his civil rights ministry from the South to the world of the ghetto underclass. His determination to limit violence increased that February when police in Orangeburg, South Carolina, shot forty peaceful black demonstrators—killing four of them. Most had been shot in the back.

King used his Ghandian principles to shape a radical critique of a political economy that oppressed the urban poor. Nonviolence, he preached, could do more to liberate the poor than wanton rioting. By strategic disruption of the cities, the poor could extract concessions from those who held power. "It didn't cost the nation anything to guarantee the right to vote," he argued, "or to guarantee access to public accommodations, but we are dealing with issues now that will cost the nation something." That message struck home to some hip young blacks who no longer looked on King as an Uncle Tom. His revolutionary message had put him in touch with the brothers.

In March 1968, King took that message to Memphis, where black street cleaners pushed city officials to recognize their union. Upon arrival, he discovered that racial hostilities ran so deep that mediation was near impossible. Violence erupted on both sides, though if anything, the excesses of Memphis police were the most disruptive. King lapsed into a self-reflective melancholy. Black people "will get to the promised land" of racial justice, he assured his followers, but "I may not get there with you." King had offered such gloomy prophesies before, and the following day he was once again energetically organizing a peaceful demonstration. That night, April 4, a sniper's bullet left him dying on the balcony of his motel. No one doubted that the assassin had been white. Many whites actually celebrated his murder. The mood in the FBI was definitely upbeat, but as an outraged Stokely Carmichael put it, "When white America killed Dr. King, she declared war on us."

The explosion was not long in coming. Out in Indianapolis, Robert Kennedy was on the campaign trail when he heard the news. Who better to pay tribute to a fallen leader and to express the sorrow of a whole nation? Kennedy asked the angry crowd before him to honor King by working to "replace that violence, that stain of bloodshed that has spread across our land, with an effort to understand, compassion, and love." But as Kennedy spoke, Stokely Carmichael strode down Pennsylvania Avenue in Washington, D.C., with a gun in his waistband. He warned the businesses that they ought to close out of respect for Dr. King. Inspired by his earnest manner, his gun, and the crowd following him, most shops locked their doors. Carmichael told his angry followers, "go home and get your guns," though whether for self-defense or to do violence he did not say. By midnight, the Washington skyline was ablaze as some 700 fires burned. The rioters were careful to distinguish black businesses from white. Similar rioting, though nowhere so severe as Washington, erupted in over 100 cities. By the time order returned, 46 people were dead, 3,000 injured, and 21,000 arrested.

Thus, King's death inspired not the racial reconciliation that he had sought or that President Johnson, Robert Kennedy, and other leaders thought would honor his memory, but a profound polarization that deepened the battle lines of the uncivil wars. As Todd Gitlin suggested, "non-violence went to the grave with him and the movement was 'free at last' from restraint." White radicals and ghetto blacks had understood, according to Gitlin, that King "stood for our better selves, and the rage and grief we felt when he died was the same sour rage blacks felt when they torched their neighborhoods the night of April 4." Cesar Chavez, leader of the movement to unionize migrant farm workers in California, spoke for many non-black civil rights groups that were then beginning to advance their own causes. He told King's widow that "the courage which we have found in our struggle for justice in the fields has had its roots in the example set by your husband." With minorities pressing ever harder for economic justice, white Americans, especially those Richard Nixon would soon identify as "the silent majority," began to express an anger of their own.

The person who sought both to capture that anger and turn it into a political movement was Alabama governor George C. Wallace. Wallace had first gained notoriety in 1963 when he personally barred African-American students from integrating the University of Alabama. "Segregation Forever!" was his battle cry. As of 1968, he remained an unregenerate racist. Among the villains in his demonology were black radicals and white fellow travelers who, Wallace charged, fomented violence in the nation's cities. Kennedy, Johnson, and the Supreme Court had forced reluctant whites to accept integration. And Wallace heaped scorn on "the overeducated, ivory-tower folks with pointed heads" and the "sissy britches" (a code term for homosexuals and effete snobs) who ran Washington. That message had a sympathetic audience outside the South. He warned, "the people of Cleveland, Chicago, and Gary and St. Louis will be so goddamned sick and tired of Federal interference in their local schools, they'll be ready to vote for Wallace."

As Wallace addressed the resentments of blue-collar America, students at Columbia University in New York City dramatized the deepening alienation among the future white-collar elite. The mood at Columbia in April 1968 was much like that at other leading universities. Student radicals had protested against the war, against Dow Chemical for manufacturing napalm, and against recruiters for the CIA and the military services. But since Columbia students also had New York City as an outlet for their political activism, the campus appeared less engaged than some other schools. That relative calm belied the growing turmoil in the student body.

Few universities were as insensitive to their surrounding community than was Columbia in the 1960s. Nor was its administration particularly sensitive toward students and their rights. The students had no role in disciplinary proceedings against those charged with infractions against antiquated rules. Many of Columbia's more distinguished faculty had little time for teaching or students. This was a research university. Much of that research was funded by the Defense Department and government intelligence agencies. Most notorious at Columbia was the Institute for Defense Research, which specialized in weapons development. Hence, radical students denounced Columbia as a central part of the postwar military-industrial-university complex.

Then there was the problem of Columbia the slumlord and bad neighbor. Over the years the university showed scant regard for the problems of nearby Harlem, which lay just below the campus. In order to expand, the university acquired buildings in the nearby neighborhood. That usually led to the eviction of tenants, almost always minorities. With similar insensitivity, the university announced plans to build a gymnasium in Morningside Park. A private institution would appropriate public land from a community with little open space. What act could better demonstrate the university's brazen disregard for blacks, Hispanics, and the poor? At a rally held by members of the Student Afro-American Society and Harlem residents, protestors carried signs that proclaimed "Gym Crow Must Go."

The decision to build a gym in Morningside Park persuaded radical students that Columbia's scholarly and aloof president, Grayson Kirk, was part of the system "which demands gross inequalities of wealth and power, a system which denies personal and social freedom and potential, a system which has to manipulate and repress us in order to exist." On April 23, an "action faction" of radical Columbia students lashed out at that system. Twenty-year-old junior Mark Rudd pressed the radicals to act. The Columbia uprising would make Rudd one of the first political celebrities from the baby boom generation. He had arrived at Columbia naive but politically engaged, and quickly began to imbibe Marxist ideas and radical rhetoric. Che Guevera, the romantic revolutionary, became his idol, while a visit to Cuba confirmed his Marxist sympathies for Third World liberation.

Rudd came to epitomize qualities that had come to define the New Left by 1968—an impatience with intellectual analysis, a gift for facile generalization, an almost overbearing sense of moral righteousness, and an absolute disdain for the conventions of civility. Egged on by Rudd, SDS disrupted Columbia's memorial service for Martin Luther King and sent a letter to Grayson Kirk guaranteed to ruffle his presidential dignity. "There is only one thing left to say," the letter concluded. "It may sound nihilistic to you since it is the opening shot in a war of liberation. I'll use the words of LeRoi Jones, whom I'm sure you don't like a whole lot: 'Up against the wall, motherfucker, this is a stick up.'" The term "motherfucker" had not then passed into common usage, much less polite conversation.

Protest began as a demonstration against the gym provoked a counter-demonstration by conservative students. They blocked the protesters who charged toward Low Library, which also housed the president's offices. Rudd was at a loss for what to do next. But then a member of the Afro-American Society spoke: "If you are talking about identifying with the Vietnamese struggle you don't have to go to Rockefeller Center, dig? There's one oppressor—in the White House, in Low Library, in Albany, New York. You strike a blow against Low Library, you strike a blow for freedom fighters in Angola, Mozambique, Portuguese Guinea, Zimbabwe, South Africa." Stirred to act but blocked from Low Library, the crowd rushed into nearby Hamilton Hall, a classroom and administration building. By the end of the day, militant Black Nationalists from Harlem had filtered into the building and ordered the white radicals out. That step marked a racial division that no amount of Marxist rhetoric would ever heal. Even as it came into its own, the action-oriented New Left was splitting into factions.

The exiled white radicals now forced their way into Low Library and President Kirk's office. Some of their actions deeply offended traditional notions of decorum. They played president at Kirk's desk, rummaged through his files, drank his sherry, and smoked his cigars. More disturbing, some students burned the notes and manuscript in a history professor's office. His book would never be published. Yet for all the crude manners and nihilistic vandalism, a giddy idealism also defined their actions. They established the kind of participatory democracy about which they so often preached. Revolutionary committees offered analysis of the system that these predominantly middle-class students of privilege had in their actions rejected. Some came to believe that within the captured buildings they had created a "new society," a "liberated area," or, perhaps, a "commune." They also smoked dope, made love, sang, and had what at times seemed like a long spring weekend.

The real chaos began only after Kirk, under enormous pressure to deal harshly with student anarchists, called in the police. And as in so many other politically charged civil disturbances, the police staged a riot. One week after the protest began, a thousand club-wielding police officers charged into the occupied buildings. Surely the lower-middle-class sons of Ireland and Italy among New York's finest could not help but be offended by the appearance of the protestors. They dragged students with heads banging down stairs; those who moved slowly were beaten, dozens were injured, and several hundred arrested. Whatever community Columbia had known was shattered that day. Under severe criticism from many moderate faculty and students for resorting to "gestapo" tactics, Kirk refused to resign. To do so would be to grant a victory "to those who are out to destroy the university." Neither Kirk nor his supporters ever addressed the issues protestors had raised—Columbia's highhanded treatment of its Harlem neighbors, the deep involvement of the university in weapons research, its role as slumlord, and its indifference to the rights of students. The issue as Kirk saw it was the incivility of student protest that threatened to mire Columbia and the nation in anarchy.

In the wake of the police assault, SDS veteran Tom Hayden called for "two, three, many Columbias." At campuses across the country and in Western Europe, student radicals tried to keep the Columbia flame burning. Whether it was a gym or parietal hours or Dow Chemical recruiters that triggered protest, the underlying source of radical discontent on campus was the growing sense that university officials saw students as cogs in a machine to be managed and manipulated, not educated.

The Death of Liberal Hope

The unrest that shut down Columbia persuaded the leaders of the political establishment that anarchy threatened. Richard Nixon saw in that anxiety an issue that might propel him into the White House. On the election trail in May 1968, he warned that the disruptions were "the first skirmish in a revolutionary struggle to seize the universities of this country and transform them into sanctuaries for radicals and vehicles for revolutionary political and social goals." Nixon pressed Kirk to take a hard line to "rid the campus now [of] anarchic students." He characterized radicals as "hotheads who assume they know all truth." Failure to take immediate steps against them "invited student coups on other campuses all over this country."

The criticism of universities as incubators of radical politics and bohemian social behaviors was just one way in which Nixon embraced the conservative agenda. In addition to protest, he attacked "centralizing and domineering" government—a code phrase for liberal social programs. Nixon, by contrast, favored individual initiative and entrepreneurship. For blacks that would mean reduced "handouts or welfare" and more "black capitalism." In this way, Nixon played the race card that he hoped would draw southern conservatives into the Republican camp. By 1968, white Americans increasingly saw Great Society programs in general, and welfare programs in particular, as advantaging blacks at their expense. In attacking welfare, Nixon could establish the Republicans as the party of white America without overt appeal to racist sentiments. He constantly argued that neither protest nor massive federal spending programs would redress the problems of poverty and racial injustice. Such arguments appealed to those who saw "law and order" as the alternative to anarchy.

In wooing Southerners, Nixon sensed that the Democrats had become hopelessly split. Eugene McCarthy appealed almost exclusively to campus activists and suburban liberals. Hubert Humphrey, Johnson's designated heir apparent, commanded the loyalty of regular machine Democrats like Mayor Richard Daley of Chicago and the leaders of organized labor. But Humphrey's continued support for Johnson's Vietnam policy outraged much of the liberal wing. His past record on civil rights alienated many southern Democrats. They were more inclined to bolt to the insurgent campaign of George Wallace unless Nixon succeeded in capturing them. Only one candidate showed any capacity to pull together the increasingly fractious Democrats, and that was Bobby Kennedy. The Kennedy name still had magic for many of the nation's voters. No one showed more passion for the minority and poor, yet Kennedy also excited the enthusiasm of blue-collar workers and ethnic Catholics.

To win the nomination, Kennedy faced two problems. Humphrey held a commanding lead among delegates committed prior to the Chicago convention, and Eugene McCarthy's loyalists could not forgive Kennedy for jumping so late into a campaign in which their candidate had shown the way. Even though it was clear that McCarthy could not win in November, his followers remained intensely loyal; nor could Kennedy persuade his rival to withdraw. Yet for all his supposed convictions, McCarthy proved a remarkably indifferent campaigner. Civil rights and the problems of the poor were not issues that animated him as they did Kennedy. One of his staff members recalls wondering "whether McCarthy had the executive ability to be president. He seemed to pay no attention to the campaign." What did seem to keep McCarthy going was not the remote prospect of becoming president, and certainly not a love of politics, which he in fact disdained, but a deep resentment of Bobby Kennedy and his family's ruthless brand of politics. "I think what [McCarthy] most wanted," Kennedy ruefully acknowledged, "was to knock me off. I guess he may hate me that much."

Bruised by an unexpected primary defeat in Oregon, Kennedy stormed into California to win its primary by a 46 to 40 percent margin. The victory gave his campaign a boost it desperately needed. He told a celebrating crowd at the Ambassador Hotel in Los Angeles, "we can work together [to] end the divisions between blacks and whites, between the poor and more affluent, or between age groups or on the war in Vietnam." He held out the olive branch to McCarthy, who had made "citizen participation a new and powerful force in our political life." For one brief moment it seemed possible that all of those people demanding racial justice, authentic politics, and an end to the war in Vietnam might coalesce around the Kennedy candidacy. But as Kennedy left the reception, Sirhan Sirhan, a young Palestinian émigré, shot and killed him.

A white supremacist, an angry conservative, a crazy radical, maybe a Black Nationalist—in the fractious climate of 1968, such an assassin might have made some sense, but a Palestinian nationalist? Yet like so many young people in the 1960s, Sirhan believed he had a grievance. A week earlier he had seen Kennedy on television leaving a Jewish synagogue in Oregon with a yarmulke on his head. Kennedy had reiterated a central theme of his campaign: "we are committed to Israel's survival." Only a year before, the Israelis had won a smashing six-day victory over the Arab states. The future for the Palestinian people seemed bleak and Sirhan had taken these events personally. His brother recalls that the sight of Kennedy at the synagogue drove him from the room weeping. In his dairy, Sirhan described as "an unshakable obsession" his determination to kill Kennedy. The day of the assassination he had practiced target shooting before heading to the Ambassador, where he mingled with the crowd, waiting for Kennedy to pass by.

The murder of King and then Kennedy killed the promise of reconciliation in a nation deeply divided along lines of race, class, gender, ethnicity, and values. Tom Hayden, who had once dismissed Kennedy as a "little fascist," openly wept at his death. Hayden confessed that he was personally drawn to Kennedy and believed he might have made the system work. The assassination convinced Hayden "that our society was even worse in terms of the opportunities for peaceful change" than he had thought. Even though Kennedy's death boosted his campaign, Eugene McCarthy simply lost heart and virtually withdrew from the race. Now it seemed inevitable that in November, voters would get to choose between Nixon and Humphrey, two traditional politicians committed to positions that had divided the nation. Or worse yet, there was George Wallace, peddling his blend of populism and racism. Many young activists could only conclude that the system would destroy any person who championed the cause of peace, hope, and justice. Some retreated from the political fray, while a small minority turned to violence.

The major beneficiary of the Democrats' disarray was Richard Nixon, the man they hated most. After his losses to Jack Kennedy in 1960 and Pat Brown in the California governor's race in 1962, Nixon had spent a period in political self-exile. He made money as a Wall Street lawyer until his undying passion for the presidency drew him back into politics. For years he traveled the rubber chicken circuit, raising funds for Republican candidates, pressing the Republican flesh, and rebuilding his Republican following. Goldwater's smashing defeat in 1964, having undermined the political viability of the party's right wing, allowed Nixon to capture the middle. Long before the Republican convention met in Miami, Nixon had wrapped up the nomination. The delegates who chose him to lead the party were almost exclusively wealthy, white, and male. They paid little attention when blacks rioted in nearby Liberty City. While Nixon reached out to middle-class blacks, his real audience was "the forgotten Americans, those who did not indulge in violence, those who did not break the law, people who pay their taxes and go to work, people who send their children to school, who go to their churches, people who are not haters, people who love their country."

The Spirit of Chicago

As the Republicans preached the politics of Middle America, the Democrats prepared to self-destruct in Chicago. A number of ironies attended that process. McCarthy's popularity among Democrats rose in the wake of Kennedy's death, but McCarthy lost interest in the nomination. He left the command of his campaign to squabbling lieutenants who could not agree on what direction to take. His delegates arrived in Chicago backing a candidate who appeared determined not to win. Many of the blue-collar voters energized by Robert Kennedy's crusade gravitated neither to McCarthy, the antiwar candidate, nor to Humphrey, the voice of New Deal liberalism, but to George Wallace and Richard Nixon.

Hubert Humphrey came to Chicago with the nomination locked up. That involved yet another irony. To win the nomination, he had accepted conditions imposed by Lyndon Johnson that virtually guaranteed he would lose the election. Despite advice to distance himself from Johnson, especially on the war, Humphrey repeatedly asserted his loyalty to a person who in private treated him with undisguised contempt. Humphrey accepted Johnson's claim that the election hinged on efforts to negotiate with Hanoi. If the president achieved a breakthrough in the negotiations, Humphrey would win. But if Humphrey broke ranks, Hanoi would not negotiate. Since in reality Hanoi had no intention of accepting Johnson's terms, Humphrey was doomed. Yet the president held him captive to his determination to vindicate his decisions on the war, even if it cost the party the election.

Though he was not a candidate, Johnson dominated the convention, even though he had become so unpopular that he dared not attend. His political machine ran the proceedings under the watchful eye of Chicago's mayor, Richard Daley. Party officials arranged that the California and New York delegations, with large antiwar factions, be isolated at the back of the convention hall. Johnson loyalists also insisted that the party platform praise the president's Vietnam policies rather than adopt the McCarthy forces' antiwar plank or even a moderate statement Humphrey favored. Humphrey's ambition to be president outweighed whatever impulse he might have had to be his own person. That display of spinelessness further eroded his already dim prospects.

That Richard Daley, political czar of Chicago and Democratic kingmaker, should have been the target of the frustrated antiwar Democrats offers a final irony in this bizarre melodrama. Daley may have been the embodiment of old-fashioned machine politics, but, unlike J. Edgar Hoover, to whom radicals often compared him, he was not a person given to confrontation. Instead, he practiced the politics of accommodation. Whenever possible, he co-opted potential enemies with favors rather than struggle with them for power. And his political instincts told him the Vietnam War was a loser. Unbeknownst to the antiwar protestors, who made the mayor a target of their frustration, Daley had privately informed Johnson that he opposed the war.

Opposing the war in private was not, however, the same as supporting antiwar protest. Daley despised radicals and hippies. He publicly derided them as "hoodlums and Communists." As a former Catholic altar boy, he found their behavior morally offensive and their extremist politics un-American. More important, he knew that the city's conservative ethnic and minority population shared his contempt for what he thought of as spoiled, rich brats. If his police cracked a few heads, most Chicago voters would support him. In April, Daley let those who had notions of disrupting the convention know that Chicago was an inhospitable town. When the ghettos erupted in violence after King's assassination, Daley ordered his police "to shoot to kill" arsonists. Three weeks later, his police maced and clubbed a crowd of peaceful antiwar marchers. Daley prepared a suffocating blanket of security for the convention hall. He created an army of 12,000 police, with an equal force of National Guardsmen and regular soldiers in reserve, and hundreds of police, FBI, and other agents working undercover to monitor radical plans. Some delegates would complain that they felt trapped in a prison fortress.

Just as determined as the mayor was that radicals and hippies would not disrupt his city and his convention, antiwar factions were convinced they would. Planning for Chicago had begun almost as soon as the bedraggled "armies of the night" left the Pentagon in October 1967. Among the largely unorganized forces opposing the war, three groups stood out. Chief among them was the National Mobilization Committee to End the War in Vietnam (MOBE), the coalition of antiwar groups who organized the march on the Pentagon. Tom Hayden and Rennie Davis, former founders of SDS and veteran community organizers, saw protest in Chicago as a step toward a student revolution, potentially worldwide in scope. "A new international was formed without a comintern," Hayden told a sympathetic interviewer, "without a bureaucracy, reaching around the world to students in France, West Germany, Cuba, Venezuela, Quebec. Vietnam was the internationalizing force," he added, "and SDS was the inspiration." Hayden remained one of the most visible and controversial radicals. He had visited North Vietnam, had advised the mayor of Newark during the riots, and had taken a prominent role in the Columbia uprising. Encouraged by student revolts in Paris and Prague, he and Davis were convinced by the summer of 1968 that the system was tottering and a well-timed student push might knock it down. Chicago might just offer the moment.

Davis and Hayden took their plans for Chicago to David Dellinger, MOBE national chair. Dellinger had roots in the pacifist movement of the 1930s. He remained dedicated to nonviolence and, along with many liberal opponents of the war, had grown concerned about the violence creeping into the antiwar movement. At the same time, he recognized that his coalition would come unglued unless it found an effective way to protest the war. Davis and Hayden, no matter what their broader revolutionary goals, at least had a plan. They hoped to organize huge crowds for three days of protest in Chicago that would "delegitimize" the Democratic Party. Following the convention they would turn their energies to organizing antiwar protest at the community level.

That plan was naive at best. MOBE had neither the personnel nor financial resources to undertake a major organizational drive. And as weary as the American people were with the war, few were prepared to come to Chicago to protest. That was not, however, why the gathering of radicals, antiwar liberals, Black Nationalists, and yippies refused to adopt the Davis-Hayden plan. Rather, each faction had its own reservations. Liberals suspected that Hayden and Davis had no intention of keeping the protests "nonviolent and legal." Radicals assumed liberals would sell out to the system, especially if Kennedy or McCarthy received the nomination. Blacks suspected that during demonstrations, they would become the primary targets of the police.

The yippies, of course, disdained the whole proceeding. Even the name of their party began as a joke—it meant nothing but sounded stoned. Abbie Hoffman informed the gathering that the yippies demanded the abolition of pay toilets as the central tenet of their revolutionary platform. Rubin insisted that if the yippies came to Chicago, they would come for revolution and fun. Besides, Hoffman and Rubin already had plans for Chicago—while the Democrats held their "Convention of Death," the yippies would sponsor a "Festival of Life." "Chicago is LBJ's stage and we are going to steal it," they announced. They hoped that by recruiting forty rock bands, they would attract a half a million young protestors. At a minimum they would sponsor a "nude-in" at a Lake Michigan beach, hold workshops on draft resistance, offer drug and poetry seances, and discuss visions for a new social order. Beyond that, they disagreed about how to proceed.

After the aborted planning meeting in March, MOBE and the yippies went their separate ways. Both had written Chicago off as a waste of their energies. But once Johnson withdrew and Kennedy had been murdered, protest took on renewed importance. Elements in SDS threatened revolutionary mayhem in Chicago. MOBE, disavowing any link with SDS, began organizing in earnest for what Dellinger hoped would be a massive protest. Davis lined up legal defense teams, medical care, housing, and meeting spaces. To keep his pledge that the protests would be legal, Davis asked for permits to parade, hold demonstrations, and use city parks for sleeping spaces. Daley's representative, David Stahl, frustrated those efforts by refusing the permits. Finally, MOBE sued, but a Daley crony, Judge Lynch, dismissed the suit. So as the convention approached, Stahl and Lynch (an irony not lost on the antiwar groups) had denied MOBE any legal basis for gathering in Chicago or demonstrating during the convention.

The yippies spent much of their energy hectoring Mayor Daley. They threatened to put LSD in Chicago's water system and run naked through the streets. Mingling the political with the theatrical, they demanded an end to the war, legalized marijuana, a money-less society, and recognition "that people should fuck all the time, anytime, whomever they want." No political platform could have been better designed to provoke Chicago's puritanical mayor. Determined to intimidate the protestors, his police began systematic harassment of Chicago yippies. When the yippies failed to acquire permits for their Festival of Life, almost every musician who had promised to perform backed out.

But Daley had no way to block the yippies ultimate put-on: three days before the convention they chose "Pigasus" as their candidate for the presidency. "They nominate a president and he eats the people," they explained. "We nominate a president and the people eat him." Pigasus had a simple platform, "Garbage," and a slogan: "Why take half a hog when you can have the whole hog?" Before a crowd of TV cameras and reporters, Rubin released Pigasus in Chicago's Civic Center Plaza. The police were not amused. They captured the pig and arrested Rubin and five other yippies. Three days before the convention officially opened, the battle for Chicago had begun in the theater of the absurd.

Besides MOBE and the yippies, a third group came to Chicago determined to upset the convention, from inside, not outside, the system. These were the increasingly frustrated McCarthy delegates. With no hope of nominating an antiwar candidate, they could at best hope to influence the party platform. McCarthy, fearing potential violence, urged his young supporters to stay away. Most came anyway in hopes that somehow they could derail the Humphrey express. Allard Lowenstein, who orchestrated the dump Johnson movement, had since organized the Coalition for an Open Convention. Well aware that McCarthy would never be chosen, Lowenstein wanted to deny Humphrey the nomination. An open convention might opt for a compromise candidate. When Lowenstein sought permission to hold a march and rally as an outlet for moderate, nonviolent antiwar factions, Daley officials refused him as well. Lowenstein warned that party leaders "seem determined to have a confrontation that can only produce violence and disruption." The convention, he admitted, filled him "with a sense of dread." To add a final layer to the confusion, Senator George McGovern sought to rally the Kennedy followers by announcing that he would be an antiwar candidate for the nomination.

The Democrats went on to choose Humphrey and sure defeat in November. MOBE and the yippies did protest. And whatever damage the Democrats did to themselves inside the convention hall, Mayor Daley compounded on the streets of Chicago. A national television audience was treated to repeated scenes of violence as the police set upon the yippies, then upon the nonviolent MOBE, and finally upon McCarthy organizers at the Hilton Hotel. The violence that erupted was no accident, since both sides had planned for it. The protestors wanted to expose the harsh hand of repression that upheld the system; Daley wanted to show the people of America that long-haired freaks and radicals, or "outside agitators," as he viewed them, could not disrupt his convention and his city.

Despite all the furor, only a few thousand protestors actually came to Chicago. Their numbers, abetted by a significant number of curious locals, tourists, and police agents, probably never reached 10,000. Some historians have estimated that as many as 1 in 6 protestors in Chicago was actually a government agent or informer. The first yippie concert in Lincoln Park attracted only a few thousand and a single band (John Sinclair's MC-5). Scattered incidents erupted throughout the day as the police sought to disrupt the music. The yippies responded with cries of "Fuck the Pigs." More-sustained violence occurred on Sunday night as the police moved in to enforce the curfew. Eager to "Kill the Commies," officers made no effort to distinguish demonstrators from spectators as they clubbed away. Once the convention opened on Monday, police harassed a peaceful MOBE gathering outside the convention headquarters at the Hilton Hotel. A few demonstrators raised North Vietnamese flags; the police arrested them with notable force. Some demonstrators threw stones; the police broke a few heads.

After sporadic rioting and police assaults on Tuesday, events climaxed on Wednesday. That was the day the convention coronated Humphrey as its candidate and the day demonstrators were determined to express their sense of betrayal. That day also gave the Chicago police a chance to vent all the rage they felt toward the snot-nosed kids who shouted obscenities, abused the flag, and called them "Pigs." At a rally held Wednesday afternoon in Grant Park, David Dellinger announced that a march on the convention would begin at 4:30. Some 10,000 protestors had already gathered to join the march for which Rennie Davis had received a permit. Dellinger knew, however, that the city authorities, urged on by the Secret Service, had rescinded the permit. Daley also called in National Guard units to reinforce the police, who were under orders to use any means necessary to block the marchers from the convention hall.

Around 4:00, a protestor tore the American flag off a pole. Police immediately rushed in with clubs swinging. Under a barrage of stones, bricks, and garbage, they arrested the flag snatcher. The nonviolent Dellinger pleaded for order while Davis circulated through the crowd, seeking to cool people off. Suddenly, Davis went down in a pool of blood, the victim of a blindside assault from a policeman. The crowd erupted. Police and demonstrators frantically traded blows, with the police inflicting far more pain. After twenty frantic minutes, the violence subsided and Dellinger was able to organize the crowd for what he hoped would be an orderly march to the convention hall. The police would have none of it. They blocked the exits from the park, forcing marchers into a sit-down strike while Dellinger negotiated.

They were not the only frustrated protestors. Outside the Hilton, several thousand McCarthy supporters had gathered. Some 600 National Guard troops separated them from the marchers sitting down in Grant Park. Finally, protestors began to find their way in smaller groups out of the park and to the Hilton. As the marchers dispersed, the police fired tear gas that filtered into the hotel air conditioning system, causing tears in the eyes of Hubert Humphrey, the champion of the "politics of joy." By about 7:00, some 5,000 protestors had converged outside the Hilton. What followed was later described by an investigating commission as "a police riot." Under bright lights set up by television news crews, one police force waded into the crowd while another blocked any chance of either escape or access to the convention center. "The whole world is watching," protestors chanted. Senator Eugene McCarthy, looking on from his hotel room, compared the police tactics to past treatment of the Indians. "They told them they could march, and they've surrounded them," he remarked to an aide.

One McCarthy organizer found himself trapped on the street outside the hotel as the police assaulted the crowd. "They started beating people," he remembered, "and then they'd continue to beat them . . . as they fell on top of each other." Outraged protestors kept yelling "Seig Heil! Seig Heil!" at the police. As a McCarthy staffer bent down to help a woman beaten unconscious, police pushed them through a plate glass window into the hotel cocktail bar. Police also knocked Tom Hayden through the bar window. All he remembered were policeman jumping in after him, tables crashing, and patrons scattering toward the exits. Determined to discourage the media from exposing their violence, police saved some of their most savage beatings for reporters. The police riot, captured on television for a national audience, lasted only seventeen minutes.

The consequences reverberated far longer. George McGovern, watching from the fourth floor, was blunt: "Do you see what those sons of bitches are doing to those

Almost no one who protested at the Democratic Convention in Chicago in 1968 understood that Chicago's law-and-order mayor, Richard Daley, privately opposed the war in Vietnam. (Source: Associated Press)

kids down there?" Around 9:30, the networks piped news footage into the convention center. Antiwar delegates were outraged. Senator Abraham Ribicoff of Connecticut used his nominating speech for McGovern to condemn Daley. "With George McGovern we wouldn't have Gestapo tactics on the streets of Chicago," he told the delegates. In the uproar that followed, no one could hear what a beet-faced Mayor Daley shouted back, but those who read lips claimed that he said, "Fuck you, you Jew son-of-a bitch." Americans who saw these scenes on television were aghast. Here was a party and a nation at war with itself. Those attacked by the police were not angry ghetto blacks and many were not long-haired hippies, but rather neatly dressed delegates, reporters, and bystanders. Just one week before, Americans had watched Soviet tanks rumble into Prague to crush a nascent democratic movement. No matter how disturbing those scenes might be they at least made sense, since repressive dictatorships had no tolerance for dissent or civil liberties. But what did it mean to have the streets of America awash with violence between citizens and their government?

And that was not the end of the police brutality. Probably the most disturbing of a string of police assaults was an unprovoked attack late that night on McCarthy headquarters. Defeated McCarthy workers had gathered at the Hilton to regret their defeat, comfort themselves for fighting the good fight, and say good-bye after a grueling campaign. Around 5:00 that morning, police and National Guard soldiers, on the flimsiest of pretexts, burst into the fifteenth floor gathering. They indiscriminately beat and clubbed the defenseless workers. Richard Goodwin, a former Kennedy staffer and McCarthy aide, confronted the police as they herded their bloody victims into the lobby. He summoned both McCarthy and Humphrey, but predictably only McCarthy appeared. Visibly angered, he defied the police and told his people to return to their rooms.

What happened in Chicago reveals much about the nature of the uncivil wars. Jerry Rubin later admitted that while "nothing happened as we planned," that what the Chicago police had done was exactly what the yippies had wanted. "We wanted to show that America wasn't a democracy, that the convention wasn't politics," he explained. "The message of the week was of an America ruled by force. That was a big victory." The yippies had wanted to further polarize the nation. In that regard, Rubin was undoubtedly correct to claim victory. But what exactly had they won? The mayhem in the streets of Chicago did not hasten the end of the war. It did destroy any hope that Humphrey's candidacy would survive. As political observer Teddy White noted, "the Democrats are finished." So in attacking Humphrey, the yippies and their allies opened the White House to Richard Nixon.

Humphrey certainly contributed to his own demise. In failing to offer any concession to the McCarthyites, Humphrey turned them into enemies. He underscored his subservience to Johnson by defending Daley and his police and condemning the protestors, who believed, he claimed, that "all they have to do is riot and they'll get their way." As for the police excess, Humphrey suggested it was time to "quit pretending that Mayor Daley did anything that was wrong." To that the mayor himself added that those who criticized him "missed the point. No one was killed." Daley was probably wrong. Much of the hopefulness that had been a central part of the 1960s rebellion died in Chicago. Events there drove both the Left and Right into more extreme positions.

In the wake of Chicago, the only interesting question left in the 1968 presidential campaign was how many votes George Wallace might attract. Could he prevent either Nixon or Humphrey from winning a majority? His appeals to "law and order" seemed to many conservatives the antidote for leftist anarchy. Then Wallace made a fatal error. He chose former SAC commander General Curtis LeMay as his running mate. LeMay had a solution for the Vietnam War—"bomb the North Vietnamese back to the Stone Age." Once this nuclear cloud drifted into the Wallace campaign, Humphrey dismissed his opponents as "the bombsy twins." The subsequent decline in Wallace's fortunes gave the Humphrey campaign a desperately needed lift. Through September, Humphrey had attracted little money and small crowds. Antiwar demonstrators disrupted his rallies with shouts of "Dump the Hump." Not until September 30 did he move to become his own man. He told a Salt Lake City campaign audience that as president "he would stop the bombing" as a step in the peace process and that he would move to "de-Americanize the war." With that his polls climbed, while Wallace and Nixon began to slide. And on the Thursday before the election, Johnson made a surprise announcement of a total bombing halt and the promise of a negotiate settlement.

Had that agreement held, Humphrey might have pulled off an upset equal to Harry Truman's in 1948. Instead, major South Vietnamese figures with encouragement from Nixon repudiated the agreement. On election day, Nixon polled some 2.3 million votes fewer than he had in his 1960 race with Kennedy. That was, however, enough to give him the victory by a shockingly thin margin of just 510,000 votes. Had Lyndon Johnson allowed Humphrey some independence in framing a position on Vietnam, the outcome might have been different. Or if Humphrey had chosen to break with his patron, he might have won back some of the liberals, whose low turnout on election day cost him the election. The 57 percent of voters who chose Nixon or Wallace certainly had rejected Lyndon Johnson, his war, and his Great Society. That vote marked a political turn to the Right that was a major legacy of the uncivil wars.

∾

The election of 1968 brought to a close a very bad year that had in actuality lasted over sixteen months. It began with the flowering of the counterculture, erupted into racial violence, saw the Vietnam War destroy Lyndon Johnson and his party, and ended with the collapse of the cold war consensus. The decision to seek an end to the war through negotiations rather than further escalation was a tacit admission of defeat. That long year also marked a deterioration of the prosperity that had been an essential ingredient in the optimism that inspired both the vision of American as the leader of the free world in its struggle with Communism and the belief that Americans possessed both the will and the means to eliminate social injustice at home. Stagflation, a combination of recession and inflation, was one price the nation paid for the excess of the 1960s. For the next three decades, conservatives would dominate the White House and increasingly define the national public agenda. That outcome was not at all obvious in November 1968. If anything, the voices of protest would ring louder over the next few years. The war would drag on and sporadic violence would upset the domestic scene. The uncivil wars had entered their final phase.

Part Three

THE RISE OF
ESSENTIALIST POLITICS
AND THE FALL OF
RICHARD NIXON
1969–74

12

The Rise of Gender and Identity Politics

During the Democratic convention, surprisingly few African Americans had demonstrated in Chicago's streets. Mayor Daley's threats had discouraged local blacks who, if only out of curiosity, might have joined the rumpus. Black Nationalist leaders stayed away for another reason. Chicago, they decided, was not their fight. African Americans would stake their future on a movement without whites and identified more with the struggles of Third World peoples of color. The decision of Black Nationalists to segregate their movement coincided with the disintegration of key organizations like SNCC. After 1968, more-extreme elements like the Black Panthers redefined race politics with confrontational tactics that agitated the press, menaced the police, and angered politicians. Most significant, the Panthers, unlike SNCC or CORE, did not inspire moderate whites to join them or to follow their example. Many whites who had participated in the civil rights struggle now found expression in a host of alternative minority rights and social movements.

Also absent in significant numbers from the streets of Chicago were women. Male protestors had outnumbered females by possibly as much as eight to one. That too presaged a new direction for the protest movements of the 1960s. During the period from 1964 through 1968, women had been closely associated with both civil rights and antiwar protest. But at the same time, women, like other key elements in the movement, had begun to define an agenda of their own. So if Chicago stands as the apotheosis of the second phase of the 1960s, the Miss America Pageant, held in Atlantic City barely a month later, marked the opening of the third.

The pageant was as American as apple pie. Richard Nixon once claimed it was the only show that he let his daughters, Julie and Tricia, stay up late to watch. Each year a group of celebrity judges chose the lucky winner from among a bevy of leggy, toothy, and breasty women who fixed their faces into permanent smiles. They played piano, twirled batons, and gave innocuous answers to insipid questions. At the climax, unctuous emcee Bert Parks placed the crown on the new queen's head. "There she is—Miss America. There she is—our ideal," Bert would croon.

That September, Robin Morgan organized several busloads of women to attend the 1968 pageant in Atlantic City. Morgan had once enthralled early TV audiences as the youngest daughter, Dagmar, in a popular series called I Remember Mama. No longer a young innocent, Morgan was angry. So were the New York Radical Women, who joined her excursion. They came not to cheer the new Miss America, but to condemn the pageant for its blatant exploitation of women as sex objects. They crowned a sheep as their Miss America to suggest that the contestants, like women in general, were "oppressed and judged like animals at the county fair." They swung

Until angry feminists protested the objectification of women at the 1968 Miss America Pageant in Atlantic City few Americans ever thought of the event as in any way political. (Source: Associated Press)

bras in the air while chanting "Welcome to the Miss America Cattle Auction." A particularly striking poster portrayed a nude female body divided like a side of beef in a butcher shop into cuts of meat. The protestors filled a trash can (which they dubbed "Freedom Trash Can") with what they considered various articles of torture—spiked-heel shoes, girdles, bras, curlers, and representative copies of magazines they thought exploited women, Cosmopolitan, Playboy, and Ladies Home Journal among them.

Rumors that the protestors would symbolically burn their bras brought the media in search of a hot story. To publicize the dearth of women on news beats, the protestors refused to speak to male reporters. Newspapers had to search for women on staff, which usually meant raiding the society page. A plan to burn the offending contents of a Freedom Trash Can, including brassieres, ran afoul of a local ordinance that banned open fires on the boardwalk. So in fact no bras were burned that day. Yet the image of militant feminists as "bra burners," with all the sexual innuendoes the term implied, remained a fixture of media rhetoric about the feminist movement. As historian Susan Douglas observed, "No one had ever seen anything quite like it."

For Douglas, the feminist protest at Atlantic City "marked a watershed in American history, a watershed virtually ignored in retrospectives on the 1960s and 1968 in particular." Historians are forever marking events as "watersheds," but in this instance Douglas makes a strong case. The Miss America protest marked the opening of a new era in gender relations. On a symbolic level, what happened at the 1968 pageant did anticipate the future direction of the uncivil wars. In exposing the sexist content of the show as an insult to women, the protestors had politicized this event, no matter how much the organizers and the national television audience might resist the message. Feminists thereby served notice that no cow was too sacred to provide a target for protest.

The Sixties: Phase Three

By 1968, feminists were a major element among activists who had been driven out of civil rights organizations or were frustrated by their inability to stop the war or were simply no longer willing to dedicate themselves to someone else's cause. They turned their energies to new fronts. On one front were those who participated in what might be called value politics. These reformers had strong ties to the muckrakers of the early twentieth century and to New Deal liberalism. Chief among those were consumer advocates and environmentalists. On a second front were more numerous and disparate groups who engaged in what have come to be called gender and identity politics. These new civil rights activists established a host of movements seeking to redress the inequalities not just of blacks, but also of women, gays, Latinos, Asian Americans, and American Indians. The new identity politics would take up causes that the political establishment had ignored or dismissed as private matters: religion, family values, gender, and sexual orientation. The "personal became the political."

Though they seldom acted together, the movements of the late 1960s transformed American politics. They brought into public debate issues once seen primarily as social or cultural. Their activism provoked groups like Christian fundamentalists, ethnic Americans, and conservative club women, who had never thought of themselves as oppressed or particularly stigmatized, to adopt identity and value politics in their own defense. As has generally been the case with new social and political movements, sharp disagreements arose over goals and strategies. The moderate or accomodationist ideas of the founding members faced challenges along conservative, liberal, and radical lines. That in turn accelerated the fragmentation that was such a central consequence of the uncivil wars.

With no broad areas of agreement about the public agenda, with political symbols contested and defamed, and with traditional authority under constant attack, American politics would become after 1968 an arena for division rather than consensus. That may explain why in the 1968 presidential campaign, when Richard Nixon noticed a sign saying "Bring Us Together," he adopted it as his campaign theme. Yet Nixon had been, and would continue to be, one of the most divisive political figures of the modern era. His constant effort to battle those he saw as enemies—hippies, liberals, the media, the eastern establishment, campus radicals, Jews (the list was long)—would further polarize the nation. It caused Nixon to use the FBI and CIA as well as the Plumbers, a secret White House political action team, to destroy those he saw as a threat to the nation and his own political fortunes.

The emerging battles over value and identity politics distinguished the third and final phase of the uncivil war. That is not to say that antiwar and civil rights protests disappeared or that Americans rejected countercultural values. In fact, during this period the Vietnam War entered its most violent phase as American bombing intensified. All the same, the news media concentrated their coverage on the withdrawal of American troops from Vietnam and on the stuttering peace talks between American and North Vietnamese delegates in Paris. Antiwar and radical protest became more sporadic, if occasionally more violent. At the same time, countercultural values penetrated the mainstream as Americans increasingly grew their hair long, adopted hippie fashions, and celebrated the joys of sexual liberation, mind-altering drugs, and rock music. Having entered the commercial mainstream, the counterculture lost much of its capacity to shock and disturb.

Instead it was the new value and identity politics that most roiled the waters of domestic tranquillity. They continued the destruction of consensus that the antiwar, civil rights, and countercultural movements had begun. From the early protests of the 1960s, the newest political activists had learned how small advocacy groups could use civil disobedience and outrageous behavior to capture media attention. Against this new assault on traditional values, Richard Nixon tried to mobilize what he called "the silent majority." These were middle-class Americans who valued God, family, and country but who did not protest. The silent majority might condemn the tactics of identity and value political groups, but they could not ignore them. And, as often as not, the silent majority shared or sympathized with at least some of their goals.

Women Fight for Liberation

Those who read Betty Friedan's The Feminine Mystique in 1963 would not have expected that five years later feminism would be resurgent. As we have seen, Friedan's message, despite its call to action, was not a hopeful one. The media, according to Friedan, had so trivialized, marginalized, and sexualized women that they seemed quite helpless or even willing to mount a major public movement. Her favored prescriptions—equal work and equal pay—were hardly the stuff to capture the hearts and minds of radical female activists who, from the antiwar and civil rights battlefields, condemned the system Friedan urged them to join.

Nonetheless, by 1966 Friedan had launched the National Organization for Women (NOW), with the goal of bringing "American women into full participation in the mainstream of American society now." Drawing on the arguments Friedan had made in The Feminist Mystique, NOW insisted that the media redress "the false image of women now prevalent," that women receive equal pay for equal work, and that marriage become a union of equals. No longer would women assume that their place was in the home and that a man was responsible to "carry the sole burden of supporting himself, his wife, and family." Nor should women have to make the traditional choice "between marriage and motherhood, on the one hand, and serious participation in industry or professions on the other." In place of the current gender inequities must emerge "a fully equal partnership of the sexes, as part of a worldwide revolution of human rights."

The women of NOW had found their voice not in older organizations like the League of Women Voters, but in civil rights politics. In the 1954 Brown case, the Supreme Court had accepted evidence that discrimination eroded self-esteem. NOW similarly argued that "all policies and practices [that] not only deny opportunities but also foster in women self-denigration, dependence, and evasion of responsibility, undermine their confidence in their own abilities and foster contempt for women." NOW also had links to the Old Left and its involvement with labor organization. Several founding members had union backgrounds. In that spirit NOW rejected the notion that dissatisfaction was an individual problem. As historian Nancy Woolloch noted, "NOW contended that women's problems were society's problems" to solve. That message found a receptive audience. NOW's membership rose from 1,000 in 1967 to 48,000 by 1974. The anthem it informally adopted, "I Am Woman (Hear Me Roar)" by Helen Reddy, became a major hit record in 1972.

NOW, however, was too mainstream to suit more radical feminists. Friedan had created the organization as a political action group with pragmatic goals—a national system of day-care centers, job retraining programs to bring women back into the workforce, and support for equal opportunity. That agenda shared the liberal spirit of Lyndon Johnson's Great Society. Indeed, NOW had come into being intent on pressing the federal government to enforce the 1964 Civil Rights Act's ban on sex discrimination.

Radical women saw feminism as more about liberation than equality. As we have seen, Casey Hayden's confrontation with SNCC leadership in 1965 was an early sign of women's discontent within the New Left. The female veterans of antiwar and civil rights protest had wearied of fighting to liberate others from an oppression that they increasingly recognized in their own experience. By 1967, a number of activist women were ready to divorce themselves from politics determined by men. One radical feminist contrasted the "ecstasy of discussion" she discovered among liberated women with the "blank and peripheral" feelings she had felt when part of the male-dominated movement. To speak of the oppression of women was to speak about one's own life. "There was nothing distant about it," she recalled.

While many radical women objected to the sexism of New Left males, they shared the conviction that oppression, whether of women, of the poor, or of people of color, was systemic in origin. The same welfare/warfare state that projected American hegemony in Vietnam and other Third World areas promoted second-class citizenship at home. New Leftists came to see liberalism as the enemy of their movement. The Great Society, they believed, sought not to ease inequality or promote equality so much as to co-opt discontent and thereby stifle dissent. Nothing short of revolution could bring an end to classism, racism, and sexism.

The sharp differences between NOW and more radical liberationists became obvious soon after the Miss America demonstration. Early leaders of the women's liberation movement associated NOW with the liberal reformism they had vowed to overthrow. Robin Morgan, who besides organizing the Miss America protest wrote the best-selling 1970 feminist book *Sisterhood Is Powerful*, dismissed NOW as "essentially an organization that wants reforms [in the] second-class citizenship of women—and this is where it differs drastically from the rest of the Women's Liberation Movement." Radical feminist Ti-Grace Atkinson condemned NOW liberalism as seeking for "women to have the same opportunity to be oppressors, too." Atkinson wrote as a disillusioned former member of NOW who left the New York City chapter when it rejected her efforts to democratize its structure. Betty Friedan, in turn, missed few opportunities to denounce radicals as "man haters" who waged "sex-warfare." Their "bedroom war," Friedan charged, diverted feminists from what was the essential battle for equality in the public sphere.

Where NOW saw exclusion from equal participation in the public sphere as the major problem confronting women, women's liberationists saw patriarchy as a critical aspect of the systems they found oppressive. As one feminist writer explained, "the American system consists of two interdependent but distinct parts—the capitalist state, and the patriarchal family." Because women held a subordinate position in the family which was traditionally "dominated by men," they were vulnerable to exploitation as low-wage labor and consumers in a capitalist economy also run by and for men. Feminist Adrienne Rich denounced patriarchy as "the power of fathers: a familial-social, ideological, political system in which men—by force, direct pressure, or through ritual, tradition, law and language, customs, etiquette, education, and the division of labor, determine what part women shall or shall not play, and in which the female is subsumed under the male." Radical feminists saw gender inequality as so deeply engrained in the structures of society that only the destruction of capitalism and patriarchy could succeed in eradicating it.

The Feminist Agenda

One of the most remarkable aspects of feminism was the speed with which it developed into a major social movement. When the New York Radical Women protested at the Miss America Pageant, few women, and few Americans in general, thought much about the politics of gender. By the early 1970s, feminism had emerged as a social force. At the national level and especially within university communities, the issues feminists raised had begun to redefine the political and social agenda. Gender relations, feminists argued, could no longer serve the particular interests of men. Rather, they had to be reconstituted to free women to realize their destinies as autonomous beings. Whether liberal or radical feminists, they demanded full equality as persons and citizens that translated into equality in education and jobs. No longer would women accept gender differences as inevitable reflections of biological destiny. Most could be better understood as socially constructed.

Assertion of these general principles translated into specific demands. Most obviously, they buttressed the argument for equal pay and equal job opportunities.

They also reinforced demands for sexual equality, whether that meant readily available information on birth control, access to contraception, and legalized abortion or an end to the sexual double standard and an increased understanding of women's sexual wants and needs. In the workplace, women sought an end to "old boys' networks" that favored men in finding jobs, earning promotions, and gaining power. Placement would be determined by public procedures open to all. So, too, women would no longer face sexual harassment as an everyday feature of work.

Feminists had advanced that agenda despite the condescending and often hostile reaction of the media. Mainstream media did generally support what it treated as the legitimate demands of feminists who sought redress through traditional political channels. But when feminists moved into the personal realm, the media balked. Issues that affected the home, marriage, family roles, or sexuality were forbidden territory. Commentators tended to dismiss as psychologically unstable, physically unattractive, or sexually frustrated the women who made the personal political. Male commentators (and virtually all were male) were generally dismissive of women as "completely incompetent as politicians, tacticians, and organizers" and suggested that women "had proved, again and again, that they didn't deserve to be anywhere but the kitchen, the bedroom, and the nursery."

No matter how condescending the news media might be to feminist demands, they could not resist a good story, and, as the Miss America protest showed, the women's movement generated human interest. So even as they disparaged feminists' more radical demands, the media did give the movement widespread coverage. One good example is the 1970 Women's Strike for Equality, called to commemorate the fiftieth anniversary of the women's suffrage amendment. The strike offered women an opportunity to step out of their ordinary roles to protest against sexism, whether in the workplace or at home. After much difficult negotiation, strike organizers agreed on three demands that would become the core feminist agenda: equal opportunity in work and in education, the right to childcare, and the right to abortion. More radical feminists went further to call for abortion on demand and twenty-four-hour childcare centers.

Organizers also saw the event as a way to combat the media's tendency to treat "the women's movement as a joke." Betty Friedan recognized that hostile coverage caused many women to fear "identifying themselves as feminists or with the movement at all. We needed an action to show them—and ourselves—how powerful we were." If numbers meant anything, the event succeeded. The strike mobilized the largest number of women since the suffrage movement. In New York City, somewhere between 20,000 and 50,000 women left work to join the march up Fifth Avenue. Signs like "Don't Cook Dinner—Starve a Rat Today" and "Don't Iron While the Strike Is Hot" caught the attention of news photographers and television news crews. Those signs also suggested the depth of feminist anger toward male domination.

Editorial and news coverage of the strike, mostly provided by men, was predictably dismissive. All three networks featured a story about West Virginia senator

Jennings Randolph, who had labeled feminists "bra-less bubbleheads." Howard K. Smith of ABC, who quickly established himself as a man feminists loved to hate, opened his story with a line from the Nixon administration's designated media heavy, Spiro Agnew: "Three things have been difficult to tame: The oceans, fools, and women. We may soon be able to tame the oceans, but fools and women will take a little longer." That comment was only a little more demeaning than that of Eric Sevareid at CBS, who dismissed feminism as the work of an "aroused minority" and likened feminism to a contagious disease that would spread like Communism as women's libbers indoctrinated innocent housewives. Susan Douglas has argued that in that way "the news media of the 1970s played an absolutely central role in turning feminism into a dirty word, and stereotyping the feminist as a hairy-legged, karate-chopping commando with a chip on her shoulder the size of China, really bad clothes, a complete inability to smile—let alone laugh."

Douglas also recognized, as did feminist leaders at the time, that whether sympathetic or hostile, the coverage by the news media was vital to the movement. In the wake of the Women's Strike for Equality, polls revealed that 80 percent of women over eighteen had heard of women's liberation. Membership in NOW doubled over the following year. The strike and the subsequent coverage broke down the isolation that had prevented many women from identifying their sense of common grievance.

Consciousness Raising

Of even more importance in drawing women into the movement were informal networks of women's groups who participated in a process that came to be known as "consciousness raising." The term referred to the practice of women gathering to discuss the political dimensions of their personal lives. Consciousness raising blended the democratic processes of New Left and Marxist politics with the communal aspects of the civil rights movement. The person credited with coining the term, Kathie Sarachild, had impeccable New Left and radical feminist credentials. Her odyssey had taken her from Harvard peace advocate in the early sixties to civil rights work in Mississippi, after which she joined the New York Radical Women and eventually became a member of Redstockings. Once she discovered feminism in the mid-1960s, she embraced her maternal lineage by changing her name from Amatniek to Sarachild.

In their Manifesto, the Redstockings rejected NOW's program "to bring women into full participation in the mainstream of American society now, exercising all the privileges and responsibilities thereof in truly equal partnership with men." Unlike NOW, these radical feminists saw women "as an oppressed class." Intimacy with men in isolation from other women prevented them from recognizing their "personal suffering as a political condition." The conflicts between individual men and women, they concluded, "are political conflicts that can only be solved collectively." Consciousness raising was an essential step by which women could come to understand the collective nature of their oppression and begin the process of liberation.

Sarachild had first encountered the process during a policy planning session of New York Radical Women. Discussion of their "next step" led one woman to remark that she thought they had "a lot more to do just in the area of raising our consciousness." After some uncertainty about how that might occur, they decided they would study core issues in women's lives such as childhood, work, and mothering. Their starting point "would be the actual experience we had in these areas." Gathering in small groups, they might research key issues but would concentrate on sharing their stories and questioning the "natural order of things." Once women became aware that oppression in their lives was not personal but political in nature, they would be prepared "to organize and to act on a mass scale."

Sarachild offered an agenda that would allow women to "see their condition through their own eyes." She urged consciousness-raising groups to explore family roles, education, work, health, and sexuality. Why, women began to ask, did men have "a night out with the boys" while women stayed home with the kids? Why could women keep the family books but not business accounts? Why did women get up in the night with sick children so their husbands would be ready for work the next day? Why did schools steer women away from high-powered careers as doctors or lawyers into low-paying service jobs such as nurses and secretaries?

Mainstream organizations like NOW avoided issues that delved into such private realms. In practice, as NOW leaders were to learn (and as Douglas has argued), those were precisely the issues that appealed to many women who had never before thought of themselves as political. Women who had not yet experienced the widespread discrimination in the workplace or who had not been involved in civil rights or antiwar politics knew full well the gendered inequities of family life. They readily accepted the notion that the personal was political and could understand the idea that women everywhere faced a form of discrimination every bit as disabling as racism was for African Americans. "Sexism," as Robin Morgan put it, was "all pervasive," "the definition of and discrimination against half the human species by the other half." The worst practitioners of gender oppression were what feminists identified as "male chauvinist pigs."

By 1969, consciousness raising began to generate political action, some of it meant to attract attention to feminist issues. WITCH, the Women's International Terrorist Conspiracy from Hell, placed a hex on the stock exchange and protested a bridal fair at Madison Square Garden. Singing "Here comes the slave, off to her grave" and distributing free "shop-lifting bags," they waved signs with slogans like "Always a Bride, Never a Person." These tactics may have been outrageous, but WITCH was far from alone in its actions. By 1969, feminists had formed a network of organizations across the country. Some continued to use consciousness raising to recruit new members to their cause. Most addressed the range of issues feminists had identified. Even NOW began to see the need for more direct action. Betty Friedan had at first dismissed consciousness raising as a form of "navel gazing." In

February 1969, she led a sit-in to desegregate the all-male Oak Room Bar at New York's Plaza Hotel. NOW also co-sponsored with the more radical Redstockings public meetings on the issue of abortion.

Feminists won an important linguistic victory when they established a widely accepted preference for "Ms." as the proper term of address for women, both married and single. Where "Miss" or "Mrs." acknowledged marital status, the term "Mr." did not. In such ways, the feminists came to argue, seemingly trivial matters of everyday life served to mark the separate and unequal circumstances of men and women. The notion of dramatizing the term as the title of a magazine came from Gloria Steinem. Steinem discovered feminism somewhat later than the movements' leaders. After graduating from Smith College in 1956, she won a fellowship that took her to India to study. A year later, she returned to New York where she began a career in journalism, writing occasionally for *Esquire* and the *New York Times Sunday Magazine*. One assignment inspired her to work undercover as a Playboy bunny. Decked out in the puffy tail, black stockings, spiked heels, and a tight, strapless costume that revealed the cleavage essential to the bunny image, she spent three weeks at one of Hugh Hefner's Playboy Clubs. In the process, she discovered the demeaning and sometimes sordid conditions the bunnies faced every day. Decent wages, not glamour, kept them at this work.

By 1968, Steinem had wearied of assignments that focused largely on such trivia as sex kitten Zsa Zsa Gabor's bed or a day at the beach. When a good friend founded *New York* magazine, he gave her an opportunity to do substantive political writing. One assignment brought her to a Redstockings' speakout on abortion rights. For twelve years, Steinem kept secret that she had had an abortion. Now from a dozen women she heard stories that were very much like her own. A "great blinding lightbulb" went off in her head. She knew from that point out what it meant to be a feminist. She confessed to being disturbed with herself for her "capitulation to the small humiliations, and my own refusal to trust what was going on, or even trust my own experience." For too long she had tolerated discrimination that gave less-qualified male reporters the choice stories.

In 1971, Steinem found the opportunity to voice her newfound feminism. An editor at *New York* offered to finance a single edition of a magazine she chose to call *Ms*. The inaugural issue included stories entitled "Sisterhood," "Raising Kids without Sex Roles," and "Women Tell the Truth about Their Abortions," along with feature articles entitled "Welfare Is a Woman's Issue" and "Why I Want a Wife." These articles aimed to raise the consciousness of women not already committed to the feminist cause. "Why I Want a Wife" made the telling point that wives created opportunities for men that few women ever experienced.

Ms. had an immediate impact. As Steinem's biographer has suggested, "Here was, written down, what [women] had not yet admitted that they felt, had always feared to say out loud, and could not believe was now before their eyes, in public, for all to read." The demand for the inaugural issue persuaded Steinem that *Ms*. filled an important need. In July 1972, she launched it as a full-time publication. CBS anchor

Harry Reasoner typified male broadcasters when he remarked that in six months Ms. would "run out of things to say." He was wrong. Steinem had correctly sensed that millions of middle-class women were eager to learn, as had the founders of the feminist movement, that they were not alone. Historian Ruth Rosen has suggested that the letters section of the magazine "functioned as a national consciousness-raising group," much in the manner of electronic bulletin boards. Rosen added, "Voluminous letters to the editors, whether furious or grateful, document the tremendous impact Ms. had on the lives of its readers."

With the coming of Ms., feminists succeeded in placing their issues in the forefront of the nation's political agenda. Veterans of consciousness raising spoke out against child and spousal abuse, pornography, and sexual violence. They established centers for rape crisis, battered women, day care, abortion counseling, and women's health. They lobbied successfully on college campuses for courses in women's studies and for revision of existing curriculum to address issues important to women. And by 1972, feminists had successfully pressed Congress to adopt an Equal Rights Amendment to the Constitution. In 1973, the Supreme Court in *Roe v. Wade* would remove legal barriers to a woman's right to abortion.

One Movement Divisible

Many feminists had as their ultimate goal the uniting of all women as sisters. By the early 1970s, that vision was proving as elusive as the hope of Martin Luther King, Jr., to organize civil rights under the banner of equality or of MOBE to unify antiwar protest. Despite its many successes, the feminist cause suffered from divisions common to most movements of the era. Disunity was not a consequence of what Susan Douglas has identified as the news media's conviction that "women were constitutionally incapable of cooperating with one another." Rather, women split along many of the same fault lines that divided other political movements—chiefly, class, race, and ideology—as well as the inevitable clash of ambitions.

The feminist movement of the 1960s was led by and appealed most powerfully to middle-class, white, and often college-educated women. Ms., for example, did include articles aimed at minority and working-class women, but unlike most of its readers, lower-class women often worked out of necessity, not out of a desire for a career or economic independence. Working-class women would have gladly traded their entry-level and unskilled jobs for the domestic prisons their middle-class sisters sought to escape. Access to the all-male world inhabited by fathers, husbands, and brothers held little allure. "If your husband is a factory worker or a tugboat operator, you don't want his job," Congresswoman Barbara Mikulski observed. And, having limited education, few had the experience needed to assume "the independent, assertive, self-determined, equal role put forward for the liberated woman." Indeed, many working-class women identified with the ideals of female domesticity. The feminist attack on sexism devalued the lifestyle they embraced.

Race deepened the class divide. African-American women shared many of the concerns of lower-class whites. The majority who worked sought ways to spend more, not less, time with their families. Where white feminists identified marriage and family "as the roots of women's oppression," civil rights activist Maxine Williams observed that middle-class black women found that idea "abhorrent." Lower-class black women, Williams added, saw race more than gender as the barrier to their aspirations. "Their oppression is completely racial," she argued. Writer Celestine Ware observed that "poor black women are too occupied struggling for essentials—shelter, food, clothing—to organize themselves around the issue of women's rights."

The real problem of race lay in the apartheid systems that barred African Americans, both male and female, from gaining skills and finding high-paying jobs. Blacks, and especially young black males, suffered from a far higher unemployment rate than whites, whether middle or working class. Joblessness eroded the stability of black family life. The feminist agenda, rather than promoting gender equality, threatened to exacerbate the problem of female dominance within the black community. Many prominent African Americans believed that advances for the race depended more on improved status for black men than on equality for black women. "If the Negro woman has a major underlying concern," a prominent African American told the Kennedy Commission on the Status of Women in 1963, "it is the status of the Negro man." Black civil rights activists often made the same point. They were most determined to see "black men get ahead."

On a number of issues the feminist movement did appeal to black women. Feminists supported school integration and civil rights while opposing the war in Vietnam. But those were issues working-class white women saw as threatening. On such key issues as birth control and abortion, black feminists were often ambivalent. Celestine Ware, an African-American writer, explained that "feminist goals, like abortion on demand and easily obtainable birth control, are viewed with paranoid suspicion by some black militants at a time when they are literally fighting for their lives and looking everywhere to increase their numbers." Religion also tended to divide women. For the large masses of black and white working women, the church was at the center of family and community. Those churches were conservative on most social issues. In particular, they opposed the feminists' agenda on the ERA, abortion rights, and lesbian feminism. In the face of that opposition, feminists had difficulty attracting significant support across racial and class lines.

Core issues like the ERA and abortion rights also divided women, even though in the late 1960s the amendment appeared to be a unifying issue. Feminists from across the political spectrum supported it as a critical means to counter the pervasive sexism of American society. The Johnson administration had responded with a series of executive orders banning gender discrimination on the part of federal contractors. The Labor Department by 1970 had issued "affirmative action" guidelines. Women became far more visible in the political arena. Pat Nixon, the president's wife and a person seldom tied to feminism, privately put intense pressure on her husband to name a woman to the Supreme Court. When the Democrats met in 1972, some 40 percent of the delegates were women. Congress acknowledged women's new political clout when it passed the ERA with overwhelming majorities. And within a year, twenty-eight states had voted to adopt it. There the amendment stalled.

What had seemed a virtual certainty to succeed aroused a potent backlash. Beginning in 1971, Phyllis Schlafly, a conservative professional woman and mother of six children, began organizing opposition to the amendment. Schlafly recognized that while many Americans supported "equal rights" for women, they resisted the conception of redefined gender roles they associated with the amendment. Many women worried as well that the ERA would invite government interference in the private realm or restrict rules protecting women in the workplace.

A major irony attended Schlafly's success in helping to defeat the ERA. Given her public visibility, she could have served as a model of the liberated woman. Besides raising her six children, she had a career in politics and public policy. In 1964, she wrote *A Choice, Not an Echo* to promote Barry Goldwater's presidential crusade. In public she came across as self-possessed and articulate. Goldwater's crushing defeat had pushed conservatives, Schlafly among them, to the periphery of the GOP. Before Congress passed the ERA in the early 1970s, feminism was not on her agenda, even though she believed that women's liberation threatened family values and that feminists were wilfully misguided. Conservative friends urged her to get into the emerging debate over the amendment. She soon became a staunch opponent and in the process gave her political career new life.

Backers of the ERA viewed it as a significant step toward true gender equality. To Schlafly, the ERA constituted a direct assault on traditional values and especially the family. She charged that it would liberate men from their obligations to support families, force women out of the home into the labor market, and destroy "the legal bonds that tend to keep the family together." Schlafly's assault on the ERA reflected deep popular reservations about how feminists redefined gender roles. Those reservations were deepest in the southern states that uniformly rejected the amendment. Blue-collar women shared Schlafly's concern that the ERA would eliminate rules that protected women on the job. Many alumna of women's colleges heeded her warning that the ERA might spell the end of single-sex education.

By 1973, Schlafly's Stop ERA organization had mobilized enough opposition to doom the amendment. Her success went well beyond defeating the ERA. Rather than mark the triumph of liberal reformism of the 1960s, the politics of the ERA gave new life to Goldwater conservatism. The coalition which Schlafly helped pull together to defeat the ERA—traditional conservatives, unliberated women, blue-collar ethnics, Southerners, libertarians, religious fundamentalists—would become the backbone of the "Reagan Revolution" in the 1980s.

While the politics of the ERA received wide attention, the debate over abortion would prove even more divisive. Feminists saw abortion as a fundamental right. Without it, women could not control their own reproduction. Unwanted pregnancies forced many to undergo illegal operations that often left them scarred for life.

Feminists in the late sixties began to call for the repeal of all laws that restricted access to abortion. One of their most effective and effecting tactics was the public "speak-out." Women, many of them recognized public figures, admitted to past abortions, explained their reasons for choosing this course, described the often shady and even life-threatening circumstances under which they were performed, and confessed the emotional price of carrying this dark secret. The speak-out, as a participant noted, "informed the public that most women were having abortions anyway. People spoke their hearts. It was heart-rending."

Before the feminists could successful mobilize legislative support for abortion reform, the Supreme Court handed them what appeared a resounding victory. Having said little on reproductive issues, the Court ruled in 1965 in *Griswold v. Connecticut* that the right to privacy barred the states from legislating against the use of contraception. And the question of privacy was at the heart of the Court's decision in January 1973 when it handed down *Roe v. Wade*. Justice William Brennan, one of the Court liberals, wrote that "we recognize that the right of the individual, married or single, to be free from unwanted intrusion into matters so fundamentally affecting a person as the right of a woman to decide whether or not to terminate her pregnancy." The issue, as defenders of the Court's ruling would argue, was not so much a woman's right to abortion, but her "right to choose" on matters affecting her own body. The decision struck down all state laws restricting abortion and left the decision about terminating pregnancy during the first two trimesters (six months) up to a woman and her doctor.

Feminists assumed that the Court had settled the matter. No longer would women seeking abortions face the terrifying trip down dark alleys. What they had won, however, proved to be a legal, not a political, victory. In many ways parallel to Stop ERA, a national network of small but highly organized and emotionally committed "right-to-life" organizations emerged. They set out to overturn *Roe v. Wade* in the courts by seeking the appointment of sympathetic justices or to defeat it through legislation and civil disobedience. Right-to-life organizations often attracted adherents who had not been politically active before. Conservative Catholics were among the most outspoken foes, but fundamentalist Jews and Protestants and Mormons were equally passionate on the issue. As historian Rosalind Rosenberg has suggested, housewives committed to traditional family values formed the backbone of the anti-abortion movement. For them, "abortion, like equal rights, seemed to set selfish individualism above family responsibility and to challenge women's traditional conception of themselves as nurturing caretakers." Many foes equated abortion with murder.

With both sides of the abortion debate so deeply committed to their moral positions, no basis for consensus existed. How does one reconcile a "woman's right to choose" with the belief in the sanctity of all life? And because abortion rights rested on a Supreme Court ruling, opponents could argue that the pro-choice position had never achieved legitimization through the legislative process.

Gay Rights

Issues of sexuality created divisions of another kind. In 1970, Kate Millett, author of the widely read *Sexual Politics*, admitted to a university audience that she was a lesbian. Such an acknowledgment from a major feminist figure brought the issue of lesbian feminism into open public debate. At this time, too, a group who called themselves "Radicalesbians" declared they had become the vanguard of the feminist movement. They defined their sexuality as a political choice. In their view, women who had sexual relations with men committed themselves to reactionary politics. The true woman could find her political voice and discover personal freedom and sexual gratification only through relations with other women.

Differences over sexuality were not the sole source of conflict. Robin Morgan suggested the degree to which the lesbian vanguard divided feminists: "There were lesbians, lesbian-feminists, dykes, dyke-feminists, dyke-separatists, 'old dykes,' butch dykes, bar dykes, and killer dykes. . . . There were divisions between Political Lesbians and Real Lesbians and Nouveau Lesbians. Heaven help a woman who is unaware of these fine political distinctions and who wanders into a meeting for the first time, thinking she maybe has a right to be there because she likes women." Morgan was obviously exaggerating to make a point. Yet the divisions were real enough. Lesbian women were addressing a problem they did not share with their heterosexual sisters. They were stigmatized as much or more for their sexuality as for their gender.

Where heterosexual women had always had some measure of social acceptance and legal rights, male and female homosexuals faced socially and legally sanctioned discrimination. The mere hint that a person was gay could lead to social ostracism and the loss of a job. Betty Friedan reflected those traditional prejudices. To her lesbianism, which she disdained as "the lavender menace," was a grave threat to the feminist movement. If the feminists championed lesbians, she feared that conventional Americans would see the movement as dominated by man-hating women.

Media reaction to Millett gave credence to Friedan's concern. *Time* magazine suggested that Millett no longer qualified as a feminist spokesperson. According to *Time*, her sexuality "cast further doubt on her theories, and reinforced the views of those skeptics who routinely dismiss all liberationists as lesbians." Rather than risk such denigration, Friedan urged NOW to purge lesbians from its leadership. Many radical feminists saw the "bourgeois" Friedan as the menace to the movement, not their lesbian sisters. They deserted NOW rather than reject lesbianism. Ruth Rosen noted that "by 1972, a 'gay-straight' split had affected nearly every women's liberation group."

Homophobia was deeply embedded in American culture and had been a core element of the cold war consensus. Anti-Communists, whether conservatives or liberals, thought homosexuality was equally if not more pernicious than Communism. The homophobic implications of Senator Joseph McCarthy's sneering references to the "perfumed notes" and "silk pants" of the diplomatic corps were typical.

Among all the essentialist rights groups, gays and lesbians had the most difficulty finding a collective public voice. (Source: JP Laffont/Sygma/ CORBIS)

Many of those fired from government positions during the loyalty crusades were dismissed not as Communists but as homosexuals. The chair of the Republican National Committee warned that "sexual perverts . . . have infiltrated our Government" and were "perhaps as dangerous as actual Communists."

The stigma attached to homosexuality was so great that most gays dreaded having their sexual orientation exposed. Over the 1950s, efforts intensified to discharge homosexuals and to prevent their hiring both in government and the private sector. President Eisenhower signed an executive order that banned all gays and lesbians from government jobs. Local police turned gay bashing into a virtual shakedown racket. Targeting the bars and other public places where homosexuals gathered, the police would conduct periodic raids. Many victims preferred to pay bribes than to face exposure in the local press. Doctors compounded the stigma by treating homosexuality as a disease. One historian noted that throughout the twentieth century "some physicians did not hesitate to remove ovaries from women and castrate men in their war against 'perversion.'" The American Psychiatric Association listed homosexuality as a pathology in its diagnostic manual. Just as the authority of the medical establishment legitimized legal discrimination against homosexuals, so did the crusades led by moral reformers. Their success in criminalizing same-sex practices gave police the legal basis for arresting gay men or lesbians who engaged in consensual sex.

The emergence of lesbians as a force in the feminist movement was one sign that homosexuals were taking up the liberationist politics of the 1960s. The time had come, many decided, to stop internalizing society's norms and to accept same-sex love as a legitimate alternative to heterosexuality. The general redefinition of sexual standards, the spirit of greater tolerance inspired by the civil rights movement, more liberal Supreme Court rulings on privacy, contraception, and obscenity standards, and growing acceptance of alternative lifestyles all contributed to a more favorable social and legal climate. Small groups of gay men and lesbian women had by the late 1960s laid some groundwork for a more aggressive campaign to achieve civil rights and wider social acceptance.

That new climate helped to trigger the Stonewall riot of 1969. For one long June weekend, gays battled police in the streets of New York City. The rioting erupted on the night of June 27 after the police launched one of their regular gay-bashing raids at the Stonewall Inn, a Mafia-controlled nightclub in Greenwich Village. Under normal practice the police, having received generous payoffs, notified the management that they would be conducting a raid. They usually struck early so the bar could reopen in time for the heavy late-night crowds. Arrests were limited to Stonewall employees, patrons without proper identification, and those dressed in the clothes of the opposite gender.

This raid did not take the normal course. The police arrived late and without prior warning. They also made many more arrests. Outside a crowd gathered and, as the police began loading patrons into the waiting paddy wagons, violence erupted when some of those arrested attempted to escape. Then the crowd began pelting the police with whatever debris lay at hand, including bricks from a nearby construction site and trash baskets. The stunned officers retreated into the Stonewall for protection. Word spread to the press and to the wider gay community that something big was up. The police called in riot-control units seasoned by their confrontations with rioters and antiwar protestors. Despite the squad's fearsome demeanor, the crowd refused to disperse. Not until well after 3 A.M. was an uneasy calm restored.

The following night, a jubilant throng gathered outside the Stonewall, chanting "Gay Power." When the police moved to clear the streets, they realized the crowd was too big. Barrages of rocks and bottles flew. Intermittent violence lasted until almost 4 A.M., at which point the police units withdrew. One gay participant described the event as "a public assertion of real anger by gay people that was just electric." Several days of rain brought an uneasy calm, but on Wednesday the police were back and so were the crowds. Another round of violence ensued until the police once again pulled back. Though the riots ended that night, the gay community would never be the same. One police observer noticed a marked change in attitude among gays. "Suddenly, they were not submissive anymore," he remarked.

Stonewall would not have proved so catalytic had the gay community not already become more politically assertive. Younger gays did not share the same sense of caution that had limited the effectiveness of earlier organizing. The Mattachine Society established in Los Angeles in 1951 and the Daughters of Bilitis begun in San Francisco in 1955 had each taken an accomodationist approach. Both published magazines stressing educating the public and gay community to achieve more toleration, but they never campaigned for gay rights.

Just as the civil rights movement had inspired feminists, it also energized gay rights activists. One group began to challenge the medical establishment's treatment of homosexuality as an illness. The members embraced their sexuality as a healthy alternative and took legal steps to overturn the federal ban on employing homosexuals. In San Francisco in 1965, the Council on Religion and the Homosexual brought together local clergy with the gay community. Through this organization, the public began to understand the harassment and legal abuse to which the police routinely subjected gays.

By the time homosexual outrage exploded outside the Stonewall, gays and lesbians had created a network of activist organizations. They adopted as their primary goals an end to employment discrimination, a repeal of sodomy laws, and a revision of the medical definition of homosexuality. After Stonewall, younger gays and lesbians adopted many of the tactics of the New Left. Under the banner of groups like the Gay Liberation Front (GLF) and Radicalesbians, they organized boycotts, sat-in on university campuses, marched against police harassment, and protested at meetings where doctors persisted in stigmatizing homosexuality as a disease.

"Coming out of the closet" proved to be the boldest new strategy. In the past, the desire for anonymity had long barred homosexuals from effective organizing and political action. Few people had been willing to acknowledge publicly their sexual orientation. After Stonewall, activists challenged gays and lesbians to embrace openly their sexuality as a first step on the road to personal liberation. From feminists they adopted consciousness raising to free themselves from the self-recrimination and heterosexual standards that had ruled their lives. No longer would they accept the ideal that, in historian Barry Adam's words, "confined sexuality to heterosexual monogamous families." Sexuality would exist along a continuum rather than in mutually exclusive categories of homo- and heterosexuality.

By 1970, gay protestors were highly visible at demonstrations for causes pursued by a variety of New Left and identity politics groups such as feminists, Chicanos, and Native Americans. The number of gay and lesbian organizations grew from around 50 in 1969 to over 800 just four years later. A public network of businesses, social centers, and community services catering to homosexuals emerged in the nation's major cities. Faced with pressure from gay organizations, the American Psychiatric

Association in 1974 eliminated homosexuality from its list of mental disorders. One year later, the U.S. Civil Service Commission removed its prohibition of federal jobs for lesbians and gays. Many states eliminated their laws against sodomy.

Yet for all these successes, gay liberation, like feminism, failed to unify the movement or to achieve consensus. There was not one homosexual community but many. Moderate gays rejected the radicalism of the GLF with its revolutionary ethos, and in 1969 founded the Gay Activists Alliance (GAA). GLF members saw the GAA as disturbingly close to the accomodationist strategy they had rejected. The conservative tide that had thwarted the ERA and contested abortion rights pushed many gay and lesbian activists toward reform rather than revolution. Where the GLF struggled to build community and consensus in the spirit of the New Left, the GAA focused on issues of discrimination that they saw as central to their cause. The GLF, like so many New Left groups, burned out, while the more moderate GAA survived as civil rights became more important than the idea of redefining the nation's sexual values.

The FBI and Movement Discord

Radical gays and feminists failed in large part because they overestimated the appeal of their ideas. Groups like NOW and GAA developed more-effective organizational structures and fundraising. But the fault lines that existed within the gay and feminist movements, especially between radicals and moderates, were compounded by FBI harassment. The Bureau did not simply monitor these political activists. It planted agents in their ranks, often with the goal of fomenting discord and embarrassing the movements. As one memo on the New Left proposed, "whenever possible, agents and informers were to expose, disrupt, misdirect, discredit, or otherwise neutralize individuals and groups." The FBI also developed close working relations with local police, who often had their own "red squads." Historian Ruth Rosen estimates that the Bureau paid hundreds of informants to spy on feminist organizations.

By the early seventies, most of that spying produced reports so modest in their conclusions that no further surveillance should have been warranted. True to his anti-Communist obsessions, J. Edgar Hoover rejected that possibility. By this time, Hoover had become more erratic in his behavior and something of a liability, even to staunch conservatives in the Nixon administration. He clung tenaciously to power and persisted in his belief that the women's movement was tightly linked to dangerous radical groups. Moreover, he made the mistake of seeing feminism as a monolithic movement. When the San Francisco office of the FBI recommended ending its surveillance activities, Hoover ordered them to continue. He concluded, "it is absolutely essential that we conduct sufficient investigation to clearly establish the subversive ramifications of the WLM [Women's Liberation Movement] and to develop the potential for violence presented by the various groups connected with this movement as well as any possible threat they represent to the internal security of the United States." The FBI in general aggravated weaknesses within gay and

feminist organizations, especially in their formative stages, when they were struggling to establish their identities and political credibility.

∼

Sexual and gender politics in many ways encapsulate the last phase of the uncivil
war. Neither feminists nor gays succeeded in their more radical ambition to destroy
the ideal of monogamous heterosexual marriage as a national norm. Nor were they
able to articulate an agenda that unified gays or women in a single national movement. They could not transcend the divisions of class, race, and ideology that have
made consensus among Americans near impossible to achieve. What is then supris-
ing is not that feminists and gays failed in their larger ambitions, but that they
achieved as much unity as they did. No other movements of the era more successfully crossed the fault lines that divide Americans. They made the personal political.
They did so despite government harassment and the prejudices of a culture that had
traditionally stigmatized both groups.

Of the two movements, feminism was by far the larger and provoked more sustained political opposition. In a single decade, from *The Feminist Mystique* to *Roe v.Wade*,
feminists had redefined the American political agenda. "Sexism" and "gender inequality" became widely used measures of social injustice. Few issues more powerfully roused conservative ire than abortion rights, radical lesbianism, and the ERA.
Given the force of that opposition, it is not surprising that the feminists achieved
only limited success in advancing their core issues. Inequalities, especially in economic opportunity and wages, remained glaring.

All the same, over the next decades women would invade many once largely exclusive male bastions, such as the military service academies and graduate professional schools. No longer would Americans be surprised to see women holding important positions in the private and public sphere. Of course, many of the gains that
accrued to women affected gays as well. Together, they challenged Americans to
make diversity in sexuality and gender an essential part of the nation's social fabric.
And both movements survived the conservative backlash of the 1970s that sought
to reverse their gains and to keep gays and feminists isolated from the mainstream
of American economic and political life. Subsequent conservative efforts to stigma-
tize these movements succeeded largely in perpetuating the polarization that created the uncivil wars.

13

Identities of Race and Ethnicity

Las Vegas: Caesar's Palace, 3 A.M., the bar. The dark-skinned person was big, barrel chested, wearing an expensive suit. His ethnicity was unclear—could have been a Pacific Islander, maybe a Filipino, possibly Latino. He nursed a glass of Tequila with lemon and salt. Next to him sat an Anglo decked out in safari hat and sneakers, smoking a cigarette and drinking. Even by Las Vegas standards, this pair made an odd couple. At the moment they were subdued, but they had treated this sin city to a spree of debauchery from which legends were made. The Anglo later recalled, "we took enough speed to keep Hitler awake in the bunker for fifty days and enough acid to make him think he was in the Austrian Alps."

They first met in summer of 1967 at the Daisy Duck Saloon in Aspen, Colorado. The dark one, Oscar Acosta, was at that time a truly lost soul. Zeta, as he was sometimes known, had quit his job as a legal aid lawyer in Oakland, California, had a nervous breakdown, and suffered from ulcers. A friend directed him to Aspen and the Anglo, a man with a cure. The Anglo was actually a journalist then doing an article on police violence against the Chicano community in East Los Angeles. Zeta had done a stint in L.A. defending poor Chicanos. His work brought him into contact with Marxist professor Angela Davis, labor leader Cesar Chavez, and leading Chicano civil rights activists. Those connections made him an ideal source for the Anglo, who was on assignment with *Rolling Stone*, a nationally circulated journal of the counterculture and rock music. Out of this unusual collaboration had come "Strange Rumblings in Aztlan," published in the April 1971 issue.

The essay focused on the violent death, most likely the murder, of Ruben Salazar, a Chicano reporter for the *Los Angeles Times* and radio station KMEX. Salazar had been a voice for Brown Power in L.A. Like pioneers for African-American civil rights, he had helped bring Mexican Americans a new sense of pride. He defined the increasingly popular term "Chicano" as "a Mexican-American with a non-Anglo image of himself" who found his identity in his Mexican-Indian past. Growing Chicano militancy provoked intense police repression. Los Angeles County sheriff Peter Pritchess was infamous in the East L.A. barrio for his brutal treatment of Mexican-American prisoners in the county jail. His deputies also did what they could to destroy the Brown Berets, a group that modeled itself after the Black Panthers. Acosta had become so embittered that in 1970 he ran as La Raza Unida (the Race United) candidate for sheriff. Even though he was trounced, he managed to win a half million votes, largely from disgruntled minorities.

At the time of his death in 1970, Salazar was in a bar with friends. Outside at nearby Laguna Park, the Brown Berets had attracted some 30,000 Chicanos to protest the war in Vietnam and particularly the high casualty rates for Mexican Americans. La Raza Unida, a political party dedicated to the creation of an autonomous Chicano homeland, had helped organize the event. In the midst of the Laguna Park demonstration, rioting broke out. Without provocation, a deputy fired a tear gas canister into the bar, killing Salazar. His friends and the East L.A. community believed he had been assassinated. Was it mere coincidence he had been working on an exposé of the Los Angeles police at the time of his death? The deputy who fired the projectile was never charged. The community was so outraged that Salazar became a martyr to the cause of Brown Power, and for months after crowds protested.

The Anglo who wrote this story for Rolling Stone was Hunter S. Thompson, the originator of "Gonzo journalism." Acosta had invented the term to describe a style that recreated in prose the mind-bending contours experienced under the influence of drugs. Thompson gained even more notoriety in 1971 when he published his raucous opus, Fear and Loathing in Las Vegas. Much of the inspiration came from Acosta, whose insatiable appetite for drugs and alcohol made him an ideal complement to the Anglo's Dr. Roul Duke. Thompson portrayed him as the 300-pound Samoan attorney, also known as Dr. Gonzo.

For their trip, the two filled the trunk of the large red convertible with a "mobile police narcotics lab." It contained "two bags of grass, seventy-five pellets of mescaline, five sheets of high-powered blotter acid, a salt shaker half full of cocaine, and a whole galaxy of multicoloured uppers, downers, screamers, and laughers." And that was just the more illicit stuff. They had added to that "a quart of tequila, a quart of rum, a case of Budweiser, a pint of raw ether, and two dozen amyls (amyl nitrate). All this and more they consumed during their first Las Vegas odyssey.

Although a lawyer and sometimes civil rights advocate, Acosta had been drawn to Thompson because he wanted above all to be a writer. When he first read Fear and Loathing he was aghast. "My God," he told his editor, "Hunter has stolen my soul! He has taken my best lines and has used me. He has wrung me dry for material." Acosta felt so exploited that he threatened to sue Random House, Thompson's publisher. Rather than face potentially damaging legal hassles, Random House offered Acosta a contract for two books. The tumultuous relationship with Thompson had in this bizarre fashion allowed Acosta to realize his ambition.

Acosta's biographer, Ilan Stavans, described him as a distinctive Latino literary voice, "ambiguous at best, in large part because of his confusing identity." Stavans added that "his style is slangy, his language erratic." That is not surprising, since Acosta admitted to Thompson that his first book, The Autobiography of a Brown Buffalo, had taken him just five weeks to write. His manic personality and stream of consciousness style makes clear why one critic described him as a "Chicano Kerouac." Prior to the publication of Brown Buffalo, many Chicanos had dismissed Acosta with considerable justification as "crazy, a drug-taking hippie." Brown Buffalo established him as a leading advocate of Chicanismo. Historian Manuel Gonzales wrote, "The mood of the radical sixties is nowhere better evoked than in this erratic figure, who combined in his personality elements of the vato loco (literally, 'crazy guy') and the Chicano intellectual."

Acosta's path into the Chicano literary canon was idiosyncratic. Growing up in El Paso, Texas, and Riverbank, California, a rural community near Modesto, he had followed the second-generation immigrant's path toward assimilation. His father, Manuel, was a naturalized citizen who served in the navy during World War II. His mother had been raised in a blue-collar family in Texas. Manuel Acosta was a severe, hard-working, hard-drinking man, often away from home. That left Oscar to deal with a mother who "was going crazy. She ate nothing but aspirins and oranges, drank black coffee and beat us with belts, rubber hoses, ice-hooks." While Zeta loved and respected his parents, he sometimes referred to his father as an "indio," a term Stavans defines as "exemplifying the divided collective self everywhere in Latin America, it is often used to offend someone, referring to him as uncivilized, uneducated, and unmannered."

Acosta struggled all his life to define his identity. Manuel insisted that his son speak English so he would fit into the Anglo world, but Oscar saw himself as an outsider. He was not black, but brown—"a fat, brown Chicano." His were the Brown Buffalo people, or as he put it, "we do have our roots in our Mexican past, our Aztec ancestry, that's where we get the brown from." Despite his insecurities, he was generally successful through high school, excelling in music and sports. His teachers did observe in him a rebellious streak that would come to define him as an adult. Acosta dealt with his feelings of alienation by playing the wild street dude and drinking heavily. At eighteen he developed ulcers. His senior year he turned down a music scholarship to the University of Southern California and joined the air force instead. A failed relationship with an Anglo woman led him to leave the Catholic Church and become a Baptist. While stationed in Panama, he became a minister in a leper colony, organized missions, and preached to the local people. Six months before his discharge, he suffered a crisis of faith that resulted in a failed suicide attempt.

Thus began a cycle of psychiatric care, deep depression, and drug abuse, amidst bursts of creativity and political activism. During this period of struggle he married, finished law school, passed the California bar, and published his first short story—"Perla Is a Pig." His identification with his Mexican roots and Chicano activism blossomed in 1968. He moved to East L.A., where he adopted the name Buffalo Z. Brown and became an outspoken legal advocate for the community's poor. It was at that time the Brown Berets organized the National Chicano Moratorium Committee to protest the high casualty rates for Chicanos fighting in Vietnam. Brown Buffalo began a legal action to challenge the exclusion of Mexican Americans from California grand juries. All the while, his personal life continued to unravel. By 1971, the combination of substance abuse and intense political activism left him burned out. He hooked up with Thompson and in that way launched his brief literary career.

Zeta chronicled his rebirth into Chicanisimo in his second autobiographical book, *The Revolt of the Cockroach People*. It opens on Christmas eve 1969 with 300 "brown-eyed children of the sun" trying to enter Saint Basil's Roman Catholic Church "to drive the money-changers out of the richest temple in Los Angeles." Saint Basil's was a monument in concrete, marble, and steel to the religious vanity of Cardinal James Francis McIntyre and his parishioners from Beverly Hills. Acosta had contempt for the congregation with "pearls in hand, diamonds in their Colgate teeth." The socially and politically conservative McIntyre punished any priest in his archdiocese who became involved in the city's civil rights politics. Nor would he support the social justice cause of labor leaders like Cesar Chavez. So he had no sympathy with the demands of these demonstrators from Catolicos por la Raza, who insisted that the church use some of its wealth for projects in the barrios.

On hand that Christmas eve were the legions from the city's tactical riot squad to protect the service from "a gang of cockroaches from east of the Los Angeles River, from a Mexican-American barrio there called Tooner Flats." "Viva la Raza" the Chicanos shouted before climbing the concrete steps to the church. They had an agreement they could enter so long as they left their "demonstration" outside. Neither the police nor the archbishop intended to honor that agreement. When the crowd reached the church, they found the heavy glass doors locked As sounds of struggle interrupted the service, a priest exhorted the faithful to "pay no attention to the rabble rousers out there." One young protestor, a street nun who had adopted the Chicano cause, managed to reach the front of the church. "People of St. Basil's," she cried to the congregation, "please come and help us. They're killing the poor people out in the lobby." Buffalo Z. Brown stood in the midst of the mayhem. The police spared him from the violence because the officer in charge recognized him as a lawyer. These protestors and their cause would consume him over the next three years.

In 1974, just a year after he published *The Revolt of the Cockroach People*, Oscar "Zeta" Acosta disappeared from a boat off the coast of Mexico and was presumed dead. The national media took little notice, but for Chicanos he had become, in Stavans's words, "a symbol of his people's agony and energy, hope and despair. A leader with too much of an inferiority complex. . . . A role model who often lost control of his impulses." His legacy as a writer stood less on literary merit than on the conviction he gave "that once we can use the language of our oppressors, we can become part of the system, and change it from within." For all his flaws, Brown Buffalo gave his people hope.

Latinos and Identity

Had Zeta Acosta pursued his ambitions in another decade, he might have assimilated into the Anglo world. Many Mexican Americans with his abilities (though not his erratic nature) did move into the Anglo middle class. In the 1960s, however, the emergence of the black civil rights movement encouraged Latinos across the

United States to identify more closely with their own people and to challenge the inequities they experienced in an Anglo nation. Acosta's years as a legal advocate for the Chicanos of East Los Angeles are but one example of that new consciousness. A variety of established Latino organizations and host of new ones, often more racially conscious and radical, initiated a struggle to achieve greater equality and opportunity. A parallel movement among American Indians emerged at the same time.

To explain the rise of Brown and Red Power in the late sixties as simply an off-shoot of the African-American civil rights movement oversimplifies a complex social phenomenon. Certainly after World War II, veterans among all three groups had played a vital role in creating new political activism. Latino and Indian leaders found inspiration in the successes of African Americans in achieving greater political and legal equality. The 1964 Civil Rights and 1965 Voting Rights Acts, while inspired by African-American protests, had benefited the three communities alike. Much in the rhetoric of African-American leaders such as Martin Luther King, Jr., or the more radical Malcolm X addressed the grievances and aspirations of other minorities. Yet in many critical ways, the Latino and Indian struggles to establish political rights and ethnic identity were separate and independent phenomena. Put another way, differences were as defining as similarities.

Take for example the issue of race. Latinos had an even more complex racial heritage than did African Americans. After the Moorish conquests in Iberia (modern Spain and Portugal), North African and European people had mingled freely. That meant that many of the Iberian migrants to the New World were themselves from mixed racial backgrounds. In the New World, an even more complex pattern of race mixing evolved. Historian Juan Gonzalez marvels at the racial variety in Latin America. Along with *mestizos* and *mulatos*, he notes, "there were *zambos* (Indians and Blacks), *coyotes* (mestizo and Indian), *salta-atras* (those with Negroid features born of white parents), *chinos* (offspring of Indians and *salta-atras*), *cuareterones* (quadroons), and even more exotic distinctions." Only a small white elite strove for racial purity, though more to maintain inheritance lines and class status than from fear of miscegenation. Nor did the Spanish and Portuguese colonies adopt the rigid racial code that used the Anglo definition of blackness as the inheritance of even a single drop of black blood. The *mestizos* and *mulatos* in Latin America, according to Gonzalez, "no matter how dark, were invariably treated as part of white society, although admittedly second-class citizens."

The Latino settlers who came into southwestern Anglo-America were largely *mestizos*. They entered a world marked by a rigid racial caste in which whites seldom if ever acknowledged their mixed racial offspring. By the twentieth century, Jim Crow defined the social status of most Latinos. They suffered from economic discrimination, segregation in housing and schools, prohibitions against voting and service on juries, and lack of access to social services. Their second-class citizenship mirrored that of African Americans in all but one important particular. The law in southwestern states where the large majority resided recognized only two categories of race—black and white. Since most Mexican Americans were not black according to Jim Crow practices, the law treated them as whites. That meant that they could not sue under the doctrine of "separate but equal" adopted in *Plessy v. Ferguson,* even though by social and legal custom they experienced all the inequalities African Americans faced.

After World War II, Mexican-American civil rights activists began a series of court cases to end this legal limbo. By establishing Latinos as a distinct class of people, they could fight discrimination through the courts as the NAACP was doing. They found their opportunity in the case of Pete Hernandez. An all-white Texas jury had convicted Hernandez of murder. Indeed, as Gus Garcia, the lawyer who appealed his conviction recognized, no Mexican American had served on a local jury in the past twenty-five years. The state of Texas defended its system by arguing that since Mexicans were white, a jury without Mexicans was still a jury of peers. Among the arguments Garcia made before the Supreme Court, one proved particularly compelling. The courthouse in which Hernandez was convicted had two men's rooms. As Garcia informed the court, one had a sign that said simply "men." The other had a crudely lettered sign that said "colored men," and beneath that in Spanish "Hombres Aqui [Men Here]." The point was clear: "In the jury pool, Mexicans may have been white, but when it came to nature's functions they were not."

Two week before it banned racial segregation in the *Brown* case, the court ruled that Latinos in Texas, like African Americans, constituted a discrete group afforded the full protection of the law. Speaking for the majority, Chief Justice Earl Warren argued that "the Fourteenth Amendment is not directed solely against discrimination due to a 'two-class theory,' that is, based upon differences between 'white' and 'Negro.'" The 1954 decision in *Hernandez v. Texas* gave Latino activists a basis for broadening their attack against discrimination.

The ambiguities of race complicated problems of Latino identity. Most African Americans found in slavery a common racial heritage. They could trace their roots to Africa and link the inequalities of the modern era to the legacy of the peculiar institution. By the 1960s, they had struggled for equality for over a century. For better or worse, Latinos had no such common heritage. Some Mexican Americans could trace their American ancestry back to the seventeenth century. Yet the large majority of Latinos had entered the United States during the twentieth century, and most of that influx had come after World War II. The greatest numbers had arrived in three separate streams from Cuba, Puerto Rico, and Mexico. They settled in discrete areas—Cubans in and around Miami, Puerto Ricans in the northeast and especially in New York City, and Mexicans in a belt across the southwest from Texas to southern California. Isolated by geography, culture, and history, the three groups were linked only by their common language, Catholicism, and minority status in their adopted land.

Discrimination was seldom a major problem for the Cubans. The refugees who fled Castro's revolution came from an elite with close ties to the United States. Prior to 1959, they often represented American interests in Cuba and traveled freely between the two countries. By 1963, over 200,000 had come to the States.

Sociologist Alejandro Portes has observed that "few immigrant groups have commenced their economic adaptation to American life from a position of such relative advantage." While some had left their wealth behind, they brought with them the advantages of education, technical skills, and experience in business, government service, and the professions. Most settled around Miami, where they formed a distinct Cuban community.

The U.S. government extended a host of benefits to them under the 1966 Cuban Adjustment Act. As Juan Gonzalez observed, these were programs that "Mexicans, Puerto Ricans, and other Latinos never received." The state of Florida added additional benefits that facilitated their economic readjustment. Around Miami the Cubans created a largely self-contained economy. Small Cuban banks financed Cuban-operated businesses. Cuban employers hired fellow Cubans when they had jobs available. Cuban consumers did their shopping in Cuban-owned businesses. And when the community thought about politics, it focused largely on the overthrow of Castro and a return to their native soil. All those factors help explain why Cubans, who might have provided much-needed support, played almost no part in the emergence of the wider Latino identity movement.

Puerto Ricans by contrast struggled to make a place for themselves on the mainland. Unlike the prosperous Cubans, the majority of post–World War II Puerto Rican migrants became an impoverished underclass. Why their adjustment should have been so difficult is not readily apparent. Puerto Rico had commonwealth status within the United States. In skin color, the Puerto Ricans were not so different from the Cubans. As historian Clara Rodriguez points out, Puerto Ricans "entered the United States as citizens, served in the U.S. armed forces, had accessible transportation to their country of origin, came from a strategic base of the United States, and had a Caribbean (as opposed to a European) cultural and racial background." Moreover, they came to the States with a relatively high level of literacy, though most were Spanish speaking and raised in what was a foreign culture.

Race proved to be one determining factor. The Puerto Rican immigrant wave came from a racially integrated society with a long history of racial mixing. Cultural categories, more than racial ones, determined position in society. Light-skinned children of mixed racial couples were treated as white, especially in middle- or upper-middle-class families. Dark-skinned Puerto Ricans who were economically or social successful could also be accepted as "white." In the United States, they confronted the strict two-race theory (white/non-white) based on the "one drop" rule. Thus, when Puerto Ricans came to the States, mainlanders ignored their ethnicity and treated them simply as colored. Writer Jesus Colon tells some poignant stories that suggest the wrenching adjustment many Puerto Ricans had to make. After arriving in the States in the 1950s, Colon found himself entering a nearly deserted railway station. With him on the platform was a single white woman with a child and heavy luggage. His first impulse was to offer assistance, but this was the mainland, not Puerto Rico. Fearful that she might be frightened if he, a Negro man, approached her, he left her to struggle alone. After settling in the States, Colon sought employment as a writer. One publisher to whom he sent his resume did offer him a job. But when he entered the office, they rescinded the offer because he was not white as they had thought.

Economic circumstances compounded the problem of race. After World War II, the small peasant agriculture of the island collapsed. Many displaced farm families migrated to the island's cities, where they faced stagnant urban economies. The presence of earlier migrants, cheap direct flights, and a robust job market led many on to New York City as well as to smaller communities in Chicago, Philadelphia, Ohio, and around the Northeast. Lighter-skinned newcomers could often pass for white and find housing in established Italian or Irish neigborhoods. Darker-skinned newcomers settled either in all Puerto Rican areas or in African-American ghettos. Between 1945 and 1960, over a million came to the States.

While jobs were plentiful, first-generation Puerto Rican newcomers had devoted their energies to securing an economic place in the States, not to asserting their ethnic identity. Few actively voted, and only a few politicians tied to the local Tammany Hall Democratic machine actually held elective office. About the only issue the community actively debated was the question of Puerto Rican independence. Not until 1965, when a coalition of Jewish liberals and African-American reformers backed Herman Badillo in his successful race to win the Bronx Borough presidency, did an independent Puerto Rican politician hold a major city office. Until then, the one significant display of ethnic pride was the annual Puerto Rican Day Parade.

Identity politics did not flourish in the Puerto Rican community until the late 1960s. Although similar in many regards to Black Nationalism, ethnic pride in this case proved more unifying than divisive. Inspired in part by the Black Panthers, Juan Gonzalez helped found a radical organization called the Young Lords. Like the Panthers, the Lords rejected the integrationist strategy of established community organizations and identified powerfully with Third World liberationist movements. Puerto Rico, they came to believe, could be a free and prosperous nation once liberated from American shackles. Such assertions of nationalist pride evoked widespread sympathy, not animosity, from older Puerto Ricans. As Gonzalez recalled, "unlike white America, where New Left activism divided father and son, mother and daughter, the new nationalism brought the two Puerto Rican generations closer together." Most significantly, it transformed a sense of being a stigmatized "other" into a more assertive ethnic identity.

That sense of unity proved transient. More extreme Marxists groups like Los Macheteros and FALN (Fuerzas Armadas de Liberacion Nacional) aligned themselves with fringe New Left groups. When they resorted to sporadic acts of terrorism, they alienated much of the community. More moderate nationalists concentrated on issues that affected daily life—voting rights, access to public services, welfare rights, job opportunities, and better education. Veterans of the Young Lords helped create the Puerto Rican Legal Defense and Education Fund and *Aspira*, a youth organization that offered leadership training.

Despite such efforts, time and circumstances held back the rising tide of community assertiveness. The recession of the early 1970s led many of the more prosperous community business and professional families to return to the island, taking with them much-needed human capital. Reverse migration actually exceeded the inflow of newcomers. The community further dispersed as families migrated out of the New York region in search of better job prospects. At the same time, a more diverse Latino migration eroded community solidarity. In addition to much poorer migrants from the island, the new wave included Cubans, Dominicans, Panamanians, Nicaraguans, and other Central Americans. As Gonzalez concluded, economic adversity combined with the conservative backlash against identity politics led Puerto Rican leaders to adopt a more "muted" militancy. Their sense of ethnic pride remained, but concern with "nationalistic independent politics" gave way to a more accomodationist agenda focused on bread and butter issues.

Mexican Americans established a parallel but independent and nationally more visible Latino identity movement. After all, the two communities occupied two geographically distant corners of the country. Moreover, they were historically, culturally, and ethnically distinct. In the 1960s, Mexican Americans constituted the nation's second largest minority after African Americans. The vast majority of the official census total of 3.85 million lived in the Southwest, particularly in Texas and California. About 85 percent of those were American born, and at least half qualified as second or third generation. Despite the stereotype of Mexicans as rural farm workers, about one-third lived in four cities (Los Angeles, San Antonio, San Francisco, and El Paso), and many more lived in smaller cities across the region. The 1950s brought significant advances in politics, as indicated in the *Hernandez* case, in economics, with rising household income, and in education, with a 75 percent increase in those completing high school.

Such improvements could not mask the persistence of second-class citizenship. In the vital areas of income, occupation, and education, Mexican Americans stood far below Anglos and below African Americans. Just 6 percent had some college education, as opposed to 12 percent of African Americans and 25 percent of Anglos. Lack of education locked Mexican Americans out of the primary, high-skill, high-paying labor market. Twice as many were unemployed as Anglos. One-third of the families fell below the poverty level (in Texas it was over half). Efforts to organize and advance the community were often eroded by the influx of illegal workers. Even where Mexican Americans made economic and social gains, they advanced less rapidly than Anglos did. Thus by the 1960s, Mexican Americans had reason to challenge the prevailing order in the American Southwest.

Those promoting ethnic identity in the 1960s could draw on a long history of labor organizing. Radical labor groups like the IWW (International Workers of the World) had periodically attempted to organize immigrant workers in the Southwest. Moreover, mutual-aid societies, or *mutualistas*, became vital centers of the Mexican community and often played a central role in the efforts to improve conditions for farm laborers. So did the socialist Mexican government, which opened some fifty-eight consulates across the region. From this tradition of labor activism emerged two people who came to personify the Chicano movement— Dolores Huerta and Cesar Chavez. There is irony in this because Chavez never adopted the term "Chicano." Huerta, a social as well as a labor activist, more fully embraced the spirit of "Chicanisimo" than her socially conservative collaborator.

Chavez achieved among Mexican Americans much the same stature as Martin Luther King, Jr., had among African Americans. Born in 1927, three years before King, he was part of the generation of minority leaders that emerged from World War II. Chavez knew the world of migrant workers from first-hand experience. His grandfather had lost the family farm in the North Gila River Valley of Arizona during the Depression. The uprooted Chavez family drove an old Chevy to California, where they followed the crops. Regular schooling was a luxury the family could ill afford. Young Cesar managed to attend school on a sporadic basis until forced to quit after the eighth grade. His father became an activist among farm workers in the Imperial Valley. Chavez never got over the feeling that came when the growers crushed a strike. "Some people put this out of their minds and forget it," he later recalled. "I don't." During World War II, he served in the navy until discharged in 1946. Married with a young family, he once again became a migrant laborer until he, his wife, Helen, and their children settled in San Jose. Like his father, he joined a farm labor union which in the late 1940s conducted a series of ill-fated strikes intended to win concessions from the large growers.

In 1952 he met Fred Ross, a local leader, who persuaded him to join the Community Service Organization (CSO). Through Ross, Chavez discovered his gift for organizing, but he grew increasingly uncomfortable with the CSO's elite orientation. Most of the CSO leadership saw their role as gaining concessions for middle-class and professional Mexicans. Chavez thought the organization should take up the cause of the farm workers. Unable to reorient its agenda, he quit to form the Farm Workers Association, which would eventually become the United Farm Workers.

He could not have succeeded in his crusade without the dedicated support of Dolores Huerta. Like Chavez, Huerta had learned her organizational skills through Fred Ross and the CSO, where the two first met. She, however, came from the middle class that organization chose to serve. In the mid-1930s her mother, recently divorced, brought her family to Stockton, California. There she operated a successful hotel. Much of Huerta's life was spent like Oscar Acosta's, in an integrated world. She first married an Anglo and, after earning a college degree, became an elementary school teacher.

Her passion, she soon discovered, was not for teaching but for advocating the rights of the poor. Ross schooled her in the techniques of the radical activist Saul Alinsky, who preached a concept of empowering the poor and minorities through community organization. Alinsky's programs discovered and developed leadership from within the community. That became a guiding force for both Huerta and Chavez. When he left CSO in 1961 to found the Farm Workers Association in Delano, she came with him. Where the twice-divorced and independent Huerta was a modern woman, Chavez was in all matters save his labor activism a social conservative. The UFW welcomed women like Huerta into its leadership not because it was liberated in its social outlook, but because Chavez saw the family as the building block for the union. Whatever its motive, the UFW had a number of outstanding women leaders, and within the union, Huerta functioned more as a partner than as a lieutenant.

The moment of truth came for the UFW in 1965 when a Filipino union, the Agricultural Workers Organization Committee (AWOC), struck against grape growers around Delano in Kern County. Chavez had settled in Delano in part because its large year-round population of migrant workers offered a fertile prospect for organizing. The UFW had barely begun to make inroads when the AWOC demanded that the growers recognize their union and raise wages. The AWOC leaders understood

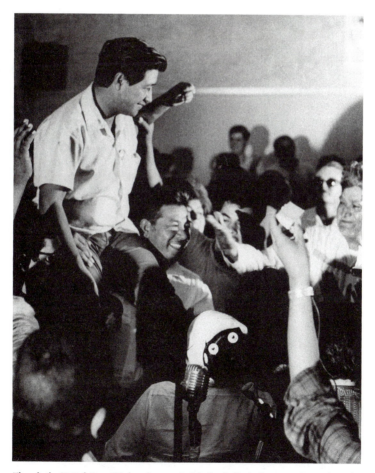

Though the United Farm Workers he organized had only limited success, Cesar Chavez became for Mexican-Americans a leader every bit as revered as Martin Luther King, Jr. was for African-Americans. (Source: Associated Press)

that they could not win without the participation of Mexican migrant workers, who made up over two-thirds of the region's field hands. To that end, they turned to Chavez and the UFW. Chavez entered the strike with understandable reluctance. The UFW had scant resources other than its dedicated leadership, but Chavez did have an acute sense of the historical moment. From the civil rights movement, he had learned that moderate Americans would support nonviolent protest on behalf of the poor. He extended the union's resources by attracting the support of activist churches, student radicals like SDS, civil rights veterans, and the AFL-CIO, with which the UFW had affiliated.

To give La Huelga (The Strike) wider visibility, Chavez also tapped into a growing consumer consciousness. In 1968, the UFW called for a nationwide boycott of non–union picked grapes and lettuce. Never before had a boycott been attempted on this scale. Historian Manuel Gonzalez estimates that about 17 million Americans, or 12 percent of the population, respected the boycott. In 1970, facing a mounting threat to their profits, the growers accepted the strikers' demands, including recognition of the UFW. The boycott and subsequent victory made Chavez a celebrity not only among Mexican Americans, but also across the nation. Fame was not, however, something he sought, for it brought with it much unwanted controversy. Liberal Americans admired Chavez's dedication to the poor, his commitment to labor activism, his nonviolent philosophy, and his ascetic personal style. Conservative Mexicans opposed the politicizing of ethnicity that many liberals applauded. Having tried to gain acceptance into the Anglo world as business and professional leaders, they now found their ethnicity making them into highly visible symbols of a social movement. They preferred accommodation to confrontation. Conservatives objected as well to the close ties Chavez had forged with radical student and labor groups.

Despite those ties, Chavez was not immune from radical criticism. Young Chicanos and Chicanas often dismissed his pragmatic union goals in much the same way Black Nationalists opposed Martin Luther King's integrationist agenda. Just as King drew inspiration from the teachings of the church, Chavez used Catholic symbols to attract support from poor migrants. Chicanos found more inspiration in Marx than in Jesus. By the early 1970s, political consciousness among Mexican Americans lay more with the conservatives and radicals than with Chavez and the labor movement. As a result, efforts to export the Delano model to other regions had only limited success. In 1973, Chavez was back in Delano, fighting a losing battle with the Teamsters Union to preserve the UFW contract. Successive Republican governors undermined the effect of legislation designed to preserve peace between the UFW and Teamsters. At the time of his death in 1993, the UFW had shrunk to just 26,000 members. Despite those reverses, few Mexican Americans ever forgot the intense pride they felt for the person who became their first truly national hero.

Chavez had rejected the Chicano concept of La Raza (The Race) because he saw it as a reverse form of racism. By contrast, young Mexican Americans, especially students, embraced *La Raza* as a new form of identity politics. Most had grown resentful of the constant reminders of their second-class citizenship. Indignities large and small triggered their anger. Schools were generally segregated, with a curriculum designed to direct young Mexicans into vocational work and to suppress their Mexican-Spanish culture. Overt racism among teachers was all too common. One young woman recalled being forced to sit outside on the sidewalk because she had spoken Spanish in school. College students were the first to organize and protest openly. Certainly, the civil rights movement and growing student activism encouraged their increased militancy. Chicanos identified easily with the cause of Third World people, increasingly popular with the New Left. They, like the New Left, embraced Marxist ideals, revolutionary heroes like Che Guevera, and opposition to the war in Vietnam. But they also discovered the militant traditions of the Mexican-American labor and migrant farm workers' unions. Leaders of an older generation such as Chavez and Rodolfo "Corky" Gonzalez provided models of activism within their own communities.

Rudolfo "Corky" Gonzales believed that the real battle for Mexicano rights lay in the urban barrios, not the countryside. Demographics supported that belief. The large majority of Mexican Americans were both urban and young. Gonzales grew up among them in Denver, where he had a successful career as a boxer. He was drawn into politics first through the G.I. Forum and then as a Colorado organizer of Mexicano voters for the 1960 Kennedy campaign. The Kennedys and Johnson rewarded his service with a series of positions in poverty programs. Exposure to local machine politics took its toll. As he shifted steadily leftward along with the political climate of the 1960s, Gonzales decided that the future for Mexicanos lay outside the traditional party system. He created La Crusada para la Justicia (The Crusade for Justice) as an advocacy organization for the Mexicanos of Denver.

Initially La Crusada focused on creating community services for Denver's barrios. Gonzales became increasingly committed to the nationalist goals of the growing Chicano movement. He and other Chicano leaders began referring to the Southwest as Aztlan, the ancestral homeland for Mexicans. By violence, fraud, and legal technicalities, he charged, Anglos had wrested this land from its rightful Chicano owners. Gonzales demanded that the lands be returned and that the Southwest become an autonomous Chicano homeland. While he had initially concentrated his political energies in Denver, by the late 1960s he took his message to a national audience. He joined Martin Luther King's 1968 Poor Peoples' March on Washington as a spokesperson for Chicanos. In 1969, he helped organize the Chicano Youth Liberation Front at a convention held in Denver that attracted some 1,500 participants. To highlight the meeting, Gonzales introduced his *Spiritual Plan of Aztlan* and announced his intention to build a political party dedicated to Chicano separatism. A year later, at a second conference, the Colorado Raza Unida Party was born.

Gonzales's Colorado Party had ties to La Raza Unida from southwest Texas. La Raza brought together young Chicano activists as well as members of the middle class who had begun to embrace their Mexican roots. What most distinguished

La Raza was the youth of its membership. Perhaps its single most influential proponent, Jose Angel Gutierrez, had just entered graduate school when he embraced the idea of an independent Chicano political party. In 1967, Gutierrez had help create the student-based Mexican American Youth Organization (MAYO). MAYO initiated an Alinski-styled project to build Mexicano political activism in the Texas counties along the Rio Grande. By 1970, it had established La Raza, which for the first time managed to elected candidates to local offices. Success brought MAYO together with Gonzales in hopes that La Raza would become a national party. As part of the effort to broaden its base, La Raza had joined the antiwar demonstration in Los Angeles where Ruben Salazar was killed.

Student activists embraced the idea of "indigenismo." As historian Manuel Gonzales observed, "students were heavily committed to the idea of cultural regeneration, which, as in the case of blacks, meant a glorification of the motherland. It was the Indian legacy, however, that they found attractive, rather than the Spanish, who were doubly condemned for being white and imperialists." While much of the activism flourished on college campuses, high school students initiated some of the most newsworthy events. Student attitudes, in turn, reflected growing discontent in the urban barrios, for which the poor quality of schools was a major cause. In Los Angeles, for example, barrio schools were inferior even to those in African-American areas. Teachers openly discriminated, and nothing in the curriculum addressed Mexican heritage or student academic deficiencies. Dropout rates for Mexican-American high school students exceeded 50 percent.

Some community activists urged the students to speak out. Raul Ruiz, writing in a community newspaper, told students, "you should be angry! You should demand! You should protest! You should organize for better education." Sal Castro, a dynamic teacher from Lincoln High, suggested the students stage a "blowout" (walkout). In March 1968, some 10,000 from five largely Mexicano East L.A. schools heeded his call. Police and sheriff's deputies treated the blowout as an insurrection. They indiscriminately beat protestors and arrested many who did not follow orders with sufficient speed. A grand jury indicted Castro and other leaders for conspiracy. Two years of constant police harassment passed before an appeals court finally dismissed the charges as unconstitutional. Over the next several years, students staged blowouts throughout the Southwest, but especially in Texas and California.

The East L.A. walkouts also gave increased visibility to the Brown Berets. Sharing the Black Panther's ideal of self-help, they too sought to address the problems that plagued the urban poor—hunger, poor housing, chronic unemployment, and deficient schools. Like the Panthers, the Berets fashioned themselves as a barrio self-defense group. They kept an eye on the L.A. police, whom they thought of as an occupying enemy rather than a force for law and order. The police viewed this assertion of ethnic autonomy as a direct challenge to their authority—which it was. Their response was totally disproportionate to any threat the Brown Berets might have posed. After the blowout in March 1968, the authorities blamed the Berets, though in fact they had done little more than applaud the students' actions. Of the eleven Chicanos indicted after the walkout, seven belonged to the Berets. Police and sheriff's deputies raided meetings, planted bogus news stories, dragged members into court on trumped-up evidence, and used infiltrators and informers to stir up trouble. And the evidence in several cases, much as in the case of Ruben Salazar, suggests that they even resorted to murder.

Under that reign of constant harassment, the Brown Berets could not sustain their efforts at community building. A few members followed the path of the New Left by adopting a more radical, sometimes violent, strategy. Increased violence alienated more-conservative and established community groups, who favored assimilation over confrontation. While conservative Chicanos recognized the gross inequities between Mexican Americans and Anglos, they were less inclined to blame the system. One moderate academic leader observed, "Too many of us, however, have ignored the example Chavez and the farm workers have given us and instead resorted to rhetoric and have blamed others for all our problems." Equality, he believed, would come only when the community accepted responsibility for its own shortcomings.

Gender issues also created tensions among Chicanos. Women had a long history of participation in Mexicano labor politics. Dolores Huerta was a prime example. But in the 1960s, women in the Chicano movement reprised the experience of women civil rights activists. Where Chicano men had progressive ideas about politics and ethnicity, they held conservative views of women and family. They generally consigned movement women to domestic roles. As Manuel Gonzalez reports, male delegates at a 1969 National Youth conference in Denver resolved that Chicanas "were opposed to their own liberation!" Unable to find their own voice in male-dominated organizations, some Chicanas embraced the feminism of their Anglo sisters. A schism resulted, as it had among African Americans. Many Chicanas continued to submerge their gender grievances in order to promote group solidarity. They argued that the source of their oppression lay ultimately within the Anglo world. For them to criticize their men would weaken the movement.

Chicana feminists charged that in its identification with its Mexican roots, the Chicano movement failed to discriminate between humane traditions and those that promoted machismo and tolerated sexual abuse. Chicanas had to first liberate themselves as women and only then as daughters of Aztlan. The split between loyalists and feminists came into the open at the first national Chicana conference, Mujeres Por La Raza, held in 1971. After much heated debate, the loyalist factions left the meeting. The feminists found themselves alienated from their own community. Nor did they find receptive allies among Anglo feminists. Just as in the case of African-American women, preoccupation with gender made white feminists less receptive to the issues of race and class that animated Chicanas.

The alienation of these dynamic and politically engaged women weakened the movement. So too did the factionalism between radical and moderate elements. In September 1972, Corky Gonzales called a convention in El Paso with the hope that La Raza Unida would emerge as a viable national political party. Gonzales had envisioned the party as a means to promote a radical agenda around issues of class and gender. Moderate delegates agreed with Jose Guiterrez that the party should build political power to achieve more immediate ends. It could serve Chicanos as an alternative to the Democrats and Republicans. But if cooperation with either party meant success at the polls, Guiterrez was prepared to deal. Gonzales was not. So bitter was the acrimony between the two factions that the first La Raza convention proved to be the last. Its candidates had little success during the 1972 elections.

Among the reasons for its failings was an inability to wean moderates and labor activists like Chavez from their traditional ties to the Democrats. The new openness of the Democrats in 1972 reinforced those ties. The movement also failed to attract support from within the community of immigrants and migrant workers. As with Puerto Ricans, most migrants from Mexico avoided politics altogether. Whatever the inequities of their new home, they found far greater opportunity to make a living. Thus, when recession struck in the 1970s, Brown Power lost much of its momentum. No leader emerged who could unify the many local groups and ideological factions. The more established and assimilated leaders of the Mexican-American community generally criticized the militancy of younger activists. Infiltration by police and the FBI added to the dissension. As jobs disappeared and inflation eroded wages, the desire for economic security shifted the agenda away from issues of civil rights.

Red Power

Among the many issues La Raza raised, the return of lands lost to fraud and appropriation held a central place. The restoration of traditional lands was of even more concern to the American Indian protestors of the late 1960s. As historian Peter Iverson has observed, for many Indian people, land and identity were inseparable. Sometimes the land in dispute involved sacred places like the Blue Lake for the Taos people of New Mexico. For some sixty years, Juan de Jesus Romero, the *cacique*, or spiritual leader, of the Taos community, waged a political crusade to regain possession of the lake. Where the forest service saw the lake as part of the Kit Carson National Forest, the Taos saw it as sacred. Where the Taos worshipped the crystal blue waters, the forest service worshipped the conservation movement's "gospel of efficiency." The service did grant the Taos a use permit, but it also allowed logging in the nearby forests. The inevitable scarring of the land threatened to desecrate the site. Should the lake die, the Taos Pueblo would die with it, Romero had told Congress. "Our people will scatter as the people of other nations have scattered. It is our religion that holds us together." In 1970, Congress took heed. Both liberals and conservatives voted for a bill granting the pueblo control over the lake and 48,000 surrounding acres.

As Iverson suggests, in the past, such Indian protests had gone largely unheard. The native people were scattered across the nation and, for most Americans, were both out of sight and out of mind. Not so in the 1960s. Television, movies, and other media humanized the Indians so that Americans could not so easily ignore their grievances. The ninety-year-old Romero had become a powerful and a sympathetic image. Hollywood, having long portrayed Indians as cruel savages, began to show them in a far more human way. Rather than dramatize the defeat of the Indians as a triumph for civilization over wilderness, movies of the 1960s more often treated the conflict as a clash between cultures and the Indians as victims of white savagery.

For the New Left and the counterculture, Indians held a special status. Radicals identified the Indians with Third World people of color who had suffered under colonial rule. What Americans had done to the Indians in the nineteenth century, they were doing to the Vietnamese in the 1960s. Hippies romanticized the spiritual and nonmaterial values they discovered in Indian traditions. Many sought to emulate Indian practice in rejecting technology, returning to the land, wearing Indian-style clothing, and adopting native religious practices.

That romantic view was captured in what may have been the most potent advertising image of the era—popularly known as "the crying Indian." Keep America Beautiful, Inc., unveiled this campaign just a few months after Earth Day in April 1970. Millions of Americans recognized from television and print media his dignified gaze and tearful eye. They knew the message as well: "Pollution: it's a crying shame. People start pollution. People can stop it." Yet few Americans actually knew his name (Iron Eyes Cody), his tribe (Cree-Cherokee), or any of his history (as an actor and supporter of Indian culture). Rather, they embraced the ad and its message because it drew on the popular image of Indians as "noble savages." Where whites exploited resources and unleashed pollution, the noble savage treated nature with reverence and preserved the land. Or as Lakota writer and historian Vine DeLoria, Jr., explained, "The Indian lived with his land," while "the white destroyed his land. He destroyed the planet earth."

The counterculture discovered similar environmental and spiritual values in *Black Elk Speaks*, the autobiographic and visionary memories of a nineteenth-century Lakota holy man. The book became an underground classic and minor bestseller. Like all stereotypes, the image of the noble savage had elements of truth. Indians, especially in the pre-contact era, did generally adopt a more biocentric lifestyle than Euro-Americans.

Indian activists in the 1960s were less concerned with the accuracy of such representations than with their utility in promoting an emerging social and political agenda. For most of those activists, Indian survival was the burning issue they faced. Periodically, federal officials had determined to integrate Indians into the mainstream of American society. In the process, their identity would be destroyed as their connections to tribal customs and sacred places dissolved. One path was through urbanization. World War II had encouraged some individual Indians to move into cities where they could find work and better educate their children. Most selected cities within the region of their tribal roots. In 1950, federal officials initiated programs to encourage further urbanization. They promised assistance with job training, housing, and the cost of resettling.

Many Indians made the transition successfully. They found in city economies new outlets for skills that had little utility on the reservation. Established patterns of segregation and racism limited contact with whites but brought many Indian people of varied tribal backgrounds into regular contact. Aware that federal officials would provide scant assistance, urban Indians turned to each other for support. In the process, they broke down tribal allegiances that often divided the wider community, where old animosities lingered. The Crow, for example, still thought of the Sioux as their enemies, and the Sioux reciprocated those feelings. But as one Chicago Indian remarked, "When we get to the city we begin to think of ourselves more as Indians. Here we all stick together." Out of these urban networks came many of the leaders who would build the Indian civil rights movement.

Termination had also increased the population of urban Indians. After World War II, many officials from the Bureau of Indian Affairs (BIA) and western state politicians argued that rather than promote independence and economic self-sufficiency, the reservations perpetuated Indian dependence on the federal government. By contrast, integration and assimilation into American life would liberate the Indians. That meant moving them off the reservations and thereby reducing federal responsibility for the system. Primary responsibility rested with the BIA. It ran Indian schools, managed the lands, provided health care, and ran the legal system. As one report on Indians noted, "The BIA possesses final authority over most tribal actions as well as over many decisions made by individuals. BIA approval is required, for example, when a tribe enters into a contract, expends money, or amends its constitution." Rather than educate Indian children locally, the BIA sent them away, often over great distances to boarding schools where they were discouraged from practicing Indian customs.

Early experience confirmed fears that termination threatened Indian culture. The BIA had identified a handful of tribes it thought were prepared for an immediate end of federal protection. Among them were the Menominees of Wisconsin, the Klamath of Oregon, and the Salish-Kootenais of Montana. These were, not coincidentally, the most economically self-sufficient tribes, whose reservations held valuable lands and resources. While the Salish-Kootenais managed to stave off termination, the Klamath and Menominees suffered severe financial reversals. The government discovered that it had to provide more, not less, money, but after termination it came in the form of welfare benefits to sustain the newly impoverished people.

The efforts in the early 1960s of Klamath, Menominee, and other Indian people to reverse termination inspired much more widespread political activism. Where the government sought "to bring Indians into the mainstream," the Indians wanted something quite different in spirit. As Sam DeLoria, a lawyer and member of the Standing Rock Sioux, explained, they sought "a true recognition of a permanent tribal right to exist." As a result, Indians wanted to continue to receive federal support in health care, education, and economic development, but they were also determined to develop local autonomy. No longer would they be subjected to the authority of BIA officials.

Ironically, as the Indians pushed for more autonomy, Lyndon Johnson's Great Society made the reservations eligible for a host of new federal programs and an influx of government monies. Programs like Head Start, legal services, and job training came from agencies other than the BIA. Access to legal advice allowed Indians opportunities to confront a host of long-standing grievances over matters ranging from fishing and hunting rights to religious freedom. All the same, political activism did not always bring unity. The authority of some tribal leaders depended on their ties to the BIA. The shift of resources away from BIA occurred as Indians were gaining far more authority within the agency. These established leaders found themselves challenged and sometimes displaced by a new generation of activists, often younger and college educated. Rather than depend on the meager resources of the BIA, the new leaders brought the benefits of Great Society programs to the reservations.

Whatever suspicions Indians harbored of this sudden federal largesse dissipated as the money started rolling in and they learned that many of the programs operated under local control. Peter Iverson points out some of the unintended consequences. In establishing Head Start and other family service programs, for example, women more often had the skills needed. Job opportunities gave women a new status and turned many into social activists and community leaders.

Out of urban networks, college campuses, and the growing number of local activists emerged a greater pan-Indian consciousness. In 1961, a group of younger Indians formed the National Indian Youth Council (NIYC) to inject new energy into pan-tribal politics. Before its founding, only the National Congress of American Indians (NCAI) had served as the collective voice of Indians in their dealings with the BIA and Congress. The organization had never been especially effective. Some of its leaders were former BIA officials, and its ties to the tribes were seldom close. Money was also a problem. The NCAI depended for its funds on contributions from member tribes and prided itself on its nonconfrontational approach to politics. As late as 1967, a banner proclaiming "Indians Don't Demonstrate" flew at its annual meeting. At first the NIYC kept a low profile as it devoted its energies to organization building. The approach had much in common with the Beloved Community of the civil rights movement. Decisions were made by consensus, not by an isolated leadership. The NCAI held its annual meetings in convention centers; the NIYC gathered on Indian reservations. At the close of each meeting, delegates gathered around a drum to share tribal songs and chants. They had dedicated themselves to "attaining a greater future for our Indian people" and sustaining the "high principles derived from the value and beliefs of our ancestors."

Clyde Warrior was one of the most dynamic advocates for the new pan-Indian movement. He shared many of the same mercurial qualities that made Oscar Acosta a leader among Chicanos. Born into the Oklahoma Ponca tribe in 1939 and raised by his grandparents in the language and customs of his tribe, Warrior gained fame in his teens as a fancy dancer. Fancy dancing mixed traditional dress and dance with grace and athleticism. The dancers competed at powwows and tribal ceremonies. As a frequent champion, Warrior visited gatherings of Indian people around the country. In the process, he gained a wider sense of the native people and their traditions. His true gift, however, was for political organizing. He discovered this calling while attending an annual conference on Indian affairs at the University of Colorado. The conference persuaded him that life for his people would not improve until they had their consciousness raised. Only with the development of pride in themselves and their traditions could Indians break out of their cycle of poverty and oppression. As his friend Browning Pipestem, an Osage and Oto, remarked, Warrior took the "negative image of Indians and shoved it down people's throats." He offered in return an image of "red pride." "The sewage of Europe does not flow through these veins," he once told delegates to a youth council meeting.

Many young Indians at first resisted confrontation in favor of a more practical route to self-esteem through education and careers. Pipestem understood their reluctance. "It's painful to have to admit you'd given yourself over to self-hatred," he observed. Recognition of that idea was common to all identity politics. Every identity group, whether women, gays, African Americans, or Latinos, came to believe that until they had discarded the negative stereotypes they had internalized from the dominant male, Anglo culture, they could not liberate themselves.

By the fall of 1963, Warrior had grown impatient with the agenda of educational programs and organization building. The time had come for the NIYC to act. In 1964, he and other NIYC leaders traveled to New York City at the invitation of liberal whites who saw themselves as patrons of Indian causes. Rather than express gratitude to their hosts, the NIYC leaders used a press conference to condemn those who thought they knew what was best for Indians. They went on to chide their tribal elders, the "Uncle Tomahawks," who for decades had sold out Indian interests. And finally, they issued a call for Red Power, by which they meant power for Indians to determine their own affairs.

Historian Alvin Josephy, Jr., suggested that the militants at first used Red Power ironically. They intended to shock those who saw Indians as passive and to inspire a more activist spirit among those who had given up hope of improving their lives. In time, though, the term more accurately described what was a new form of identity politics. The NIYC rhetoric obviously drew self-consciously on the African-American civil rights movement. To send this new message, Warrior brought actor Marlon Brando to the annual NIYC meeting. Brando had recently attended the September civil rights march on Washington. Inspired by Martin Luther King's impassioned oratory, Brando told the delegates the time had come for them to join the wave of civil rights protest. While Warrior and his faction welcomed a call to arms, many of the delegates continued to resist the pressure for greater militancy. Not until the next meeting three months later was Warrior able to push his agenda, since most moderates, fearing they would be forced to take more confrontational steps, stayed away. He then persuaded the NIYC to begin organizing protests at the local level.

That was a message Hank Adams had been waiting to hear. As a young man, Adams had witnessed the corrosive impact of termination on the Quinalt reservation in Washington state. Under termination, Congress had permitted the states to impose their jurisdiction on Indian lands. One of Washington's first acts was to remove the prohibition on alcohol adopted by the Quinalt tribal council. Within a few years, alcoholism and suicide became a scourge. Even worse, the state threatened one of the Quinalts' most sacred traditions when it limited the right of Indian people to fish the annual salmon runs. Many who violated the rules were arrested and fined. From an early age, Adams had resented rules that he saw undermining his people's legal autonomy. He persuaded Brando to take part in what would become the first in a series of "fish-ins," supported by celebrity political activists. Brando joined a group of Indians who, in an act of civil disobedience, fished openly in front of state game wardens and national news media. In that way, Adams and the NIYC finally forced Americans to recognize the Indians' sense of grievance.

Though the NIYC inspired much of the early Indian activism, other Indian rights organizations began to assume a more prominent role. By the mid-sixties, the far more staid NCAI decided to replace many of the older generation of leaders with a younger, more reform-minded group. As executive director it chose Vine DeLoria, Jr., a member of the Standing Rock Sioux (and author of *Custer Died for Your Sins*) who had grown up on the Pine Ridge Reservation in South Dakota. As the NCAI gained new energy, the NIYC struggled to resolve the tension between local and pan-Indian issues that had long divided native peoples. Hank Adams left the NIYC because he thought it had not adequately supported the fishing rights movement. Warrior continued to push NIYC to confront the system, but by 1966 it was clear that moderates were once again setting the organizational agenda. He had more influence as a national spokesperson for Indian grievances than as an organizer. And he was in the process of losing a battle with alcoholism. Though he married and had two daughters, his drinking had increased to prodigious proportions. As his health declined, so did his effectiveness. He died in 1968, just a few weeks short of his twenty-ninth birthday. His death added to the tragic list of those who died that year before they could realize their dreams of racial and social justice.

By the late 1960s, leadership among Red Power activists had shifted to urban Indians. Possibly a third to a half of Indian peoples (between 200,000 and 500,000) lived in cities. With increasing militancy, their pride in their Indianness grew. Indian students formed clubs, held seminars and conferences on Indian issues, and pressed for the creation of Indian studies programs. In Minneapolis, Dennis Banks and Clyde Bellecourt were among a group of Anishinabegs who established the American Indian Movement (AIM). Many Americans equated AIM with the militant Indian movement. A series of highly visible occupations and protests gave the organization wide visibility, but in reality it shared the stage with a variety of organizations like United Native Americans in the San Francisco Bay Area and American Indians United, a national federation of Indian centers.

AIM did support, but did not organize, the event that most galvanized public awareness of Indian activism—the occupation of Alcatraz Island in San Francisco Bay.

The takeover of Alcatraz Prison made Americans more aware of the grievances of American Indians. (Source: Associated Press)

Inspiration for this action came largely from local circumstances, though the reverberations were felt nationwide. At the time of the occupation, the foreboding federal prison on the island lived largely in the popular imagination. "The Rock" had been the nation's most secure prison from which distance and swirling currents made escape virtually impossible. It had been home to such criminal luminaries as Al "Scarface" Capone, Machine Gun Kelly, and the Bird Man. The government in 1963 closed it down in a cost-saving move, leaving it to the birds and the weather. For a brief moment in November 1964, a group of Lokota men had claimed the seventeen-acre island in the name of "Indians of All Tribes," but they decided to leave.

On November 20, 1969, seventy-eight Indians landed to lay claim to the deserted island. A group of Bay Area Indians had conceived the idea over that fall. When a fire burned down the San Francisco Indian Center, the group decided to act, though they were not totally in agreement on their objectives. Some thought that in claiming Alcatraz as an Indian cultural center, they could make a case for similar centers around the country. Others saw the occupation in more symbolic terms. By taking Alcatraz, they asserted a treaty right to reclaim federal lands when the government no longer used them. In addition, the occupation of the island would draw widespread attention to a long list of Indian grievances. But on one point there was general agreement. The occupiers called themselves "Indians of All Tribes" because they saw their cause as "one of the first pan-Indian movements in the country."

Indians of All Tribes established a council to make decisions by consensus. All the same, they needed a spokesperson to present their positions. For that critical role they chose Richard Oakes, a Mohawk from New York. Oakes had spent ten years as a construction worker in New England before he decided to head to California. On his travels across the country, he stopped at a number of Indian reservations. The experience was, to say the least, sobering. He read that Indians believed in "love and friendship for your fellow man." What Oakes actually saw "was the bickering and barroom fights between Indians; the constant drinking." That did not stop him from taking a job as a bartender in San Francisco. The Bay Area happened to be home to one of the nation's largest urban Indian communities, and the bar proved to be a perfect place to meet people and learn about the problems that beset them. Oakes also enrolled at San Francisco State University, a campus embroiled in radical activism and identity politics. He began to travel the state, recruiting students for a new program in Native American studies. Charisma and imposing physical presence made Oakes a natural recruiter. So did his commanding intellect. He attracted most of the students who occupied Alcatraz from UCLA and other California colleges. Those same qualities made him the logical person to speak for Indians of All Tribes.

Despite a Coast Guard blockade limiting the flow of people and supplies, the occupation went smoothly at first. The major task was making the place liveable. Without heat, electricity, or running water, living accommodations were spartan. Some people actually chose to live in the empty cells rather than the dank apartments that once housed the guards. Sympathizers donated money, food, and clothes, while a stream of visitors and new residents braved the blockade to reach the island. Richard Oakes moved in with his wife and five children. Other families came as well. The local and national media gave the occupation considerable coverage, much of it sympathetic. The mayor of San Francisco remarked that on a trip to Europe he was repeatedly "asked about Alcatraz and the Indians." When a reporter wanted to know how they felt about the threat of armed federal intervention, one student replied that since Indians were the "invisible Americans," their enemies could never see them.

To increase their visibility, the occupiers issued the bitingly ironic Alcatraz Proclamation. Through it they informed the nation that Indians of All Tribes reclaimed Alcatraz for all Native Americans "by right of discovery." Not to be thought unfair, they offered to pay $24 in glass beads and red cloth, the same price the Dutch paid for Manhattan Island. An American Indian government would administer the island and a "Bureau of Caucasian Affairs" would "guide the inhabitants in the proper way of living" by teaching them "our life-ways in order to help them reach our level of civilization and thus raise them and all their white brothers up from their savage and unhappy state." The proclamation went on to give the top ten reasons why Alcatraz made the perfect Indian reservation:

- It is isolated from modern facilities without adequate means of transportation.
- It has no fresh running water.
- It has inadequate sanitation facilities.
- There are no oil or mineral rights.
- There is no industry and so unemployment is very great.
- There are no health care facilities
- The soil is rocky and nonproductive; the land does not support game.
- There are no educational facilities.
- The population has always exceeded the land base.
- The population has always been held as prisoner and kept dependent upon others.

Despite its sarcastic tone, the proclamation did announce five serious goals. Indians of All Tribes hoped to establish a series of centers for Native American studies, spirituality, Indian ecology, training in the arts and crafts, and finally, a memorial to the tragic events of Indian history, including the Trail of Tears and the massacre at Wounded Knee.

As the initial fervor cooled, the cold winds, fog, isolation, and boredom set in. Unresolved issues created friction and personalities clashed; fights broke out with increasing frequency. Some of those on the island had come to be part of the action or to get off the streets but had little commitment to the pan-Indian movement. Hippies and reporters came, consumed scarce supplies, and drifted away. Worse yet, a pan-Indian conference intended to draw thousands of Indians from "every tribe, every nation" drew a scant 100 participants. An optimistic press release touting the event as "the most important conference since the days of the Ghost Dance" could not mask the deteriorating situation. The occupiers now had to depend on the Coast Guard to ferry the sick and hurt off the island. When the second semester began in January 1970, most of the students returned to school.

Among those remaining, resentment built against Richard Oakes. Fund raising, recruiting, and publicizing the cause took him regularly off the island. His media fame contradicted the egalitarian ideal under which the occupiers ran their affairs. Rumors spread that he was profiting off donations and spending time off the island hanging out with celebrities. Finally, the council voted to remove him as chief spokesperson. Then tragedy struck, though some called it murder. One of Oakes's daughters sustained such severe injuries from a fall that she died five days later. Neither Oakes nor the occupation ever recovered. He left the island never to return. Six months later he too died senselessly from injuries in a vicious barroom brawl.

Early on, the White House had taken direct control of federal policy toward the occupation. Richard Nixon had little tolerance for the antiwar activists, hippies, and student radicals. Toward the Indians he showed unexpected restraint. As a Quaker, he had long opposed federal Indian policy. As president, he saw little political advantage and great potential risks in smashing the occupation. He left the handling of the crisis to his friend and political advisor Leonard Garment who did not share the paranoia that often cloaked the Nixon White House. He believed that with proper handling, the Alcatraz confrontation could serve as a means to introduce worthwhile new programs for Indians. But if the occupation ended violently, it could become a political nightmare. So Garment looked for a negotiated solution. The problem lay in reaching agreement with the Indian radicals on Alcatraz who thought of the White House as the center of white imperialism. After months of futile talks, the government offered rather generous terms. It would renovate part of the island to create a museum and cultural center. Proceeds from tourism would support the center's program. The National Park Service would manage the operations that would be staffed largely by Indians. On the prospects for a university the negotiators asked for further study, because the government believed the island was not suited for such an undertaking.

The occupiers rejected those terms. They wanted above all legal title to the island and control over its operations. Those were conditions the government refused to grant. And for many on the island, the occupation had become an end unto itself. Any tangible concessions would rob them of this symbol of their defiance. And so they rejected compromise, though their numbers steadily dwindled and conditions on the island continued to deteriorate. Apparent arson destroyed four buildings. By shutting down a lighthouse on the island, the protestors created a significant threat to navigation in San Francisco harbor. By June of 1971, the government decided to end the occupation. An armed Coast Guard force removed the last fifteen stragglers. While the occupiers had no tangible gains to show for their sacrifices, they had inspired an upsurge in Indian activism across the country. They had also reminded the nation that native people still suffered from widespread prejudice and injustice. In the wake of Alcatraz, Indian groups staged some seventy occupations across the country. They even tried unsuccessfully to reclaim Ellis Island in New York Harbor.

In the wake of these demonstrations, Vine Deloria suggested that AIM, the NCAI, and other organizations merge their efforts. Hank Adams promoted a twenty-point plan to redefine the way in which treaty rights were enforced and to restore the right of tribal groups to negotiate new treaties. Unfortunately, the leaders in these groups had lost all faith in each other. To the NCAI, AIM, the thugs who ran it, and its radical rhetoric had become the issue. To AIM, the NCAI was little more than "an inept and irrelevant collection of 'hang around the fort Indians.'" Young Indian radicals saw AIM leaders Russell Means and Dennis Banks as heroes who were fighting the colonial oppressors. Everywhere they went, the police were on alert. They arrived at the Oglala Sioux Reservation in Pine Ridge, South Dakota, to support those on the reservation who wanted to oust tribal leader Richard Wilson. Opponents accused Wilson of instituting a reign of terror or a police state. Efforts to impeach him initiated by a coalition of AIM activists and traditional full-bloods had failed. Wilson warned Means that he had better not set foot on the reservation, to which Means responded that he intended to be the next tribal president. Pine Ridge became an armed camp divided by hostile factions. Armed government agents from a special operations group reinforced BIA officials and tribal police. Two of Wilson's bodyguards attacked and beat Means the first time he came to the reservation.

Traditional leaders persuaded AIM that it was time to bring Wilson down. Together on February 27, 1973, members of the two groups seized a trading post at Wounded Knee, where they were immediately surrounded by a large coalition of federal law enforcement agents. Some eighty-three years before, federal forces had surrounded another group of Sioux at Wounded Knee. These were a starving band of Mnikowojou Lakota that U.S. Army troops, including members of the seventh Cavalry, had herded to this place, about twenty miles from Pine Ridge. During an argument, the troops opened fire with rifles and machine guns. When the shooting stopped, over 300 Lakota, many of them women and children, lay dead in the bitter cold. For most Americans then, and historians after, Wounded Knee had come to symbolize the end of Indian resistance and the disappearance of their way of life. Of the millions of native people who had populated North America in pre-Columbia times, perhaps as few as a quarter of a million survived at the end of the nineteenth century. Indian activists at Alcatraz and Wounded Knee hoped to symbolize the resilience of Indian people and their culture over the twentieth century. To the American Indian nation they announced, "We are still here."

The occupation captured widespread media coverage. As historians Paul Smith and Robert Warrior suggest, "Wounded Knee received more attention in its first week than the entire previous decade of Indian activism." The occupiers pronounced themselves the "Independent Oglala Nation." A steady stream of supplies reached them through the blockade, despite occasional bursts of gunfire. Sniper fire claimed the lives of two men. But in the end the occupation was doomed, because the site was effectively cut off from the world. As the standoff dragged on, the nation turned its attention to other issues—the rise of inflation, mounting evidence of White House involvement in the Watergate break-in, and the final withdrawal of U.S. forces from Vietnam. Seventy-one days after it began, the siege ended. The occupiers had extracted an agreement that the federal government would investigate conditions at Pine Ridge. They had also succeeded, as did the occupiers of Alcatraz, in bringing media attention to a host of issues including treaty rights, the incompetence and corruption of the BIA, and the desperate poverty and disease on many reservations.

But Wounded Knee proved to be more of an end than a beginning. It came after many other radical essentialist movements such as the Black Panthers and Brown Berets had burned out. AIM was no exception. Like those groups, it was more a loose coalition of individuals and factions than a structured organization. AIM had no coherent strategy to turn its vision of rebirth of tribal independence and autonomy into practice. When the government reneged on its promise to investigate Pine Ridge, AIM could not rekindle its movement. Richard Wilson and what his critics referred to as his "goon squad" began a systematic campaign against those who had opposed him. At least three opposition women had sons killed in gun battles with BIA and tribal police.

To destroy AIM, the government launched a massive campaign of criminal prosecutions. No charge was too far fetched nor evidence to flimsy to stop the prosecutorial machinery. Within a year, 500 activists had been arrested and over 300 were under indictment. None of Wilson's goons was ever indicted, despite government promises to do so and compelling evidence against them. The strategy was self-consciously cynical. As one official observed, "the government can win even if no one goes to prison." Even though many lawyers devoted their services to the cause, trial expenses bankrupted AIM. At the height of the prosecutorial crusade, Dennis Banks was a fugitive from justice. Russell Means had posted bond to the tune of $130,000 and faced eight separate trials. Prosecution was not the only government weapon. Agents and informers had infiltrated the movement. Banks discovered that the person he trusted to be director of security was himself an FBI informer.

The Indian civil rights movement failed only in the sense that other identity and value political crusades failed—it never came close to achieving its radical proposals. Pan-Indian unity remained elusive. Many tribes struggled to prevent further erosion of their treaty rights. Disease and poverty continued to plague the reservations—Pine Ridge, for example, is the poorest community in the nation. Under the weight of the federal government's legal assault, AIM had collapsed, as had the Black Panthers and the Brown Berets. The ease with which the government crushed these groups undermines the case that grassroots radicalism posed a serious threat to the nation. Even within their communities, more-moderate factions had far wider followings and continued to function through more traditional styles of politics.

All the same, AIM and the other activists had given the Indians of America new faith in themselves. Vine Deloria, a vigorous AIM critic, said of Russell Means, "he may be the greatest Lakota of this century and his ability to light eyes that have been dimmed so long is probably more important to us than anything that anyone else can do." Means had given his people "a strength they did not know they possessed." AIM and other activitists had also helped revived the nation's consciousness of the Indian people and their heritage. They created widespread sympathy that helped Indians expand their rights and enforce treaty provisions. Their visibility strengthened the opposition that put an end to termination and encouraged the Nixon administration to reform the BIA.

Those plans, like so many of Nixon's dreams and schemes, collapsed as the excesses of the 1960s gave way to scandal and recrimination. The United States would slide from rapid economic growth to recession and rampant inflation, from the spectacle of manned space flight to the fiasco of the Cayuhoga River catching fire, and from the sunny optimism of Woodstock to the constitutional crisis of Watergate.

14
Taking on the System

In the post–World War II era, most Americans so loved their cars they cared little about their deficiencies. General Motors, along with rivals Chrysler and Ford, had prospered in the 1950s by producing overpowered, chrome-laden, gas-guzzling behemoths. These cars were neither safe nor efficient. They spewed pollution and, despite their size, afforded little protection in an accident. But in the 1960s, some buyers began choosing smaller, more efficient imports such as the Volkswagen Beetle. Since large cars were more profitable, Detroit resisted the pressure to design compact cars.

General Motors' belated efforts to compete with the VW led to the Corvair, which, like the Beetle, had an air-cooled rear engine. Internal engineering studies indicated that the design was inherently unsafe. If a Corvair hit a bump during even moderate turns, the car tended to roll over, with potentially fatal consequences. A fix for the problem existed, but it would have added $15 to the cost of the car. So GM, with annual profits over $1 billion, ignored the problem for three years. By the time the company ordered the defect corrected, Ralph Nader had published *Unsafe at Any Speed*. The book did not simply expose the problems of the Corvair; it indicted an entire corporate culture that put profits ahead of the public good and used political influence to evade responsibility for auto safety and air pollution. Rather than address the issues Nader raised, GM hired private detectives to unearth any dirt that might sully his reputation.

GM could have saved itself a great deal of money and public humiliation. Corporate sleuths found nothing in Nader's past that could remotely embarrass him. Quite the opposite. Nader was something of a monk. He lived in a cheap rooming house in a low-rent neighborhood, read only non-fiction, ate no foods with unhealthy additives, did not own a car, and had little social life. One biographer called him "an American Pied Piper, a male Jeanne d'Arc. A Lenin some would say, or—others—a Luther." Born during the Depression, the youngest child of Lebanese immigrants, he so excelled in public school that he got into Princeton and then Harvard Law. At Princeton, he rebelled against social conformity, once going to class in a bathrobe and refusing to wear the white bucks that were all the rage. The suits and shoes he wore in the late sixties were those he had bought at discount in the army PX years before. When asked by then Senator Robert Kennedy what motivated his concern for consumers, Nader explained that the human carnage on the roads sickened him. He was convinced that a country like the United States with companies like GM should do more to protect its citizens.

In 1965, Senator Abraham Ribicoff of Connecticut, a supporter of consumer causes, called Nader to testify before a Senate subcommittee on auto safety. Nader had

Ralph Nader used his settlement from a lawsuit against General Motors to fund his Public Interest Research Groups, more popularly know as Nader's Raiders. (Source: Time Life Pictures/Getty Images)

studied the issue while in law school, and as a young lawyer handled a number of auto accident cases. For years, efforts to promote safer cars had languished under the suffocating lobbying of the Big Three automakers. When Ribicoff's staff publicized GM's campaign to smear Nader, he became an overnight hero and auto safety became a hot issue. Nader sued GM for invasion of privacy. To avoid further embarrassment, GM settled the case, and within a year Congress had passed the National Traffic and Motor Safety Act, the first in a string of consumer protection laws.

Nader used GM's settlement money to found the Center for the Study of Responsive Law. The center became home to the group dubbed "Nader's Raiders," idealistic college students who spent their summers investigating the federal agencies, such as the FTC and FDA, with primary responsibility for consumer protection. Their mission was to wake the watchdogs caught sleeping on the job and to expose those who had gotten into bed with the interests they were charged with regulating. By 1972, Nader's Raiders were darlings of the press, and Nader himself had become more popular in opinion polls than the pope and comedian Bob Hope (that era's equivalent of Billy Crystal).

～

As the antiwar and civil rights movements had begun to factionalize, two movements—consumer advocacy and environmentalism—began to attract wider support. These movements were similar in that both had links to earlier twentieth-century reformers and attracted traditional social, political, and educational elites who no longer felt welcome in organizations dominated by Black Nationalists, Marxist revolutionaries, or identity standards they could not meet. Their advocates ranged from relatively apolitical and conservative groups demanding little more than fair standards and a modicum of justice, to politically engaged activists willing to work within the system to achieve reform, to dedicated radicals persuaded that only the complete overthrow of the system would achieve meaningful change.

Over time, factionalism would beset these movements just as it had civil rights and antiwar protest. Deep ecologists promoting alternative lifestyles would chafe as traditional organizations such as the Sierra Club and Wilderness Society fought for national parks and forests. Such internal divisions prevented either environmentalists or consumer advocates from establishing a coherent agenda or attaining shared goals. Most often they could not agree on what those goals might be. Co-optation was also a problem. The system made concessions sufficient to placate moderate elements, while leaving radicals isolated within their own movements. Equally important, commercialization through advertising and new products such as Recycled Paper's Earth Notes and Celestial Seasons teas created an impression that countercultural values associated with these movements had been welcomed into the mainstream.

Consumerism

Few Americans associate consumer advocacy with the fractious politics of the 1960s. Given the antimaterialist rhetoric of the counterculture, that should not surprise us. A movement that at first glance was dedicated to creating a nation of smart shoppers would seem to be the antithesis of the counterculture's anti-commercial sensibility. Nonetheless, consumer advocates found in Ralph Nader a champion who in true David spirit took on corporate Goliaths. Along with his young Raiders, Nader brought enormous energy and hope to a movement with roots deep in the history of twentieth-century American reform. While consumer advocacy seldom inspired the passions characteristic of many social movements of the sixties, it produced significant structural and political reforms. Conservative politicians condemned consumer advocates with the same venom they lavished on hippies and antiwar radicals.

In practice, consumerism was about far more than fair prices and quality merchandise. It was probably the most broadly conceived of all the reform movements of the era. Among the issues consumer advocates took on were pollution and environmental protection, political corruption and citizen participation in the political system, urban poverty and the rights of the poor, health care, auto safety, as well as more traditional consumer concerns such as price fixing, fraudulent advertising, and product safety. Indeed, by casting its net so widely, the consumer movement ultimately undermined its own effectiveness. It made too many powerful enemies, it competed with other advocacy organizations for political and financial support, and it failed to articulate a coherent agenda or strategy.

Consumerism had a decided countercultural flair. With his simple ways and antimaterialist values, Ralph Nader struck many of his critics as a hippie in a rumpled suit. His youthful Raiders showed their corporate elders scant respect. And as much as SDS radicals, consumerists believed in "power to the people." They pioneered a host of advocacy devices like the class action law suit, which allowed individuals with modest means to seek redress from organizations with seemingly unlimited financial, legal, and political resources. Consumer advocates left behind a legacy of new legislation, revived government agencies, and watchdog organizations that gave the average citizen more rights and protections in the market economy.

The eruption of consumerism in the 1960s was in many ways the revival of a movement that had flourished twice before in the twentieth century. During the progressive era, reformers had responded to host of problems—political corruption, corporate malfeasance, slum conditions, fraud—the list was long. These issues affected the vast majority of Americans, regardless of class status. Muckraking proved the means to expose the seamy side of American society. Progressive reformers responded to revelations of wrongdoing with a mixture of moral outrage and scientific condemnation. They adopted the Pure Food and Drug and Meat Inspection Acts of 1906 to give federal agencies the power to regulate fraudulent labeling, ban harmful products, and impose sanitary conditions. The Federal Trade Commission Act of 1915 empowered the FTC to eliminate unscrupulous or predatory trade practices. Other legislation sought to improve factory safety and protect women and children in the workplace. All these reforms did not, however, create a consumer consciousness. Most Americans identified themselves with the work they did rather than their role as consumers. As a result, the first wave of consumer regulation was, as historian Robert Mayer concluded, "a more basic and in some ways reactionary critique of industrial capitalism." The intention was more to contain greed and moral turpitude than to establish a consumer-based political economy.

The 1930s brought a fundamental political transformation that profoundly influenced consumer advocacy in the 1960s. That was a revised conception of the voter/citizen. Progressives had pursued as their ideal a citizenry of independent political actors making informed choices. New Deal liberals shared that ideal, but the rise of mass propaganda during the Depression era posed a significant threat to citizen autonomy. To some degree, all the major leaders of the Western world in the 1930s—Joseph Stalin, Adolph Hitler, Benito Mussolini, Winston Churchill—recognized the power of mass media to shape public opinion. Some obviously used propaganda to control or diminish citizen participation. Though in most ways a progressive and small "d" Democrat, Franklin Roosevelt was not above exploiting the propagandistic potential of media. He was a master radio performer who used his "Fireside Chats" to sell New Deal programs. But he also saw New Deal reforms as a way to empower political participation.

Despite Roosevelt's efforts, the 1930s produced a more tawdry notion of citizen participation. In 1934, muckraker Upton Sinclair ran as a socialist candidate for governor of California on the EPIC platform (End Poverty in California). Once Sinclair won the Democratic Party primary, he seemed destined to win the governorship. Panicked conservatives were convinced that a Sinclair victory would bring Communism to California. To destroy the EPIC campaign, they perfected modern media politics. Public relations experts used radio, direct mailings, opinion polls, national fundraising, and, above all, movies to convince California voters that Sinclair was a dangerous Red. MGM, for example, produced short films showing waves of unemployed workers and Communist agitators pouring into California to cash in on Sinclair's campaign promises. One columnist wrote that he had never seen a campaign "in which fraud has been so brazenly practiced." Success in defeating Sinclair made public relations experts a fixture in California elections.

These experts tended to treat voters as political consumers whose opinions were to be managed, much as they influenced how buyers chose toothpaste. As historian Arthur Schlesinger, Jr., observed, "advertising men now believed they could sell or destroy political candidates as they sold one brand of soap and defamed its competitor." That technique soon spread eastward so that by the 1950s it had "begun to dominate the politics of the nation." By the 1960s, media treated voters as political consumers who selected candidates on the basis of image and slogans. That is one reason why both political radicals and consumer advocates of the 1960s attacked campaign advertising as a barrier to their goal of "power to the people."

The emergence of Nader as a unifying symbol of consumer advocacy masked many lines along which reformers disagreed. In reality, like all the movements of the era, consumerism had conservative, liberal, and radical elements. Conservatives continued to hold the consensus belief in the inherent benevolence of corporate consumer culture. The real problems, from their perspective, were the shyster lawyers, con men, medical quacks, and high-pressure scam artists who unscrupulously preyed upon unwary consumers. The solution was stricter policing of the bad apples who threatened to bring the system and its responsible corporate citizens into disrepute.

Liberal reformers were more inclined to find deficiencies in consumer laws and regulatory apparatus. As one reformer pointed out, the law might allow the buyer of a car deemed a "lemon" (because it required constant repair) to reimbursement or even a replacement. But what aggrieved auto owner was going to spend thousands of dollars suing GM if the company refused to honor its obligations? Indeed, many consumers did not even understand their right to sue. Hence, problems arose from inadequate access to information and to legal redress. Some classes of consumers—children, the poor, the elderly—without the sophistication to recognize false or seductive advertising became unwitting victims. Liberal reformers thus insisted on more rigorous enforcement and modification of existing laws to give consumers both adequate information and protection so that they could act competently in the marketplace.

Radicals believed that an open marketplace might be nice in theory but did not, and could not, exist in practice. Because big business dominated markets and used advertising to shape consumer decisions, individuals had no capacity to make legitimate choices about their wants and needs. Nor did the system hold corporations accountable for or restrain their excesses. Under the current system, consumers had no protection from high prices, dangerous products, and manipulative advertising. Rejecting the liberals' ideal of a sovereign consumer, radicals believed that consumers were largely victims. The most invidious mechanism of corporate domination was the oligopoly, or "shared monopoly." Among cereal companies, General Mills, General Foods, and Kellogg's had about 85 percent of the market. The Big Three automakers controlled an even higher percentage of automobile sales. Was it mere coincidence that supposedly competitively produced cars that required thousands of parts and complex manufacturing should cost the same amount? Radicals identified this price conformity as a consequence of the anticompetitive role of shared monopolies. The only way in which large firms did compete was in offering meaningless advertising claims.

Even worse, from the radical perspective, the government itself often used its regulatory powers to stifle competition. Among trucking firms, airlines, utilities, and banks, government rigged the market so that industry profited at consumer expense. Free from competitive challenge, corporations raised prices, produced shoddy goods, and resisted innovation. In some instances, like the Corvair, corporations acted without any sense they would be held accountable for their misdeeds. Radicals viewed that behavior, one historian noted, as "deliberate, criminal, and systematic." Neither consumer education nor regulation of hazardous products would fix the problem. Rather, consumers must be empowered so that their rights offset corporate domination.

Radicals offered three means to create consumer democracy. One was a consumer protection agency, which would assume the role of legal advocate. Hence, in David versus Goliath mismatches, where the deep financial resources of corporations denied consumers legal redress, the CPA would serve as an advocate. Needless to say, the business community resisted the creation of such an agency. Consumer radicals also sought to use purchasing power more systematically as a weapon. That took the form of boycotts and buying cooperatives. In that way, Cesar Chavez successfully used the consumer boycott of lettuce and grapes to win concessions from the California growers. Boycotts called in the late 1960s and early 1970s targeted high prices for coffee and milk. They could also be used for political protest, such as those aimed at Dow Chemicals for its manufacture of napalm during the Vietnam War.

Consumer cooperatives provided radicals a third option. These cooperatives promoted not only an increase in purchasing power, but also the activist mentality essential to grassroots democracy. As Ralph Nader commented, "Buyers' groups can be the early links that bond people together. Then they'll start asking questions about municipal services, the schools, pollution." Such questioning of the system was precisely the attitude conservatives found so problematic, while the cooperative spirit struck them as decidedly socialistic. Conservatives feared that organized consumer resistance would undermine the efficiency of markets. Liberals had faith that improved regulation and stricter laws would tame unruly business practices. Radicals believed that since the markets were rigged, they worked only for big business.

Nader proved too spartan in manner and radical in values to head a mass movement. His vision for a better America would have required a fundamental shift in lifestyle, beginning with a marked decline, in consumption. The combination of reduced materialism and enhanced corporate responsibility he fought for would have had environmental benefits as well. Pollution would decline, as would the wasteful exploitation of natural resources. In that way, Nader appealed as much to environmentalists as he did to consumerists. Indeed, organizations in both movements took up many of the same issues and shared many members in common. But the majority of Americans responded more to specific fears rather than the radical critique of corporate capitalism. For example, revelations in 1962 that the drug thalidomide caused severe birth defects resulted in stiffer rules regulating the effectiveness of drugs. Nader's joust with GM and its Corvair led to improved highway safety. Beyond such particular successes in response to specific fears, consumer advocacy remained stymied. More radical notions such as consumer ombudsmen or the creation of a consumer protection agency fell afoul of organized corporate resistance in Congress and state legislatures.

Hence, most of the consumer successes of the late 1960s belonged to the moderates, not the radicals. Americans had been seduced by the higher standard of living established during twenty-five years of economic growth. Consumer activists, a largely liberal, affluent, and college-educated group, did not so much want to destroy the system as to humanize it and make it more accountable; to continue to consume, but with less risk and more fairness. To that end they subjected the corporate culture to a level of criticism unheard of in the heyday of consensus. By the early 1970s, they had achieved greater product safety and quality, fairer pricing, adequate credit with full disclosure of terms, and legal redress for victims of fraud and other illicit practices. As Robert Mayer suggested, with some tongue in cheek, consumerism "expresses the traditional values of efficiency and humanitarianism while at the same time legitimizing consumption. It allows individuals to eat their cake and feel good about it too."

As the economy slid into recession in the early 1970s, consumerism lost some of its appeal. Middle- and lower-income Americans worried more about the availability of credit than its fairness, about the price of goods more than their quality, and about declining corporate competitiveness (with an accompanying loss of jobs) in the face of stiffer competition from Europe and the Pacific Rim. Conservatives often blamed the decline in competitiveness on excess government regulation. They also launched a successful attack on the movement's elite, liberal, and affluent membership. That attack struck a responsive chord among blue-collar Democrats struggling to maintain their standard of living in the face of spiraling inflation, increased unemployment, and wage stagnation. Consumer advocates would win individual battles whenever events like the 1979 accident at Three Mile Island Nuclear Power Plant aroused public fears. Some 300 to 400 state and local groups continued to fight causes like toxic waste dumps and air pollution.

A few broad-based organizations with substantial staffs continued on the national level. Common Cause, founded in 1970 as "a nationwide, independent, nonpartisan organization," sought to empower the citizen/voter by opening the political process to public scrutiny. The organization funded itself strictly on members' dues. It accepted no money from foundations or special interest groups. Over the first three years, Common Cause sued both the Republican and Democratic parties for campaign spending abuses, opposed tax bills conceived in secrecy, fought for an independent counsel to investigate the Watergate scandals, and backed the creation of the Federal Election Commission. Nader and his Raiders survived as well. He established Public Citizen, Inc., in 1971 as an umbrella organization concerned with issues as diverse as health care, tax reform, and lower airfares, while creating Congress Watch as its lobbying arm. The initiatives of both Common Cause and Public Citizen were more in the spirit of early-twentieth-century progressivism than the radicalism of the 1960s. As the recession of the 1970s deepened, enthusiasm for consumer democracy waned.

Environmentalism

Numerous factors in the 1950s and early 1960s accounted for the rise of environmentalism. By the mid-1950s, scientific data offered incontrovertible evidence that auto and truck exhausts, in combination with fossil fuel–burning power plants, produced a brown, acrid smog that often filled the skies of Los Angeles. Other cities faced their own problems with air and water pollution. Outmoded sewer systems spewed human wastes and industrial discharges into local waters. Soapy scum from phosphate-based laundry detergents and fertilizer runoffs turned once clear waters a soupy brown. Sudden inversion layers would occasionally trap gases with sometimes fatal consequences. Most of the 1950s pollution problem stemmed from postwar prosperity and the industrial boom that accompanied it. Americans had powered that boom with cheap fossil fuels and a host of plastics, fertilizers, pesticides, and other products derived from petrochemicals. Nuclear advocates held out the promise that atomic energy offered a pollution-free source of cheap and abundant energy.

The nuclear arms race, however, produced another, more invidious kind of pollution—atomic fallout. Operating in complete secrecy, the Atomic Energy Commission denied that the radioactivity from its tests exceeded innocuous levels found in nature. But on April 26, 1953, a cloudburst drenched Troy, New York. Scientists at nearby Rensselaer Polytechnic Institute (RPI) noticed a sudden surge in background radiation. High clouds had captured radioactive debris from nuclear tests in Nevada and dumped unusual concentrations on Troy. That fallout contained a threat previously unknown to most scientists—strontium 90, a radioactive isotope. In nature the isotope posed no threat, since it could barely penetrate the skin. But when taken up through the food chain it attached to bones, especially in children, where it increased the risk of cancer. That became painfully evident in March 1954 when a surprise squall drenched a Japanese fishing boat that strayed into a Pacific Ocean nuclear test site. Shortly after, many crewmembers became sick from radiation poisoning and several died.

From those events, scientific awareness of the dangers of radioactive fallout rapidly grew. As biologist Barry Commoner recalled, "the meaning of the environment and its importance to human life was suddenly brought to light." Adlai Stevenson raised the fallout issue during the 1956 presidential campaign. Commoner formed an organization of scientists and local leaders called the Saint Louis Committee for Nuclear Information. The committee's research demonstrated the link between fallout and high levels of strontium 90 in babies' teeth. In an era that venerated family and motherhood, that information shocked normally apolitical women to protest against aboveground nuclear tests. They discovered a veil of official secrecy that allowed the government to deceive its own citizens. Further, they came to understand that national defense through nuclear weapons was no defense at all. In any nuclear war, fallout would harm all peoples of the world. In response to growing world pressures, John Kennedy and Nikita Khrushchev negotiated the Nuclear Test Ban Treaty of 1963. Hailed by members of the peace movement, it was also a triumph for environmental awareness because it advertised the profound ecological deficiency of nuclear weapons. As one historian noted, for the first time concern with environmental impacts took precedence over cold war ideology.

The campaign against fallout coincided with the publication of Rachel Carson's Silent Spring in 1962. We have seen how this iconoclastic book challenged many of the central assumptions of the cold war consensus. It brought into question the beneficence of corporate culture, it exposed the manner in which wanton use of pesticides threatened life without the consent of an informed public, and it educated the public to the ecological concept of the web of life. As one historian concluded, "[Carson's] work inspired a global environmental consciousness." Beyond the banning of DDT, however, the immediate political impact of her writing was less clear. As with consumer issues like thalidomide, Americans did react to particular problems of pollution or threats to animal life. But until 1965, the New York Times did not even list the term "environment" as a discrete category.

When it did come of age in the late 1960s, the environmental movement, like consumer advocacy, could draw on a rich history. Numerous organizations formed long before the 1960s—the Sierra Club, Wilderness Society, Ducks Unlimited, the National Audubon Society among them—already lobbied on behalf of what would become core environmental issues. What was different in the 1960s was a greater awareness of the science of ecology. Ecology was biocentric in outlook. It demonstrated that all living things, including humans, are tied into one continuous web. The earlier environmental movement had been far more anthropocentric (human centered) in outlook. It, like consumer advocacy, had its main roots in the Progressive Era.

At that time, two broad strategies emerged—conservation and preservation. Conservationists applied the concept of efficiency to the resource problem. During the late nineteenth century, bountiful resources were wasted because those who used them thought only about profit and ignored the interests of other potential users. In the West, for example, hydraulic mining fouled streams with silt to the detriment of cattle ranchers, irrigation farmers, and municipalities along river-banks. Clear-cutting of timber in the Adirondack and Catskill Mountains in upstate New York threatened the water supply of New York City.

Conservationists adopted the idea of multiple resource use. Rather than look at a forest as a single resource (timber), conservationists saw it as a single resource with multiple uses—recreation, protection of watershed, game management, as well as timber. Scientific management allowed foresters to arbitrate among conflicting claims for this resource. Judicious cutting practices turned forests into renewable resources. That in turn increased profitability in the long run while accommodating other claims to forest resources. Just as consumerism flourished in both the Progressive and New Deal eras, so did conservation. The Soil Conservation Service, the Tennessee Valley Authority, and the Taylor Grazing Act were among the New Deal conservation initiatives.

Where conservation stressed the idea of efficient use, preservation sought to protect wilderness and unique geographic areas. Yellowstone and Yosemite National Parks were among the first successful preservation initiatives. Preservationists shared with conservationists a certain anthropocentric perspective. For them, a central measure of the value of nature was the benefits it confirmed on human society. Conservationists believed those benefits could be measured largely in economic terms. Preservationists joined Henry David Thoreau and other Romantics in believing that nature had spiritual and aesthetic value. John Muir, the patron saint of preservation and a founder of the Sierra Club, became the chief propagandist for the ideal that nonmaterial values should have equal standing with economic ones.

Readers of Rachel Carson could see that she had links to both the conservation and preservation traditions. Like conservationists, Carson marshalled the authority of science to make her case that pesticides had a destructive impact on natural habitats and human health. She also acknowledged a debt to John Muir and Thoreau, with whom she shared the conviction that humans needed to reestablish their connection to the nonhuman world. Hence, her approach was both practical and spiritual. She warned of "the possibility of the extinction of mankind by nuclear war" and of the "contamination of man's total environment with such substances of incredible potential harm" that they threatened "the very material of heredity upon which the shape of the future depends."

Along with its apocalyptic tone, this critique had an ethical perspective that combined the science of ecology with the older preservation and conservation traditions to define the modern environmental movement. Carson condemned the spirit of conquest that had led to the wanton destruction of vital ecosystems. "The 'control of nature' is a phrase conceived in arrogance born of the Neanderthal age of biology and philosophy," she wrote, "when it was supposed that nature existed for the convenience of man." The time had come, Carson believed, for humans to live in, not over, nature. Or as Adlai Stevenson said in his last public speech, "We travel together on a little space ship, dependent on its vulnerable supplies of air and soil. . . . Preserved from annihilation only by the care, the work, and I will say the love, we give our fragile craft."

Carson's critique of science run amok found a responsive audience in the emerging New Left. Her argument that pesticides made little biological or economic sense complemented the radicals' condemnation of rampant consumerism. The movie *The Graduate* (1967) had encapsulated that point of view in a single word: "plastics." The artificially induced compulsion to acquire meaningless goods had created "a false consciousness which is immune against its own falsehood," wrote Herbert Marcuse, a German-born Marxist intellectual. This American materialist way of life, Marcuse believed, produced "one-dimensional thought and behavior." Murray Bookchin, another Marxist critic of consumer society, argued that escape from this materialist trap lay in a reconstitution of society into affinity groups and social ecology—direct-action political associations built around personal ties and spontaneous associations of people committed to ecologically harmonious lifestyles.

Environmental awareness and the desire for individual empowerment linked affinity and social ecology groups to Ralph Nader's consumer cooperatives and counterculture communes. Marcuse, Bookchin, and Nader, along with numerous others on the Left, believed the promise of science and technology to create a healthy world order had been hijacked in the cause of meaningless consumption. Having eliminated the material scarcity of the premodern world, modern society had become addicted to wasteful abundance. As mindless consumers, people had no power to direct their own lives toward constructive goals. The most pressing goal, as Carson had so passionately argued, was to restore the health of nature. New communities with a social purpose, by helping people escape the compulsion to consume, would afford the possibility of placing spiritual goals ahead of material ones. New, nonmaterial lifestyles would make fewer demands on nature.

A series of events made more credible the environmentalist warning that the destruction of nature threatened human survival. A study released in 1965 revealed that within the entire United States, only one river near a major urban area (the Saint Croix between Minnesota and Wisconsin) remained unpolluted. That same year (the year of the Watts riots) a strike by New York City sanitation workers nearly crippled the city. Huge piles of uncollected garbage stood as fetid symbols of society's wastefulness. Then, in November, a massive power failure blacked out seven Northeast states and two Canadian provinces. The outage hit New York at the height of the rush hour, stranding hundreds of thousands of people in elevators and subways. These events exposed the fragile infrastructure on which the modern social order rested. They also suggested that the web of life in nature had its counterpart in human society. As in nature, the interdependent systems that supported life now appeared vulnerable to cataclysmic disruption.

Several ecological disasters heightened public awareness. In 1969, the unthinkable happened. The Cuyahoga River in Cleveland, long an industrial sewer and toxic waste dump, burst into flames. Yes, a river caught fire. The irony prompted singer Randy Newman to croon, "Burn on, big river, burn on." The Cuyahoga became a symbol for the long-term pattern of environmental abuse. Oil spills dramatized the danger of ecological accidents. In 1969, Californians learned firsthand about that threat. For some affluent Californians, Santa Barbara was an earthly paradise, with white sand beaches and ocean views. Unfortunately, modern paradise ran on oil. One of America's richer reserves lay in the channel stretching between Santa Barbara and Los Angeles 90 miles to the south, where oil companies had drilled some 925 wells. Santa Barbara city officials worried about the possibilities of pollution, but the oil companies had frustrated state efforts to impose stricter regulations. Federal officials assured local leaders they had "nothing to fear." How wrong they were. On January 28, Union Oil's well A-21 blew a billow of gooey crude into the channel. Crews quickly capped the well, only to discover that the pressure had opened a fissure in the channel floor. Natural gas and crude seeped to the surface. "It looked like a massive, inflamed abscess bursting with reddish-brown pus," one observer remarked. Given the nature of ocean tides and currents, the disaster quickly spread. Within days, heavy oil tar covered five miles of Santa Barbara beaches. An oil slick extended some 800 miles south to San Diego. "All along the mucky shoreline, birds lay dead or dying, unable to raise their oil-soaked feathers," a reporter wrote.

Few Santa Barbarans were surprised to learn that Union Oil was operating below state and federal standards when the well blew. Twice in the recent past the company had been fined for polluting California waters. Its president, Fred Hartley, had dismissed the leak as "Mother Earth letting some oil come out." He later told a group of Senate conservationists that he was "amazed at the publicity for the loss of a few birds." Such callous disregard for the environment confirmed some of the movement's worst fears. The Santa Barbara blowout, at least, helped inspire the U.S. Senate to pass a bill imposing fines for oil spills.

Even with such repeated warnings, far more Americans thrilled to technological marvels such as the American space program than worried about the destruction of the environment. Nineteen sixty-nine was, after all, the year in which humans first walked on the moon. In launching the space program, John Kennedy had invoked the spirit of cold war liberalism. Success in the race to the moon would affirm both the wondrous possibilities of free market technology as well as the power of democracy to achieve great things. As Kennedy told the nation, "we must go into space because whatever men must undertake, free men must fully share." Some skeptics questioned whether this space extravaganza was necessary at all. Former president Eisenhower thought Kennedy was "nuts" to commit billions to a quest promising little in the way of scientific advances. Other critics thought the billions could be far better spent on more worldly problems.

Whatever doubts skeptics raised, the public thrilled to an endless string of space firsts. In February 1962, Colonel John Glenn circled the earth three times in what he called a "fireball of a ride." The *Telstar* satellite began relaying television broadcasts around the earth, opening up a new era of global mass communications. In May 1965, astronaut Ed White took the first space walk. White called the order to return to his space module "the saddest moment in my life." Even the tragic death of three astronauts in a module fire in 1967 could not derail the Apollo program. On Christmas 1968, members of the *Apollo 8* crew reported live from their lunar orbit to the United States that the moon looked like a "vast, lonely and forbidding sight."

In July 1969, Americans thrilled as *Apollo 11* thundered into the heavens. Several days later, the lunar module came to rest on the moon. Over a quarter of a million miles from earth, Commander Neil Armstrong, followed by Buzz Aldrin, stepped down the ladder to the moon's white, chalky surface in what he called "one small step for a man, one giant leap for mankind." It seemed almost like a moment from *Star Trek*, the popular 1960s series, conceived in the same spirit of New Frontier's liberalism. Trekkies followed Captain James T. Kirk and his international and interplanetary crew on its quest "to boldly go where no man had gone before."

No matter how spectacular its success, the Apollo program, much like the Miss America Pageant, could not escape the political currents of the era. Reverend Ralph Abernathy, seeking to revive Martin Luther King's dream, had led his "poor people's march" and its mule-cart procession to Cape Kennedy (Canaverale) to force Americans to recognize the persistent problems of poverty. Instead, the *Saturn* rockets' fiery ignition had so overwhelmed Abernathy that he knelt to pray for the safe return of the crew. President Richard Nixon hailed the moon landing as the best day's work since the creation. Evangelist Billy Graham privately chided him for his irreverent disregard of Christmas, Good Friday, and Easter. Some environmental scientists saw *Apollo 11* as liberation of another kind. Now, no matter how badly people abused the earth's ecology, they at least had a means to escape to other worlds.

The emerging struggle over environmental renewal took place against the backdrop of a Vietnam War that seemed destined to go on forever. By 1969, however, Vietnam had become as much an environmental battle as a military one. Critics of the war viewed it as one of the great ecological disasters of the modern age. As early as 1965, campus protesters had targeted companies such as Dow Chemicals, which produced napalm. When used as a bomb, napalm, a jellied gasoline, burned with ferocious intensity, often maiming and killing civilians. More devastating were herbicides such as Agent Orange. Frustrated by the thick jungle canopy that afforded cover to the Vietcong, American generals decided to make war on the land as well as its people. They sprayed huge volumes of Agent Orange, which killed the vegetation and crops in an area roughly the size of Connecticut. Agent Orange also proved dangerous to the American troops who handled it and people exposed to it on the ground.

Environmental destruction in Vietnam seemed to antiwar protestors an extension of the misguided effort to conquer nature. The terms "ecocide" and "ecotastrophe" described not only the assault on Vietnam's ecology, but a more general demonstration of the anthropocentric American way of life. Marxists linked environmental destructiveness to corporate profits. A California group published a pamphlet entitled "Where There's Pollution, There's Profit." One radical environmentalist argued that the "deterioration of the natural environment all around us [was] clearly the product of the nature of production and consumption . . . that today holds sway in technological society—American or Soviet." By 1969, many in the New Left saw ecological politics as a way to revitalize protest.

Two events symbolized that convergence. Not surprisingly, one arose on the West Coast, at (where else?) Berkeley. That was People's Park. Former House speaker Tip O'Neill once remarked that "all politics is local," and the circumstances leading to the confrontation over People's Park arose from local issues. The university had begun destroying low-rent apartments that attracted hippies, druggies, and dropouts to areas south of the campus. For several years one vacant lot stood overgrown with weeds and littered with rubble. Neighbors and members of the university community proposed to reclaim it as a much-needed park. Administrators ignored their requests. When a reporter for the local underground press chastened the university for neglecting the site, the administration immediately laid plans to convert the area into a soccer field and parking lot.

Local activists had no intention of waiting for the university to act. They believed that nature expressed through flowers and trees would brighten this bleak urban landscape. The park project also created an opportunity to unify hippies and radicals. Thus, the park linked issues of community and university governance to the growing ecology movement. Radicals hoped to use it to broaden their base and force a confrontation with the Board of Regents and California's combative conservative governor, Ronald Reagan. As one radical predicted, with Abbie Hoffman at his side, the park issue would "suck Reagan into a fight." Other radicals, led by Tom Hayden, wanted Berkeley to become a model for a future revolutionary America. Pride in the park would inspire the community to defend itself. Marxist radicals, reflecting the growing factionalism on the Left, dismissed the park issue as "bourgeois reformism" or as irrelevant to the coming class struggle.

Stew Albert, a former FSM activist who now called himself "Robin Hood's Park Commissioner," informed the community through the *Berkeley Barb* that they should come to the site armed with picks, shovels, and hoes to fashion a green space out of the muddy debris. "The University has no right to create ugliness as a way of life," Albert asserted. And true to the libertarian and anarchist spirit of the New Left, no one would supervise or offer a plan, for "the trip belongs to whoever dreams." That Sunday, to Albert's amazement, several hundred people showed up ready to work. Someone even produced a tractor. The site was too large, however, to tame in just one day, so most of the park builders agreed to return the next Sunday. All week, the neighborhood was abuzz with talk about People's Park. Black Panther leader Bobby Seale dropped by and expressed his amazement that "you just took the land without asking anyone?" The next Sunday so many people arrived, each with an idea of what the park might be, that chaos threatened. One man tried to dig a barbecue pit while another filled it in. Since no one was in charge, no one could resolve the conflict. Some neighbors complained to police about the noisy festival spirit that had invaded the park.

News of the park also reached the University Regents, many of them handpicked Reagan conservatives, among them Ed Meese, who had earlier prosecuted the free speech dissidents. Viewing the park as a flagrant assault on property rights, they insisted that University Chancellor Roger Heyns reclaim the site. Heyns, with no stomach for unnecessary confrontation, believed the issue and the park would wash away with the fall rainy season. Besides, his budget had no money for the project. While the regents pressed him to act, the park builders planted trees and grass, put in swings, and began a vegetable garden. One conservative paper warned, "Commie illegal takeover of property is the first step of a planned confrontation." Meanwhile, a local minister consecrated the park. In reality, Reagan and his allies wanted the confrontation even more than the park activists, because the conflict allowed the university to reassert its authority. Just before the regents were to meet on the Berkeley campus, Heyns ordered the park site fenced. No sooner did work crews post "No Trespassing" signs than park supporters tore them down and burned them in the communal fire pit. Four hundred students announced they would defend the park.

With battle lines drawn, a contingent of California State Police drove community members off the site while bulldozers cleared a trench for the fence. Several thousand protestors joined a noon rally on the Sproul Hall steps. Once again they believed the administration had shown arrogant disregard for the community. One angry law student compared the university desecration of the park to U.S. policy in Vietnam. "Let's go down and take over the park," he urged. Several thousand students began to march but ran into the police. Amidst the resulting turmoil, a radio station managed to contact John Lennon of the Beatles, who with his wife, Yoko Ono, was conducting a "bed-in" to protest the Vietnam War. Lennon urged the students to avoid violence in favor of peace and sanity.

Despite Lennon's plea, the battle continued. Stray bullets and birdshot struck several bystanders. One activist was killed. Some police, for unknown reasons, gassed the university campus, making hundreds of students sick. Dissidents hurled junk and rocks from surrounding rooftops. That evening, Governor Reagan ordered in the National Guard. Once again, the Guard managed to make a difficult situation worse. Soldiers stopped people without significant cause, frisked them, and sometimes beat them for no apparent reason. For days protestors held rallies and police broke them up with tear gas. One group planted flowers; the police followed and tore them out. A state of near anarchy persisted until Reagan finally ordered the Guard off the streets. On Memorial Day, moderates organized a march in which tens of thousands of people proclaimed their commitment to People's Park. There, the crisis ended. Months later the university built a parking lot in which no one dared leave a car. Eventually the weeds, the dogs, the hippies, and the drugs returned. A year later, a mob tore down the fence. People's Park proved a victory for no one, but it suggests that environmentalism had become central to the revolutionary spirit of the uncivil war.

Even more than People's Park, Earth Day, April 22, 1970, expressed the new prominence of environmental awareness. The impetus for Earth Day came from Senator Gaylord Nelson of Wisconsin, who suggested an environmental teach-in to inform Americans about the dangers of pollution. Nelson had two goals in mind. First, he sincerely believed that the environmental crisis was "the most critical issue facing mankind." Second, he thought the teach-in might forge an environmental political constituency without the confrontational style of either the New Left or the counterculture. The person most responsible for defining what Earth Day might be was Harvard Law School student Denis Hayes. Hayes embodied the divided sensibility of environmental activism. On the one hand, he shared much of the New Left's conviction that government and business colluded to maintain an industrial order hostile to nature. "Ecology is concerned with the total system—not just the way it disposes its garbage," he told a press conference. On the other hand, Hayes believed that the New Left's confrontational style alienated mainstream Americans, whose sympathies were essential if the environmental movement was to succeed. "We didn't want to lose the 'silent majority' just because of style issues," Hayes explained. So the event would be critical of the system, but it would also be celebratory.

Needless to say, New Leftists viewed Earth Day with a mix of suspicion and open hostility. Radicals understood the intention of moderates to channel environmental activism away from confrontational politics. They recognized that Earth Day planners wanted to focus on lifestyle issues rather than the Left's critique of the capitalist system. Efforts to forge a consensus with the media, public officials, and corporate leaders struck radicals as selling out. Reformist efforts to reduce pollution would do nothing to alter present power relations. "When conservationists argue that everyone is in the same boat (or on the same raft)," an eco-radical wrote, "that everyone must work together . . . they are in fact arguing for the further consolidation of power and profit in the hands of those responsible for the present dilemma."

Many of the more traditional environmentalists sensed that the spirit of the new movement and of Earth Day was not simply "a relabeled Conservation movement." They feared that the new preoccupation with lifestyle and ecological issues would distract attention from the conservation agenda. "We cannot afford to let up on battles for old-fashioned wilderness areas, for more preservation of forests and streams and meadows and the earth's beautiful and wild places," a Sierra Club official argued. Instead, organizations should continue to focus on those strategies and goals that "the traditional movement has pioneered and knows best." Thus, some of the mainstream conservation and preservation organizations including the Sierra Club, Wilderness Society, and National Audubon steered clear of Earth Day involvement.

So, too, did many government agencies. The White House actually urged public support for Earth Day, but few agencies were willing to modify their long commitment to development and resource exploitation. Most problematic was Secretary of the Interior Walter Hickel from Alaska. His department was best positioned to take up the environmental mantle because it exercised sovereignty over much of the nation's public lands and natural resources. And Hickel did express considerable sympathy for environmental reform. Yet on Earth Day he went to the University of Alaska to announce his support for the 800-mile trans-Alaska oil pipeline, one of the most environmentally hostile projects of the era. So environmentalists remained skeptical about the professed greening of the Nixon administration. Three months before Earth Day, the president devoted a significant part of his state of the union address to environmental issues. His motives were, as always, exquisitely political. At that time, his most likely challenger in 1972 was Senator Ed Muskie of Maine, who was an ardent Earth Day supporter.

On April 22, 1970, some ten million Americans, and millions more around the globe, reclaimed city streets, planted trees, hiked, and in various ways protested the pollution of the environment. Yet what seemed on the surface as a harmonious celebration of nature reflected the usual fault lines of the uncivil war. Conservatives, moderates, and radicals could agree neither on what a pollution-free environment might be nor on how to achieve it. The media celebrated the new environmentalism as a broad-based movement dedicated to stopping litter, cleaning the air and water, and preserving the wilderness. The news cameras ignored the protestors at the University of Alaska who booed Interior Secretary Hickel as he laid out plans for the oil pipeline. Nor did the media give any play to anti-nuclear activists in Denver who gave the Colorado Environmental Rapist of the Year Award to the Atomic Energy Commission.

At the University of Pennsylvania, Senator Muskie explained that the political and environmental issues of the day were entwined. "Those who believe we are talking about the Grand Canyon and the Catskills, but not Harlem and Watts, are wrong," Muskie told his audience. "And those who believe that we must do something about the SST [supersonic transport jet aircraft] and the automobile, but not ABM's [anti-ballistic missiles] and the Vietnam War are [also] wrong." One historian of the environmental movement identified Earth Day as a transitional event. It drew much of its style and energy from the teach-ins and other protest strategies of the 1960s. Many who demonstrated that day shared the idea of alternative lifestyles and utopian visions that inspired earlier reform movements. Yet environmentalism did not briefly flourish and then die as upheavals of the 1960s gave way to the conservative backlash of the 1970s. A host of old and new environmental organizations continued to fight pollution, advocate the rights of all living things, and fight against the anthropocentric assumptions that assumed the superiority of humans over nature.

∿

Earth Day was noteworthy more for its symbolism than its enduring impact on the immediate political scene. Opposition and confrontation, not accommodation and compromise, remained the order of the day. Less than three weeks after environmentalists celebrated the earth with new trees and cleaner streets, state police opened fire on students at Jackson State University in Mississippi and National Guardsmen fired into a crowd at Kent State University in Ohio. The uncivil wars were far from over.

15
The Uncivil Wars:
Woodstock to Kent State

In the summer of 1969, rowdy crowds had marred a number of rock festivals. Conservatives liked to charge that such behavior was inevitable whenever you mixed degenerate music with radicals, druggies, hippies, and freaks. Given that atmosphere, Woodstock Music Festival could have and should have been a disaster. Still, the success of Monterey had convinced promoters that even a small festival could make big money, and some of the festivals that summer had been peaceful. Almost 150,000 people gathered without incident in Atlanta to hear Janis Joplin, Creedence Clearwater, Led Zeppelin, and Paul Butterfield. So the promoters of Woodstock had some reason to believe they too could stage a successful three-day concert. Town authorities in Walkill, New York, were less confident. One month before the festival, they refused to issue the necessary permits.

The promoters then turned to farmer Max Yasgur, who agreed to lease them his 600 acres in Bethel, New York, some sixty miles south of Woodstock. They expected that 50,000 people would pay $18 to listen to a mix of famous and not-so-famous performers. No visible police presence would incite the crowd. Instead, they hired members of the Wavy Gravy Hog Farm commune on the theory that hip security would have a calming effect and could deal with drug ODs and other likely emergencies. To be on the safe side, the Hog Farm planned food, portable toilets, and medical facilities for 150,000 people. Should matters get out of hand, promoters arranged to have 300 specially trained New York City police officers on standby. They built a raised wooden platform with a canopy and hired helicopters to ferry performers to and from the site.

The fans came in numbers far beyond the wildest imaging of the promoters who had planned the festival. By the evening of August 14, the roads in the region were so clogged that state police urged motorists to stay away. And the fans kept coming for three days, at least 400,000 and possibly half a million. No one could tell for sure because they stopped collecting tickets. The New York City special police did not show up, however. Apparently the department brass worried about the stigma of police associating with the counterculture. The rains did come, turning the pastures into a quagmire. Food ran out early on and the crowds overwhelmed the toilet facilities. And somehow it all worked. This event was not about comfort, but about music. And by the accounts of those who could hear the performers, it was fabulous. "It didn't matter what time of day it was," one fan said. "We're talking about two o'clock in the morning, five o'clock in the morning. There was always something going on." Crosby, Stills, and Nash called Woodstock a "rock and roll fantasy."

While a few performers sang about social injustice or the war in Vietnam, the event was largely apolitical. It spoke little if at all to the emerging identity and value politics of the day. Indeed, most of the performers (and a large percentage of the fans) were white and male. At one point yippie leader Abbie Hoffman took the stage to ask for donations for the Chicago Eight, who were on trial for conspiracy in the Chicago riots of 1968. An impatient Peter Townsend of the Who, eager to start his set, hit Hoffman upside the head with his guitar to get him off the stage.

If the music brought the fans to Woodstock, the crowd stole the show. The festival demonstrated to the world, in the words of Max Yasgur, "that half a million kids can get together for fun and music and have nothing but fun and music." On Friday night, with the threat of anarchy looming, a PA announcer appealed to the crowd, "We are going to need each other to help each other work this out, because we are taxing the systems we've set up. We are going to be bringing the food in. But the one major thing that you have to remember tonight is that the man next to you is your brother." The fans took that message to heart. Despite the rain, the mud, the overflowing toilets, the food shortages, the bad trips, and the crowding, not one single act of violence was recorded. Three people died from accidental causes, but three were born. So widespread was the sense of community that people began to see themselves as the "Woodstock Nation," suffused in peace and harmony.

Many people came away persuaded that Woodstock signaled a revolution in consciousness. The counterculture was winning the struggle for the nation's soul. LSD guru Timothy Leary wrote to a friend that "the loving and the peaceful are the majority. The violent and authoritarian are the minority." The staid *New York Times* referred to the spirit of Woodstock as a cultural "declaration of independence." For Yale law professor Charles Reich, Woodstock signaled a new level of consciousness—Level III, as he defined it in his 1970 bestseller *The Greening of America*. Reich believed that people at Consciousness I still clung to the nineteenth-century beliefs "that success is determined by character, morality, hard work, and self-denial." Those in Consciousness II were locked into a corporate ethos dictated by organizations and technology. For them "richness, the satisfactions, the joy of life, are to be found in power, success, status, . . . and the rational . . . mind." Those who attained Consciousness III, by contrast, were "unaggressive, nonviolent, uninterested in the political game." For them the defining issues were cultural— "unrestricted" drug use, an end to legal restraints on private sexual behaviors, the right to dress and look as they pleased, and a preference for communal living. Reich believed that Consciousness III had blossomed at Woodstock and "was sweeping all before it."

Such optimism was understandable given the aura that surrounded the founding of the Woodstock Nation, but it was more than a little naive. For one thing, Woodstock could not easily be repeated. It worked in part because nothing like it had ever happened before. The fans were more likely familiar with festivals spoiled by no-show performers, lousy sound systems, unruly crowds, and hostile police. The transcendental joy of Woodstock raised expectations to unrealistic heights. Future promoters on the other hand were more likely to be motivated by the commercial potential Woodstock had shown rather than the spirit of harmony. So would many of the performers. In the end, the festival proved to be unique.

The difficulty of replicating the experience became clear at Altamont in California four months later. Many Californians were eager to stage a Woodstock west. The Rolling Stones were looking for a way to cap off a commercially successful U.S. tour. Some critics complained that the high ticket prices for Stones concerts undermined the egalitarian spirit of rock. They suggested the Stones could give a free concert to restore their countercultural credentials. After some frantic last-minute negotiations, the Stones settled on Altamont Speedway. It was far from an ideal choice. On its biggest night, Altamont had once attracted 6,500 race fans. The Stones expected about 100,000. With little time to prepare, construction crews managed to build only crude facilities. The low stage could easily be invaded by overeager fans. To assure security, the Stones offered the Hells Angels motorcycle gang $500 worth of beer to guard the stage.

A lineup including the Grateful Dead, Santana, and the Jefferson Airplane guaranteed the one-day concert would be well attended. By show time, some 300,00 fans had descended on Altamont, a site about one-sixth the size of Yasgur's farm. Most people tried to duplicate the Woodstock experience. They ringed the hillside above the stage, got high, and tried to hear the music. Up close it was a different story. People pushed and shoved to get near the stage. At one point Jefferson Airplane guitarist Marty Balin tried to restrain an overzealous Angel who was beating a fan. Another Angel then coldcocked Balin. Tension filled the crowd by the time the Stones came on. During their performance of "Sympathy for the Devil" a small-time street hood named Meredith Hunter pulled a gun. He was immediately surrounded by Angels, who beat him with pool cues before one stabbed him to death.

It has become a historical cliché to contrast the good vibes of Woodstock with the dark mood of Altamont. That has more to do with the manipulation of symbols than reality. Not that much had changed in the four months since the founding of the Woodstock Nation. Most of those who attended Altamont recall it as a great musical experience. Critics, however, saw in Altamont and in the aura of the Stones more sinister forces at work. Police had recently charged a psychotic hippie named Charles Manson and his harem of flower children with a series of murders, including actress Sharon Tate, who was pregnant at the time. Hippies condemned Manson and his violent acts, but many conservatives saw him as a byproduct of the counterculture. How distant, after all, was Mick Jagger's strutting sexuality from Manson's predatory sexual appetites? More than a few critics drew direct links between Altamont and Manson. Worried state and local officials took steps to ban future rock festivals. As rock historian Ed Ward noted, "Meredith Hunter died at Altamont, but a generation's faith in itself was mortally wounded." Altamont became, whether fairly or not, a symbol for the end of the Woodstock Nation.

The bad vibes from Altamont were in reality symptoms of far deeper forces. Take the most obvious example—the music. Most of those who performed at Monterey in the summer of 1967 played for nothing more than expenses, since they assumed the profits would go to charity. Many of them were not then well-enough known to command high fees. At be-ins, the performers and the crowd were part of the same show. "By the time they got to Woodstock," rock concerts had become elaborately staged and expensive affairs. Most bands had left behind the garage style pioneered by the Grateful Dead, who often played be-ins for free food and drugs. Performers like Jimi Hendrix and the Who could command large fees and huge record contracts. The fans had become simply an audience; the performers were celebrities. Rock had left the counterculture to become big business.

In that way commercialization, the most defining quality of American culture, had done much to destroy the spirit that created the Woodstock Nation. Even before the crowds gathered at Yasgur's farm, the world that hippies had created was being co-opted by the commercial society they had rejected. Staples of the hip diet like granola, yogurt, and herbal teas appeared on supermarket shelves. Miniskirts had become high fashion for women. Middle-aged men had started wearing their hair long, sporting jewelry around their necks, and trading suit coats for Nehru jackets popularized in 1968 by Johnny Carson on his *Tonight Show*. Some went so far as to adopt a "trans-sexual fashion" that included "flowing scarves and look-alike vests, psychedelic prints, and perhaps even he/she caftans, serapes, djellabahs, and burnooses." Advertisers had helped to promote that trend. They understood that "the youth market has become the American market. It now includes not only everyone under 35, but most people over 35."

A more disturbing shift had occurred in the world of drugs. Once upon a time, in the heyday of Timothy Leary, drugs had been about transcendence and feeling good. The hip community considered drug suppliers like Owsley Stanley to be public-spirited citizens. By the late sixties, much of that good feeling had dissipated. Seeing new opportunities for profit, organized crime had muscled in on the drug scene. Violence and even murder became more commonplace. Charles Manson was not as much of an aberration as most hippies liked to think. Inevitably, hip communities like Greenwich Village in New York and the Haight in San Francisco had attracted all manner of rip-off artists, crazies, criminals, and, possibly worst of all, tourists. Some of the newcomers were simply psychotic. "Rape is as common as bullshit on Haight Street," one underground publication warned.

Historians Martin Lee and Bruce Schlain have linked the growing violence of hippie communities not just to the intrusion of crazies and criminals, but also to new fashions in drugs. Beginning around 1967–68, amphetamines, primarily Methedrine, or speed, swept through the counterculture. Unlike acid or grass, speed was highly addictive and took a terrible toll physically and mentally. So did heroin, which became the high of choice for increasing numbers. In the wake of these new addictions came near epidemics of hepatitis and VD, spread by dirty needles and addicts prostituting themselves to score drugs. By the time Altamont rolled around, hip communities like the Haight had become battle zones and the vibrations had lost their good feeling.

Most of those who attended Woodstock or Altamont had avoided the worst excesses of this new drug culture. They were more often part-time hippies, sympathetic to the values of the counterculture, who went to college or held jobs during the week so they could "hang loose" on the weekends. Part-time citizens are not the people who make great and enduring nations.

～

The celebratory spirit of Woodstock reflected the commitment to human betterment that had energized the Left and counterculture since the early 1960s. Political activists and hippies had shared the dream Martin Luther King had so eloquently evoked in his speech to civil rights marchers in 1963. By 1969, that dream was fading with the echoes of Woodstock. Commercialization of the counterculture and the new drug scene were just two factors eroding the spirit of peace and love. We have already seen the ways in which value and identity politics fragmented what many people had once seen as a "movement." Each had their particular agendas for reform. That particularism tended to dissipate energies and, as in cases like the environmental and consumer movements, create rivalries among groups that might have worked more effectively in concert. Racial tensions divided Black Power advocates from liberal integrationists, who in turn faced the ire of diehard segregationists and conservatives opposed to affirmative action programs such as school busing. Feminists, including those in the antiwar, Chicano, Indian, and Black Power movements, rejected the macho values of their brothers. Official repression, whether by the FBI, local authorities, or secret government organizations, accelerated the growing fragmentation of 1960s social movements. That repression would increase with Richard Nixon in the White House. Calling for "law and order" and catering to what he called the "silent majority," he intensified the polarization of American society.

Less personal forces were at work as well. The combination of spending on Lyndon Johnson's Great Society and the costs of the war in Vietnam sent the economy into an inflationary spiral. Recession and rising unemployment eroded the prosperity that had made alternative lifestyles seem so affordable. No longer would government fund the vast range of programs launched to solve a host of social problems like urban blight, chronic unemployment, underperforming schools, or the plight of the poor. But of all the factors at work dividing Americans and eroding the promise of the Great Society, none was more corrosive than the war in Vietnam. Radicals on the Left saw the war as a symptom of deeper ills inherent in a capitalist system. Conservatives viewed those who opposed the war as traitors to their country and dupes of the international Communist conspiracy. They called for a return to more traditional values and respect for law and order. Both saved their most strident condemnation for the liberal center, which radicals charged with sponsoring the war and conservatives accused of failing to win it. Together, radicals and conservatives destroyed the consensus Lyndon Johnson had struggled to sustain. In the process, the uncivil wars reached their climax.

Nixon and the Divided Nation

Richard Nixon brought a burning ambition to the White House. "He wanted to be the Architect of his Times," observed Elliot Richardson, a Boston patrician who served Nixon in three cabinet posts. As president, Nixon believed that history, not to mention voters in the next presidential election, would judge him on how well he healed the nation's wounds. He embraced that challenge, confident he could bring unity out of discord. Unrest at home and abroad would afford him the opportunity he sought to move the United States in bold new directions. His political life, he believed, had prepared him for the task. Though determined to appear tough, he also thought of himself as an idealist, a member of a generation that proved its capacity for sacrifice during the Great Depression and World War II. On most domestic matters he was a pragmatist willing to accommodate his opposition in order to save his political capital for what he truly loved—foreign relations. As biographer Richard Reeves has suggested, Nixon was a right-center conservative, small-minded only in the sense he had few interests. Foreign policy, political campaigns, sports, and bedeviling his enemies were his consuming passions. As a consequence, liberals loathed him and conservatives never fully trusted him.

What is perhaps most striking about Richard Nixon is that he ever became president at all. Politicians instinctively like people; Nixon was a loner. During crises he retreated to the executive office where he could be alone with his yellow legal pads. There he would jot down inspirational thoughts and orders for his assistants to carry out. Often he recorded notes to and about himself. These addressed qualities he felt the public did not adequately understand or appreciate. "Compassionate, Bold, New, Courageous . . . Zest for the job (not lonely but awesome). Goals—reorganized govt . . . Each day a chance to do something memorable for someone. Need to be good to do good . . . Need for joy, serenity, confidence, inspiration." Nixon in reality possessed few of these qualities. He was innately secretive, obsessive, awkward, and suspicious rather than inspired.

Socializing came hard to him. He often memorized topics of conversation when preparing to meet new people. H. R. Haldeman, who ran the Nixon White House and spent more time with the president than anyone else, believed that Nixon had no idea or any interest in how many children Haldeman had or what their names were. Where Ike radiated a sense of warmth and integrity, Nixon struck some who knew him as a person "who is acting like a nice man rather than being one." In the wake of Watergate, Henry Kissinger, his former national security adviser, drew a devastating portrait of the man he once worked for:

> He was a very odd man. . . . He is a very unpleasant man. He was so nervous. It was such an effort for him to be on television. He was an artificial man in the sense that when he met someone he thought it out carefully so that nothing was spontaneous, and that meant he didn't enjoy people.
>
> People sensed that. What I never understood is why he became a politician. He hated to meet new people. Most politicians like crowds. He didn't.

Nixon overcame his defects through the sheer force of will. His law school class-mates nicknamed him "iron pants" because he studied so long and hard. In the end he graduated third in his class and was president of the Student Bar Association. A tour of duty in the navy during World War II gave him the opportunity to learn how "to be one of the boys," though he continued to be awkward in social situations. His awkwardness often caused his political foes to underestimate him. That was a mistake most came to regret. Nixon was a determined and, at times, ruthless, even unscrupulous, campaigner. Few opponents ever equaled his mastery of the issues. In his campaign for Congress in 1946 and the Senate in 1950, he established his reputation as a Red-baiter, referring to his Senate opponent, Helen Gahagan Douglas, as the "Pink Lady." Douglas reciprocated by calling Nixon "Tricky Dick," a label that he never lost. Even Nixon's supporters acknowledged that the 1950 campaign was one of "the most hateful" in California history. They applauded "the adroitness and calmness with which Nixon and his people executed their hyperbole and innuendo."

The resilience Nixon demonstrated in facing personal crises was another defin-ing trait. After crushing political defeats to Kennedy in 1960 and in the 1962 California governor's race, many pundits wrote his political obituary. Through dogged determination he reconstructed his public image. By 1968, he had styled himself into a "new Nixon," more candid, mature, and statesmanlike than "Tricky Dick." The successful makeover helped him edge out Hubert Humphrey to win the election.

In his campaign, Nixon spoke about healing the nation's wounds. As president, he tended to exploit them instead. On the domestic front he sought to forge a new Republican majority. During the New Deal era, Franklin Roosevelt had built a Demo-cratic coalition of northern liberals, unionists, intellectuals, African Americans, and southern conservatives. For almost forty years, that coalition dominated the politi-cal system. Nixon's new majority would include such traditionally Democratic groups as white Southerners, blue-collar unionists, and what he called "the silent majority." Opposition to school busing would help him woo disgruntled southern Democrats into the Republican fold. In the wake of the Civil Rights Act and Great Society affirmative action programs, many conservative Democrats were ready to switch parties. On value and identity issues, Nixon chose to be pragmatic, backing reform where it gained him votes, but cracking down on protest, pot, pornography, and permissiveness in favor of a "law and order" agenda popular with unionists and Middle Americans. He would also turn loose the forces of law and order on his enemies in a campaign that would be noteworthy for its lawlessness.

Finding a politically acceptable way out of Vietnam posed Nixon's most daunt-ing challenge. Nixon understood the war was a liability, though he never said so publicly. True to his devious nature, he confessed to an election aide, "I've come to the conclusion that there's no way to win the war. But we can't say that, of course. In fact, we have to seem to say just the opposite." So throughout the campaign he indicated that he had a secret plan to end the war, while steadfastly refusing to divulge it. Behind the scenes he sabotaged Johnson's peace initiatives by secretly urging South Vietnam's president Nguyen Van Thieu not to negotiate until after the U.S. election. Thus, Nixon inherited a war he knew was a losing proposition. His determination to construct a new American foreign policy rested in large part on getting the United States out of Vietnam with its credibility in tact. "I'm not going to end up like LBJ," he assured his staff, "holed up in the White House afraid to show my face on the street. I'm going to stop that war. Fast."

Henry Kissinger, his chief foreign policy advisor, concluded that of all the potential candidates in 1968, Nixon was the one least likely to find a compromise solution to the Vietnam problem. "Seeing himself in any case as the target of a liberal conspiracy to destroy him," Kissinger later wrote, "he could never bring himself to regard the upheaval caused by the Vietnam War as anything other than a continuation of the long-lived assault on his political existence." Nixon looked bitterly on Johnson advisors such as Robert McNamara, who having supported escalation had become outspoken opponents of the war. Rather than reach out to those among the antiwar forces with whom he had some sympathy, Nixon treated them as enemies. Kissinger concluded that "in the process he accelerated and compounded" the bitterness of the domestic struggle.

The desire for an "honorable" peace proved a formidable barrier to extracting the United States from the war. For Nixon and Henry Kissinger, an honorable peace meant the survival of an independent non-Communist regime in South Vietnam. For Hanoi, peace would come only when all foreign forces had left the South. American withdrawal must be unconditional. Since the South could not survive without American support, Hanoi's condition meant a Vietnam unified under a Communist government. To force Hanoi to compromise its demands, Nixon resorted to strategies that had been tried and failed. On the one hand, he continued to strengthen South Vietnamese armed forces. On the other, he bombed the North in order to force Hanoi to negotiate. "A fourth rate power like North Vietnam" must have "a breaking point," Kissinger believed. To that end, he and Nixon applied maximum pressure. And in an attempt to deny the northern forces sanctuary in neutral Laos and Cambodia, Nixon secretly expanded the war into South Vietnam's neighbors. His search for an honorable peace thus brought on the bloodiest phase of the war and provoked continued divisiveness at home.

Nixon chose secrecy in part because it suited his political style, and in part because he did not wish to provoke the antiwar movement. Despite protests at the inauguration, in early 1969 the movement was demoralized, disorganized, and relatively inactive. At the same time, opposition to the American role in the Vietnam War was the one issue on which political activists were broadly united. The president believed that opposition, if aroused, might frustrate his plans to end the war. As long as Hanoi sensed that American support for the war was dwindling, it had little incentive to negotiate. On Easter 1969, several hundred thousand marched in cities across the nation. Nixon and Kissinger asked for their forbearance. "Give us six months and if we haven't ended the war by then, you can come back and tear down the White House fence," Kissinger told one group of peace advocates. Moderates were inclined to give the new administration a reasonable time to carry out its plans.

To further defuse opposition, Nixon adopted "Vietnamization," under which South Vietnamese forces would begin to replace Americans in combat roles. In June of 1969, Nixon called 25,000 troops home. His critics dismissed this step as no more "than changing the color of the corpses," but the public came to believe the war was winding down. The television networks reinforced that view. No longer would they feature scenes from the battlefield on the nightly news. Since 1965, combat footage had appeared three to four times weekly. In the spring of 1969, ABC decided it would shift from the battlefield "to themes and stories under the general heading: We Are on Our Way Out of Vietnam." After that, combat scenes aired once or twice a month. As one journalist remarked, "the war was over, because you didn't see it on the tube anymore." In reality, the war had grown more savage.

So had dissent at home. By 1969, all of the value and identity political groups had begun to assert their claims for political and social recognition. Tactics such as the Chicano high school "blowouts," eco-terrorism by radical environmentalists, or the Indian takeover of Alcatraz offended traditional views of political behavior. College and university campuses produced some of the sharpest clashes. During the 1968–69 academic year, some 4,000 students were arrested for acts of political violence. That number almost doubled for the next academic year. Much of the unrest had more to do with campus issues than with the war. At San Francisco State University, for example, radical students called for a "Third World revolution." The radical Black Student Union (BSU) became a center for Black Power. It demanded the university establish a black studies program and restricted its meetings to "Third World students." During one demonstration, 100 black students chanted, "revolution has come. Off the pig. Time to pick up the gun." That aggressive posture reflected the influence of the Black Panther Party. George Murray, a lecturer and BSU advisor, also served as the Panther's minister of education.

The BSU's confrontational style provoked the anger of the state's university trustees, many of them aroused by the battle over People's Park. When radical blacks stalked the campus, interrupting classes and vandalizing campus facilities, the president called in police. That decision offended many faculty and students, who called a strike to close down the university. The president then resigned. In his place, the board appointed S. I. Hayakawa, a distinguished linguist better known for his conservative politics and ties to Ronald Reagan. Hayakawa insisted the campus remain open and threatened to fire faculty who supported the student strike. Efforts to repress dissent further angered demonstrators and attracted more faculty and students to their ranks. For some two months, 600 police guarded the campus and made hundreds of arrests. An uneasy calm returned only after Hayakawa agreed to create a black studies program, admit more "Third World students," and increase minority financial aid. The authorities did not, however, drop charges against 700 arrested students or rescind the firing of several dozen faculty. George Murray spent six months in jail.

San Francisco State was an urban university in the midst of the revolution in identity politics. Cornell University in upstate New York was by contrast the rural "cow college" of the elite Ivy League. Out of 14,000 students, only 250 were black. Yet Cornell was not immune to the Third World politics sweeping the nation's campuses. Militant black students had renamed the Afro-American Society the Cornell Black Liberation Front. They accused the university of promoting a white, racist curriculum and called for the creation of a black studies program. Some middle-class black students came to support the demands for curriculum revision. As Tom Jones, a black student body leader and self-styled integrationist, recalled, "I was appreciative of the Black Power thrust for making me want to inquire into these subjects. I had to go outside the curriculum to read those books, and I thought there was something wrong in that process." That revelation converted Jones to the cause of black studies. The Black Liberation Front wanted more. It pressed the university to drop disciplinary actions against six students who in December had damaged a building after seizing it for a black studies center. The students called it a political act; the university disciplinary committee ruled it was vandalism. In April, the university rescinded its ruling and agreed to create a black studies program.

That decision escalated campus tensions. Some white fraternity students and conservative faculty objected to what they saw as a double standard. One white student complained that "we're tired of them getting everything they want and doing everything they please." An unidentified group burned a cross on the lawn of a black women's cooperative, called Wari House (Swahili for home). Jones sensed that the university's concessions had not satisfied the need that many black students felt to be confrontational. Ed Whitfield, leader of the Black Liberation Front, agreed: "It seemed as though the student organization would fall apart if not for some ability on our part to act on concert instead of just talking. So occupying a building was something to do at the time, and we did it." Claiming they feared the hostility of many whites, they felt the "need to stand up to it." On parents' weekend, 100 black militants seized Willard Straight Hall, the student union building, and forced 30 guests out into a cold spring rain.

By that time, the takeover of buildings had become common practice in campus protests. That same weekend, militant students at the black Atlanta University (former campus of W. E. B. DuBois) freed 22 trustees they had held hostage in the administration building. The students demanded the university rename itself after Martin Luther King, Jr. At Rutgers University in New Jersey, black high school students and Job Corps trainees from New Brunswick invaded a campus fraternity party. An ugly brawl resulted. Even high schools were not immune. The *New York Times* reported politically charged incidents at two city schools. In Northern Ireland violence had erupted as Catholics marched to claim their civil rights from the Protestant-dominated government. So the takeover at Cornell reflected a pattern of racially and politically charged confrontations across the nation and beyond.

In Ithaca, the Cornell administration moved quickly to negotiate an end to the occupation. It granted key demands, including amnesty for those who had taken over Willard Straight and a revision of the university's judiciary proceedings. But no one was prepared for the scene that occurred when the militants left the building. The *New York Times* headline declared: "Armed Negroes End Seizure: Cornell Yields." A picture accompanying the story showed the occupiers leaving the building. Brandishing rifles and shotguns, a few with bandoliers of shells draped around their necks, they looked like Third World guerillas. Indeed, some had self-consciously affected that look, though they claimed the guns were strictly for self-defense. During the occupation, a group of white fraternity jocks had entered the building through a broken window. Fighting broke out until police removed the new invaders. Rumors spread among the occupiers that the jocks planned to return and drive them out of the building. At that point they collected their guns. The image stunned the nation. If radicals could resort to "armed self-defense" at an elite university like Cornell, what steps might they take next?

That was precisely the fear the Weathermen tried to promote. A largely privileged group of college radicals disaffected with SDS formed this extremist splinter group. They dismissed "so called movement people" as "a kind of right wing force" preoccupied with pacifism. The Weathermen called instead for a campaign of revolutionary violence. When SDS held its 1969 meeting in Chicago the following June, the Weathermen were prepared to destroy the organization. On hand to record and even to help encourage the growing discord were hundreds of Chicago police and undercover FBI agents. The time had come, one manifesto declared, for "anti-imperialist action in which a mass of white youths tear up and smash wide-ranging imperialist targets such as the Conspiracy Trial, high schools, draft boards

The image of armed African-American protestors emerging from the student union of the elite Ivy League Cornell University, stunned Americans.   (Source: Associated Press)

and induction centers, banks, pig [police] institutes, and pigs themselves." After increasingly bitter debate, the Weathermen led their followers and Third World Chicano and Black Panther allies out of the convention. Here was irony with a vengeance. National membership in SDS had grown rapidly over the past year. Yet at what could have been the beginning of new era of radical politics, the organization disintegrated into feuding factions. It would never again hold a national meeting.

The Weathermen, however, made good their pledge to instigate a more confrontational brand of politics. Over the summer they tried with little success to recruit tough city kids to join their battle against "pigs." They disrupted July 4th parades by waving National Liberation Front flags. At Harvard, a small cadre descended on a center that specialized on counterinsurgency research. They broke windows, vandalized offices, and beat up several professors. These guerilla forays were little more than a preview for their big revolutionary target: Chicago. The Weathermen predicted 20,000 supporters would show up in October; about 300 actually did. They gathered at Lincoln Park, a site of rioting during the 1968 convention, to launch "Days of Rage." Calling themselves the "Americong," they wanted to "bring the war home." These radical street fighters intended not "to make specific demands, but to destroy this imperialist and racist society." Charging into the streets of Chicago's fashionable shopping district, they shattered windows, smashed cars, and assaulted people at random. Then the police arrived. When the punching and clubbing ended, scores of police and rioters had been hurt, 6 Weathermen had been hit with buckshot, and 250 arrested. After Chicago, the Weathermen became increasingly isolated and extreme. Most of their members went underground.

Radical protest played into Nixon's hands. James Reston, a widely respected columnist for the *New York Times*, noted that the picture of armed blacks leaving Willard Straight "sent a shudder through this country." Reston found it "paradoxical" that leftist students and faculty acted in ways that encouraged "the political authorities they oppose to use the political power and police power they hate." In the end, he concluded, "Some authority must oppose anarchy." Richard Nixon was all too eager to be that authority. He sensed that the Left's strident demands, vulgar language, slovenly dress, and disruptive tactics offended the vast majority of the American people. Racial tensions added to the distress. Most whites found the posture of militant Black Nationalists particularly disturbing. In one poll, 84 percent of the whites surveyed agreed that protestors were treated too leniently. As one blue-collar worker explained, "What I don't like about the students, the loudmouthed ones, is that they think they know so much they can speak for everyone, because they think they're right and the rest of us aren't clever enough and can't talk like they can."

To help promote the growing disarray on the Left, Nixon initiated operations by various intelligence and police agencies as well as highly politicized federal prosecutions. A provision of the 1968 Civil Rights Act gave the federal government (as opposed to local or state officials) authority to prosecute those who crossed state lines to incite a riot. The act was inspired by antiwar protests and the racial violence in Newark and Detroit, but in March 1969 the Justice Department used it to indict eight radicals for inspiring the rioting at the 1968 Democratic Convention. They included peace advocate David Dellinger and MOBE leader Rennie Davis, SDS veteran Tom Hayden, yippies Abbie Hoffman and Jerry Rubin, as well as Black Panther Bobby Seale. The case against Seale indicated the politically charged purpose of the prosecution. During the Chicago rioting, he had been in the city for less than twenty-four hours, in which time he gave two unmemorable speeches.

Some defendants like Tom Hayden preferred to play the trial straight. By seeking to win over the jurors, they hoped to create a political forum that would expose the nation to their ideas. By contrast, Rubin and Hoffman welcomed the trial as "the academy awards of protest." Turning the courtroom into a theater of the absurd surprised no one who followed the trial. That was standard yippie practice. Rubin and Hoffman wore outrageous costumes, blew kisses to the jury, and even placed a North Vietnamese flag on the defense table. They frequently taunted the judge and prosecutor both inside and outside the courtroom. What was unexpected was the equally outrageous behavior of the presiding judge, Julius Hoffman. Hoffman made no attempt to mask his contempt for the defendants. On every point of law or procedure, he ruled against them. Their lawyers submitted questions to test the cultural bias of potential jurors: "Do you know who Janis Joplin and Jimi Hendrix are?" "Would you let your son or daughter marry a Yippie?" He rejected all but one.

Against Bobby Seale, Judge Hoffman became overtly enraged. The judge rejected Seale's demand to represent himself or to have a continuance until his lawyer recovered from surgery. In response, Seale called Hoffman a "fascist dog," a "pig," and a "racist," among other things. Hoffman then had Seale bound to a chair and gagged. Finally, on November 5, Hoffman separated Seale from the case and sentenced him to four years in prison for contempt. Without Seale's angry outbursts, the trail lost some of its edge. Hoffman showed more composure as the defendants focused their efforts on winning over the jurors once they realized the weakness of the prosecution's case. The jurors were generally hostile. One later commented that the defendants "should be convicted for their appearance, their language, and lifestyle." Another remarked that the demonstrators in Chicago "should have been shot down by police."

During the last two weeks, the trial erupted into what one reporter called the "barnyard epithet phase." The defendants and their attorneys showed ever more impatience and disgust with Judge Hoffman. He, in turn, became virtually irrational, issuing forty-eight contempt citations. Once the jury left to deliberate, Judge Hoffman extracted his revenge on both the defendants and their attorneys. He cited them on some 159 instances of criminal contempt. The charges ranged from disrespect to the court for failure to stand when the judge entered to doubting the integrity of the court by calling him a "liar," "fascist dog," and "hypocrite." Attorney William Kunstler drew the judge's special wrath and a jail term of four years, thirteen days. An appeals court later threw out all the contempt convictions.

On the conspiracy and intent to incite riot charges, the jury struggled to a compromise verdict. Jurors acquitted all the defendants on the conspiracy charge and found five—David Dellinger, Davis, Hoffman, Rubin, and Hayden—guilty of crossing state lines to incite a riot. Once again, Judge Hoffman proved unforgiving, sentencing each defendant to five years in prison and a $5,000 fine. A year later, the appeals court reversed all those verdicts. The appellate court chastened Judge Hoffman for his "deprecatory and often antagonistic attitude towards the defense." It also learned that the judge and prosecutors had been complicit in an FBI operation to bug the offices of the defense attorneys. The "wrong doing of F.B.I. agents would have required reversal of the convictions on the substantive charges," the justices concluded.

Who had won in Chicago? Probably both sides could claim a victory of sorts. The defendants had gained far more fame and notoriety from the trial than from the riots that led to their arrests. Almost every night of the trial they went off to give speeches and raise defense funds from sympathetic audiences. And in so far as they used the trial to expose the ruthlessness and arbitrary behavior of "the system," they had succeeded in that as well. As writer Norman Mailer commented, they showed "you didn't have to attack the fortress anymore." Instead, you simply "surround it, make faces at the people inside and let them have nervous breakdowns and destroy themselves." Certainly Judge Hoffman had made himself an embarrassment to the courts. Yet the government knew it could win even by losing. Many Americans were appalled at the disrespect that the defendants showed the court. The costumes, the party atmosphere, the slovenly appearances, and foul language offended Middle American sensibilities. In that way, the defendants gained little sympathy for the causes they claimed to represent. Most of all, they lived for over two years with the threat of major prison sentences hanging over their heads. Energy and money that could have gone to stop the war, fight social injustice, or expose the system went instead to their defense. In that way, the prosecutorial strategy proved one of the major weapons in the government's efforts to repress dissent.

Vietnam and Protest

By the fall of 1969, the war in Vietnam triggered new outbursts of domestic protest. Support for the war steadily eroded after doves made significant gains in the 1968 congressional election. Newspapers across the nation routinely carried antiwar petitions signed by distinguished community leaders, educators, and cultural figures. The nation's clergy were especially outspoken. Public impatience grew as American combat deaths increased despite the introduction of Vietnamization.

Richard Nixon actually did have a plan to end the war, though not as quickly as he had promised during the election. In dealing with Hanoi, he and Kissinger would play good cop / bad cop. In secret overtures, Kissinger offered what they considered generous peace terms. At the same time, he warned Hanoi that failure to compromise would be dangerous. Kissinger hinted that only with great difficulty could he keep the mad dog anti-Communist Nixon on his leash. To his assistant H. R. Haldeman, Nixon explained the strategy as his "madman theory": "I want the North Vietnamese to believe that I've reached the point where I might do anything to stop the war. We'll just slip the word to them that, 'for God's sake, you know Nixon is obsessed about Communists. We can't restrain him when he's angry—and he has his hand on the nuclear button'—Ho Chi Minh himself will be in Paris in two days begging for peace." Hanoi had a deadline of November 1, 1969. If the peace process remained stalled, the United States would escalate violence with a vengeance. To that end, Kissinger's staff in the National Security Council began to plan Operation Duck Hook, for which Kissinger ruled out few options. The planners weighed bombing of North Vietnam's dikes to destroy food supplies, an invasion, or even nuclear weapons to seal the border with China.

Whether Duck Hook was a serious plan or a ruse to pressure the North Vietnamese has never been clear. Nor did the death of Ho Chi Minh on September 2 change strategy in Washington or Hanoi. Nixon remained determined that Hanoi take his "madman theory" seriously. He leaked some of the details of Duck Hook to a selected group of senators, knowing they would never keep them secret. He also authorized missions into Laos and bombing in neutral Cambodia. Kissinger and Nixon kept those incursions secret because they feared provoking the wrath of the media and antiwar movement. Who would believe that escalation of violence was a strategy for peace? Antiwar groups had already been planning a national moratorium for October 15. Nixon worried less about the moratorium affecting domestic opinion than about the possibility that it would convince Hanoi American will was weakening.

As a result, the president took steps to limit the moratorium's appeal. The White House began leaking disinformation to the press that linked the moratorium's organizers to the Communist Party and other radical groups. Yet neither the CIA nor the FBI had ever produced any credible evidence of foreign influence over domestic protest. A month before the moratorium, Nixon announced that Lewis Hershey would step down as the head of the Selective Service Board. During the first era of antiwar demonstrations, Hershey politicized his position by ordering local boards to review protestors' draft deferments. The idea of using the draft to silence protest outraged student dissidents. Hershey came to stand side by side with LBJ, Nixon, and J. Edgar Hoover in the radical gallery of villains. His departure, along with the troop withdrawals, seemed to suggest that the war was winding down.

To further defuse protest, Nixon announced in September that "under no circumstances" would he be influenced by demonstrations. Despite such efforts, the administration could not blunt the moratorium's appeal. For one thing, the organizers did not simply round up the usual cast of antiwar malcontents. Instead, these veterans of Eugene McCarthy's campaign targeted mainstream Americans. Clergy, prominent congressional Democrats, and a few Republicans endorsed the event. A number of senators and congressmen introduced antiwar resolutions. So did the faculties and presidents of major colleges and universities. Rather than schedule the moratorium for a weekend, the organizers planned it for a weekday to emphasize the idea of no more business as usual. Nor was the event limited to Washington and a few major cities. Instead, on October 15, several million Americans in communities across the nation gathered to call for an end to the war. Some 600,000 peace advocates joined a candlelight procession from the Mall in Washington to the White House. For a brief moment, the president observed them from behind a curtained window.

The *Boston Globe* described the moratorium as a "Political Woodstock." Historian Melvin Small later called it "the single most important one day demonstration in the history of the war." Small speculated that while Duck Hook may well have been a bluff, the outpouring of peace sentiment made it near impossible for Nixon to unleash new violence on November 1 as he had threatened. The moratorium's success inspired organizers to announce they would stage monthly events so long as the United States remained in Vietnam. The New Mobilization Committee to End the War in Vietnam called for a major march on Washington over the weekend of November 13.

The administration fought back. On one front it sought to reduce media attention to antiwar demonstrations. Some observers noted that the television networks had given the moratorium little live coverage during prime time, even though in size and middle-class makeup it was an extraordinary event. The network's caution followed hostile remarks from Vice President Spiro Agnew. Agnew had once been a modestly progressive governor of Maryland. Racial disturbances in his state turned him into a law-and-order man whose tough talk caught the attention of the Nixon campaign. Still, the decision to name him to the GOP ticket came as a shock, for he was a virtual unknown outside of Maryland. The *Washington Post*, which had more closely followed Agnew's career, called his choice "perhaps the most eccentric political appointment since the Roman emperor Caligula named his horse as consul." Once elected, Nixon had little idea what to do with Agnew. He discovered that his vice president was a deeply ignorant man with little grasp of major issues. Two of his most aggressive and conservative speechwriters believed they had a solution. Pat Buchanan and William Safire proposed that Agnew become the administration point man in its war against the "liberal" media.

The opening attack came three weeks before the moratorium. Agnew chided the television news networks for their sympathetic coverage of antiwar demonstrations. Quite possibly, his criticism led the networks to curtail their moratorium coverage. As the November mobilization approached, Nixon joined the media offensive. Ever since his days as a college debater, he had an abiding belief in the power of political oratory to change the course of events. For several long days and nights he worked over his thoughts on the war. The question he posed was stark: Should the United States launch Duck Hook to force Hanoi to the bargaining table or should the United States cut its losses and bail out?

For Nixon, this was no choice at all. On November 3, he told a national television audience that the easiest course for him might be "the immediate withdrawal of all American forces." In that way he could "avoid allowing Johnson's war to become Nixon's war." Where the previous administration had "Americanized the war in Vietnam," his administration was "Vietnamizing the search for peace." Should Hanoi decide to escalate, he would "not hesitate to take strong and effective measures to deal with the situation." Failure of the United States to stem Communist aggression would lose America the confidence of its allies, encourage recklessness on the part of its enemies, and spark violence "wherever our commitments help maintain the peace."

Having justified both Vietnamization of the war and a continuation of the American presence in Vietnam, Nixon then sought to undermine the growing appeal of the antiwar movement while notifying Hanoi that American resolve was firm. A decision to withdraw, as the demonstrators demanded, would lead to "inevitable remorse and divisive recrimination." So Nixon reached out "to you, the great silent majority of my fellow Americans—I ask for your support." He had used the phrase "silent majority" before, but never with such clear intent to define the fault line between those "united for peace" as opposed to those who would accept defeat. "North Vietnam cannot defeat or humiliate the United States," Nixon assured the nation. "Only Americans can do that." As one news commentator concluded in his analysis, "The President tonight has polarized attitude in the country more than it has ever been into groups that are either for him or against him." Nixon had anticipated such hostile reactions. Even before it came, he ordered Haldeman to have letters sent to the media complaining about the negative analysis. "I want dirty, vicious ones to the [New York] Times and the Washington Post about their editorials," he insisted. An outpouring of praise for the president's position turned his bitterness into euphoria. "We've got those liberal bastards on the run now," he gloated.

News corporations like the Times and Post, as well as the TV networks, all owned local affiliate stations that required licenses issued by the FCC. Should presidential pressure lead the FCC to revoke those licenses, the owners would suffer major financial losses. Thus the media was especially anxious when Vice President Agnew renewed his attacks. Agnew would gain wide notoriety for his alliterative broadsides. News commentators became "nattering nabobs of negativism" and "troubadours of trouble." Agnew held them largely responsible for "creeping permissiveness that afflicted America." He dismissed antiwar protestors as "an effete corps of impudent snobs." On November 14, as the antiwar forces gathered in Washington to protest the war, Agnew delivered his sternest rebuke of the media. What bothered him most, he told a group of Iowa Republicans and a national television audience, was that no sooner had President Nixon finished his thoughtful speech on Vietnam, than a "small band of network commentators and self-appointed analysts," with minds "made up in advance," subjected the president's words "to instant analysis and querulous criticism."

Worse yet, "a small group of men numbering no more than a dozen anchormen, commentators, executive producers" had assigned to themselves through no democratic procedure "a concentration of power over American public opinion unknown in history." That dirty dozen all lived within the Washington Beltway or New York City. One of their numbers, Agnew complained, had said of Richard Nixon on the eve of the 1968 election that he would give into "his natural instinct to smash the enemy with a club or go after him with a meat axe." In reality, most people who knew Nixon would have agreed. Agnew characterized the comment as partisanship disguised as "an objective statement." Then he issued a thinly veiled threat that chilled media headquarters. Was it not fair to question the wisdom of leaving this "concentration in the hands of a tiny fraternity of privileged men elected by no one and enjoying a monopoly sanctioned and licensed by Government?" The media, of course, heard "licensed by Government." Middle America heard "elite fraternity," "privileged men," "concentration of power," and "monopoly," the traditional populist bogymen. With this speech, Agnew became an apostle of the politics of resentment.

On the eve of the Mobilization, public opinion remained conflicted. A majority supported the president's efforts to achieve an honorable peace. Yet even more saw the war as a mistake and some 80 percent were "fed up and tired of the war." They also believed demonstrators hurt prospects for peace. Besides its attack on the media, the Nixon administration also tried dirty tricks to limit the impact of the Mobilization. Attorney General Mitchell had approved an FBI plan to wiretap the organizers and again leaked stories about their links to foreign radicals and Communists. Many New Yorkers discovered that at the last minute bus companies had canceled their charters to Washington. That did not prevent a crowd estimated between 700,000 to 800,000 (the White House claimed about half that number) from descending on Washington to demand "Peace Now." The Mobilization was at that time the largest single demonstration in American history.

Attendance may have been swollen by a story that broke in the New York Times on November 12. Seymour Hersh reported that in March 1968, a company of soldiers had slaughtered over 400 Vietnamese civilians, including women and children, in the hamlet of My Lai. An army photographer witnessed the event. His efforts to initiate an official inquiry ran into a stone wall until Hersh broke the story. For those who condemned the immorality of the war in Vietnam, My Lai provided stark evidence. Moral outrage fueled the protest in Washington. Over two days and nights in the "March against Death," some 40,000 people walked single file by the White House. Each carried a candle and a sign bearing the name of a soldier killed in Vietnam.

The media reported quite another story. CBS news, for example, ignored the candlelight march and the massive crowd gathered at the Mall, and focused instead on the actions of a small radical element organized by the Weathermen with help from Abbie Hoffman and Jerry Rubin. The radicals led several thousand protestors to the steps of the Justice Department, where they replaced the "Amerikan" flag with the NLF banner. Then they rampaged through the streets, building barricades and setting fires. In just a few hours they accomplished what the Nixon administration had failed to do in a month—discredit the antiwar movement. Nixon and Agnew could not have been more pleased, especially when Time magazine concluded "that those who want an immediate end to the war, regardless of the consequences, still represent a minority." Nixon's public approval rating reached 68 percent.

In general, the public welcomed the combination of peace talks, gradual troop withdrawals, and Vietnamization. With popular support, Nixon felt less pressure to end the war immediately. That support remained firm into the following spring, as the antiwar movement failed to mount significant opposition. In March 1970, an explosion in a Greenwich Village townhouse killed three members of the Weathermen. Police investigation revealed that they had been running a bomb factory. Three days later, a bomb killed two SNCC members who were in Maryland for the arson trial of H. "Rap" Brown. Whether the two had been killed by their own carelessness or murdered was never determined. All the same, those explosions destroyed whatever romance was left in the image of the radical fringe. Efforts to repeat the moratorium drew such small crowds that by April, the Vietnam Moratorium Committee disbanded. Nixon built upon that momentum by announcing the future withdrawal of an additional 150,000 troops. He also defused the draft issue. Convinced that the fear of being drafted inspired many students to protest, Nixon instituted a lottery system. Students with a high number no longer had the same incentive to protest against the war.

On April 22, possibly as many as thirty million people did demonstrate, not to protest the war, but to celebrate Earth Day,. The pragmatic Nixon had already co-opted some of the environmentalists' fervor by signing the Clean Air and Clean Water Acts along with a bill creating the Environmental Protection Agency. In that way, a demonstration conceived in the spirit of protest ended largely in celebration. With the trees in bloom, the national mood seemed to brighten. Neither the public nor the antiwar movement was prepared for April 30.

That day Nixon told a stunned nation that he had ordered American troops into Cambodia. Exactly why he did so requires a complex conjecture. Nixon told the American people the invasion would protect the lives of Americans in Vietnam. Yet the military situation in Cambodia had changed little over the past months. No new circumstances seemed to justify the invasion. On the other hand, Nixon always delighted in confounding his enemies by doing the unexpected. He likened it to the "big play" in football. The Senate had recently rejected two of his nominations for the Supreme Court. Now he could show his Senate foes "who's really tough." Besides, he told an aide, "We'll catch unshirted hell no matter what we do, so we better get on with it." This bold stroke would let his enemies know that he was still in charge.

Nixon had military and diplomatic goals as well. He believed the Cambodian invasion sent a clear signal—the United States was not backing down. Once in Cambodia, American forces could help protect the new pro-American government of Lon Nol from a possible North Vietnamese takeover. Even more important, the military convinced Nixon the North had a major base area across the Cambodian border. By destroying this center and sanctuaries in Cambodia, the United States could severely limit Hanoi's ability to resupply in the South. A dramatic military success would vindicate an unpopular policy.

The invasion failed to justify Nixon's high-risk strategy. Damage to North Vietnamese supply routes may have bought time for Vietnamization and briefly shorn up Lon Nol's shaky government. But the North Vietnamese nerve center proved to be little more than a few huts. American bombing and troops forced North Vietnamese units into the heart of Cambodia, where they supported a rebel group called the Khmer Rouge. The civil war that swept Cambodia produced a tragedy of epic proportions. Bombing left much of the country in ruins, and the victorious Khmer Rouge began a violent campaign that left as many as two million people dead and another two million refugees.

The reaction across the United States was immediate and negative. Three of Henry Kissinger's top aides resigned in protest, even before Nixon publicly announced the invasion. Soon after, 200 State Department officers resigned as well. Nixon had gambled that college campuses would remain relatively quiet because he had reduced both the draft and U.S. casualty levels. Instead, students and antiwar groups felt betrayed. They had accepted Nixon's pledge that he was winding down the war. Within days, demonstrations swept the nation's campuses. Angry protestors trashed or destroyed hundreds of buildings, including some used for military training programs. An angry Nixon dismissed the protestors as "bums blowing up campuses." The New Mobilization Committee to End the War called for demonstrations in Washington over the weekend of May 9.

Kent State University, southeast of Cleveland, was one of several Ohio campuses torn by rioting. With over 20,000 students, Kent had flourished in the post–World War II era. More than the prestigious Ohio State campus in Columbus, it catered to blue-collar and lower-middle-class Ohio students. While protests had erupted on both campuses, the demonstrations at Kent State were less intense. Still, by Saturday Kent was in turmoil—an ROTC building lay in ruins and local businesses had been damaged. Thousands of demonstrators threatened to overwhelm the small local police force. Unbeknownst to university administrators, the town's mayor had called the governor for help. That Saturday night a contingent of the Ohio National Guard arrived. By social background, the Guardsmen were not so very different from the students they had come to police. They were largely white and from blue-collar families. Many of them had chosen the Guard, rather than college, to avoid a trip to Vietnam. They resented students who had privileges they could not achieve or afford. Having spent several days policing a strike in Akron, they arrived in Kent tired and eager to get home.

The Guard first confronted demonstrators at the smoldering ROTC building. A few Guardsmen used their bayonets to inflict superficial wounds on fleeing students. Witnesses saw their commanding officer, General Sylvester Corso, hurling rocks at students and yelling, "If these goddam kids can throw rocks, I can too." A local official who sensed that the situation was dangerous urged the university to shut down, but Governor James Rhodes pressured the school administration to stand pat. Facing a difficult gubernatorial election on Tuesday, Rhodes saw the Kent protests as an opportunity to showcase his tough law-and-order posture. He told

Few of the students shot at Kent State University by the National Guard were actually protesting. No one yet knows what prompted the shooting. (Source: Associated Press)

reporters that closing down the campus "would be to play into the hands of all the dissent elements" who were trying to shut it down. Those who led the protests were, he charged, "worse than the Brown Shirts and Communist element and also the night riders and vigilantes. They're the worst type we harbor in America."

Rhodes polarized a situation that was already teetering on anarchy. Sunday began with relative calm and ended in angry skirmishes that left both students and Guardsmen hungering for a confrontation. By late Monday morning, after thousands of students had returned from the weekend, a crowd gathered to protest Cambodia. The Guard ordered them to disperse, though it had no authority to do so. When the jeering students refused to move, the Guard put on gas masks and began to fire tear gas canisters. As the soldiers advanced, the protestors retreated. "Whenever the Guard came near us we backed away," one of their leaders recalled, and added, "the Guard had already stabbed people with bayonets, and nobody was foolish enough to stand there." Then, in the midst of the confusion, one troop of sixteen Guardsmen suddenly knelt and aimed their rifles at the protestors. After several tense minutes they rose and gathered for a brief meeting. No one has ever admitted what was said, but they must have decided the time had come to teach the students a lesson. It was as if at that moment they saw themselves standing up against all the hippies, radicals, protestors, and children of privilege who criticized America. They were going to make the uncivil wars into a real fight. After marching back to the top of a hill, they stopped, turned, raised their rifles, and opened fire.

The shooting lasted no more than thirteen seconds. When it stopped, four students lay dead and nine wounded. Of those killed, two had been protestors; two had been walking far from the scene of the shooting. One student who was shot some 730 feet away would be paralyzed for life. Richard Nixon expressed no sympathy for any of the victims. Rather, he told a stunned nation, "when dissent turns to violence it invites tragedy." His callousness only highlighted the profound divisions that had inspired Kent State. A majority of Americans actually supported the president's decision to invade Cambodia, and an even larger percentage agreed that the students, not the Guardsmen, bore responsibility for the shootings. College students and faculty had quite another view. Some 450 colleges closed or went on strike. Well over two million students participated in demonstrations. The following weekend, almost 100,000 descended on Washington to protest against Cambodia. Several hundred armed soldiers forming a protective ring around the White House.

The administration moved to restore some measure of calm. Nixon assured the demonstrators that he understood their frustration and was determined to end the war in Vietnam and bring American troops home. Most of the students viewed his remarks as cynical. To his staff, the president appeared very much at ease in the face of this crisis; privately, he was a man in turmoil. In one of the more bizarre episodes of his presidency, Nixon left the White House Saturday morning around 4:30 A.M. and arrived at the Lincoln Memorial accompanied only by his driver and valet, Manolo Sanchez. There he engaged eight to ten students in conversation: Where were they from? They should get out and travel; see the world. He assured them that their goals were his goals. "I know most of you probably think I'm an S.O.B.," he said at one point, "but I want you to know that I understand just how you feel." After about half an hour, he finally turned to leave and urged them, "Don't go away bitter." At the moment, he most likely meant what he said.

The bitterness was far too deep on both sides to make reconciliation a possibility. In New York City, Mayor John Lindsay, a liberal Republican, memorialized Kent State's victims by flying the City Hall flags at half-staff. Students from Hunter College and NYU marched through Wall Street to protest those deaths and the Cambodian incursion. Several hundred construction workers attacked them with fists, hammers, and lead pipes. "Kill the Commie Bastards," a few yelled. New York City's "finest" had been warned the attacks would take place. Sympathetic to the construction workers, they stood by and watched approvingly. When the "hard hats" held a patriotic parade through the streets three days later, the financial community showered them with ticker tape—an honor conferred on the nation's heroes. *Time* magazine linked the outpouring of patriotic fervor to "a resentment that doubtless runs deep across the nation." Far away at Jackson State University in Mississippi, that resentment took another deadly turn. Without provocation, local and state police suddenly fired into a crowd of student protestors outside a dormitory. The shooting left two students dead and twelve injured.

The animus that police and blue-collar workers showed toward demonstrators sprang more from class antagonisms than from support for the war. Poll data indicated that almost half of all blue-collar workers favored immediate withdrawal from Vietnam. That was a greater percentage than among the middle class. What the hard hats resented most were those who spat on the flag and condemned their country. As one city worker said, "I think we ought to win that war or pull out. What the hell else should we do—sit and bleed ourselves to death, year after year?" But then he added, "I hate those peace demonstrators. Why don't they go to Vietnam and demonstrate in front of the North Vietnamese? . . . The whole thing is a mess. The sooner we get the hell out of there the better."

In none of these events were Guardsmen, construction workers, or police ever charged with a crime. The state of Ohio eventually brought charges, not against the Guard but against demonstrators. A federal grand jury failed to charge the Mississippi police. Nonetheless in October, a commission appointed by the president to investigate campus unrest, while finding much to blame in the protestors' actions, pointed a finger directly at the authorities. It described police behavior in Jackson as an "unreasonable, unjustified, overreaction" and determined the police had fired because they knew they would never be accountable for shooting at black protestors. Unable to extract testimony from any Ohio Guardsmen, the commission never learned what had caused the shooting at Kent. Still, the commissioners determined that, despite provocation from students, the Guard's action was "unnecessary, unwarranted, and inexcusable."

Those conclusions went largely unheeded. By the time the commission issued its report, the sense of imminent crisis had passed. Richard Nixon showed his disdain for its conclusions by simply ignoring it. The irrepressible Spiro Agnew disparaged it as "pablum for permissiveness." Although the war would drag on, the demonstrations following Kent State proved to be the final sustained outpouring of anti-war protest.

16

Watergate: The Last Battle

Through 1970 Americans battled over the Vietnam War, racial integration, the environment, popular culture, and the rights of women, gays, consumers, Latinos, and Native Americans. The Scranton Commission warned, "we are now in grave danger of losing what is common among us through growing intolerance of views on issues and on diversity itself." Despite such fears, both the war in Vietnam and the wars at home were beginning to wind down. No longer would the nation face the level of civic disorder it had from the summer of 1967 to the spring of 1970. Skirmishes would break out, demonstrators would march, but the shootings at Kent and Jackson State introduced a more sober tone. So did the continued Vietnamization of the war and the draft lottery. Protest now seemed more localized, less sustained. The siege at Wounded Knee, for example, did not disturb the nation in the way Kent State did.

As civil strife diminished, Richard Nixon looked forward to reelection. Most Americans continued to support his efforts to extract the United States from the war with its honor intact. Secretly, he planned foreign policy overtures to China and the Soviet Union that would drive Vietnam from the front pages of the news. The excesses of radicals and antiwar protestors left the White House in control of both the conservative and the all-important middle sectors of the American electorate. Nixon could anticipate that his "southern strategy" would win the Republicans even greater inroads in the once solidly Democratic southern states. By polarizing the country over the war, race, and radicalism, he seemed to have assured his own political success. Yet the "Tricky" side of Dick Nixon was far from dead. He still hungered to destroy those he believed conspired to destroy him. In trying to avenge himself against antiwar protestors, radicals, Jews, and the liberal media, he destroyed himself and in that unintended way brought the uncivil wars to an end.

Final Skirmishes

Two protests in the period after Kent State exposed most painfully the wounds that the Vietnam War had inflicted—the Vietnam Veterans against the War (VVAW) and the publication of the Pentagon Papers. They would also provoke the White House to lawless behavior that led to Richard Nixon's downfall. VVAW came into being in 1967 when a group of veterans banded together to retrieve some meaning out of what now seemed lost years of their lives. Their wounded psyches and maimed bodies offered silent proof of their sacrifice. As activist Tom Hayden observed, "They carried with them a credibility that could perhaps be ignored—as indeed it was—but never refuted." Wheelchair-bound Ron Kovic discovered VVAW in the wake of

Kent State. After returning from Vietnam, Kovic had gone back to school. He still felt bitterness toward hippies and protestors, who in his eyes disparaged the sacrifices he and his comrades had made. News of the campus shootings transformed him. For the first time, his Vietnam experience and the antiwar movement came together. That weekend he joined the protest in Washington. "In the war," he remembered thinking, "we were killing and maiming people. In Washington on that Saturday afternoon in May we were trying to heal them and set them free."

The trial of Lieutenant William Calley in early 1971 provoked VVAW to take the lead in protesting the war. Calley's platoon had committed the atrocities at My Lai in March 1968. Many vets felt that Calley had become the "fall guy" for all that was wrong with the war. Responsibility, they believed, went up the chain of command to the president. "My Lai was not an isolated incident," one VVAW officer said, but "only a minor step beyond the standard official United States policy in Vietnam." To drive home that point, VVAW organized what they called "The Winter Soldier Investigation." They borrowed the phrase from the Revolutionary War propagandist Tom Paine, who chided the "summer soldier and sunshine patriot." At a meeting in Detroit, a string of witnesses confessed to all manner of atrocities they had either seen or committed. As one soldier explained, "once the military has got the idea implanted in you that these people are not humans . . . it makes it a little easier to kill 'em."

By 1971, plunging morale among the troops in Vietnam created a military crisis. Reports of "fraggings" became commonplace. The term referred to fragmentation grenades used to silence overzealous officers and NCOs. A yellow smoke grenade warned the target to ease off. Red smoke meant the next one would be for real. One especially arrogant and incompetent officer chose to ignore both. "The last one was a hand grenade, and he was eliminated and replaced," one witness recalled. "Grenades leave no fingerprints. Nobody's going to go to jail." Drug use and abuse, including opium and heroin, reached epidemic proportions. Soldiers reported whole battalions wandering around hopelessly stoned. As many as 20 percent of the soldiers sent to Vietnam became addicted. African-American soldiers increasingly segregated themselves as the racial conflicts that had divided the nation infected the military as well. The antiwar movement encouraged dissent and occasional insubordination. Underground newspapers, protest organizations, coffeehouses, and demonstrations became common on and around military bases. Desertion rates soared. Some officers feared the military now lacked the means to fight effectively in Vietnam. As historian Marilyn Young commented, by 1971, "Vietnamization was a matter not of choice but of necessity."

VVAW found an especially poignant way to express the futility and immorality of the war. In February 1969, a marine division had undertaken a secret incursion into neutral Laos code named "Dewey Canyon I." In February 1971, the ARVN (Army of the Republic of Vietnam) had been bloodied in Dewey Canyon II, a second incursion into Laos. In April 1971, VVAW organized Dewey Canyon III. For five emotional days Vietnam vets demonstrated in Washington against the war they had fought. Many wore the fatigues they had brought home from the war. Some lobbied Congress. Former swift boat skipper John Kerry explained to a congressional panel that their current mission was an effort "to search out and destroy the last vestige of this barbaric war, to pacify our hearts, to conquer the hate and fear that have driven this country these last ten years and more, so when thirty years from now our brothers go down the street without a leg, without an arm, or a face, and small boys ask, 'why,' we will be able to say 'Vietnam' and not mean a desert, not filthy obscene memory, but mean instead the place where America finally turned and where soldiers like us helped in the turning." More memorably still, the vets gathered before a barrier erected to keep them away from the capitol and threw away medals, insignias, and campaign ribbons, all of which had become to them symbols of shame, not heroism and service to their country.

The vets left Washington on April 23. The following day, 500,000 protestors descended on the city for one more effort to end the war. They insisted that the war had not only devastated Vietnam, but added to the insufferable burdens of the poor at home. Some 30,000 stayed on, determined to bring the city to a halt. On May 30, they blocked the flow of government workers commuting to their jobs. The Nixon administration called out the police and the military to stop them. Over three days, police arrested some 10,000 people, often without a semblance of due process. Once again arbitrary arrests served to control dissent. Attorney General John Mitchell boasted that the government had kept the traffic flowing. To that Senator Ted Kennedy remarked, "the city may have been safe for cars at the time, but it was very unsafe place for citizens." In the end the courts threw out the charges against all but 200 of those arrested.

Among those who came to protest was a former aide to Henry Kissinger, Daniel Ellsberg. Ellsberg had compiled a brilliant record as a student at Harvard, worked on his doctorate with Kissinger, and served a tour in Vietnam as a captain in the Marine Corps. In 1964, the government had selected him to be a spokesman at a university teach-in. After his government service, Ellsberg joined the RAND Corporation, a private consulting firm with close ties to the Defense Department. The prior September he had been startled to learn that the army had dropped its case against six green berets accused of assassinating a Vietnamese intelligence officer. When the CIA refused to let its agents testify, the army had no case. Ellsberg was convinced (correctly) that the White House was behind what he saw as a miscarriage of justice. His doubts about the war and his anger at what he saw as a pattern of official deception pushed him into action. He knew the RAND Corporation possessed a top-secret report on the origins of the Vietnam War, commissioned in 1967 by an increasingly disillusioned defense secretary Robert McNamara. That night, Ellsberg and his friend Anthony Russo began photocopying some 7,000 pages.

On June 13, 1971, a *New York Times* headline declared, "VIETNAM ARCHIVE: A CONSENSUS TO BOMB DEVELOPED BEFORE '64 ELECTION, STUDY SAYS." Nixon was not at first much concerned about what became known as the Pentagon Papers. "This is really rough on Kennedy, McNamara, and Johnson," he told Bob Haldeman.

"The key for us is to keep out of it." The report made clear, for example, that Kennedy and Johnson had both escalated the war while convinced it could not be won. Both had misled the American people about the level of American involvement. Johnson had, as a *Times* reporter noted, deliberately deceived "the public on the most important issue facing the country at the moment it was choosing its President." Nixon was more concerned about the leaking of the report than the content. He assumed that someone on Henry Kissinger's staff was responsible or else some "fucking Jews."

Henry Kissinger massaged the president's paranoia. Kissinger was in the midst of secret negotiations to arrange Nixon's surprise visit to China. The leak, he warned the president, "shows you're a weakling." Unless the leaks were controlled, other countries "will not agree to secret negotiations." Kissinger may well have feared the culprit would be traced to his staff, which in effect he was. After someone mentioned Ellsberg, Kissinger disparaged him as "a little unbalanced," a sexual pervert, a murderer of peasants in Vietnam, and a drug user. To that, Nixon replied, "maybe it's him or maybe it's Gelb [Leslie Gelb, a Kissinger staffer], one of the two, either's a radical. Somebody's got to go to jail for that." The president also conceived schemes to use the Papers to further embarrass Democrats. Could Kennedy be linked to the assassination of Diem? Had Johnson ordered the 1968 bombing halt solely to derail Nixon's reelection? When Haldeman mentioned that there might be an incriminating file in the Brookings Institution, Nixon told his staff to "get in there and get those files. Blow the safe and get it." The president had ordered his staff to commit burglary.

The struggle over the Pentagon Papers was waged largely in the courts. On Tuesday, June 15, Attorney General John Mitchell asked the *Times* to cease publication on the grounds of national security. Privately, Nixon told his staff to end all contact with the *Times* and in particular its Washington bureau chief, "that damn Jew Frankel." A federal judge in New York then granted the government, a restraining order to prevent further publication until it could investigate possible espionage charges. Unfortunately for the government, the *Washington Post* also began to publish installments. When the courts enjoined the *Post* from publishing, other papers picked up the story. Ellsberg had been busily spreading the Papers around the country, while the FBI tried futilely to hunt him down. He even appeared on national television before turning himself in to federal authorities. On June 30, the U.S. Supreme Court resolved the legal wrangling. By a 6-3 vote, the Court ruled that the government had failed to demonstrate that a sufficient threat to national security justified a restraint against publication of the Pentagon Papers.

Even though the government lost the Pentagon Papers case, Nixon won the battle for public opinion. A majority of Americans thought the *Times* had been unpatriotic in deciding to publish them. The revelations about the government's duplicity damaged Kennedy and Johnson, not Nixon. Nor did the evidence in the Papers that the war had been a mistake do anything to revive antiwar demonstrations. As historian Melvin Small concluded, by the summer of 1971, "the life had gone out of the movement." Organizers could no longer persuade themselves or their followers that protesting would substantially alter the course of the war. The draft lottery had certainly made the war a distant reality for many college males. Vietnamization further defused opposition. By 1972, troop levels had dropped to 157,000, and battlefield deaths that peaked at a six-month high of almost 9,600 in June of 1968 had fallen to 276 by December 1971. The peace talks, not combat, dominated the news about Vietnam. Activist Tom Hayden speculated that by then his comrades had "burned out."

The Final Battle

Despite the economic and political turmoil in his first term, by 1972 Richard Nixon seemed firmly in command. He confounded those who dismissed him as an unregenerate cold warrior by becoming the first president to visit either Beijing or Moscow. His triumphant visit to China in February 1972 followed three months later by a trip to the Soviet Union opened new possibilities for easing cold war tensions. The media hailed him as a great statesman. At home, the Democrats had yet to recover from their 1968 debacle in Chicago. Their best prospect to face Nixon was Senator Ed Muskie from Maine. Muskie had handled himself with considerable dignity as Humphrey's running mate and had a strong record on environmental issues. But in February, his campaign self-destructed. Responding to a vicious attack on his wife from New Hampshire's leading right-wing newspaper, Muskie began to weep. In the politics of the day, real presidential candidates didn't cry. Support among Democrats shifted to North Dakota senator George McGovern, a staunch liberal whose outspoken opposition to the war made him a weaker candidate.

With the war in Vietnam winding down, the economy strengthening, and the Democrats in disarray, Nixon had every reason to expect another term in the White House. Yet Nixon's insecurities and bitterness toward his enemies would prove his undoing. In 1970, shortly after Kent State, he ordered Tom Huston, a junior White House aide, to develop a plan to coordinate domestic intelligence operations. Nixon believed the FBI and CIA had been so consumed with political infighting they had failed to link domestic dissent to foreign influence. Nor had the FBI been effective in discrediting such radical groups as SDS, the Black Panthers, and the Vietnam Veterans against the War. As a former member of Young Americans for Freedom, Huston shared the president's hostility to dissent. He told a meeting of high-level intelligence officials, including J. Edgar Hoover and CIA director Richard Helms, "we are now confronted with a new and grave crisis in our country—one which we know too little about. Certainly hundreds, perhaps thousands, of Americans—mostly under 30—are determined to destroy our society."

To meet this threat, Huston proposed a plan breathtaking in both its scope and its illegality. The primary purpose was to centralize control over domestic intelligence in the White House. Its most daring recommendations called for increased electronic eavesdropping, mail interception, informants on college campuses, and fewer restrictions on "black bag jobs," also known as breaking and entering (B&E). Huston acknowledged that B&E was "clearly illegal" and posed great risk of exposure, but it promised to produce information unobtainable in any other way. On July 14, Richard Nixon approved the Huston Plan. So had the intelligence directors for the CIA, the military branches, and several top-secret agencies.

There was one holdout. On July 26, J. Edgar Hoover invited Huston to his office. At age seventy-six, Hoover had served his government for over a half-century. Now, though in failing health and increasingly irrational, he still recognized in Huston's Plan a scheme to circumvent the FBI. That he would not tolerate. Hoover warned Huston that the old methods had become "too dangerous." Should any of the intelligence operatives be caught, surely the press and civil liberties organizations would subject the government to extreme embarrassment. Worse yet, they might expose the recent history of illegal surveillance. After the *New York Times* had revealed the secret Cambodian bombings in May of 1969, for example, Nixon and Kissinger ordered taps placed on the home phones of thirteen NSC staff members and four reporters. Hoover thus informed his nominal boss, Attorney General John Mitchell, that the FBI would cooperate only if the president signed the orders. Since Nixon wanted to avoid any direct involvement, that condition spelled the death of the Huston Plan. The president understood that a disgruntled Hoover sooner or later would reveal White House operations to the press. So the president left Hoover in charge of domestic intelligence, both legal and illegal.

The demise of the Huston Plan did nothing to quiet the paranoia that inspired it. Publication of the Pentagon Papers put the president back on the warpath. Once again, he was persuaded the FBI was not doing what was needed to find the sources of the leaks and silence them. "If we can't get anyone in this government to do something about the problem that may be the most serious one we have, then, by God, we'll do it ourselves," he told John Ehrlichman. Ehrlichman knew that to fix a leak, you call a plumber. Thus, in June 1971 was born the White House unit known as The Plumbers, a clandestine group staffed by zealous junior staffers and right-wing veterans of the CIA and FBI. Their first target was Daniel Ellsberg, though their larger purpose was to find evidence of a "counter government." Nixon suspected that Ellsberg was part of a group dedicated to undermining American foreign policy. Determined "to paint Ellsberg black," the Plumbers in August 1971 broke into his psychiatrist's office. When they found no useful evidence, they trashed the office to cover up their crime.

With the existence of the Plumbers, the White House acquired the ability to undertake covert operations against its enemies. The Plumbers and their contacts also provided Nixon's reelection committee (the Committee to Reelect the President, or CREEP) a means to damage potential Democratic opponents and party officials. Given this new resource, Nixon found the temptation to attack his enemies too great to resist. He especially wanted to discredit Democratic National Committee chairman Lawrence O'Brien. O'Brien had faithfully served both John Kennedy and Lyndon Johnson. Like Nixon, O'Brien had financial links to the reclusive billionaire Howard Hughes. Where the Democrats had sought to use the Hughes link to embarrass Nixon, O'Brien's ties were largely unknown. At one point Nixon told Haldeman, "the time is approaching when Larry O'Brien is held accountable for his retainer with Hughes."

Even after disbanding the Plumbers, the White House continued to employ its key operatives. Among them was G. Gordon Liddy, the former FBI agent who led the team that broke into Ellsberg's psychiatrist's office. Along with several other Plumber alumni, he had taken his fertile imagination to work for CREEP, where he conceived Operation Gemstone. The plan was as flamboyant and bizarre as Liddy himself. As an assistant D.A. in Dutchess County, New York (home of Franklin Roosevelt), Liddy had first come to national attention when he orchestrated a raid on Timothy Leary's commune in Millbrook. Once, to dramatize his toughness and loyalty, he burned his hand in the flame of a candle.

Gemstone had all the earmarks of a bad James Bond movie. To prevent demonstrations at the GOP's August convention, Liddy planned to use former CIA "street fighting squads" that would conduct "surgical relocation activities." That was spook-speak for kidnapping. "If, for example, a prominent radical comes to our convention," Liddy explained, "these teams can drug him and take him across the border." Another Gemstone operation would embarrass key Democrats. It involved a luxury yacht, "wired for sight and sound" and staffed by "the finest call girls in the country." Lest anyone doubt their ability to seduce Democratic delegates, Liddy assured his audience, "they are not dumb broads, but girls who can be trained and programmed." Other elements of the plan included surveillance, wiretapping, and break-ins. Attorney General John Mitchell thought that both the plan and Liddy were more than a little off-the-wall, not to mention that the million dollar budget was rather pricy. "It's not quite what I had in mind," he told Liddy.

But Nixon was determined to expose O'Brien's relationship to Hughes. He told Haldeman, "We're going to nail O'Brien on this one, one way or the other." One aide complained to CREEP headquarters, "Why don't you guys get off the stick and get Liddy's budget approved?" John Mitchell, the newly named head of CREEP, then accepted a modified version of Gemstone. It included plans to bug the Democratic National Headquarters in Washington and a break-in at a newspaper office in Las Vegas to determine what evidence its editor, Hank Greenspun, had on Hughes and O'Brien. And in August 1972, burglars did break into Greenspun's office but failed to open the safe.

In May, Liddy's operatives bugged O'Brien's office at the Watergate office complex only to have the listening device fail. On Saturday morning, July 17, 1972, they were back, but this time Washington police arrested the five men who had broken in. These men were no ordinary burglars. They wore business suits and carried sophisticated electronics equipment, including bugging devices. Among them they had $2,300 in cash—largely in the form of $100 bills with sequential serial numbers. Bob Woodward, a new reporter on the crime beat for the *Washington Post*, attended their arraignment. When the judge asked their spokesman, James McCord, his occupation, McCord replied, "security consultant." Who had he worked for most recently, the judge wanted to know. The "CIA," McCord confessed. Later the next day, Woodward learned something even more puzzling. Among the suspects' belongings, the police discovered two address books. Each listed a Howard Hunt, followed in one by "W.H." and in the other by "W. House." So Woodward called Hunt to ask him what he had to do with these burglars. "Good God," he replied and hung up.

The White House was almost equally terse. Nixon press secretary Ron Ziegler dismissed the break-in as "a third-rate burglary attempt" and complained "certain elements may try to stretch this beyond what it is." Behind the scenes, however, a cover-up operation began immediately. Nixon's aides understood that McCord could be linked to Liddy and Hunt, and thus to the White House. John Dean, legal counsel to the president, had Hunt's White House safe cleaned out. Hunt and Liddy started shredding documents. And the president and several aides talked about raising money to guarantee that the burglars would remain silent. The media meanwhile treated the whole matter as little more than an election caper gone awry. In this instance, according to journalist Anthony Lukas, the campaign to intimidate the media worked to protect Nixon. Until after the election, almost no newspapers except the *Washington Post* investigated the break-in or the White House links to the burglars. Even when the McGovern campaign sued CREEP and raised such questions as "Who ordered this act of political espionage?" and "Who paid for it?" the press showed little interest. Why should the media want to embarrass Nixon when over 753 out of 809 daily papers endorsed him?

With Watergate seemingly under control, the president focused on winning the largest electoral victory in history, larger even than Lyndon Johnson's defeat of Barry Goldwater in 1964. The threat that George Wallace might derail his southern strategy ended in May when would-be assassin Arthur Bremer shot the segregation candidate four times at close range and left him paralyzed. Bremer had no political motive; he simply wanted to be famous. The Democrats for their part seemed determined to complete the political self-immolation they had begun in Chicago. Their convention represented the triumph of identity and value politics over the politics of coalition building. George McGovern, the likely candidate in November, supported stringent environmental rules, busing for school desegregation, higher taxes on the wealthy, cuts in defense spending, amnesty for those who fled to Canada to avoid the draft, and an immediate end to the Vietnam War. So in tune was McGovern with the Left that one editorial suggested that he would be "essentially a fourth-party candidate." Hubert Humphrey, his primary opponent and the candidate favored by party regulars, ridiculed those positions. He predicted that moderate Democrats would vote Republican in record numbers. Richard Nixon was possibly McGovern's most enthusiastic supporter.

When the Democratic convention met in Miami in July, McGovern won. His backers had reformed the party rules so that the delegates would include more women, minorities, and young people. Over half of the delegates who came to

Miami had never been to a convention before. Thirty-eight percent were women. Civil rights activist Jesse Jackson headed an Illinois delegation that successfully unseated the one chosen by party kingmaker Richard Daley, boss of Chicago. Labor leaders also lost much of their power. Vocal elements booed Hubert Humphrey and any mention of Lyndon Johnson. Some thirty-nine candidates received vice presidential nominations, including such irreverent choices as Mao Tse-tung and John Mitchell's blunt-spoken wife, Martha.

Never before had women or minorities played such a prominent role at a major party convention. The National Women's Political Caucus forced debate on the issue of abortion and a woman's right to control her own body. Jean Westwood replaced Nixon nemesis Larry O'Brien as chair of the Democratic National Committee. Frances "Sissy" Farenthold, a liberal Texas congresswoman, became a serious prospect for vice president. And finally, the party platform supported the appointment of a woman to the Supreme Court and endorsed the Equal Rights Amendment. Beyond that, the platform called for immediate withdrawal from Vietnam, abolition of the draft, amnesty for draft resisters, and a guaranteed income for the poor. As Nixon biographer Stephen Ambrose wrote, "The Democrats gave an appearance of being anti-religion and pro-drugs, anti-profit and pro-welfare, anti-family and pro-abortion, anti-farmer and pro-migrant worker, anti-Saigon and pro-Hanoi, anti–armed forces and pro–draft dodgers." Prominent Democrats lined up to pledge their support to Nixon.

Behind the scenes, Nixon operatives had been working to assure that no protests would mar his convention when the Republicans came to Miami in August. Vietnam Veterans against the War had been a special target. Plumber Howard Hunt had infiltrated informers into the group. One of the informers told police in Tallahassee, Florida, that a VVAW group planned to disrupt the convention with firebombs and shootings. The police arrested six. In July, a grand jury indicted them and two others on conspiracy charges. A Florida jury later found them all innocent, but while they were tied up in court, Richard Nixon was reelected.

The Republican convention convened what were, in symbolic ways, the last encampments of the uncivil war. In one camp gathered the mostly white, well-to-do, and conservative male delegates who represented the Republican Party. On hand to support them were the Young Voters for the President. These young politicos, also largely white and male, camped in motel rooms, wore their hair short, dressed in neat khakis and button-down shirts, and called their elders "m'am" or "sir." At Flamingo Park, several miles away, Miami police had set aside a campground for the 3,000 people who had come to protest. Flamingo Park distilled the remnants of uncivil war dissent into a single space. Curious tourists who entered the campground walked down Ho Chi Minh trail. Along the way they passed tents housing the Free Gays, feminists, Neo-Americans, the Society for the Advancement of Non-verbal Communication, yippies, and Vietnam Veterans against the War, their numbers thinned by the arrests in Tallahassee. The end of the Trail led into People's Pot Park.

Miami city leaders had no intention of having the debacle of Chicago mar the playground image of their city. They would contain protest by tolerating it. Only a few VVAW protestors actually made their way into the convention hall. Bothered only by a few brief interruptions and some skirmishes on the street, the Republicans celebrated Nixon and "four more years." Not only were they going to win the election, they had every reason to believe they were winning the uncivil wars. They and their clean-cut youth brigade, not the scruffy protestors in Flamingo Park, represented the future.

Watergate

Nixon's smashing victory in November confirmed Republican hopes, but it did little to quiet the demons that haunted Richard Nixon. Having won in forty-nine out of fifty states (only Massachusetts and the District of Columbia went to McGovern), Nixon was determined to use his power ruthlessly. He was convinced that those who supported McGovern remained a menace to America. By opposing busing and dismantling Great Society programs, he could continue to build the Republican base in the South and woo disgruntled Democrats. The "bunch of bastards" in the federal bureaucracy offered another inviting target. Nixon believed federal agencies housed liberals and Democrats scheming to sabotage his programs. By reorganizing the bureaucracy, Nixon aimed to bring it directly under his control.

The day after the election, he perfunctorily thanked his staff for their work in the campaign and left. Bob Haldeman then informed them that they were all to tender their resignations immediately. He sent a similar message to the Cabinet. The independent members like Defense Secretary Melvin Laird and Secretary of Commerce Peter Peterson were gone. In their place, Nixon wanted men of unquestioned loyalty. Henry Kissinger, though assured he would become secretary of state, was stunned by "the frenzied, almost maniacal sense of urgency about this political butchery."

Washington Post reporters Bob Woodward and Carl Bernstein had frustrations of their own. Ever since the Watergate break-in, they had been trying to piece the story together. What they discovered linked the burglary to officials at CREEP. One burglar had opened a checking account with $89,000 that Woodward and Bernstein traced back to funds raised by the reelection committee. Finance chief Maurice Stans had laundered the money through Mexican bank accounts so it could not be linked to the donors. CREEP had created a $350,000 slush fund to finance clandestine operations. Senior White House officials had authorized the use of those funds. And the break-in appeared to be just one among numerous efforts to discredit leading Democrats. Woodward and Bernstein had identified Donald Segretti as the mastermind of the "dirty tricks" campaign. His minions had been "following members of Democratic candidates' families; assembling dossiers of their personal lives; forging letters and distributing them under the candidates' letterheads; leaking false and manufactured items to the press [such as the letter that provoked Senator Muskie's tears]; throwing campaign schedules into disarray; seizing confidential campaign files and investigating the lives of dozens of Democratic campaign workers." Segretti was not merely a prankster. He had been hired directly by Dwight Chapin, the personal appointments secretary for the president.

All the stories Woodward and Bernstein broke had little impact on the election. In August, Nixon had dismissed any implication that the White House "was involved in this very bizarre situation." Following his orders, White House legal counsel, John Dean, had done a thorough investigation. "What really hurts in matters of this sort is not that they occur," Nixon added. "What really hurts is if you try to cover it up." As the election approached, the White House accused the *Post* of conducting a vendetta. Press Secretary Ron Ziegler charged, "This is a political effort by the *Washington Post*, well-conceived and well-coordinated, to discredit this administration and individuals in it." By election time, Woodward and Bernstein had run out of leads; their story had gone dry. Ben Bradlee, their editor, recalled that he had been "ready to hold both Woodward's and Bernstein's heads in a pail of water until they came up with another story."

The courts, not the press, cracked the case. By January 1973, prosecutors had enough evidence to charge Gordon Liddy, Howard Hunt, and the five burglars. The trial lasted one month and the jury took just an hour and a half to convict all seven defendants. Presiding judge John Sirica (called "Maximum John" for his stiff sentences) was unhappy with the prosecution's handling of the case. None of the defendants explained what they were doing at the Watergate or where they got their money. "These hundred dollar bills were floating around like coupons," Sirica complained. He was thus convinced that the prosecution had failed to uncover all the pertinent facts. To break the defendant's code of silence, he threatened them with harsh sentences. That was too much for James McCord. In March, he admitted to Sirica that the defendants had been under political pressure to remain silent, that some witnesses had perjured themselves, and that others had been involved with the conspiracy.

What until then had been a trickle of evidence and accusations now became a flood. Nixon's White House staff and CREEP officials scrambled to hire lawyers. Patrick Gray, acting head of the FBI [Hoover had died in May 1972], admitted to a Senate hearing in February that he had given the White House access to FBI files on Watergate. With new revelations that Dean and Ehrlichman had persuaded him to burn evidence from Howard Hunt's safe, Gray resigned his post. On April 17, Nixon announced that "major new developments" had brought about further inquiry into the Watergate case. Ron Ziegler told reporters that the president's earlier statements denying the involvement of White House staff in Watergate or the cover-up were now "inoperative." On April 30, Watergate claimed its first major White House victims. Denying any personal role, Nixon told a national television audience that he had reluctantly accepted the resignations of his two most trusted aides, John Ehrlichman and Bob Haldeman. Reporters learned the president had also forced out Attorney General Kleindienst and fired his legal counsel, John Dean. Dean, it seems, had promised to cooperate with prosecutors.

Other problems arose from the Pentagon Papers trial. A Justice Department memo acknowledged that Hunt and Liddy had burglarized the office of Ellsberg's psychiatrist. John Ehrlichman had even tried to influence Judge William Byrne by suggesting he might become the new FBI director. Worse yet, the government had tapped Ellsberg's phone but had lost the records. Byrne was so outraged by the government's misconduct that he dismissed all charges. "Bizarre events have incurably infected the prosecution of this case," he concluded. Six days later, the Senate select committee to investigate Watergate headed by Sam Ervin of North Carolina opened its televised hearings. On the second day, James McCord testified that a White House aide had offered him executive clemency to remain silent. Nixon then admitted that he had limited the Watergate investigation for reasons of "national security," but denied prior knowledge of the burglary or efforts of his aides to cover it up. On May 25, he appointed Solicitor General Archibald Cox, a Democrat, to be the special Watergate prosecutor.

As spring turned to summer, television audiences flocked to watch the latest from the Ervin committee. With his folksy manner and deep respect for the Constitution, the North Carolina senator cast an air of propriety over the proceedings. A parade of witnesses testified that Attorney General John Mitchell had attended meetings where Gordon Liddy discussed Gemstone, that McCord, Liddy, and Hunt had worked directly for Ehrlichman, that they had operated the clandestine "Plumbers," and that the Plumbers had broken into Ellsberg's psychiatrist's office to find damaging information. And then came John Dean. Boyish and unassuming in manner, Dean spoke in a quiet, often monotonous voice.

The boyish-looking John Dean seemed an unlikely figure to bring down a president. His testimony, confirmed by the White House tapes, linked Richard Nixon to the cover-up of the Watergate burglary.   (Source: Associated Press)

Howard Baker, the senior Republican on the committee, got to the heart of the matter. "What did the president know and when did he know it," Baker asked Dean. Over four days in a statement 245 pages long, Dean painted a damning picture of White House complicity. Ehrlichman and Haldeman had been the architects, but the president, Dean claimed, had been involved in the cover-up from the beginning. He had met with the president at one point to discuss "hush money" to buy the burglars' silence. The figure of one million dollars had been mentioned. The president also had maintained what was popularly known as an "enemies list" that included well-known celebrities like Bill Cosby, Paul Newman, and antiwar activist Jane Fonda. These figures were subject to harassment, including special IRS tax audits. Dean speculated that Watergate was the product of the president's "excessive concern" with political opponents and antiwar protestors and a "do-it-yourself White House staff" that had scant regard for the law.

The committee seemed skeptical about Dean's accusations. Republican members did what they could to shake his credibility. After all, it was Dean's word against the president's—that is, until July 13. On that day, committee counsel Donald Sanders interviewed Alexander Butterfield, an aide to Bob Haldeman. Sanders had served ten years in the FBI before becoming a congressional staffer. He saw the hearings as a way to exonerate the president. The precise recollections of several key presidential aides convinced him that their testimony "had to have been made from verbatim recordings." Since the president "would never have said anything incriminating on the record," Sanders assumed that if tapes existed, they "would prove the president's innocence." One point was troubling him all the same. If the recordings would clear Nixon, "why hadn't the president revealed the system and used it to his advantage?"

Hence, Sanders questioned Butterfield with considerable caution. Why might the president have taken Dean into a corner and spoken to him in a whisper, as Dean had testified? "I was hoping you fellows wouldn't ask me that," Butterfield replied. Reminded he was under oath, Butterfield then admitted, "Well, yes, there's a recording system in the White House." When he testified publicly to that effect, the revelation stunned virtually everyone in America, from the committee members to the millions watching on television to the president himself. After all, Nixon had assumed that the secret of the tapes was safe. Now, it was no longer Dean's word against the president's. The tapes could reveal all.

Well, not everything. As revelation tumbled over revelation and followers of the Ervin hearings believed they had heard it all, Vice President Spiro Agnew admitted he was under criminal investigation. As executive of Baltimore County, as governor of Maryland, and even as vice president, Agnew had been receiving bribes and kickbacks. Rather than subject the nation to a potential constitutional nightmare, the Justice Department allowed him to plead no contest to a single charge of tax evasion. For that he was fined, placed on three years probation, and on October 10 resigned his office. The alliterative apostle of law and order turned out to be a common crook.

Watergate prosecutor Cox meanwhile realized that discovering the tapes was one thing, hearing them was quite another. When he subpoenaed the relevant tapes, the

White House refused to supply them, citing "executive privilege." After the courts ruled for Cox, Nixon fired him on Saturday, October 20, 1973. Reaction to the news was furious. Rather than carry out Nixon's order, Attorney General Elliot Richardson resigned, as did his assistant. Nixon then appointed Solicitor General Robert Bork as acting attorney general, and Bork fired Cox. Reporters called these events "the Saturday Night Massacre." Congress produced twenty-two separate bills calling for the possible impeachment of the president.

Finding himself cornered, Nixon appointed a new special prosecutor, Leon Jaworski from Texas, and turned the subpoenaed tapes over to Judge Sirica. Actually, he turned over most of the tapes. The White House counsel informed Sirica that some of the tapes were missing and others had mysterious gaps. One critical tape contained an eighteen-and-a-half-minute erasure. Asked if the erasure could have been caused by human error, an expert explained, "it would have to be an accident that was repeated at least five times." By April 1974, Jaworski and the House Judiciary Committee asked the White House to produce additional tapes. Once again, the president refused, but then agreed to supply edited transcripts instead. White House secretaries typed up over 1,200 pages. Even the expurgated versions proved damaging to the president. As a public figure, Nixon presented himself as the soul of propriety. The transcripts, laced with "expletive deleted" to remove profanity, revealed a man who in private was vain, vindictive, vulgar, and petty. The tape for March 21, 1973, largely confirmed John Dean's testimony. Nixon discussed in detail how they might, as he phrased it, "take care of the jackasses who are in jail." When Dean said it might cost a million, the president replied, "You could get a million dollars. And you could get it in cash. I know where it could be gotten. I mean it's not easy, but it could be done."

As damning as that statement was, it was not the smoking gun the Republicans demanded. Speculating about hush money was not the same as providing it. Jaworski thus appealed to the Supreme Court to get the originals. In July, a unanimous court ordered Nixon to turn over the subpoenaed tapes. The House Judiciary Committee also produced three articles of impeachment that accused the president of obstructing justice, misusing the powers of his office, and refusing to comply with the committee's request for evidence. With that, the president's own lawyers insisted that he turn over the June 23, 1972, tapes. These contained his conversation with Chief of Staff Bob Haldeman six days after the Watergate break-in.

The June 23rd tapes produced the smoking gun. No one could doubt that the president had been in on the cover-up from the beginning. Haldeman warned that the "FBI is not under control." Its agents had "been able to trace the money" found on the burglars. The two decided they could stymie the investigation by playing the CIA off against the FBI. "The FBI agents who are working the case, at this point feel that's what it is. This is CIA," Haldeman suggested. Nixon ran with that idea. Since four of the burglars were Cuban, he thought the FBI would see the matter as a "Cuban thing," carried out as part of a covert CIA operation. Why not tell the FBI, he suggested, "'Don't go any further into this case,' period." These tapes answered

Senator Baker's question: The president knew pretty much everything, and he had known it right from the beginning. Not even the most diehard of Nixon's supporters could protect him any longer. Impeachment had become inevitable. On August 9, 1974, Richard Nixon resigned as the thirty-seventh president of the United States. His successor, Gerald R. Ford, told the nation, "our long national nightmare is over."

The Uncivil Wars Are Over

Historians have as much difficulty understanding why and how wars end as they do in explaining why and how they begin. When can we truly say a war is over? Take Vietnam, for example. American forces had almost completely withdrawn from Vietnam by 1973, but Saigon did not fall to northern forces until 1975. In 1976, Congress forbade any foreign assistance to Indochina, forcing Hanoi to turn increasingly to the Soviet Union. The American insistence on learning the fate of its MIAs (missing in action in Vietnam) became a new source of tensions. The United States supported China in 1979, when it briefly invaded North Vietnam. Was the war with Vietnam over? Or think about the civil rights conflict. The Civil Rights and Voting Rights Acts (1964 and 1965) eliminated the worst forms of racial discrimination. Yet in 1974, disputes over school busing, job discrimination, and affirmative action programs kept the struggle over racial equality very much alive.

The end of the uncivil wars is even more difficult to identify. Americans fought with each other in every part of the nation and on many fronts, ranging from civil rights to popular culture to the war in Vietnam to value and identity politics. Not only did Americans divide over race, class, and gender, such apolitical matters as the acceptable length of a boy's hair or of a girl's skirt had become equally divisive. Certainly no single event, no matter how consequential, could fully explain either the origins or end of such a complex phenomenon. Altamont, Kent State, Wounded Knee, and *Roe v. Wade* all marked endings of a sort, but only after Watergate did the uncivil wars seem to be over.

The impact of Watergate was both tangible and symbolic. Richard Nixon was after all the man the Left most loved to hate. As president, he had made no secret of his disdain for hippies, radicals, and dissidents. His resignation thus removed from public life perhaps the most polarizing personality of the uncivil wars era. In some ways he was the last of the great dividers. Many of the controversial sixties figures over whom Americans had deeply conflicted feelings were gone before him. Assassins had murdered John and Bobby Kennedy, Martin Luther King, Medgar Evers, and Malcolm X. A number of Black Nationalist leaders had gone into exile like Stokely Charmichael or into jail like H. "Rap" Brown. George Wallace was a paraplegic. Government harassment silenced many leaders of the New Left, drug gurus like Timothy Leary, and activists in the antiwar movement. Excess claimed the lives of rock icons such as Jimi Hendrix, Janis Joplin, and Jim Morrison of the Doors. By choosing not to seek reelection, Lyndon Johnson ceased to be a target for his enemies, though conservatives would spend the next three decades trying to dismantle his Great Society programs. Johnson died on January 22, 1973, just one day before Henry Kissinger and Le DucTho signed the Paris Agreements, ending what many historians still think of as "Johnson's war."

And J. Edgar Hoover was dead as well. Had he not died in May 1972, he might well have extracted Nixon from the scandal that drove him from office. With Nixon still in the White House stalking his enemies, the uncivil wars would certainly have gone on. Evidence suggests that he and Kissinger had seen the Paris peace accords as a cloak behind which they laid plans to continue the war in Vietnam. Nixon's civil rights policies also aroused old passions. Nixon entered the White House as a racial moderate, but his southern strategy pushed him toward his party's conservatives and states' rights advocates. Two of his early Supreme Court nominees (both rejected) had poor records on desegregation. The Nixon administration also opposed busing, the remedy favored by the courts and civil rights groups to achieve school desegregation. In fact, busing had come to be the issue that most inflamed white voters, and not only in the South. In Boston in 1974, busing to integrate schools provoked widespread demonstrations. Since race and Vietnam were the two issues that most provoked the uncivil wars, Nixon's approach to those issues would most certainly have kept public passions inflamed.

Watergate was not only a consequence of White House criminal behavior and a cover-up. It revealed significant flaws in the structure of the federal government. In 1973, historian Arthur Schlesinger, Jr., drew attention to what he described as *The Imperial Presidency*. It was a consequence of a long era in which successive presidents, beginning with Franklin Roosevelt and intensifying during the cold war, consolidated power in the executive branch. Such concentrations of power seldom go long unchallenged. In the aftermath of wars, Congress and the Supreme Court often seek to restore balance among the three branches of government. After the Civil War, Congress impeached President Andrew Johnson; after World War I, Senate isolationists rejected the Treaty of Versailles. In some ways, the post–World War II Red scare and McCarthyism represented the efforts of congressional Republicans to undermine the New Deal presidency. Dwight Eisenhower was more of a caretaker president, but in the uncivil wars era Kennedy, Johnson, and Nixon were all activists who expanded the powers of their office.

Certainly, Nixon took the imperial presidency to extremes. He reveled in the trappings of his office and the powers it afforded. Where previous presidents had seemed content to retreat on weekends to Camp David or their enclaves at Gettysburg, Hyannis, or Johnson City, Nixon had a compound in Key Biscayne, Florida, and another in San Clemente, California. He complained that the presidential yacht *Sequoia* was not sufficiently luxurious for such a powerful head of state. His predecessors had of course used *Air Force 1* and other military aircraft to travel about the country. Nixon had a fleet of thirty-six aircraft assigned to ferry members of his family and the White House entourage wherever they might want to go. And having been impressed by the ceremonial troops who guarded other national leaders, Nixon decided to dress the White House security forces in frilly uniforms better suited for Italian light opera.

Watergate, and all the scandals related to it, painted a picture of a White House out of control. Problems extended beyond the presidency into the executive branch. In the wake of Watergate, both the Senate and House appointed committees to investigate intelligence abuses by the CIA, FBI, military services, IRS, and other federal agencies. Such activities did not begin with Richard Nixon. Franklin Roosevelt was the first president to bug the oval office. Trading political favors for campaign support was a practice as old as the republic. Every president from Roosevelt to Nixon had relied on J. Edgar Hoover to dig up dirt on political enemies. Hoover was reputed to possess extensive files on most prominent public figures. These amounted to a kind of blackmail that insulated Hoover from political accountability. Whatever files that existed disappeared after his death.

Congressional investigation did confirm the widespread illegal infiltration and harassment of political groups. During the 1960s, political activists routinely claimed that their phones were bugged. Skeptical observers assumed they were inflating their own sense of importance. Why, after all, would the government take the trouble to spy on small fish like them? Well, in fact, investigation revealed that the FBI had been determined to link the New Left to foreign Communist sources. When that failed, Hoover had ordered the creation of COINTEL-PRO–New Left. So most likely those phones were tapped. The investigations also disclosed that agents had opened mail, harassed dissident groups, spied on citizens, and encouraged acts of violence. The government even had contingency plans in case of a domestic insurrection to imprison over 26,000 people it had identified as potential subversives.

As a result of these varied and widespread abuses, Watergate provoked Congress and the Supreme Court to curb presidential power. In the Pentagon Papers case and in the presidential tapes cases, the courts rejected the president's sweeping claims to executive privilege. In 1973, both houses overrode Nixon's veto of the War Powers Act that limited to sixty days the president's ability to commit troops without congressional authorization. Budget reform gave Congress greater control over spending. A campaign finance law sought to eliminate many of the practices that CREEP had used in the 1972 election. The Freedom of Information Act gave the public far greater access to government documents. And the Senate created the Permanent Select Committee on Intelligence to monitor the CIA, FBI, and other agencies.

In the long run, most of those reforms would prove ineffective as future presidents developed new ways to extend their power. In the short run, at least, Congress had sought to make the presidency less imperial and more accountable. The excesses of Watergate, combined with America's defeat in Vietnam, had undermined the imperial presidency that Kennedy, Johnson, and Nixon, all abetted by J. Edgar Hoover, had constructed. That process completed the destruction of the cold war consensus that provided a major rationale for consolidating power in the executive branch. Such an outcome constituted a modest victory for those on the Left who struggled for a more participatory democracy and a less interventionist American foreign policy.

Watergate also coincided with what proved to be a major downturn in the American economy. The chief culprit was inflation unleashed by spending on Great Society programs and the war in Vietnam. During the 1950s and 1960s, income levels for almost all Americans rose substantially. Many historians assumed that the resulting prosperity made the uncivil wars possible. Lyndon Johnson argued persuasively that the nation could afford both "guns and butter." Freed from the necessity of finding jobs or worrying about the future, cultural and political rebels had plenty of time to protest. After Watergate, that economic cushion was gone. Real earnings stagnated or fell for most lower- and middle-class workers. Foreign competition wiped out high-paying jobs in the blue-collar sector. The AFL-CIO worried that the United States might become "a nation of hamburger stands, a country stripped of industrial capacity. . . , a nation of citizens busily buying and selling cheeseburgers and root beer floats."

The teetering economy suffered another serious blow when the Arab members of OPEC organized an oil boycott in the wake of the 1973 Yom Kippur War, in which Syria and Egypt launched a surprise attack on Israel. The OPEC boycott was doubly disturbing. Americans learned for the first time how deeply dependent they were on foreign sources of energy. Combined with defeat in Vietnam, dependence on foreign oil signaled a new sense of the limits to American power. Rising oil prices increased the recessionary pressures that threatened prosperity. Shortages forced Americans to wait in long lines in hopes of buying a few extra gallons of gas. Those lines suggested that the United States was no longer the hegemonic giant the New Left had sought to humble.

Recession flattened the economy as the rebels of the uncivil war began to settle down and raise children. The teens who had swooned when Elvis sang "Heartbreak Hotel" were in their thirties and early forties. The young girls who mobbed the Beatles when they first came to New York had graduated from college. With greater maturity came more awareness of the naivete and excessiveness of their youthful behavior. Families brought new responsibilities. The major protest of 1973 was not over the Vietnam War or civil rights but over the price of meat. In response to rapidly rising food prices, housewives and consumer groups organized a national meat boycott.

Epilogue:
Who Won?

As with most wars, the uncivil wars ended without resolving the issues over which they were fought. Conservatives would win the political battle, dissenters would win the cultural battle; no one would win the wars.

By the time Richard Nixon resigned, the counterculture's celebration of sex, drugs, and rock and roll had entered the mainstream. Americans expressed this new freedom in varied ways—in the more casual ways they dressed, the informal ways they entertained, and the acceptance of formerly taboo subjects in films, literature, art, and even television. In particular, most Americans were more open to free sexual expression. Rejecting the double standard, they accepted the greater sexual equality women had achieved since the introduction of the birth control pill. That equality also included, for a majority, a woman's right to choose an abortion and growing sensitivity to sexual harassment, rape, and other forms of violence against women. Over time, Americans would become more accepting of gay and lesbian as well as mixed racial couples. Couples living together before marriage or marrying across ethnic and religious lines became commonplace.

Most conservatives resisted that new freedom. They saw abortion as murder, casual and gay sex as a threat to traditional family values, and the explicit depiction of sex in the media as morally corrosive. To them, drug use was equally corrupting. Ronald Reagan would make the war on drugs the centerpiece of the conservative assault on the legacy of the 1960s. Yet by the late 1970s, the majority of Americans at least tolerated if they did not adopt the recreational use of marijuana and LSD. This hedonism was a far cry from the transcendental vision of Timothy Leary and his acolytes, but it did reflect a permanent change in American cultural norms.

Even more than drugs and sex, rock and roll entered the American cultural mainstream. Where rock had once defined the counterculture, historian Ken Tucker observed, "in the 1970s and on into the 1980s, this music was the culture." And it became both more commercial and more eclectic. In 1974, the year Richard Nixon resigned, the Beatles as individual performers had three of the year's top songs: Paul McCartney and Wings, "Band on the Run," John Lennon and Yoko Ono, "Whatever Gets You through the Night," and Ringo, "You're Sixteen." The acid sounds of Jimi Hendrix, the Who, and the Grateful Dead had given way at the top of the charts to pop balladeers like Barbra Streisand, John Denver, Cher, and Roberta Flack. Punk, heavy metal, and disco were on the horizon.

Some sixties diehards saw these new trends as proof that rock had lost its ability to define an adversarial culture. It had become to them, in Tucker's words, "family entertainment only slightly more daring than [a Borscht-belt comedian's] night-club act." For many other fans, however, the new eclecticism represented the maturing of the music. Rock had proven to be an artistic medium with the capacity to appeal to its old adherents while attracting a new generation of fans. Rock and roll was here to stay. Most conservatives remained convinced that rock and roll corrupted the nation's youth. In 1992, the wives of both vice presidential candidates tried to promote censorship of lyrics in popular music.

The history of rock suggests the degree to which what had once seemed controversial and confrontational had lost its shock value. In that way, radical cultural and political dissent declined not so much because it failed to make a difference, but because it had succeeded. The American war in Vietnam was over. Racial integration was the law of the land. In the realm of popular culture, Americans now accepted much that seemed outrageous only a few years before. During the uncivil wars, the advocates of identity politics had removed much of the stigma that consigned women, blacks, gays and lesbians, teenagers, Latinos, and Native Americans to second-class citizenship. Even if equality remained elusive, Jim, Jane, and José Crow were dead. Law, medicine, and other professions ceased to be exclusive enclaves for white males. The glass ceiling in both private and public sector employment which once limited women and minorities to low-level positions cracked noticeably, even if it had not broken.

Further, dissenters had succeeded in restricting the power of government and large bureaucratic organizations to determine the choices people made on how to live their lives. After the uncivil wars, the instruments by which the government asserted its authority—the police, the National Guard, the IRS, the military services, and the FBI—became less intrusive and increasingly integrated by race and gender. So, too, did the nation's colleges and universities, including the service academies. Students gained new rights and a wider role in university governance. Consumer advocates had armed ordinary citizens with new ways to challenge the power that large, impersonal organizations exercised over the marketplace. Environmentalists had acquired more ability to hold the government and private interests responsible for the degradation of nature. Watergate had been the last great battle, and Richard Nixon the last dragon left to slay. The uncivil wars ended in part because dissenters had run out of new battles to fight.

Dissent in the post–uncivil wars era shifted from Left to Right. Despite the debacle of Watergate, conservatives had already begun to set the nation's political agenda. Their success owed much to the New Left. The radicals had taught them about organizing grassroots protest, capturing media attention, and setting the terms of public debate. By the 1970s, they were putting the lessons to use. Over the next decades, conservatives would try to undo what they saw as the worst features of a permissive society. They fought to eliminate welfare, restrict immigration, end affirmative action, make war on drugs, recriminalize abortion, make business less accountable to bureaucrats, and redefine environmental rules to favor economic development. They embraced a Christian evangelical approach to spiritual redemption and championed traditional family values while denouncing the liberal bias of the media. To overcome the crippling effects of "Vietnam syndrome," they asserted American power in Nicaragua, the Caribbean, and the Persian Gulf.

It did not take the conservative backlash to remind dissenters of the fragility of their achievements. In many ways, they were their own harshest critics. Rather than see peace in Vietnam as a victory, they mourned the lives lost and regretted that their efforts to end the war had not been more effective. They recognized, too, that the end to legal discrimination did not end de facto segregation or remove many of the stereotypes and prejudices that perpetuated inequality for minorities and women. Even in the short run, neither Woodstock nor Earth Day marked a shift to Consciousness III. Americans continued to embrace a consumer culture with its polluting technologies that threatened the environment. The evangelical preoccupation with individual salvation and the self-help therapies of the 1970s in many ways repudiated the spiritual quest at the heart of almost all 1960s social and political movements. As a result, few veterans of the uncivil wars have ever claimed victory.

That sense of a revolution stillborn may account for the defensiveness with which many former rebels faced the postwar conservative onslaught. In the 1992, election Bill Clinton presented an exaggerated version of their ambivalence. When asked if he had ever smoked marijuana, he admitted that he had held a joint "but never inhaled." Sixties veterans found the answer laughable. In smoke-filled rooms, everyone inhaled. They were truly dismayed, however, when Clinton discounted his efforts to avoid service in Vietnam and his opposition to the war. His equivocation demonstrated the degree to which conservatives had discredited the legacy of the 1960s. In order to hold the center of the political spectrum, Clinton believed he had to repudiate positions he had embraced just twenty years before.

Conservatives found Clinton's denials morally indefensible. Clinton was to them a classic product of the sixties, a person who flouted authority but refused to assume responsibility for his behavior. Thus they saw Bill and, by extension, his wife, Hillary, as the embodiment of moral, political, and spiritual bankruptcy. Congressman Newt Gingrich, the apostle of the new conservative creed, dismissed them as "Counterculture McGoverniks." Gingrich believed that in attacking the cold war consensus, the Clintons and their ilk had undermined essential America values—traditional religious faith, family, community, neighborhood schools, law and order, hard work, and simple love of country. Clinton's early attempt to integrate gays into the military confirmed the conservatives' worst fears. Yet during his presidency, Clinton advanced no social policy worthy of "Countercultural McGoverniks." His primary achievements were both conservative—welfare to workfare reform and a federal budget surplus. On most social issues, Clinton could do little more than frustrate the conservative assault on affirmative action, abortion rights, and environmental protection.

Conservatives were as intolerant toward the moral defects of their enemies as were the radicals of the sixties. Out of that sense of moral outrage came the 1997 attempt to impeach Clinton. The attacks on the Clintons and, by extension, 1960s values sounded curiously like the jeremiads of the 1930s Liberty Leaguers who fulminated over the evils of Franklin Roosevelt and his New Deal. What had Roosevelt done that so aroused their ire? He had reached out to people on the margins of American society and vastly expanded the elite culture. His elite included ethnics, Catholics, Jews, organized labor, intellectuals, artists, and women. The New Deal also shifted responsibility for meeting the vicissitudes of life—war, economic hard times, sickness, injury, or death—from the individual or family to the federal government. For being a traitor to his class, the Liberty League condemned Roosevelt.

By the 1990s, many New Deal liberals had become Reagan Democrats. They, like the more traditional conservatives, felt threatened by the culturally libertarian, economically egalitarian, and socially inclusive ethos of the Woodstock Nation. They saw those who championed the rights of minorities and the poor, who demanded cultural freedom, and who argued the United States should lead the world by moral example rather than by the force of arms as subversives. Leftists, hippies, women's libbers, and their ilk had been free to make such demands not because of their moral righteousness or patriotic sacrifice, but because they were the heirs of social and economic privilege. In that way, conservatives laid claim to the populist legacy once held by the New Deal coalition.

Long after they ended, the uncivil wars continue to provoke powerful emotions. Like all wars, they have had their revisionists, who reinterpret the reasons for which they were fought and what they meant. George Will, a conservative journalist, recognized a similarity to the Civil War. "So powerful were—are—the energies let loose in the sixties," he observed, "there cannot now be, and may never be, anything like a final summing up. After all, what is the 'final result' of the Civil War? It is too soon to say."

Both conflicts raised fundamental questions about the nature of American society and its values. Before the Civil War, Abraham Lincoln had warned his countrymen that the union could not endure "half slave, half free." At Gettysburg, he spoke of a nation "conceived in Liberty, and dedicated to the proposition that all men are created equal." He concluded by calling on Americans to dedicate themselves to making certain "that this nation, under God, shall have a new birth of freedom—and that government of the people, by the people, for the people shall not perish from the earth." In ending slavery, the Civil War did indeed give new meaning to freedom and equality, but it did not resolve the inequalities of race, gender, ethnicity, and age. It was left for later generations to take up those battles.

The generation who shaped the cold war consensus believed they were carrying out Lincoln's charge. In defending the American way of life from godless Communism, they were keeping alive the spirit of liberty, equality, and freedom to which Lincoln gave such noble purpose. They acknowledged that connection by adding "under God" to the Pledge of Allegiance. The cultural and political radicals of the 1960s disputed that claim. To them, the enemy of American ideals could be found not abroad but at home, in the impersonal structures of government, corporations, and universities controlled by elite white males. Beginning with their support for civil rights and their opposition to the war in Vietnam, the rebels dedicated themselves to the proposition that all men and women regardless of race, religion, or creed should have freedom from want, freedom of opportunity, and freedom of personal self-expression. Such sweeping claims were anathema to conservatives. They associated freedom from want as freedom from responsibility, freedom of opportunity as reverse discrimination, and freedom of personal self-expression as self-indulgence and moral depravity.

Both conservatives and dissenters of the 1960s can look back with regret on their uncivil wars. For conservatives, the sixties left a legacy of so much to be undone; for dissenters, so much was left undone. The uncivil wars generation had no Lincoln to consecrate its battlefields or find a common meaning in its differences, though possibly Martin Luther King, Jr., came closest. For his efforts, King earned the scorn and hostility of combatants on both sides, as did Lincoln. In that spirit, it is most appropriate that King is the one uncivil wars leader for whom Americans observe a national holiday. Equally fitting, the great memorial of the uncivil wars dedicated to those who died in Vietnam was conceived by Maya Lin, a young Asian-American woman. Her somber design evoked the fault lines of the uncivil wars. Its abstraction aroused the ire of those Americans who believed commemoration should be expressed in traditional aesthetics. That same abstraction has moved the nation more than any classical marble columns. Through Lin's vision, those soldiers whose names appear on the memorial did not die in vain. As she insisted, "you cannot ever forget that war is not just a victory or loss. It's really about individual lives." In her memorial, she gave power to the people.

The conservative assault on the Woodstock Nation misses an essential quality of the uncivil wars—the buoyant optimism and hopefulness with which the rebels went to war. Think of what it was like to stand on the Washington Mall in August of 1963 when Martin Luther King's dream still seemed a living possibility. Consider the sense of mission young people felt as they headed off to Freedom Summer in 1964. Or the sense of personal liberation when they headed to the Haight in the Summer of Love. After two decades of McCarthyism and cold war, it took idealism and courage for young men to burn their draft cards in Washington in October of 1967. How vibrant the world must have seemed for hippies who drove their VW Beetles up the New York Thruway toward Woodstock in August 1969. And what could have done more to confirm the sense of a government at war with its people than the revelations of Watergate?

Like all wars, the uncivil wars bred excesses on both sides, but looking back reminds Americans that for this nation to long endure, each generation must contest the meaning of its common values.

Notes on Sources

These notes are intended to reflect my debts to those historians and other writers from whom I have drawn much of the material for this book. Since *Uncivil Wars* is not a monographic work, these are not endnotes in the formal sense, but references that should guide interested readers to the appropriate sources and reflect my obligations. Two works merit special attention because they are invaluable to anyone writing on the 1960s. Rita Lang Kleinfelder, *When We Were Young: A Baby-Boomer Yearbook* (New York, 1991), covers the period from 1947 to 1975. For each year, she highlights significant news events, science and technology, obituaries, the arts, major works of fiction, new words or phrases, fashion, popular music, movies, television and radio, and sports. Second, David Farber and Beth Bailey, eds., *The Columbia Guide to America in the 1960s* (New York, 2001), include a brief history, topical essays, an annotated bibliography, and interesting information about sports, popular culture, and other topics to warm the hearts of Trivial Pursuit fans—even the most popular male and female names.

Introduction

The opening Buchwald anecdote and jokes come from Ronald Shafer, "President as Punch Line," *Wall Street Journal Europe*, September 27, 2004. Kenneth Cmiel's thoughtful essay "The Politics of Civility" can be found in David Farber, ed., *The Sixties: From Memory to History* (Chapel Hill, NC, 1994). Another important study of the impact of civility is William Chafe, *Civilities and Civil Rights: Greensboro, North Carolina, and the Black Freedom Struggle* (New York, 1980). The religious side of this movement is covered in Mark Silk, *Spiritual Politics: Religion and America Since World War II* (New York, 1988). For the broad trends in American religion and the fracturing in the church, see Sydney Ahlstrom, *A Religious History of the American People* (New Haven, CT, 1972). See also Winthrop Hudson and John Corrigan, *Religion in America: An Historical Account of American Religious Life* (Upper Saddle River, NJ, 2004). Three important sources on the conservative movement and the rise of the New Right are Godfrey Hodgson, *The World Turned Right Side Up: A History of the Conservative Ascendancy in America* (New York, 1996), John Andrews III, *The Other Side of the Sixties: Young Americans for Freedom and the Rise of Conservative Politics* (New Brunswick, NJ, 1997), and Lisa McGirr, *Suburban Warriors: The Origins of the New American Right* (Princeton, NJ, 2001). On civil rights and its impact on politics, see Thomas Edsall and Mary Edsall, *Chain Reaction: The Impact of Race, Rights, and Taxes on American Politics* (New York, 1992). The classic early study is Kirkpatrick Sale, *Power Shift: The Rise of the Southern Rim and Its Challenge to the Eastern Establishment* (New York, 1975). The discussion of generational patterns is in Arthur Schlesinger, Jr., *The Cycles of History* (New York, 1986), especially his essay "The Cycles of American Politics." For Baltzell's theory of class and caste politics, see his *The Protestant Establishment: Aristocracy and Class in America* (New York, 1964). Peter Braunstein and Michael William Doyle make a parallel case for treating 1964–68 as a discrete phase within in the larger frame of the sixties. See their edited collection *Imagine Nations: The American Counterculture of the 1960s & 70s* (New York, 2002).

Chapter 1 The Consensus

pp. 13–14 The opening reflections on school are drawn from my experience at PS 64 in Buffalo in the 1950s. On the amending of the Pledge of Allegiance, see Mark Silk, *Spiritual Politics: Religion and America since World War II* (New York, 1989). On the secular, material culture of the consensus from 1955 to 1964, see Thomas Hine: *Populux: The Look and Life of America in the '50s and '60s, from Tailfins and TV Dinners to Barbie Dolls and Fallout Shelters* (New York, 1986).

pp. 14–16 Good sources on the National Security Council and the cold war consensus are Walter LaFeber, *America, Russia, and the Cold War*, 9th ed. (New York, 2002), and Melvyn Leffler, *A Preponderance of Power* (Stanford, CA, 1992). The National Security Council information is available in NSC-7, "The Position of the United States with Respect to Soviet Directed World Communism" (1948), NSC-20, "United States Objectives with Respect to Russia" (1948), and NSC-68, "United States Objectives and Programs for National Security" (1950), all available through the National Archives in Washington, though NSC-68 is online. On Eisenhower, see John Andrew III, *The Other Side of the Sixties* (New Brunswick, NJ, 1997).

pp. 16–17 In discussing civil rights and desegregation, I have found Robert Weisbrot, *Freedom Bound: A History of America's Civil Rights Movement* (New York, 1990), particularly cogent and useful. On J. Edgar Hoover in the 1950s, see Stephen Whitfield, *The Culture of the Cold War* (Baltimore, 1991). Whitfield is probably the best single source on 1950s culture. Also on Hoover, see Athan Theoharis and John Stuart Cox, *The Boss: J. Edgar Hoover and the Great American Inquisition* (Philadelphia, 1988).

pp. 17–19 Eric Barnouw, *Tube of Plenty* (New York, 1977), discusses *I Led Three Lives*.

pp. 19–25 On conservatives and Senator McCarthy, see Andrew, *The Other Side of the Sixties*, Whitfield, *Culture of the Cold War*, and Godfrey Hodgson, *The World Turned Right Side Up: A History of the Conservative Ascendancy* (New York, 1996). Also see Richard Rovere, *Senator Joe McCarthy* (New York, 1959), and Nicholas Von Hoffman, *Citizen Cohn* (New York, 1988). On Edward R. Murrow, see Barnouw, *Tube of Plenty*. The documentary by Emile de Antonio, *Point of Order* (1964), is another excellent source.

Chapter 2 The Cultural Cold War

pp. 26–28 Two excellent general sources on teen culture in the 1950s are James Gilbert, *A Cycle of Outrage: America's Reaction to the Juvenile Delinquent in the 1950s* (New York, 1986), and Thomas Doherty, *Teenagers and Teenpics: The Juvenilization of American Movies in the 1950s* (Boston, 1988). See also Whitfield, *Culture of the Cold War*, and William Graebner, *Coming of Age in Buffalo: Youth and Authority in the Postwar Era* (Philadelphia, 1994). Graebner makes clear the varieties of teen styles and cultures.

pp. 29–30 Gilbert, *Cycle of Outrage*, is the source for Frederick Wertheim and the furor over comic books.

pp. 30–32 The story of Bill Gaines and his encounters with censorship is told with vivid illustrations in Maria Reidelbach, *Completely Mad: A History of the Comic Book and Magazine* (Boston, 1991).

pp. 32–39 The most comprehensive source on rock and roll is Ed Ward, Geoffrey Stokes, and Ken Tucker, *Rock of Ages: The Rolling Stone History of Rock & Roll* (New York, 1986). Ed Ward wrote the section on the 1950s. Other interesting perspectives come in Carl Belz, *The Story of Rock* (New York, 1972), Charlie Gillett, *The Sound of the City: The Rise of Rock and Roll* (New York, 1970), and Colin Escott, *Good Rockin' Tonight: Sun Records and the Birth of Rock and Roll* (New York, 1991). Brian Ward, *Just My Soul Responding: Rhythm and Blues, Black Consciousness, and Race Relations* (Berkeley, 1998), traces the connection between music and civil rights. In a similar vein, Glenn Altschuler, *All Shook Up: How Rock 'n' Roll Changed America* (New York, 2003), explores the cultural controversies. For the roots of Elvis Presley, see Peter Guralnick, *Last Train to Memphis: The Rise of Elvis Presley* (Boston, 1994). I was fortunate to direct the senior thesis of Chris O'Brien, "The Wages of Spin: Disk Jockeys, the Payola Scandals and American Music" (Bard College Library, 1986).

pp. 39–42 Gilbert, *Cycle of Outrage*, describes elements of teen culture. On teen flicks see Doherty, *Teenagers and Teenpics*. Also good on movies is Peter Biskind, *Seeing Is Believing: How Hollywood Taught Us to Stop Worrying and Love the Fifties* (New York, 1983).

pp. 42–43 This anecdote comes from Lawrence Wright, *In the New World: Growing Up with America* (New York, 1988). Wright's is a wonderfully told tale of how a conservative Texan came to grips with the youth culture of the 1960s. See also Ward, *Rock of Ages* and Todd Gitlin, *The Sixties: Years of Hope, Days of Rage* (New York, 1987).

Chapter 3 Cracks in the Consensus

pp. 44–45 One of the best places to start on the politics and culture of the 1950s is Morris Dickstein, *Gates of Eden: American Culture in the Sixties* (New York, 1977), especially the first three chapters. Whitfield, *Culture of the Cold War*, is another rich source. Also good are Alan Brinkley, *Liberalism and Its Discontents* (New York, 1998), John Diggins, *The Proud Decades: America in War and Peace, 1941–1960* (New York, 1988), and David Halberstam, *The Fifties* (New York, 1993).

pp. 45–47 J. D. Salinger, *The Catcher in the Rye* (Boston, 1951).

pp. 47–48 Halberstam, *The Fifties*, is good on Hefner and *Playboy*.

pp. 48–51 On the Beats see Dickstein, *Gates of Eden*, Whitfield, *Culture of the Cold War*, and Diggins, *Proud Decades*. See also Allen Ginsberg, *Howl and Other Poems* (San Francisco, 1956), and Jack Kerouac, *On the Road* (New York, 1957). A good anthology is Anne Waldman, ed., *Beat Book* (Boston, 1999).

pp. 51–57 Gitlin, *The Sixties*, is good on the dissenting culture. William Whyte, *The Organization Man* (New York, 1956), is a classic sociological critique of corporate and suburban culture. John Kenneth Galbraith, *The Affluent Society* (Boston, 1958), set the tone for liberal critics. C. Wright Mills, *The Power Elite* (New York, 1959), defies easy labeling. Gitlin gives a sense of Mills's impact on the New Left.

pp. 57–60 Rachel Carson, *Silent Spring* (New York, 1962), deserves special mention not simply as a woman making an impact in a man's world, but also because of her impact on popular ecological thought. On that influence, see Donald Worster, *Nature's Economy*, 2d ed. (New York, 1994), and Robert Gottlieb, *Forcing the Spring: The Transformation of the American Environmental Movement* (Washington, D.C., 1993). Worster is especially effective in placing Carson in the context of evolving ecological ideas. Charles Rubin, *The Green Crusade* (New York, 1994), supports the recurring critique of Carson's science. In fact, her critics do have a point in so far as she set out not to do research as such but to build a case against the abuse of DDT and other pesticides. The best single source on Carson is Linda Lear, *Rachel Carson: Witness for Nature* (New York, 1997). The article in *Science* magazine is dated May 24, 1963, p. 878, and in the *Saturday Review of Literature* is dated June 1, 1963, p. 45. The *New York Times* is another source. American Experience produced *Rachel Carson's Silent Spring*, available through PBS Video (Los Angeles, 1992).

pp. 60–62 Dickstein, *Gates of Eden*, explains the concept of black humor. Betty Friedan, *The Feminine Mystique* (New York, 1963), is the obvious source. Ruth Rosen, *The World Split Open: How the Modern Woman's Movement Changed America* (New York, 2000), places Friedan in a larger context, as do Susan Douglas, *Where the Girls Are Growing Up Female with the Mass Media* (New York, 1994), Rosalind Rosenberg, *Divided Lives: American Women in the Twentieth Century* (New York, 1992), and Nancy Woloch, *Women and the American Experience* (New York, 2000). A corrective to Friedan's view of women in the 1950s is Joanne Meyerowitz, ed., *Not June Clever* (Philadelphia, 1994).

pp. 63–64 Thomas Frank, *The Conquest of the Cool: Business Culture, Counterculture, and the Rise of Hip Consumerism* (Chicago, 1997), advanced the novel (and convincing) notion that advertisers and clothing manufacturers anticipated the hip style and absurdist sensibility before the counterculture emerged. Hine, *Populux*, is another source, as is James Twitchell, *ADCULTusa* (New York, 1996).

pp. 64–67 Joseph Heller, *Catch-22* (New York, 1961). Again, see Dickstein, *Gates of Eden*, for the context of black humor.

pp. 67–70 The story of Robert Sprague, the Gaither Commission, and General LeMay is told in Fred Kaplan, *Wizards of Armageddon* (New York, 1983). On the bomb and sixties culture, see Margot Henrikson, *Dr. Strangelove's America: Society and Culture in the Atomic Age* (Berkeley, 1997). Henrikson contends, "It was in particular the new cultural products and genres—film noir and roman noir, science fiction films, pulp crime literature, beat poetry, rock 'n' roll, and black humor—that illustrated the revolutionary and explosive cultural impact of the atomic bomb." The reviews of *Dr. Strangelove* are *New York Times*, February 2 and 16, 1964; *Newsweek*, February 3, 1964.

p. 70 Gar Alperowitz, *Atomic Diplomacy: Hiroshima and Potsdam: The Atomic Bomb and American Confrontation with Soviet Power*, rev. ed. (New York, 1985).

Chapter 4 The New Generation

pp. 72–73 The best source for SANE is Milton Katz, *Ban the Bomb: A History of SANE, the Committee for a Sane Nuclear Policy, 1957–1985* (New York, 1987). Gitlin, *The Sixties*, is also a valuable source, especially on the connections to the Left. Gitlin discusses the HUAC demonstrations in San Francisco, as does William Rorabaugh, *Berkeley at War: The 1960s* (New York, 1989).

pp. 73–74 This early episode in the creation of YAF is discussed in Andrew, *Other Side of the Sixties*. See also Hodgson, *World Turned Right Side Up*.

pp. 74–76 The Greensboro story is told in William Chafe, *Civil Rights and Civilities: Greensboro, North Carolina, and the Black Struggle for Freedom* (New York, 1980), one of the best books on the early civil rights era. Additional detail comes from Robert Weisbrot, *Freedom Bound: A History of America's Civil Rights Movement* (New York, 1991), an excellent survey of the whole movement.

pp. 76–77 Andrew, *Other Side of the Sixties*, draws some interesting comparisons.

pp. 77–80 In addition to Weisbrot, I drew heavily on Clayborne Carson, *In Struggle: SNCC and the Black Awakening of the 1960s* (Cambridge, MA 1981). On Martin Luther King, Jr., see Taylor Branch, *Parting the Waters: America in the King Years, 1954–1963* (New York, 1989), certainly one of the finest biographies of the past decades. Another good source on King is David Garrow, *Bearing the Cross: Martin Luther King, Jr., and the Southern Christian Leadership Conference* (New York, 1986). On Robert Moses, see Eric Burner, *And Gently He Shall Lead Them: Robert Parris Moses and Civil Rights in Mississippi* (New York, 1994). Terry Anderson, *The Movement and the Sixties: Protestyn In America From Greensboro to Wounded Knee* (New York, 1995) is also good on Civil Rights.

pp. 80–88 At the core of this discussion of SDS are Tom Hayden, *Reunion: A Memoir* (New York, 1988), Kirkpatrick Sale, *SDS* (New York, 1973), and Gitlin, *The Sixties*. See also Todd Gitlin, *The Whole World Is Watching: The Mass Media in the Making and Unmaking of the New Left* (New York, 1981). Gitlin and Hayden look on these events as participants as well as observers. A much underappreciated early book is Milton Viorst, *Fire in the Streets: America in the 1960's* (New York, 1979). Two other valuable works are James Miller, *"Democracy Is in the Streets": From Port Huron to the Siege of Chicago* (New York, 1987), and Maurice Isserman, *If I Had a Hammer: The Death of the Old Left and the Birth of the New Left* (New York, 1987). Additional materials are available in the excellent reader (which includes excerpts from the *Port Huron Statement*) edited by Alexander Bloom and Winnie Breines, *"Takin' it to the streets"* (New York, 1995). Rorabaugh, *Berkeley at War*, provides background on the West Coast student movement. Another perspective, this time on Texas, is Doug Rossinow, *The Politics of Authenticity: Liberalism, Christianity, and the New Left in America* (New York, 1998). Maurice Isserman and Michael Kazin, *America Divided: The Civil War of the 1960s* (New York, 2004), also place the New Left into a wider context.

pp. 88–95 Hodgson, *World Turned Right Side Up*, and Andrew, *Other Side of the Sixties*, are the major sources for this section. Isserman and Kazin, *America Divided*, also have an interesting discussion of the conservative political movement. Lisa McGirr, *Suburban Warriors: The Origins of the New American Right* (Princeton, 2001), has focused historians' attention on the conservative politics that were a central legacy of the 1960s. A number of authors address the spiritual dimensions of both conservative and countercultural movements: Robert Wurthow, *The Restructuring of American Religion* (Princeton, 1988), and *After Heaven: Spirituality in America since the 1950s* (Berkeley, 1998); Robert Ellwood, *The 60s: Spiritual Awakening* (New Brunswick, NJ, 1994); and John T. McGreevy, *Catholicism and American Freedom* (New York, 2003).

Chapter 5   The Cold War on the New Frontier

pp. 96–104 A basic source for the 1960 election is the classic by Theodore White, *The Making of the President 1960* (New York, 1961). Norman Mailer's essay on John Kennedy, "Superman Comes to the Supermarket," appears in the editors of *Esquire*, *Smiling through the Apocalypse: Esquire's History of the Sixties* (New York, 1987). Wright, *In the New World*, comments on the sectional implications of the election. On Kennedy and his approach to politics, Thomas Reeves, *A Question of Character: A Life of John Kennedy* (New York, 1992), is good. Also see David Burner and Thomas West, *The Torch Is Passed: The Kennedy Brothers and American Liberalism* (Saint James, NY, 1984). On Richard Nixon before his presidency, see Stephen Ambrose, *Nixon: The Education of a Politician, 1913–1962* (New York, 1987), Tom Wicker, *One of Us: Richard Nixon and the American Dream* (New York, 1991), and Gary Wills, *Nixon Agonistes: The Crisis of the Self-Made Man* (New York, 1970). The "kitchen" and presidential debates as well as Kennedy's telegenic appeal are discussed in White, *Making of the President*, Barnouw, *Tube of Plenty*, and Karal Ann Marling, *As Seen on TV: The Visual Culture of Everyday Life in the 1950s* (Cambridge, MA, 1994). Wright, *In the New World*, is the source of the story of the Johnsons in Dallas. For a broader picture of Johnson, see Robert Dallek, *Lone Star Rising: Lyndon Johnson and His Times, 1908–1960* (New York, 1991).

pp. 104–108 On the Kennedy administration and the creation of Camelot, see Reeves, *A Question of Character*, and Burner and West, *The Torch Is Passed*. John Blum, *Years of Discord: American Politics and Society, 1961–1974* (New York, 1991), is judicious on Kennedy, Johnson, and Nixon. Richard Reeves, *President Kennedy: Profile of Power* (New York, 1994), follows the day-by-day flow of events that offers insight into the swirl of issues surrounding the president. David Halberstam, *The Best and the Brightest* (New York, 1972), captures the dynamism and hubris that surrounded Kennedy, especially in the person of Robert McNamara. Kennedy's inaugural address is widely available in print and audio versions on the Web.

pp. 108–113 For an overview of Kennedy's foreign policy and its cold war context, see LaFeber, *America, Russia, and the Cold War, 1945–2002*. On the Bay of Pigs, see Trumbell Higgins, *Perfect Failure: Kennedy, Eisenhower, and the Bay of Pigs* (New York, 1991). On how the nuclear arms race stirred the peace movement, see Charles DeBenedetti and Charles Chatfield, *An American Ordeal: The Antiwar Movement of the Vietnam Era* (Syracuse, NY, 1990), and Amy Swerdlow, *Women's Strike for Peace: Traditional Motherhood and Radical Politics in the 1960s* (Chicago, 1993). On the Peace Corps, see Elizabeth Cobbs Hoffman, *All You Need Is Love: The Peace Corps and the Spirit of the 1960s* (Cambridge, MA, 1998).

pp. 113–115 The best history of the crisis itself is Aleksandr Fursenko and Timothy Naftali, *"One Hell of a Gamble": Khrushchev, Castro, and Kennedy, 1958–1964* (New York, 1997), and Ernest May and Philip Zelikow, *The Kennedy Tapes: Inside the White House during the Cuban Missile Crisis* (Cambridge, MA, 1997). An intriguing earlier analysis of Kennedy's policymaking is Graham Allison, *Essence of Decision* (Boston, 1971). Gitlin, *The Sixties*, and Hayden, *Reunion*, draw a vivid picture of how the missile crisis impacted the Left.

Chapter 6   The Second Civil War

pp. 115–118 The primary source for the Dawson story is Sara Evans, *Personal Politics: The Roots of the Women's Liberation in the Civil Rights Movement and New Left* (New York, 1980). See also Rossinow, *The Politics of Authenticity*, for more background. Anne Moody tells her own story in the powerful *Coming of Age in Mississippi* (New York, 1968).

pp. 119–121 To view the civil rights movement in the broad national picture, as spokespersons such as Billy Graham did, go to Whitfield, *Culture of the Cold War*, and Halberstam, *The Fifties*. Weisbrot, *Freedom Bound*, is also good for the big picture. Juan Williams, *Eyes on the Prize: America's Civil Rights Years, 1954–1964* (New York, 1987), is both an interesting read and richly illustrated. It served as the companion to the powerful PBS series. On the role of clergy, see James F. Findlay, Jr., *Church People in the Struggle: The National Council of Churches and the Black Freedom Movement, 1950–1970* (New York, 1993). The FBI's passive role is explored in Frank Donner, *The Age of Surveillance: The Aims and Methods of America's Political Intelligence System* (New York, 1980). Gitlin's reactions are in Todd Gitlin, *The Sixties*.

pp. 121–126 Juan Williams, *Eyes on the Prize*, gives a vivid account of the Freedom Rides. Mark Stern, *Calculating Visions: Kennedy, Johnson, and Civil Rights* (New Brunswick, NJ, 1992), explodes many myths about Kennedy's liberalism. Hugh Graham Davis, *Civil Rights and the Presidency* (New York, 1992), is similarly sobering.

pp. 126–128 The best place to learn about events in Mississippi is John Dittmer, *Local People: The Struggle for Civil Rights in Mississippi* (Champaign-Urbana, IL, 1994). On SNCC's role, see Carson, *In Struggle*, Burner, *Gently He Shall Lead Them*, Evans, *Personal Politics*, and Moody, *Coming of Age in Mississippi*.

pp. 128–134 Once again, Weisbrot, *Freedom Bound*, Dittmer, *Local People*, Stern, *Calculating Visions*, and Williams, *Eyes on the Prize*, are good for these events. On King's role, see Branch, *Parting the Waters*. See also David Goldfield, *Black, White, and Southern: Race Relations and Southern Culture* (Baton Rouge, 1990).

pp. 134–137 Williams, *Eyes on the Prize*, and Branch, *Parting the Waters*, describe the march on Washington. Carson, *In Struggle*, gives a sense of the struggle between SNCC and the march organizers.

pp. 138–140 I was nineteen years old when Kennedy was assassinated. All the same, my memories of that day remain vivid. Cornell at that time was just becoming politicized, though my friends were generally strong supporters of civil rights and liberal values. Blum, *Years of Discord*, gives a good account of the politics, while Wright, *In the New World*, shows how Texans experienced that event.

Chapter 7 1964: Welcome to the 1960s

pp. 143–147 The major source for rock and roll was the section by Geoffrey Stokes in *Rock of Ages*. Kleinfelder, *When We Were Young*, catalogs the performers and hits year by year. Other sources include Gillett, *The Sound of the City*, Greil Marcus, *Mystery Train: Images of American Rock 'n' Roll Music* (New York, 1990), Herbert London, *Closing the Circle: A Cultural History of the Rock Revolution* (Chicago, 1985), Robert Palmer, *Rock and Roll: An Unruly History* (New York, 1995), and Suzanne Smith, *Dancing in the Streets: Motown and the Cultural Politics of Detroit* (Cambridge, MA, 1999). The 2003 documentary Film of the Funk Brothers, *Standing in the Shadow of Motown* (2003), is a tribute to the unsung studio band. George Lipsitz, "Who'll Stop the Rain?" is in David Farber, ed., *The Sixties: From Memory to History* (Chapel Hill, NC, 1994). On the Beatles, see Hunter Davies, *The Beatles* (New York, 1984), and Martin Goldsmith, *The Beatles Come to America* (New York, 2004). On Bob Dylan, see Bob Spitz, *Dylan: A Biography* (New York, 1988), and Robert Shelton, *No Direction Home: The Life and Music of Bob Dylan* (New York, 2003).

pp. 147–148 The episode at the World's Fair is in Hine, *Populux*. On urban unrest see, U.S. Riot Commission, *Report of the National Committee on Civil Disorders* (New York, 1968). This is popularly known as the Kerner Commission. For a detailed look at the Watts riot, see Gerald Horne, *Fire This Time: The Watts Uprising and the Meaning of the 1960s* (Charlottesville, VA, 1995).

pp. 148–152 Weisbrot, *Freedom Bound*, is a good general source on Johnson and civil rights politics as is Stern, *Calculating Visions*. The Miller Center at the University of Virginia has also provided transcribed materials in Jonathan Rosenberg and Zachary Karabell, *Kennedy, Johnson,* and the Quest for Justice: The Civil Rights Tapes (New York, 2003). Other Johnson tapes are transcribed in Michael Beschloss, ed., Taking Charge: The Johnson White House Tapes (New York, 1997), and Reaching for Glory: Lyndon Johnson's Secret White House Tapes, 1964–1965 (New York, 2001). Robert Caro has waged a vendetta against Johnson in a series of biographies, most recently Master of the Senate: The Years of Lyndon Johnson (New York, 2002). A more balanced view of Johnson can be found in Robert Dallek, Lyndon B. Johnson: Portrait of a President (New York, 2003), and Doris Kearns Goodwin, Lyndon Johnson and the American Dream (New York, 1991).

pp. 152–163 The best general sources on freedom summer and the Mississippi Freedom Democratic Party are Dittmer, Local People, and Charles Payne, I've Got the Light of Freedom: The Organizing Tradition and the Mississippi Freedom Struggle (Berkeley, 1995). On the northern volunteers, see Doug McAdam, Freedom Summer (New York, 1988). Moody, Coming of Age in Mississippi, offers an African-American perspective as does Burner, Gently He Shall Lead Us. Weisbrot, Freedom Bound, and Carson, In Struggle, also provide important perspectives. See also Anthony Lewis, Portrait of a Decade: The Second American Revolution (New York, 1964).

pp. 163–166 The best concise overviews of the United States in Vietnam are George Herring, America's Longest War, 3d ed. (New York, 1996), Robert Schulzinger, A Time for War: The United States and Vietnam, 1941–1975 (New York, 1997), and Marilyn Young, The Vietnam Wars, 1945–1990 (New York, 1991). On the process of early U.S. involvement and Johnson's escalation, see David Kaiser, American Tragedy: Kennedy, Johnson, and the Origins of the Vietnam War (Cambridge, MA, 2000), and Fredrik Logevall, Choosing War: The Last Chance for Peace and the Escalation of War in Vietnam (Berkeley, 1999). Three historians who focus on Johnson and his escalation of the war are Larry Berman, Lyndon Johnson's War: The Road to Stalemate in Vietnam (New York, 1989), Michael Hunt, Lyndon Johnson's War: America's Cold War Crusade in Vietnam (New York, 1996), and George Herring, LBJ and Vietnam: A Very Different Kind of War (Austin, 1994).

pp. 166–168 McAdam, Freedom Summer, and Carson, In Struggle, discuss the difficulties that beset the group after the summer of 1964. Evans, Personal Politics, explores the issues raised by women and the gender difficulties that arose.

pp. 168–173 Rorabaugh, Berkeley at War, is the obvious source for the free speech movement. Anderson, The Movement and the Sixties, covers this topic well.

Chapter 8 Teach-in, Strike Out

p. 174 On YAF, see Andrews, The Other Side of the Sixties.

pp. 174–176 Philip Caputo, A Rumor of War (New York, 1977).

pp. 176–178 This section on Vietnam draws on Herring, America's Longest War and LBJ and Vietnam; Young, The Vietnam Wars; Berman, Lyndon Johnson's War; Kaiser, American Tragedy; and Logevall, Choosing War.

pp. 178–179 John M. Blum, Years of Discord: American Politics and Society, 1961–1974 (New York, 1991); David Farber, The Age of Great Dreams: America in the 1960s (New York, 1994); and Alan Matusow, The Unraveling of America: A History of Liberalism in the 1960s (New York, 1984), are all useful on LBJ's domestic politics.

pp. 179–184 For Berkeley and antiwar protest, see Rorabaugh, Berkeley at War. SDS and the war is covered in Sale, SDS, and Gitlin, The Sixties. For a more general treatment of the antiwar movement, see Melvin Small, Johnson, Nixon, and the Doves (New Brunswick, NJ, 1987), and Covering Dissent: The Media and the Anti–Vietnam War Movement (New Brunswick, NJ, 1994), and DeBenedetti and Chatfield, An American Ordeal.

pp. 184–185 On religion generally and also on Vatican II, see Ellwood, The Sixties Spiritual Awakening, Wuthnow, After Heaven, and McGreevy, Catholicism and American Freedom.

pp. 185–190 Taylor Branch, Pillar of Fire: America in the King Years, 1963–65 (New York, 1998), continues King's biography through the voting rights phase. Weisbrot, Freedom Bound, and Harvard Sitkoff, The Struggle for Black Equality, 1954–1992 (New York, 1993), are good sources for the broad picture on the emergence of Black Power as well as the Nation of Islam and Malcolm X. See also Marable Manning, *Race, Reform, and Rebellion: The Second Reconstruction in Black America, 1945–1990* (Jackson, 1991), Rod Bush, *We Are Not What We Seem: Black Nationalism and Class Struggle in the American Century* (New York, 1999), and William Van Deburg, *New Day in Babylon: The Black Power Movement and American Culture, 1965–1975* (Chicago, 1992). Carson, *In Struggle*, is another useful source. Two classics are also worth revisiting: Kwame Ture (Stokely Carmichael) and Charles Hamilton, *Black Power: The Politics of Liberation in America*, rev. ed. (1967; New York, 1992), and Malcolm X with Alex Haley, *The Autobiography of Malcolm X* (New York, 1965). On the riots, see James Button, *Black Violence: Political Impacts of the 1960s Riots* (Princeton, 1978), as well as the Kerner Commission, *Report of the National Committee on Civil Disorders*.

pp. 190–193 Herring, *America's Longest War*, and Young, *The Vietnam Wars*, are the major sources, as is Small, *Johnson, Nixon, and the Doves*, on antiwar protest. Two terrific sources on journalism and news management in Vietnam are Neil Sheehan, *A Bright Shining Lie: John Paul Vann and America in Vietnam* (New York, 1989), and Michael Herr, *Dispatches* (New York, 1977). See also Daniel Hallin, *The "Uncensored" War: The Media and Vietnam* (New York, 1986), and Clarence Wyatt, *Paper Soldiers: The American Press and the Vietnam War* (New York, 1993).

Chapter 9 The Great Freak Forward

pp. 194–198 Tom Wolfe, *The Electric Kool-Aid Acid Test* (New York, 1967), is both the account of Kesey and the Pranksters on their journey and a pioneering example of the new journalism. Lee and Schlain, *Acid Dreams*, provides background on the development of LSD, the counter-culture, and Leary as an acid guru.

pp. 198–205 Wolfe and Lee and Schlain are major sources for this section as well. Gitlin, *The Sixties*, Anderson, *The Movement and the Sixties*, and Ed Morgan, *The 60s Experience: Hard Lessons about Modern America* (Philadelphia, 1991), are general sources. For an excellent source on hippies and their values, see Timothy Miller, *The Hippies and American Values* (Knoxville, TN, 1991). An original celebration of the counterculture is Theodore Roszak, *The Making of a Counter-culture* (New York, 1969). For more original flavor of the sixties, see Hunter Thompson, *Fear and Loathing in Las Vegas* (New York, 1971), another new journalist and the pioneer of gonzo journalism.

pp. 205–209 The general source for rock music and its trends is the Geoffrey Stokes section in Ward et al., *Rock of Ages*. Spitz, *Dylan*, Shelton, *No Direction Home*, and Davies, *The Beatles*, are other sources. A particularly good essay on rock and the youth movement is George Lipsitz, "Who'll Stop the Rain? Youth Culture I, Rock 'n' Roll, and the Social Crisis," in Farber, ed., *The Sixties*.

pp. 209–211 General information about popular culture is available in Kleinfelder, *When We Were Young*, and in Farber and Bailey, *America in the 1960s*. Lee and Schlain, *Acid Dreams*, describe the political and cultural assault on acid and the head culture.

pp. 211–216 In addition to Lee and Schlain, *Acid Dreams*, Anderson, *The Movement and the Sixties*, offers a good account of the "first wave." The life of one of the era's more curious figures and a force behind the Diggers is Emmett Grogan, *Ringolevio: A Life Played for Keeps* (London, 1972). While Grogan is fascinating, he is not the most reliable source. Peter Coyote, *Sleeping Where I Fall: A Chronicle* (Washington, D.C., 1999), is probably a better source. Breines, *"Takin' it to the streets"* has interesting material, including the Perry story. Gitlin, *The Sixties*, provides insight into the tension between "heads" and "fists."

Chapter 10 A Very Bad Year Begins

pp. 217 David Caute, *The Year of the Barricades* (New York, 1988); Mark Kurlansky, *1968: The Year That Rocked the World* (New York, 2003); and Irwin Unger and Debbie Unger, *1968: Rip Tides*

(New York, 1988), are but three of many titles. For a good political discussion see Geoffrey Hodgson, *America in Our Time* (New York, 1995).

pp. 218–224 Some of this information comes from the CD liner notes for *Sgt. Pepper*. Davies, *The Beatles*, Palmer, *Rock and Roll*, Lipsitz, "Who'll Stop the Rain?" in Farber, ed., *The 60s*, and Stokes in Ward et al., *Rock of Ages*, are useful. Stokes provides much of the background detail on the Monterey Pops Festival. A number of Web sites also offer recollections of the event and some of the critical reaction. See, for example, www.retroactive.com/July 1997. You can see the highlights of the festival in D. B. Pennebaker's landmark documentary, *Monterey Pops* (1969). For a general sense of trends in film consult Robert Sklar, *Movie Made America: A Social History of the American Movies*, rev. ed. (New York, 1994). A source for plot summaries, production information, casts, and critical reviews is the Internet Movie Data Base www.IMDB.com.

pp. 224–227 The best source on Hoover, the FBI Cointelpros, and illegal activities is William Keller, *The Liberals and J. Edgar Hoover: Rise and Fall of a Domestic Security State* (Princeton, 1989). Theoharis, *Boss*, is also useful as is David Garrow, *The FBI and Martin Luther King, Jr.: From "Solo" to Memphis* (New York, 1981). For additional perspectives, see Clayborne Carson, *Malcolm X: The FBI File* (New York, 1991), and Kenneth O'Reilly, *"Racial Matters": The FBI's Secret Files on Black America, 1960–1972* (New York, 1989).

pp. 227–230 Weisbrot, *Freedom Bound*, and Viorst, *Fire in the Streets*, both cover this story well. Van Deburg, *New Day in Babylon*, is also good.

pp. 230–239 The bulk of material for this section came from the Kerner Commission, *Report of the National Committee on Civil Disorders*. Gary Wills, *The Second Civil War: Arming for Armageddon* (New York, 1968), is provocative and insightful. On the change in SNCC leadership, see Carson, *In Struggle*. Allen Matusow, *The Unraveling of America*, has important insights, especially on the Black Panthers. Hodgson, *America in Our Times*, also gives a general sense of the impact of Black Nationalism.

Chapter 11 A Bad Year Gets Worse

p. 240 On King and the war, see Garrow, *Bearing the Cross*.

pp. 240–246 The anecdote from the Johnson Cabinet meeting can be found at the LBJ Library, Cabinet papers, Cabinet meeting, September 18, 1968, 1 of 3, box 15. On the general debate over the war, see Herring, *America's Longest War*, Young, *The Vietnam Wars*, and Small, *Johnson, Nixon, and the Doves*. Another excellent source is Tom Wells, *The War Within: America's Battle over Vietnam* (Berkeley, 1994). If you can get around Norman Mailer's intrusive persona, his book *Armies of the Night* (New York, 1968), is enormously powerful and full of insights into ideological and cultural conflict. It may be the best single work of new journalism ever written.

pp. 246–250 This section also draws heavily on Herring, *America's Longest War*, Young, *The Vietnam Wars*, and Small, *Johnson, Nixon, and the Doves*. On the reaction to Tet, see Peter Braestrup, *Big Story: How the American Press and Television Reported and Interpreted the Crisis of Tet in Vietnam and Washington* (Washington, D.C., 1977), and Hallin, *"Uncensored" War*.

pp. 250–254 Garrow, *Bearing the Cross*, is good on King. Anderson, *Movement and the Sixties*, also covers this well. Blum, *Years of Discord*, and Geoffrey Hodgson, *America in Our Time*, explore the politics. Dan Carter, *The Politics of Rage: George Wallace, the Origins of the New Conservatism, and the Transformation of American Politics* (New York, 1995), is the best source on the Alabama governor. On Columbia, Breines, "*Takin' it to the streets*," has good documentary materials. The obituary of Grayson Kirk is another source: *New York Times*, November 27, 1997. Gitlin, *The Sixties*, has other insights. I also experienced events at Columbia through two of my neighbors in New Haven, both recent graduates who knew many of the participants and visited the scene. Their observations often differed markedly from what the *Times* reported.

pp. 254–257 Jules Whitcover, *The Year the Dream Died: Revisiting America in 1968* (New York, 1998), does the politics of 1968 well. See also Gitlin, *The Sixties*, and Blum, *Years of Discord*. Hayden, *Reunion*, has a sympathetic view of Robert Kennedy.

pp. 257–268 David Farber, *Chicago '68* (Chicago, 1988), provides a vivid and detailed account of events surrounding the Democratic convention. Additional materials are in Viorst, *Fire in the Streets*, Blum, *Years of Discord*, Whitcover, *The Year the Dream Died*, and Abbie Hoffman, *Autobiography of Abbie Hoffman*, rev. ed. (New York, 2000).

Chapter 12 The Rise of Gender and Identity Politics

pp. 269–271 On the thinking of Black Nationalists, see Weisbrot, *Freedom Bound*, and on the aftermath of Chicago, see Farber, *Chicago '68*. The Miss America story is widely known but best contextualized in Douglas, *Where the Girls Are*. I think many historians have failed to appreciate the importance of Douglas's book. She describes how large numbers of essentially apolitical young women began to encounter feminism. In that way she explains the way in which the movement gained traction outside its politicized sectors.

pp. 271–272 On the patterns of protest against the war, see Small, *Johnson, Nixon, and the Doves*. For a good general treatment of gender and identity politics, see Stewart Burns, *Social Movements in the 1960s* (Boston, 1990).

pp. 272–282 Friedan, *The Feminine Mystique*, is an obvious source. Background material is in Evans, *Personal Politics*. For a broad view, see Woloch, *Women and the American Experience*, and Rosenberg, *Divided Lives*. A very useful essay by Alice Echols, "Nothing Distant about It: Women's Liberation and Sixties Radicalism," appears in Farber, ed., *The Sixties*. Possibly the best single source on feminism in this era is Rosen, *The World Split Open*. Rosen has the virtue of being both a participant and a historian. Another participant who writes about the movement is Susan Brownmiller, *In Our Time: A Memoir of a Revolution* (New York, 1999). Susan Hartmann, *From Margin to Mainstream: American Women and Politics since 1960* (Philadelphia, 1989), is a good source. The creation of Ms. is told in Amy Erdman, *Yours in Sisterhood: Ms. Magazine and the Promise of Popular Feminism* (New York, 1993). Elizabeth Watkins, *On the Pill: A History of Oral Contraception, 1950–1970* (Baltimore, 1998), is a social history. On Pat Nixon and the Supreme Court appointment, see Richard Reeves, *Richard Nixon: Alone in the White House*. David Garrow, *Liberty and Sexuality: The Right to Privacy and the Making of Roe v. Wade* (New York, 1994), explores the constitutional basis for the case.

pp. 283–287 A good general source is Barry Adam, *The Rise of the Gay and Lesbian Movement* (Boston, 1987). Rosen, *The World Split Open*, tells the Robin Morgan story. Martin Duberman, *Stonewall* (New York, 1993), is most informative and a good read. John D'Emilio, *Sexual Politics, Sexual Communities: The Making of a Homsexual Minority in the United States* (New York, 1983), is good on background.

pp. 287–288 Rosen, *The World Split Open*, discusses the FBI surveillance of feminists. Her stories are amusing and sobering. Duberman, *Stonewall*, provides some poignant examples of the FBI using abusive strategies to investigate gay activists.

Chapter 13 Identities of Race and Ethnicity

pp. 289–292 The primary sources for this opening are Ilan Stavans, *Bandido: Oscar "Zeta" Acosta and the Chicano Experience* (New York, 1995), a compelling biography of Acosta, and Thompson, *Fear and Loathing in Las Vegas*. Oscar Acosta wrote two autobiographical works—*The Revolt of the Cockroach People* (New York, 1973), and *The Autobiography of a Brown Buffalo* (New York, 1972). Additional sources include Manuel Gonzales, *Mexicanos: A History of Mexicans in the United States* (Bloomington, IN, 1999), and Peter Skerry, *Mexican Americans: The Ambivalent Minority* (New York, 1993).

pp. 292–304 In addition to Skerry and Manuel Gonzales, the following were sources for this section: Juan Gonzales, *Harvest of Empire: A History of Latinos in America* (New York, 2000); Roberto Suro, *Strangers among Us: How Latino Immigration Is Transforming America* (New York, 1998)—Suro alerted me to the importance of the *Hernandez* case; Clara Rodriguez, *Puerto Ricans: Born in the U.S.A.* (New York, 1989), and *Changing Race: Latinos, the Census, and the History of Ethnics in the United*

States (New York, 2000); Andres Torres, "Explaining Puerto Rican Poverty," *Boletin del Centro de Estudos Puerto Riquenos*, 2, no. 2, winter 1987–88, 9–21; Rudolfo Acuna, *Occupied America: A History of Chicanos*, 4th ed. (New York, 2000); Ignacio Garcia, *Chicanismo: The Forging of a Militant Ethos among Mexican-Americans* (Tuscon, 1997); Richard Griswold del Castillo and Richard A. Garcia, *Cesar Chavez: A Triumph of Spirit* (Norman, OK, 1995); and last, but far from least, Carlos Munoz, Jr., *Youth, Identity, Power: The Chicano Movement*, rev. ed. (London, 2000).

pp. 304–315 Two sources were especially valuable in constructing this section, Robert Allen Warrior and Paul Chaat Smith, *Like a Hurricane: The Indian Movement from Alcatraz to Wounded Knee* (New York, 1996), and Peter Iverson, *We Are Still Here: American Indians in the Twentieth Century* (Wheeling, IL, 1998). Shepard Krech III, *The Ecological Indian: Myth and History* (New York, 1999), has the story of the "Crying Indian." In addition, I drew on Alvin Josephy, Jr., *Red Power: The American Indian Fight for Freedom* (Lincoln, NE, 1999), Stephen Cornell, *The Return of the Native: American Indian Political Resurgence* (New York, 1988), Peter Mathiessen, *In the Spirit of Crazy Horse* (New York, 1983), and John William Sayer, *Ghost Dancing the Law: The Wounded Knee Trials* (Cambridge, MA, 1997).

Chapter 14 Taking on the System

pp. 316–318 Robert Mayer, *The Consumer Movement: Guardians of the Marketplace* (Boston, 1989), and Ralph Nader, *Unsafe at Any Speed: The Designed-in Dangers of the American Automobile* (New York, 1972). Almost no one is aware of Nader's subtitle that makes much clearer the real subject of the book.

pp. 318–323 Mayer, *The Consumer Movement*, is the best general source. Greg Mitchell, *Campaign of the Century* (New York, 1992), chronicles the intrusion of mass media into political campaigning. Ambrose, *Nixon: The Triumph of a Politician*, and Reeves, *Nixon: Alone in the White House*, are additional sources.

pp. 323–333 On the postwar American economy and its impact on the environment, see Barry Commoner, *The Closing Circle* (New York, 1971), Otis Graham, *Limited Bounty: The United States since World War II* (New York, 1996), and John McNeill, *Something New under the Sun: An Environmental History of the 20th Century World* (New York, 2000). Donald Worster, *Nature's Economy: A History of Eoclogical Ideas*, 2d ed. (New York, 1994), explores the development of ideas about the human-nature relationship. Carson, *Silent Spring*, criticized the dangerous use of pesticides and herbicides, as well as human irresponsibility toward the natural world. Two works that deal with the environmental movement across the twentieth century are Philip Shabecoff, *A Fierce Green Fire: The American Environmental Movement* (Washington, 2000), and Gottlieb, *Forcing the Spring*. Gottlieb is especially good on the environmental movement in the 1960s. Kirkpatrick Sale, *The Green Revolution: The American Environmental Movement, 1962–1993* (New York, 1993), is another useful study. One source that frames much of the conservative critique of environmentalism is Rubin, *The Green Crusade*; Irene Diamond and Gloria Feman Orenstein, eds., *Reweaving the World: The Emergence of Ecofeminism* (San Francisco, 1990), provide a cross section of eco-feminist ideas. Edward Abbey, who rivals Hunter Thompson for curmudgeonliness, draws a vivid picture of eco-radicals in his novel *The Monkey Wrench Gang* (New York, 1975). Roderick Nash, *The Rights of Nature: A History of Environmental Ethics* (Madison, WI, 1989), discusses a movement to invest animate and inanimate beings with legal and moral rights. On the battle over People's Park, see Rorabaugh, *Berkeley at War*, and Anderson, *The Movement and the Sixties*.

Chapter 15 The Uncivil Wars

pp. 334–338 The background for both Woodstock and Altamont can be found in Ward et al., *Rock of Ages*, and numerous Web sites contain participant memories. Michael Wadleigh's *Woodstock* (1970) and Albert and David Mayles's *Gimme Shelter* (1970) are documentaries of these two concerts. One of my more interesting sources was a former Hells Angel who wrote me to challenge the conventional condemnation of the group's actions at Altamont. On the levels of consciousness, see Charles Reich, *The Greening of America* (New York, 1970). For a good discussion of Reich, see Blum, *Years of Discord*. The impact of commercial culture on the counterculture is discussed in Frank, *The Conquest of the Cool*. Lee and Schlain, *Acid Dreams*, describe the criminal intrusion into the drug scene.

pp. 338–347 Reeves, *President Nixon*, follows the administration through an almost daily account. That allows readers to follow the interplay of issues. Blum, *Years of Discord*, and Ambrose, *Nixon: Triumph of a Politician*, are good general sources. Ambrose is quite sympathetic. A much darker view comes in Stanley Kutler, *The Wars of Watergate* (New York, 1990). An excellent though unflattering portrait of Henry Kissinger is Walter Isaacson, *Kissinger* (New York, 1992). Further background and bibliography are available in James West Davidson and Mark Hamilton Lytle, "Breaking into Watergate," in *After the Fact: The Art of Historical Detection*, 5th ed. (New York, 2004). On Vietnam, see Herring, *America's Longest War*, and Young, *The Vietnam Wars*. The Kissinger recollection comes from Robert McMahon, ed., *Major Problems in the History of the Vietnam War*, 2d ed., (Lexington, MA, 1995). On efforts to deal with antiwar protest, see Small, *Johnson, Nixon, and the Doves*. On the media and Vietnam, see Melvin Small, *Covering Dissent: The Media and the Anti–Vietnam War Movement* (New Brunswick, NJ, 1995), and Chester Pach, "And That's the Way It Was," in Farber, ed., *The Sixties*. Anderson, *The Movement and the Sixties*, has background on the troubles at San Francisco State. Most of the material on Cornell came from the *New York Times*, conversations with faculty who were involved, and recollections in Joan Morrison and Robert K. Morrison, *From Camelot to Kent State: The Sixties Experience in the Words of Those Who Lived It* (New York, 2001). The Weathermen's "Days of Rage" is covered in Gitlin, *The Sixties*. The Nixon administration's reaction is in Reeves, *President Nixon*, and David Farber, "The Silent Majority and Talk about Revolution," in Farber, ed., *The 60s*. An excellent source for the Chicago Seven trial is Douglas Linder, "The Chicago Seven Conspiracy Trial," www.law.umkc.edu/faculty/projects/ftrials/Chicago7/Account.html.

pp. 347–356 Young, *The Vietnam Wars*, is good on Duck Hook, and Herring, *America's Longest War*, is also helpful. Small, *Johnson, Nixon, and the Doves* and *Covering Dissent*, looks at the antiwar protest as does Wells, *The War Within*. On Nixon, Agnew, and war protest, see Reeves, *Nixon: Alone in the White House*. Additional coverage is in Gitlin, *The Sixties*, and Anderson, *The Movement and the Sixties*. Many books discuss Kent State, but Milton Viorst, *Fire in the Streets*, has gathered some participant accounts. Reeves and Kutler both tell the story of Nixon's early-morning foray to the Lincoln Memorial.

Chapter 16 Watergate

pp. 357–361 Tom Hayden, *Reunion*, discusses the sympathetic view of the veterans. Ron Kovic, *Born on the Fourth of July* (New York, 1976), is a sometime searing autobiography of this veteran's transformation into an outspoken opponent of the war. Vietnam Veterans against the War published *The Winter Soldier Investigation: An Inquiry into American War Crimes* (Boston, 1972). Young, *The Vietnam Wars*, is good on declining morale. Small, *Johnson, Nixon, and the Doves*, covers the demonstrations.

pp. 361–366 A good place for background, though a hostile source, is Stanley Kutler, *The Wars of Watergate* and *Abuse of Power: The New Nixon Tapes* (New York, 1997). Daniel Ellsberg tells his story in *Secrets: A Memoir of Vietnam and the Pentagon Papers* (New York, 2002). The Nixon side is well covered in Reeves, *President Nixon*. One of the best inside views of the White House is John Dean, *Blind Ambition: The White House Years* (New York, 1976). The most riveting account is Carl Bernstein and Bob Woodward, *All the President's Men* (New York, 1976), in which they reveal their efforts to crack the story of the Watergate break-in. See also J. Anthony Lukas, *Nightmare: The Underside of the Nixon Years*, rev. ed. (New York, 1988). On the administration's reaction to demonstrators and approach to the convention, see Stephen Ambrose, *Nixon: Ruin and Recovery, 1973–1990* (New York, 1991).

pp. 366–371 Considerable material for this chapter came from Davidson and Lytle, "Breaking into Watergate," and another version from earlier editions of *After the Fact*, "Footnoting the Final Days." That essay has a bibliography containing many books on Watergate. A few worth emphasizing are Carl Bernstein and Bob Woodward, *The Final Days* (New York, 1976), Kutler's two books, *The Wars of Watergate* and *Abuse of Power*, Theodore White, *Breach of Faith: The Fall of Richard Nixon* (New York, 1975), and more recently Fred Emery, *Watergate* (New York, 1995). Ambrose, *Nixon: Ruin and Recovery*, follows out Nixon's post-Watergate career. Reeves, *President Nixon*, is also valuable, as is Blum, *Years of Discord*.

pp. 371–374 The speculation about Nixon's plans for Vietnam are discussed in Larry Berman, *No Peace, No Honor: Nixon, Kissinger, and Betrayal in Vietnam* (New York, 2001). On the institutional crisis of the presidency, see Arthur Schlesinger, Jr., *The Imperial Presidency* (New York, 1973). A particular good study of America in the 1970s is Bruce Schulman, *The Seventies: The Great Shift in American, Culture, Society, and Politics* (New York, 2001).

Epilogue

pp. 375–378 For the situation of women in the 1970s, see Rosen, *The World Split Open*, and Schulman, *The Seventies*. For the conservative reaction, see Hodgson, *The World Turned Right Side Up*, and Tucker, *Rock of Ages*.

p. 378 George Will's comment appears in his introduction to Stephen Macedo, ed., *Reassessing the Sixties: Debating the Political and Cultural Legacy* (New York, 1997).

Index